Windows® Scripting Secrets®

Windows° Scripting Secrets°

Tobias Weltner

Hungry Minds™

Best-Selling Books • Digital Downloads • e-Books • Answer Networks • e-Newsletters • Branded Web Sites • e-Learning

New York, NY ◆ Cleveland, OH ◆ Indianapolis, IN

Windows® Scripting Secrets®

Published by
Hungry Minds, Inc.
909 Third Avenue
New York, NY 10022

Copyright © 2000 Hungry Minds, Inc. All rights reserved.
No part of this book, including interior design, cover
design, and icons, may be reproduced or transmitted in
any form, by any means (electronic, photocopying,
recording, or otherwise) without the prior written
permission of the publisher.

ISBN: 0-7645-4684-8

Printed in the United States of America

10 9 8 7 6 5 4 3 2

1B/RY/QT/QS/FC

Distributed in the United States by Hungry Minds, Inc.

Distributed by CDG Books Canada Inc. for Canada; by
Transworld Publishers Limited in the United Kingdom; by
IDG Norge Books for Norway; by IDG Sweden Books for
Sweden; by IDG Books Australia Publishing Corporation
Pty. Ltd. for Australia and New Zealand; by TransQuest
Publishers Pte Ltd. for Singapore, Malaysia, Thailand,
Indonesia, and Hong Kong; by Gotop Information Inc. for
Taiwan; by ICG Muse, Inc. for Japan; by Intersoft for South
Africa; by Eyrolles for France; by International Thomson
Publishing for Germany, Austria and Switzerland; by
Distribuidora Cuspide for Argentina; by LR International
for Brazil; by Galileo Libros for Chile; by Ediciones ZETA
S.C.R. Ltda. for Peru; by WS Computer Publishing
Corporation, Inc., for the Philippines; by Contemporanea
de Ediciones for Venezuela; by Express Computer
Distributors for the Caribbean and West Indies; by
Micronesia Media Distributor, Inc. for Micronesia; by
Chips Computadoras S.A. de C.V. for Mexico; by Editorial
Norma de Panama S.A. for Panama; by American
Bookshops for Finland.

For general information on Hungry Minds' products and
services please contact our Customer Care Department
within the U.S. at 800-762-2974, outside the U.S. at 317-572-
3993 or fax 317-572-4002.

For sales inquiries and reseller information, including
discounts, premium and bulk quantity sales, and
foreign-language translations, please contact our
Customer Care Department at 800-434-3422, fax
317-572-4002, or write to Hungry Minds, Inc., Attn:
Customer Care Department, 10475 Crosspoint Boulevard,
Indianapolis, IN 46256.

For information on licensing foreign or domestic rights,
please contact our Sub-Rights Customer Care Department
at 212-884-5000.

For authorization to photocopy items for corporate,
personal, or educational use, please contact Copyright
Clearance Center, 222 Rosewood Drive, Danvers, MA
01923, or fax 978-750-4470.

For information on using Hungry Minds' products and
services in the classroom or for ordering examination
copies, please contact our Educational Sales Department
at 800-434-2086 or fax 317-572-4005.

Please contact our Public Relations Department at 212-
884-5163 for press review copies or 212-884-5000 for
author interviews and other publicity information or fax
212-884-5400.

Library of Congress Cataloging-in-Publication Data

Weltner, Tobias, 1962-
    Windows Scripting secrets/Tobias Weltner.
        p.   cm.
    ISBN 0-7645-4684-8 (alk paper)
    1. Microsoft Windows (Computer file) 2. Progamming
languages (Electronic computers) I. Title.
    QA76.76.O63 W   2000
    005.4'469--dc21   00-023392

About the Author

Dr. Tobias Weltner is a best-selling computer book author who has published more than 30 books on Windows operating systems, Active Server Pages Internet technology, and topics such as Unix and PostScript. He regularly contributes to a number of European computer magazines and works as senior developer consultant for Microsoft Germany. However, Tobias doesn't limit himself to computer science. In 1996, he earned his medical degree and did some research on multi-organ failure in trauma patients before returning to the computer arena. Tobias prefers an easy-to-understand writing style and concentrates on the practical aspects of his work.

When time allows, Tobias enjoys crew rowing and his friendship with his former host family in Arizona as well as his many friends in the West Coast region. You may contact him at Tob@compuserve.com.

Credits

Acquisitions Editors
Sherri Morningstar
John Osborn

Project Editors
Kurt Stephan
Luann Rouff

Technical Editor
Chris Stone

Copy Editor
Julie M. Smith

Media Development Specialist
Jake Mason

Permissions Editor
Lenora Chin Sell

Media Development Manager
Stephen Noetzel

Project Coordinator
Linda Marousek
Joe Shines

Graphics and Production Specialists
Robert Bihlmayer
Jude Levinson
Michael Lewis
Ramses Ramirez
Victor Pérez-Varela
Dina F Quan

Quality Control Specialist
Laura Taflinger

Book Designer
Murder By Design

Illustrator
Mary Jo Richards

Proofreading and Indexing
York Production Services

To Claudia, my wife! You supported me in any way imaginable. And to Carol and Dave Mansfield, who welcomed me to the States more than a decade ago, made me appreciate the American way of life, and still are caring friends.

Preface

Windows Scripting is exciting! Today, most professional software suites offer extensive script support, enabling you to tailor software functions exactly to your needs. The most important piece of software, however, the operating system itself, doesn't even bother supplying a similar useful way of automating routine tasks. Instead, Windows left you with the old-fashioned and ugly DOS batch files.

Not anymore! Microsoft has released Windows Scripting Host, and although its name doesn't sound heroic, it may well be one of the most important innovations Microsoft has released in the past years. And it's one of the most unknown and undocumented techniques, too. This is why you are reading *Windows Scripting Secrets*.

The Windows Scripting Host gives you the ability, for the first time, to talk directly to Windows — without having to resort to sophisticated programming environments. You don't need to knock yourself out just to get a list of broken links or find all files that you didn't use within the last two months. In fact, you don't even need to know much about programming at all. Script languages are easy, fault-tolerant, and fun to use.

Why Should You Use Windows Scripting?

So what can *Windows Scripting Secrets* do for you? A lot! This book is like an exciting adventure game and hundreds of scripts provide you with ready-to-run examples. Get live demonstrations of what is possible rather than just reading about it, and use the source codes as solid foundation for your very own scripts and programs. You will see results in a matter of minutes rather than having to study theoretical background for weeks.

This book won't just scratch the surface, either. It goes deep into subjects such as DLLs, COM objects, the Windows API, TypeLibraries, IDispatch Interfaces, and more. And unlike some other books, you'll learn these details almost casually. There's no need to dig your way through theoretical overhead. Instead, go ahead and do things: look into real DLL files, retrieve secret type library information, call API functions from your own scripts, and see what happens.

Have a look:

- **Writing little time savers:** As a warm up and comfortable start, you can stick entirely to one of the Script languages like VBScript and build little time savers that calculate mortgages or find out the day of the week of your next birthday party. This is an excellent and fun way to get accustomed to the script language itself. Knowledge you gain here can be used for the more sophisticated scripting projects you find in this book. It's also a perfect foundation for your personal career since many other Microsoft technologies are based on exactly the same scripting language. Whether you plan to get into Internet programming and e-commerce using Active Server Pages, or would like to move on to professional application development and Visual Basic—feeling at home with the script language VBScript is an excellent starting point.

■ **Extending the scope of your scripts:** Software companies develop applications filled with zillions of functions, desperately trying to please virtually any customer need. The results are huge applications that sometimes overwhelm users with choices they never need. On the other hand, even the best software engineers will never be able to guess all of your needs and wishes, so many times there's just no application available that does exactly what you want it to do. Scripting can help out because the Windows Scripting Host has the ability to "borrow" functions from other applications so you can pick out those you really need. Even better, your scripts can act like software glue and tie together software functions from different applications. In Chapter 21, for example, you will see how to glue together a TWAIN-scanner driver with your printer. This way, you get a powerful Xerox copy machine—absolutely free!

■ **Developing your own Script extensions:** You are not a programmer? Why not? Too complicated? No development environment available? Don't limit yourself! Instead of spending a great deal of money on shareware and commercial software, you can do it yourself. You'll be amazed on how many ready-to-use components are already installed on your system—just waiting for you to take advantage of them. It's only a very small (and very undocumented) step to develop your own Scripting Host extensions. And best of all it's free, and very easy to master. Microsoft gives away the Microsoft Control Creation Edition. This software is a full-fledged Visual Basic 5 development environment. Although Microsoft has stripped out the ability to develop "real programs," the Scripting Host secretly brings back everything you need to develop your own Scripting Host Extensions— which you can even sell to others. Inside of the MS CCE, you don't use much more than what you already know: VBScript, your scripting language, is a subset of the full-flavored Visual Basic language. So there's very little to learn to transform you into a versatile and powerful software developer.

■ **Untapping the real Windows power:** Using the MS CCE, you blast away the last scripting limitations. The MS CCE can access any of the basic Windows API functions, even those that are heavily undocumented. With some special tricks, you can also use functions that were originally designed for the "elite" C programmers. So no matter whether you already have programming experience or whether all of this still sounds like black magic, by the end of this book you will know how to boss around Windows in any way you please—knowledge that also comes in handy for any Visual Basic programmer.

■ **Administering Windows and the Network:** Are you responsible for software updates or work as a system administrator? Then chances are great that scripting will get you a couple of extra weeks of vacation. The

Scripting Host has full access to all important information stores: scripts can access the entire file system and network. Scripts can also look inside of the magic Windows Registry, the central information database. And with the advent of Windows 2000, scripts have full access to the Active Directory and can change thousands of user accounts and profiles in a couple of minutes. The interface ADSI (Active Directory Service Interface) is even available for Windows NT and 9x and is discussed in great detail in Chapter 24. If this is not enough, the MS CCE allows you to add on any additional windows functionality you need to administer your system: shutting down machines remotely, checking available disk spaces, and sending messages across the network.

Who Can Use Windows Scripting?

Everyone can use scripting. You. Your neighbor. Your entire company. Scripting is everywhere, and chances are it will become very popular. So far, Microsoft has concentrated efforts on making scripting available on all 32-bit Windows platforms. Windows 98 and Windows 2000 already come with it. Windows 95 and Windows NT can be easily updated to include it. On all of these Windows platforms, you can run the same Scripting Host and the same scripts — without changes, tweaks, or adjustments. It's a brave new world!

This Book's Structure

Windows Scripting Secrets is loaded with powerful and undocumented information, divided into five parts:

Part I: Scripting Kickstart

Start your journey with a VBScript "guerilla session" that shows you all the highlights and professional tweaks you need to know to write great scripts. You will learn how to use the undocumented Script Debugger to find errors quickly and step through your code. Learn how to use Visual Basic or the free Visual Basic Control Creation Edition to write your own script extensions. Discover how to use undocumented Windows API functions to display any of the standard dialog windows, and find out how DLL files are internally organized. As a special highlight, you will learn how to use scripts to untap the secret TypeLibraries and list all the methods and properties undocumented components provide.

Part II: Conquering the File System

Employ numerous sample scripts to control files and folders, create your own incremental backup utility, find broken links, and create new text files from scratch. Discover how to use the Windows API to get access to completely undocumented copy functions.

Part III: Starting and Controlling Other Software

Learn how to launch any software, enumerate all the running programs, and send key strokes to specific windows to remote-control dialog boxes and entire programs. Find out how to switch between program windows and close programs at will.

Part IV: Accessing the Operating System

Discover how to read and write to the Windows Registry, control numerous undocumented Windows settings, and change screen resolution or refresh rate. Learn all about events and how to use them to communicate between programs and scripts.

Part V: Accessing Hidden Components

Take advantage of the many COM objects already installed on your system. Access TWAIN scanners, synchronize your local hard drive with Web servers using FTP, access databases and design your own HTML-based custom dialog windows. As a special highlight, use ADSI and the windows API to completely administer Windows NT and 2000 by script.

Scripting: A Detailed View of Its Architecture

There has been a lot of confusion about what scripting really is — and in which scenarios you can use it. So let's take a quick look at the general concept.

There are only two parts required for scripting and they include the script language itself and a host in which the scripts are executed.

Script languages: Your options

Microsoft provides two scripting languages: VBScript and JScript (the Microsoft version of JavaScript). It is completely up to you which one you prefer, and since the entire scripting architecture is highly modular, you can also plug in other scripting languages like PERLScript or REXX.

Scripting Hosts: There's more than one!

Scripting languages themselves can't do much. They are designed as "in-process" DLLs, so they require a host application that loads and executes the DLL. Just consider scripting languages to be plug-ins.

Where do you plug them in? You need a host application! Microsoft has developed the Windows Scripting Host, which resides in `WSCRIPT.EXE` and `CSCRIPT.EXE`.

Secret

`WSCRIPT.EXE` is the "default" script host and runs as a Windows program. `CSCRIPT.EXE`, in contrast, executes scripts within a DOS window. Your scripts can then act like DOS- or UNIX-commands and use the DOS windows for input and output.

Whenever you store a VBScript in a file with the extension VBS, it will be executed by `WSCRIPT.EXE` using the VBScript engine. If you store a script in a file with the extension .JS, it will be interpreted using the JScript engine. And if you use the file extension .WS, you can mix different script languages and use XML-tags for advanced options.

The Windows Scripting Host isn't the only suitable host, though. Originally, scripting languages like VBScript and JScript were developed for Web designers. They can use both script languages inside of HTML pages to add dynamic functionality. So Internet Explorer may be considered just another scripting host.

Secret

Although it is perfectly possible to embed any of the example scripts you find in this book into a HTML page, it's not always a good idea. Scripts are extremely powerful, and a malicious script can easily trash the entire system, so you don't want to have your browser execute just any script from any Web site. This is why Microsoft implemented security settings into Internet Explorer. As a default in most versions, advanced scripts won't be executed or will pop up a warning message first. Therefore, the Windows Scripting Host is a much better alternative to run scripts locally.

Applications that act as Scripting Host

Even regular applications like a word processor or spreadsheet program can act as script hosts. Here, the intention is to use one of the script languages to control the software and design macros.

Actually, many professional software packages use another scripting language called Visual Basic for Applications (VBA). This language is more powerful than VBScript and JScript, and VBA also includes a sophisticated development environment. However, VBA is not free.

The scripting host and its script languages are free of charge, and you can easily integrate script capabilities into your own software by using the script control. By placing the free script control into your own software projects, you essentially transform them into scripting hosts. They now can host script languages and use them to control software functionality.

The important thing to remember is that you need a Scripting Host to execute script languages. The Windows Scripting Host is the most versatile script host because it's an independent application that can control an unlimited number of other applications simultaneously. The Windows Scripting Host can, for example, control the Kodak Imaging Tools to scan in an image and then feed it to WinWord. Also, the Windows Scripting Host requires very little memory, making it the perfect choice for administrative scripts and script tools.

A special Scripting Host: Active Server Pages

Whether you execute a script with `WSCRIPT.EXE` or one of the other scripting hosts, the script will always run locally. You can't start a script remotely on another machine.

However, there is another Microsoft technology called Active Server Pages (ASP). It's part of the Internet Information Server and enables you to embed server-side scripts into your HTML pages.

Server side scripts will be executed on the Web server, and only the result is transferred to the person who calls the Web site. ASP is just another host application, and uses the exact same scripting engine. So you can place any of the example scripts in this book into an ASP Web page and have them executed remotely just by calling the ASP page from some remote browser. For example, you can use the command extension from Chapter 16 to find out the available physical memory, then use it as an ASP page to easily find out the memory statistics of your Web server.

Scripting Host from the inside

The Scripting Host is nothing more than a shell in which COM objects can be executed. The kind and number of commands you can use in your scripts depends only on the COM objects you "plugged in."

As a safe start, the Windows Script Host always plugs in one of the scripting languages. If you store your script in a VBS file, it will be VBScript, and if you use a JS file extension, it will be JScript. This scripting language provides you with the basic set of commands.

You don't need to stick to this command set, though! Scripting is modular, and to be able to do more, you just need to plug in more COM objects. Plug in as many additional objects as you need! For example, to use the WinWord spelling checker, just plug in the Winword COM object. Your scripting command set will now not only include the scripting language commands but also all of the WinWord commands, including the spelling checker. In Chapter 4, you will get detailed information about all the COM objects available on your system and how to retrieve the commands stored inside of them.

Even if a particular software program does not come with a COM interface, you can still control its functions. Either use SendKeys to send key strokes to the program window, or develop your own COM object that "translates" between scripts and the software. This is a very powerful concept, and it's far less complicated than it seems. Chapter 11 shows you how to do this.

Get your system "scripting-ready"

Microsoft gives away the Scripting Host for free. You just need to install it on your system. In addition, there are many other free software products that help you develop scripts.

What's the story about the "new" Scripting Host?

Windows Scripting Host was introduced with Windows 98. You can find it either on the Windows 98 CD-ROM or on the Windows NT Option Pack. However, both sources only deliver the old WSH version 1.0. There are many good reasons not to use this version. Most importantly, the latest version (2.0) comes with many new and important features.

There's an easy rule — if you are in doubt whether or not the latest version of WSH is installed on your system: just go ahead and install the latest version anyway. It will update your system if necessary, and at the end you can be sure you're using the new WSH 2.0 with all of its improved power and speed. To download the latest version of WSH, go to:

`http://www.microsoft.com/msdownload/vbscript/scripting.asp?id=01`

On Windows 95 and Windows NT, make sure you install Internet Explorer 4 or above first. If you want to take advantage of the secret `Shell.Application` object covered in Chapter 8, you do need Internet Explorer 4. IE5 won't install this object.

Updating Windows 2000

Windows 2000 is already up-to-date! You don't need to do anything special. Don't install any updates. Just happily move on to the first chapter!

Obtaining the Visual Basic Control Creation Edition

If you want to open the source codes for all of the script extensions, use internal Windows API functions, or change the script extensions provided on the companion CD, you need the Visual Basic development environment. You don't need to purchase Visual Basic, though. Just download the free Visual Basic Control Creation Edition: `http://msdn.microsoft.com/vbasic/downloads/cce/`. All the samples in this book have been created and compiled with the VB CCE.

The security hole — and how to fix it

Will scripts endanger your system?

There's currently a lot of discussion about this important topic, and even Microsoft recommends turning off ActiveX components inside of IE4.

Why you need to protect your system

Scripting is not evil at all. And it's not dangerous, either. Installing the Scripting Host will do your system no harm. It might, however, make it more sensitive to other related security issues.

In order to wreak havoc, evil scripts need to be able to talk to your computer. It's the only way a script can do something bad (such as convince the CPU that it would be better to erase the entire hard disk first thing in the morning). An e-mail that contains foul content can sit on your system for years and not bother anyone.

However, there are two major groups of potentially evil (i.e., dangerous) objects: programs and ActiveX controls. They are equally dangerous because they are equally powerful.

Obviously, you should never download software from an unknown source and run it right away. It's common practice to first check the software using a virus scanner. But even if the software does not contain a virus, it can still crash your system. Any program can do this if it contains errors or does things differently than you thought it would.

ActiveX controls are just as powerful as regular programs. The only difference is that ActiveX controls need to be hosted by some other program, most commonly a Web browser. This makes them comparably small, so they can be easily embedded into Web pages. Therefore, opening a Web page and allowing any ActiveX control to be executed without checking it would be just as irresponsible as starting unknown software without a virus check.

This is the whole story. All that people currently talk about is the advice not to run ActiveX components without a check, and since the built-in check inside of IE4 has proven to be weak, some recommend to not allow ActiveX components to run at all — inside of IE4 browser, that is!

The good news is that your scripts — that is, all the scripts covered in this book — don't run inside of IE4, so they are not subject to this caveat about ActiveX. They are not limited by anything you turn on or off inside of IE4. They have nothing to do with the Internet and are not subject to any dangers that might arise from using it.

A safe solution

I do think you should check your Internet Explorer security settings before you get started. You should make sure no Web page has the potential to activate COM objects on your computer. To do this:

1. Open the Control Panel, and open the Internet module. Then, click on the Security tab.

2. In the Zones List, select Internet Zone.

3. Choose Custom to customize the Security settings. You now have the choice which things can be run by your browser. One of the entries applies to ActiveX components that might be unsafe.

4. Next, choose Disable.

Potentially unsafe ActiveX components should never be allowed to run on a Web page. They can do virtually anything on your system, and allowing them to run would, in essence, allow the Web author to take over your entire machine.

Conventions Used in This Book

Seven icons appear throughout this book. You should know their meanings before proceeding:

Secret

Secrets are the very core of this book; the Secret icon indicates valuable extra information not commonly found elsewhere. Secrets tell you more about extra functionality, hidden commands, powerful workarounds, and little-known productivity gainers.

Undocumented

The Undocumented icon marks technical information and background you should know about, but won't find in the official documentation.

Note

Notes highlight information you shouldn't overlook, so your scripts run smoothly and as intended.

Tip

Tips are my personal recommendations. They may not be as valuable as Secrets, but still toss in ideas what to do next and how to further exploit what you have just read about.

Caution

Caution indicates information you should definitely take into consideration. Most of the scripting samples in this book are friendly and benign. If you see a Caution icon, though, hold on for a second, have a sip of coffee, and make sure you understand the side effects and consequences the Caution information outlines for you.

Cross-Reference

A Cross-Reference helps to tie together related topics of this book. A Cross-Reference icon makes it easy to jump to a topic that further enhances what you have just read about.

CD

This icon indicates material found on the companion CD.

Tell Us What You Think

Since scripting is a lot about communication between COM objects and recycling code that's already installed on your system, expect to discover even more secrets and opportunities than those revealed by this book. At the same time, also expect to run into little problems every now and then. Working with scripting is not always like working a major appliance – you can't expect to push a button and have it work all the time.

By that, I mean you will most likely have to develop your own solutions and work-arounds for known issues. Likewise, as you read and refer to this book, you'll undoubtedly think of ways in which this book can be improved.

That said, I want to hear from you. If you are interested in communicating with me directly to ask questions, share tips, and so on, send e-mail to tob@compuserve.com. Be patient, and I'll try to answer your e-mails within a few business days.

Acknowledgments

This book would never exist without the caring help of a number of very special people. Writing a book like this requires lots of support, both from the family for the many months of testing and exploring, as well as from the IDG team of editors.

First and foremost I'd like to thank Claudia Wolters for her patience, and for supplying me with love, food, and cheer even during the most stressful parts of our lives.

I'd also like to thank John Osborn from IDG Books Worldwide for his tremendous work in getting the project started. Together, John and I carefully planned this book and brought together everything needed to make it possible. Thanks also to project editor Kurt Stephan, copy editor Julie Smith, acquisitions editor Sherri Morningstar, and freelance development editor Luann Rouff. I worked closely with them during the development and production of this book, and their comments and suggestions were always welcome. I appreciate their great skills and outstanding commitment. Finally, many thanks to tech editor Chris Stone, who spent numerous hours testing the code and double-checking that everything ran smoothly.

Contents at a Glance

Preface ix
Acknowledgments xix

Part I: Scripting Kickstart 1
Chapter 1: Script Development with Ease 3
Chapter 2: VBScript Guerilla Session 31
Chapter 3: Kidnapping Objects 85
Chapter 4: Developing Your Own Script Components 117
Chapter 5: Using Internet Explorer as the Output Window 155
Chapter 6: Using System Dialog Boxes 185

Part II: Conquering the File System 217
Chapter 7: Accessing the File System 219
Chapter 8: Advanced File System Tricks 249
Chapter 9: Mastering Links 289

Part III: Starting and Controlling Other Software 321
Chapter 10: Launching Any Program By Script 323
Chapter 11: Controlling Running Software 355
Chapter 12: Gaining Full Control Over Any Window 367
Chapter 13: Starting Scripts Automatically 393

Part IV: Accessing the Operating System 405
Chapter 14: Getting Access to the Registry 407
Chapter 15: Registry Tweaks 423
Chapter 16: Getting System Information 483
Chapter 17: Working with Events 509
Chapter 18: Developing Unix-like Commands 529

Part V: Accessing Hidden Components 537
Chapter 19: Using the WebBrowser Control 539
Chapter 20: Internet and Communications 559
Chapter 21: Fax, Printer, Scanner, and Graphics 581
Chapter 22: Fun, Tricks, and Multimedia 607
Chapter 23: Using Databases 645
Chapter 24: Managing Windows NT/2000 Server 669

Appendix A: When Bad Things Happen...........................697

Appendix B: About the CD-Rom 701

Index 707

End-User License Agreement 752

CD-Rom Installation Instructions 756

Contents

Preface...ix

Acknowledgments xix

Part I: Scripting Kickstart 1

Chapter 1: Script Development with Ease 3

Writing Your First Script 3
    Editing the contents of a script 5
    Conveniently starting new scripts 6
    Automatically renaming and opening new scripts 8
Getting Help When Scripts Misbehave 11
    Finding the right parts of your scripts 11
    Canceling run-away scripts 15
    Invoking the Script Debugger 15
Executing Scripts Line by Line 19
    Repairing script errors 20
    When the Debugger stops answering 21
    Setting breakpoints 21
Logging Your Script's Activity 21
    Logging events on NT 24
    Choosing the kind of log entry 25
Handling Errors Yourself 26
    Preventing errors from happening 26
    Dealing with unpredictable errors 28
    Turning off error handling the smart way 29

Chapter 2: VBScript Guerilla Session 31

Getting Input and Showing Results 32
    Asking questions 32
    Checking information type 34
    Asking simple yes-or-no questions 36
    Asking questions with a time-out 38
Passing Arguments to Scripts 40
    Dragging files onto your script icon 40
    Using DOS input and output streams 42
The Truth About VBScript Variables 46
    Finding out the variable subtype 46
    Converting variables 48
    Using variable arrays 51

Dissecting strings 56
Converting text formats 59
Using Random Numbers 61
Encrypting files using random numbers 62
Decrypting files 62
Have Your Scripts Make Decisions 65
If...then...else 65
Select case 67
Looping: Doing Something Many Times 67
For...next 68
For each...next 68
Do...loop 70
Exiting loops prematurely 71
The Beauty of Functions and Procedures 72
Defining a procedure 72
Returning values with the help of functions 73
Common pitfalls with procedures and functions 74
Passing results using arguments 76
Using Dictionaries 80
Using case-insensitive dictionaries 81
Overview: properties and methods 82
Declaring Variables Explicitly 83
Playing safe: declaring variables 83
Declaring or not declaring: a case example 83

Chapter 3: Kidnapping Objects 85

What Objects Really Are 85
How Can I Talk To COM Objects? 86
Connecting to an Object 86
Knowing Which Objects Are Available 88
Finding Out Where Objects Are Stored 91
Finding Out Undocumented Object Information 94
Listing All Automation Objects 98
Determining Whether an Object is Scriptable 100
Auto-Documenting Undocumented Objects 105
Getting More Help On Specific Commands 108
Finding More Information About Commands 115

Chapter 4: Developing Your Own Script Components 117

Getting Accustomed to VB CCE 118
Toolbox 118
Main window 119
Project Explorer 119
Properties window 120
Form Layout window 120
Developing Your Own Script Extension 121
Assigning a name to your control 122
Compiling the COM object 123
Testing your new object 123
Advantages of COM objects 124

Calling Windows API Functions 124
    Opening and closing the CD-ROM tray..125
    How API functions really work 127
Looking Inside DLL Files..129
    Decrypting the contents of a DLL file 129
Developing Dialog Boxes 131
    Designing a form..132
    Choosing the right element order 133
    Compiling your COM object 134
    Adding code to make your window appear 134
    Adding code to make your window do something 136
Using Properties to Change Your Window's Behavior..139
    Accessing your element's properties 140
    Making properties accessible from the outside..140
Using Optional Parameters 141
    Specifying default values...142
    Detecting missing arguments 142
Uncovering Special Window Properties 142
    Changing the colors...143
    Non-resizable windows..143
    Special dialog windows...143
    Positioning windows in the center of the screen..144
Implementing Special Window Behavior 144
    Resizing the contents of your window 144
    Preselecting window elements 147
    Responding to the [Enter] key 147
Displaying OLE Error Messages as Clear Text..147
    Creating your new OLE error spy tool..148
    Finding out more about OLE errors 149
Distributing Your Self-Made COM Objects 150
    Manually registering a COM object 150
    Preparing a setup package..152
    Important caveats you must know about 153

Chapter 5: Using Internet Explorer as the Output Window 155

Finding Out the Secret Functions Inside IE 156
    Determining a program's real name...156
    Reading out secret TypeLibrary information 157
Opening Internet Explorer with Style 157
    Writing something into the IE window 158
    Dynamically changing the IE contents 159
Responding to Events 161
    Finding out which events the object supports 163
    The perfect output window example 165
    Sizing the IE window..167
Responding to Events Inside Your Documents...168
    Setting up dialog elements and buttons...168
    Stopping the script until events are fired 170
    Creating your own HTML dialog boxes 171
Getting Information About Internet Explorer DHTML Object Model...........................174

Generating HTML-formatted documentation manuals 176
Retrieving undocumented information about the screen object 182

Chapter 6: Using System Dialog Boxes 185

Where Do System Dialog Boxes Come From? 185
Opening system dialog boxes...186
Finding out more information about system dialog boxes.............................187
Using Other System Dialog Boxes 188
Managing flags and special behavior 189
Picking a color 192
Wrapping System Dialog Boxes 193
Creating your own system dialog boxes 193
Getting access to the system dialog boxes 194
Using the Folder Picker...197
Accessing Folder Picker through API functions...198
Automatically documenting all secret Folder Picker options 201
Getting Access to the Hidden Icon Picker...203
How to call undocumented shell functions 203
Displaying icons hidden in the system files 205
Displaying and Sorting Lists..207
Getting Aacess to the ListView 207
Designing and sorting lists..207
Sorting lists without dialog boxes 211
Diving into documentation and source code 212
Successfully Dealing with API Functions 213
String handling — undocumented Visual Basic commands 213
Dealing with ANSI and UNICODE...214
Cutting excess string space 215
Experimenting and getting source code for free...215

Part II: Conquering the File System 217

Chapter 7: Accessing the File System...............................219

Finding the Secret Backdoor to the File System...219
Accessing a drive 220
Finding information about properties and methods 221
Getting Details About Your Drives 221
Closely examining the Drive object 222
Is the drive ready for action?...223
Changing a drive's volume name 224
Using a drive's serial number 224
Determining drive type and file system 224
Finding out available space on drives 225
Accessing Folders...230
Examining the Folder object 231
Determining a folder's total size 232
Finding and deleting empty folders 234
Creating new folders...236

Organizing Files..237
    Accessing files 238
Mastering File Attributes..238
    Reading file and folder attributes 239
    Changing a file's attribute 240
Changing File Content..241
    Peeking into files 241
    Creating Files 246
    Renaming files 247

Chapter 8: Advanced File System Tricks 249

Using Advanced File System Methods...249
    Kidnapping the shell's copy station 250
    Getting access to the Windows file services 250
    Understanding SHFileOperation 250
Deleting Files to the Recycle Bin 253
    Emptying the recycler 255
Copying and Moving Files 256
    Backing up valuable data 256
    Copying files to multiple folders 259
Formatting Drives..259
Uncovering Extended File Version Information................................262
    Accessing file version information 262
    Finding out file versions and copyright information.....263
    Searching for 16-Bit Windows files...............................265
    Searching for DOS files...266
    Exploring Windows system files 266
Compressing (and decompressing) files 269
    Getting access to compression functions 269
    Squeezing files onto a disk...269
    Decompressing compressed files 271
    Some second thoughts about compression 272
The Secret Shell View on the File System.......................................273
    An inside view of the shell.Application object 273
    Accessing folders the shell way 274
    Finding out a folder's name 276
    Reading folder contents 276
    Retrieving secret file information 278
    Accessing special virtual Windows folders 279
    Translating between namespaces 281
    Calling a file's Property page 282
    Opening Properties windows as modal windows 284
    Accessing context menu Commands the smart way 284
    Calling Properties pages using API calls 286

Chapter 9: Mastering Links 289

Why Do I Need Links Anyway?...289
    Creating a new link file 290
    Examining the shortcut object 290

Accessing Existing Link Files 291
    Searching for invalid links...291
    Finding (and eliminating) duplicate keyboard shortcuts 293
Changing a Shortcut Icon 295
    Borrowing system icons...295
    Changing your program menu's icons...299
    Creating your own icons..300
Inserting Scripts into Special Places 300
    Starting scripts automatically 301
    Using scripts as a Send To extension 302
Advanced Shortcut Tricks..305
    Providing optional arguments 305
    Selecting a new window size 306
    Accessing the shell link object 307
    Examining the shell's link object 308
    Resolving links...309
    Background: How Windows resolves links 312
    Using the official link resolving dialog box 313
    Designing Context menu extensions 315
    Selecting a link target 318

Part III: Starting and Controlling Other Software 321

Chapter 10: Launching Any Program By Script 323

Launching Programs 323
    Launching programs directly 324
    Determining window size..327
    Waiting for a program to finish..328
Remote Controlling Running Programs 329
    Getting to know SendKeys 329
    Directing keys to the right window...332
    Telling windows to switch focus no matter what 333
    Finding out whether a window exists..335
    Safely directing keystrokes to the window of your choice..............335
    Remote controlling menus and the Start menu 338
    Shutting down all running programs...339
Executing DOS Commands 344
    Feeding DOS commands to the interpreter 344
    Reading in the DOS command results 345
    Feeding answer files to DOS commands 346
Launching Control Panel Items..347
    Where do Control Panel items live?..347
    Executing Control Panel items 348
Accessing Software Through CreateObject 349
    Remote controlling Microsoft Word 349
    Accessing the Word spell-checker 351
    A whole new universe 353

Chapter 11: Controlling Running Software.........................**355**

  Controlling Software Through ProcessIDs 355

    Accessing ProcessIDs directly..355

    Closing applications under all circumstances 356

    Closely monitoring a program 357

    Running programs synchronously..358

    Controlling window style 359

    Closing external programs 360

  Splitting Programs into Modules 360

    Which Windows version is running? 361

    Enumerating running processes 362

    Listing program modules 363

Chapter 12: Gaining Full Control Over Any Window **367**

  Full Control Over Any Window 367

    Accessing any window 368

    Bringing a window to the foreground..371

    Closing a window 372

  Making Windows Invisible 372

    Finding out the current window style 372

    Changing window style dynamically 374

  Changing Window Size and Moving Windows 375

    Finding out current window dimensions 375

    Changing window size 376

    Moving windows around 376

    Resizing windows 377

  Flashing a Window Title Bar 378

    Flashing title bars manually 378

    Flashing title bars automatically 378

  Manipulating Window Buttons 379

    Disabling minimize and maximize..380

    Disabling the window system menu 380

    Disabling window resizing 381

  Hiding and Cascading All Windows..381

    Minimizing all open windows 381

    Cascading and tiling windows 382

  Exploring Window Internals and Child Windows 382

    Accessing system windows 383

    Finding window parents 384

    Finding child windows...385

    Hiding the Start menu button 386

    Enumerating child windows 386

    Browsing through system windows...387

    Hiding the desktop 389

    Changing desktop View mode 389

  Capturing Window Content 390

    Capturing the entire screen 390

    Capturing the active window 391

    Capturing any window 391

    Displaying a window preview 391

Chapter 13: Starting Scripts Automatically **393**

Starting Scripts the Smart Way 393
    Launching scripts at logon 393
    Hiding script launch 394
    Launching scripts before logon 396
    Launching scripts in intervals 396
Inserting Scripts into Context Menus 397
    Inserting new commands into the folder context menu 398
    Inserting new commands into any file's context menu 401
    Copying the filename to the clipboard 403

Part IV: Accessing the Operating System **405**

Chapter 14: Getting Access to the Registry **407**

Getting to Know the Registry 407
    Where does the Registry live? 407
    Accessing Registry content 408
    Backing up the Registry 409
Reading and Writing to the Registry 411
    Reading the Registered Owner 411
    Changing Registry information 412
    Tricks and tips around Registry edits 413
    Deleting Registry values 414
Creating Advanced Registry Tools 415
    Enumerating subkeys 415
    Listing subkey entries 416
    Version-independent Windows settings 417
    Writing Registry scripts for specific Windows versions 418
    Finding out the variable type 418
    Reading binary data 419
    Writing binary data 419
    Deleting Registry keys and values 420
    Finding out if a key exists 420
    Additional things to remember 421

Chapter 15: Registry Tweaks **423**

The Registry: Zillions of Undocumented Features 423
    Comparing Registry snapshots 424
    Spying: Watching the Registry work 426
    Writing a script to access undocumented features 428
    Forcing Windows to recognize your new settings 430
    Max Cached Icons key 431
    Searching for interesting Registry keys 431
    Controlling program settings 434
Managing System Icons on the Desktop 434
    Changing the name of the Recycle Bin 435
    More secrets about desktop items 436
    Hiding the Recycle Bin 438

Refreshing the desktop automatically...439
Finding and restoring system icons..440
Adding commands to system context menus 443
Inserting icons into your Explorer..446
Controlling Windows Settings Through API...447
Retrieving Windows settings 448
Gaining full access to all Windows settings..450
Changing Windows settings..452
Changing icon spacing...453
Managing Active Window Tracking 454
Changing window borders 456
Controlling the system beep...457
Using Icon Title Wrap 458
Controlling Screen Savers 458
Launching screen savers..458
Temporarily disabling screen savers 459
Setting screen saver timeout 460
Finding out if a screen saver runs 461
Changing screen saver settings..461
Installing new screen savers...463
Controlling low-power screen saver features..463
Animations and Visual Effects 465
Turning off visual effects altogether..465
Overview: Visual effects built into Windows..465
Combo box animation 466
Cursor shadow 467
Gradient captions...467
List box animation 468
Menu animation..468
Menu underlines...469
Menu show delay 470
Selection fade 471
Tooltip animation...471
Full window drag 474
Font smoothing 474
Setting blinking text cursor width 475
Specifying a new desktop wallpaper 475
Enabling "Snap-To-Button"...478
More Undocumented Registry Tweaks..478
Getting rid of shortcut arrows..478
Changing the shortcut arrow..480
New icons for all system icons 481
Sizing the Cool Switch window...481

Chapter 16: Getting System Information 483

Finding Out Important Path Information..483
Retrieving special folder path names...484
Cleaning up your Documents menu 485
Finding the Windows folder...488
Reading Network Information..489

Inside view: WScript.Network 489

Listing current username 490

Managing Memory Consumption 491

Retrieving memory statistics 491

Running in physical memory only 492

Checking memory installed and memory consumed 492

Getting Miscellaneous Windows Settings 493

Querying system metrics 494

Identifying slow computers 496

Detecting mouse/wheel information 497

Is a network present? 497

Controlling boot mode 498

Managing Screen Resolution and Refresh Rate 498

Finding out all available screen resolutions 498

Determining the current video settings 499

Finding out the best frequency setting 500

Changing display frequency 500

Changing screen resolution 500

Enumerating System Fonts 501

Creating a font sample page 501

Analyzing your processor 503

Determining your processor type 503

Determining how many processors are onboard 504

Dealing with Windows Versions 504

Getting an overview: Windows version details 505

Determining Windows version 505

Extracting individual version information 506

Determining system support for specific functions 506

Chapter 17: Working with Events **509**

What's So Thrilling About Events? 509

Receiving events 510

Implementing an event sink 511

Using events 511

Defining Your Own Events 513

Creating a timer control 513

Creating a debugging timer 514

Showing icons in the tray area 516

Tray icons under the hood 517

Changing form icons dynamically 520

Responding to tray icon events 521

Creating Modeless Windows 522

Output status information to a modal window 522

Using progress bars to spice up dialog boxes 526

Chapter 18: Developing Unix-like Commands **529**

Developing Your Own Command-Line Macros 529

Creating a new command 529

Calling scripts like DOS commands 531

Detecting whether a script runs in a DOS box 531

Using piping: Feeding results to your commands 534
    Developing pipe commands 534
    Writing filters through piping 535

Part V: Accessing Hidden Components 537

Chapter 19: Using the WebBrowser Control................................539

The WebBrowser Control: Mastering Real-World Tasks 539
    Creating custom dialog boxes 540
    Getting access to template elements 542
    Revealing implementation details 545
Advanced WebBrowser Tricks 545
    Calling script procedures through your HTML template.....................546
    Communication between the HTML template and the COM object.......547
    Automatically closing the form on RETURN...550
    Hooking COM procedures to individual elements 551
    Checking for valid form entries 553
    Responding to WebBrowser control events 555
Reading Groups of Radio Buttons 555
    Creating a group of radio buttons..555

Chapter 20: Internet and Communications.................................559

Accessing the Internet 559
    Creating a universal Internet script extension 560
    Connecting to the Internet 560
    Closing the connection once the Web page is loaded.........................561
Using FTP to download and upload files 562
    General rules for accessing FTP 562
    Accessing an FTP server 562
    Retrieving an FTP directory listing 562
    Downloading FTP files 567
    Uploading FTP files 568
    Synchronizing local folders and Web folders 569
Miscellaneous Internet Methods 575
    Determining Internet connection type 575
    Determining host names 575
    Determining IP address 576
Script Extension Internet Methods 577

Chapter 21: Fax, Printer, Scanner, and Graphics 581

Say "Hi" to Kodak Imaging..581
    A closer look...582
    Getting access to the control..583
    Finding out if TWAIN support is available 584
Scanning Pictures 585
    Saving scanned pictures to disk...585
    Automated scanning...586
    Scanning large numbers of pictures 588
    Scanning pictures with the preview function.....................................589

Printing Scanned Images 590
   Your personal photocopy machine 590
   A photocopy machine with editing functions 592
Managing Pictures 593
   Loading and printing pictures 593
   Printing pictures without a dialog box 594
Converting Graphics Files 594
   Rotating pictures 594
   Scaling pictures 595
   Creating buttons and icons 596
   Generating thumbnails and preview pages 597
   Converting picture quality and color formats 599
   Saving scanned pictures with compression 601
   Choosing the right compression options 602
   Repairing pictures with damaged
      file type info 604

Chapter 22: Fun, Tricks, and Multimedia 607
Extracting Icons from Files 607
   Creating a list of available icons 608
   Selecting a file from your icon list 611
Changing Folder Icons 614
   Hiding folders 619
   Changing system icons 619
   Extracting icons to files 622
   Searching for customized DESKTOP.INI folders 623
Accessing Multimedia Devices 626
   Opening and closing CD trays 628
   Finding out if an audio CD is inserted 631
   Querying audio CD parameters 632
Remote Controlling Audio Playback 634
   Controlling position 634
   Changing time format from tracks to milliseconds 635
Dealing with Wave Audio, MIDI Files, and Miscellaneous Multimedia Types 636
   Playing back MIDI files 638
   Playing back WAV audio files 640
   Showing AVI movie files 640
   Automatically recording CD tracks to WAV audio 642

Chapter 23: Using Databases 645
Accessing Databases 645
   Checking ADO version 646
   Do I need to upgrade or install anything? 647
Getting Access to a Database 648
   Opening and querying a database 648
   Reading database contents 650
   Finding out design information 651
   Adding new data to your database table 653
   Counting the number of records 655

Deleting records 655
Creating new database tables..656
Deleting tables 657
Controlling the Index Server 658
Activating local file system indexing 658
Adding and removing folders from the index..660
Adding a new catalog...660
Querying the Index Server 661
Exploring information categories 662
Limiting searches to specific folders..664
Creating your own search dialog box 665
Fine-tuning Index Server 666

Chapter 24: Managing Windows NT/2000 Server 669

Managing Windows NT/2000 Security 669
Creating scripting extensions to manage user accounts 670
Getting ready for ADSI 670
Managing User Accounts (the API Way)...671
Enumerating users 671
Adding users..672
Deleting user accounts 673
Changing passwords...673
Listing global groups 674
Managing group membership 675
Finding the primary domain controller..675
Exploring the ADSI World 675
Is it a container? 677
Enumerating group memberships 678
Testing whether a user belongs to the group...679
Creating a new user account 679
Finding out all groups a user belongs to...680
Adding a user to the group 680
Removing a user from a group 681
Finding out secret group properties 681
Setting user passwords 684
Changing user account information 684
Forcing password changes 686
Prohibiting password changes 686
Disabling accounts..687
Managing Windows Services..688
Controlling services through the API 688
Managing services through ADSI 688
Managing individual services 689
Controlling Network Shares 690
Adding network shares..691
Accessing shared folder properties...691
Automatically Restarting and Shutting Down 692
Shutting down a local machine 692
Remotely shutting down a machine 693
Automatic logon 694

Appendix A: When Bad Things Happen.............................**697**

Appendix B: About the CD-ROM......................................**701**

Index **707**

End-User License Agreement **752**

CD-Rom Installation Instructions **756**

Part I

Scripting Kickstart

Chapter 1: Script Development with Ease

Chapter 2: VBScript Guerilla Session

Chapter 3: Kidnapping Objects

Chapter 4: Developing Your Own Script Components

Chapter 5: Using Internet Explorer as the Output Window

Chapter 6: Using System Dialog Boxes

Script Development with Ease

In This Chapter

▶ Write and edit script files

▶ Create blank script files with a mouse click

▶ Select script lines automatically

▶ Get help when scripts misbehave

▶ Execute scripts line by line

▶ Log your scripts' activity

▶ Catch errors and handle them yourself

Scripts are plain text files (see Figure 1-1), so you can use any text editor to develop them. However, most text editors are not designed to meet developers' needs. For example, they often lack the ability to mark specific lines you'd like to take a closer look at. This is unfortunate because when the Scripting Host encounters a problem, it tells you the line number that caused the hiccup — and it's nice to have a convenient way of jumping to that particular line.

In this chapter, you'll learn how easy it is to use hidden script techniques to enhance any text editor that has line-marking capabilities. You will also discover convenient ways of starting new script files with a mere right-click of the mouse button. In addition, you'll discover how scripts are executed line by line and learn about the Script Debugger, which allows you to step through your script code while it is executed. This "slow motion" execution helps you understand the script mechanics and is also perfect for finding (and resolving) script errors easily.

Writing Your First Script

Writing scripts is as easy as launching your favorite text editor. Even the simple Windows editor will suffice — Just select Run from your Start menu and enter **NOTEPAD**.

Tip

If you like, you can even use your favorite word-processing software for writing scripts, by using line-numbering or other advanced features. Remember though, word processors don't save plain text files as a default — they use their own proprietary binary format. The Scripting Host can't decipher this format, so you'll need to be sure to save your scripts as `file type plain text`. In most cases, a plain text editor is the better choice.

Now you'll see your blank text editor window. This is your playground, the place where you can start developing your scripts. The traditional first step in programming books is to greet the world. Let's do it!

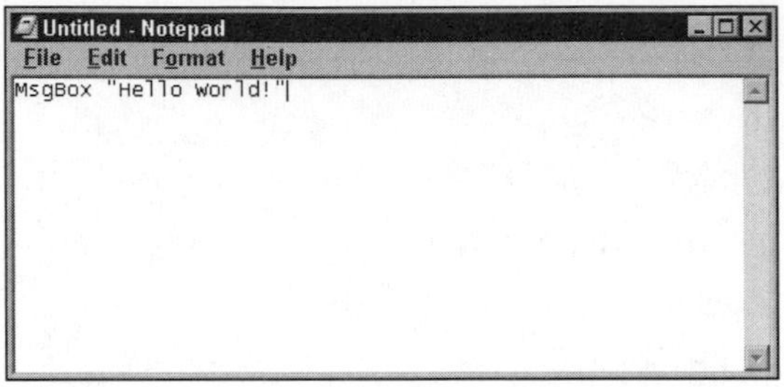

Figure 1-1: Scripts are just plain text files.

At this point, your script is a plain text file. In order to have Windows interpret it as a VBScript file and feed its contents to the Scripting Host, you'll need to save it with the file extension `.vbs` (see Figure 1-2). Choose Save As from the File Menu, change the Save in the listbox to Desktop, and enter the filename `welcome.vbs`.

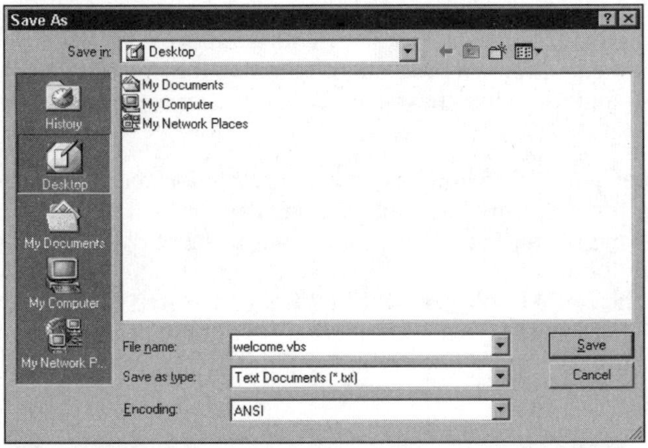

Figure 1-2: Save scripts with a .vbs file extension.

Your script will be placed right on your desktop (see Figure 1-3). If you have correctly set up the Scripting Host as outlined previously, it will have the typical script icon.

Figure 1-3: A .vbs script

To see your script, just open up the file. It will pop up a small dialog box and say hello to the world (see Figure 1-4).

Figure 1-4: It works! Your script says hello to the world.

Editing the contents of a script

During script development, you will probably edit a script many times, in order to fix errors and adopt new features (see Figure 1-5). To keep things simple, it's a good idea to break larger projects into small pieces and run the script after each step is completed. This way, it is much easier to identify and correct script errors.

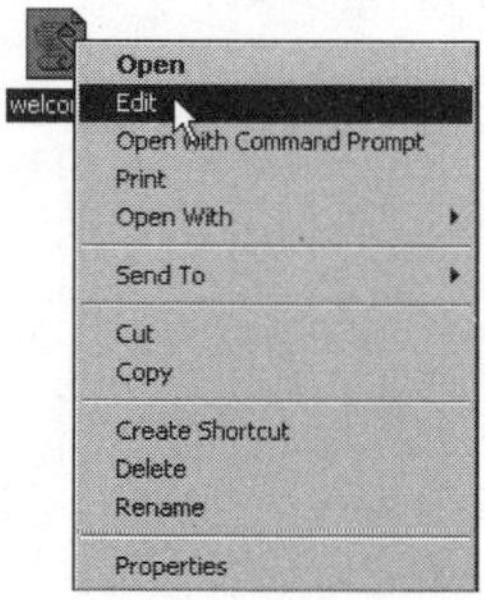

Figure 1-5: Choose Edit to change a script anytime you feel like it

To change a script, right-click its icon and choose Edit. Make whatever changes you like, and then save it again. Editing a script is like editing a letter, except that you can't open the script file to change it, because opening the file always runs the script. Use the Edit command instead, or drag the script file onto the program icon you want to use for displaying the file contents.

Conveniently starting new scripts

You don't have to go through all this clicking and renaming of file extensions just to start a new scripting project. Instead, use the scripting capabilities to place a new command into the New menu. This way, it's easy to get new script files, of the right file type, anytime you want.

To insert a new document type into your New menu, just execute the following script:

```
' 1-1.VBS

' this is the file extension the new command
' should generate:
filetype = ".vbs"

' connect to WScript.Shell for registry access:
set WSHShell = CreateObject("WScript.Shell")

' read in the name of the vbs-section:
prg = ReadReg("HKCR\" & filetype & "\")
' read in the official name for vbs-files:
prgname = ReadReg("HKCR\" & prg & "\")

' ask for a new name
ask = "What should be the name for new VBScript scripts?"
title = "New menu entry"
prgname = InputBox(ask, title, prgname)

' save the new program description:
WSHShell.RegWrite "HKCR\" & prg & "\", prgname
' add a New menu entry asking for an empty new file:
WSHShell.RegWrite "HKCR\" & filetype & "\ShellNew\NullFile", ""

' reads a registry key
' should the key be invalid, complain and stop:
function ReadReg(key)
    on error resume next
    ReadReg = WSHShell.RegRead(key)
    if err.Number>0 then
        ' key could not be read: complain!
        error = "Error: Registry-Key """ & key _
            & """ could not be found!"
        MsgBox error, vbCritical
        WScript.Quit
    end if
end function
```

This script is a great example of how powerful the Scripting Host can be. With it, you can change the official name of .vbs files and write information into the windows registry to make the .vbs files available in the New menu. Just enter a name under which VBScript files will appear in your New menu (see Figure 1-6).

Tip

It may take a few seconds before the new command becomes visible. To force Explorer to recognize the change, click an empty spot on the desktop and press [F5].

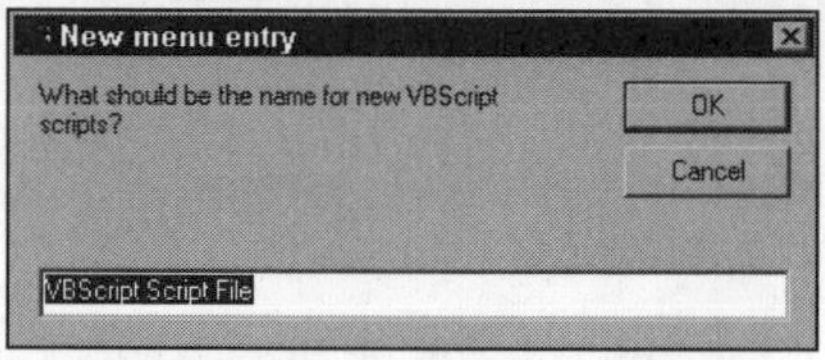

New menu entry   ✕

What should be the name for new VBScript
scripts?   OK

                                                           Cancel

VBScript Script File

Figure 1-6: Choose a name for your `.vbs` script files

To start a new script (see Figure 1-7), right-click the mouse, choose New, and then click the name you specified for `.vbs` files. That's all there is to it. Windows will generate a new and empty `.vbs` file for you.

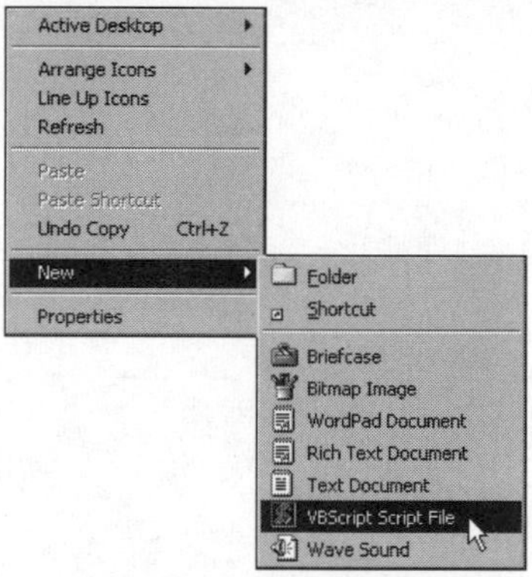

Active Desktop   ▶
Arrange Icons   ▶
Line Up Icons
Refresh

Paste
Paste Shortcut
Undo Copy   Ctrl+Z

New   ▶   📁 Folder
Properties   ☑ Shortcut

                                      📦 Briefcase
                                      🖼 Bitmap Image
                                      📄 WordPad Document
                                      📄 Rich Text Document
                                      📄 Text Document
                                      📄 VBScript Script File
                                      🔊 Wave Sound

Figure 1-7: Start new script files with the help of New.

All that is left to do is to rename the file and then right-click the file: Edit will open the empty file in your text editor, and you'll be ready to bring your script to life.

Tip

For more information about how the script accomplishes all of this, see Chapter 13. For now, it's just a convenient tool.

Getting rid of a new entry is even easier:

```
' 1-2.VBS

set WSHShell = CreateObject("WScript.Shell")
filetype = ".vbs"
```

```
WSHShell.RegDelete "HKCR\" & filetype & "\ShellNew\"
MsgBox "Command removed!"
```

Automatically renaming and opening new scripts

Scripts can help you to automate routine tasks — it's their job. Let's start with a convenient way to create new scripts from scratch!

Secret

Placing file templates into the New menu is common practice for many file types, and you have just seen how to do this with .vbs files. The New menu can do much more, though. You can also place commands into this menu, launching scripts that take over much of the work involved in getting new files.

The next script places a new command into the New menu. This command itself launches another script, and then the subsequent script takes over the responsibility of generating a new script file.

```
' 1-3.VBS

' Name of your new command:
commandname = "Get New VBScript file"

' connect to Wscript.Shell for registry access:
set WSHShell = CreateObject("WScript.Shell")

' get path to windows folder:
windir = WSHShell.ExpandEnvironmentStrings("%WINDIR%")

' name of the script to be executed by the new
' command:
script = "\newvbsfile.vbs"
command = "WSCRIPT.EXE " + windir + script + " ""%2"""

' the dummy file extension name this commands registers with:
prgextension = "vbscustom"
extension1 = "HKCR\.vbsneu\"
extension2 = "HKCR\" & prgextension & "\"

' save the command to be executed:
WSHShell.RegWrite extension1, prgextension
WSHShell.RegWrite extension1 + "ShellNew\command", command

' Name of the editor you want to open scripts with:
WSHShell.RegWrite extension2 + "Shell\open\command\", "NOTEPAD.EXE"

WSHShell.RegWrite extension2, commandname
WSHShell.RegWrite extension2 + "DefaultIcon\", "SHELL32.DLL,44"

MsgBox "Command installed.",_
  vbInformation + vbSystemModal
```

Once you run this script (see Figure 1-8), you'll discover a new entry in the New menu called Get New VBScript File.

Tip

In order to have Explorer update its menus, you may need to click an empty space on your desktop and press [F5].

Figure 1-8: Your new command launches a script, but it's missing.

Choosing this entry will raise an error—and that's good! Now you know your script is working well, because instead of placing an empty file somewhere, your command tries to execute another script, called newvbsfile.vbs. Your command looks for this script inside your Windows folder, but because you haven't placed it there yet, the command fails.

It won't fail for long. Just place the following script into your Windows folder and call it newvbsfile.vbs:

```
' NEWVBSFILE.VBS

' look for the arguments the New menu
' supplied to this script:
set args = WScript.Arguments

' no arguments? Then someone called this script directly:
if args.Count=0 then
    MsgBox "This script cannot be run directly"
    WScript.Quit
else
    ' access Scripting.FileSystemObject to get a hold
    ' of all the file system commands necessary to
    ' generate a new and empty script file:
    set fs = CreateObject("Scripting.FileSystemObject")

    ' where does the user wants the script file to be
    ' placed? Read the arguments:
    path = args(0)
    ' strip off the preliminary file name
    ' we just want the path name:
    path = left(path, InstrRev(path, "\"))

    ' ask for the name:
    do
        ask = "I am going to place a new vbs file here: """ & _
path        & """." + vbCr + vbCr
        ask = ask + "What's the name of the new script file?"
        name = InputBox(ask)
        if name = "" then
            ' oh, no file name specified!
            ' Quit!
```

```
            status = 3
        else
            ' a name was specified:
            ' generate new fully qualified path name
            ' for script file:
            filename = path + name + ".vbs"

            ' does this file exist already?
            if fs.FileExists(filename) then
                ' yes, overwrite it?
                ask = "Script """ + name _
                    + """ already exists! Replace?"
                answer = MsgBox(ask, vbQuestion + vbYesNo)
                if answer = vbYes then
                    ' delete old file
                    status = 2
                else
                    ' ask for another name:
                    status = 0
                end if
            else
                ' generate new file:
                status=1
            end if
        end if
    ' ask until a valid file name was entered
    loop while status=0

    if status = 3 then
        ' no file name was entered:
        MsgBox "Exit!", vbInformation
    else
        ' Create new text file and overwrite any
        ' existing file:
        set handle = fs.CreateTextFile(filename, true)
        handle.close
        ' open new script file automatically
        ' for editing:
        ' connect to WScript.Shell for Run-command:
        set WSHShell = CreateObject("WScript.Shell")
        WSHShell.Run "NOTEPAD.EXE " + filename
    end if
end if
```

Secret

It's easy to save this file to the Windows folder: Open the file in your editor, choose Save As from your File menu, and use %WINDIR% [Enter] as your filename. The Save As dialog box will immediately switch to your Windows folder, and you can save your file using newvbsfile.vbs as the filename. Environment variables like %WINDIR% are recognized only with the new set of dialog boxes introduced with Windows 98. On Windows 95 systems, this shortcut doesn't work.

Now try your new command again! This time, it will find the target script and execute it. Your new script, `newvbsfile.vbs`, will politely ask for a filename, and will then automatically open a new file for editing (see Figure 1-9).

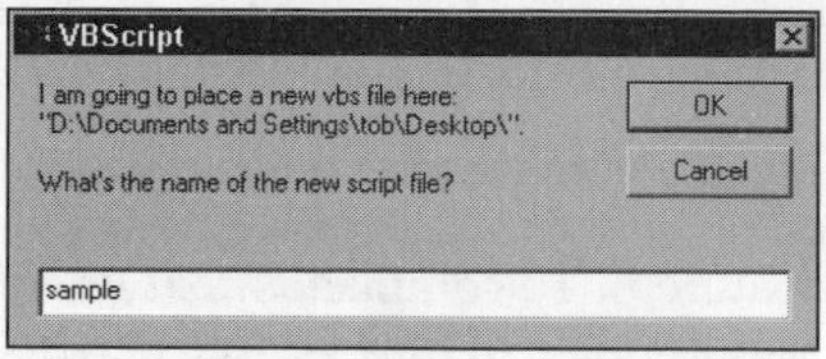

Figure 1-9: Enter the name of your new script file.

Getting Help When Scripts Misbehave

The more you experiment with scripts, the more you will encounter errors. This is absolutely normal. Errors are a great way of learning, and even the most experienced script developer will have to cope with errors every now and then.

Finding (and correcting) errors can be frustrating if you don't have the right tools and strategies to assist you. This chapter provides you with all the debugging information you need to know. Come back to this chapter whenever your scripts don't do what you expect them to!

Finding the right parts of your scripts

Whenever the Scripting Host encounters a problem, it pops up an error message (see Figure 1-10). It may look a little ugly, but it provides all the information you need, including a short description of the most probable cause and a line number. This line number indicates the script line where the error was discovered.

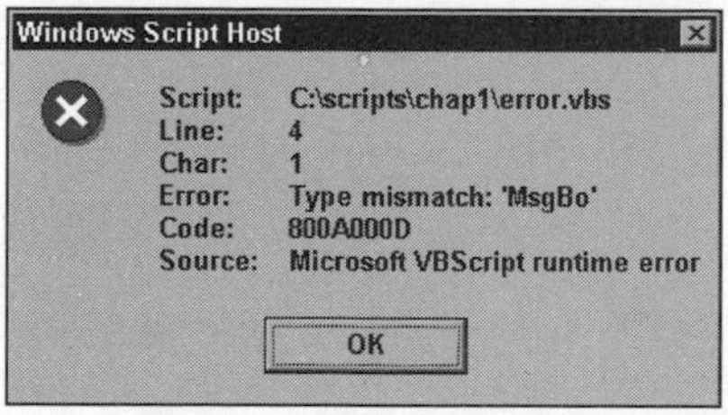

Figure 1-10: This message tells you on which line number an error occurred.

The next step is to take a look at the line. Open up the script in your editor, right-click the script icon, and choose Edit.

Tip

If your script is relatively short, it's easy to identify the line number. There's only one caveat — turn off word wrapping! Word wrapping breaks long lines into more than one line so you can view the entire line without the need for horizontal scrolling. Word wrapping, however, interferes with an editor's ability to count line numbers. Using the Notepad editor, open the Edit menu and turn off Word Wrap before you start counting line numbers!

Once your script grows, counting line numbers becomes tedious. It's just not practical to count a hundred or so lines. Unfortunately, as I've mentioned previously, most editors don't feature GoTo commands that let you jump to specific lines. Again, this is a great example of how scripts can help out. You can develop a script that controls your favorite editor and have it jump right to the line you specify.

Use the following script:

```
' 1-4.VBS

' mark a line

' Connect to WScript.Shell-Object which provides
' the SendKeys-Command
set wshshell = CreateObject("WScript.Shell")

' Ask which line number to highlight:
line = inputBox("Which line do you want to mark?")

' Check whether entry is a number:
if not isNumeric(line) then
    MsgBox "You did not specify a number!"
    WScript.Quit
else
    ' convert number to Integer:
    line = Fix(line)
    ' is line number valid?
    if line<1 then
        MsgBox "Your line number is invalid!"
        WScript.Quit
    end if
end if

' wait 200 milliseconds (0.2 sec):
WScript.Sleep(200)

'Jump to start of page: CTRL+HOME
wshshell.SendKeys "^{HOME}"

' Move to line number:
for x=1 to line-1
    wshshell.SendKeys "{DOWN}"
    WScript.Sleep 10
next

' Mark line:
' Jump to beginning of line: HOME
```

```
wshshell.SendKeys "{HOME}"
' Mark to end of line: SHIFT+END
wshshell.SendKeys "+{END}"
```

To make this script work, save it at a location on your hard drive where it can stay for the next couple of months. Then, drag the script icon onto your Start button in the left corner of the task bar (see Figure 1-11).

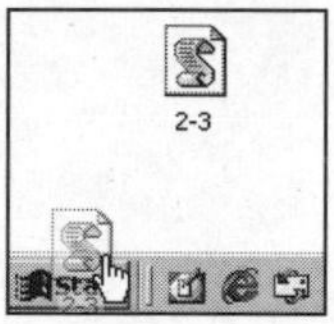

Figure 1-11: Drag scripts onto the Start button to place them in the Start menu.

Windows will place a shortcut into the Start menu. Next, open your Start menu, right-click Start, and choose Open. Windows opens the Start menu as a folder, and you see your new link to your script.

Caution

You will also see the Programs program. Don't delete or rename this folder! It contains all your program groups, and deleting it will empty the Programs command located in the Start menu.

You can either leave the shortcut inside of your Start menu, or you can store it in one of your program groups where it won't occupy valuable Start menu space. To move the shortcut there, right-click the mouse and choose Cut. Then, open up the Programs folder. You will now see all of your program groups. Open the appropriate group and choose Create Shortcut from the File menu.

Undocumented

Shortcut keys only work on shortcuts that are located in either the Start menu or in one of your program groups. This is why you need to insert a link to your line-numbering script at either one of these places.

To be able to mark lines, you just need to specify a keyboard shortcut that can run your line-marking script (see Figure 1-12). First, right-click the shortcut and choose Properties. A dialog box will open. Click the Shortcut tab.

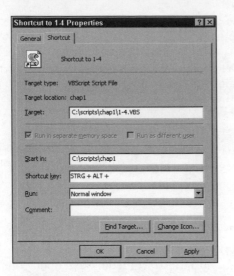

Figure 1-12: Assign shortcut keys to scripts you launch frequently.

Now all that's left to do is to choose a keyboard shortcut: Click inside the shortcut field and fill in the key combination you want to use to run this script.

Tip

Most keyboard shortcuts start with [Ctrl]+[Alt]. It's easier to remember (and use) function keys in some cases, however. Most function keys are used by Windows, but [F11] and [F12] are always available for your own purposes. If you need more available function keys, try using [Shift] plus one of the 12 function keys. Windows 2000 imposes more restrictions though—you can't use function keys alone or in combination with [Shift]. [Alt] needs to be part of your key combination.

Once you have closed all windows by clicking OK, your new keyboard shortcut is activated. Whenever you need to mark a line in the editor, just press your new shortcut key(s)!

Caution

Always make sure your editor window is in the front and receives the keyboard inputs. Your line-numbering script sends cursor control codes to the window in front no matter which window actually is receiving the cursor control codes.

Your line-marking script is now automatically invoked and asks for the line number you're interested in. Then, it can "remote-control" the Editor and mark the line.

Undocumented

Unfortunately, Windows does not check for duplicate keyboard shortcuts. This means that if you program the same keyboard shortcuts to do different things, the results will be unpredictable because Windows will choose the function at random. Chapter 9 shows you ways to list all the keyboard shortcuts and their definitions, and to resolve duplicate entries as well. Also, Windows doesn't protect the built-in Windows keyboard shortcuts. So, if you assign [F1] as a shortcut key to your own shortcut, it will no longer open up the Windows help system. And there's another thing to notice—keyboard shortcuts can get lost when you move shortcut files that contain those keyboard shortcuts. Only after a system restart will those shortcuts work again.

Canceling run-away scripts

Scripts run invisibly in the background, and if your script doesn't work the way you expected it to work, you might not immediately realize it. Chances are it's caught in some endless loop, which will run forever and tie up valuable system resources until the next time you reboot your machine.

But you don't have to wait that long, or reboot your computer every time there's a problem. To stop a script anytime, open the task list and end the scripting process manually. Here's how to do this, depending on your operating system.

On Windows 9.x, press [Ctrl]+[Alt]+[Del] simultaneously. Now you'll get a list of all the running applications. Any running script will appear as "WScript.exe" and can easily be kicked out of memory using the End Task button.

On Windows NT/2000, [Ctrl]+[Alt]+[Del] doesn't open the task list directly. You first need to click the Task List button. Next, click the Processes tab. Now you can cancel any running "WScript.exe" process.

Undocumented

If you suspect your script contains errors, you can always use a timeout, because if time is up, your script will end no matter what. To set a general timeout for all scripts, open the Start menu and choose Run. Then, enter WSCRIPT. That said, it's not always a good idea to specify a general timeout. Some scripts may run without a hitch but will still need a longer time for execution. Therefore, a better way is to tackle each script separately. Right-click the script icon and choose Properties. Next, click the Script tab and specify an individual timeout setting. It will apply to this script only.

Invoking the Script Debugger

Complex scripts are not always easy to understand. When the Scripting Host pops up its error message, it can be almost impossible to guess what caused the error. Logical errors are even trickier because they aren't caused by typos or wrong syntax, so the Scripting Host never complains. Still, if there are design flaws, the script might just take the wrong action.

Secret

The Microsoft Script Debugger is a great help for this problem. Although this program was originally developed to display script errors inside of Web pages, it also works with stand-alone local scripts and allows you to step through a script line by line. This way, it's easy to discover the true logical structure, and you can check variable contents after each step to see if the script does what you think it should.

Before you can use the Script Debugger, you need to install it as outlined in the Preface. Always make sure to install the right version of the Script Debugger (there are versions for Windows 9.x and versions for Windows NT). Also, make sure you install the correct language version.

In previous versions of the Scripting Host, the Script Debugger was invoked automatically whenever the Scripting Host encountered a problem. The Scripting Host 2.0 doesn't do this anymore, and for good reason — Microsoft wanted to prevent the complex Script Debugger from popping up in front of an innocent user, probably frightening him or her to death. Now the Script Debugger only takes over when you as a developer explicitly ask for it.

Secret

There's no way to invoke the Script Debugger directly. After all, it was developed as an extension to the Internet Explorer. To load a script into the Debugger, you need insider information in order to call the Scripting Host with a secret option (see Figure 1-13). Option //D enables the debug mode so that whenever the Scripting Host encounters a problem, it will call the Script Debugger. Option //X loads the script into the Script Debugger and waits for you to execute the script. To see all the hidden Scripting Host options, just select Run from the Start menu and enter **WSCRIPT /?**. Then hit [Enter].

```
Windows Script Host                                              ☒

 ⓘ    Usage: WScript scriptname.extension [option...] [arguments...]

      Options:
      //B             Batch mode: Suppresses script errors and
      prompts from displaying
      //D             Enable Active Debugging
      //E:engine      Use engine for executing script
      //H:CScript     Changes the default script host to
      CScript.exe
      //H:WScript     Changes the default script host to
      WScript.exe (default)
      //I             Interactive mode (default, opposite of //B)
      //Job:xxxx      Execute a WS job
      //Logo          Display logo (default)
      //Nologo        Prevent logo display: No banner will be
      shown at execution time
      //S             Save current command line options for this
      user
      //T:nn          Time out in seconds:  Maximum time a script
      is permitted to run
      //X             Execute script in debugger

                        [    OK    ]
```

Figure 1-13: Take a look at the secret options you can use to launch script files.

Obviously, it's no fun to launch a script with the complicated WSCRIPT command because you'd need to specify the exact path to the script. Don't worry; there's a much easier way. Just write a script that either launches other scripts in debug mode or loads them into the debugger for step-by-step execution (see Figure 1-14). The following script utilizes the new WSH 2.0 drag-and-drop capabilities.

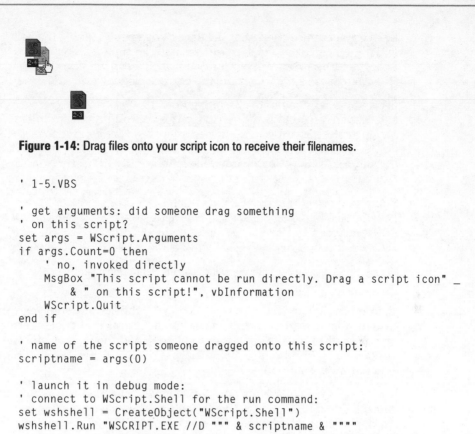

Figure 1-14: Drag files onto your script icon to receive their filenames.

```
' 1-5.VBS

' get arguments: did someone drag something
' on this script?
set args = WScript.Arguments
if args.Count=0 then
    ' no, invoked directly
    MsgBox "This script cannot be run directly. Drag a script icon" _
        & " on this script!", vbInformation
    WScript.Quit
end if

' name of the script someone dragged onto this script:
scriptname = args(0)

' launch it in debug mode:
' connect to WScript.Shell for the run command:
set wshshell = CreateObject("WScript.Shell")
wshshell.Run "WSCRIPT.EXE //D """ & scriptname & """"
```

Once you drag a script file onto this script's icon, it will be launched in debug mode. If the script contains no errors, you won't notice the difference. The script will be executed as usual, and the Script Debugger will remain hidden. If, however, your Script does contain an error, the Script Debugger will pop up and mark the line with the error.

The Script Debugger is an optional add-on—you can only use it if you have installed the software. On Windows 2000 systems, the script debugger is included on the Win2000 CD-ROM (see Figure 1-15). Just open Control Panel, open Add/Remove Programs, and choose Add/Remove Windows Components. Next, check the Script Debugger entry in the list. On any other Windows system, you should install the Script Debugger manually, as outlined in the Preface.

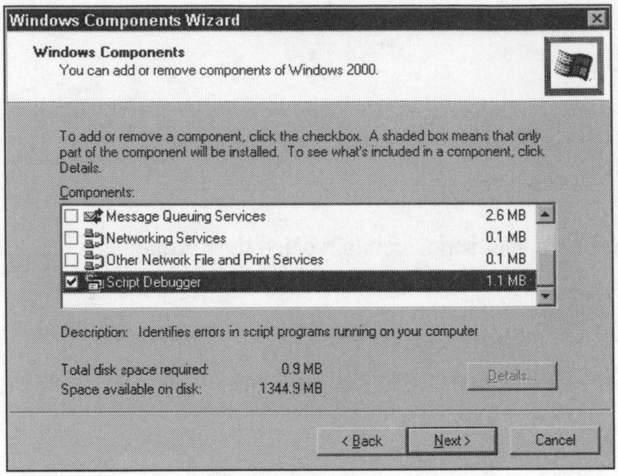

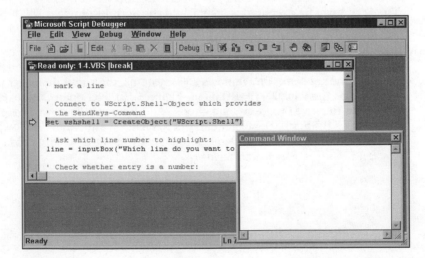

Figure 1-15: Windows 2000 already includes the Script Debugger.

Before I show you what else you can do with the Script Debugger, you should also be able to load innocent scripts into it. Scripts that contain errors are "dead" by the time the error is encountered, and though you still can examine the last variable contents, you no longer are able to step through the script to find out what went wrong.

So, in order to load scripts into the Debugger, change the previous script and replace the option //D with the option //X. Then save the changes. From now on, any script you drag onto the script icon will be loaded into the Debugger (see Figure 1-16). The first executable script line will be marked, and the Debugger will then wait for you to decide what should happen next.

Figure 1-16: Execute scripts line by line and view their internal mechanics.

Adding debugging commands into your context menus

As an alternative, you can launch the following script. It will place two new commands into the context menu of your .vbs script files—Debug and Monitor. Debug starts the Debugger right away so you can start executing your script line by line. Monitor's only job is to alert the Debugger. It remains hidden and pops up only when an error or breakpoint (stop-command) is encountered.

```
' 1-6.VBS

set wshshell = CreateObject("WScript.Shell")
vbsfile = wshshell.RegRead("HKCR\.vbs\")
master = "HKCR\" & vbsfile & "\shell\"

wshshell.RegWrite master & "debug\", "&Debug"
wshshell.RegWrite master & "debug\command\", "wscript.exe //X ""%L"""

wshshell.RegWrite master & "check\", "&Monitor"
wshshell.RegWrite master & "check\command\", "wscript.exe //D ""%L"""

MsgBox "Debugging Command Setup Successful"
```

Take a look at Chapter 14 to find out how the script did its magic.

Secret

The //X and //D options are supported by WSH 2.0 only. Make sure you updated your WSH as outlined in the Preface. In addition, debugging requires the Internet Explorer Script Debugger to be installed. Remember, Microsoft has released two different Debugger versions—one for Windows 9.x and another one for Windows NT—so if the Debugger won't debug your scripts, you may have installed the wrong Debugger version. Windows 2000 already includes the Debugger. It may still need to be installed using the Control Panel Add/Remove Software module.

Executing Scripts Line by Line

Once a script is loaded by the Debugger, you'll find all the important commands inside of the Debug menu. [F5] can run the script, but unless there's an error, this option will take control out of your hands because you won't have a way to stop the script and return control to the Debugger. A better choice is [F8], because it lets you execute line by line, returning control to the Debugger immediately.

[Shift]+[F8] is a good choice if you want to execute entire procedures without having to step through all the lines. The Debugger regains control once the procedure is completed.

Tip

All of these commands will only work if the main Debugger window has the focus. If in doubt, click its title bar. The line marked is the script line that will be executed next. The marked line hasn't been executed yet.

Stepping through a script can give you valuable information about which paths a script follows and which lines and procedures are called in which order. It does not reveal much of the internal script mechanics, though.

So, whenever the Debugger regains control, it's a good idea to examine the contents of key variables to see if everything runs the way you expect it to. Examining the internal script state is possible with the help of the Command Window. If it's not visible right away, then launch it from the View menu.

The command window is your direct connection to the script. Whatever you enter here is executed in the global script context. For example, to see which value is stored inside of a variable, just display the variable's contents using a dialog box. In the command window, enter:

```
MsgBox variablename
```

You can also output the results directly into the command window:

```
? variablename
```

The other way around works equally well: If for any reason you need to change the content of a variable, just assign the new value:

```
variablename = "new content"
```

You can even call procedures directly: Just enter the command line as you would from inside of your script.

Undocumented

The command window can only execute one line of code. Still, you are able to loop through variable arrays or do other things that involve more than one command. Just use a colon to separate individual commands. For example, to display all the character codes from 32 to 255, enter the following line inside of your command window:

for x=32 to 255: ? chr(x):next

To clear the entire command window, press [Ctrl]+[End], then [Ctrl]+[Shift]+[Home], then [Del].

Tip

The command window is an individual window that appears separate from the Debugger. Once the command window has the input focus, you cannot use the Debugger's keyboard shortcuts. Click inside the Debugger window first to give it back the focus.

Repairing script errors

The Script Debugger is a great tool to help you understand the mechanics of complex scripts and to find errors quickly. It is not a tool to correct errors, however. The Debugger always opens the script as a read-only file. You can't change the script inside of the Debugger.

So, to correct scripts, you need to exit the Debugger and open your script file in the editor. Always change scripts in the place you originally developed them.

Undocumented

The Debugger ties itself into the message chain and is displayed before the Scripting Host has any chance to display an error message. So, to find out why the Debugger displays an error, ask for the error description. In the Debuggers' command window, enter **err.description**. But, it's important to note that when you close the Debugger, you only close this tool, not the script. So, if the script isn't finished, it will continue to run, or if there is an error, the Scripting Host will display its usual error message. To prevent this from happening, stop the script in the command window before closing the Debugger, by entering **wscript.quit**. If you just want to prevent the error message from being displayed, enter **err.clear**.

When the Debugger stops answering

The Debugger's command window only works while the Debugger waits for you to take any action. During script execution, the Debugger won't respond to any of the commands entered in the command window.

The same is true once a script is done: No line is marked inside of the Debugger window anymore, and no command is available from the Debug menu. Close the Debugger. You are done.

Setting breakpoints

In large scripts, it may not be easy to examine the interesting parts of a script. Executing a script with [F5] runs the script completely until it ends, and stepping through a hundred script lines with [F8] until the interesting script part is reached is no great solution either.

This is where breakpoints come into play. Breakpoints act like errors except they do not raise an error condition. The script is still working perfectly. The breakpoint only returns control to the Debugger, so you have the option of examining variables or continuing with step-by-step execution.

Unfortunately, the built-in breakpoint mechanism of the Script Debugger doesn't work with your scripts. The Debugger just ignores those breakpoints.

Secret

Still, you can use breakpoints. Just use the secret stop command. Place it into your script code wherever you want the Debugger to stop and ask what to do next. Then invoke the Debugger and run the script with [F5]. The script will stop at the first stop command and return control to the Debugger.

Logging Your Script's Activity

Sometimes, even the Script Debugger won't be helpful. It may not be practical to step through long scripts line by line, and maybe you just don't know where to set a breakpoint because it's just not obvious where things go wrong.

Secret

The new WSH 2.0 finally supports event logging. With a single command, you can write information to a log file and view it after the script has executed. Because Windows 9.x doesn't support log files natively, WSH uses a private file on these machines. On Windows NT/2000, you can write information into the official system log. Windows 2000 Beta before Build 2128 doesn't support WSH event logging yet.

In these cases, the best approach is to make the internal script mechanics more visible. An easy way to do this is by placing MsgBox commands on all the strategic parts. MsgBox then displays the contents of key variables. While this works perfectly well on a small scale, dialog boxes can become extremely annoying when they appear each of the 10,000 times a loop executes. Dialog boxes also only give you a snapshot at one particular point. You cannot see all the messages as a whole.

A much more powerful solution is event logging. LogEvent writes a message into a log. Depending on your operating system, the information will be written either to the system log (Windows NT/2000) or into a private file called WSH.LOG, which resides inside of your windows folder (Windows 9.x).

The following examples assume you use Windows 9.x. On Windows NT/2000, you can only write information that is ill-suited for debugging purposes into the system log. See the next section, "Logging Events on NT," to learn how you can simulate Win9.x behavior on NT/2000 machines.

Undocumented

Although Windows 9.x doesn't support an official log facility, obviously there is the need for logging information. Using a private file as a workaround is nothing really new. Many programs already log events in private files with the log filetype. Just select Search from the Start menu, select Files/Folders, and search for *.LOG on your entire hard drive. You will be amazed how much useful information this search uncovers. To look inside of a log file, just open it with a text editor – it's plain text! For example, each modem connection to the Internet is logged, so your scripts could add the connect time or warn you if there have constantly been errors. For more information about this, see Chapter 20.

Take a look at the following simple script. It will log all the important states to the log file. After the script has completed, you get a detailed report on its activity that allows you a much better understanding of its behavior:

```
' 1-7.VBS

' don't use this on Windows NT/2000 as it
' writes to the system log.
set wshshell = CreateObject("WScript.Shell")
debugging=true

LogIt "Script has started."

LogIt "Loop is entered."

for x=1 to 10
    LogIt "Variable x: " & x
next
```

```
LogIt "Loop is done."

MsgBox "Done!"
LogIt "Script is done."

sub LogIt(text)
    If not debugging then exit sub
    wshshell.LogEvent 4, text
end sub
```

To be able to use event logging, your script needs to set up a connection to the `Wscript.Shell` object first because this object provides the `LogEvent` command.

Note that this script uses a self-defined procedure called `LogIt` to write information to the log. Although you could always use `LogEvent` directly, this procedure makes life much easier: It saves a lot of typing, as it automatically supplies the right arguments to `LogEvent`. Also, logging can now be controlled by the variable `debugging`: Only if this variable is set to true will the `LogIt` procedure write debug information to the disk. This way, you can turn debugging on only when needed, and turn it off while things run smoothly.

Note also that you could not name your self-defined procedure `Log`, as this is a reserved word. `Log` already refers to a mathematical function and may not be used for other things.

To view the log on Windows 9.x, you open the Windows folder, locate `WSH.LOG`, and open it in the text editor. Because you will probably need log files many times during script development, a much easier solution is the following script, which you can place inside your Start menu to assign a key shortcut:

```
' 1-8.VBS

' connect to WScript.Shell to find out the
' path to the windows folder and get access
' to the run command:
set wshshell = CreateObject("WScript.Shell")

' connect to Scripting.FileSystemObject for
' all the file system commands:
set fs = CreateObject("Scripting.FileSystemObject")

' find out the name of the windows folder:
windir = wshshell.ExpandEnvironmentStrings("%WINDIR%")

' this is the name of the log file:
logfile = windir & "\wsh.log"

' does it exist?
if fs.FileExists(logfile) then
    ' yes, display content in editor and wait
    wait = wshshell.Run("NOTEPAD.EXE " & logfile,,true)
    ' after the editor is closed, ask if file should
```

```
            ' be deleted:
            answer = MsgBox("Do you want to keep the log file?", vbYesNo)
            if answer = vbNo then
                ' delete it, no matter what:
                fs.DeleteFile logfile, true
            end if
        else
            ' no log file found:
            MsgBox "There is currently no log file available.", vbInformation
        end if
```

VBS automatically locates the log file and opens it using the editor. Once you close the editor, the script asks whether you want to keep the log. This is important to keep things simple.

Undocumented

The Scripting Host always appends new information to the log file, so if you don't delete it regularly, it constantly grows and becomes confusing. However, not deleting the log file can be a good idea to directly compare the results of two script runs after you make some alterations. Delete the log file after you are done with debugging.

Here's your script's log file (see Figure 1-17) — it documents the way your script works pretty well, don't you think?

```
 wsh - Notepad                                              _ □ ×
File  Edit  Format  Help
1/13/2000 4:53:00 PM    Information: Script has started.
1/13/2000 4:53:00 PM    Information: Loop is entered.
1/13/2000 4:53:00 PM    Information: Variable x: 1
1/13/2000 4:53:00 PM    Information: Variable x: 2
1/13/2000 4:53:00 PM    Information: Variable x: 3
1/13/2000 4:53:00 PM    Information: Variable x: 4
1/13/2000 4:53:00 PM    Information: Variable x: 5
1/13/2000 4:53:00 PM    Information: Variable x: 6
1/13/2000 4:53:00 PM    Information: Variable x: 7
1/13/2000 4:53:00 PM    Information: Variable x: 8
1/13/2000 4:53:00 PM    Information: Variable x: 9
1/13/2000 4:53:00 PM    Information: Variable x: 10
1/13/2000 4:53:00 PM    Information: Loop is done.
1/13/2000 4:53:01 PM    Information: Script is done.
```

Figure 1-17: Document your scripts' activities with a log file.

Logging events on NT

On Windows NT/2000, LogEvent always writes information into the official system log. You can view the result with the event viewer tool.

Although there are a number of good reasons to integrate information into the system log, debugging definitely is not one of them. The system log is much too important to be flooded with debugging information. Also, you can retrieve only one piece of information at a time.

To keep debugging information separate and use the same simple viewer script shown in Figure 1-17, just simulate the Windows 9.x behavior on

Windows NT! It's easy; you just need to expand the LogIt procedure just described. The following script enables logging functionality on both Windows 9.x and Windows NT without the LogEvent function, and it also works on any Window 2000 beta versions. Use script 1-9.VBS to look at the logging information.

```
' 1-9.VBS

set wshshell = CreateObject("WScript.Shell")
set fs = CreateObject("Scripting.FileSystemObject")
windir = wshshell.ExpandEnvironmentStrings("%WINDIR%")
logfile = windir & "\wsh.log"
debugging = true

LogIt "Script has started."

LogIt "Loop is entered."

for x=1 to 10
    LogIt "Variable x: " & x
next

LogIt "Loop is done."

MsgBox "Done!"
LogIt "Script is done."


sub LogIt(text)
    if not debugging then exit sub
    set output = fs.OpenTextFile(logfile, 8, true, -2)
    output.WriteLine now() & vbTab & "Information: " & text
    output.close
end sub
```

You will find a detailed description of OpenTextFile in Chapter 7.

Tip　You could integrate the CreateObject lines and the definition of the logfile path name into your procedure to better capsulate it. However, this would cost additional CPU time, because each time you call LogIt, all of these lines have to be executed again.

Choosing the kind of log entry

Each entry in the log file starts with a time stamp, followed by the word "Information." The time stamp obviously helps you see how much time was needed to execute between the steps. The word "Information" serves a different purpose, helping to structure the information you log.

If you use the original LogEvent function, you can choose the type of entry. Script 1-9.vbs uses the code 4 to insert plain information. To better structure the information, you can choose any of the codes shown in Table 1-1.

Table 1-1   Information Categories Available for Logging

Code	Type of Information
0	Success
1	Error
2	Warning
4	Information
8	Audit_Success
16	Audit_Failure

If you'd rather stick to the self-defined log function, you can insert any information. You are not bound to these predetermined categories.

Handling Errors Yourself

Usually, the Windows Scripting Host takes care of all errors. Once an error happens, it stops the script and displays its error message. This is good practice, as errors are handled automatically.

Obviously, error messages should only pop up during script development. Ready-to-use scripts should not confront the user with any errors whatsoever. So, one of the tasks to perform during script development is thorough testing and a technique called error prevention.

Errors can occur in two different contexts. One, you may have misspelled a command. You should detect this error during testing and correct it. Two, your script may encounter an environment in which it can't function correctly. For example, you asked the user to type in a number, but instead the user typed in some words. Or, your script tries to save a file, but that file already exists. These errors are much harder to detect because they only happen in certain circumstances. You won't always be able to foresee these circumstances during script testing.

Preventing errors from happening

To prevent errors from happening in the first place, your script should test all conditions that are not absolutely predetermined. If you ask for a number and your script expects to process a numeric value, then first check whether the user really entered a numeric value:

```
' 1-10.VBS

number = InputBox("Please enter a number!")
if isNumeric(number) then
    MsgBox "The square of " & number & " is " & number^2
else
    MsgBox "You did not enter a number!"
end if
```

isNumeric checks whether the input really is a number and prevents errors from happening. VBScript contains a whole group of checking functions that all start with "is" and can tell you more about the type of a variable.

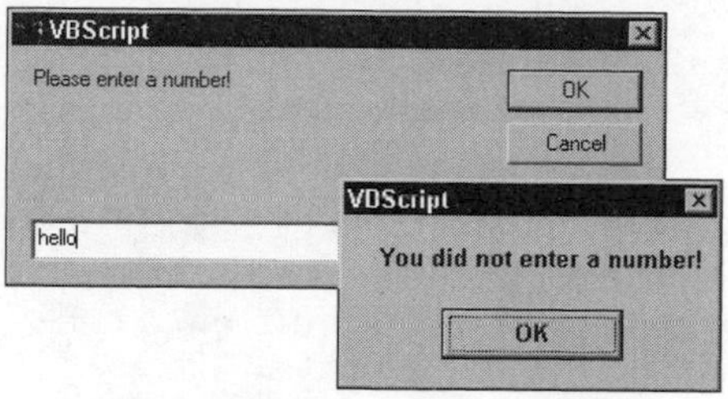

Figure 1-18: Prevent errors by checking the input type.

If, for example, you expect the user to enter a date, make sure the user does so:

```
' 1-11.VBS

mydate = InputBox("Please enter a date!")
if isDate(mydate) then
    MsgBox mydate & " is a " & WeekdayName(Weekday(mydate))
else
    MsgBox "You did not enter a date!"
end if
```

This little script tells you the weekday name of any date (see Figure 1-19). The user can enter the date as either a numeric or as a "real" date: March 18, 1968, is just as much a date as 3/18/68. isDate will sort out any input that cannot be converted to a date.

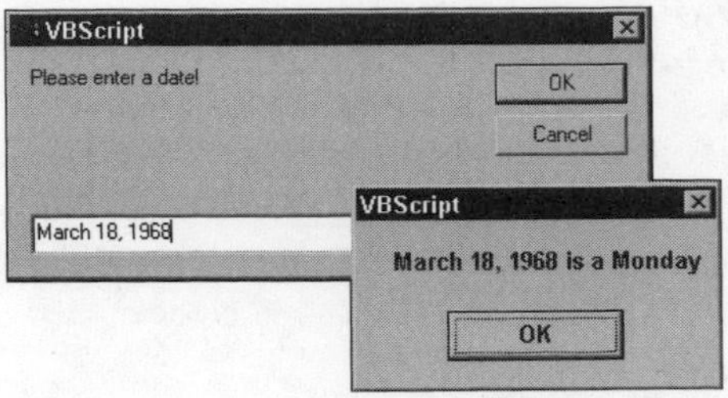

VBScript

Please enter a date!

OK

Cancel

March 18, 1968

VBScript

March 18, 1968 is a Monday

OK

Figure 1-19: Foolproof script checks for date and returns weekday information.

Likewise, in the file system, check whether files or folders already exist. The following script counts the number of files in a specific folder only if this folder really exists:

```
' 1-12.VBS

set fs = CreateObject("Scripting.FileSystemObject")
folder = InputBox("Enter the path to a folder!", "Folder", "C:\")
if fs.folderExists(folder) then
    set handle = fs.GetFolder(folder)
    filecount = handle.files.count
    MsgBox "The folder contains " & filecount & " files!"
else
    MsgBox "The folder " & folder & " does not exist!"
end if
```

You will find all the file system commands in Part II of this book.

Undocumented

The old Scripting Host 1.0 comes with a buggy `FileSystemObject`. It does not support the `Count` property and will raise an error instead. Always update to the corrected version as outlined in the Preface.

Dealing with unpredictable errors

Not all errors can be prevented beforehand, although you should make every effort to do so. Some functions just fail under certain circumstances. You cannot always predict failure.

Undocumented

For example, one of the new and undocumented functions in the `File-SystemObject` is `getFileVersion`. This function finds out the version of a file if version information is available. Should the examined file just not be version-tagged, `getFileVersion` raises an error, halting your script. Microsoft has fixed this odd behavior on Windows 2000 systems, and there will probably soon be an updated WSH for older Windows versions, too.

In these rare circumstances, it makes sense to turn off the built-in error handling. Once you do this, no error will pop up anymore, and your script will just ignore commands that cause errors.

Caution

Although this sounds appealing, it is, in fact, very dangerous. You no longer know that errors happen, and liberal use of this technique can result in scripts getting completely out of control. If, for example, a script is designed to erase empty folders and you turn off error handling, then an old version of the Scripting Host would cause an error once your script checked the number of files inside of a folder using `Count`. Because you turned off error handling, this error would never show up, and your script would assume all folders to be empty. As you can imagine, this script would free a lot of space, an unwelcome result.

Turning off error handling the smart way

Still, you can safely turn off error handling. Just be careful to stick to the following guidelines:

- Never turn off error handling in the main body of your script. Doing so would turn off error handling altogether. Instead, manually put the parts of your script that should be error-handled inside of procedures, and turn off error handling only inside of these procedures.

- Always check manually whether an error occurred. If an error was detected, take appropriate measures. For example, end your script gracefully. Don't just ignore errors.

- Never turn off error handling during script development! You will miss vital error messages and be left wondering why your script just won't do what it is supposed to.

- Turn error handling back on as soon as possible.

The following script illustrates both why it may be necessary to turn off error handling and how it is done in a safe way. The script "wraps" the `getFileVersion` function and deals with errors raised by files that do not contain any file version information.

Undocumented

The `GetFileVersion` function is already fixed in some WSH versions. Here, `GetFileVersion` doesn't raise an error. Instead, it returns a blank string if the file in question doesn't contain version information.

```
' 1-13.VBS

set wshshell = CreateObject("WScript.Shell")
' get windows folder:
windir = wshshell.ExpandEnvironmentStrings("%WINDIR%")

' read version of the explorer:
MsgBox "Explorer-Version: " & GetVersion(windir & "\EXPLORER.EXE")

' try to read a version that does not exist:
MsgBox "AUTOEXEC.BAT-Version: " & GetVersion("C:\autoexec.bat")
```

```
function GetVersion(path)
    set fs = CreateObject("Scripting.FileSystemObject")
    ' turn off error handling:
    on error resume next

    ' execute the problematic function
    GetVersion = fs.getFileVersion(path)

    ' check whether there was an error:
    if not err.Number=0 then
        ' error occurred
        cause = err.description
        if cause="" then
            cause = "unknown error, code: " & err.Number
        end if
        MsgBox "There was an error: " & cause
        ' clear error condition and continue because
        ' this error is not fatal:
        err.clear
        ' return -1: version unknown
        GetVersion = -1
    end if
end function
```

Error handling is turned off once you issue the on error resume next command. Unfortunately, there is no way to launch error-handling procedures automatically once an error occurs. You will always need to check manually.

Undocumented

The new WSH 2.0 finally contains a method to turn the build-in error handling back on. Use the command on error goto 0 to re-enable the built-in error-handling mechanisms. 0 is the only line number you can use. In contrast to other Visual Basic dialects, VBScript can't jump to specific line numbers or procedure names when errors occur. Line number 0 — which doesn't really exist — instructs VBScript to jump to its internal error handler.

After the script uses the problematic getFileVersion function, it checks whether an error occurred. Err.Number returns zero if no error was detected; otherwise, it returns the error number. If an error occurred, you can do a number of things: Depending on the nature of the error, you can shut down the script using Wscript.Quit, display the error as an informal message as above, or just silently go over the error if it's not important to script execution. In the previous example, you could, for instance, return a version of –1 for all files that cause an error, and skip any error message (see Figure 1-20).

Chapter 2

VBScript Guerilla Session

In This Chapter

▶ Get input and showing results

▶ Pass arguments to scripts

▶ Use drag-and-drop operations

▶ Write and reading in the DOS console window

▶ Create your personal VBScript command line interpreter

▶ Examine VBScript variable types

▶ Create random numbers

▶ Encrypt and decrypting files

▶ Create scripts that make decisions

▶ Loop and repeat steps

▶ Create functions and procedures

▶ Use dictionaries to look up key-value-pairs

▶ Declare variables explicitly to get error information

▶ Build loops

▶ Design functions and procedures

How can you talk to Windows? Scripts are your messengers, carrying commands directly to the CPU. So all you need is a language in which to "wrap" your wishes.

Luckily, there is a script language that is very similar to plain English. In contrast to many common programming languages, VBScript is both easy to learn and powerful. It doesn't emphasize strange symbols or hard-to-remember structures. Instead, it's friendly, fault-tolerant, and fun to use.

Tip

The Scripting Host is not tied to VBScript. If you feel more comfortable using JavaScript, then you can use this language too. In fact, the Scripting Host can easily be extended by third-party developers to support other languages like REXX or PerlScript, among others. Throughout this book, however, I concentrate on VBScript, both because it's gained the most benefits during the last update and because it's much easier to use than JavaScript. In addition, VBScript is a subset of Visual Basic, so getting comfortable with VBScript makes it easy for you to use the free Visual Basic Control Creation Edition to design your own COM objects (as shown in Chapter 4).

In this chapter, you will take a ride in the fast lane and discover everything you need to fully utilize VBScript. This is the foundation of everything to come later in this book, so you may want to come back to this chapter whenever you are in doubt about how to use a certain function.

Getting Input and Showing Results

Microsoft targets scripts primarily as background workers or parts of Web pages. This is why the Scripting Host lacks its own output window and only offers very limited support for interaction with the user.

However, the Scripting Host can do much more for you. You can develop scripts that ask questions and display results interactively — a perfect way to build little applications that can solve your problems very specifically.

In this chapter, you will see the appropriate commands at work. In Chapters 5 and 6, you will discover secret methods to supply your scripts with an output window so scripts can display results just as any regular program would do. Chapter 4 reveals methods to add any of the functions missing in the standard set of commands. You also might want to browse through Chapter 18: Here, you will see the brand-new functions integrated in WSH 2.0 that allow scripts to act like DOS or UNIX commands.

Asking questions

Before your script can start making life easier for you, it needs to ask questions. You can either prompt the user for the information required, or you can use command-line arguments to supply the required information automatically.

Prompting for information

Prompting for information is easy: Just use `InputBox` (see Figure 2-1). This function pops up a dialog box, and users can happily enter whatever you asked them to.

```
' 2-1.VBS

ask = "Hey, what's your name?"
title = "Who are you?"
default = "??"

answer = InputBox(ask, title, default)

MsgBox "Welcome " & answer & "!"
```

You only need to supply a question; the rest of the arguments are optional. Leaving out the other arguments results in an empty dialog box.

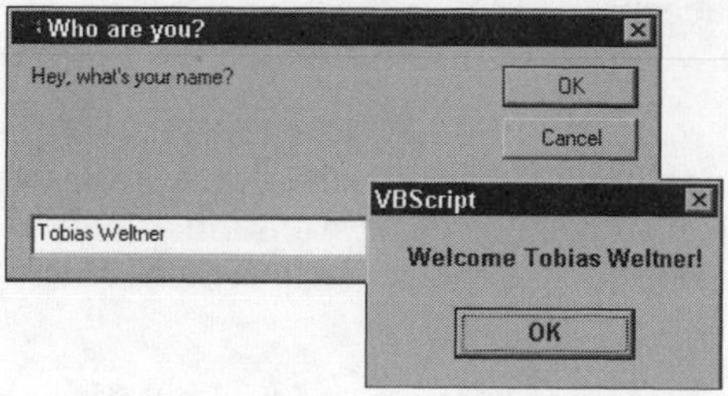

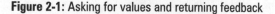

Figure 2-1: Asking for values and returning feedback

Did you notice the Cancel button on the dialog box? It doesn't seem to work at first, because clicking Cancel will just pass an empty text string. The script isn't canceled, however.

Undocumented

InputBox doesn't supply an empty string when you click Cancel. Instead, it reports an "empty" value. It's the MsgBox function that tries to deal with this empty value and converts it to an empty string. As it turns out, some WSH versions seem to contain a bug—they report an "Out Of Memory" error if you leave the InputBox dialog box empty. Always make sure you have installed the latest WSH version as outlined in the Preface.

To make Cancel work, just check whether InputBox returned an empty value. Empty values are different from empty strings. You can identify empty values with the constant vbEmpty. Have a look:

```
' 2-2.VBS

ask = "Hey, what's your name?"
title = "Who are you?"

answer = InputBox(ask, title)
if answer = vbEmpty then
    MsgBox "You want to cancel? Fine!"
    WScript.Quit
elseif answer = "" then
    MsgBox "You want to stay incognito, all right with me..."
else
    MsgBox "Welcome " & answer & "!"
end if
```

This script is smart enough to detect whether the user supplied a name, left the input box empty, or hit Cancel (see Figure 2-2).

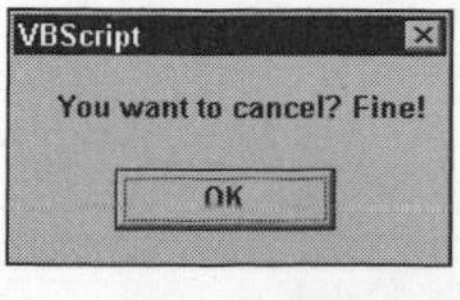

Figure 2-2: Responding to the InputBox Cancel request

Checking information type

Prompting for information doesn't necessarily mean you'll get it. You can ask politely, because InputBox accepts anything the user types in. Therefore, after asking for information, you should check the entered information to make sure it is valid.

VBScript has a whole armada of functions that can do the job. They all start with "is" and will return true if the pieces of information are of the desired type. In Chapter 1, you saw an example that checks for a date and returns the weekday name.

Once you've checked the entered information and find out it's of the wrong kind, you can do either of two things — either stop the script and complain with an error message, or inform the user that he or she did something bad, and give him or her another chance.

The following script shows how to do this. It asks for some information, checks the type of information, and keeps on asking until the user either enters the right information or clicks Cancel.

```
' 2-3.VBS

' asking for a date
ask = "What's your birthday?"
title = "Let's see how old you are!"

' start a loop:
do
    birthday = InputBox(ask, title)
    ' check whether the user wants to quit:
    if isEmpty(birthday) then
        MsgBox "Hey! You could always lie to me to hide " _
        & " your age! But ok, I quit!"
        WScript.Quit
    elseif not isDate(birthday) then
        ' check whether birthday is really a date!
        ' complain and give another chance:
        MsgBox "You didn't enter a valid date! Try again!"
    end if

' loop until a valid date was retrieved
loop until isDate(birthday)


' at this point, we have a valid date, good!
' do some fun calculations:

age_in_days = DateDiff("d", birthday, date)
age_in_months = DateDiff("m", birthday, date)
age_in_years = DateDiff("yyyy", birthday, date)
day_born = WeekdayName(Weekday(birthday))
```

```
' calculate this year's birthday
date_day = Day(birthday)
date_month = Month(birthday)
' use current year:
date_year = Year(date)

this_years_birthday = DateSerial(date_year, date_month, date_day)

' use Abs to convert to positive numbers in case the birthday's
' already over:
days_to_birthday = Abs(DateDiff("d", date, this_years_birthday))
day_celebrating = WeekdayName(Weekday(this_years_birthday))

' already over?
if this_years_birthday<date then
    message = "you celebrated your birthday " & days_to_birthday _
& " days ago"
elseif this_years_birthday = date then
    message = "Happy Birthday!!!"
else
    message = days_to_birthday & " days to go!"
end if

' output Information

msg = "This is your birthday analysis:" & vbCr
msg = msg + "You are born on " & birthday & vbCr
msg = msg + "You are " & age_in_years & " yrs old. That's" & vbCr
msg = msg & age_in_months & " months or " & age_in_days _
& " days!" & vbCr
msg = msg + "You were born on a " & day_born & vbCr
msg = msg + "This year's birthday is on " & this_years_birthday & vbCr
msg = msg + "It's a " & day_celebrating & vbCr
msg = msg + message

MsgBox msg
```

For now, concentrate on the first part of the script. Here, a loop block keeps on asking for a date until the user either supplies it or cancels. You can easily adjust this part to your needs and ask for all kinds of information (see Figure 2-3).

Tip

Whenever you ask questions in a loop, always supply a way to cancel. The user may be unable to supply the correct answer, so you better provide a way out. In general, loops always need an exit condition. Otherwise, they'll run forever.

Did you notice that this loop has two exit conditions? The loop will exit whenever isDate finds a valid date. The loop will also exit when the user hits Cancel. In this case, isEmpty detects an empty value and exits the entire script: Wscript.Quit does the job.

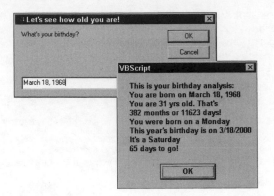

Figure 2-3: Use VBScript date functions to calculate interesting information.

Undocumented

Empty variables can be checked with `isEmpty` or compared against `vbEmpty` (the prototype of an empty variable). Either way works equally well, and in either case, an empty variable is not equal to an empty text string.

The second part shows how the date could be utilized. VBScript contains a rich set of date and time functions. In this example, they are used to calculate all kinds of birthday statistics. In reality, though, they can just as easily be used to run disk tools every Wednesday or to check how long it's been since you last defragmented your hard drive.

You won't find a detailed discussion of these time and date functions in this book. Instead, refer to a VBScript entry-level book. Or even simpler, install the VBScript online documentation, which you'll find on the companion CD (`msrelated\vbsdoc.exe`).

Asking simple yes-or-no questions

In many cases, you don't need text input. You just need a simple Yes-or-No decision. VBScript contains a very versatile tool that allows you to ask all kinds of simple questions. It's called MsgBox—you've already used this function to display plain text information.

Secret

You can call a function using parentheses, and it will return a value. If you call a function as a procedure, without using parentheses, it will not return a value. MsgBox is a function. When you use it as a procedure, it will simply output information. If you want to base decisions on MsgBox dialog boxes, then use it as a function, and check which value MsgBox returned.

The easiest way to call `MsgBox` as a function looks like this:

```
result = MsgBox("Do you agree?")
```

The resulting dialog box wouldn't leave much room for decision-making though, as the standard dialog box only includes an OK button.

This is where the second (and optional) parameter comes into play. Use it to generate all the important buttons you need:

VbOkOnly/0	**OK**
VbOKCancel/1	**OK, Cancel**
VbAbortRetryIgnore/2	**Abort, Retry, Ignore**
VbYesNoCancel/3	**Yes, No, Cancel**
VbYesNo/4	**Yes, No**
VbRetryCancel/5	**Retry, Cancel**

The VBScript constants already indicate which buttons they show. And likewise, you can use named constants to evaluate the result that MsgBox delivers. Have a look:

```
' 2-4.VBS

result = MsgBox("Do you want to continue?", vbYesNo)

if result = vbYes then
    MsgBox "We'll continue..."
else
    MsgBox "OK, enough..."
end if
```

Note the different use of MsgBox: In the first line, it's used as a function and delivers a result. In the rest of the script, MsgBox is called as a procedure without parentheses, to just output information.

Because you did not specify a button constant here, the default 0 is assumed, showing an OK button.

Tip
You always need to decide whether you want to use a function with parentheses, or whether you want to use it as a procedure. Calling a function without reading its return value is okay as long as you eliminate the parentheses. As an alternative, use the command call to explicitly call the function as a procedure. MsgBox "Hello!", retval=MsgBox("Hello!"), and call MsgBox("Hello!") are all fine. MsgBox("Hello!") or retval=MsgBox "Hello!" are not.

These built-in constants make it easy to handle MsgBox results. If you display a dialog box of type vbAbortRetryIgnore, then you know that the result is vbAbort, vbRetry, or vbIgnore.

Undocumented
You can also choose a button to be *preselected*. This button is then chosen if the user hits [Enter]. Just add one of the following constants: vbDefaultButton1, vbDefaultButton2, or vbDefaultButton3.

To emphasize the severity of your dialog box message, you can also display one of the four system state icons. To display an icon, add its constant to the other constants you want to use:

vbInformation	Information-Symbol
vbQuestion	Question mark
vbExclamation	Warning-Sign
vbCritical	Highest level of alert

Undocumented

MsgBox dialog windows behave just like regular windows. If they're buried under other windows, and your script either doesn't have the initial focus or has lost it to some other program, MsgBox dialog boxes might not pop up at all. Instead, they may just announce their presence by a flashing button in the task bar. To prevent a dialog box from being hidden, add the special constant vbSystemModal to your other constants. That way, the box will always be above the other windows and stay there until the question is answered.

You can even write text in the dialog box title bar. MsgBox will always display VBScript in front of your text. Specify the title as the third parameter:

```
result = MsgBox("Continue?", vbYesNo+vbQuestion, "What now?")
```

Asking questions with a time-out

Asking questions using MsgBox always halts your script. Scripts are modal and can only do one thing at a time. So unless the user answers the question, your script doesn't do a thing. It will patiently wait for years if it has to.

This limitation is fine for user-attended script execution, but it can be devastating if you also want to be able to run your script unattended. Here, the Popup function can help. Popup behaves in many aspects like MsgBox's big brother. It's not part of VBScript though — it's provided by the Wscript.Shell object, an integral part of the Scripting Host.

Secret

Popup is a perfect example of a function enhancement. MsgBox suffers from various limitations, so developers designed a new function and placed it into the Wscript.Shell-object. Your scripts can access the new function whenever the regular MsgBox command reaches its limits. Throughout this book, I'll show you much more add-on functionality that's already installed on your system and is just waiting to be discovered. Read Chapter 4 for all of the information necessary to develop extensions like Popup by yourself.

To make Popup work, you first need to have a connection to Wscript.Shell. Next, you need to feed basically the same arguments to Popup that you would feed to MsgBox. Unfortunately, Popup expects the parameters in a different order. It does, however, accept the same vb constants and can display icons just like MsgBox does.

The following script asks a simple question and waits five seconds for a response. If there is no response, the question is revoked, and the script assumes a default (see Figure 2-4). This way, your script runs even if there's nobody around to answer the question. Obviously, this strategy only works if there is a safe default your script can assume.

```
' 2-5.VBS

' get access to WScript.Shell
set wshshell = CreateObject("WScript.Shell")

' ask question and wait 5 seconds for answer:
ask = "Your system needs to restart!"
timeout = 5
title = "Installation complete!"
constants = vbExclamation + vbOkCancel
result = wshshell.Popup(ask, timeout, title, constants)
if result = vbCancel then
    MsgBox "OK, I do not restart the system!"
elseif result = true then
    MsgBox "You did not respond! I could now restart anyway!"
else
    MsgBox "The system could now be restarted!"
end if
```

This example could be part of an installation script asking the user if it is okay to restart the system. If the user doesn't respond, the script could go ahead and restart anyway. In Chapter 24, you'll find the necessary functions to turn this example into a working script and really restart your system.

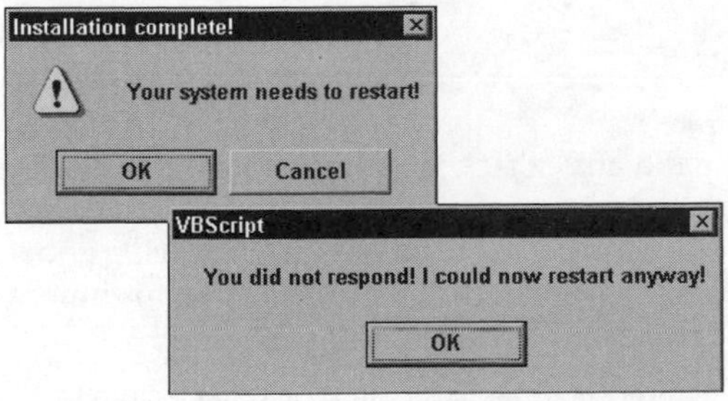

Figure 2-4: Specify a timeout so your script can continue if your question isn't answered.

Popup has other things going for it besides a built-in timeout. Unlike MsgBox, which has a limit of 1,000 characters, Popup displays any number of characters. Popup doesn't show the annoying VBScript in its title bar, and it leaves the entire title bar to your text. Most importantly, the Popup window will always get the focus no matter what — the window always pops up, whereas MsgBox windows will only flash its button in the task bar under certain circumstances.

Undocumented

Passing Arguments to Scripts

Asking for parameters through `InputBox` and `MsgBox` may not always be suitable. You might want to supply the information as command-line parameters, calling your script like a DOS or UNIX utility.

Not interested in command-line arguments? You like the drag-and-drop Windows way? Read on, this part is still right for you! In order to make your scripts drag-and-drop-capable and to place scripts into one of the Windows context menus, you use exactly the same technique.

Dragging files onto your script icon

To make your script recognize any passed arguments, all you need to do is ask for the arguments collection. It's an object that stores all the arguments. Here's a script that shows the general concept:

```
' 2-6.VBS

' get arguments as collection object
set args = WScript.Arguments

' check whether there are any arguments:
if args.Count = 0 then
    ' no arguments
    MsgBox "You called this script directly, no arguments specified!"
else
    for each argument in args
        list = list & argument & vbCr
    next
    MsgBox "Here's the list of arguments:" & vbCr & list
end if
```

This is all you need to make any script arguments-aware. If you launch this script, it won't show any arguments. Try dragging another file's icon onto your script icon (see Figure 2-5). This time, your script will report the name of the dragged file because it was fed to the script as an argument.

Figure 2-5: Drag files onto your script icon to test its drag-and-drop capabilities.

Next, try moving a couple of files onto your script's icon. Hold down [Ctrl] to select more than one file. This time, all the filenames will be reported.

There is a limit to how many arguments a script can read. This limit is based on the maximum number of characters allowed in a path. If your arguments occupy more space, an error will be raised. In addition, drag-and-drop operations are only supported by the new WSH 2.0. Drag-and-drop doesn't work on Windows 2000 beta less than Build 2128.

The arguments collection is the general script interface to arguments passed to the script. Arguments are not only passed by drag-and-drop operations. When placing scripts into the Send to, or one of the context, menus, they will also automatically receive arguments — the name(s) of the objects that invoked the script. You can also specify the arguments manually.

Try the following steps to supply arguments manually:

1. Choose Run from the Start menu and delete the command box contents by pressing [Del].

2. Drag your script icon into the command field. Windows automatically fills in the correct path name.

3. Click in the command box, add a space, and then supply your arguments. Type whatever you like and then press [Enter].

Both the Windows Run command inside the Start menu and the DOS window support an unusual type of drag-and-drop operation: You can drag a file or folder onto them, and Windows automatically fills in the path name. Likewise, both support environment variables. Windows stores the path to the DOS command line interpreter inside of COMSPEC, so calling %COMSPEC% always launches the DOS window. This feature isn't supported on Windows 95.

Once again, your script reports the arguments you specified. However, you may have noticed that spaces divide your arguments. Whenever you use a space, WSH assumes a new argument, and the script places all arguments onto individual lines.

This is a very important concept. In order for your scripts to correctly read arguments that contain spaces — long filenames, for example — you need to place them into quotes.

In everyday situations, the command line use of scripts is impractical because you just can't expect anybody to type in the script's full path name. Chapter 18 shows you a couple of strategies for calling scripts without the need for path names, allowing you to use scripts just as you would use DOS or UNIX commands.

Calling script files directly, either with Run or inside of a DOS box, can be annoying because you need to specify the exact path name. Beginning with Windows 2000, however, script files can act like program files. So if you have a Windows 2000 system, place a script file into the windows folder or any other folder that is part of the PATH environment variable. From that point on, you won't need to specify the path anymore. Windows 2000 is smart enough to find script files automatically as long as they are stored in one of the system folders. You don't even have to specify the file type extension. This technology is very important because it sets the foundation for using scripts as DOS and UNIX command replacements.

Using DOS input and output streams

Thanks to WSH 2.0, your scripts can tie themselves into the input and output streams of a DOS window. They can read what you type in and write to the DOS window — they can act just like any DOS or UNIX command!

This concept is discussed in detail in Chapter 18. Still, I'll give you a little taste right away because the DOS input stream is a powerful alternative to command-line arguments and builds the foundation of important tools you need to better understand VBScript.

Command-line arguments are supplied to the script the moment you launch it. They have a size limit, and once the script starts, you can't change or add anything.

The DOS input stream is different. Information is read in interactively while the script runs, and you can supply as much information as needed. You can literally "talk" to your script while it runs.

Try out the following script:

```
' 2-7.VBS

' get access to input and output stream:
set output = WScript.StdOut
set input = WScript.StdIn


do until input.atEndOfStream
    ' read in lines:
    line = input.ReadLine
    ' exit condition: stop loop once someone enters "exit":
    if lcase(line)="exit" then
        exit do
    else
        ' else echo input in upper case characters:
        output.WriteLine ucase(line)
    end if
loop
```

Don't be surprised if Windows raises an error message once you try to start this script: It uses the DOS input and output streams (see Figure 2-6).

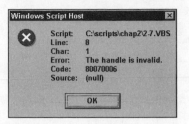

Figure 2-6: Input and output streams are only valid inside DOS windows.

To be able to do that, this script needs to be launched inside DOS. In fact, you need to start this script explicitly with CSCRIPT.EXE, the DOS version of the Scripting Host. You could open a DOS box manually, type in CSCRIPT.EXE, and supply your script's full path name as an argument. However, there's a much easier way. Right-click your script icon and choose Open with Command Prompt (Open With MS-DOS Prompt on Windows 9.x systems). Your script is launched by CSCRIPT.EXE and appears in a DOS box automatically.

This time, no error message pops up. Instead, your script hooks itself into the input stream. Try typing in something. It will be echoed back into the window using the output stream. To prove that the script processed your input, it converts all characters to uppercase.

Type in exit [Enter] to stop the script.

The following script demonstrates how powerful and versatile this concept really is. With only a few changes, it will turn a dull echo script into a fully functional VBScript command-line interpreter. This tool is perfect for trying out small VBScript examples without the need to start a new script file all the time.

Undocumented

In addition, this script demonstrates how to automatically switch to CSCRIPT.EXE. The script detects if accessing StdIn caused an error. If so, the script will launch itself in CSCRIPT.EXE and then quit WSCRIPT.EXE.

```
' 2-8.VBS

' check whether script is run in CSCRIPT (DOS-Environment)
host = WScript.FullName
hostexe = lcase(mid(host, InstrRev(host, "\")+1))
if not hostexe = "cscript.exe" then
    ' error! We run in WSCRIPT, so let's re-launch in CSCRIPT!
    set wshshell = CreateObject("WScript.Shell")
    wshshell.run "CSCRIPT.EXE """ & WScript.ScriptFullName & """"
    'quit
    WScript.Quit
end if

' get access to input and output stream:
```

```
set input = WScript.StdIn
set output = WScript.StdOut

output.Write "> "
do until input.atEndOfStream
    ' read in lines:
    line = input.ReadLine
    ' exit condition: stop loop once someone enters "exit":
    if lcase(line)="exit" then
        exit do
    else
        ' interpret the command:
        ' replace ? with output command
        line = Replace(line, "?", "output.WriteLine")
        ExecuteIt line
        output.Write "> "
    end if
loop

sub ExecuteIt(command)
    ' Execute is a separate procedure because it turns off
    ' build-in error handling
    ' This is necessary to keep the script running even if
    ' invalid commands are entered:
    on error resume next
    ' execute statement:
    ExecuteGlobal command
    ' did an error occur?
    if not err.Number=0 then
        ' yes, report cause:
        output.WriteLine "Error: " & err.description
        err.clear
    end if
end sub
```

You'll probably launch this script frequently to try out the examples provided on the following pages, so try this handy shortcut:

1. Right-click your script icon and choose Create Shortcut. A new shortcut appears.

2. Right-click the new shortcut and choose Properties. Next, click the target field and move to the first character. The target field contains the full path name of your script.

3. To make your link use CSCRIPT.EXE as a host, enter CSCRIPT.EXE and a space, and leave the script path name as an argument. Then click OK.

Tip

Click Change Icon if you want to assign an eye-catching icon to your link. Leave the Filename field empty and press [Enter] to get the default Windows icon selection.

In the future, whenever you want to try out a little VBScript magic, just launch your link. You can also provide it with a handy key shortcut as outlined in Chapter 1.

The scripting host starts inside a DOS window. Now, you can enter any valid VBScript statement, as shown in Figure 2-7. Use ? to print out messages. For example, you could assign a value to a variable:

```
> a="Test" [Enter]
>
```

Next, you could print out this variable:

```
> ? a [Enter]
test
>
```

Wondering what kind of variable type VBScript used to store your text? Find out:

```
> ? TypeName(a) [Enter]
String
>
```

You can even tie commands together using the colon. To find out all of the character codes between 32 and 255, use this line:

```
> for x=32 to 255:list = list & x & "=" & chr(x) & " ":next [Enter]
```

Now it's easy to output the key codes:

```
> MsgBox list [Enter]
> ? list [Enter]
```

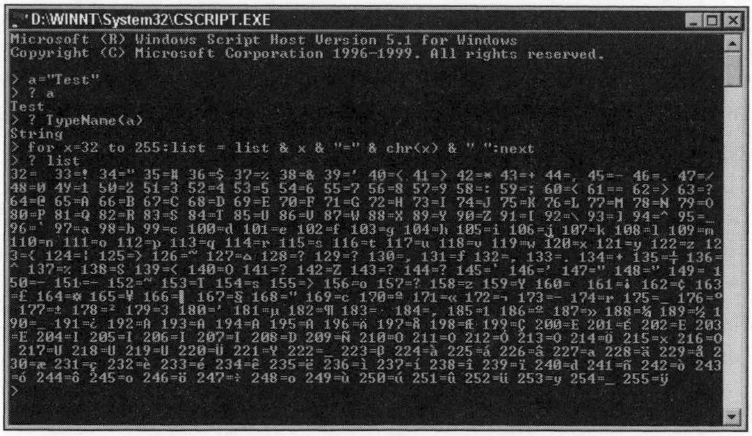

Figure 2-7: Experiment using your homemade VBScript command line interpreter.

The script will even intercept error messages, so causing an error will just display the error message:

```
> MsgBo "Hello!"
Error: Type mismatch
>
```

Once finished, just type in exit [Enter]. This time, the DOS window disappears automatically.

Secret

If you launch a script in a DOS window and the script ends, the DOS window will still be there. It was there in the first place, so why should it disappear? In contrast, if you launch CSCRIPT.EXE directly, you omit the DOS command line interpreter. This time, when your script ends, CSCRIPT ends, and because CSCRIPT opened the DOS window, it will close the window automatically.

The Truth About VBScript Variables

Variables are placeholders for your data. While most programming languages require you to define specific variable types, VBScript is very liberal. It uses only one variable type called *Variant*. This type can store any kind of data — numbers, text, objects, you name it. There's no need to define the variable beforehand. Just use it, and VBScript takes care of the rest.

This liberal concept is very easy to use. Still, there's no single perfect solution, and because VBScript doesn't complain much, it doesn't help much either when trying to find a script error or typo.

For example, if you accidentally misspell a variable name, VBScript just initializes a new variable. It doesn't complain, and you might never get a clue why your script is misbehaving. In the same way, if you assign values to the wrong variable, VBScript won't suspect an error. It just assigns the value. If there were the need to declare variable types, you'd get an error message if the assigned variable type wouldn't match the declared variable type.

Tip

You can force VBScript to accept only declared variables by placing the command option explicitly on top of your script code. Now, variables need to be declared using Dim before they can be used. You will find more information about this at the end of this chapter.

Therefore, VBScript variables are perfect for small and simple scripts. Scripts that go beyond a couple of lines of code, however, need careful planning. The following part will show you how to play it safe.

Finding out the variable subtype

Although Variant variables can store any kind of data, VBScript contains two important functions that help identify what type of data is actually stored inside of a variable. These are TypeName and VarType.

The best way to get accustomed to Variant variables is by playing with them. Playing around is easy enough; just launch your VBScript command line interpreter as described, then assign a value to a variable. For help, see Table 2-1.

```
> a="Hello!" [Enter]
> ? TypeName(a)
String
> ? VarType(a)
8
>
```

TypeName returns a text description of the variable type.

Secret

TypeName will reveal the internal name of the object. In Chapter 3, TypeName helps you to understand the structure of unknown objects.

VarType, in contrast, returns a code that corresponds to one of the Variant subtypes.

Table 2-1   Variable Types and Constant Names

Value	Constant	Description
0	vbEmpty	Uninitialized variable
1	vbNull	No valid data
2	vbInteger	Integer (0-32767)
3	vbLong	Long integer
4	vbSingle	Single-precision floating point number
5	vbDouble	Double-precision floating point number
6	vbCurrency	Currency
7	vbDate	Date
8	vbString	String
9	vbObject	Automation object
10	vbError	Error
11	vbBoolean	Boolean
12	vbVariant	Array of variants
13	vbDataObject	Data-access object
17	vbByte	Byte
8192	vbArray	Array

Try it out! Assign a whole number below 32,768 to a variable and check its type:

```
> a=567 [Enter]
> ? TypeName(a) [Enter]
Integer
>
```

Repeat this example, using a larger number this time:

```
> a=668543 [Enter]
> ? TypeName(a) [Enter]
Long
>
```

Without any declaration, VBScript always automatically chooses the most efficient storage type. You don't need to be aware of the difference between Integer and Long. This is the concept of Variants.

Converting variables

Sometimes, it is necessary to change the type of a variable. For example, if your script finds out how many files are stored in some folder, you might want to output this information to the user. Therefore, you need to transform the numeric value into a text value that you can display.

Again, VBScript does most of the job automatically. The following example reports the number of files in the root folder of drive C:\:

```
' 2-9.VBS

set fs = CreateObject("Scripting.FileSystemObject")
files = fs.GetFolder("C:\").files.count

MsgBox "Variable type: " + TypeName(files)
MsgBox files
' this line will cause an error:
MsgBox "C:\ contains " + files + " files."
```

Launching this script reveals many interesting details:

- First, the script finds out the number of files in the root folder of C:\. It uses GetFolder to get access to the folder, asks for a files collection, and calls Count. By the way, all of the file system functions are covered in detail in Chapter 7.

- The result is a variable of subtype Long. You may be thinking, shouldn't this be Integer? No. To be able to handle a virtually unlimited number of files, Count always uses Long variables. VBScript will choose the most efficient variable subtype only when it assigns variables. In this case, Count assigned the variable, so Count controls the variable subtype.

- MsgBox then outputs the number of files. Although files are of subtype Long, this works perfectly well because MsgBox automatically converts the number to a text.

- The third `MsgBox` command fails however. WSH reports a type mismatch error (see Figure 2-8), and this is the first time you run into variable type conflicts. Your script tried to combine text with a number. This doesn't work. You first have to manually convert the number to text.

Windows Script Host

Script:	C:\scripts\chap2\2-9.VBS
Line:	9
Char:	1
Error:	Type mismatch: '[string: "C:\ contains "]'
Code:	800A000D
Source:	Microsoft VBScript runtime error

OK

Figure 2-8: Sometimes it's necessary to change variable type manually.

To repair the line, you have two options: One, you manually convert the number to text using the appropriate conversion function:

```
MsgBox "C:\ contains " + CStr(files) + " files."
```

`CStr` transforms the variable to text:

```
MsgBox TypeName(CStr(files))
```

Or two, you use another nice VBScript trick: &.

Secret

Many authors use + and & synonymously. Don't do that! + and & are very different. Use + if you want to add together variables of the same or compatible type. You can add texts, or you can add numbers, but you can't mix variable types. In contrast, & adds text and other variable types by automatically converting them to text. The result is always a string variable.

The & operator concatenates variables and produces a text string. It automatically converts variables to subtype `String` as needed:

```
MsgBox "C:\ contains " & files & " files."
```

Using variable conversion functions

Almost all of the conversion functions start with a "C." These are your helper functions to explicitly switch to another variable type:

Table 2-2   VBScript Conversion Functions

Conversion function	Resulting variable type
CBool	Boolean
CByte	Byte
CCur	Currency

Continued

Table 2-2   *(continued)*

Conversion function	Resulting variable type
CDate	Date
CDbl	Double
CInt	Integer
Int	Integer
Fix	Integer
CLng	Long
CSng	Single
CStr	String

Secret

There are three different functions to convert a variable to Integer: CInt, Int and Fix. Although in most documentations, CInt is used, this is dangerous. All three functions behave differently when converting negative numbers. Only Fix limits itself to stripping the decimal places of a number. CInt and Int both automatically round negative numbers to the next lower or next higher integer. This can cause a lot of confusion and errors. Therefore, always use Fix to convert numbers to Integer.

In addition, you can use functions to format a variable:

Table 2-3   Manipulate Variable Content

Function	Description
Abs	Returns absolute number; always positive
Asc	Returns character code of a text character
Chr	Returns character represented by a character code
Hex	Returns hexadecimal format of a number
Oct	Returns octal format of a number
Round	Returns a number that is rounded to a specified number of decimal places
Sgn	Returns a number indicating the sign of a number
FormatNumber	Formats a number displaying a specified number of decimal places
FormatPercent	Formats a number as percentage
FormatCurrency	Formats a number according to the currency settings of the control panel

Using variable arrays

Variable arrays are just groups of variables that can be accessed using an index number. This is especially useful if your script needs to look up information stored in variables.

Variable arrays always need to be declared so that VBScript knows how much storage space it should reserve. You can declare variable arrays using Dim or ReDim.

Secret

VBScript variable arrays always start with index number 0. In contrast to Visual Basic and other programming languages, there is no way to change the "base" of an array. The function Lbound, which reports the first index number of an array, is therefore useless because it always reports 0.

Dim initializes a variable array of fixed size. You need to specify the number of elements the array should hold, and you cannot expand or shrink the array afterwards.

Undocumented

Using Dim, you need to specify the number of entries as a constant or absolute number. You are not allowed to use a variable to feed the size of the array to Dim. ReDim will also accept variables.

```
' 2-10.VBS

dim myarray(5)

myarray(0)="Unknown"
myarray(1)="Removable"
myarray(2)="Fixed"
myarray(3)="Remote"
myarray(4)="CD-ROM"
myarray(5)="RAM-Drive"


' find out the type of drives

set fs = CreateObject("Scripting.FileSystemObject")

' get all drives:
set drives = fs.Drives

for each drive in drives
    letter = drive.DriveLetter
    kind = myarray(drive.DriveType)
    list = list & "Drive " & letter & " is of type " & kind & vbCr
next

MsgBox list
```

This script displays a list of all drives available on your computer (see Figure 2-9). It uses the Drives collection and queries the DriveType property to find out the type of drive. Because this property just returns a number, a variable array is used to store the meaning of those numbers. The script then can use the type number to index the variable array and return a user-friendly description.

```
VBScript                          ×

Drive A is of type Removable
Drive C is of type Fixed
Drive D is of type Fixed
Drive E is of type Fixed
Drive F is of type Fixed
Drive G is of type Fixed
Drive J is of type Fixed
Drive K is of type Fixed
Drive L is of type Fixed
Drive M is of type Fixed
Drive N is of type CD-ROM

              OK
```

Figure 2-9: Your script reports all drives and their drive types.

Secret

There are two hidden functions that can make life a lot easier — Join and Split. Join converts a text variable into an array using a delimiter you specify. Split does exactly the opposite and converts an array into a text variable, allowing you to display entire array contents at once.

Using Split, you can greatly simplify the previous script. Split is perfect to fill variable arrays with text variables:

```
' 2-11.VBS

myarray = "Unknown;Removable;Fixed;Remote;CD-ROM;RAM-Drive"
myarray = Split(myarray, ";")


' find out the type of drives

set fs = CreateObject("Scripting.FileSystemObject")

' get all drives:
set drives = fs.Drives

for each drive in drives
    letter = drive.DriveLetter
    kind = myarray(drive.DriveType)
    list = list & "Drive " & letter & " is of type " & kind & vbCr
next

MsgBox list
```

Note

In this example, you do not need Dim. Split automatically generates an array. There is no need for a declaration anymore. Use Dim only to generate a new array from scratch.

Using dynamic variable arrays

Dim and Split always generate fixed-size arrays. A much more versatile approach is ReDim. ReDim behaves just like Dim except that the resulting array is dynamic and can be expanded or shrunk at a later time.

Undocumented

Even if you do not plan to take advantage of dynamic array features, ReDim might be a better alternative. Often, it makes sense to first calculate the size of an array based on what your script wants to store in it. ReDim accepts a dynamically calculated size that you pass as a variable, so you can specify the size of the array at run-time. Dim does not accept variables, so you need to know the size of the array at design-time.

The following script reads in all the .exe files in the Windows folder and stores them inside an array. Because the script can determine the number of files only at run-time, it uses a dynamic array:

```
' 2-12.VBS

set fs = CreateObject("Scripting.FileSystemObject")
set wshshell = CreateObject("WScript.Shell")

' find out location of windows folder
windir = wshshell.ExpandEnvironmentStrings("%WINDIR%")

' get access to windows folder:
set winfolder = fs.GetFolder(windir)

' find out how many EXE-files there are:
counter = 0
for each file in winfolder.files
    ' find out extension name:
    ext = lcase(fs.GetExtensionName(file.name))
    ' is it an EXE file?
    if ext = "exe" then
        ' count it!
        counter = counter + 1
    end if
next

' get appropriately sized array
' since base of array is 0, substract 1:
Redim filenames(counter-1)

' store names of EXE files in array:
for each file in winfolder.files
    ' find out extension name:
    ext = lcase(fs.GetExtensionName(file.name))
    ' is it an EXE file?
    if ext = "exe" then
        ' store it!
        counter = counter - 1
        filenames(counter) = ucase(file.name)
```

```
        end if
next

' now your array contains all the EXE files. How many?
MsgBox "I found " & UBound(filenames)+1 & " executable files!"

' Show list of files:
' transform array to text variable:
text = Join(filenames, vbCr)
MsgBox text
```

Note

UBound **reports the highest index number of an array. Because arrays start with index 0 and are consecutive, the number of array elements is reported by** UBound(array)+1.

If you need to deal with text variables such as filenames, you can also use Split **to create a dynamic array at run-time:**

```
' 2-13.VBS

set fs = CreateObject("Scripting.FileSystemObject")
set wshshell = CreateObject("WScript.Shell")

' find out location of windows folder
windir = wshshell.ExpandEnvironmentStrings("%WINDIR%")

' get access to windows folder:
set winfolder = fs.GetFolder(windir)

' list all EXE-files:
for each file in winfolder.files
    ' find out extension name:
    ext = lcase(fs.GetExtensionName(file.name))
    ' is it an EXE file?
    if ext = "exe" then
        ' add it!
        list = list & ucase(file.name) & vbCr
    end if
next

' strip off the last delimiter:
if len(list)>0 then
    list = left(list, len(list)-1)
end if

MsgBox list

' if needed, convert list to dynamic array:
filenames = Split(list, vbCr)
MsgBox "There are " & UBound(filenames)+1 & " executables!"
```

This script is much simpler (and faster) because there is no longer a need to find out the number of .exe files beforehand.

Dynamically shrinking or expanding arrays

Arrays defined by ReDim can be shrunk or expanded. The following script introduces a self-defined procedure called CompressIt that eliminates all empty fields:

```
' 2-14.VBS

' define an array dynamically:
redim myarray(100)

' only use part of the space:
myarray(1) = "Hello!"
myarray(3) = 3.1415926
myarray(18) = 2000

' a lot of space is wasted. Compress array by
' eliminating all empty fields:

MsgBox "Before compression: array contains " & UBound(myarray)+1 & "
fields."
CompressIt myarray
MsgBox "After compression: array contains " & UBound(myarray)+1 & "
fields."

for each entry in myarray
    list = list & TypeName(entry) & ":" & vbTab & entry & vbCr
next

MsgBox list


sub CompressIt(array)
    ' field used to store data:
    counter = 0

    ' loop through all fields:
    for each entry in array
        if not isEmpty(entry) then
            ' store this entry
            array(counter)=entry
            counter = counter + 1
        end if
    next

    ' counter now contains the number of
    ' fields that contain data. Resize the
    ' array:

    ReDim Preserve array(counter-1)
end sub
```

Note

CompressIt can only work because the array was initially defined dynamically by ReDim. Trying to compress a static array will cause an error.

This example reveals many interesting details:

- Compression is done by looping through the array elements. A counter is incremented each time a valid entry is found, and the valid entry is copied into the array at the position of the counter. This way, all valid entries are moved to the beginning of the array.

- Once all valid entries are concentrated at the beginning of the array, ReDim cuts off the remainder. By using Preserve, the contents in the remaining fields of the array are preserved.

Secret

Note that the resulting array still contains the same data and data type as before. VBScript arrays consist of Variants, so the array elements can contain all kinds of data types. Array contents need not be of the same type.

Using multiple dimensions

Arrays can use more than one index. If you need to, you can declare arrays of up to 60 dimensions. Using multiple dimensions requires a lot more memory, though. Multiply all dimensions (plus one for the 0-based field) to get the true number of array fields:

```
dim multi(60,5,12)
```

This line declares a static three-dimensional array. You now need to use three index numbers to access each array element. The total number of array fields can be calculated as $(60+1) \times (5+1) \times (12+1) = 4758$.

Secret

Multidimensional arrays are really no different from regular arrays. VBScript just changes the way you specify the array elements. In the preceding example, VBScript would just multiply the index numbers you specified and calculate the true (one-dimensional) index number of the field.

Dissecting strings

A lot of information is handed to your script as plain text. It's important to be able to locate and extract specific parts or to make sure text is formatted the right way.

Fortunately, VBScript contains many very useful functions to handle texts. You can automatically replace text or pick out valuable information.

The basic text manipulation functions are listed in Table 2-4:

Table 2-4 Text String Manipulation Functions

Function	Description
Len	Length of a string
Left	Returns characters from the beginning of the text
Mid	Returns characters from inside the text
Right	Returns characters from the end of the text
Instr	Finds the first occurrence of a text template
InstrRev	Finds the last occurrence of a text template
Replace	Replaces part of the text with another text or eliminates characters
Trim	Removes spaces from either end of the text
LTrim	Removes spaces from the beginning of the text
RTrim	Removes spaces from the end of the text
LCase	Converts text to lowercase
UCase	Converts text to uppercase

Text commands can help you deal with two important tasks:

- Extracting information
- Converting text formats

Extracting information

Your scripts need to deal with filenames and paths all the time. So how can you extract the path name from a filename? Suppose you want to open the folder a script resides in:

```
' 2-15.VBS

fullname = WScript.ScriptFullName

' get the path
' first, find the last "\"
pos = InstrRev(fullname, "\")

' next, extract the part with the path:
path = left(fullname, pos-1)
MsgBox "This script is stored in: " & path

' you now got the path! Now let's get the filename:
```

```
filename = mid(fullname, pos+1)
MsgBox "This script: " & filename

' open an explorer window
set wshshell = CreateObject("WScript.Shell")
command = "EXPLORER.EXE " & path
wshshell.run command
```

`ScriptFullName` returns the fully qualified path name of your script. `InstrRev` finds the position of the last "\" that divides the path and filename (see Figure 2-10).

VBScript

This script is stored in: C:\scripts\chap2

OK

VBScript

This script: 2-15.VBS

OK

Figure 2-10: Find out your script's name and storage location.

Secret

Naming implies that `Left` and `Right` are cousins. This is not true. `Left` and `Mid` are the real cousins and return at the beginning or the end of the text. `Right` also returns the end of the text but counts text position backwards. With `Right`, position 1 represents the last character of the text.

`Left` can then extract the path, and `Mid` can extract the filename. To open up the script folder, you now just need to call the Explorer and supply the path name.

Secret

Another way of opening a folder without first needing to find out the path name is /select,. This hidden Explorer option opens a folder and marks a file at the same time. Note the comma. Unfortunately, the selection feature does not always work. You can at least use the option to open folders that contain a specific file.

```
' 2-16.VBS

set wshshell = CreateObject("WScript.Shell")
command = "EXPLORER.EXE /SELECT," & WScript.ScriptFullName
wshshell.run command
```

`Mid`, `Left`, and `Right` are friendly functions — should you specify a text position that is greater than the text length, they return whatever text is left in the range. However, all three functions raise errors if you specify a zero or negative position. Therefore, if you calculate positions, always make sure the result is valid. This is especially true when using `Instr` or `InstrRev`: Both functions return zero if the specified search string is not found.

Converting text formats

Your scripts can pick out any character and convert it into any other character. This is the basis of conversion tools. Whether you want to convert DOS-ASCII to Windows-ANSI or just encrypt/decrypt files, the string manipulation functions are the right tools.

DOS commands, for example, use the ASCII character code. It is very similar to the Windows ANSI code but not identical. Special characters are mapped to different character codes. The same is true for plain text and HTML: To display text files as HTML pages, it's necessary to convert spaces and any characters that could be confused with HTML tags.

The following script shows the basic architecture of a conversion tool: It generates a DOS folder listing using the DIR command and then converts the result to HTML (see Figure 2-11):

```
' 2-17.VBS

' connect to these objects:
set WSHShell = CreateObject("WScript.Shell")
set fs = CreateObject ("Scripting.FileSystemObject")

' files to store information in:
raw = "c:\temp.tmp"
html = "c:\temp.html"

' DOS command used to get directory listing:
command = "%COMSPEC% /C DIR ""C:\"" > """ & raw & """"

' execute DOS-command
result = WSHShell.Run(command,0,true)
' in case of trouble, use this line instead to see what
' is happening with DOS command:
' result = WSHShell.Run(command,,true)

' read in DOS result and convert to HTML
ConvertFile raw, html

' open HTML file in browser
cmd = "iexplore.exe """ & html & """"
wshshell.Run cmd


' converts a DOS-text into HTML
sub ConvertFile(dir, output)

    ' does the input file exist?
    if fs.FileExists(dir) then
        ' open source file for reading:
        set source = fs.OpenTextFile(dir)
        ' create output file from scratch:
        set dest = fs.CreateTextFile(output)
```

```
' write HTML body tags:
dest.WriteLine "<html><head><style>p {font: " _
& "12pt Courier}</style></head><body><p>"

' read one character at a time and convert as appropriate:
do until source.atEndOfStream
    char = asc(source.Read(1))
    select case char
        case 132:    '⅙
            charnew = chr(228)
        case 129:    '◆
            charnew = chr(252)
        case 142:    'Ž
            charnew = chr(196)
        case 154:    'ŧ
            charnew = chr(220)
        case 153:    'Ÿ
            charnew = chr(214)
        case 148:    '‼
            charnew = chr(246)
        case 225:    'ß
            charnew = chr(223)
        case 60:     '<
            charnew = "["
        case 62:     '>
            charnew = "]"
        case 13:     'CR
            charnew = "<BR>"
        case 32:     'Space
            charnew = " "
        case else:
            charnew = chr(char)
    end select
    ' write converted character into output file:
    dest.Write charnew
loop

' close DOS input:
source.close
' finalize HTML:
dest.WriteLine "</p></body></html>"
' close output file
dest.close
' delete temporary DOS file
fs.DeleteFile dir, true
end if
end sub
```

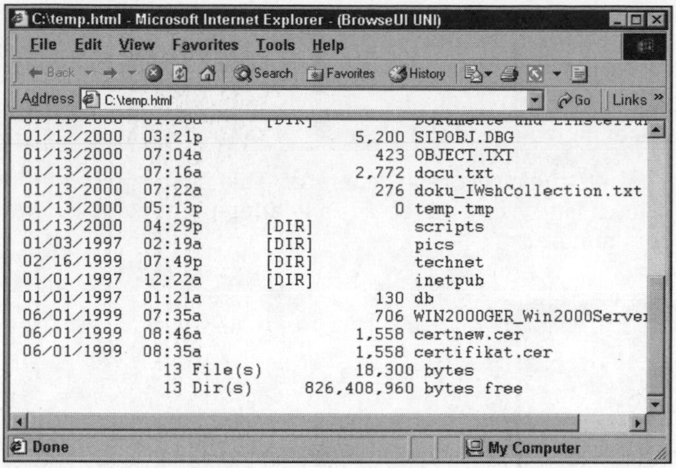

```
01/12/2000  03:21p              5,200  SIPOBJ.DBG
01/13/2000  07:04a                423  OBJECT.TXT
01/13/2000  07:16a              2,772  docu.txt
01/13/2000  07:22a                276  doku_IWshCollection.txt
01/13/2000  05:13p                  0  temp.tmp
01/13/2000  04:29p     [DIR]           scripts
01/03/1997  02:19a     [DIR]           pics
02/16/1999  07:49p     [DIR]           technet
01/01/1997  12:22a     [DIR]           inetpub
01/01/1997  01:21a                130  db
06/01/1999  07:35a                706  WIN2000GER_Win2000Server
06/01/1999  08:46a              1,558  certnew.cer
06/01/1999  08:35a              1,558  certifikat.cer
              13 File(s)       18,300  bytes
              13 Dir(s)   826,408,960  bytes free
```

Figure 2-11: Convert DOS-ASCII to Windows-ANSI and display DOS command results.

Using Random Numbers

VBScript contains a random number generator that can supply random numbers in any range. The next script shows the random number generator in action (see Figure 2-12):

```
' 2-18.VBS

' get a series of 10 random numbers between 1 and 6
do
    for x=1 to 6
        list = list & GetRandomNumber(1, 6) & " "
    next
    list = list & vbCr
    response = MsgBox(list & "More?", vbYesNo + vbQuestion)
loop until response=vbNo

function GetRandomNumber(fromnr, tonr)
    ' initialize random number generator to get
    ' new random numbers:
    randomize

    ' calculate the random number
    GetRandomNumber = Fix(rnd*(tonr-fromnr))+fromnr
end function
```

The random number generator is controlled by `randomize` and `rnd`.

Secret

Always call `randomize` at least once before using `rnd`. This way, the base of the random number generator is set to the system time, a "random" number itself. This will guarantee that you get different random numbers each time you run your script. You can also supply your own random number seed, which is useful if you need the same set of random numbers again.

`Randomize` sets the base of the generator. This base number influences all subsequent calls to `rnd`. `Rnd` returns a floating-point value between 0 and 1, the random number.

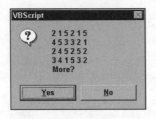

Figure 2-12: Generate arbitrary sets of random numbers.

To get a random integer of a certain range, you just need to transform the floating-point value. Multiply it by the desired range (max-min), then add the minimum random number. Cut off any decimal places using `Fix`.

Encrypting files using random numbers

Random numbers not only serve as electronic dice. They can also be used to effectively encrypt a file, too!

The strategy is simple and adopts the principle of file conversion discussed above: Your script reads in a file character by character and then adds a random number to the character code. Because character codes need to be values between 0 and 255, the script then subtracts 256 until the code is of valid range.

Decrypting files

In order to be able to decrypt the file at a later time, it's necessary to reproduce the exact same set of random numbers. Therefore, both for encryption and decryption, you need to set the base of the random number generator to the same value. This is your decryption key.

Secret

To get the exact same set of random numbers over and over again, you need to call `rnd` with a negative number just before you initialize the random base using `randomize`.

You can also determine the encryption strength by specifying how many random numbers should be used for encryption. The more numbers you use, the harder it will be to decrypt the file.

The following script shows the basic principle and encrypts a file. Specify the filename, the encryption key, and the encryption strength. The file content will be encrypted as shown in Figure 2-13.

```vbscript
' 2-19.VBS

set fs = CreateObject("Scripting.FileSystemObject")

name = InputBox("Which file do you want to encrypt?")
if not fs.FileExists(name) then
    MsgBox name & " does not exist!"
    WScript.Quit
end if

key = InputBox("Enter your encryption key!",,"12345")
if not isNumeric(key) then
    MsgBox "Your key needs to be a number!"
    WScript.Quit
end if
key = Fix(key)

sec = InputBox("Enter encryption strength!",,"500")
if not isNumeric(sec) then
    MsgBox "This needs to be a number!"
    WScript.Quit
end if
sec = Abs(Fix(sec))

rnd -1
randomize key

set readIt = fs.OpenTextFile(name, 1,,-2)
set writeIt = fs.CreateTextFile("C:\coded.txt", true)

do until readIt.atEndOfStream
    writeIt.write Encrypt(readIt.Read(1))
loop

readIt.close
writeIt.close

MsgBox "Result stored in C:\CODED.TXT" & vbCr & _
    "Your key is """ & key & """, your strength is """ & sec & """"

function Encrypt(char)
    code = asc(char)
    randomnr = Fix(rnd*sec)+1
    code = code + randomnr
    do while code>255
```

```
            code=code-256
    loop
    Encrypt = Chr(code)
end function
```

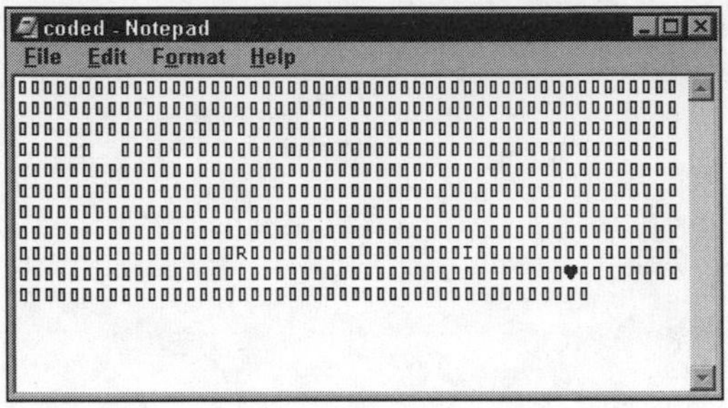

Figure 2-13: Example of an encrypted file's contents

Decryption works just the same way. All you need is the original encryption key and the encryption strength:

```
' 2-20.VBS

set fs = CreateObject("Scripting.FileSystemObject")

name = InputBox("Which file do you want to decrypt?")
if not fs.FileExists(name) then
    MsgBox name & " does not exist!"
    WScript.Quit
end if

key = InputBox("Enter your encryption key!",,"12345")
if not isNumeric(key) then
    MsgBox "Your key needs to be a number!"
    WScript.Quit
end if
key = Fix(key)

sec = InputBox("Enter encryption strength!",,"500")
if not isNumeric(sec) then
    MsgBox "This needs to be a number!"
    WScript.Quit
end if
sec = Abs(Fix(sec))

rnd -1
randomize key

set readIt = fs.OpenTextFile(name, 1,,-2)
set writeIt = fs.CreateTextFile("C:\decoded.txt", true)
```

```
do until readIt.atEndOfStream
    writeIt.write Decrypt(readIt.Read(1))
loop

readIt.close
writeIt.close

MsgBox "Result stored in C:\DECODED.TXT"

function Decrypt(char)
    code = asc(char)
    randomnr = Fix(rnd*sec)+1
    code = code - randomnr
    do while code<0
        code=code+256
    loop
    Decrypt = Chr(code)
end function
```

Tip

VBScript has no built-in support for binaries. Still, you can encrypt binaries like program files or pictures. Because the script reads the file byte-by-byte, it is capable of preserving the binary file structure. However, these scripts take much too long to encrypt large files such as pictures.

Have Your Scripts Make Decisions

To effectively automate tasks, you need to be able to delegate decisions to your scripts. VBScript contains two different decision-making functions — if...then...else and select case.

If...then...else

If...then...else checks for a condition, and depending on the result, it executes the appropriate script parts.

Secret

Actually, the if function doesn't check anything. Instead, it wants to be fed with either true or false. So, you are free to use whatever function (or variable) suits you best as long as the result is either true or false.

To check the available disk space, you can use one of the functions from the Scripting.FileSystemObject and have your script issue a warning if disk space drops below a threshold.

```
' 2-21.VBS

set fs = CreateObject("Scripting.FileSystemObject")

freespace = fs.GetDrive("C:\").AvailableSpace
```

```
' less than 100 MB available?
if freespace<(100*(1024^2)) then
    response = MsgBox("Drive C:\ is almost full. " _
& "Do you want to empty the Recycler?", _
vbQuestion + vbYesNo)
    if response=vbYes then
        MsgBox "Here, you could launch a function to empty " _
& "the recycle bin!"
    end if
else
    MsgBox "There's more than 100 MB Space available " _
& "on Drive C:\!", vbInformation
end if
```

Tip

This script won't actually empty the recycle bin. There are numerous ways to throw away recycle bin contents, and you can find detailed descriptions on how to do this in Chapter 8.

Note that if bases its decision on the statement freespace<(100*(1024^2)). This comparison returns either true or false, so it's a valid input for if. Try it!

```
MsgBox freespace<(100*1024^2))
```

Undocumented

Sometimes, you'll see strange lines such as if ok then.... Here, the variable ok contains the result of some comparison. As long as the variable contains either true or false, it's perfectly fine to feed it to if. In fact, the variable could even be a number. False is internally represented by 0, and if checks for 0. So if you supply a number to if, it will be executing any commands as long as the number is not 0.

If is a very flexible function and can be used in a number of ways:

```
if condition=true then
    ' do stuff
elseif othercondition=true then
    ' do something else
elseif yetanothercondition=true then
    ' do something different
else
    ' should no condition be met,
    ' do this
end if
```

If can check for many different conditions. The first condition that equals true (or is not 0) will execute the block of code that follows it. Should no condition be met, then VBScript executes the block after else. If you omit else altogether, code will only be executed if at least one condition equals true (or is not 0). Code that follows end if will be executed in either case.

The shortest way to call if looks like this:

```
if condition=true then dosomething
```

This if statement is contained within one line of code and doesn't need any end if delimiter.

Select case

Especially when there's the need to check various conditions, it becomes impractical to use numerous `elseif` statements. In this case, `select case` might be a good alternative.

`Select case` checks the contents of one variable. You then can check this variable as many times as needed.

Tip

Note however that `select case` cannot check for larger- or smaller-than values. `Select case` always checks whether a variable is equal to some value.

```
city = "New York"
select case city
    case "Washington":
        do this
    case "San Francisco":
        do that
    case "New York":
        do yet another thing
    case else:
        do this if no condition is met
end select
```

`Select case` is just another special subset of the `if` statement. It's there only to save you time. It's not really necessary. You could easily rephrase the example from above:

```
city = "New York"
if city="Washington" then
    do this
elseif city="San Francisco" then
    do that
elseif city="New York" then
    do yet another thing
else
    do this if no condition is met
end if
```

Tip

The `If` statement is much more powerful than `select case` because you can choose any comparison function. `Select case` is limited to checking whether a variable is equal to something.

Looping: Doing Something Many Times

Repeating steps is one of the most efficient ways scripts can ease your life. You can ask your script to repeat something a hundred or a thousand times — it's just a matter of changing the looping variable.

VBScript contains two looping mechanisms: `for...next` and `do...loop`.

For...next

`For...next` is right if you know beforehand how many times your script should execute something. You can specify a looping variable that will be automatically incremented (see Figure 2-14):

```
' 2-22.VBS

for x=1 to 100
    list = list & "Hello World!(" & x & ") "
next
MsgBox list
```

Figure 2-14: Loops cycle through your script to do routine tasks more than once.

The `MsgBox` function can display only 1,000 characters. Therefore, it only shows part of the result. Use `Popup` if you need to output more.

Tip VBScript delimits a loop with the keyword `next`. In contrast to other programming languages, you may not specify the variable name of the counting variable after `next`. Just use `next`.

You can even specify an increment. If you want your loop to increment the counter variable by 4, then change the script and add `step 4`: `for x=1 to 100 step 4`.

`For...next` sets the increment to 1 by default. This is why you are forced to use `step` when counting backwards. To count backwards, use statements like this: `for x=100 to 1 step -1`.

For each...next

`For each...next` is a special way to loop through a collection of items. You don't get a counter variable this time, and you don't set start and end points.

Instead, VBScript automatically loops through all the items of a collection and returns the item name (see Figure 2-15).

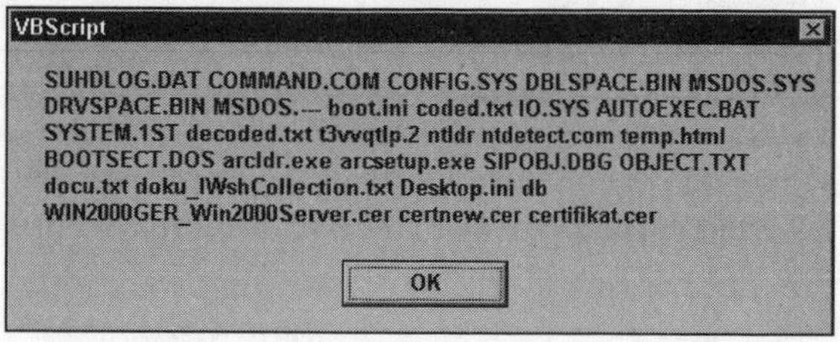

Figure 2-15: Use `for each...next` to retrieve all files in a folder.

This loop is very important when accessing third-party components. For example, the next script gets access to a folder and enumerates all files:

```
' 2-23.VBS

' get access to file system:
set fs = CreateObject("Scripting.FileSystemObject")

' get handle to folder C:\
set folderc = fs.GetFolder("C:\")

' get collection of all files:
set files = folderc.files

' prepare list with all filenames:
for each file in files
    list = list & file.name & " "
next

' present list:
MsgBox list
```

Although `for each...next` is just another special form of `for...next` and many times you can choose between both, there are cases where you depend on `for each...next`. You can't always determine the number of elements inside a collection or access the elements by index number. In these cases, `for each...next` is the only solution.

Variable arrays, for example, can be enumerated either way:

```
' 2-24.VBS

' define array with names:
names = Split("Frank,Michael,Barbara,Erin", ",")

' enumerate elements the "classical" way:
for x=0 to UBound(names)
```

```
    MsgBox names(x)
next

' enumerate elements the "elegant" way:
for each name in names
    MsgBox name
next
```

Many `FileSystem` objects, in contrast, can only be accessed with the help of `for each...next` because there's no way to use an index number to access individual collection members.

Undocumented

It's important to notice that `for each...next` returns a copy of the actual collection element. You can change this copy without changing the collection content. `For...next`, in contrast, references the collection elements directly. Changes will apply to the original collection elements.

Do...loop

You'll know that `do...loop` is right for you if it's not obvious how many times your script should repeat a step. You can use `do...loop` to read a file of unknown size or to ask questions until the user enters the correct answer.

Because `do...loop` has no built-in limit, it will continue looping happily for years if the exit condition is never met. Never-ending loops hang your script and consume considerable amounts of CPU resources, so it's a good idea to carefully plan the exit condition to make sure it will always be reached at some point.

```
' 2-25.VBS

set fs = CreateObject("Scripting.FileSystemObject")

filename = "c:\autoexec.bat"
set inputhandle = fs.OpenTextFile(filename)

do until inputhandle.atEndOfStream
    content = content & inputhandle.ReadLine & vbCr
loop

MsgBox content
```

This script reads in a text file's content. A loop continues to read lines until the input object signals its end — `atEndOfStream` returns true.

Undocumented

You can place the `exit` condition either behind `do` or behind `loop`. You can also specify no exit condition at all. In this case, define an exit condition inside of the loop that calls `exit do` to exit the loop.

This script places the exit condition right after `do`. You can also specify the exit condition after `loop`; both ways work fundamentally different.

In the example, the exit condition is checked before the loop is entered, making sure the end of the file is not reached. If you place the exit condition at the end of the loop, an empty file will raise an error.

On the other hand, there are good reasons for placing exit conditions at the end of the loop, too:

```
' 2-26.VBS

randomize
do
    dice = Fix(rnd*6)+1
    answer = MsgBox("Random number is " & dice & vbCr _
        & "Do you want to continue?", vbYesNo)
loop while answer=vbYes
MsgBox "Thanks for playing!"
```

This loop will be executed at least once. Also, this time the exit condition uses the keyword `while` instead of `until`.

Undocumented

`While` and `until` are really the same—they just interpret the result in the opposite way. `While` will continue looping until the condition returns false, while `until` will continue looping until the condition returns true. `While not condition` equals `Until condition`, and `Until not condition` equals `While condition`. It's nice to have the choice, but you really only need one of the two.

Exiting loops prematurely

Don't waste time! Whenever a loop searches for some information and finally gets it, there's no need for it to continue running. In these cases, stop the loop. Use the keyword `exit` and the type of loop you want to stop, either `exit for` or `exit do`.

You can even use `exit do` as the main exit condition. Consider the following example:

```
' 2-27.VBS

do
    text = InputBox("Enter a name")
    if text=vbEmptyString then exit do

    list = list & text & vbCr
loop

MsgBox list
```

Here, `do...loop` doesn't use an exit condition at all. The loop would run forever if there wasn't an `exit do`.

The loop prompts you to input names until you hit Cancel. Cancel returns an empty string the script can detect. It then terminates the loop from inside.

Just consider what would happen if you placed the exit condition at the top or end of the loop. The empty string would be attached to the name list before the loop would detect the Cancel button. By checking the input right away, you can leave this loop at the earliest possible time.

Tip

Again, make sure your loop will exit at some time. If you misspelled `vbEmptyString`, this loop would run forever. An easy rule to remember is this: Inside of loops, whenever you display dialog boxes of any kind, always supply a Cancel button and make sure the logic behind it exits the loop. This not only prevents runaway scripts, it also allows the user to stop lengthy operations. If your loop doesn't display dialog boxes, runaway scripts are less problematic. You can then always use the task list to stop the script (see Chapter 1).

The Beauty of Functions and Procedures

You already know the fundamental mechanics of VBScript by now. Let's put them together and define new commands.

Functions and procedures tie VBScript commands together to deliver more complex results. This not only eliminates redundancy, but also helps keep scripts straightforward and easy to understand. Functions and procedures are also the only way to define private variables.

Defining a procedure

Procedures execute a set of VBScript commands. They do not return any values. Procedures are defined by `sub...end sub`. They can be called from anywhere inside your script.

```
' 2-28.VBS

message = ""

Say "This is an easy way"
Say "to design multi-line"
Say "messages."

MsgBox message

sub Say(text)
    message = message & text & vbCr
end sub
```

The new procedure `Say` adds text to the message variable and automatically inserts a line wrap. This makes it very easy to display messages that consist of more than one line (Figure 2-16).

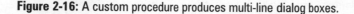

Figure 2-16: A custom procedure produces multi-line dialog boxes.

Secret

Variables inside functions and procedures are private variables. They are only valid inside the function or procedure. However, if the variable was already defined in the main part of the script, the variable has global scope. It's owned by the entire script and is valid everywhere. The only way to define private variables therefore is to use variables inside procedures or functions that have not been previously used in the main script.

Try taking out the first line of the script. You'll see that the script doesn't work anymore. This is because the message wasn't defined inside the main part of the script, and it's not a global variable anymore. Instead, the message is now a private variable that lives inside the procedure. Therefore, the MsgBox command cannot access it.

This is a very important concept, and you will learn more about it below.

Returning values with the help of functions

All functions work in a very similar way. Basically, they are spiced-up procedures that have the ability to return a value. Take a look how easy it is to add a custom function to your script:

```
' 2-29.VBS

MsgBox ReadFile("C:\AUTOEXEC.BAT")

function ReadFile(name)
    set fs = CreateObject("Scripting.FileSystemObject")
    if fs.fileExists(name) then
        set handle = fs.OpenTextFile(name)
        ReadFile = handle.ReadAll
        handle.close
    else
        MsgBox "The file " & name & " does not exist!"
    end if
end function
```

With only a couple of lines of code, you gain a powerful new function that reads in the contents of text files. All the necessary mechanics are nicely hidden inside the ReadFile function, and the main script structure remains clear and straightforward. You can even read in a bunch of files without redundant code. In addition, you can store functions like this one in your private script library and paste them into your projects as needed.

Take a look at how the function actually returns the value: All you need to do is assign the return value to a variable that has the same name as the function itself. In the previous example, the `ReadFile` function assigns the return value to the `ReadFile` variable. Pretty easy, huh?

Common pitfalls with procedures and functions

Procedures and functions are easy and powerful. Yet they can cause very tricky errors if global and private variables are not clearly separated.

Never use variables inside procedures and functions that are used by the main part of your script if you do not want to explicitly return values in them. Take a look at the following script: It demonstrates the bad side effects:

```
' 2-30.VBS

for x = 1 to 10
    MsgBox ExpandText("Hello World!")
next

function ExpandText(text)
    for x=1 to len(text)
        character = mid(text, x, 1)
        ExpandText = ExpandText & character & " "
    next
end function
```

This script looks pretty straightforward as a loop displays a `MsgBox` ten times and the function `ExpandText` returns spaced-out text. Once you run this script, it will show the dialog box only once, though. Why?

Your function accidentally uses a global variable. The loop variable x is used in the main script as well as inside the function. So whenever the script calls `ExpandText`, it will set x to the maximum length of your text: 12. 12 is larger than `the for...next-exit` condition, so the loop will exit right away. The text is displayed only once, and then the puzzle is solved. Exchange x with y inside the function, and everything will work as intended.

However, this little experiment shows how dangerous an accidental double-use of variables really is. If you tried to display text of less than ten characters, for example, x would always be set to less than 10, thus the `for...next-loop` would never exit — you would end up with a runaway script.

To make things even worse, there's another tricky source of errors — the arguments you pass to procedures and functions are global variables by default. If you change an argument inside a function, you also change the variable that was passed to the function. You now end up with two different variables storing data at the same place and affecting each other.

```
' 2-31.VBS

text = "Hello World!"

for x = 1 to 10
    DisplayText text
next

sub DisplayText(showwhat)
    showwhat = "[" & showwhat & "]"
    MsgBox showwhat
end sub
```

This cute script *should* just display a little greeting ten times and wrap it in brackets. It does, but it adds new brackets each time the procedure is called. Why?

The argument is a global value, so the text variable outside the procedure and the showwhat variable inside the procedure are the same. They have different names, but they refer to the same data. When the procedure adds brackets to this variable, it adds them permanently. The next time the main script calls the procedure, it supplies text that already is framed by brackets.

There are some easy ways out, though. You can even leave the arguments the way they are. If you need to make changes, then first assign the argument to another variable, preferably a private variable that's not used in the main script. This is the most common approach, but it's not the best.

Usually, procedures and functions use arguments, but with ByRef they share the same physical data storage and just call the variable differently. However, there's another way. You can pass arguments with ByVal. This way, only the value of the variable is passed, and the procedure or function stores the value into a different variable. To pass arguments with ByVal, just place them into parentheses. In the preceding example, use DisplayText (text).

By placing arguments into parentheses, they are passed as values and stored in different variables. You can use this naming convention with procedures and functions equally well. Calling a function, you would include all arguments in parentheses and then put parentheses around each argument you want to pass through ByVal.

Passing results using arguments

Functions can only return one value; procedures cannot return values at all. This is not so good. What if you need to return more than one value? What if you want to indicate whether a certain operation succeeded?

Luckily, there are numerous ways out of this limitation. One of the easiest is using arguments in the opposite direction!

You just saw that arguments are passed through ByRef by default, connecting a global variable with some procedural variable. In effect, this is all you need. Arguments passed through ByRef work in both directions, and what was a cause of complaint just a page ago can be of great help if used wisely.

Take a look at the ReadFile function again. This function can only return data if the specified file exists. It's not a good idea to pop up a dialog box in case of an error because your script would be unable to response to this error. A better way is to use a status variable:

```
' 2-32.VBS

' file found?
if ReadFile("C:\AUTOEXEC.BAT", content) then
    ' yes, display content:
    MsgBox content
else
    ' no, complain:
    MsgBox "File not found!"
end if

function ReadFile(name, text)
    set fs = CreateObject("Scripting.FileSystemObject")
    if fs.fileExists(name) then
        set handle = fs.OpenTextFile(name)
        text = handle.ReadAll
        handle.close
        ReadFile = true
    else
        ReadFile = false
    end if
end function
```

This time, your main script remains in control: ReadFile will not display any dialog boxes but instead will report directly whether it was able to open the file or not. The file's contents are sent to the main script using the second argument in the "wrong direction": Instead of receiving data, it uses this argument to pass back data.

It's now up to your main script to decide what to do if something goes wrong. You could even expand this concept and use a third variable to return detailed error information.

Tip

It's completely up to you which piece of information will go through which channel. However, the best approach is to return status information using the function's return value, and to pass all other information through arguments. This way, the caller can check immediately whether things went wrong.

For this concept to work, you need to pass arguments through ByRef (the default). Also, you need to specify real variables so the function can return something. If you specify constants or quoted text, your main script will never be able to receive the returned information.

Tip

Windows uses this way of data transfer very often. Many of the internal API functions return a status value indicating success. The real data is returned through arguments. You call API functions in Chapter 4.

Returning more than one value

There's a limit of one return value per function. But is this the final answer? No! It's true: Functions can only return one value. But it's up to you to determine the kind of variable your function returns.

You can return a variable array that in turn contains as many return values as you like. Or, you can return an object. It's just a variable. If you use the dictionary object, you can easily return thousands of individual values. Another way is to use a String as a return value that contains delimiters. Each of these ways has individual advantages. Have a look!

```
' 2-33.VBS

if EnumDir("C:\", list) then
    MsgBox list
else
    MsgBox "folder does not exist"
end if

if EnumDir("C:\", list) then
    list = Split(list, vbCr)
    MsgBox "folder contains " & ubound(list)+1 & " files."
    MsgBox "file #1 is called: " & list(0)
else
    MsgBox "folder does not exist"
end if

function EnumDir(dirname, result)
    ' get file system functions:
    set fs = CreateObject("Scripting.FileSystemObject")

    ' does folder exist?
    if fs.FolderExists(dirname) then
        ' yes, open:
        set dir = fs.GetFolder(dirname)

        ' enum files and store in string:
```

```
        result = ""
        for each file in dir.files
            result = result & file.name & vbCr
        next

        ' strip off last vbCr
        if len(result)>0 then
            result = left(result, len(result)-1)
        end if

        EnumDir = true
    else
        ' folder not found: error!
        EnumDir = false
    end if
end function
```

In this example, EnumDir enumerates all files in a directory. It returns true
if this is successful; otherwise, it's false. The list of filenames is returned
through an argument. It's a String that uses vbCr as the delimiter. This way,
you can easily display the list using MsgBox, and there is no danger of vbCr
interfering with filename characters.

Secret

Always set the argument to zero before you start storing your return values
in it. Otherwise, you might keep return values from previous calls and
accidentally add new values to existing ones.

You can also access filenames individually. To do this, the script uses Split
to convert the file list into an array. This is easy because you know vbCr is
the delimiter. Your script can now easily determine the number of files, and
it can access each file by index.

Here's another way:

```
' 2-34.VBS

if EnumDir("C:\", list) then
    for each file in list
        filelist = filelist & file & vbCr
    next
    MsgBox filelist
else
    MsgBox "folder does not exist"
end if

if EnumDir("C:\", list) then
    MsgBox "folder contains " & list.Count & " files."
    MsgBox "Is MSDOS.SYS contained in this dir? " &
list.Exists("MSDOS.SYS")
else
    MsgBox "folder does not exist"
end if
```

```
function EnumDir(dirname, result)
    ' get file system functions:
    set fs = CreateObject("Scripting.FileSystemObject")

    ' get dictionary object
    set result = CreateObject("Scripting.Dictionary")

    ' does folder exist?
    if fs.FolderExists(dirname) then
        ' yes, open:
        set dir = fs.GetFolder(dirname)

        ' enum files and store in string:
        for each file in dir.files
            result.add file.name, file.path
        next

        EnumDir = true
    else
        ' folder not found: error!
        EnumDir = false
    end if
end function
```

This script uses a dictionary object. I will present its anatomy at the end of this chapter. You can store key-value pairs inside a dictionary using Add.

Have a look at your main script. This time, it's not so easy to display the file list because you need to assemble the list using for each...next first. In contrast, finding out the total number of files or even checking whether a certain file is part of the directory now is very easy. The dictionary object offers the property Count and the method Exists.

So, your choice of method largely depends on what you want to do with the results.

There is one limitation—either solution deals with string values. It's not possible to return a number of different variable types. In this case, you might want to use variable arrays, as they can hold any number of variables of any type. The next example shows how to do this. It uses a two-dimensional array and stores filename and file size:

```
' 2-35.VBS

if EnumDir("C:\", list) then
    for x=0 to UBound(list)
        filelist = filelist & list(x,0) & ", " & list(x,1) & " bytes."
& vbCr
    next
    MsgBox filelist
else
```

```
        MsgBox "folder does not exist"
end if

if EnumDir("C:\", list) then
    MsgBox "folder contains " & ubound(list)+1 & " files."
    MsgBox "file #1 is called: " & list(0,0) & " and of size: " &
list(0,1)
else
    MsgBox "folder does not exist"
end if

function EnumDir(dirname, result)
    ' get file system functions:
    set fs = CreateObject("Scripting.FileSystemObject")

    ' does folder exist?
    if fs.FolderExists(dirname) then
        ' yes, open:
        set dir = fs.GetFolder(dirname)

        ' how many files are there?
        filenum = dir.files.Count

        ' reserve storage
        redim result(filenum-1,1)

        ' enum files and store in string:
        counter =0
        for each file in dir.files
            result(counter, 0)=file.name
            result(counter, 1)=file.size
            counter = counter + 1
        next

        EnumDir = true
    else
        ' folder not found: error!
        EnumDir = false
    end if
end function
```

Tip

If you use a one-dimensional array, then you can easily convert it to a String for quick display. Just use Join and specify vbCr as the delimiter. Join doesn't work with multidimensional arrays.

Using Dictionaries

The basic VBScript language set can easily be expanded, and in fact this book is going to show you numerous ways to add new and exciting capabilities to your scripts. One of the extensions that is already part of VBScript is the Dictionary object. It does exactly what its name implies; you can store unique key-data pairs in it and retrieve the information later through its keyword.

Dictionary objects are very efficient and powerful. Take a look at Script
2-36.vbs — it uses a Dictionary object and fills in data. Next, you can search
for data by keyword and even add new data to the dictionary.

```
' 2-36.VBS

set dict = CreateObject("Scripting.Dictionary")

dict.Add "san francisco", "Hyatt Regency"
dict.Add "new york", "Mariott"

do
     city = InputBox("Please enter a city!")
     if city = vbEmpty then exit do
     if dict.Exists(city) then
         MsgBox "Result for " & city & ":" & vbCr & dict(city)
     else
         result = MsgBox("No result for " & city _
             & ". Do you want to add a reference?", _
             vbYesNo + vbQuestion)
         if result = vbYes then
             info = InputBox("Add information for " & city & "!")
             if not info=vbEmpty then
                 dict.Add city, info
                 MsgBox "Information added!"
             else
                 MsgBox "You cancelled!"
             end if
         end if
     end if
loop
```

Using case-insensitive dictionaries

You may have noticed that your dictionary is case-sensitive. If you enter a
city in capital letters, it refers to a different key-value pair, and you may not
always want this. If so, you can instruct your Dictionary object to ignore
cases. However, you have to make up your mind before you start using the
Dictionary. Add the following line right after you create the Dictionary using
CreateObject:

```
dict.CompareMode = 1
```

A CompareMode of 0 enables case-sensitive comparision. It's the default
behavior, so you need to set this property only if you want to disable case-
sensitive comparision.

With this small change, your script now accepts city names and finds the
corresponding information no matter how you capitalize the city name.

Using more than one dictionary

Dictionary objects are individual objects. You can use as many simultaneously as you want (or need). However, the data stored in the Dictionary object is lost the moment your script ends. To conserve the Dictionary contents, you can enumerate its contents and save the results to a file. Chapter 7 shows how to save data in text files, or, alternatively, you can also save the data using a database (Chapter 23). Here's how to enumerate the contents of your Dictionary object:

```
for each item in dict
    list = list & item & "=" & dict(item) & vbCr
next
MsgBox list
```

Overview: properties and methods

You may not need Dictionary objects right away. They are valuable tools, though, and if you'd like to do some more experimenting, here is the complete list of properties and methods that the Dictionary object supports:

Table 2-5 Dictionary Object — Properties and Methods

Property/Method	Description
dict.Add key, value	Adds the key-value pair to the Dictionary object.
dict.CompareMode = (0/1)	Controls whether the Dictionary is case-sensitive (0) or not (1). Needs to be set before you store any values in your Dictionary object.
dict.Count	Returns the number of key-value pairs stored in the Dictionary object.
dict.Exists(key)	Checks whether a specified key exists in the Dictionary object.
dict.Item(key) dict.Item(key) = newvalue	Retrieves the value stored under the specified key, or changes the value.
dict.Items	Returns an array with all the values stored in the Dictionary object.
dict.Key(key) = newkey	Changes the name of a key.
dict.Keys	Returns an array with all the key names stored in the Dictionary object.
dict.Remove(key)	Removes the key and its associated value from the Dictionary object.
dict.RemoveAll	Empties the entire Dictionary object.

Declaring Variables Explicitly

VBScript doesn't force you to declare the variable names you use. Instead, it creates the variables as you use them. This is convenient because declaring variables involves a lot of bookkeeping and code-writing.

For small scripts, it is perfectly okay not to declare variables. However, the luxury of using variables without prior declaration comes at a price: VBScript won't warn you if you misspelled a variable. Misspelling a variable name can easily trash the complete script and lead to hard-to-find errors.

Playing safe: declaring variables

To play it safe, include the option-explicit statement as the first statement in your scripts. From now on, VBScript will only accept variables that have been declared using either `Dim` or `Public/Private`.

This serves a dual purpose:

■ VBScript will warn you if you misspelled a variable name because you never declared such a variable.

■ Variable declarations force you to review your script structure and eliminate redundant variables. In fact, it is a good idea to comment the purpose of each variable as you declare it. This way, you and others will be able to better understand your script design.

Declaring or not declaring: a case example

Take a look at the following two script examples. The first script doesn't use declarations. Therefore, the script is much shorter and will run without errors even though it does contain an error: A variable name was misspelled, and the script doesn't really do anything useful anymore.

```
' 2-37.VBS

start = 1
max = 30
text = "Hello World! "

for x=start to max
     list = list & text
next

' here's the typo:
MsgBox lizt
```

The second example does use declarations. You will get an error message indicating the problem with the misspelled variable name. As a nice side effect, the declarations provide extra information on the purpose of the variables.

```
' 2-38.VBS

option explicit

dim start.....' start counter
dim max.....' increment to this number
dim text.....' text to repeat
dim x.....' looping variable
dim list.....' contains the resulting text

start = 1
max = 30
text = "Hello World! "

for x=start to max
     list = list & text
next

MsgBox lizt
```

Note   Throughout this book, you will find variable declarations only in `COM` object code samples. I do not provide variable declarations for the plain script files because most of them are very short and well-documented. The declarations would have taken additional space, which I decided to spend on additional secrets and code samples instead.

Summary

VBScript is a powerful base language that you can use to both display messages and ask for input. In addition, you can easily design decisions and loops, or define your own custom functions and procedures. Because VBScript can access both input and output streams in DOS windows, you can design scripts to act as command-line tools.

Chapter 3

Kidnapping Objects

In This Chapter

▶ Find out more about objects

▶ Connect to objects and list all available objects on your system

▶ Analyze the inner structure of objects

▶ Read secret TypeLibrary information to retrieve the commands stored in objects

W hy should you deal with objects? Well, because VBScript is merely software glue. You can write little scripts that do useful things, but to really accomplish powerful automation tasks, VBScript is definitely not enough.

In this chapter, all you need to do is sit back and enjoy the ride. This tour will show you how to get all the information you need to understand script development—and I'll show you how to find out the names of all the hidden methods stored inside objects.

Eventually, all of this information will fall into place without much brainwork.

Tip

You want action fast? Then fast forward to Part II. You already know everything you need to execute scripts. Part II is loaded with everyday examples you can try out and use as a foundation for your own experiments. Do come back later, though, to find out all about hidden COM objects and how to access their methods.

What Objects Really Are

VBScript only delivers the basic infrastructure. You can define decisions, functions, and procedures, but VBScript has no command to access any of the interesting parts of your computer. These include reading values from the Windows Registry, for example, or checking for available disk space. The real work has to be done by someone different.

Fortunately, VBScript contains one very powerful command—`CreateObject`. This command can access COM components installed on your system and "borrow" all the commands stored inside of this component. This is an incredible source of power.

Undocumented

There is a lot of confusion about the technical terms. COM objects store functionality in a language-independent format. Some books refer to COM objects as ActiveX objects; others use the old term OLE2. Just think of COM objects as black boxes that contain useful stuff. You don't need to know how the COM object achieves its results. As you will see, almost any modern software stores its functionality in a number of COM objects. These modules can be accessed by anyone.

Basically, through the use of COM objects, your scripts can do just about everything a regular program can do. There aren't limits anymore. And even better, you don't need to waste your time programming all of these functions yourself. In fact, you don't even have to know much about programming. Chances are there are already predefined ActiveX objects on your system, be they database access, Internet FTP transfer, or scanner control. Just pick the right ActiveX component and have your script boss it around. That's the fun part about scripting—you get incredible power, yet you don't have to invent all the programs and functions yourself. Instead, borrow whatever functionality you need from what's already installed on your system. Recycle your software, and use its power to suit your needs.

How Can I Talk To COM Objects?

How do you identify a COM object? COM objects come in two flavors—either `OCX` or `DLL` files. To get a taste of how many potentially useful resources are waiting for you, do a quick search: Open your Start menu, choose Find, and do a search on files and folders. In the filename box, type in `*.DLL *.OCX`. Make sure you choose your hard drive as the search target. Hundreds of files will be listed, leaving you wondering which secrets await you inside.

Undocumented

`OCX` files are ActiveX controls. They were originally designed to be hosted by Web pages. `DLL` files are dynamic link libraries. They help to split programs (and Windows itself) into modules. Each `DLL` file stores some functionality, and whenever more is needed, Microsoft and other companies add more `DLL`s. Both file types may or may not be suitable for scripting. In order for scripts to access the functions inside, the file needs to offer a special interface called `IDispatch`. In addition, the file needs to be registered. You will learn more about this later in this chapter.

COM objects work pretty much like VBScript command extensions. Plug them in, and you get an extra set of commands. Plug in as many objects as you need simultaneously. It's really that easy.

Connecting to an Object

You want proof? Take a look at the following example. VBScript has no file system commands whatsoever, so it would be pretty useless if you wanted to design your own disk utility. That's why Microsoft added a special object to the scripting host called `Scripting.FileSystemObject`. Plug it in, and you get all the file system commands you could possibly ask for:

```
' 3-1.VBS

' get access to the ActiveX object:
set fs = CreateObject("Scripting.FileSystemObject")
' call a method to make the object do something:
set drive = fs.GetDrive("C:\")
MsgBox "Available Space on C:\:" &
FormatNumber(drive.AvailableSpace/1024^2) & "MB"
```

This script determines the free space on drive C:\ (see Figure 3-1). To be able to do that, the script needs to borrow some functions from `Scripting.FileSystemObject`. So, the first thing the script does is call for help. It uses `CreateObject` to get a reference to the object it wants to help out — `Scripting.FileSystemObject`.

Figure 3-1: Find out available space on a drive with the help of `Scripting.FileSystemObject`.

Your scripts will call for help all of the time. Their cries will be answered by many different objects throughout this book, so it's a good idea to fully understand this mechanism. `CreateObject` returns a reference to the object. Because this reference is not a regular variable, like a number or a text string, you need to use the key word `Set` to assign it to a variable. The variable then acts like the object, and the script above can use the variable `fs` to access methods and properties of the new object.

> **Tip** `Set` is a very important key word. VBScript doesn't need it, but you do. Use `Set` whenever you want to store an object reference in a variable.

Whenever you want to access the inside of the object, you just use your newly created reference. The script wants to get a hold of a drive, so it calls `GetDrive`. `GetDrive` is part of the `Scripting.FileSystemObject`; it's not a VBScript command. So, in order to call this function, you need to use your reference stored in `fs`. This is why the script calls `fs.GetDrive` instead of `GetDrive`. Your script now has successfully called its first foreign function.

`GetDrive` returns another object called `IDrive`. This object represents the drive with all its technical details. You will see much more about these functions in Chapter 8. Because `GetDrive` returns an object, your script again uses `Set` to store the object reference in a variable.

To find out the available space on the drive, the script asks for the drive property `AvailableSpace`. Because this information is stored in the `IDrive` object, the script again uses the correct object reference. It asks for `drive.AvailableSpace`. Either `AvailableSpace` alone or `fs.AvailableSpace` would fail because this property only exists in the `IDrive` object — and nowhere else.

If you're wondering how to find out which object contains which information, it's not black magic; it's just a matter of information and documentation. You will see in a moment how easy it is to find out which objects are returned and what information is contained in them.

The `FormatNumber` command just serves cosmetic purposes. It formats the raw number, which is divided by 1024^2 to get megabytes instead of bytes.

Secret

What's all this fuss about "methods," "properties," and "functions?" Actually, a method is just a new term for either "function" or "procedure." "Method" refers to some built-in mechanics inside an object that does something for you. Properties, in contrast, are information stores that act like variables.

This example provides all you need to know. It shows you all the steps that are necessary to access an object. As you see, much of it involves getting object references and calling the right object methods.

Knowing Which Objects Are Available

How did I know there was an object like `Scripting.FileSystemObject` anyway? And how can you find out if there are more?

Easy. `Scripting.FileSystemObject` is part of the scripting host, and it's fully documented. If you are curious, just take a look at the book's CD and install `msrelated/vbsdoc.exe`. This file contains the official VBScript help file, and `Scripting.FileSystemObject` is part of it.

It's not the only object the WSH brings along, either, as you can see in Table 3-1.

Table 3-1   COM objects included with the Scripting Host

Object Name	Description
`Scripting.FileSystemObject`	A rich set of file system functions.
`Scripting.Dictionary`	Returns a dictionary object that stores key-value pairs.
`WScript.Shell`	A rich set of functions to read system information: Read and write to the Registry, find out path names to special folders, read DOS environment variables, and read the settings stored in links.

Object Name	Description
WScript.Network	Functions to manage network connections and remote printers: Find out the name of the currently logged-in user.

Secret

Wondering why object names often share part of their name with other objects? If object names start with the same name like "Scripting" or "Wscript," they are part of the same physical object file. So, both Scripting.FileSystemObject and Scripting.Dictionary live inside SCRRUN.DLL. Consider the first part of the object name as the "Company name" and the second part as the "Department."

All the Scripting Objects live inside SCRRUN.DLL, and all the WScript Objects are stored inside WSHOM.OCX. You can view both files in the Windows system folder.

Let's use this new freedom and borrow some external methods to check both files and find out their file versions (see Figure 3-2).

```
VBScript                                                    [X]
   (i)   wshom.ocx is stored here: D:\WINNT\system32\wshom.ocx
         Version: 5.1.0.4411

         VBScript                                              [X]
            (i)   scrrun.dll is stored here: D:\WINNT\system32\scrrun.dll
                  Version: 5.1.0.4411

                        [    OK    ]
```

Figure 3-2: Retrieve location and version information of important COM objects.

```
' 3-2.VBS

Check "wshom.ocx"
Check "scrrun.dll"

sub Check(filename)
    if LookFor(filename, path) then
        ' if file exists in either system folder,
        ' path now contains the pathname

        ' find out file version:
        version = GetVersion(path)

        ' display results
        msg = filename & " is stored here: " & path & vbCr
        msg = msg + "Version: " & version
        MsgBox msg, vbInformation
```

```
        else
            MsgBox filename & " was not found."
        end if
end sub

function LookFor(filename, path)
    ' returns true if filename was found
    ' in either of the two possible system folders
    ' win9x only has one.
    ' path returns the full path name

    ' we need this object to find out
    ' the windows folder using
    ' ExpandEnvironmentStrings:
    set wshshell = CreateObject("WScript.Shell")

    ' we need this object to find out
    ' whether the file exists:
    set fs = CreateObject("Scripting.FileSystemObject")

    ' find out windows folder path:
    ' environment variable %WINDIR% contains the
    ' windows folder path:
    windir = wshshell.ExpandEnvironmentStrings("%WINDIR%")

    ' construct names of both file paths to check:
    path1 = windir & "\system\" & filename
    path2 = windir & "\system32\" & filename

    if fs.FileExists(path1) then
        ' file exists in path1
        LookFor = true
        path = path1
    elseif fs.FileExists(path2) then
        ' file exists in path2
        LookFor = true
        path = path2
    else
        ' file not found:
        LookFor = false
        path = ""
        exit function
    end if
end function

function GetVersion(path)
    ' accepts a filename and returns
    ' file version

    ' we need this object to get access to
    ' the file version number:
    set fs = CreateObject("Scripting.FileSystemObject")
```

```
' needs to turn off error handling
' because error will be raised if
' no file version info is available
' (fixed in newer WSH versions)
on error resume next

GetVersion = fs.GetFileVersion(path)
' file version available? Error raised?
if not err.number=0 then
    ' clear error
    err.clear
    ' set return value to -1
    GetVersion = -1
end if
end function
```

Tip

Don't try to understand all the details of this script. It's there for your convenience only. Take one step at a time!

Finding Out Where Objects Are Stored

How do you know that WScript.Shell lives inside WSHOM.OCX? You can look it up in the Windows Registry. It's easy to do, and then you'll see how important it is to know the name of a file that stores an object. Later in this chapter, you'll use this information to uncover all the undocumented commands stored in an object.

Undocumented

Any object name you supply to CreateObject — like Scripting. FileSystemObject or WScript.Shell — is really a ProgID, or program identifier. You will always find a Registry key in HKEY_CLASSES_ROOT\ with the same name. This is the central store telling CreateObject how to access the object. If the Registry key is missing, you will no longer be able to access the object.

Let's do the first step and spy on objects! Find out the real filename of WScript.Shell.

1. Choose Run from the Start menu and launch the Registry Editor: REGEDIT [Enter].

2. In the left pane, you'll see all the keys. Keys work like folders and in fact share the same icon. They can contain subkeys and values, the real data. Values are displayed in the right pane.

3. To open a key and look at what's inside, click the plus sign or double-click the key. Open the key HKEY_CLASSES_ROOT. This key stores all information about file associations and ActiveX objects.

4. Now enter the beginning of the object name you are looking for. Enter WScript. The cursor jumps to the first key that starts with the characters you entered. Most likely, it will be WScript.Network (see Figure 3-3). Scroll down a little farther until you see WScript.Shell.

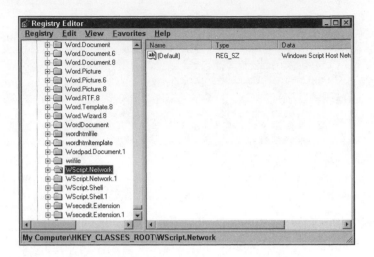

Figure 3-3: COM objects are registered as individual keys.

Tip

Once you have accustomed yourself to the Registries' architecture, you can "beam" yourself to the right places. Just select the Edit menu and choose Find. Then, activate the key option only because you are looking for a key. Enter the name of the key, WScript.Shell, and start the Search.

5. Open the key WScript.Shell. In the right pane, you'll find the official name of this object. You'll also discover two subkeys called CLSID and CurVer (see Figure 3-4).

The most important subkey is called CLSID. Click on it to see its contents in the right pane. The (standard) value contains a very large number, known as the Class-ID. The reason this number is so large is because it's the unique identifier of your object. It's always the same, no matter in which country of the world you installed the current version of the object. It's a global nametag. Write down this number somewhere — it's the official name of WScript.Shell, and you will need this number soon.

Secret

The compiler that produced the run-time object generates the Class-ID. Whenever you install the object, the Class-ID is read from the object file and written to your Registry. So, it's a one-way street, and you can't manually change the Class-ID by changing Registry values. If you did, you could no longer access the object because the Registry Class-ID needs to match the Class-ID stored inside the object. The same is true if you update an object file. Because the new version has a new Class-ID, you need to register the new object. Just replacing the file would disable the object. You could no longer access it because the Class-IDs inside the Registry and the Class-IDs stored in the object would be out-of-sync. Registering an object updates the Registry.

Because different versions of the same object may be installed on your system, the subkey CurVer informs you which version is most up-to-date.

Most likely, `CurVer` will contain something like `WScript.Shell.1`. This is the name of another Registry key, just beneath `WScript.Shell`. This key contains a `CLSID`-subkey, and this key points to the most up-to-date Class-ID for the object you are interested in. Don't worry too much: Either take a look into your Registry and see for yourself, or lean back and let Windows handle the technical details.

Now let's get to the real object information (Figure 3-4).

Undocumented

The Registry key `HKEY_CLASSES_ROOT\CLSID\` stores all the detail information about any installed object.

1. Press [Home] to go back to the start of the Registry. Now type in `CLSID`. A key named `CLSID` will be marked. Open it.

2. It's full of Class-IDs. The key is the main storage room for ActiveX detail information. Scroll down the list until you reach the Class-ID you just found out. If you followed all the steps correctly, Windows Script Host Shell Object will appear in the right pane.

3. Open the key. It contains a lot of subkeys.

Figure 3-4: Each COM object is identified by a unique Class-ID.

Take a closer look at this wealth of information.

`InProcServer32` contains the name of the physical file. It's `WSHOM.OCX`.

Secret

`InprocServer32` reveals that this COM object is to be used as an "in-process" server. It can't run alone or remotely—it always needs a host that loads the COM object into its private address space. In contrast, COM objects with a `LocalServer32` key indicate that they are independent programs. They can run without anyone's help. They can even be invoked remotely from another machine using DCOM. Most COM objects are "in-process" servers, though.

`ProgID` contains the `Program Identifier` you can use to access this object by script. It's the name of the latest version of this object. The version-independent (generic) object name is stored in `VersionIndependendProgID`, and you should always use this name in your scripts if it is available.

Using a version-dependent `ProgID` can cause problems once you upgrade objects with newer versions.

`TypeLib` tells you where to look for the secret documentation of all the methods contained in the object. If there is no `TypeLib` key, then the function information is most likely contained in the object file itself. `InProcServer32` tells you the filename. `TypeLib` again contains a Class-ID. This time, it's the Class-ID of the `TypeLibrary` file.

You can find out the physical filename of the `TypeLibrary` with the help of the `TypeLib` key. It's located below the `CLSID` key, and it's `HKEY_CLASSES_ROOT\TypeLib\`.

`ImplementedCategories` tells you what this object was designed for. You can easily find out whether it is suitable for scripting.

`ImplementedCategories` contains Class-IDs that link to `HKEY_CLASSES_ROOT\Component Categories\` and tells you more about the abilities a certain object has. You can find out whether it can be inserted into a Web page or whether it supports automation. Before Microsoft invented the `ImplementedCategories` key, information about the nature of a COM object was stored as a separate subkey — and it's still there! The subkey `Programmable` informs you that this COM object can be used as a program extension. Likewise, you can find subkeys for any of the categories found in `ImplementedCategories` — `Insertable` being only one of them.

Undocumented

In some cases, an object requires some functionality to be there before it can do its job. In these cases, you find an additional subkey called `Required Categories`. Just like `Implemented Categories`, it refers to the central Categories definition located in `HKCR\Component Categories\`.

Finding Out Undocumented Object Information

Now that you know how much valuable undocumented information is stored right in your Registry, let's develop a tool that automatically extracts all this information for you. After all, jumping back and forth in the Registry is not very convenient.

To be able to run this script, you need access to a custom Registry function because VBScript has no way to enumerate Registry subkeys. Make sure you installed the Registry toolkit found on the companion CD — `\install\ registry\setup.exe`.

```
' 3-3.VBS

' we need this object for registry access!
set wshshell = CreateObject("WScript.Shell")

' we need this CUSTOM object to enumerate
' subkeys. Make sure you installed the COM object
' as outlined in the book.
set registry = CreateObject("regtool.tob")

' we need this object to create a text file and
```

```
' output the findings:
set fs = CreateObject("Scripting.FileSystemObject")

name = InputBox("Type in the ProgID of the Object you are interested
in!")
keyA = "HKCR\" & name & "\"

' Check whether this Object is registered:
objectname = ReadKey(keyA, ok)
if not ok then
    MsgBox name & " was not found."
    WScript.Quit
end if

' create a log file:
outputfile = "C:\OBJECT.TXT"
set output = fs.CreateTextFile(outputfile, true)
Print name & ": " & objectname

' find out current version
curver = ReadKey(keyA & "CurVer\", ok)
clsid = ReadKey(keyA & "CLSID\", ok)


keyB = "HKCR\CLSID\" & clsid & "\"
physfile = ReadKey(keyB & "InprocServer32\", ok)
vidpid = ReadKey(keyB & "VersionIndependentProgID\", ok)
typelib = ReadKey(keyB & "TypeLib\", ok)

Print "Generic ProgID: " & vidpid
Print "Physical File: " & physfile
Print "File Version Information: " & GetVersion(physfile)
Print "Current Version: " & curver
Print "Class-ID: " & clsid
Print "TypeLibrary ClassID: " & typelib

keyC = "HKCR\Component Categories\"

Print "Kind of Object:"

cats = ReadKey(keyB & "Implemented Categories\", ok)
if ok then
    set categories = registry.RegEnum(keyB _
        & "Implemented Categories\")
    for each cat in categories
        catKey = keyC & cat & "\"
        if KeyExists(catKey) then
            set entries = registry.ListChildNames(catKey)
            for each entry in entries
                if entry<>"" then Print ReadKey(catKey _
                    & entry, ok)
            next
        else
```

```
                        Print "Category information is missing!"
                end if
        next
else
        Print "No Category Information"
end if

cats = ReadKey(keyB & "Required Categories\", ok)
if ok then
        set categories = registry.RegEnum(keyB _
            & "Required Categories\")
        for each cat in categories
            catKey = keyC & cat & "\"
            if KeyExists(catKey) then
                set entries = registry.ListChildNames(catKey)
                for each entry in entries
                    if entry<>"" then Print ReadKey(catKey _
                        & entry, ok)
                next
            else
                Print "Category information is missing!"
            end if
        next
else
        Print "No Required Categories"
end if

keyD = "HKCR\TypeLib\" & typelib & "\"
if typelib="" then
        Print "No TypeLib available. Use physical file " _
            & "and search application folder."
else
        set typelibs = registry.RegEnum(keyD)
        for each typelib in typelibs
            if typelib<>"" then Print "TypeLib Version " _
                & typelib & ": " & ReadKey(keyD & typelib _
                & "\0\win32\", ok)
        next
end if

' close log and show
output.close
wshshell.run outputfile

function KeyExists(key)
        on error resume next
        check = wshshell.RegRead(key)
        if not err.Number=0 then
            KeyExists = false
        else
            KeyExists = true
        end if
end function
```

```
function ReadKey(key, status)
    on error resume next
    ReadKey = wshshell.RegRead(key)
    if not err.Number=0 then
        value=""
        err.clear
        status=false
    else
        status=true
    end if
end function

sub Print(text)
    ' writes information into log file
    output.WriteLine text
end sub

function GetVersion(path)
    on error resume next
    GetVersion = fs.GetFileVersion(path)
    if not err=0 then
        err.clear
        GetVersion = -1
    end if
end function
```

Don't be too puzzled about the mechanics of this script. It basically follows the same steps you already did manually to extract the information from the Registry (see Figure 3.5).

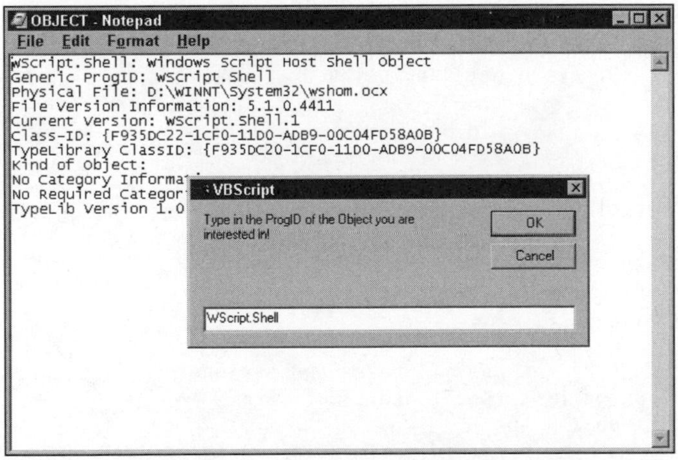

Figure 3-5: Script automatically retrieves hidden detail information.

Because the Scripting Host lacks some important Registry functions, this script uses additional custom commands defined in registry.tobtools to enumerate subkeys and values. Make sure you have installed the book toolkit.

Tip

This script is a perfect example of how to add custom commands. The book toolkit delivers methods to enumerate Registry keys because the WScript. Shell object lacks them. In this chapter, you'll only put those custom commands to work. In Chapter 4, however, you see how easy it is to program your own custom commands. And in Chapter 14, you see how the Registry command extension works.

The result is a handy text file that supplies all the hidden information about a COM object. Just type in the object's name: for example, WScript.Shell.

Listing All Automation Objects

So far, you have examined only those objects the Scripting Host brought along. What about all the other objects that might be installed on your system? How can you find out their names?

It's easy! Just take a look inside the Registry. Every accessible automation object is stored inside HKEY_CLASSES_ROOT. This key holds a lot of additional information, too. To filter out the names of automation objects, just look for keys that have a dot somewhere in their name. Keys that start with a dot represent file types. Skip those!

Again, you can delegate this work to a script:

```
' 3-4.VBS

' get advanced registry functions:
' make sure the book toolkit is installed!
set registry = CreateObject("regtool.tob")

' get a dictionary object to store key names in
set dict = CreateObject("Scripting.Dictionary")

' enumerate all keys in HKEY_CLASSES_ROOT
set allkeys = registry.RegEnum("HKCR\")

' sort out all key names that have a dot in the name:

for each key in allkeys
    ' where's the first dot (skipping initial dots)?
    pos = Instr(2, key, ".")
    if pos>0 then
        ' there's a dot. Is there another one?
        pos2 = Instr(pos+1, key, ".")
        if pos2>0 then
            ' yes, so this name is version specific
            'check whether we already have a
            ' version-independent progid!
            independent = left(key, pos2-1)
            if not dict.Exists(independent) then
                ' no, store it
                dict.Add key, 0
            end if
```

```
        else
            ' this one is version-independent.
            ' do we already have a version-dependent
            ' progID in store?
            vdpid = ""
            for each element in dict
                if len(element)>len(key) then
                    if left(element, len(key)+1)=key & "." then
                        ' yes, return name
                        vdpid = element
                        exit for
                    end if
                end if
            next
            ' any version dependent progID found?
            if vdpid="" then
                ' no, add to store
                dict.add key, 0
            else
                ' yes, replace
                dict.Remove vdpid
                dict.add key, 0
            end if
        end if
    end if
next

MsgBox dict.Count & " Objects found!"
for each key in dict
    list = list & key & vbCr
next

MsgBox list
```

Try it out! Be patient, the script takes some seconds to execute. Then it reports the number of objects it found and lists their names (see Figure 3-6).

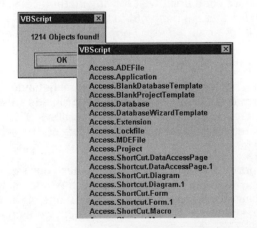

Figure 3-6: Automatically build a list of all installed COM objects.

The script automatically takes care of multiple-version objects. It reports the version-independent ProgID, if available; otherwise, it reports the version-specific ProgID.

Most likely, there will be hundreds of objects, and they won't all fit into the dialog box. That's okay, though. So far, the list of objects is interesting but still not refined enough. Most of the objects serve internal purposes and cannot be used as script components.

The ProgID consists of two parts. The first part represents the "server" object. The second part is the name of a section inside this server object. ProgIDs that share the first part are related and live inside the same object file.

Determining Whether an Object is Scriptable

To get a real useful list of objects that can serve as Script extensions, you need to further test the objects. It's easy—just call CreateObject on each of the objects and see what happens. Should there be an error, then you know for sure that this object is unsuitable for scripting.

Calling CreateObject on an object usually only establishes a connection to this object. Sometimes, however, the object will respond with some action. You then know that these objects have defined code in the Initialize code segment. This code is executed immediately upon object initialization.

However, calling CreateObject on an unknown object is a brute-force approach. If the object is generally unsuitable for scripting, CreateObject will simply fail. This is okay because the script uses the on error resume next safety net.

If the object is generally suitable for scripting, CreateObject will launch the code inside the object. Usually, nothing exciting happens—most objects just get initialized and patiently await your commands. There are some objects, though, which start right away and don't wait for any method calls. Calling CreateObject is enough for them to jump out in the open. Should this happen to you, then you'll see some windows pop up or messages appear. Just click them away.

In very rare circumstances, calling CreateObject can even crash your script (or your entire machine). This is obviously neither normal behavior nor by design. It indicates some malfunction inside the object or inside some other component the object relates to. COM objects are executables. They can fail just as any regular software program can crash. So, before starting the spy-script, save any valuable information and close all your programs!

It's very useful to know more about why an object crashes your system. To find out, install Dr. Watson, a little utility that comes with Windows. It will tell you more about the cause of a crash. For example, on one of the test systems, three objects crashed the script. All three objects were innocent, though! It turned out that in all three cases, the Adobe Type Manager caused the fault by changing system files it wasn't supposed to. On systems without this software, no crashes occurred.

The test script checks all objects and records a log file. If something goes wrong and your script breaks, then just start it over again. It'll skip the last object and start where it left off. So even if some exception errors do occur, you will eventually get a list of all suitable scripting objects — and warnings about the ones that aren't stable.

Caution

On Windows NT/2000, there may be numerous COM objects responsible for business logic or advanced server features. It's common for them to raise errors when called directly. Try generating the list only on systems that are not crucial to your business. They might stop responding and need a restart. You must be sure your system can safely crash. If in doubt, use the files on the companion CD I've prepared for you instead of generating your own.

I have prepared sample files for both Windows 98 and Windows 2000. They represent objects available on my test systems and may not be completely identical to what's available on yours. However, should you have trouble generating the list on your system, they provide information about most standard COM objects. You can find both samples here — `\info\win98.txt` and `\info.win2000.txt`.

```
'3-5.VBS

' get advanced registry functions:
' make sure the book toolkit is installed!
set registry = CreateObject("regtool.tob")

' get a dictionary object to store key names in
set dict = CreateObject("Scripting.Dictionary")

set fs = CreateObject("Scripting.FileSystemObject")
set wshshell = CreateObject("WScript.Shell")

' enumerate all keys in HKEY_CLASSES_ROOT
set allkeys = registry.RegEnum("HKCR\")

' sort out all key names that have a dot in the name:

for each key in allkeys
    ' where's the first dot (skipping initial dots)?
    pos = Instr(2, key, ".")
    if pos>0 then
        ' there's a dot. Is there another one?
        pos2 = Instr(pos+1, key, ".")
        if pos2>0 then
            ' yes, so this name is version specific
            'check whether we already have a
' version-independent progid!
            independent = left(key, pos2-1)
```

```
                            if not dict.Exists(independent) then
                                ' no, store it
                                dict.Add key, 0
                            end if
                    else
                        ' this one is version-independent.
                        ' do we already have a version-dependent
                        ' progID in store?
                        vdpid = ""
                        for each element in dict
                            if len(element)>len(key) then
                                if left(element, len(key)+1)=key & "." then
                                    ' yes, return name
                                    vdpid = element
                                    exit for
                                end if
                            end if
                        next
                        ' any version dependent progID found?
                        if vdpid="" then
                            ' no, add to store
                            dict.add key, 0
                        else
                            ' yes, replace
                            dict.Remove vdpid
                            dict.add key, 0
                        end if
                    end if
            end if
next

MsgBox dict.Count & " Objects found! Now checking if suitable" _
& " for scripting!"

' open log file
logfile = "C:\SCRIPTOBJECTS.TXT"

' open crash recovery file
crash = "C:\CRASH.TXT"
if fs.FileExists(crash) then
    set input = fs.OpenTextFile(crash)
    crashedAt = Fix(input.ReadLine)
    input.close
    MsgBox "Crash detected: skipping Object!"
    ' open for append!
    set output = fs.OpenTextFile(logfile, 8)
else
    crashedAt = 0
    set output = fs.CreateTextFile(logfile, true)
end if

' check every object
for each key in dict
```

```
        crashcount = crashcount + 1
        LogCall crashcount
        if crashCount = crashedAt then
            MsgBox "This Object caused a crash: " & key
            Print "WARNING" & vbTab & key & " caused a crash!"
        elseif crashcount>crashedAt then
            if CheckObject(key) then
                Print key
            end if
        end if
    next

    ' delete crash log
    fs.DeleteFile crash, true

    ' open file

    wshshell.run logfile

    sub Print(text)
        output.WriteLine text
    end sub

    function CheckObject(name)
        ' turn off error handling
        on error resume next
        ' try to access object
        set dummy = CreateObject(name)
        ' check whether error was raised:
        if not err.Number=0 then
            ' object unsuitable
            err.clear
            CheckObject=false
        else
            ' add Object Information:
            name = name & vbTab & TypeName(dummy) & vbTab _
                & ProcessInfo(name)

            ' Object ok for scripting
            CheckObject=true
        end if

        ' release Object
        WScript.DisconnectObject dummy
    end function

    sub LogCall(crashcount)
        set recovery = fs.CreateTextFile(crash, true)
        recovery.WriteLine crashcount
        recovery.close
    end sub

    function ProcessInfo(name)
```

```
        clsid = ReadKey("HKCR\" & name & "\CLSID\", ok)
        keyA = "HKCR\CLSID\" & clsid & "\"
        physicalname = ReadKey(keyA & "InprocServer32\", ok)
        if physicalname = "" then
            physicalname = ReadKey(keyA & "LocalServer32\", ok)
        end if
        if physicalname="" then
            physicalname = "unknown object file location"
        end if
        typelib = ReadKey(keyA & "TypeLib\", ok)
        if typelib<>"" then
            set typelibs = registry.RegEnum("HKCR\TypeLib\" _
                & typelib & "\")
            for each typelibid in typelibs
                if typelibid<>"" then lib = lib _
                    & ReadKey("HKCR\TypeLib\" & typelib _
                    & "\" & typelibid & "\0\win32\", ok) & vbTab
            next
        else
            lib = "no typelib" & vbTab
        end if
        ProcessInfo = physicalname & vbTab & lib
end function

function KeyExists(key)
    on error resume next
    check = wshshell.RegRead(key)
    if not err.Number=0 then
        KeyExists = false
    else
        KeyExists = true
    end if
end function

function ReadKey(key, status)
    on error resume next
    ReadKey = wshshell.RegRead(key)
    if not err.Number=0 then
        value=""
        err.clear
        status=false
    else
        status=true
    end if
end function
```

Note

Go ahead and sip your coffee. The script takes many minutes to check all the available objects. Even though it works behind the scenes, it's still alive. You'll either get the final list of object names or some sort of reaction to the test call. Close all program windows that might appear, and restart the script if Windows reports an exception fault. Once the list is generated, restart your system — just to make sure. The list will still be there. It's stored in C:\SCRIPTOBJECTS.TXT.

This list includes the `ProgID` (the object name tag you pass to `CreateObject` to get a hold of the object) and the object `Type`. Most of the time, the object `Type` will only be "Object", but some objects reveal their true names. This is valuable information because it helps to identify the object's inner structure once you tap into the `TypeLibrary`.

In addition, the list reveals the physical name of the object and the names of any type libraries associated with this object. This information will come in handy throughout the rest of this book.

Reading Secret TypeLibrary Information

Now that you know how many potentially useful objects reside on your machine, you just need a way to access the functions stored inside. This is where the fun comes to an abrupt end because most objects are undocumented.

However, there are ways to auto-document hidden object functions yourself. Most objects come with a TypeLibrary, and inside this TypeLibrary, you find detailed information about all functions, events, and constants defined in the object.

Secret

Type Libraries are used by program development environments like Visual Basic to check the syntax and give clues to the programmer. This is why many objects "involuntarily" contain very detailed documentation, even if they did not intend to supply this information to you. It's all a matter of accessing the information stored in the TypeLibrary.

Under normal conditions, a TypeLibrary is of no great use. The Scripting Host has only limited abilities to "look inside" and report the hidden information. This is why I have developed a little add-on. It uncovers any useful information found in any TypeLibrary and helps to get very detailed documentation about any object you might be interested in. Just make sure you install the book toolkit.

Auto-Documenting Undocumented Objects

Above, you constructed a list of all the potentially useful objects installed on your system. All the information is stored in `C:\SCRIPTOBJECTS.TXT`. Next, extract the "owners manual" for any of these objects with the help of the TypeLibrary.

To be able to do so, your scripts again need a command extension. Make sure you install `\install\typelib\setup.exe`, found on the on the companion CD, before trying to launch the following script.

Pick out an object you would like to know more about. Let's start with `WScript.Shell`. The list states that the real name is `WSHOM.OCX`. This file resides in the Windows system folder.

Let's check out which objects really live inside this file (see Figure 3-7):

```
' 3-6.VBS

obj = InputBox("Object?",,"wshom.ocx")
set wshshell = CreateObject("WScript.Shell")

set tl = CreateObject("typelib.decoder")
set erg = tl.GetInterfaces(obj)
for each interface in erg
    list = list & interface & vbCr
next
MsgBox list
```

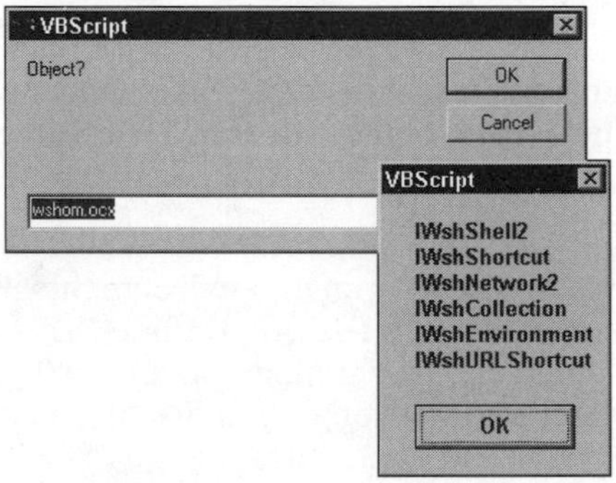

Figure 3-7: Peek into COM objects and find out names of internal objects.

It works! The script reports a number of object names, and you can see two things immediately. First, you'll notice that wshom.ocx contains the IWshShell2 object, which belongs to WScript.Shell. It also contains IWshNetwork2, which belongs to WScript.Network. In addition, wshom.ocx contains a number of other objects.

Object files contain many different objects. Some of them refer to objects that scripts can instantiate using CreateObject. These are "Start-Objects." Other objects cannot be created directly. For example, a CreateObject on WScript.Shell returns an IWshShell2-Object. One of the hidden functions inside IWshShell2 is called CreateShortcut, and this function returns either IWshShortcut- or IWshURLShortcut-Object. Both objects cannot be created directly using CreateObject.

If you use WSH 2.0, then WScript.Shell returns IWshShell2-Object. If you use WSH 1.0, then you get the original object called IWshShell. Take a look at your SCRIPTOBJECTS.TXT list: It tells you exactly which object type your system returns.

Now that you know the internal name of the object, you can take a look inside and retrieve the internal "owner's manual." Just supply the filename of the

TypeLibrary and the name of the object you are interested in: for example,
wshom.ocx and IWshShell2 (see Figure 3-8).

```
' 3-7.VBS

' make sure you installed the custom object
' as shown in the book.

set tl = CreateObject("typelib.decoder")
set fs = CreateObject("Scripting.FileSystemObject")
set wshshell = CreateObject("WScript.Shell")

typelib = InputBox("Please enter the name of the" _
& " type library!",,"wshom.ocx")
object = InputBox("Please enter the name of the" _
& " object!",,"IWshShell2")

docu = "C:\docu.txt"
set output = fs.CreateTextFile(docu, true)

set ifc = tl.EnumInterface(typelib, object)
for each info in ifc
    infos = split(info, vbTab)
    output.WriteLine infos(0)
    if len(infos(1))>0 then
        output.WriteLine infos(1)
    else
        output.WriteLine "no description available"
    end if
next
output.close
wshshell.Run "IEXPLORE.EXE " & docu
```

Wow! The script lists all the functions and procedures stored in IWshShell2,
and you now know the exact syntax of any command available through
WScript.Shell. That is, you know the names of the commands, the number
and kind of arguments to supply, and the type of return value, if any.

Undocumented

If you are using the "old" WSH 1.0, there is no IWshShell2 object. Use
IWshShell instead.

What you do not get is background information on the commands.
wshom.ocx does not supply this kind of information. Instead, the list just
states "no description available."

Check out what happens if you list the commands stored in
Scripting.FileSystemObject. To do this, take a look in your
C:\SCRIPTOBJECTS.TXT list and search for Scripting.FileSystemObject.

Immediately, you know that this object is stored in scrrun.dll and that the
TypeLibrary is stored in the same file. You also know that you need to look
for an object called FileSystemObject. Supply this information to your
script above.

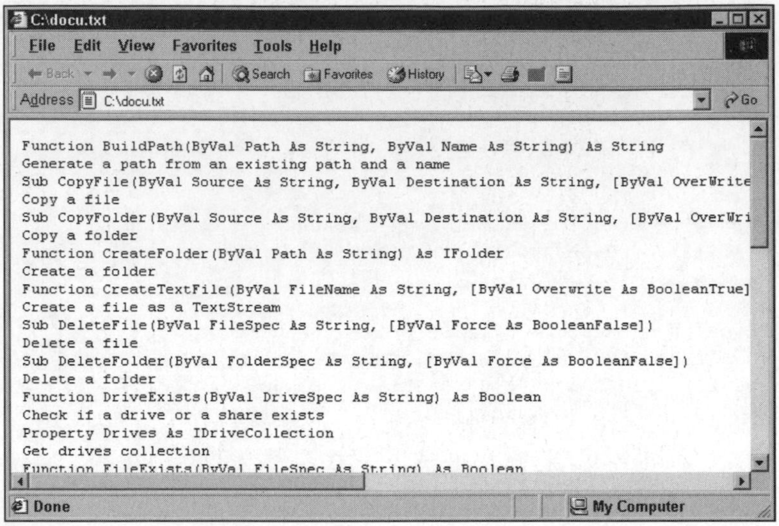

Figure 3-8: Often, the TypeLibrary even includes documentation about the use of functions.

This time, the list includes a short description of each command that tells you what the command is supposed to do. There's no law that requires an object to supply additional descriptive information, but many objects deliver such information voluntarily.

Getting More Help On Specific Commands

In everyday life, you need some sort of information source that tells you more about available commands and their purposes. There are numerous ways to get this information.

Maybe you need to quickly look up the syntax of some command. To do so with the help of the TypeLibrary, you would need to know a lot of information: You would need to know the object file and the object name. In addition, you would obviously need to know the exact name of the command you are looking for.

This is too much work—let your scripts do the dirty stuff. The following script returns any command that contains your search word anywhere in its name, and the script automatically searches the most common object files and all objects inside them.

```
' 3-8.VBS

' make sure you installed the custom object
' as shown in the book.

set ti = CreateObject("typelib.decoder")
```

```
list = Split("wshom.ocx;vbscript.dll;scrrun.dll;" _
& "shdocvw.dll;wscript.exe", ";")
searchword = InputBox("Please enter the command name you are looking
for!")
for each library in list
    result = ti.Search(searchword, library)
    if not result="" then
        endresult = endresult & "(" & library & ")" & vbCrLf & result
    end if
next
MsgBox endresult
```

Test this script! Just enter some command name: GetDrive, for example. Immediately, the script opens a dialog window and displays the calling syntax. It also tells you which object file contains the command: for example, scrrun.dll. Even the name of the internal object that supplies this command is provided: in this case, FileSystemObject (see Figure 3-9).

This script is not limited to external objects. It also queries the files vbscript.dll and wscript.exe, so you can also search for intrinsic VBScript commands like MsgBox and InputBox or commands provided by the scripting host like Sleep (WSH 2.0 only).

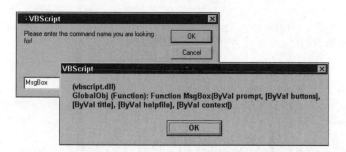

Figure 3-9: Search for function syntax using key words.

Tip The script automatically searches the most common objects. You can always append the list of filenames to include more objects. If objects are stored outside the system folders covered by the PATH environment variable, then you need to provide the full path name.

Interesting, don't you agree? The InputBox command features some undocumented arguments to specify the position. Check this line out:

```
answer = InputBox("Question",,,10,10)
```

This line opens an InputBox dialog window, but this time, you can specify its upper-left corner position on your screen.

Note that optional arguments are enclosed by square brackets. You immediately see that the prompt is the only argument InputBox requires.

Even more interesting: The search function returns any command that includes your search word anywhere in its name. So, if you don't know the exact command name, just type in part of it. For example, type in **Drive**! Now you get a list of all kinds of commands that relate to drives (see Figure 3-10).

Note also that some functions are provided by more than one object, so there may be duplicate entries. This is normal behavior.

```
VBScript                                                    [X]

(wshom.ocx)
IWshNetwork (Function): Function EnumNetworkDrives As IWshCollection

IWshNetwork_Class (Function): Function EnumNetworkDrives As
IWshCollection
(scrrun.dll)
FileSystemObject (Property): Property Drives As IDriveCollection
IFileSystem (Property): Property Drives As IDriveCollection
(wscript.exe)
FileSystemObject (Property): Property Drives As IDriveCollection
IFileSystem (Property): Property Drives As IDriveCollection

                        [    OK    ]
```

Figure 3-10: Find any function related to "Drives."

If you want to limit the search result to only those commands that start with your search text, then just replace one line of code:

```
result = ti.Search(searchword, library, false)
```

To be able to use a specific command, you should carefully look at the object name that provides this functionality. Let's suppose you have searched for the key word Drive. The dialog box shows all commands with "drive" in its name.

Maybe you are interested in EnumNetworkDrives. As you see, this command is provided by IWshNetwork, so take a look in your C:\scriptobjects.txt file and search for IWshNetwork. As you see, WScript.Network provides this object. Next, take a look at the command syntax. The function EnumNetworkDrives returns IWshCollection. This name is no standard variable type, so you can safely assume it's another object; therefore, you need to store the function result using Set. This is all you need to know:

```
' 3-9.VBS

' get access to IWshNetwork-Object
set iwshnetwork = CreateObject("WScript.Network")
' call unknown command:
set iwshcollection = iwshnetwork.EnumNetworkDrives
MsgBox TypeName(iwshcollection)
```

The script works and no error is raised. Nothing exciting happens either, though. EnumNetworkDrives has retrieved an iwshcollection object, and you need to know more about this object before you can do something with it.

The previous script can't help you much. IWshCollection is an object, not a command, so you can't search for it. Try the next script! It searches both for commands and for objects, and because the result can be a lot of information, it displays the information as a text file:

```
' 3-10.VBS

' make sure you installed the custom object
' as shown in the book.

set fs = CreateObject("Scripting.FileSystemObject")
set wshshell = CreateObject("WScript.Shell")

set ti = CreateObject("typelib.decoder")
list = Split("wshom.ocx;vbscript.dll;scrrun.dll;" _
& "shdocvw.dll;wscript.exe", ";")
searchword = InputBox("Please enter the command name you are looking
for!")

for each library in list
    result = ti.Search(searchword, library)
    if not result="" then
        endresult = endresult & "(" & library & ")" _
& vbCrLf & result
    end if
next

for each library in list
    set iflist = ti.GetTypeInfos(library)
    for each interfacename in iflist
        if Instr(lcase(interfacename), lcase(searchword))>0 then
            set result = ti.EnumInterface(library, interfacename)
            if result.Count>0 then
                endresult = endresult & "(" & library & ")(" _
                    & interfacename & ")" & vbCrLf
                for each infoset in result
                    info = Split(infoset, vbTab)
                    endresult = endresult & info(0) & vbCrLf
                    if not info(1)="" then
                        endresult = endresult & info(1) _
                            & vbCrLf
                    end if
                next
            end if
        end if
    next
next

file = "C:\doku_" & searchword & ".txt"
set output = fs.CreateTextFile(file, true)
output.WriteLine endresult
output.close
wshshell.run file
```

Now search for `IWshCollection`! You will get a complete reference of all its methods and properties (see Figure 3-11).

```
doku IWshCollection - Notepad
File  Edit  Format  Help
(wshom.ocx)(IWshCollection)
Function _NewEnum As Unknown
Function Count As Long
Function Item(pvarIndex)
Property length As Long
(wshom.ocx)(IWshCollection_Class)
Function _NewEnum As Unknown
Function Count As Long
Function Item(pvarIndex)
Property length As Long
```

Figure 3-11: Build complete function lists for future reference and research.

As it turns out, the `IWshCollection` object is a generic object used to store any kind of information. This is all you need to know in order to complete your script:

```
' 3-11.VBS

' get access to IWshNetwork-Object
set iwshnetwork = CreateObject("WScript.Network")
' call unknown command:
set iwshcollection = iwshnetwork.EnumNetworkDrives
' get detail information
if iwshcollection.Count>0 then
' how many network connections exist?
MsgBox "Network connections: " & (iwshcollection.Count/2)
    for x = 0 to iwshcollection.Count - 1 step 2
        connect = "Connection Name: """ & iwshcollection.Item(x)
        connect = connect & """ UNC: " & iwshcollection.Item(x+1)
        MsgBox connect
    next
end if
```

`Count` tells you how many pieces of information are stored inside the collection. You can retrieve the actual information with `for...next` using `Item(x)` and using index number 0 for the first collection element, or you can use `for each...next`.

Tip

The helper tools can provide information about the structure of commands and objects. They cannot tell you all the details, though. So, it's up to you to find out which information `EnumNetworkDrives` actually returns. This is part of the adventure game. Fortunately, you just need to look at the returned data to find out what it stands for.

`EnumNetworkDrives` happens to store two pieces of information per network connection: the name of the connection (if any) and its UNC path name. This is why the script divides `Count` by 2 to retrieve the number of actual network connections, and this is also the reason why the script uses for...next with step 2. It wants to retrieve two pieces of information at a time.

Undocumented

EnumNetworkDrives lists all currently active network connections. This includes permanent connections as well as temporary connections. For example, you could use Run from the Start menu and type in a valid UNC path like \\10.10.1.5 [Enter]. This would establish a temporary connection to the server 10.10.1.5, and EnumNetworkDrives would report this connection. Because it's a temporary connection, it does not carry a name tag.

Getting access to hidden help files

It's amazing: Many object functions are extremely well-documented, but the documentation is stored away in some help file deep down on your hard drive. Again, here comes the TypeLibrary to the rescue. It contains help context information that specifies not only the name of the help file but also the "page" that contains the information about the specific function you wonder about.

Secret

The help information provided by the TypeLibrary isn't supposed to help you out. Instead, it's provided for programming environments: They can pop up the right help file whenever the programmer hits [F1]. Luckily, this help information is available to your scripts, too!

Check out the following script. It wants you to type in the exact name of some command. This time, it won't be enough to just specify part of the name. Your input doesn't need to be case-sensitive, though. See what happens if you type in MsgBox!

```
' 3-12.VBS

' make sure you installed the custom object
' as shown in the book.

set ti = CreateObject("typelib.decoder")
set fs = CreateObject("Scripting.FileSystemObject")
set wshshell = CreateObject("WScript.Shell")

list = Split("wshom.ocx;vbscript.dll;scrrun.dll" _
& ";shdocvw.dll;wscript.exe", ";")
searchword = InputBox("Please enter the command name you are looking
for!")
helpfile = ""
for each library in list
    result = ti.SearchHelp(searchword, library)
    if not result="" then
        helpfile = result
    end if
next
if not helpfile="" then
    filename = mid(helpfile, InstrRev(helpfile, " ")+1)
    if fs.FileExists(filename) then
```

```
        msg = searchword & " is covered in " & filename & vbCr _
& "Do you want to open help file?"
        if MsgBox(msg, vbYesNo)=vbYes then
            wshshell.Run helpfile
        end if
    else
        msg = searchword & " is covered in " & filename & vbCr _
& "The file does not exist on your computer."
        MsgBox msg
    end if
else
    MsgBox "No help file associated with this item."
end if
```

Darn. There isn't a help file associated with this command. Try a different command: for example, GetDrive. Hey, this time a help file is specified! You can open the help file right away if it's installed on your computer. This way, you get immediate help and some example code. In my case, the documentation is in German because on my system, the German version of the MSDN library was installed (see Figure 3-12).

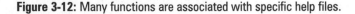

Figure 3-12: Many functions are associated with specific help files.

Tip

Should the script report that the help file is missing on your computer, then manually search your hard drive using Search from the Start menu. Sometimes, help files do exist but are misplaced. Always search for the filename without extension, so if the file VBENLR98.CHM is missing, search for VBENLR98 only. Help files can consist of more than a single file, and you want to find all parts of it. Then, copy all found files into the appropriate folder. Should the file be missing, then surf to one of the internet search pages like www.altavista.com and look for the file someplace else. Maybe you can download it somewhere.

Why are help files sometimes missing? It's by design. Remember that help context information is provided mainly for programming environments like Visual Basic. So, sometimes the help files are also part of these software packages and are only available if you install them.

Still, you are not required to buy expensive programming software just to get help information. Both WScript- and Scripting-Objects are well-documented. The help files are provided on the book CD. They will not match the internal help context IDs, but it's easy to look up the information manually using the index page.

Most of what you have discovered in this chapter is useful primarily to access undocumented objects. These objects bring their own help files (if available), so there's no need for any programming environment anyway.

Just install the Kodak Imaging tools on your system to see how this concept works! They are free, and they are part of any Windows version (see Chapter 22 for details). Then, extend your search scripts by adding the new object filenames:

```
Split("wshom.ocx;vbscript.DLL;scrrun.DLL;shdocvw.DLL;wscript.exe;imgad
min.ocx;imgedit.ocx;imgscan.ocx;imgthumb.ocx", ";")
```

Now try it out! Search for the command ScannerAvailable. The command is found in no time, and you get a reference to its help file. Open it. Automatically, the script jumps to the right page of the file, and you get all the official documentation available for ScannerAvailable.

Undocumented

In Windows 2000, for some reason, Microsoft decided to take out both the help information and the help file for the imaging controls. Still, you can use the free version. This chapter provides the tools to reveal the internal methods, and Chapter 21 provides a lot of sample scripts!

There are two types of help files: Old Windows help files carry the extension .hlp. You can open those files using WINHELP.EXE and jump to a specific page using option -n. Current help files come in a different flavor — they carry the extension .chm and consist of HTML pages. You can open those help files with HH.EXE and jump to individual pages using the hidden option -mapid.

Finding More Information About Commands

If you need additional information about a specific command, search this book's index. It contains hundreds of examples. If you are still hungry for more, then surf to one of the Internet search sites like www.altavista.com and enter the command name as a search phrase. You will be amazed how much useful information will pop up in your browser.

Summary

Hundreds of potentially useful automation objects are installed on your system, and most of them are valuable add-ons to your scripts. It only takes some hidden tools and techniques to uncover the important hidden information inside these objects. Tools provide you with the detailed "owner's manual" of any automation object you find interesting. With the help of this information, you can immediately start accessing the internal functions.

Chapter 4

Developing Your Own Script Components

In This Chapter

- ▶ Get accustomed to the free Visual Basic Control Creation Edition
- ▶ Develop your own script extensions using Windows API functions
- ▶ Open and close the CD-ROM tray by script
- ▶ Look at Windows API functions and DECLARE in-depth
- ▶ Examine functions stored in DLL files
- ▶ Develop your own dialog boxes
- ▶ Discover properties and design your own
- ▶ Create optional parameters and default values
- ▶ Change window style
- ▶ Make windows resizable
- ▶ Distribute self-made COM objects to others

COM objects work like command extensions and provide all the functions missing in VBScript. In the previous chapter, you saw how useful it is to access COM objects.

You are not limited to the COM objects other people have developed. You can design your own. It"s very easy, and it's free, too. Microsoft provides all the necessary development tools, and you can find them on the companion CD.

Developing your own COM objects allows you to access even the most basic Windows Application Programming Interface (API) functions. COM objects can do anything a "C" or Visual Basic programmer can do.

In this chapter, I'll show you how to develop your own COM objects. It's easy, because you can use Visual Basic to develop COM objects. Visual Basic is very similar to VBScript. In fact, VBScript is just a subset of Visual Basic, so you already know most of what is needed.

Tip

COM development is the second step, not the first. Before you start developing your own COM objects, browse through Part II and get familiar with VBScript and the script examples. Once you feel comfortable with VBScript, it's only a small step to COM development.

You don't need to buy Visual Basic in order to develop COM components. Microsoft has created a special version of Visual Basic called Visual Basic Control Creation Edition. It's a full Visual Basic development environment. Microsoft has just disabled some options so you can't create "regular" programs. You can, however, easily create COM objects, and that's all you need. The VB CCE is included on the companion CD. You just need to install it.

Undocumented

Microsoft has released the VB CCE primarily to promote the use of ActiveX Internet controls. So, the primary target group is Web developers. However, ActiveX controls are not a good choice to spice up Web pages, primarily because of security concerns outlined in the Preface. Fortunately, ActiveX controls are not limited to Web pages. They can act as COM objects, too.

Getting Accustomed to VB CCE

After installation, you'll find a new program group called Visual Basic 5.0 CCE. Inside, you'll find the VB CCE program and an Application Wizard. The Application Wizard helps you to produce setup files so you can distribute your COM objects to others.

Once you start VB CCE, the New Project window opens. Pick ActiveX Control to start a new ActiveX control project.

Tip

Other project types are available, too. However, VB CCE can't compile a Standard .exe, so the only useful option is ActiveX Control.

You get a new project. At first, the menu bars and window panes are a little overwhelming, but not for long. Take a look at Figure 4-1.

Toolbox

On the left side, you'll see the toolbox. It contains controls that you can place inside your project. You need the toolbox only if you plan to design a window. For now, you won't need controls, so you can safely turn the toolbox off. To get it back later, open the View command and choose Toolbox.

Tip

All Toolbars (this includes Toolbox window as well as all the other toolbars) are dockable. It's up to you whether you want to use them docked or as floating windows. You can even stack a couple of toolbars on top of each other or dock them at another side of the main window.

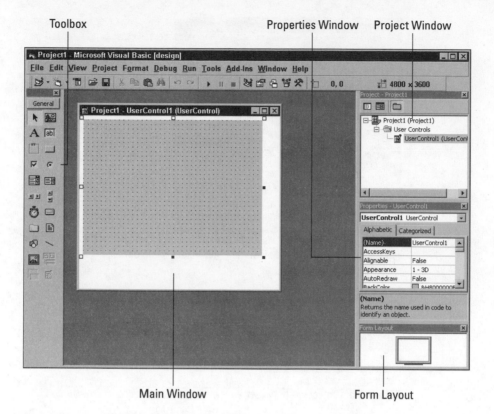

Figure 4-1: Discover the anatomy of Visual Basic Control Creation Edition.

Main window

The main window shows the object you are developing. There are two different views, and Object View is enabled by default. In Object View, you see the user interface. It's just a gray square, but you can easily place controls on it — just double-click a control in the toolbox window.

In Code view, you will see the "inside" of your object. Code view is much more important than Object view because in Code view you can develop the internal mechanics of your object. To switch between both view modes, just right-click somewhere inside the main window and choose View Code (see Figure 4-2). You can also open the View menu and choose Code to switch to Code view.

Project Explorer

On the right side, you'll see three individual helper windows. One of them is the Project Explorer. It works like a table of contents and lists all the components your object consists of. At the beginning, there is only one object — UserControl. It's stored in the virtual User Controls folder, which is part of your project, most likely called Project1 (see Figure 4-3).

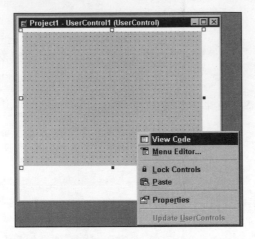

Figure 4-2: Switch to Code view to enter Visual Basic code.

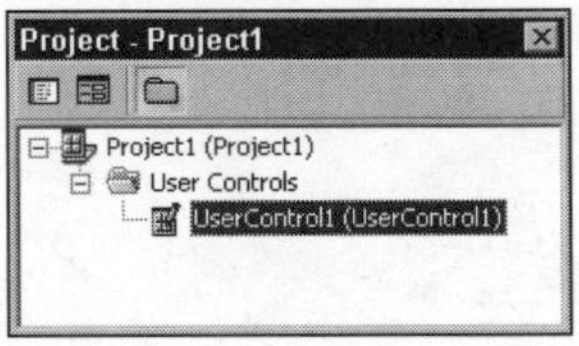

Figure 4-3: Project window lists your projects' elements.

You can always turn this window off if it's in the way. You can get it back later by opening the View menu and choosing Project Explorer. Leave this window open, though, because you need it to assign a name to your project.

Properties window

The Properties window displays all the properties of a control. Because there is only one control called UserControl, it shows the properties of your control form. You can always close this window and get it back later by opening the View menu: Choose Properties Window. Leave the window open, though, because you will need it in a second to change your control's name.

Form Layout window

The last helper window displays any forms you may have developed — it's a chance for you to judge their looks. But, you're not going to design any forms now, so just turn the window off. You can always get it back by opening the View menu and choosing Form Layout Window.

Developing Your Own Script Extension

Once you have closed all unnecessary windows and switched to Code view, your VB CCE window looks a lot friendlier. In fact, it almost looks like the text editor you used to develop scripts. And it works much the same, too.

Before you start, rethink what you are going to do. You are going to develop a script add-on. You aren't going to develop a stand-alone program. So, at this stage, all you want to do is define functions and procedures, which can then be called by your scripts. Don't write a main script body.

For example, write something like this:

```
Sub SayHello(text)
    MsgBox "This is my message: " & text
end sub
```

This code is just plain script code, so you can just as easily use it inside of a VBScript file. This time, however, you are designing a COM component. One of the first differences you'll notice is the professional development environment. VB CCE automatically adds the End Sub statement, and once you type in MsgBox, an info box opens and assists you by providing the syntax information (see Figure 4-4).

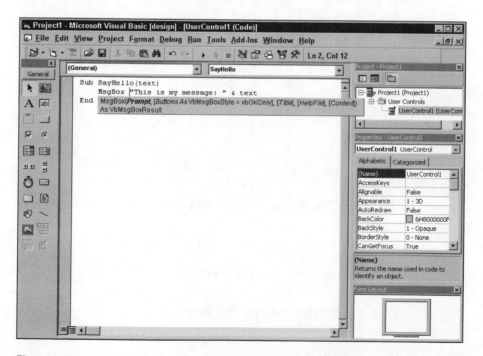

Figure 4-4: You can design your own COM objects using plain VBScript.

You can't execute your code, though. If you click the Play button, you'll just get an error message stating that controls can't run independently. Always remember that controls are designed to be add-ons to script hosts like the Windows Scripting Host or the Internet Explorer. They can't run independently.

Assigning a name to your control

The next important step is to assign a name to your control. This name is very important because it will be used as ProgID inside your scripts to access your new component.

First, assign a name to your project. Switch to the Project Explorer and click the Project1-entry. In the Properties window, you now see the only property available — Name (see Figure 4-5). Click in this field and assign a new name.

Tip Be careful choosing a name. Never use a name already taken by some other object installed on your system. In this example, use test.

Figure 4-5: Mark your project and assign a name in the Property window.

Next, you need to assign a name to your control. Switch to the Project Explorer window and click UserControl1. Now the Properties window shows the properties of your control. Click the Name field and choose a name (see Figure 4-6).

Tip You cannot use the same name you already used for your project. In this example, use module.

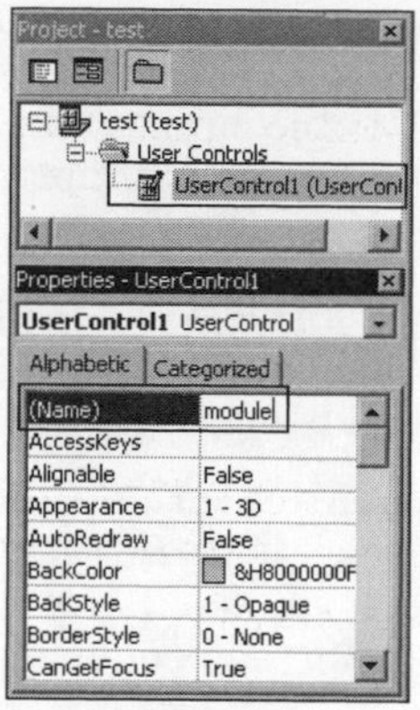

Figure 4-6: Mark your user control and assign a name in the Property window.

Your control is now named `test.module`.

Compiling the COM object

You are almost finished. You just need to compile your code, transforming it into a real COM object. Open the file menu and choose Make `test.ocx`. Write down the name of the `OCX` file somewhere so you know where your component will be stored.

Testing your new object

Once you have compiled your object, it's ready for use by your scripts. You can access it just like any other COM object. Try the following script code. Enter it into a text editor and save it with the .vbs file extension:

```
' 4-1.VBS

set myobj = CreateObject("test.module")
myobj.SayHello "Hi World!"
MsgBox TypeName(myobj)
```

It works. Your script accesses your new COM object using `CreateObject` and the name you assigned to both your project and your user control. Then it calls the `SayHello` procedure.

`TypeName` reveals the name of the object you accessed. It's "module," just as expected.

Advantages of COM objects

Why go through the hassle of developing a COM object if you can just as easily implement the same functionality directly into your script? There are a number of sound reasons:

- Hide your code: If you want, you can place it inside a COM object to hide it. COM objects always work like black boxes. You can use them, but you can't look inside them once they are compiled.

- Reuse code: You can easily design comprehensive script extensions and include them in any script file you feel like. Because the complex mechanics are stored inside the COM object, you don't need to clutter your script code. It will only use one `CreateObject` command to access all the functionality inside your COM object.

- Language independence: COM objects are language-independent because the COM interface uses a common standard. Any script language can use COM objects. So if you prefer to solve a problem using Visual Basic, but you like JavaScript as a script language, then develop a COM object using MS CCE and plug it into your JavaScript script. You can even use your COM objects inside Visual Basic for Applications scripts, so you can add functionality to WinWord macros.

- Advanced functions: VB CCE uses Visual Basic, not VBScript. So far, your COM object is limited to the VBScript subset of commands. But not for much longer. Visual Basic is able to access any of the basic Windows API functions, so you can write script enhancements that offer completely new functionality not available to VBScript.

- Forms and dialog windows: COM objects can neither run independently nor open multiple windows. COM objects can, however, display one single window, so you can design a graphical user interface for your scripts. For example, you can develop an enhanced `InputBox` function that hides what a user enters — perfectly suited for password checks. You can even develop stand-alone disk tools that just need to be called by a script.

Calling Windows API Functions

Most of the time, software packages are not monolithic blocks of code. Instead, they contain many different modules, and each module serves a specific purpose. In real life, whenever you start such an application, the individual components start to communicate with one another, sending commands and requests back and forth.

This is good news. Nothing prevents you from talking to the modules as well. You can access a component and call its functions, and the component won't realize that you're an outsider. It will do whatever it's supposed to do.

In fact, to make Windows software development easier, Microsoft provides hundreds of DLL files stuffed with internal Windows functions that you would never be able to invoke from any dialog box. They're there for internal purposes, and almost any software you buy makes heavy use of them. This set of basic Windows commands is called the application programming interface (API).

Originally, this API was developed for "serious programmers" using a complicated programming language like C. However, Visual Basic can access those API functions as well. And this is where COM objects come into play.

VBScript has no way of accessing API functions because it doesn't have a built-in command to specify DLL files and call certain functions within it. Visual Basic, in contrast, sports the declare command, and because VB CCE uses the full language set of Visual Basic, you can easily access API functions from inside your COM object and then repackage them so your scripts can access the functions.

Opening and closing the CD-ROM tray

Take a look at your CD-ROM drive, for example. Right-click the CD-ROM drive icon in the Explorer window, and you see the Eject command (see Figure 4-7). Using it, you can open and close the CD-ROM tray without having to climb under your desk and search for the button on the drive.

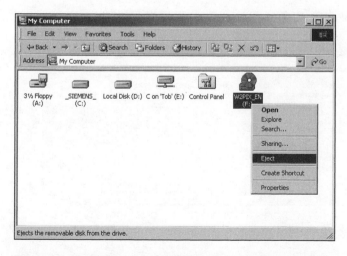

Figure 4-7: The Explorer supports an Eject command for CD-ROMs and ZIP drives.

Your scripts can't remote control the CD-ROM tray yet, though. Obviously, there needs to be some built-in Windows functionality that opens and closes the CD-ROM tray. But how can you access it?

CD

The following project is available on the companion CD: \components\ cdtray. Provided you have installed the VB CCE or your own Visual Basic, you just need to copy this folder to your hard drive and open the vbp-Project file.

Start a new VB CCE project. Then enter the following code (see Figure 4-8):

```
Private Declare Function mciSendString Lib "winmm.DLL" Alias _
"mciSendStringA" (ByVal lpstrCommand As String, ByVal _
lpstrReturnString As String, ByVal wReturnLength As Integer, ByVal _
hCallback As Integer) As Long

Sub closeTray()
call mciSendString("Set CDAudio Door Closed Wait", 0&, 0, 0)
End Sub

Sub openTray()
call mciSendString("Set CDAudio Door Open Wait", 0&, 0, 0)
End Sub
```

This is all you need to remote control the CD-ROM tray. Before you can compile your COM object, assign a new name to it. In the project window, click the uppermost entry (Project1). Then, assign a name to your project using the name property in the Property window. Next, in the project window, click your user control. It's the lowest entry. Then, assign it a name using the name property in the Property window.

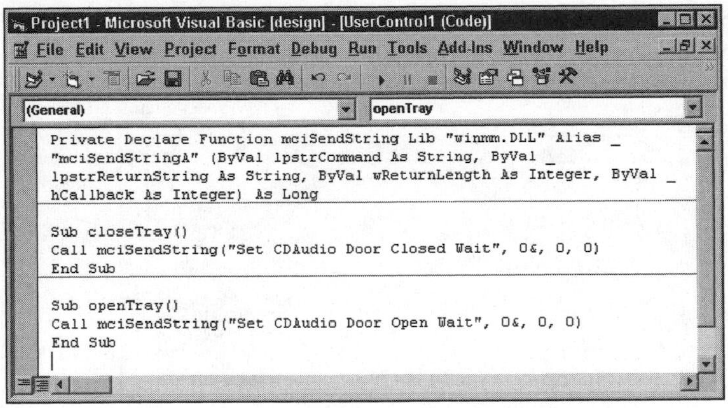

Figure 4-8: Wrap CD-ROM tray API functions as COM objects.

Tip

You do not have to assign a name to your project and your user control if you don't feel like it. However, the standard name Project1.UserControl1 is not very thrilling. You might want to choose something you'll remember. Even more important, using the default name for more than one project would register only the last project. All the other projects you have compiled previously would no longer be accessible.

Once you have assigned a name like cd.tools to your project and control, you can compile it. Open the file menu and choose Make. Done.

To remote control your CD-ROM tray, just write a little script:

```
' 4-2.VBS

set tool = CreateObject("cd.tools")
tool.openTray
MsgBox "CD-ROM Tray is open!"
tool.closeTray
MsgBox "CD ROM Tray is closed!"
```

Tip

Make sure your script uses the correct COM object name. If you have called your new COM object something else, change the ProgID that CreateObject uses.

The script can now open and close the CD-ROM tray. You can call the methods openTray and closeTray.

Secret

If there is a CD-ROM in the drive, once you open and close the tray, an AutoPlay program may start. Every time you insert an AutoPlay-enabled CD-ROM, it automatically launches the program specified in the file AUTORUN.INF.

How API functions really work

How did your COM object get access to the CD-ROM tray? It used a Windows API function called mciSendString. This function sends commands to multimedia devices. You can do many things with this command. For example, you can remote control VCRs or play back sound files. CD-ROMs are multimedia devices, so they are also controlled by mci. In Chapter 23, you will find many more examples and learn how to access multiple CD-ROM drives.

To be able to use mciSendString, your COM object needs to declare this function. Declaring a function is just like teaching Visual Basic all it needs to know to call the function.

First, it needs to know how you want to refer to the command. Just pick a name. In this example, the COM object wants to refer to the function as mciSendString. You can pick a different name if you like, as long as you use this different name throughout the rest of your code to access the function. However, when calling API functions, it's a good idea to use the standard names so others will recognize the standard API functions.

Next, it needs to know where it can find the function. The lib statement declares the name of the DLL file that contains the function. In this example, it's winmm.dll, and because this file is stored in one of the Windows system folders, you do not need to specify the full path name.

Then, it needs to know the internal name of the function. This information is preceded by Alias. This information is crucial, and it's case-sensitive. The official name of the multimedia function is mciSendStringA.

You don't need an Alias statement if you have called your function by the official name in the first place. In the preceding example, if you call your function mciSendStringA instead of mciSendString, then you can skip the Alias statement. Be careful, though, and remember that the official function names are case-sensitive.

Secret

Windows operating systems have two different ways of storing strings. On Win9.x, strings are stored as ANSI, using one byte per character. On Windows NT/2000, strings are stored as Unicode, using two bytes per character. To make life easy for you, most API functions are available both as ANSI ("A") and as Unicode ("W" for "wide"). This example uses mciSendStringA because although Visual Basic stores strings as unicode internally, it always converts them to ANSI. However, you can just as well use mciSendStringW. Then you would have to convert the command string to Unicode, though. Take a look at the following code example. The important thing to keep in mind is that the "A" API functions are much easier to handle than the "W" API functions.

```
Private Declare Function mciSendString Lib "winmm.DLL" Alias _
"mciSendStringW" (ByVal lpstrCommand As String, ByVal _
lpstrReturnString As String, ByVal wReturnLength As Integer, ByVal _
hCallback As Integer) As Long

Sub closeTray()
Call mciSendString(StrConv("Set CDAudio Door Closed Wait", _
vbUnicode), 0&, 0, 0)
End Sub

Sub openTray()
Call mciSendString(StrConv("Set CDAudio Door Open Wait", _
vbUnicode), 0&, 0, 0)
End Sub
```

In addition, declare states which arguments the API function expects to receive and which information it returns.

The declare statement is extremely powerful because it imposes virtually no restrictions on you. It's entirely up to you to define the communication between Visual Basic and the API function, and there is often more than one way you can "talk" to an API function. On the other hand, declaring an API function correctly is fundamentally important. While Visual Basic and VBScript safeguard each of your steps, this safety net does not apply to declare — it opens a door to the hostile "C" programming world, and if you declare the wrong variable types, you can easily crash your entire machine.

So why risk brain damage trying to understand all this strange stuff at once? You don't need to. All that you need to access core Windows functionality are declare statements, and I have prepared them for you. Once you feel comfortable with the hundreds of examples in this book, there's still plenty of time to dive into variable types, pointers, and all the other details Visual Basic usually takes care of for you. If you're still hungry for more at the end of this book, I'll show you how to access just about any API function by developing your own declare statements.

Looking Inside DLL Files

To fully understand the concept of .dll files and the functions stored inside, just take a look at what's stored inside .dll files. Most use a fixed structure called Microsoft Portable Executable and Common Object File Format. Part of this structure is an export table. This table reveals all the names of the stored functions.

Note DLL stands for "dynamic link library", and .dll is also the extension name. To find .dll files, just search for *.dll. There are hundreds of them stored on your computer. Each file is actually a library of predefined functions. And each program (or script) can dynamically link to the library it needs for a specific purpose. This is what makes the concept of .dll files so powerful.

Decrypting the contents of a DLL file

To peek inside .dll files, you just need to know the exact structure they use to organize their content. The following script reveals all the hidden information stored in a PE-compliant .dll file. It uses a COM object I developed to decipher the PE-DLL-file format (see Figure 4-9). You'll find full source code on the companion CD. Just make sure you install the COM object on the companion CD before you launch the script: \install\ dll\setup.exe.

```
' 4-3.VBS


set wshshell= CreateObject("WScript.Shell")
set dll = CreateObject("dll.tobtools")

windir = wshshell.ExpandEnvironmentStrings("%WINDIR%")
dllname = windir & "\system\winmm.dll"

set coll = dll.GetDLLFunctions(dllname)
for each member in coll
    list = list & member & vbCr
next

MsgBox list
```

As you see, winmm.dll contains hundreds of functions, mciSendStringA being only one of them. Also, you now see all the "A" and "W" versions mentioned above.

Unfortunately, the PE file format is no type library. It only contains the function names so the declare statement can reference a function. The .dll file does not contain syntax information. You can't find out the arguments or return types.

Tip If you find a specific function interesting, just surf to one of the Internet search sites like www.altavista.com and search for the function name. Chances are you will find a lot of examples showing the function in action. Most of these examples will be written in "C" though. In order to use those examples for own COM objects, you will need to translate "C" into Visual Basic, which is not a trivial task.

Replace "system" with "system32" if you are working on an NT/2000 system.

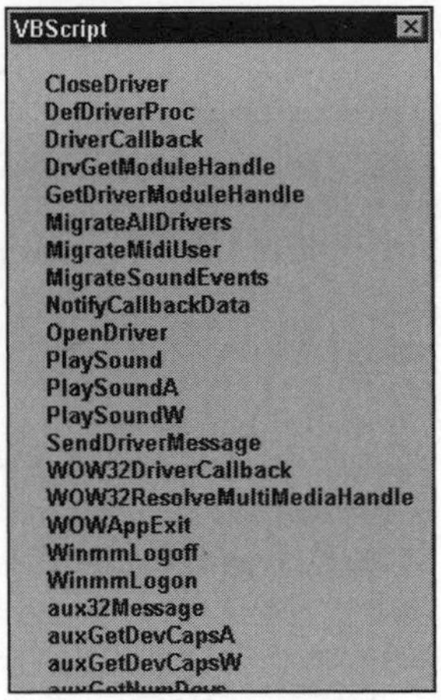

Figure 4-9: Uncover all the hidden functions stored in a .dll file.

To get a nicely formatted list of exported functions, you can easily spice up this script and have it output the information as an HTML file:

```
' 4-4.VBS

set wshshell = CreateObject("WScript.Shell")
windir = wshshell.ExpandEnvironmentStrings("%WINDIR%")
dllfile = windir & "\system\winmm.dll"

outputfile = "C:\dll.htm"

GetDLLInfo dllfile, outputfile
wshshell.run "IEXPLORE.EXE " & outputfile

sub GetDllInfo(dllname, outputname)
    set dll = CreateObject("dll.tobtools")
    set coll = dll.GetDLLFunctions(dllname)
```

```
set fs = CreateObject("Scripting.FileSystemObject")
set output = fs.CreateTextFile(outputname, true)

dim colors(1)
colors(0)=" bgcolor=""#EEEEEE"""
colors(1)=" bgcolor=""#DDDDDD"""

output.WriteLine "<html><head><style>td {font: " _
    & "10pt Arial}</style></head><body>"
output.WriteLine "<table border=0><tr><td><b>" _
    & fs.GetBaseName(dllname) & "</td><td>" & coll.Count _
    & " functions</b></td></tr>"
for each name in coll
    counter = counter + 1
    output.WriteLine "<tr " & colors(counter mod 2) & "><td>" _
        & name & "</td><td>" & coll(name) & "</td></tr>"
next
output.WriteLine "</table></body></head>"
output.close
end sub
```

The list contains the name and the ordinal number of each .dll function that is accessible.

Secret

Actually, the ordinal number is the important part. The ordinal number is the real name of a function. Whenever you call a .dll function by name, Windows looks up the name in the export list and translates it to the ordinal number. Then it looks up the base offset and knows at which byte position in the .dll file the function code starts. You can call a .dll function directly by ordinal number, too. Instead of the name, just use a # and then the ordinal number. Instead of mciSendStringA, you could just as well write #52. If you did, your COM object wouldn't work on Windows 2000 systems anymore, though. Here, mciSendStringA has a different ordinal number. By using the function names, you leave it to the operating system to determine the correct ordinal number. However, there are times when you must use the ordinal number. Undocumented Windows functions have no text entry so you can't call those functions by name. You can only access these functions through the ordinal number. Because ordinal numbers are consecutive, just take a look at your .dll function list. If there are any ordinal numbers missing, you can safely assume that these ordinal numbers represent undocumented hidden Windows features. Some .dlls don't contain any, while others contain mostly undocumented functions.

Developing Dialog Boxes

So far, your COM objects have contained commands only. COM objects can do a lot more, though. If you want to, they can also pop up dialog windows for you. And because you are free to design the window content, you can easily create all the dialog boxes you might need for a special project.

Secret

Many authors are convinced that an ActiveX control can't open a window. Instead, they believe ActiveX controls can only become visible as an embedded object on a Web page. This is definitely wrong. Although ActiveX controls were originally designed as Web page add-ons, they can also pop up regular windows. There are only two things you need to know to make this work. One, the user control itself can only be embedded on Web pages, but if you add forms to your project, you can view those as windows. And two, because ActiveX controls are not independent programs, they can't open modeless windows. This means they can't open more than one window at a time, and while the window is displayed, your script stops. However, even this limitation can be overcome. In Chapter 17, I'll show you how to use events to turn modal windows into modeless windows.

Start the VB CCE and create a new project. Next, assign a name to both your project and your `UserControl` as outlined above. Call it `dialog.test`.

Now you can start developing your dialog box.

Designing a form

Visual Basic calls dialog windows forms. In order to develop a COM function that pops up a window, you just design a form.

In the main window, you see your user control. Most likely, it looks like a gray square. However, this user control can never act as a dialog window. User controls are always invisible and can only appear as part of a Web page. To create a real window, you need to add a form to your project.

In the Project window, right-click on your project, then choose Add and Form. The Add Form window appears. Click Open.

You now get a new form. It appears in your project window and looks like a gray, empty window. This is your dialog window. In order to design it, you just open the Toolbox window — open the View menu and select Toolbox.

Tip

Always make sure you are working with the form. The user control looks just the same. If in doubt, take a look at your Project window and click your form.

The Toolbox window contains the design elements. To place a design element on your window, just double-click it in the Toolbox window. It appears on your form. Now you can drag it to the correct position and adjust its size.

CD

The complete `InputBox` project is also available on the CD-ROM. Just open `\components\inputbox\dialog.vbp`. You can also install the pre-compiled project: `\install\inputbox\setup.exe`.

Let's assume you want to design a new input box. You need a label and a text field. Double-click on both elements, then position the elements. If you feel like it, you can also add a frame. In addition, you need a button element so the user can close the dialog box.

Selecting the right elements

Putting together the elements is easy once you know some tricks:

■ Double-click elements in the Toolbox window to place a copy on your form. You can't drag elements onto your form. Once the elements are placed on your form, you can drag them into position and change sizes.

■ Having trouble selecting an element? Take a look at the Properties window. It sports a drop-down list. Just select the element in this list, and it will be selected on the form as well.

■ Some elements act like containers. The frame element is a container. You need to place elements into the frame; otherwise, the frame will cover them. To place elements into the frame, select the element and then cut it to the clipboard using [Ctrl]+[X]. Next, select the frame and insert the element using [Ctrl]+[V].

Next, explore the properties of your elements. Select the element on the form and see which properties the Properties window has to offer. For example, change the label of the frame. Most elements offer the caption property. To change the caption of your button, click the button on the form, then switch to the Properties window and change the caption property.

Secret

You can even assign keyboard shortcuts to your elements. Just insert the & character into your caption. Windows automatically underlines the following character and uses it as a keyboard shortcut. To use "O" as a shortcut for OK, write &OK.

Every element you place on your form has a name property. This property is very important because you need it to access the element from your program code. Either write down the standard element names for reference once you develop the logic behind your dialog window or assign your own names to the elements.

Note

You should play around with the elements and properties available. One of the first "serious" things you need to do, though, is assign a name to your form. To do so, in the Project window, click your form and then switch to the Properties window. In the drop-down list of elements, choose the form. Then assign it a name using the name property. In this example, call your form window1.

Choosing the right element order

You can place as many elements on your form as you want. As soon as elements start to overlap, though, things become tricky. You now need to specify the element in order to make sure that elements don't bury other elements under them.

To change the order of elements and determine which ones are on top of others, you first select the element you want to move up or down in the pile.

Tip

If you can't click the element, then use the drop-down list in the Properties window.

Next, you open the Format menu and choose Order. Now you can move the selected element up or down.

Compiling your COM object

You have designed your form? Great! Just assign a name to both your project and your `UserControl`, as shown above. Call your project dialog and your `UserControl` test.

Next, compile your COM object — open the File menu and choose `Make dialog.ocx`.

Caution

Should your `Make` command report a name other than `dialog.ocx`, then you probably did not assign names to your project and your `UserControl` yet. It's easy; just follow the rules above. Using names other than those I recommended will cause trouble because the sample scripts expect your COM object to be named `dialog.test`.

Now it's time to test your COM object. Open the text editor and save the following file with the `.vbs` extension:

```
' 4-5.VBS

set dialog = CreateObject("dialog.test")
MsgBox "Done."
```

Provided you have called your COM object `dialog.test`, your script will run perfectly well, and no error will be raised. However, you should note that your window did not appear either.

Initially, all forms are invisible. To show your dialog window, you need to explicitly call it. So, switch back to your project and add some code.

Adding code to make your window appear

Your COM object needs an additional method that you can call to show your window. All the public methods that are visible from the outside live inside your user control. So take a look at your Project window and right-click on your user control. It's located inside the User Controls folder. In the context menu, choose View Code.

Your user control is completely empty (see Figure 4-10). Add the following procedure:

```
sub ShowWindow()
    window1.Show vbModal
end sub
```

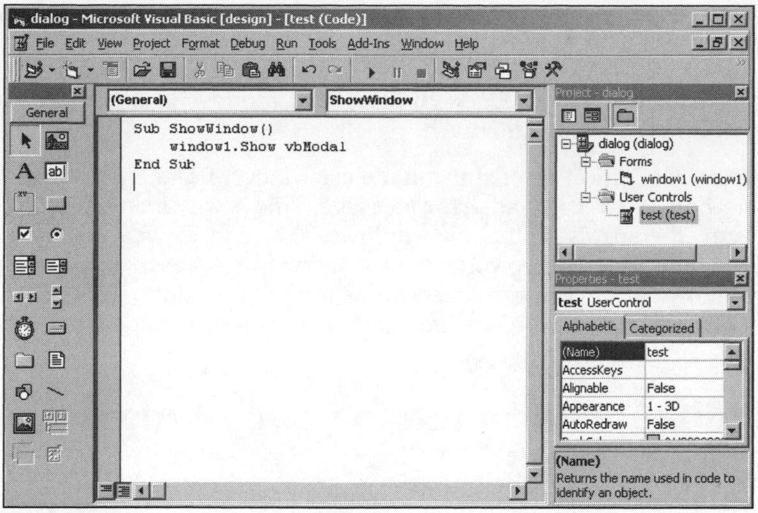

```
dialog - Microsoft Visual Basic [design] - [test (Code)]                    _ □ x
File  Edit  View  Project  Format  Debug  Run  Tools  Add-Ins  Window  Help    _ 8 x

(General)                        ShowWindow

Sub ShowWindow()
     window1.Show vbModal
End Sub
```

Figure 4-10: "In-process" COM objects can only display modal dialog windows.

Your new procedure calls the Show method that's built into any form. Because Show is supplied by your form, you need to also supply the name of the form. This is nothing new — in order to call a method, always specify the name of the object first. For the procedure to work correctly, you have to name your form window1. If you have named your form differently, then use that name instead. If you haven't named your form at all, then your form's default name is Form1.

Next, recompile your COM object — open the File menu and choose Make dialog.ocx.

You can't recompile your COM object while it is in use. Always make sure you have stopped any script that accesses your object. Right now, this is probably of no concern. Once your script is able to open your dialog window, however, you need to make sure that your dialog window is closed before you recompile your object. Because your dialog window can be hidden behind other windows, press [Win]+[M] to see all open dialog windows. Also, while your script is executed in the Script Debugger, your object is considered to be in use. Close the Script Debugger before you recompile your object.

Now you just need to call the new method to open your window. Change your script accordingly:

```
' 4-6.VBS

set dialog = CreateObject("dialog.test")
dialog.ShowWindow
MsgBox "Done."
```

It works. Your window appears exactly the way you designed it.

The elements you placed on your form may work, but they are not really functional. For example, if you click the button, nothing exciting happens. No wonder — so far, you have only designed the window layout. You haven't yet defined any logic. Once you close the window, your script continues and displays the MsgBox message.

Undocumented

Your COM object can't show modeless windows. Once you call a form's Show method, you receive an error message. This is why many people believe ActiveX controls can't show windows. They can. However, they're limited to modal windows, so you need to supply the vbModal parameter. Modal windows halt script execution for as long as the window is displayed, and this is also the reason why you can only open one window at a time.

Adding code to make your window do something

So far, you can make your dialog window appear, but the window isn't really useful. Just add some code to your form to educate it.

Switch back to your VB CCE project. Because you want to add functionality to your form, take a look at your Project window and right-click on your form. It's located in the Forms folder. In the context menu, choose View Object. Now you see your window in design mode.

First, you want to add code to the OK button so the window is closed once someone clicks this button. Double-click on the button. The window changes its appearance, and now you see the forms' Code view. You could have switched to this view by right-clicking on the form and choosing View Code, but by double-clicking the button element, Visual Basic automatically adds the appropriate procedure framework (see Figure 4-11).

Visual Basic adds a sub procedure. This new procedure is special. You don't need to call it. It will be automatically called whenever someone clicks the button. And what makes it special? Its name. The name starts with the name of the element it will be responsible for. In the case of the button, the procedure name will start with Command1, the default name of the button. If you have changed the button's name, the procedure name will start with the name you chose for the button element. Next, there is an underscore. After the underscore, you will see Click. Command1_Click() translates into "execute this procedure whenever the element Command1 raises the Click-event."

Secret

There are many events an element can respond to. Above your Code view, you will see two drop-down lists. The left list contains all available elements on your form, while the right list reveals all the events this element can possibly respond to. Press [Esc] to close the list. If you want to insert code that executes once someone presses a button, you simply choose the MouseDown event. The Click event, in contrast, is raised only after someone has released the mouse button while the mouse pointer is located over the element.

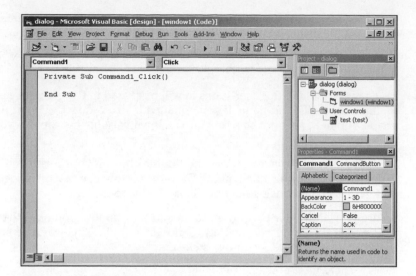

Figure 4-11: Add event handlers to your dialog box to respond to button clicks.

In order to close the dialog window, your procedure needs to call the appropriate method of the form. You can either unload the form from memory or hide the form. Unloading the form from memory is the better alternative for dialog windows. Hide windows only if you plan to make the window invisible temporarily.

Undocumented

If you hide a window and call `Show vbModal` at a later time, the exact same window will reappear. Anything you have typed into the window previously will still be there. If you unload a window and then call `Show vbModal` later, you get a new instance of the window. It will not contain old data. Hiding a window will keep it in memory until your script ends or until you explicitly close the connection to your COM object by assigning `Nothing` to your object reference.

To close the window, add this procedure to your form:

```
Private Sub Command1_Click()
    Unload me
end sub
```

To hide the window, add this procedure:

```
Private Sub Command1_Click()
    me.Hide
end sub
```

Secret

`me` is a special reference to the current object. Because your procedure is located inside the form, `me` represents the form. You can now either use the `Unload` function or provide `me` as an argument. Because `Unload` is a function provided by your COM object, you can use it directly. Alternatively, you can call the `Hide` method, which is built into your form. Here, you use `me` as an object reference. Instead of `me`, you can also use the official name of the form.

Recompile your COM object and then run your script code. This time, you can close the dialog window by clicking the button.

This is good, but not good enough. How can you read what the user has typed into the dialog window?

It's easy. Everything the user types in will be stored in the element `Text1`. (It can have a different name if you renamed it.) To return the input to your script, you need to store this text into a global variable just before you close the window.

So, switch to the Project window and double-click on your form. You see your dialog window. Double-click on the OK button. Now you see the procedure that gets executed once someone clicks the button.

Before you allow your procedure to unload the window, you read the contents of the `Text1` element into a global variable. This way, the user input is still around when the window is closed:

```
Public enteredText as String

Private Sub Command1_Click()
    enteredText = Me.Text1
    Unload Me
End Sub
```

Now, when someone clicks the button, your procedure first stores the contents of `Text1` into the string variable `enteredText`. Then the window is closed. To be able to read the variable `enteredText` from other procedures, you just declare the variable as global using the Public key word (see Figure 4-12).

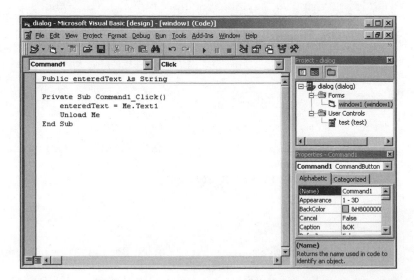

Figure 4-12: To automatically close the window, hide it or unload it from memory.

Next, you return the variable to your script. In the Project window, right-click on your user control and choose View code. Then change your ShowWindow procedure to a function because you want to return something—replace sub with function.

Now you just need to define the return value. Assign a value to the variable ShowWindow, then use the variable enteredText, which is part of the form. In doing so, specify the name of your form and then the name of the variable. That's all, and although it seems a little complex, it is very straightforward.

Tip

Again, there is only one thing you need to remember—always specify the object you want to talk to. Because it's the form that stores the enteredText variable, talk to the form when retrieving the variable.

To use your new functionality, change your script accordingly:

```
' 4-7.VBS

set dialog = CreateObject("dialog.test")
MsgBox dialog.ShowWindow
MsgBox "Done."
```

This time, dialog.ShowWindow opens the window and returns whatever the user has typed in (see Figure 4-13).

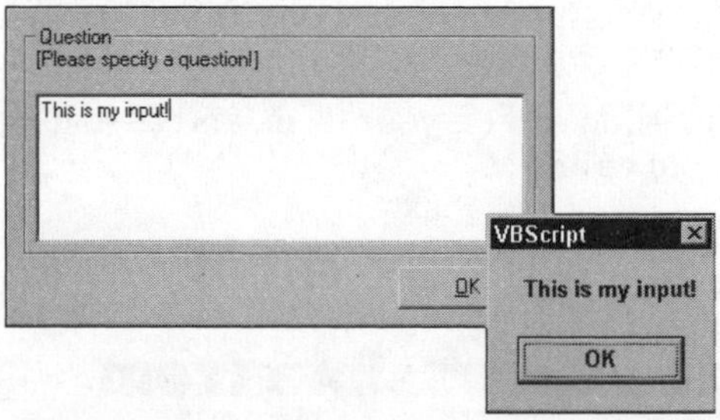

Figure 4-13: Your window reports entered text back to your script.

Tip

Maybe there's default text in the text box Text1. To start with an empty text box, just select your form in the Project window and select your text-box element in the Properties' window drop-down box. Then look for the text property and delete its default text.

Using Properties to Change Your Window's Behavior

So far, you have worked with functions and procedures. Both make your COM object do something, and functions can return values. There's a third element you can use—properties. Properties don't start action. They just control parameters.

Take a look at your dialog window. There are many aspects you probably would like to control. First of all, it would definitely be good to be able to set the label text for both the frame and the label so you can ask questions. You can set this label text using the caption property of the elements from within the COM object, but hard-coding those properties doesn't make much sense. You want your script to be able to ask any question.

If you want to be able to do that, just define some properties. In the VB CCE project, switch to the Project window and right-click your user control. In the context menu, choose View code.

Accessing your element's properties

The Properties window lists all the properties a specific object offers. Just select the element in the drop-down list, and you can see all the properties available. The Properties window is a convenient tool for setting properties during design-time. However, you need another way of accessing the properties if you choose to change properties during run-time.

You can access any object property by code. Let's assume you have placed a frame element on your form and this element's name property is Frame1. To change the label, you need to change the caption property of the Frame1 object:

```
Frame1.Caption = "New Label"
```

Because the Frame1 object is located on your form, and assuming your form is called window1, you would write:

```
window1.Frame1.Caption = "New Label"
```

Making properties accessible from the outside

You now know how to change properties during run-time. However, you can only access your elements' properties from within your COM object. Your script can't access the internal properties. Not yet. To be able to change properties from the outside, you just need to "publish" the property in exactly the same way you already used to "publish" functions and procedures. Instead of function and sub, this time you use the keyword Property.

Add the following lines to your user control code:

```
Property Let Label(ByVal text As String)
    window1.Label1.Caption = text
End Property

Property Let Frame(ByVal text As String)
    window1.Frame1.Caption = text
End Property
```

```
Property Let Default(ByVal text As String)
    window1.Text1.text = text
End Property
```

Now your script can control label text, frame text, and the default text in the text box:

```
' 4-8.VBS

set dialog = CreateObject("dialog.test")
dialog.Frame = "Question"
dialog.Label = "Enter something!"
dialog.Default = "This is the default!"
MsgBox dialog.ShowWindow
MsgBox "Done."
```

Secret

`Property Let` defines a write-only property. You can assign values to this property, but you can't read the current content. `Property Get` defines a read-only property. You can't set its value, but you can read it. To implement a read/write property, you use both `Property Let` and `Property Get`.

Using Optional Parameters

Properties are great, but they require additional lines of code. Take a look at the official `InputBox` function. This function doesn't expose properties. Still, you are able to supply additional arguments if you want to. You don't need to. Most arguments are optional:

```
' 4-9.VBS

text = InputBox("Enter something!")
text = InputBox("Enter something!", "Titlebar Text")
text = InputBox("Enter something!", "Titlebar Text", "The Default")
```

Can your dialog box use optional arguments, too? Yes. Just change your `ShowWindow` function to include the optional parameters:

```
Function ShowWindow(ByVal question As String, _
Optional ByVal frametext As String - "Question", _
Optional ByVal titletext As String, _
Optional ByVal defaulttext As String = "") As String
    window1.Label1.Caption = question
    window1.Frame1.Caption = frametext
    window1.Text1.text = defaulttext
    If Not IsMissing(titletext) Then
        window1.Caption = titletext
    End If

    window1.Show vbModal

    ShowWindow = window1.enteredText
End Function
```

Once you compile your COM object, you can call your dialog window using a number of alternatives:

```
' 4-10.VBS

set dialog = CreateObject("dialog.test")
MsgBox dialog.ShowWindow("Enter something!")
MsgBox dialog.ShowWindow("Enter something!", "May I ask?")
MsgBox dialog.ShowWindow("Enter something!", "May I ask?",,"Default!")
MsgBox dialog.ShowWindow("Enter something!", "May I ask?", _
"Titlebar under control", "Default!")
MsgBox "Done."
```

Only the first argument is mandatory. The following three arguments are optional. You can omit them, but you can't change their order. If you don't want to specify an argument, just leave it blank.

Specifying default values

To make an argument optional, you use the optional key word. Once you declare an argument as optional, you can't add mandatory arguments. Mandatory arguments must be declared before you start declaring your optional arguments.

Take a look at the arguments frametext and defaulttext. Both are optional, and both receive a default value should they be omitted.

Detecting missing arguments

titletext works differently. There is no default value defined, and if the user omits this argument, titletext is undefined. To check whether an argument was specified or not, just ask isMissing. This function returns true if the argument was omitted. In the example, isMissing determines whether the user specified an argument for titletext. If an argument was specified, it changes the form's title bar text. If the argument is missing, it doesn't change the title bar text.

Uncovering Special Window Properties

You now know much about the inside mechanics of dialog windows. All of what you have done so far happens inside the window, though. The window is just the container for all your elements and your code.

It's a good idea to also take a look at the window container itself. This container offers many useful properties you may want to use for your dialog window project.

To access these properties, click on your form in the Project window. Then take a look at the Properties window. Select your Form in the drop-down list.

Changing the colors

`BackColor` sets the background color of your form. You don't need to use gray dialog windows. You can even make them blue or yellow if you like. However, you will also need to set the `BackColor` property of elements you placed on your form.

Non-resizable windows

`BorderStyle` presents a rich set of window border settings. By default, Visual Basic uses the sizable window border. The user can resize your dialog window, and if you didn't provide the appropriate sizing mechanisms, the window will become larger but your elements will stay where they were. I'll show you more about sizing in a moment, but in most cases, it doesn't make sense to resize dialog boxes anyway. Select Fixed Dialog to get a non-resizable dialog window frame.

`MaxButton` controls whether your window displays a maximize button in its title bar. This setting has an effect only if the window is resizable. `MinButton` controls the minimize button.

If you set `Movable` to false, then your dialog window can no longer be dragged. You can achieve the same effect by hiding the title bar (see the following section).

Special dialog windows

As a default, your windows look like regular windows. They have a title bar and share the same 3D look you are used to from other software. If you want to, you can completely change this look and feel. Just change `ControlBox` to false. Now your window has no title bar anymore (see Figure 4-14), and if you select Fixed ToolWindow as BorderStyle, you will even lose the 3D effect.

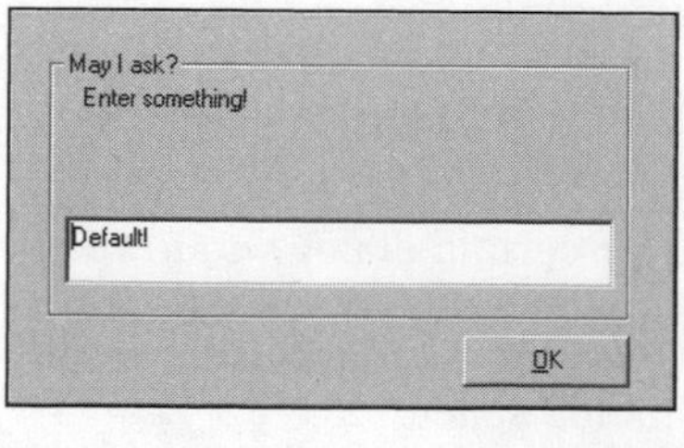

Figure 4-14: Strip off your dialog box title bar.

Undocumented

If you specify caption text for the form, you will get a title bar even if you turned off `ControlBox`.

Positioning windows in the center of the screen

Many programmers place a lot of custom code into their COM objects just to make a window appear centered on the screen. It's a good idea to center dialog windows so they catch attention. However, you don't need extra code for this. Just set `StartUpPosition` to `CenterScreen`. This will take care of everything.

As a default, Visual Basic uses Windows Default. With this setting, each new window is placed on the screen using a small offset from the position of the previously opened window. Windows Default is best when you plan to open a number of windows, so the windows don't completely overlap. Because you can't open multiple windows anyway from within an ActiveX control, you are better off using `CenterScreen`.

Implementing Special Window Behavior

You can now control both the inside and the outside of your window. Sometimes, however, it may become necessary to control the way Windows treats your window. For example, if your script has launched another program or used another COM object, then this program gets the focus and your script looses the focus. Any custom window you open afterwards may not appear on the screen. Instead, it may appear hidden underneath other windows. This is bad. But luckily, there are ways you can change this — and a lot of other things that may ruin your day at first.

Resizing the contents of your window

Default windows are resizable. Unfortunately, Windows only resizes the *window,* not its contents. If you resize your dialog window, it will become larger, but your elements inside of the window stay where they are.

The easiest way to deal with this is to turn off the resize capability altogether. This way, you don't have to deal with it. Just set the `BorderStyle` property to a fixed border, as outlined above.

While this may work perfectly well for certain dialog windows, it may limit the fun in other cases. The `InputBox` function, for example, takes the easy route and doesn't allow resizing. That's too bad because it would be nice to enlarge the dialog window for additional space.

To make your window content resizable, you need to react to the form's resize event. This event is triggered anytime the size of the window is changed.

Undocumented

The form's resize event will be triggered at least once — the moment you display your form. So if you provide a resize procedure, you no longer need to specify the height and width of your form's elements. Don't spend hours trying to align form elements during design-time. The elements will be straightened out by your resize procedure anyway.

The tricky part is to respond to this event. You will have to manually resize all the elements on your form. This is not a trivial thing.

Take a look at the following procedure. It will resize all the elements of your new InputBox dialog window:

```
Private Sub Form_Resize()
Const OFFSET = 100

Dim frmRealWidth As Integer
Dim frmRealHeight As Integer

On Error Resume Next
frmRealWidth = Me.ScaleWidth
frmRealHeight = Me.ScaleHeight

Me.Frame1.Move OFFSET, OFFSET, frmRealWidth - 2 * OFFSET, _
frmRealHeight - 3 * OFFSET - Me.Command1.Height
Me.Label1.Move OFFSET, 2 * OFFSET, _
Me.Frame1.Width - 2 * OFFSET, 300
Me.Text1.Move OFFSET, 3 * OFFSET + Me.Label1.Height, _
     Me.Frame1.Width - 2 * OFFSET, _
Me.Frame1.Height - Me.Label1.Height - 4 * OFFSET
Me.Command1.Move frmRealWidth - OFFSET - Me.Command1.Width, _
2 * OFFSET + Me.Frame1.Height
End Sub
```

For this to work, you need to place this procedure into your form. Right-click your form in the Project window, then choose View Code. Next, choose Form in the left drop-down list and choose Resize in the right drop-down list.

To be able to resize the window contents, your procedure needs to know the new size of the window. ScaleWidth and ScaleHeight provide this information. Next, the procedure moves the four elements on the form. This is the rather abstract part. The constant OFFSET determines the space between the elements.

Tip

Moving the elements in response to the resize event is a dynamic process. You don't want to use fixed sizes. Instead, always refer to the new window dimensions stored in frmRealWidth and frmRealHeight. In addition, you can use the height and width information of those elements you already resized. Use fixed sizes only for those elements you do not want to scale. In the example, the Label1 element receives a fixed height of 300 because it doesn't make sense to dynamically scale the label text. Also, use me rather than the real name of your form. This way, you can cut and paste your resize procedure and reuse it in other forms with only minor adjustments.

Your key to resizing maneuvers is the Move method. Move can be called for any form element. It accepts four parameters — left, top, width, and height. You only need to specify two if you don't want to change the size of the element. In the example, the Command1 command button is moved this way, but it is not resized.

Undocumented

Elements can be parts of other elements. In this example, both Label1 and Text1 are embedded in the Frame1 element. When using Move on Label1 and Text1, you need to specify the dimensions relative to the Frame1 dimensions.

Take a look at the Command1 element. You want to move it so it aligns at the right side of the window. Look at the first parameter calculation. The entire width of the window (frmRealWidth) minus the window margin (offset), minus the width of the command button itself, results in the left (starting) position of the command button. If you wanted to align the button on the left side, then you would replace all of this with offset.

Tip

Automating the positioning of all your form elements is rather abstract. Don't feel bad if your resize algorithm doesn't work at first. It's almost normal if your resizing procedure places the form elements all over the place at first. Start with a simple form and only a few elements. Trial-and-error is sometimes the best way to go. However, always try to keep your algorithm as simple as possible. Use constants like offset for window margins and to define the distance between the elements.

You may be wondering why the procedure turns off error handling. This is just a simplification. A window can be shrunk as well as enlarged, and whenever your window becomes too small to display all the elements inside, Visual Basic raises an error. To prevent this error, you have to double-check whether your window size is too small for additional resizing. Turning off error handling doesn't solve the cause, but it prevents the error. If your window becomes too small, then your form elements will start to overlap, and users will get immediate feedback, forcing them to re-enlarge the window.

Tip

If you plan to open your window more than once, you should hide it instead of unloading it from memory. Hiding a window preserves its current size. If you unload the window, it will always pop up with the predefined size, and your users may not like to resize it again and again. However, when hiding a window, always make sure you initialize all the important variables each time you show the window. The example in this chapter always resets the label texts and text box values as part of the ShowWindow procedure. This way, you always get an empty text box even if you have used the window before.

Preselecting window elements

The main purpose of your COM object is to present a window for input. So, it makes a lot of sense to preselect the text box element. This way, you can start typing in text right away. You don't need to grab the mouse first and click into the text box element.

To preselect the text box, just place one more line into your resize procedure:

```
me.text1.SetFocus
```

Responding to the [Enter] key

The official InputBox can do something your COM object can't — once the user has finished his input and presses [Enter], the window automatically closes. There is no need to grab the mouse and click OK.

You can implement the same service, too. All you need to do is scan the key codes entered into the text box. This is easy because every key pressed raises the KeyPress event. Should you detect code 13, then you know that the [Enter] key was pressed:

```
Sub Text1_KeyPress(KeyAscii As Integer)
    If KeyAscii = 13 Then
        DoEvents
        enteredText = Me.Text1
        Me.Hide
    End If
End Sub
```

Just place this procedure on your form. Anytime the user presses [Enter] inside the text box element, KeyAscii reports code 13. DoEvents completes the event processing, and then the procedure executes the same steps as the click-procedure of your OK button.

In fact, instead of repeating the commands both in this procedure and in the Click procedure responsible for your OK button, it would be more modular to place the exit commands into a separate sub and call this sub from both the Click and the KeyPress procedures. Try to avoid redundant code.

Displaying OLE Error Messages as Clear Text

Now that you know how to develop your own COM objects, let's move on to a short but very useful add-on for your scripts.

Let's develop a component that returns the clear text error message of any OLE error number you or your script might run into. OLE error messages are very important — they are raised by the components that handle communication between your scripting components.

Undocumented

As a rule of thumb, OLE errors indicate sloppy error handling. The component that caused the OLE error should have taken care of it in the first place, so in a perfect world, you would never encounter any OLE errors. In reality, however, OLE errors do happen. In the WSH 2.0 beta version, for example, `GetFileVersion` raised an OLE error whenever you tried to retrieve the file version of a file that did not contain version information. Microsoft has fixed this problem in the Windows 2000 version and will probably fix it in the other WSH versions, as well.

Take a look at the following example script — it uses `GetFileVersion` to retrieve a file's version information. Depending on the WSH version you use, `GetFileVersion` may or may not raise an error whenever you try to retrieve version information of a file that does not contain such information:

```
' 4-11.VBS

set fs = CreateObject("Scripting.FileSystemObject")

on error resume next
version = fs.GetFileVersion("C:\AUTOEXEC.BAT")
if not err.Number=0 then
MsgBox "Error Message: " & err.description
MsgBox "Error Code: " & err.Number
else
    MsgBox "No error occured."
    MsgBox "File Version Information: " & version
end if
```

Older versions of `GetFileVersion` report an unhandled OLE error. OLE errors are easy to recognize — error numbers are huge and negative (see Figure 4-15). Another indicator is `err.Description` — it doesn't return a clear text description.

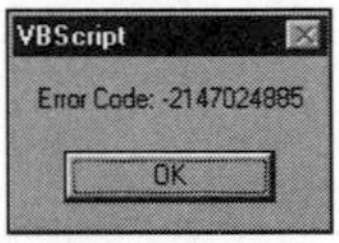

VBScript

Error Code: -2147024885

OK

Figure 4-15: OLE errors display huge negative error codes.

Creating your new OLE error spy tool

To find out more about the reason for a specific OLE error, just write a little script extension. As always, you find the complete source code on the companion CD — just open `\components\oleerror\oleerror.vbp`. If you wish, you can also install the precompiled component, or `\install\oleerr\setup.exe`.

Launch the VB CCE, call your project `ole.err`, switch to Code view, and enter the following code.

```
Option Explicit

Const FORMAT_MESSAGE_FROM_SYSTEM = &H1000

Private Declare Function FormatMessage Lib "kernel32" Alias _
        "FormatMessageA" (ByVal dwFlags As Long, _
        lpSource As Long, ByVal dwMessageId As Long, _
        ByVal dwLanguageId As Long, ByVal lpBuffer As String, _
        ByVal nSize As Long, Arguments As Any) As Long

Public Function OLEError(ByVal number As Long) As String
    Dim returnmessage As String
    Dim returnedchars As Long

    returnmessage = Space$(256)
    returnedchars = FormatMessage(FORMAT_MESSAGE_FROM_SYSTEM, 0&, _
        number, 0&, returnmessage, Len(returnmessage), 0&)
    If returnedchars > 0 Then
        OLEError = Left$(returnmessage, returnedchars)
    Else
        OLEError = "Error not found."
    End If
End Function
```

Next, compile the project — open the File menu and choose `Make ole.ocx`. Done.

Finding out more about OLE errors

Now you are ready to ask Windows what the heck error code –2147024885 actually means. Use the following script and enter the error number you need information about:

```
' 4-12.VBS

set ole = CreateObject("ole.err")

number = InputBox("Enter Error Number!",,"-2147024885")
reason = ole.OLEError(number)
MsgBox number & " = " & reason
```

Now you know — `GetFileVersion` failed because an attempt was made to load a file that did not contain version information (see Figure 4-16).

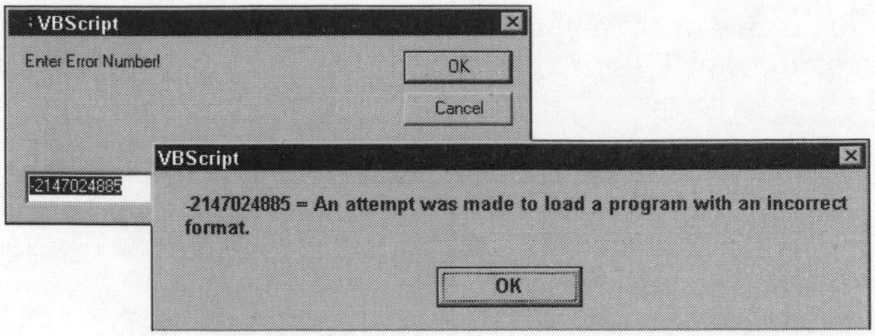

Figure 4-16: Retrieve hidden OLE error descriptions using API functions.

Distributing Your Self-Made COM Objects

Anytime you compile a COM object using the `Make` command, Windows automatically registers the component in the Registry. This is fundamentally important. In Chapter 3, you saw the keys necessary for your scripts' `CreateObject` command to find and access the component. Without those, you can't access your COM object.

Registering a component automatically builds all Registry keys necessary to access the component. Registration service is built directly into your COM object and just needs to be called.

Manually registering a COM object

Each COM object contains built-in functions to register itself. You can see those hidden registration functions with the help of the following script:

```
' 4-13.VBS


set wshshell= CreateObject("WScript.Shell")
set dll = CreateObject("dll.tobtools")

dllname = InputBox("Please enter full path to COM object!")

set coll = dll.GetDLLFunctions(dllname)
for each member in coll
    list = list & member & vbCr
next

MsgBox list
```

No matter whether you view a system `.dll` file or a custom-made `.ocx` control, there will always be a standard set of functions available to register and unregister your component.

Let's assume for a second you have developed a COM object and compiled it as cd.ocx. To be able to use its functionality on another computer, copy the .ocx file to the computer's system folder. Next, you need to register the component.

Tip

You do not have to place the .ocx file in one of the official system folders. If you don't, though, you need to specify the full path name. Also, you need to make sure that the .ocx file will stay where you put it. Should you place it on your desktop and delete it later on, you will no longer be able to use its functions. Therefore, it's a good idea to place it somewhere safe.

Open the Start menu and choose Run. Then enter this command — regsvr32 cd.ocx (see Figure 4-17).

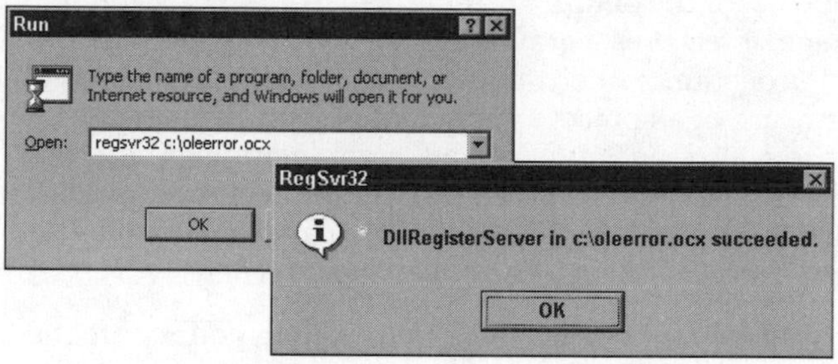

Run window:

Type the name of a program, folder, document, or Internet resource, and Windows will open it for you.

Open: regsvr32 c:\oleerror.ocx

RegSvr32

DllRegisterServer in c:\oleerror.ocx succeeded.

OK

Figure 4-17: Manually registering COM objects using REGSVR32

Regsvr32.exe actually doesn't do much. It just calls the DLLRegisterServer function inside the file you specify. Regsvr32.exe complains if the file wasn't found or if it doesn't offer the DLLRegisterServer functionality. That's all.

DLLRegisterServer internally takes all steps necessary to introduce the COM object to the local Registry, and once it's registered, you can access your component.

COM objects are also smart enough to remove their Registry keys once they are not needed anymore, so they automatically contain a deinstallation feature. This is invoked by DLLUnregisterServer. Just use /U in conjunction with Regsvr32.exe to call DLLUnregisterServer instead of DLLRegisterServer. To be able to remove a component, call its DLLUnregisterServer function before you physically delete the .ocx file. Once you've deleted the file, you will have no way to automatically remove the component's Registry entries anymore.

This is a common reason for garbage and malfunctions in general, because what applies to your COM objects also applies to the many COM objects that commercial software brings along. Never delete a program before calling its uninstall functions.

Undocumented

To view all command lines available, just choose Run from the Start menu and call Regsvr32 without arguments.

Preparing a setup package

Manually registering a component is straightforward, but it requires some technical poking around. It's not the best idea if you plan to distribute your COM objects commercially or to beginners.

In addition, registering a COM object may not be enough. Once you start developing complex COM objects, they may require additional objects, and then it becomes hard to keep track of which components need to be distributed. Even worse, COM objects designed with the Visual Basic CCE require the Visual Basic run-time objects to be available. Installing a naked COM object on a machine without those run-time files won't work.

Fortunately, there is an easy way out. The Visual Basic Control Creation Edition comes with the Setup Wizard. This wizard helps you to prepare a setup package. It features a graphical user interface and does all the technical registration procedures safely hidden in the background. In addition, the wizard takes care of all objects your COM object needs to have around and integrates them into the Setup package @em including the Visual Basic run-time files. In essence, you can then distribute the entire package, and the recipient just needs to call SETUP.EXE. You can even create a setup file for interactively installing the package over the Internet.

Secret

The setup package also takes care of uninstalling your component(s). It places an entry in the Windows software list and provides an uninstall component that calls DLLUnregisterServer for each of your components. It also removes the files. The user can deinstall your package just like any other software using the Add/Remove Programs module in the Control Panel. Nice.

Start the Setup Wizard, then choose the project file. Next, select the way you want to distribute the package. If needed, the wizard can split up the content on many floppy disks or store everything in one directory (see Figure 4-18).

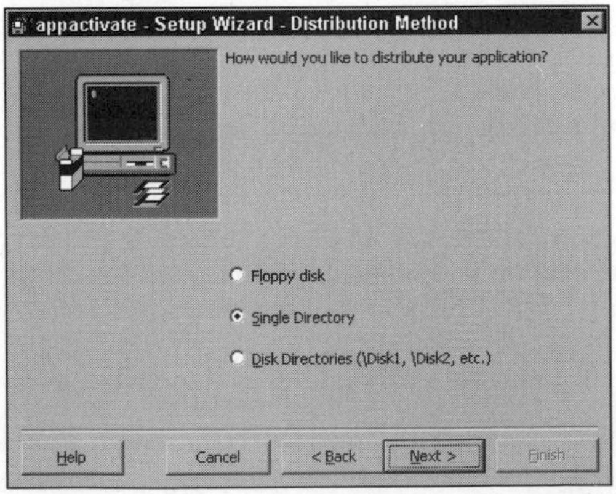

Figure 4-18: Setup Wizard automatically generates distribution packages.

The wizard may ask whether you want to include environment files. If in doubt, just click Yes. Then the wizard prepares a list of files needed to be integrated into your package and builds the package (see Figure 4-19).

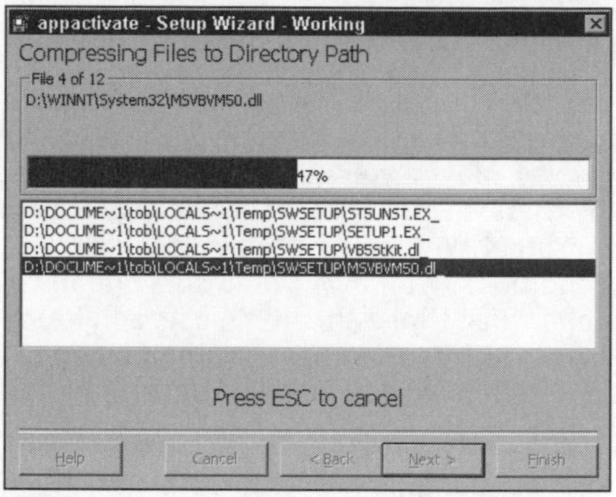

Figure 4-19: Setup Wizard automatically includes all necessary files and objects.

To make your COM object as compatible as possible, compile the COM objects on the latest Windows version available. For example, it may be necessary to compile your COM objects on a Windows 2000 machine for it to run on all Windows versions. Compiling on a Windows 98 machine may produce COM objects that do not run on Windows 2000.

Once your software package is created, you should open the file `setup.1st` in your text editor. It contains the list of files the package will install. You can manually fine-tune the list and take out files you don't want to distribute (the run-time files, for example). You can also combine more than one distribution package — prepare software packages for all of your COM objects, then combine the `setup.1st` entries of all packages and copy all distribution files in one folder. Now, your setup package installs all COM objects in one step. Be careful not to include a file reference more than once. Make sure any file that needs `DLLRegisterServer` registration is marked as `DLLSelfRegister`.

Important caveats you must know about

The Setup Wizard is a nice thing to have, but it will not always cause pure joy. One of the most important limitations of the setup package that it creates is its inability to overwrite files. Let's assume for a moment you have previously created a COM object and saved it as `test.ocx`. Whenever you try to install a newer version (or a completely different COM object) that also uses this file name, you must deinstall the old file first. You can't go ahead and install the new component on top of the old one. If you did, everything would seem to install smoothly and the setup package would even report success. The bitter truth, however, is that the new COM object isn't copied to your hard drive and isn't registered at all.

So, whenever you suspect this issue, find out the `.ocx` filename you are about to install and do a search for it. If you find it is already installed on your system, make sure it can be safely replaced and then delete the file. Now you are ready to install the new component. Note also that the Setup package the Setup Wizard creates can always be deinstalled using the Add/Remove Programs module in your Control Panel.

There's another issue, though. The Setup Wizard does take care that any file your COM project references is included with your package. It can't check, however, whether this is legal. Maybe you referenced some third-party tool that can't be supplied to others. Even worse, your package may contain system files unsuitable for other Windows systems. This definitely is a bug, because under normal conditions, Windows would sort out any system file with a lower version number than those already in use, and it does. Unfortunately, the Microsoft "DLL hell" — the mixture of different system components and versions — often leads to instabilities even if you only replace system files with newer versions.

The problem outlined is by far not limited to your COM object packages. It applies to any software installation. In contrast to most other software, you do have an option, though. First of all, you can always edit the `SETUP.LST` file and determine for yourself which files are actually installed by your package. Second, you can always choose the purist way and only distribute your `.ocx` file — it's small and handy. Just make sure that on the target system, the Visual Basic 5 Runtime Files are installed, and that you register your `.ocx` file using `regvr32.ocx` as outlined above.

Summary

The freely available Visual Basic CCE allows you to easily create script extensions. Script extensions are fully distributable COM objects that can be called from any program. Use hidden Windows API functions and form elements to create completely new scripting commands or to display custom-made dialog boxes.

Chapter 5

Using Internet Explorer as the Output Window

In This Chapter

▶ Find out the secret Internet Explorer scripting commands

▶ Open and size the IE window by script

▶ Write text into the IE window

▶ Change Internet Explorer content dynamically

▶ Respond to IE events such as onQuit

▶ Design your own HTML dialog boxes

▶ Halt scripts and enable event processing

▶ Get detailed information about the IE DHTML object model

▶ Generate color-coded documentation manuals automatically

▶ Learn to "walk" the Object hierarchies and retrieve hidden information

▶ Print Web pages using hidden IE script commands

How can you display results to the user? Your Scripting Host has no window, so the built-in communication paths use the MsgBox and Popup functions.

Both functions may be sufficient for outputting simple messages, but they don't allow much room for your own designs. Even worse, they are part of the script engine. They can't run independently and output results while your script runs.

Secret

Both MsgBox and Popup are functions defined in COM objects that serve "in-process." MsgBox lives inside vbscript.dll, and Popup resides in wshom.ocx. In-process means the COM object is loaded into your host's address space. To you, this means your script needs to wait for those functions. In order to output results while your script runs, you need "out-of-process" COM objects. Those objects are .exe files that can run outside your host.

There's an easy way out, though. Just use an independent .exe file to display results. On any WSH-enabled Windows system, you should find at least Internet Explorer Version 4.0.

Internet Explorer has two faces — it can run independently as a regular program to surf the Internet, and it also acts as a COM object. You can completely control all its features by script.

Finding Out the Secret Functions Inside IE

Before you can access a foreign program like Internet Explorer by script, you need a lot of information. Fortunately, you have already prepared all the tools necessary. Soon, you'll retrieve full documentation of the hidden safely methods and properties available inside Internet Explorer. Even better, the strategies outlined work with any program. So, if you are hungry for more, apply them to any other program you find interesting and see if and how it makes its internal functions available to your scripts.

Determining a program's real name

The first step in accessing any program is to find out its real name. That's easy, by the way; just look for the program's icon, right-click it, and choose Properties. In the Properties window, click the Shortcut tab. The Target field reveals the technical name (see Figure 5-1). Internet Explorer hides in iexplore.exe, for example.

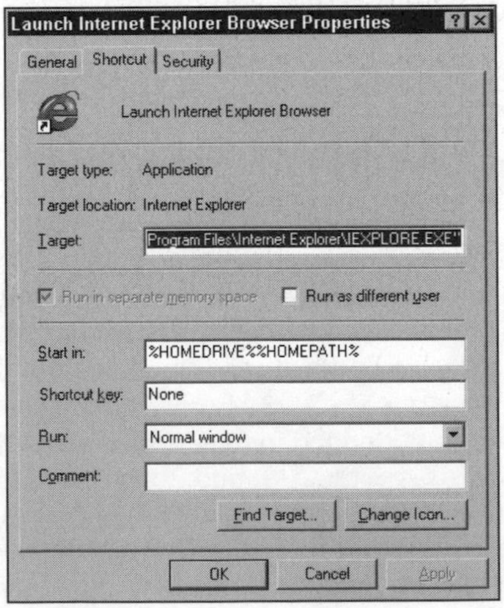

Figure 5-1: Find out a program's real name.

Next, you need to find out whether it's a COM object and whether you can access it remotely. This is also easy — just open the `scriptobjects.exe` file you generated in Chapter 4 and search for `iexplore.exe`.

Immediately, you find that `iexplore.exe` is indeed a COM object and can be called by script, referred to as `InternetExplorer.Application` and returning an `IWebBrowser2` object. You also see that its TypeLibrary is stored in `shdocvw.dll`. That's all you need to know.

Reading out secret TypeLibrary information

Next, you generate the undocumented owner's manual. Launch script 3-7.VBS and provide it with the information you just found out.

A couple seconds later, you receive the automatically generated owner's manual as a handy HTML file (see Figure 5-2). The TypeLibrary provides you not only with the syntax of all the hidden methods and properties, it also includes short descriptions. Print out this file for future reference.

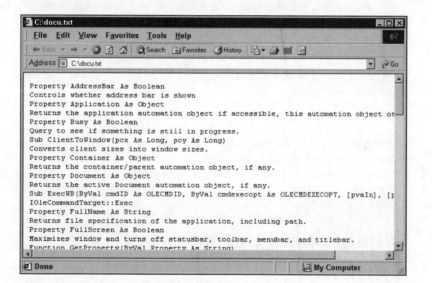

Figure 5-2: Scripts generate detailed lists of internal functions for printout and research.

Opening Internet Explorer with Style

Now you can get access to Internet Explorer easily, because you now know its `ProgID` (`InternetExplorer.Application`); you just need to call `CreateObject`. You receive a `IWebBrowser2 Object` and can start calling all its methods and properties listed in your freshly generated "owner's manual."

The following script opens Internet Explorer remotely:

```
' 5-1.VBS

set ie = CreateObject("InternetExplorer.Application")
MsgBox "Object Type: " & TypeName(ie)
ie.visible = true
MsgBox "Internet Explorer is visible now!"
ie.visible = false
MsgBox "Now it's hidden!"
ie.Quit
```

The script gets a reference to Internet Explorer and reports the object name — IWebBrowser2, just as expected.

Secret

If you use an older version of Internet Explorer, the object name may also be IWebBrowser. This version of Internet Explorer lacks some methods and properties, but you can use it as well. Just replace IWebBrowser with IWebBrowser2 in all the examples.

Now the scripts will start to use some of the properties and methods listed in the "owner's manual" you just created. The visible property controls whether or not the window is visible. Note that the window button appears in the task bar only when visible is set to true. visible is false by default.

Once the script is done, it calls the Quit method to close Internet Explorer altogether.

Undocumented

Closing an object is not really mandatory. The Scripting Host closes objects anyway once the script is done. However, "out-of-process" COM objects like Internet Explorer run as independent programs. They may not react to the WSH's close request because they are not located inside the WSH's address space. In contrast to "in-process" COM objects, the WSH can only kindly ask the object to go away. It can't use force. Therefore, it's safer to close such objects explicitly.

Writing something into the IE window

So far, Internet Explorer is completely empty. How can you access (and change) its contents? Again, this is surprisingly easy once you find the hidden door. Under normal conditions, Internet Explorer displays HTML pages, so the inside is just an HTML environment that can host and display HTML. To display an HTML page, use the navigate method.

```
' 5-2.VBS

set ie = CreateObject("InternetExplorer.Application")
scriptname = WScript.ScriptFullName
path = left(scriptname, InstrRev(scriptname, "\"))
filename = path & "showme.htm"
```

```
MsgBox "Now loading " & filename
ie.navigate filename
ie.visible = true
MsgBox "Internet Explorer is visible now!", vbSystemModal
MsgBox "Type of document: " & TypeName(ie.document)
ie.Quit
```

Just make sure you prepared an HTML file the script can load. This script looks for a file named `showme.htm`. It needs to be located in the same folder the script is stored in.

Launch your text editor and type in the following simple HTML tags:

```
<html>
<body>
<h1>Hello World!</h1>
</body>
</html>
```

Next, save it as SHOWME.HTM.

Undocumented

`WScript.ScriptFullName` always returns the full path name of your script. With this information, it's easy to retrieve the folder name. You can append the folder name to any resource filename. This way, the resource file just needs to be located in the same folder the script is stored in. You don't need to specify any fixed path names anymore.

Now Internet Explorer will display your HTML file. This isn't too exciting, though. You could have just as easily opened your HTML page with the Run command in the Start menu:

```
IEXPLORE.EXE SHOWME.HTM [Enter]
```

The real fireworks start once the page is loaded and once your script queries Internet Explorer's property document. It returns an object. This object actually represents your HTML file. This simple object reference is all you need to dynamically change the appearance of the HTML page.

Tip

If you start Internet Explorer for the first time, the Internet Wizard might pop up, asking you to set up the Internet connection. You don't need a connection for these examples, but you do need to get rid of the wizard before you can control the IE contents by script. So, just set up a connection first or specify a LAN connection.

Dynamically changing the IE contents

Using Internet Explorer as output window shouldn't require you to provide an external HTML file. After all, your script should supply all the information you want to display. But how can you initialize Internet Explorer contents?

Just use this little trick: Call `navigate`, but don't supply an HTML filename. Instead, use the undocumented JavaScript: keyword. This way, you can synthetically open a Web page.

The following script shows how this works, and it also includes another important feature. A loop delays the script until the HTML page is actually displayed. This is extremely important. Should you try to access the document property before the document is properly initialized, you will get an error. You can't change Internet Explorer content dynamically before it is fully loaded.

```
' 5-3.VBS

set ie = CreateObject("InternetExplorer.Application")
title = "My Output Window"
page = "JavaScript:'<html><head><title>" & title _
    & "</title></head><body></body></html>'"
ie.navigate page

' wait for the page to be fully initialized:
do
loop while ie.ReadyState<>4

' show page:
ie.visible = true

' now you can dynamically change content:
content = InputBox("Please enter some text!")
ie.document.body.innerHTML = "<h1>" & content & "</h1>"
MsgBox "I will now list all files on drive C:\!"

' list all files
set fs = CreateObject("Scripting.FileSystemObject")
set folder = fs.GetFolder("C:\")
for each file in folder.files
    ie.document.body.insertAdjacentHTML "beforeEnd", _
file.name & "<BR>"
next
```

The script prompts you for text and displays it in the IE window. Next, it enumerates all files on drive C:\ and displays them dynamically (see Figure 5-3).

Secret

You can even set the title bar text of your window. Just add a <head></head> section in your HTML code and provide a <title></title> section.

This is possible only because your script owns a reference to the embedded Web page. It can replace the body of the page with innerHTML, and it can add text to the body tag using insertAdjacentHTML. In fact, your script can now use any DHTML command supported by Internet Explorer.

Figure 5-3: Change text in the window dynamically.

Responding to Events

As many advantages as independent "out-of-process" COM objects offer, problems can still arise. What if someone closes the IE window while your script is still trying to access it? You will receive an automation error. No fun.

Therefore, it's necessary to inform your script about any important conditions inside the IE window. Your script needs a way to respond to events fired by the IE window. Events are messages a COM object sends as soon as something important happens, so your script needs some kind of receiver to listen to those events.

Fortunately, the Scripting Host contains such a receiver. It's called event sink, and it automatically calls a custom procedure the moment the event that the event sink listens to is fired.

The following script activates its event receiver and responds to the onQuit event. This event is fired just before the IE window is closed.

```
' 5-4.VBS

' this statement invokes the event sink feature:
set ie = WScript.CreateObject("InternetExplorer.Application", _
 "event_")

title = "My Output Window"
page = "JavaScript:'<html><head><title>" & title _
    & "</title></head><body></body></html>'"
ie.navigate page

' wait for the page to be fully initialized:
do
```

```
loop while ie.ReadyState<>4

' show page:
ie.visible = true

' now you can dynamically change content:
content = InputBox("Please enter some text!")
ie.document.body.innerHTML = "<h1>" & content & "</h1>"
MsgBox "I will now list all files on drive C:\!"

' list all files
set fs = CreateObject("Scripting.FileSystemObject")
set folder = fs.GetFolder("C:\")
for each file in folder.files
    ie.document.body.insertAdjacentHTML "beforeEnd", _
file.name & "<BR>"
next

' this procedure executes once the IE Quit event is fired:

sub event_onQuit
    MsgBox "Hey! You closed my output window!", vbExclamation
    WScript.Quit
end sub
```

The script works almost like its predecessor. Again, you can insert text dynamically into the IE window, but this time, the moment you close the IE window, your script pops up a warning message and quits. If you tried the same thing with 5-3.VBS, you would have raised an automation error.

How does the magic work? This time, the script uses CreateObject not only to get a reference to InternetExplorer.Application, but to also establish an event sink. It's the second argument, "event_." You can call your event sink something else as long as the name ends with an underscore.

Secret

There are actually two different CreateObject methods. One is part of VBScript and can be called directly. This method does not support event sinks. Instead, it allows access to remote COM objects on other machines. The Scripting Host offers its own CreateObject method. This method can't call COM objects remotely, but it supports event sinks. To call this method, you need to specify the Scripting Host explicitly, using WScript.CreateObject.

To be able to establish an event sink, you must use the Scripting Hosts' version of CreateObject. You can't use the VBScript command. This is why the script uses WScript.CreateObject instead of CreateObject.

The event sink listens to all events fired by the object. Once an event is fired, the event sink looks for a procedure that starts with the name of the event sink and ends with the name of the event. Because the script has called its event sink "event_," the procedure event_onQuit is executed each time the onQuit event is fired.

Undocumented

IE fires `onQuit` anytime its window is closed. This can happen because someone closed it with the mouse, or if your script calls the IE `Quit` method. So if you want to close the IE window by script, you should disable the event procedure first. Just call `WScript.DisconnectObject ie`. You can also build a control variable into your event procedure and set the variable appropriately. For example, display the warning message only if your control variable is set to `true`, and set it to `false` anytime you don't want event processing.

Finding out which events the object supports

How did I know Internet Explorer supports the `onQuit` event? I just looked it up in the IE TypeLibrary. You could, too.

The `IWebBrowser2` object really is just a module. It contains only the methods and properties, but no events. Events are handled by another module, so the first thing you need to do is get a clear picture of which modules there really are:

```
' 5-5.VBS

set typelib = CreateObject("typelib3.decoder")

' use a dictionary to keep track of duplicate entries:
set dict = CreateObject("scripting.dictionary")

' check interfaces defined in this file:
typelibfile = "shdocvw.dll"

' enumerate available interfaces:
set interfaces = typelib.GetInterfaces(typelibfile)

list = "Interfaces in " & typelibfile & ":" & vbCr & vbCr

' read all interfaces and put into list:
for each interface in interfaces
    ' check whether entry is a duplicate entry:
    if not dict.Exists(interface) then
        ' add to list only if new entry
        dict.Add interface, 0
        list = list & interface & vbCr
    end if
next

MsgBox list
```

The script lists all the modules mentioned in the TypeLibrary (see Figure 5-4). There are more than just `IWebBrowser2`.

Figure 5-4: Retrieve objects stored in IE TypeLibrary to find out about events.

As a good investigator, you notice that some of the module names contain "events" in their names. One might assume that DWebBrowserEvents2 contains the IE event list. To make sure, and to find out about the events, take a look inside DWebBrowserEvents2:

```
' 5-6.VBS

set typelib = CreateObject("typelib.decoder")
set wshshell = CreateObject("WScript.Shell")

' This is the Type Library responsible for IE:
module = "shdocvw.dll"

' This is the module we are interested in:
interface = "DWebBrowserEvents2"

' list content:
set result = typelib.EnumInterface(module, interface)

for each entry in result
    entry = Split(entry, vbTab)
    list = list & entry(0) & vbCr & "[" & entry(1) & "]" & vbCr
next

wshshell.Popup list
```

Because there are a lot of events, the script uses the Popup method. MsgBox wouldn't be able to show all the results. If you'd rather save the output to a file for future reference, take a look at Chapter 8 and the file system methods. You can also use script 5-13.VBS.

Right again—DWebBrowserEvents2 contains the onQuit procedure, and its secret comment states Fired when the application is quitting. In addition, you now have a complete list of all the other events the IE supports.

Tip
You could also go the opposite direction. Just use your handy lookup tool 3-8.VBS and enter `onQuit`. Immediately, you know which objects support `onQuit` (see Figure 5-5).

```
VBScript                                              [X]

(shdocvw.dll)
InternetExplorer (Function): Sub Quit
IWebBrowserApp (Function): Sub Quit
ShellBrowserWindow (Function): Sub Quit
WebBrowser (Function): Sub Quit
InternetExplorer (Event): Sub OnQuit
ShellBrowserWindow (Event): Sub OnQuit
WebBrowser (Event): Sub OnQuit
WebBrowser_V1 (Event): Sub Quit(Cancel As Boolean)
(wscript.exe)
IHost_Class (Function): Sub Quit([ByVal iExitCode As Long])
IHost2 (Function): Sub Quit([ByVal iExitCode As Long])

                    [    OK    ]
```

Figure 5-5: Search for key word `onQuit`.

The perfect output window example

By now, you have all the building blocks necessary to prepare a generic output window. Just bundle the code and put it into an easy-to-use function. In addition, the following script also disables all the IE toolbars so the window doesn't look like an IE window anymore:

```
' 5-7.VBS

' Open IE Window without scroll bar
set window = OpenWindow("My Output Window", false)

' use window:
content = InputBox("Please enter some text!")
PrintNew window, "<h1>" & content & "</h1>"
MsgBox "I will now list all files on drive C:\!"

' list all files
set fs = CreateObject("Scripting.FileSystemObject")
set folder = fs.GetFolder("C:\")
for each file in folder.files
    Print window, file.name & "<BR>"
next

sub event_onQuit
    MsgBox "Hey! You closed my output window!", vbExclamation
    WScript.Quit
end sub

function OpenWindow(title, scrolling)
set ie = WScript.CreateObject("InternetExplorer.Application", _
```

```
"event_")

    ' add attribute to body-tag to hide scroll bar if appropriate:
    if scrolling then
        scroller = "scroll = no"
    end if

page = "JavaScript:'<html><head><title>" & title _
        & "</title></head><body " & scroller & "></body></html>'"
ie.navigate page

' turn off toolbars
    ie.Toolbar = false

    ' turn off status bar
    ie.Statusbar = false

do
loop while ie.ReadyState<>4

ie.visible = true

' return reference to IE object:
    Set OpenWindow = ie
end function

sub PrintNew(obj, text)
    obj.document.body.innerHTML = text
end sub

sub Print(obj, text)
    obj.document.body.insertAdjacentHTML "beforeEnd", text
end sub
```

The function `OpenWindow` handles all the IE opening and returns the object reference. As always with references, remember to use `Set` whenever you assign the reference to another variable.

Note also the use of `scroll=no`. The script inserts this statement into the `<body>` tag to disable the vertical scroll bar whenever you supply false as a second argument. In this example, because of the missing scroll bar, you can't see the end of the file listing. So, in this case, it would be a good idea to enable the scroll bar. In other cases where you just want to design a dialog box, it's better to turn the bar off — the choice is yours.

Undocumented

Finally, Microsoft has fixed the scroll bar issue. Beginning with Internet Explorer 5, you can specify `scroll=auto`. Now, the IE will display the vertical scroll bar only when needed.

Sizing the IE window

You can even size and center your IE window. The window size is determined by the IE properties Width and Height. The current position is determined by Left and Top.

In order to center the window onscreen, you also need information about the current screen resolution so you can calculate the offsets. This information is provided by the `screen` object—part of any `HTMLDocument` object.

```
' 5-8.VBS

set window = OpenWindow("My Output Window", 400, 200)

content = InputBox("Please enter some text!")
PrintNew window, "<h1>" & content & "</h1>"
MsgBox "I will now list all files on drive C:\!"

' list all files
set fs = CreateObject("Scripting.FileSystemObject")
set folder = fs.GetFolder("C:\")
for each file in folder.files
    Print window, file.name & "<BR>"
next

sub event_onQuit
    MsgBox "Hey! You closed my output window!", vbExclamation
    WScript.Quit
end sub

function OpenWindow(title, width, height)
set ie = WScript.CreateObject("InternetExplorer.Application", _
"event_")

page = "JavaScript:'<html><head><title>" & title _
       & "</title></head><body scroll=auto></body></html>'"
ie.navigate page

    ie.Toolbar = false
    ie.Statusbar = false
do
loop while ie.ReadyState<>4

    screenWidth = ie.document.parentWindow.screen.availWidth
    screenHeight = ie.document.parentWindow.screen.availHeight

    ' limit size to max avail space
    if width>screenWidth then width=screenWidth
    if height>screenHeight then height=screenHeight

    ie.Width = width
    ie.Height = height
```

```
    ie.left = Fix((screenWidth - width)/2)
    ie.top = Fix((screenHeight  - height)/2)

ie.visible = true

' return reference to IE object:
    Set OpenWindow = ie
end function

sub PrintNew(obj, text)
    obj.document.body.innerHTML = text
end sub

sub Print(obj, text)
    obj.document.body.insertAdjacentHTML "beforeEnd", text
end sub
```

Responding to Events Inside Your Documents

So far, IE can only display information. What if you want to create a real dialog window? How can you send keystrokes, inputs, and button clicks from inside your HTML document back to your script?

Easy. You already discovered events. Whenever something exciting happens inside your HTML document, it also raises events. Responding to those events is just a matter of setting up the right receiver. Then your script can listen to these events.

In contrast to CreateObject, this time you are not going to create a new object. The HTMLDocument object is already there so you can't use CreateObject to set up an event sink the way you did for the Internet Explorer window.

You don't have to set up event sinks. It's much easier, because your HTML document already contains event-handling functions. Modern DHTML Web pages use events every day.

Setting up dialog elements and buttons

Before you can start listening to events fired by your HTML page, you first need to set up a page that contains form elements. Otherwise, there won't be any events your script can respond to.

So, start your text editor and hack in the following simple page:

```
<html>
<head>
<title>My Dialog!</title>
<body scroll=no>
```

```
<input type="text" name="myInput" size="30"><BR>
<input type="button" name="myButton" value="Read This!">
</body>
</html>
```

Save it as `dialog.htm`, and open the file to check whether it will display correctly.

Next, use the following script to display the dialog box:

```
' 5-9.VBS

' global variable will report entered text:
enteredText = ""

' open window:
set window = OpenWindow("dialog.htm", 400, 300)

' hook up event handler:
window.document.all.myButton.onClick = GetRef("buttonclick")

' display MsgBox to halt the script and wait for input
WScript.Sleep 2000
MsgBox "Press OK to read dialog box...", vbSystemModal

' see what the user has typed in:
MsgBox "This is what you entered: " & enteredText

' event procedure responds to button click:

sub buttonclick
    ' someone clicked the button!
    ' read entered text
    enteredText = window.document.all.myInput.value
    ' close window
    window.Quit
end sub

function OpenWindow(filename, width, height)
set ie = CreateObject("InternetExplorer.Application")
scriptname = WScript.ScriptFullName
path = left(scriptname, InstrRev(scriptname, "\"))
filepath = path & filename

ie.navigate filepath

    ie.Toolbar = false
    ie.Statusbar = false
do
loop while ie.ReadyState<>4

    screenWidth = ie.document.parentWindow.screen.availWidth
    screenHeight = ie.document.parentWindow.screen.availHeight
```

```
' limit size to max avail space
if width>screenWidth then width=screenWidth
if height>screenHeight then height=screenHeight

ie.Width = width
ie.Height = height

ie.left = Fix((screenWidth - width)/2)
ie.top = Fix((screenHeight  - height)/2)

ie.visible = true

' return reference to IE object:
    Set OpenWindow = ie
end function
```

Unfortunately, this script won't work yet. It does display your dialog box, but it doesn't wait for your response. Instead, right after the dialog box is shown, your script reads out the text field and finds — nothing.

Stopping the script until events are fired

So, you need a way to halt your script until either the IE window is closed or the button inside your page is clicked. You could use a `do...loop` and constantly check for either condition. However, this loop would consume so much computing power that it would slow down your entire machine. The events would have no chance to ever fire.

Visual Basic has a better solution — and it's called `DoEvents`.

Secret

`DoEvents` allows any pending events to fire, and this keeps your system responsive even if you are executing a loop. In essence, you are not only pausing your script for some milliseconds, but also forcing Windows to actively process any pending events. `WScript.Sleep`, in contrast, just pauses. Events still can't get through.

Unfortunately, VBScript doesn't support `DoEvents`.

This is a typical example where the Visual Basic CCE comes to the rescue. Should you need a little refresher, go back to Chapter 5. To use `DoEvents` from inside your scripts, just start the VB CCE, create a new project and name it `iehelper.tools`. Next, in Code view, enter this simple wrapper procedure (see Figure 5-6):

```
sub HandleEvents
    DoEvents
end sub
```

Compile your project using `Make iehelper.ocx` in the File menu. Done.

You can find the project on the companion CD: open `\components\`
`iehelper\iehelper.vbp`. Or install the precompiled package: `\install\`
`iehelper\setup.exe`.

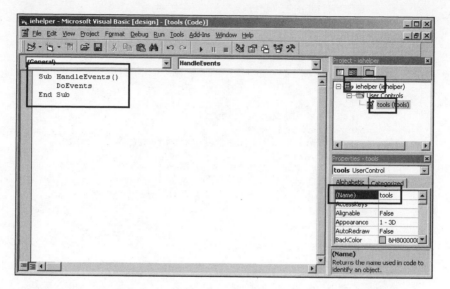

Figure 5-6: Wrap `DoEvents` for use in scripts to allow events to be handled.

Undocumented

Unfortunately, you can't call your procedure `DoEvents`. Because Visual Basic commands are reserved key words, you need to find a similar name for your wrapper function.

Creating your own HTML dialog boxes

Now that you can loop and process events at the same time, you can finally create useful dialog boxes:

```
' 5-10.VBS

' get access to your wrapped DoEvents command
set helper = CreateObject("iehelper.tools")

' global variable will report entered text:
enteredText = ""

' open window:
set window = OpenWindow("dialog.htm", 400, 300)

' hook up event handler:
window.document.all.myButton.onClick = GetRef("buttonclick")
```

```
' go to bed until either button is clicked or window is closed:
wakeup = false
do
    ' allow events to fire:
    helper.HandleEvents
loop until wakeup

MsgBox "This is what you entered: " & enteredText

' event procedures:

sub buttonclick
    ' someone clicked the button!
    ' read entered text
    enteredText = window.document.all.myInput.value
    ' close window
    window.Quit
end sub

sub event_onQuit
    wakeup = true
end sub


function OpenWindow(filename, width, height)
set ie = WScript.CreateObject("InternetExplorer.Application", _
"event_")
scriptname = WScript.ScriptFullName
path = left(scriptname, InstrRev(scriptname, "\"))
filepath = path & filename

ie.navigate filepath

    ie.Toolbar = false
    ie.Statusbar = false
do
loop while ie.ReadyState<>4

    screenWidth = ie.document.parentWindow.screen.availWidth
    screenHeight = ie.document.parentWindow.screen.availHeight

    ' limit size to max avail space
    if width>screenWidth then width=screenWidth
    if height>screenHeight then height=screenHeight

    ie.Width = width
    ie.Height = height

    ie.left = Fix((screenWidth - width)/2)
    ie.top = Fix((screenHeight  - height)/2)

ie.visible = true

' return reference to IE object:
    Set OpenWindow = ie
end function
```

It works perfectly well. Your script waits patiently until either the button is clicked or the window is closed. It then reads out whatever you have typed into your HTML page and displays the results (see Figure 5-7).

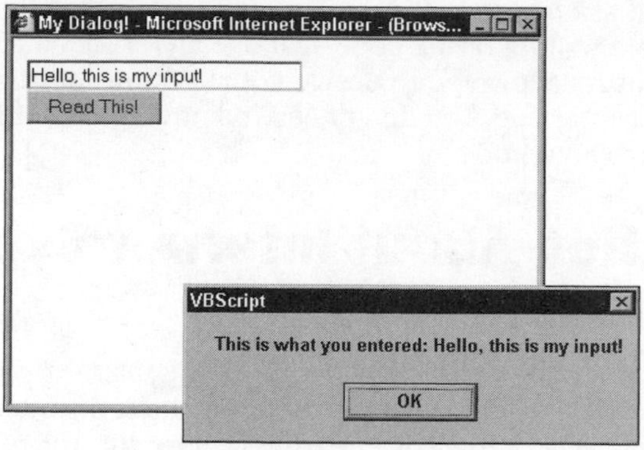

Figure 5-7: Design your own HTML dialog boxes and wait for entered text.

How does it work?

There are actually two events your script listens to. First, event_onClick checks whether someone closed the IE window. If so, the procedure changes wakeup to true. This causes the loop to exit, and your script comes back to life.

buttonclick is another event receiver. This procedure is executed when someone clicks the button on your Web page. Your script has hooked up the buttons' event procedure to its own procedure.

First, your script accesses the button element on the HTML page. window.document.all.myButton represents the button.

Always make sure you assign a name= to your HTML elements. Only with this name can your script access the element. Elements without names can't be controlled by your script.

Next, it assigns a value to the button's onClick property using GetRef. GetRef is a new WSH 2.0 function. It returns the internal address of any script procedure. This way, you can link your script procedures to other objects.

Whenever someone clicks on the button, Internet Explorer now actively calls the address it received from GetRef.

buttonclick first stores the text field value in some global variable. Again, your script accesses the text field using the same syntax as with the button. Next, the procedure closes the IE window using its Quit method. Because this automatically fires the onQuit event, immediately thereafter event_onQuit is called and exits the do...loop delay.

Tip

This technology is extremely powerful! It allows you to design just about any dialog box, even if your dialog boxes consist of many different form elements or dynamic HTML. Your script can easily respond to different buttons and read out more than just a text field. This way, you can design input forms for databases as well as complex windows for disk tools you create. If you don't feel comfortable writing HTML code, just use an HTML editor such as FrontPage. HTML editors allow you to design your window interactively and with a graphical user interface. You don't need to know HTML, although it sure helps to optimize your code.

Getting Information About Internet Explorer DHTML Object Model

Every HTML page is internally represented as an HTMLDocument object. You have already seen how useful it is to know more about the internal structure of this object. This knowledge helps to remote control an HTML page by script, and it also reveals much about how DHTML works. If you're a Web designer, the following pages will probably provide useful information you haven't seen elsewhere.

A secret TypeLibrary contains the entire documentation about the IE DHTML object model. You can look up any object and explore the entire structure of DHTML pages.

To be able to read the secret TypeLibrary information, you need a script extension. Make sure you have installed \install\typelib\setup.exe on the companion CD.

Undocumented

The secret DHTML TypeLibrary is called mshtml.tlb. However, it wasn't intended for you to see. Instead, mshtml.tlb was designed to assist in professional development environments like Visual Basic. It may or may not be available on your system.

Take a look at all the objects defined in mshtml.tlb:

```
' 5-11.VBS

' make sure you have installed the custom COM object
' as outlined in the book

outputfile = "C:\Interface.txt"
set typelib = CreateObject("typelib.decoder")
set fs = CreateObject("Scripting.FileSystemObject")
set wshshell = CreateObject("WScript.Shell")

set output = fs.CreateTextFile(outputfile, true)

' use a dictionary to keep track of duplicate entries:
set dict = CreateObject("scripting.dictionary")

' check interfaces defined in this file:
typelibfile = InputBox("Type lib name",,"mshtml.tlb")
```

```
' enumerate available interfaces:
set interfaces = typelib.GetInterfaces(typelibfile)

output.WriteLine "Interfaces in " & typelibfile & ":" & vbCrLf &
vbCrLf

' read all interfaces and put into list:
for each interface in interfaces
    ' check whether entry is a duplicate entry:
    if not dict.Exists(interface) then
        ' add to list only if new entry
        dict.Add interface, 0
        output.WriteLine interface
    end if
next

output.close
wshshell.Run outputfile
```

Tip This script can list the available object names of any TypeLibrary. Just enter the name to receive a list of the objects documented in the TypeLibrary. If the TypeLibrary file is not located in any of the system folders, you need to specify the full path name.

To find out more about individual objects, just use script 3-7.VBS. Enter the name of the TypeLibrary (mshtml.tlb) and the name of the object you are interested in. Try HTMLDocument.

Your script now reveals every detail — more than you could possibly find in even the most sophisticated reference books (see Figure 5-8). Because this information is automatically generated on the basis of your current TypeLibrary, you will get the most up-to-date information available.

```
Interface - Notepad                                    _ |□| X
File  Edit  Format  Help
Interfaces in mshtml.tlb:

DispHTMLStyle
IHTMLStyle
IHTMLStyle2
DispHTMLRuleStyle
IHTMLRuleStyle
IHTMLRuleStyle2
DispHTMLCurrentStyle
IHTMLCurrentStyle
IHTMLFiltersCollection
DispHTMLDOMAttribute
IHTMLDOMAttribute
DispHTMLDOMTextNode
IHTMLDOMTextNode
IHTMLDOMNode
DispHTMLAttributeCollection
IHTMLAttributeCollection
DispDOMChildrenCollection
IHTMLDOMChildrenCollection
DispHTCDefaultDispatch
IHTCDefaultDispatch
DispHTCPropertyBehavior
```

Figure 5-8: Retrieve all hidden IE functions and properties.

Generating HTML-formatted documentation manuals

But there's more. Your script can easily query all information sections and automatically build nicely formatted HTML documentation files for convenient reference. The following script generates your personal information library, and you can add any TypeLibrary information you find interesting:

Too lazy to generate the documentation yourself? Take a look at the companion CD: \info\documentation\. I have put some sample documentations on it. Still, it's much better to generate the documentation yourself so it adequately reflects the current program versions of your COM objects.

```
' 5-12.VBS

' make sure you have installed the custom COM object
' as outlined in the book

' change this path to the folder you want to store
' your documentation in:
docu = "C:\documentation"

' change this to false if you don't want a shortcut
' to your documentation folder on your desktop:
link = true

' we need access to a couple of COM objects:
set typelib = CreateObject("typelib.decoder")
set fs = CreateObject("Scripting.FileSystemObject")
set wshshell = CreateObject("WScript.Shell")
set dict = CreateObject("scripting.dictionary")

' ask which type library to decode:
lib = InputBox("Which Type Library do you want to decode?", _
    , "mshtml.tlb")

' do some checks:

' does the folder name end with "\"?
if not right(docu,1)="\" then docu = docu & "\"

' does the typelib file exist and is it a valid typelib?
if not isTypeLib(lib) then
    MsgBox "Error: " & err.description
    WScript.Quit
end if

' does the documentation folder exist?
if not fs.FolderExists(docu) then
    result = MsgBox(docu & " does not exist. Create?", vbYesNo _
        + vbQuestion)
    if result=vbYes then
```

```
            fs.CreateFolder docu
        else
            MsgBox "Can't continue.", vbCritical
            WScript.Quit
        end if
    end if
end if

' open status window:
set window = OpenWindow("Querying TypeLib", 600, 400)
windowavailable = true
PrintNew window, "Decoding " & lib & " Type Library<BR>"

' enumerate typelib interfaces
set interfaces = typelib.GetInterfaces(lib)

' enumerate other information contained in typelib
set modules = typelib.GetTypeInfos(lib)

' find out number of information blocks to show progress
allelements = interfaces.Count + modules.Count
allcounter = 0

' create auto-documentation files
autodocument interfaces
autodocument modules

' close status window:
closeisok=true
window.Quit

result = MsgBox("Do you want to open documentation folder?", _
    vbYesNo + VbQuestion)
command = "EXPLORER.EXE /e,/root," & docu
if result = vbYes then
    wshshell.Run command
end if

' place a link to documentation on desktop
' where's the desktop?
if link then
    desktop = wshshell.SpecialFolders("desktop")
    set scut = wshshell.CreateShortcut(desktop & "\script host
docu.lnk")
    scut.TargetPath = "explorer.exe"
    scut.Arguments = "/e,/root," & docu
    scut.IconLocation = "wscript.exe,0"
    scut.save
end if

sub autodocument(collection)
    ' create subfolder for this type library:
    foldername = docu & fs.GetBaseName(lib) & "\"
    if not fs.FolderExists(foldername) then
```

```
            fs.CreateFolder foldername
end if

' decode entire collection:
for each section in collection
    ' update status window:


    ' generate safe file name
    safename = Replace(section, "\", "")
    safename = Replace(section, ".", "")

    ' create file:
    set output = fs.CreateTextFile( _
        foldername & safename & ".htm")

    ' insert html framework like style sheets:
    output.WriteLine "<html><head><title>" _
        & "TypeLib-Information " & module
    output.WriteLine "</title><style>"
    output.WriteLine "td {font: 10pt Arial}"
    output.WriteLine "h2 {font: 14pt Arial; font-weight: bold}"
    output.WriteLine "h3 {font: 12pt Arial; font-weight: bold}"
    output.WriteLine ".c1    {color: gray}"
    output.WriteLine ".c2    {color: black; font-style:normal;" _
        & " font-weight:bold}"
    output.WriteLine ".c3    {color: green; font-style:normal}"
    output.WriteLine ".c4    {color: green; font-style:normal}"
    output.WriteLine ".c5    {color: red}"
    output.WriteLine ".c6    {color: gray}"
    output.WriteLine ".c7    {color: blue; font-style:normal;" _
        & " font-weight:bold}"
    output.WriteLine ".c8    {color: green; font-style:normal;" _
        & " font-weight:bold}"
    output.WriteLine ".c9    {color: gray}"
    output.WriteLine ".c10   {color: black; font-weight:" _
        & " bold; font-style: normal}"
    output.WriteLine ".c11   {color: gray}"
    output.WriteLine ".c12   {color: red}"
    output.WriteLine "</style></head><body>"
    output.WriteLine "<h2>" & lib & "</h2>"

    ' check whether duplicate entry:
    if not dict.Exists(section) then
        ' add to list only if new entry
        dict.Add section, 0
        allcounter = allcounter + 1
        percent = Fix(allcounter * 100/allelements)
        Print window, "[" & percent & "%] Querying " _
            & section & "...<br>"

        ' retrieve section information, preformatted as HTML
        html = typelib.EnumInterfaceHTML(lib, section, 255)
```

```
                    output.WriteLine "<table border=0 width=""100%""" _
                        & " bgcolor=""#EEEEEE"">"
                    output.WriteLine "<tr><td width=""60%""><b>" _
                        & section & "</b></td><td" _
                        & " width=""40%"">Description</td></tr>"
                    output.WriteLine html
                    output.WriteLine "</table><BR>"
                end if

                ' close this file
                output.WriteLine "</body></html>"
                output.close
            next
        end sub

        sub event_onQuit
            windowavailable = false
            if not closeisok then
                MsgBox "Hey! You closed my output window!", vbExclamation
                WScript.Quit
            end if
        end sub

        function OpenWindow(title, width, height)
            set ie = WScript.CreateObject("InternetExplorer.Application", _
                "event_")

            page = "JavaScript:'<html><head><title>" & title _
                & "</title></head><body scroll=auto></body></html>'"
            ie.navigate page

            ie.Toolbar = false
            ie.Statusbar = false
            do
            loop while ie.ReadyState<>4

            screenWidth = ie.document.parentWindow.screen.availWidth
            screenHeight = ie.document.parentWindow.screen.availHeight

            if width>screenWidth then width=screenWidth
            if height>screenHeight then height=screenHeight

            ie.Width = width
            ie.Height = height

            ie.left = Fix((screenWidth - width)/2)
            ie.top = Fix((screenHeight  - height)/2)

            ie.visible = true

            Set OpenWindow = ie
        end function
```

```
sub PrintNew(obj, text)
    if windowavailable then obj.document.body.innerHTML = text
end sub

sub Print(obj, text)
    if windowavailable then
        obj.document.body.insertAdjacentHTML "beforeEnd", text
        set textrange = obj.document.body.createTextRange
        textrange.scrollIntoView false
    end if
end sub

function isTypeLib(lib)
    on error resume next
    set interfaces = typelib.GetInterfaces(lib)
    if err.Number=0 then
        isTypeLib=true
    else
        isTypeLib=false
    end if
end function
```

Note

By default, the script stores the documentation in `C:\documentation`. Change the script if you want to store it elsewhere. `mshtml.tlb` is an exceptionally large TypeLibrary. It can take some minutes for the script to decode all the information.

You can actually watch the script retrieve the information: It uses an IE window to report progress information (see Figure 5-9). This gives you a rough estimate of how much information is already processed. However, it's very likely that the script will be finished before 100 percent is reached. There are many duplicate entries, and the script eliminates those.

```
Querying TypeLib - Microsoft Internet Explorer - (BrowseUI UNI)     _ □ ×

Decoding mshtml.tlb Type Library
[0%] Querying DispHTMLStyle...
[0%] Querying IHTMLStyle...
[0%] Querying IHTMLStyle2...
[0%] Querying DispHTMLRuleStyle...
[0%] Querying IHTMLRuleStyle...
[0%] Querying IHTMLRuleStyle2...
[0%] Querying DispHTMLCurrentStyle...
[0%] Querying IHTMLCurrentStyle...
[0%] Querying IHTMLFiltersCollection...
[0%] Querying DispHTMLDOMAttribute...
[0%] Querying IHTMLDOMAttribute...
[0%] Querying DispHTMLDOMTextNode...
[1%] Querying IHTMLDOMTextNode...
[1%] Querying IHTMLDOMNode...
[1%] Querying DispHTMLAttributeCollection...
[1%] Querying IHTMLAttributeCollection...
```

Figure 5-9: Script automatically scans all TypeLibrary objects.

The script uses the `textrange` object to automatically scroll to the last line inside the IE window. This way, you always see the latest progress information.

Once all information is retrieved, the script offers to open your documentation library. In addition, it places a shortcut on your desktop. Both not only open your documentation folder but also use hidden Explorer options to set it as root. In the left Explorer pane, you now can only see your documentation subfolders—and nothing else (see Figure 5-11).

Tip

Call your script a couple of times and have it generate documentations for all the other important TypeLibraries too. These include `vbscript.dll`, `scrrun.dll`, `wshom.ocx`, `shdocvw.dll`, and `comdlg32.ocx`. Each TypeLibrary gets its own subfolder in your documentation view. It's now easy to search for information. You can even give this documentation to friends and colleagues or put it on your Web site: The documentation files are plain DHTML, ideally suited for Internet publishing. Maybe you want to restructure the information, too. Go ahead; it's all contained in individual files, and you can easily create another folder named `FileSystemObject` and feed it any file that relates to the `FileSystemObject` object.

Now lean back and see what you can do with this wealth of information. `TypeName` has revealed that HTML documents are of type `HTMLDocument`. So, in your documentation folder, open subfolder `mshtml` and look for `HTMLDocument`. Open the file.

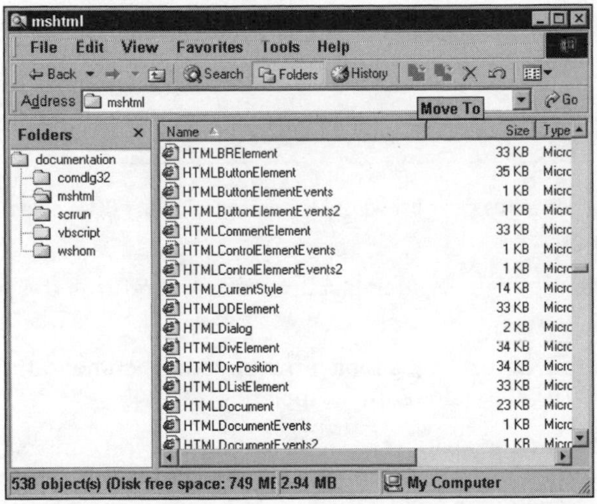

Figure 5-10: Create your personal information library of undocumented COM object functions.

It contains all the properties and methods supported by HTML documents displayed in the IE window. Obviously, this documentation is no tutorial, just technical data. However, it's a great starting point for your own research.

Retrieving undocumented information about the screen object

For example, the scripts above have used this line to determine the horizontal screen resolution:

```
screenWidth = ie.document.parentWindow.screen.availWidth
```

`ie.document` **represents your** `HTMLDocument` **object. Look up** `parentWindow` in your documentation—what you see will look like the window shown in Figure 5-11.

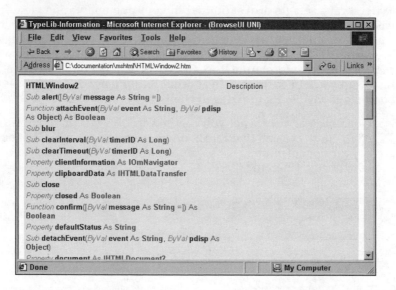

Figure 5-11: Script generates color-coded HTML references of any COM object.

You now know that `parentWindow` is a property and returns the reference to another object: `IHTMLWindow2`.

You don't know this object? Let's look it up. In your documentation folder `mshtml`, **look for** `IHTMLWindow2.htm`. Open it.

Tip

Open the View menu and switch to Details view. Now you can sort the filenames with a click on the column header. [Ctrl] + [+] (on the numeric keypad) resizes the column widths so everything is nicely in view.

Unfortunately, it's empty. `IHTMLWindow2` just refers to the interface. This is why it starts with "I." To see the real description, look for `HTMLWindow2` and open this file instead. As you see, pioneering in Windows secrets is a lot like an adventure game.

Undocumented

From now on, whenever you look for an object name starting with "I," also look for it without the "I." Whenever you look for an object name not starting with an "I," also look for the "I" version.

Look up the screen property used in the scripts above:

```
Property screen As IHTMLScreen
```

Figure 5-12: Screen property returns a reference to `IHTMLScreen` object.

Interesting: Screen opens yet another door, this time referring to an object named `IHTMLScreen`. Search for `HTMLScreen` in your documentation folder, and you finally see all the screen information available (see Figure 5-13).

```
HTMLScreen
Property availHeight As Long
Property availWidth As Long
Property bufferDepth As Long
Property colorDepth As Long
Property fontSmoothingEnabled As Boolean
Property height As Long
Property updateInterval As Long
Property width As Long
```

Figure 5-13: `HTMLScreen` object contains useful information about screen.

There it is: `availWidth`, a long integer. And it's not the only information. The screen object has a lot more to offer, and you now know how to "walk" the object hierarchy until you reach the information you need.

Undocumented

The screen object actually uses two different properties for the screen resolution. `availWidth` and `availHeight` report the available space (minus any docked bars like the taskbar). `width` and `height`, in contrast, return the physical screen resolution.

It may take some time before you fully appreciate the scope of what you have just discovered. The information you just retrieved and the strategies you learned apply to any COM object you may stumble into. In addition, you can use all the `HTMLDocument` features in regular Web pages, too. Just wrap your script code into `<script language="VBScript">...</script>` blocks (see the example below). Provided your customers use the IE to view your page, you can now determine their current screen resolutions and scale your Web page accordingly. However, always remember that different browsers use their own object models.

I'd love to dive into more DHTML, but will leave this to you instead. You now know all the necessary tools and strategies to continue discovering secrets on your own, so feel free to experiment. As a final treat, take a look at the following scripts. They take advantage of the undocumented print feature that Internet Explorer 5 and above brought along. While it will remain undocumented to most others, you now have automatically generated documentation for even the most hidden away function.

```
' 5-13.VBS

url = InputBox("Enter name of web page!",,"http://www.microsoft.com")
```

```
' surf to website:
set ie = CreateObject("InternetExplorer.Application")
ie.navigate url

' wait for page to be loaded
do
loop while ie.ReadyState<>4

ie.visible = true

answer = MsgBox("Do you want to print this page?", vbYesNo)
if answer=vbYes then
    ie.document.parentWindow.print
end if
```

Even more valuable: the exact same technique works in plain HTML files, too:

```
<html>
<body>
<H1>Hello World!</H1>
<input type="button" name="myButton" value="PrintMe!"
onclick="doPrint()">
<script language="VBScript">
sub doPrint
    on error resume next
    document.parentWindow.print
    if not err.Number=0 then
        MsgBox "Can't print! " & err.description
    end if
end sub
</script>
</body>
</html>
```

So, you finally can add a convenient Print button to your Web pages. It will only work when viewed with Internet Explorer 5 and above, so you may want to generate the print button dynamically inside a script procedure to make sure it will only appear when printing is supported.

Summary

Internet Explorer is a perfect script companion and can serve as the Scripting Host output window. It's easy to open an IE window and output text into it while the script runs. HTML elements can also be tied to script procedures so a button click invokes some script functionality. All this is possible only with a deep understanding of the IE DHTML object model. This chapter showed you how to automatically extract all details from the TypeLibrary and search for more undocumented commands. You can, for example, print Web pages by providing the appropriate print button.

Chapter 6

Using System Dialog Boxes

In This Chapter

▶ Take advantage of the built-in system dialog boxes to ask for file names, colors, and fonts

▶ Get access to the hidden Folder Picker dialog box and use it to ask for folders and files

▶ Get access to the hidden Icon Picker and display icons stored in any file

▶ Create your own dialog boxes and display custom lists for selection

▶ Use the internal `ListView` element to quickly sort lists

▶ Learn how to call undocumented API functions

▶ Convert strings between `ANSI` and `UNICODE`

▶ Write code that runs on all Windows versions

Windows already contains a rich set of system dialog boxes to ask for file names, colors, fonts, and more. To spice up your arsenal of dialog boxes, all you need is a way to access those dialog boxes.

In addition, Visual Basic contains very versatile dialog box elements. The `ListView` element, for example, allows you to display lists and sort them in a matter of seconds. The `ProgressBar` element graphically indicates the progress. All you need to do is wrap those functions to make them accessible by script.

In this chapter, you'll build your own COM objects that provide access to all of these cool features whenever your scripts need them.

Where Do System Dialog Boxes Come From?

Did you ever wonder why standard dialog boxes always look almost the same, no matter which software you use? They are provided by Windows to give all software the same look and feel.

Secret

It's completely up to you—you can happily accept the offer and use the built-in system dialog boxes, or you can be an individualist and design your dialog boxes from scratch (as outlined in Chapter 4). It may be a good idea to stick to the system dialog boxes whenever possible, though. Your users appreciate the professional look, and your scripts also automatically use the most up-to-date dialog boxes. This means that if users run your script on a Windows 2000 machine, they'll get the new Windows 2000 look and feel without a single change in your script code. Even the most sophisticated self-defined dialog boxes start looking dull and ugly after a couple of years, and they lack important features added to later system dialog boxes.

Microsoft has provided a COM object to easily access the standard dialog boxes. It's called `MSComDlg.CommonDialog`. Unfortunately, this object is not part of Windows. Instead, software packages like Microsoft Office or Visual Basic Control Creation Edition bring it along. Just take a look in the scriptobjects.txt file you generated in Chapter 3 to see whether this object is installed on your system. You can also use the following script to find out:

```
' 6-1.VBS

' turn off error handling:
on error resume next

' try to access common dialogs:
set comdlg = CreateObject("MSComDlg.CommonDialog")

' check whether error was raised:
if err.number=0 then
    MsgBox "Common Dialog COM object available!"
else
    MsgBox "Common Dialog COM object missing!"
end if
```

Undocumented

`MSComDlg.CommonDialog` is not absolutely necessary to display the system dialog boxes. It's just a wrapper that takes care of all the dirty API handling usually involved when calling system dialog boxes directly. You can display system dialog boxes without `MSComDlg.CommonDialog` when you provide your own wrapper. Below, you'll find examples for custom wrappers that provide access to other system dialog boxes.

Opening system dialog boxes

Is the `Common Dialog COM` object available on your system? Great! Then you can open any system dialog box entirely by script.

Tip

Even if `MSComDlg.CommonDialog` isn't registered on your system, it might still be there. Visual Basic CCE brings it along and redistributes it with all your COM objects. A little later in this chapter, I'll show you how to open system dialog boxes using your own COM objects. However, the following scripts do require `MSComDlg.CommonDialog` to be registered on your system.

To ask for a filename, use the following script:

```
' 6-2.VBS

whichone = OpenFile("Choose a File!", "C:\", _
"Everything|*.*|Text Files|*.TXT|Word-Documents|*.DOC", 2, 0)
MsgBox "Your choice: " & whichone

function OpenFile(title, dir, filter, index, flags)
    set comdlg = CreateObject("MSComDlg.CommonDialog")
    if filter = "" then
        filter = "All Files|*.*"
    end if

    ' initialize all dialog properties:
    comdlg.filter = filter
    comdlg.FilterIndex = index
    comdlg.Flags = flags
    comdlg.MaxFileSize = 260
    comdlg.CancelError = false
    comdlg.DialogTitle = title
    comdlg.InitDir = dir

    ' open dialog box
    comdlg.ShowOpen

    ' return selection
    OpenFile = comdlg.filename
end function
```

Windows will pop up its official Open dialog box and allow you to select a file. You'll see that the Files of type list contains the file types your script specified. This way, your script can easily limit the selection of available files to any file type you want.

Secret

You can even combine file types. If you want the dialog box to show both WinWord documents and plain text files, use *.doc;*.txt as the selector.

The dialog box may look different on your system. Windows always uses its standard dialog boxes, and their appearance varies with the Windows version.

Finding out more information about system dialog boxes

System dialog boxes support many hidden flags and features. This means it's a good idea to decode all the hidden information necessary to control the dialog boxes. Just take a look in the scriptobjects.txt file you generated in Chapter 4 and search for MSComDlg.CommonDialog. It reveals where the common controls are stored—in this case, comdlg32.ocx. You can now easily generate the hidden "owner's manual" using script 5-12.VBS (see Figure 6-1). Just supply comdlg32.ocx as the name of the TypeLibrary.

CD

You'll find sample documentation on the CD-ROM, at \info\documentation\ comdlg32. Use it if you can't generate the documentation yourself.

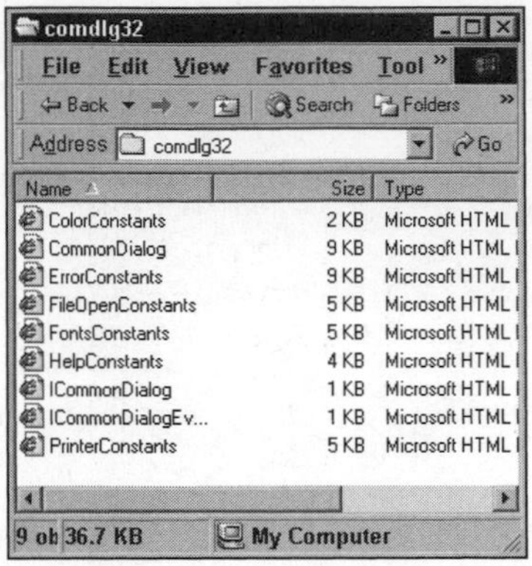

![comdlg32 window showing a list of Microsoft HTML files]

Figure 6-1: Scripts generate full CommonDialog documentation for you.

Using Other System Dialog Boxes

The Open dialog box is just one of many system dialog boxes. To find out about the others, search for commands that start with Show, as shown in Table 6-1:

Table 6-1	Common Dialog Box Scripting Commands
Command	*Dialog Box*
ShowOpen	Open File
ShowSave	Save File
ShowFont	Select Font
ShowColor	Select Color
ShowPrinter	Select Printer
ShowHelp	Show Help File

Each dialog box has its own set of flags you can use to fine-tune its behavior. The documentation file you just created lists different constant sections and provides all the documentation.

Managing flags and special behavior

The section `FileOpenConstants`, for example, applies to both the Show-Open and ShowSave dialog boxes. To get rid of the Read Only check box, use `HideReadOnly` alias 4 as a flag. To switch to `Multiselect` mode, use flag `AllowMultiselect` alias 512 or &H200. Figure 6-2 lists all available constants.

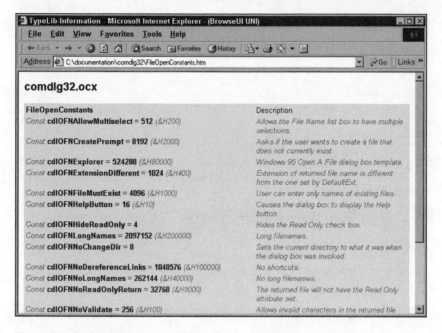

Figure 6-2: Find out all about the hidden dialog box flags.

Secret

You can't use the constant names in your scripts. Your scripts have no way of looking inside the TypeLibrary. Instead, use the numeric values. It's up to you whether you prefer decimal or hexadecimal (&h...) notation.

Add all the flags' values you want to use — 4 + &h200 opens a multiselect dialog box without the Read Only check box.

Undocumented

Flags work in both ways. You can specify values to fine-tune the dialog box before you display it and read flag values after display to find out about selections the user has made. For example, to find out whether the user checked the `Read Only` check box, you can query the flags value. It will only contain interesting information if the user has selected a file. Not all of the flags in the `FileOpenConstants` section apply to both Open and Save As dialog boxes.

This script opens a multiselect dialog box and returns all the selected files. It also reports whether or not the user has selected the Read Only check box:

```
' 6-3.VBS

flag = &h200
whichone = OpenFile("Choose a File!", "C:\", "Everything|*.*|Text
Files|*.TXT|Word-Documents|*.DOC", 2, flag)
MsgBox "Raw data returned: " & whichone

' Split up multi selection result:
' space is used as separator:
whichone = Split(whichone, " ")

' field index 0 contains path information:
path = whichone(0)

' list all the files:
' how many files were selected?
filecount = UBound(whichone)

if filecount=0 then
    ' just one file selected!
    MsgBox "You selected one file: " & whichone(0)

    ' check status of Read Only checkbox
    ' is bit 1 set or cleared?
    ' works only if just one file was selected!
    MsgBox "Returned flag: " & flag
    if (flag and 1) then
        ' (flag and 1)<>0, transforms to true
        ' bit is set!
        MsgBox "ReadOnly selected!"
    else
        MsgBox "ReadOnly not selected!"
    end if

    ' check whether selected file is of default type (txt)
    if (flag and 1024) then
        MsgBox "selected file is no txt file!"
    else
        MsgBox "selected file is of default type!"
    end if
else
    ' more than one file selected!
    MsgBox "You selected " & filecount & " files!"

    for x = 1 to UBound(whichone)
        list = list & path & whichone(x) & vbCr
    next

    MsgBox list
end if
```

```
function OpenFile(title, dir, filter, index, flags)
    set comdlg = CreateObject("MSComDlg.CommonDialog")
    comdlg.filter = filter
    comdlg.FilterIndex = index
    comdlg.Flags = flags
    comdlg.MaxFileSize = 260
    comdlg.CancelError = false
    comdlg.DialogTitle = title
    comdlg.InitDir = dir

    ' set txt as default
    comdlg.DefaultExt = "txt"

    comdlg.ShowOpen
    OpenFile = comdlg.filename

    ' important: return flag status so your main script can
    ' check it:
    flags = comdlg.Flags
end function
```

This script demonstrates many things at once. Most important, it uses the returned flag value to check whether certain conditions are met. For example, the script checks whether or not the user has selected the ReadOnly check box. This check box is handled by value 1 (ReadOnly). However, you can't go ahead and check whether flag equals 1. After all, flag contains a sum of many possible values. Therefore, you need to check the bits.

Checking bits is much easier than it sounds. To find out whether 1 is set in flag, check (flag and 1). If 1 isn't set (and the ReadOnly checkbox wasn't selected), the result is 0.

0 always equals false, and any other number always equals true, so you can write:

```
if (flag and 1) then
    MsgBox "1 is set, ReadOnly is checked!"
end if
```

Both the ReadOnly and the ExtensionDifferent flags are only used when exactly one file is selected. If more than one file is selected, the flags are useless.

In addition, the script demonstrates how to react to multiple file selections. Flag AllowMultiselect (512/&h200) allows you to select more than one file. Windows now uses a special version of the dialog box.

In Multiselect mode, spaces are used as separators between file names. Because long filenames can contain spaces, too, the dialog box converts any file name with spaces to short (DOS) file names. Windows 2000 works very differently—filenames are enclosed in quotes, and the multiselect Open dialog box looks just like the regular Open dialog box. You need to change your script code to correctly interpret the Windows 2000 results returned in multiselect mode.

Picking a color

The Color dialog box uses a completely different set of flags. They are specified in the `ColorConstants` section. The flags now control whether the detailed color picker is visible and whether you can specify an initial color (see Figure 6-3).

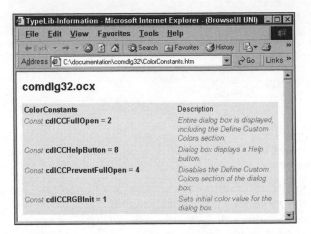

Figure 6-3: Take advantage of special color flags to adjust the Color dialog box.

Undocumented

The easiest way to provide a color is by using hexadecimal notation. Just use `&h`. This way, you can easily specify the color values for red, green, and blue separately. Use `00` to `FF` for each color component, and add the values in the following order: red, green, and blue. To use `CC` as red and `8C` as green and `35` as blue, write `&hCC8C35`. The higher the values, the brighter the color.

This is all you need to pick a color:

```
' 6-4.VBS

flag = 1+2
initialColor = &hff32ea
color = OpenColor(initialColor, flag)
MsgBox "Selected color: " & hex(color)

function OpenColor(initColor, flags)
    set comdlg = CreateObject("MSComDlg.CommonDialog")
    comdlg.Color = initColor
    comdlg.Flags = flags
    comdlg.ShowColor
    OpenColor = comdlg.Color
end function
```

Flag 1 allows you to predefine the color, and flag 2 instructs the dialog box to open the detail color picker (see Figure 6-4).

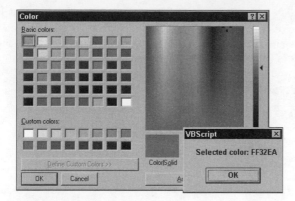

Figure 6-4: Control the color picker from your scripts.

Undocumented

If you don't specify an initial color, the brightness slider on the right side is set to dark black by default. Because all colors are now black, it appears as if you couldn't select a color. In truth, you just need to increase the brightness. It's a lot more elegant to set an initial brightness of above 0. To change brightness, use gray values as initial color. Gray values always use the same numbers for red, green, and blue. So, choose &h888888 or &hCCCCCC or &h3D3D3D as the initial color.

Wrapping System Dialog Boxes

There are a number of good reasons why you should wrap system dialog boxes in self-defined COM objects instead of using MSComDlg.CommonDialog directly. For one, wrapping dialog boxes will make them work even on systems where MSComDlg.CommonDialog is not yet installed. Second, you now can define optional parameters. This way, you can call your dialog boxes with defaults or specify as many details as you want. Wrapping dialog boxes makes them much easier to use and more dependable, too.

Tip

Wrapping system dialog boxes has two more advantages. First, your script isn't cluttered with dialog box-related code. It looks a lot cleaner. Second, you don't need to worry anymore about variables you used inside your dialog box procedures. Recall from Chapter 3 the discussion about private and public variables and how they can interfere with each other.

Creating your own system dialog boxes

To wrap system dialog boxes, just start the Visual Basic CCE (refer to Chapter 4 if this sounds unfamiliar to you).

CD

You'll find the entire project on the companion CD. Just open \components\ comdlg\comdlg.vbp. Too lazy to create the COM object yourself? Kick back and call \install\comdlg\setup.exe.

Create a new ActiveX Project. Next, you need to insert a reference to the common dialog boxes before you can start using them. Open the View menu and choose Toolbar to open the toolbar window. Right-click the toolbar, and choose Components (see Figure 6-5).

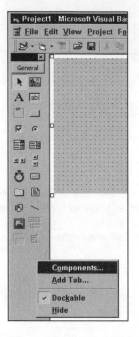

Figure 6-5: Include additional control elements in your VB CCE toolbox.

You now see a list of optional components. Look for Microsoft Common Dialog Control and click the check box. Then click OK.

Tip

Is Microsoft Common Dialog Control missing in your list? Click Browse and search for comdlg32.ocx manually.

The CCE inserts a new control into the toolbox window: the common controls. Double-click the new icon to place a copy on your UserControl (see Figure 6-6).

Now it's time to assign a name to your project and your UserControl. You might call them dlg.tools. (For tips on how to name your project, refer to Chapter 4.)

Getting access to the system dialog boxes

You're all set. Just start to develop the functions you want to make available through your COM object. You don't need CreateObject anymore. The common controls are already placed on your UserControl, and you can access them by name. It's CommonControls1 by default.

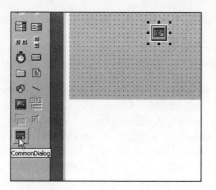

Figure 6-6: Place a copy of the `CommonControl` wrapper on your user control.

Secret

Actually, your wrapper uses the same COM object that `MSComDlg`. `CommonDialog` used, too. However, because its functions are now integrated into your COM object by "early binding" (this is what you did when you inserted the component into your toolbar window), there need not be any `MSComDlg.CommonDialog` Registry entries anymore. You still need `comdlg32.dll`, though. If you plan to distribute your dialog box wrapper control, make sure you also distribute `comdlg`. The best way is to use the Application Wizard as outlined in Chapter 4.

First, let's develop an easy function wrapper for `ShowOpen`:

```
Option Explicit

Function ShowOpen(Optional ByVal initdir As String, _
Optional ByVal title As String, Optional flags As Variant, _
Optional ByVal filter As String = "all files|*.*", _
Optional ByVal index As Long = 1) As String

    If Not IsMissing(flags) Then
        CommonDialog1.flags = flags
    End If

    If Not IsMissing(initdir) Then
        CommonDialog1.initdir = initdir
    End If

    If Not IsMissing(title) Then
        CommonDialog1.DialogTitle = title
    End If

    CommonDialog1.filter = filter
    CommonDialog1.FilterIndex = index

    CommonDialog1.ShowOpen
    ShowOpen = CommonDialog1.filename
```

```
    If Not IsMissing(flags) Then
        flags = CommonDialog1.flags
    End If
End Function
```

Your COM object makes heavy use of optional arguments. A little later in the chapter, you'll see how much easier they make your life. Note that some optional arguments have default values; others do not. Always use `isMissing` when dealing with arguments without default value. Also note how the function returns flag values. Changed flag values will only be returned if the user has supplied a flag variable in the first place. To be able to return the changed flags through the flag arguments, they need to be declared as `ByRef`. This way, script and COM object both share the same variable.

Secret

Whenever you use `ByRef`, use `Variant` as variable type. If you don't, you will need to convert variable types before you can call your COM functions. Remember, VBScript always uses variants if not told otherwise. To use an argument `ByRef`, either specify `ByRef` instead of `ByVal`, or don't specify either one. `ByRef` is the default.

Compile your project: Open the File menu and choose `Make dlg.ocx` (see Figure 6-7). Next, enjoy your new command:

```
' 6-5.VBS

set dlg = CreateObject("dlg.tools")
MsgBox dlg.ShowOpen
```

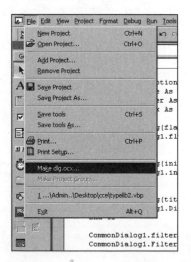

Figure 6-7: Design your dialog box wrapper and then compile, using `Make`.

Just for the fun of it, compare this script to the previous ones. How much cleaner and more straightforward things are now. And thanks to the optional arguments, you are still able to do all the tweaking you discovered above:

```
' 6-6.VBS

set dlg = CreateObject("dlg.tools")

flag = 0
whichone = dlg.ShowOpen("C:\", "Choose a File!", _
flag, "Everything|*.*|Text Files|*.TXT|Word-Documents|*.DOC", 2)

MsgBox "Selected file: " & whichone
MsgBox "Returned flags: " & flag
```

Using the Folder Picker

Did you notice that none of the system dialog boxes managed by the common controls allows you to select a folder? This is bad, but fortunately Microsoft has added another dialog box just for this purpose. It's part of Windows 98 and Windows 2000.

On older Windows versions, just install Internet Explorer 4 . It brings along the Shell.Application COM object. This object contains the Folder Picker. However, for some strange reason, Internet Explorer 5 doesn't bring along the Shell.Application-Object.

Check out the new dialog box:

```
' 6-7.VBS

set shell = CreateObject("Shell.Application")
set result = shell.BrowseForFolder(0, "Select a folder!", 0, "C:\")
MsgBox TypeName(result)
MsgBox "You selected: " & result.Title
```

The script calls the hidden BrowseForFolder method to open the dialog box (see Figure 6-8). In return, it receives an object reference to a Folder2 object (it's called Folder on older Windows versions). You can retrieve the name of the selected folder using the Title property.

This all looks a bit strange. Even worse, there is no way to retrieve the full path name. So, this dialog box seems pretty useless.

The more common system dialog boxes are managed by a COM object called comdlg32.ocx, or the common dialogs. This object wraps a lot of the internal techniques necessary to handle the dialog boxes. Shell.Application offers a wrapper for the Folder Picker dialog: BrowseForFolder. However, this wrapper was never intended for public use. It's targeted towards the internal Web view requirements of the Windows shell, and it's not suited for general path inquiries. Therefore, you need to write your own Folder Picker wrapper and access the dialog box directly using very basic API functions.

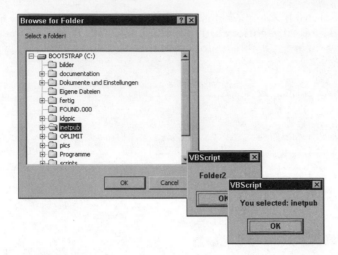

Figure 6-8: BrowseForFolder is a special dialog box wrapper used by the shell.

Accessing Folder Picker through API functions

To fully exploit all the fascinating functions hidden in the Folder Picker, you just need to wrap it as a COM object. So, start your VB CCE and create a new ActiveX Project (refer to Chapter 4 if this sounds unfamiliar to you).

As always, you can find the complete project on CD by looking at \components\folderpicker\pickfolder.vbp. If you are not interested in the internal mechanics and just want to use the Folder Picker, install the prepared software package—\install\folderpicker\setup.exe. This is the "wrapper" code:

```
Option Explicit

' define a custom structure
Private Type BrowseInfo
    hwndOwner As Long
    pIDLRoot As Long
    pszDisplayName As Long
    lpszTitle As Long
    ulFlags As Long
    lpfnCallback As Long
    lParam As Long
    iImage As Long
End Type

' declare API functions we need:
Private Declare Function GetDesktopWindow Lib "User32" () As Long
Private Declare Function SHBrowseForFolder Lib "shell32" _
(lpbi As BrowseInfo) As Long
Private Declare Function SHGetPathFromIDList Lib "shell32" _
(ByVal pidList As Long, ByVal lpBuffer As String) As Long
```

```vb
Private Declare Function SHGetSpecialFolderLocation Lib _
"shell32" (ByVal hwndOwner As Long, ByVal nFolder As Long, _
ListId As Long) As Long
Private Declare Function SHSimpleIDListFromPath Lib "shell32" _
Alias "#162" (ByVal szPath As String) As Long
Private Declare Sub CoTaskMemFree Lib "ole32.dll" (ByVal hMem As Long)

Public Function BrowseForFolder(ByVal initdir As Variant, _
Optional ByVal message As String = "Choose!", _
Optional ByVal flags As Long) As String
    Dim rootID As Long
    Dim PIDL As Long
    Dim Path As String
    Dim nullPos As Integer
    Dim BInfo As BrowseInfo
    Dim myMessage As String

    ' convert the message string to ANSI code:
    myMessage = StrConv(message, vbFromUnicode)

    ' check whether user specified a path or a code
    If VarType(initdir) = vbString Then
        ' it's a path!
        ' use undocumented function to create IDList
        ' convert path string to Unicode:
        rootID = SHSimpleIDListFromPath(StrConv(initdir, vbUnicode))
    Else
        ' it's a virtual system folder code
        ' get "real" path
        SHGetSpecialFolderLocation GetDesktopWindow, initdir, rootID
    End If

    ' fill out the BrowseInfo structure:
    BInfo.hwndOwner = GetDesktopWindow
    BInfo.ulFlags = flags
    ' fill in the address of your ANSI message string:
    BInfo.lpszTitle = StrPtr(myMessage)

    ' is there a valid rootID? Fill it in!
    If rootID <> 0 Then BInfo.pIDLRoot = rootID

    ' open the dialog box, retrieve a PIDL
    ' PIDL is internal identifier for selected folder:
    PIDL = SHBrowseForFolder(BInfo)

    ' was there a PIDL returned? Transform to path:
    If PIDL <> 0 Then
        ' reserve space for path name
        Path = String(260, 0)

        ' return path name from PIDL:
        SHGetPathFromIDList PIDL, Path

        ' manually release the memory:
        Call CoTaskMemFree(PIDL)
        Call CoTaskMemFree(rootID)
```

```
        ' cut off string at char 0:
        nullPos = InStr(Path, vbNullChar)
        If nullPos <> 0 Then
            Path = Left(Path, nullPos - 1)
        End If
    End If

    ' return path:
    BrowseForFolder = Path
End Function
```

Next, assign a name to your project. Call it `folder.tools`. Now you can compile it: Open the File menu and choose `Make folder.ocx`.

I'll show you in a minute how all of this works. This wrapper employs all the hidden techniques necessary to call internal system functions. Let's first concentrate on the practical aspects, so you can safely steal yourself away to the next chapter anytime you feel like it.

Now, it's extremely simple to access the Folder Picker. Look for yourself:

```
' 6-8.VBS

set picker = CreateObject("folder.tools")
result = picker.BrowseForFolder("C:\", "Hey, select a folder!")
MsgBox "You selected: " & result
```

This time, you receive the full path name (see Figure 6-9).

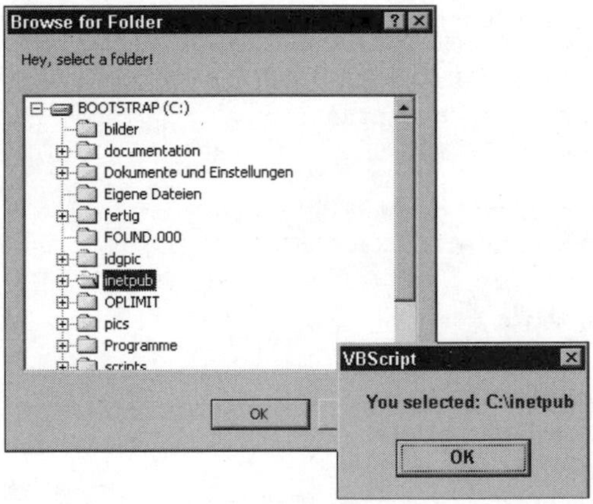

Figure 6-9: Your own `BrowseForFolder` wrapper finally returns the correct filename.

There's a lot more you can do with your new function. Instead of specifying a path name, try using a number. BrowseForFolder can also open any virtual system folder, and BrowseForFolder(2) would open your program groups. The next script lets you play around.

Caution

Your wrapper only puts a thin layer around the hostile API world. For example, the wrapper does not check whether the path you specify really exists. Specifying illegal path names may produce strange results — to say the least.

```
' 6-9.VBS

set picker = CreateObject("folder.tools")
do
    showwhat = InputBox("Enter number or path!",,2)
    if not showwhat = vbEmpty then
        if isNumeric(showwhat) then
            idnr = Fix(showwhat)
            result = picker.BrowseForFolder(idnr, "ID-Number: " _
                & idnr)
            answer = MsgBox(result & vbCr & "Again?", vbYesNo)
        else
            result = picker.BrowseForFolder(showwhat, _
                "Showing Path")
            answer = MsgBox(result & vbCr & "Again?", vbYesNo)
        end if
    else
        answer = vbNo
    end if
loop until answer = vbNo
```

You'll soon discover that BrowseForFolder can access just about any virtual Windows folder. However, because the dialog box can only display folders, you can't see files or individual content.

Not yet. You need two things to fully exploit BrowseForFolder. First, you need a list of all the codes and available virtual folders. Next, you need a list of all the special flags BrowseForFolder supports. But where do you get them?

Automatically documenting all secret Folder Picker options

Just ask the appropriate TypeLibrary. The API functions that your wrapper uses doesn't have a TypeLibrary, but the Shell.Application object uses the same fundamental API functions, so you can find a lot of the information in the Shell.Application TypeLibrary. Take a look into the scriptobjects.txt file you generated in Chapter 3. You'll quickly discover that Shell.Application stores type information in either shdocvw.dll or shell32.dll.

Undocumented

Not too long ago, `Shell.Application` and the Web view were just cute add-ons to Windows. Web view wasn't really integrated into Windows at this stage—instead, it was left to Internet Explorer to handle it. Windows 98 featured the integrated Internet Explorer, but it was still up to the integrated Internet Explorer to take care of Web view. Back then, Web view was handled internally by `shdocvw.dll`. Beginning with Windows 2000, Microsoft has incorporated Web view into the core system functionality. For this reason, on Windows 2000, Web view (and its `TypeLibrary`) is integrated into `shell32.dll`. Nobody would dare kick this `.dll` out of the system. It's the core of the Windows user interface.

If you haven't done so already in Chapter 5, launch script 5-12.VBS and let it create the documentation for you. On Windows 2000, enter `shell32.dll`. On all other Windows versions, enter `shdocvw.dll`.

Next, in your documentation folder, look for `ShellSpecialFolderConstants.htm`. There you'll find your list of available virtual folders.

Now you just need the Folder Picker flag values. Unfortunately, `Shell.Application` doesn't make use of the special flags, so it doesn't mention them. Here's a table of them for you.

Table 6-2   Folder Picker Special Flags

Flag	Description
1	Accept only file system folders
2	No network folders
8	Accept only file system objects
&h10	Show text field for direct entry
&h1000	Show only computers
&h2000	Show only printers
&h4000	Show files or individual entries

This is all you need to also display individual files or other elements. The following script displays your Desktop and then your Control Panel content:

```
' 6-10.VBS

set picker = CreateObject("folder.tools")
result = picker.BrowseForFolder(0, "Desktop", &h4000)
MsgBox "You selected: " & result
result = picker.BrowseForFolder(3, "Control Panel", &h4000)
MsgBox "You selected: " & result
```

Everything seems to work fine. Once you select a control panel item, though, your `BrowseForFolder` function won't return a value. After some rethinking, this is no surprise—your wrapper function explicitly uses the `BrowseFor-Folder` dialog box to retrieve file names. Since Control Panel items are not files, `BrowseForFolder` correctly returns an empty value.

Your new `BrowseForFolder` function is smart enough, though, to translate virtual objects to their path names if it's possible. For example, choose the Desktop entry in the first dialog box. Although Desktop is a virtual folder, your `BrowseForFolder` correctly identifies the folder your desktop content is stored in.

Getting Access to the Hidden Icon Picker

There's one more system dialog box, and it's an important one: The Icon Picker can display icons stored in files. It's your only way to present icon selections to your users. To see the dialog box in action, just follow these steps:

1. Search for any link, then right-click it and choose Properties.

2. Next, click the Change Icon button. There it is: your Icon Picker dialog box (see Figure 6-10). It may look a little different depending on your Windows version.

Figure 6-10: Getting to know the hidden Icon Picker dialog box.

How to call undocumented shell functions

Windows desperately tries to keep its Icon Picker dialog box to itself. It's not documented anywhere, and there's not even a named API function to call the dialog box. But, with a couple of tricks, you can make it work. After all, it must exist or else Windows wouldn't be able to use it either.

After some research, it turns out that the Icon Picker dialog box is contained in shell32.dll. Its function uses ordinal #62 throughout all the 32-bit Windows versions, so it's fairly easy to design an appropriate declare statement to call the Icon Picker.

Undocumented

However, because this function is undocumented, Microsoft doesn't take any effort to keep things consistent. On Windows 9.x and Windows NT, the Icon Picker accepts ANSI strings as arguments. With the advent of Windows 2000, many of the undocumented functions switch to Unicode strings without warning. So, it's up to your wrapper to determine the Windows version and convert the string arguments appropriately.

I've done all of this for you. The source code is a vivid example of developing cross-Windows-version COM objects, and the isWin2000 function can be useful for other projects, as well. Just install iconpicker.tool from the CD at \install\iconpick\setup.exe. You can also load the complete project and compile it yourself by using \components\iconpick\iconpick.vbp.

```
Option Explicit

' structure needed to retrieve OS version:
Private Type OSVERSIONINFO
    size As Long
    majorver As Long
    minorver As Long
    build As Long
    platformid As Long
    CSDVersion As String * 128
End Type


' declare undocumented icon dialog function:
Private Declare Function IconDialog Lib "shell32.dll" _
Alias "#62" (ByVal hwnd As Long, ByVal lpStrFile As Long, _
ByVal maxfilelen As Long, IconIndex As Long) As Boolean

Private Declare Function ExtractIconEx Lib "shell32.dll" _
Alias "ExtractIconExA" (ByVal lpszFile As String, _
ByVal nIconIndex As Long, phIconLarge As Long, _
phIconSmall As Long, ByVal nIcons As Long) As Long
Private Declare Function GetVersionEx Lib "kernel32.dll" _
Alias "GetVersionExA" (lpVersionInfo As OSVERSIONINFO) As Long


Public Function PickIcon(ByVal path As String, _
Optional ByVal index As Long = 0) As String
    Dim ok As Boolean
    Dim filestr As String
    Dim convert As Boolean

    ' build a string of 260 characters (max path len)
    ' that contains the path of the icon library
    ' you want to display
    filestr = path & Chr(0) & String(260 - Len(path) - 1, 0)

    ' if not Win2000, string needs to be ANSI:
```

```
         If Not isWin2000 Then
             filestr = StrConv(filestr, vbFromUnicode)
         End If

         ' call undocumented dialog box:
         ok = IconDialog(0&, StrPtr(filestr), 260&, index)

         ' did user select an icon?
         If ok Then
             ' if not Win2000, ANSI-string needs to be reconverted
             ' back to Unicode
             If Not isWin2000 Then
                 filestr = StrConv(filestr, vbUnicode)
             End If

             ' resize string - cut off anything beyond terminating
             ' chr(0) character:
             filestr = Left(filestr, InStr(filestr, Chr(0)) - 1)

             ' add index of selected icon:
             PickIcon = filestr & "," & index
         Else
             PickIcon = ""
         End If
End Function

Public Function CountIcons(ByVal path As String) As Long
    ' counts number of icons in given file:

    CountIcons = ExtractIconEx(path, -1, 0, 0, 0)
End Function

Public Function isWin2000() As Boolean
    ' checks whether OS is Win2000:

    Dim osinfo As OSVERSIONINFO

    osinfo.size = Len(osinfo)
    GetVersionEx osinfo
    If (osinfo.platformid >= 2 And osinfo.majorver >= 5) Then
        isWin2000 = True
    Else
        isWin2000 = False
    End If
End Function
```

Displaying icons hidden in the system files

The new Icon Picker is extremely versatile, and you'll find many useful examples in Chapter 23. For now, the following script examines all your system files and displays the icons in the Icon Picker dialog box (see Figure 6-12). Now select an icon. The script tells you the exact syntax of how to access the icon you selected. This syntax becomes important once you assign icons via Registry keys or script commands.

```
' 6-11.VBS

set fs = CreateObject("Scripting.FileSystemObject")
set icon = CreateObject("iconpicker.tool")

' get access to system folder
set sysfolder = fs.GetSpecialFolder(1)

' enumerate all files
for each file in sysfolder.files
    ' how many icons are stored in file?
    icons = icon.CountIcons(file.path)

    ' more than 2 files? Show them!
    if icons>2 then
        selection = icon.PickIcon(file.path)
        ' did the user select an icon?
        if selection="" then
            msg = "You did not select an icon."
        else
            msg = "This is how you access the icon: " & vbCr
            msg = msg & selection
        end if
        msg = msg & vbCr & "Continue?"
        answer = MsgBox(msg, vbQuestion + vbOkCancel)
        if answer = vbCancel then exit for
    end if
next

MsgBox "Done!"
```

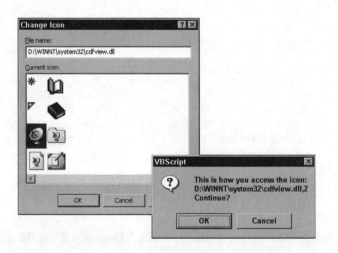

Figure 6-11: Display icon resources stored in system files.

Displaying and Sorting Lists

VBScript is unable to display lists, not to mention sort them. Although sorting is an important functionality, you are left alone and need to resort to slow custom VBScript procedures.

Do you really have to live with these limits? No way. A look at the Windows Explorer proves that there must be some kind of List view and sorting capability built into Windows. How else would the Explorer be able to display folder contents as Details view and allow you to sort those lists in any way you please?

The answer is contained in the `ListView` dialog box component. This component can easily display huge lists and sort them by any category you specify. All you need is a way to access the `ListView` element.

Undocumented

The `ListView` element was originally designed to display lists. You don't need to, though. It's up to you—if you prefer, you can use the hide the `ListView` element entirely. In this case, it will only serve to sort lists.

Getting Aacess to the ListView

VBScript has no way of accessing the `ListView` element directly. You can, however, wrap the `ListView` element as a COM object. I have done it for you. The full source code is provided on the companion CD. Just open `\components\listview\listview.vbp`.

Either open the project and compile it yourself, or run `\install\listview\setup.ocx`. Both ways will register the `listview.tool` component.

Designing and sorting lists

Check out how powerful the new `ListView` element really is. The following script reads in all files stored in the root folder of drive C:\. Then, the files are displayed in the `ListView` element. You can sort each column by clicking on the column heads. Another click sorts in the opposite direction.

You can even find out which file(s) the user has selected. Just select one or more files in the `ListView` and then click OK. Your script will report the file details.

```
' 6-12.VBS

set fs = CreateObject("Scripting.FileSystemObject")
set lview = CreateObject("listview.tool")

' open sample folder:
set folder = fs.GetFolder("C:\")
```

```
' scale dialog box
lview.width = 600
lview.height = 400

' design some column headers
' AddHeader name, size in percent, alignment
' 0 - left (default)
' 1 = right
' 2 = center


lview.AddHeader "File name", 50
lview.AddHeader "Size", 20, 1
lview.AddHeader "Type", 30

' read files into ListView:
for each file in folder.files
    lview.AddItem file.name
    lview.AddSubitem 1, AlignNumber(file.size)
    lview.AddSubitem 2, file.type
next

' sort result
' 0 = first column
' 1 = second column...
lview.Sort 0

' enable multiselect
lview.MultiSelect = true

' show ListView Form
set result = lview.Show("Files on Drive C:\")

list = "Selected items: " & result.Count
for each entry in result
    list = list & entry & vbCr
next

MsgBox list

function AlignNumber(number)
    size = len(CStr(number))
    AlignNumber = Space(20-size) & number
end function
```

The new ListView dialog box allows for both single- and multiselection. Use the MultiSelect property to determine whether the user will be able to select more than one file.

Undocumented

The ListView stores String values. To be able to sort numeric content, the script uses the function AlignNumber to pad the numeric strings with spaces. This way, numbers will be sorted correctly. It's easy to get rid of the padding spaces: Once a number is returned, just use LTrim to eliminate the leading spaces.

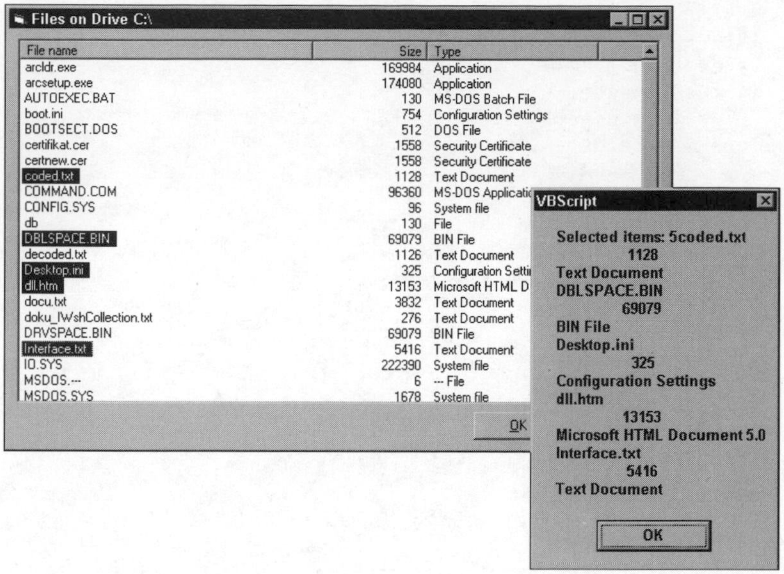

Figure 6-12: Using your own dialog boxes to display lists and select entries.

Your new `listview.tool` component offers a rich set of options. Use the `labelOK` and `labelCancel` properties to change the labels on the buttons. You can manually sort columns before you display the dialog box by using Sort. With the help of the `MultiEdit` property, you can even display the same dialog box more than once and delete entries.

Tip

When defining column headers using `AddHeader`, you can specify up to three arguments: the name of the column header, its size in percent, and the alignment type as documented in the script. The first column always has to be left-aligned, which is also the default.

The next script demonstrates the advanced options. It will delete the selected entry from the list and continue to display the list until the user hits Cancel.

Whenever you select an entry and either click OK or press [Enter], the script displays detailed information about this file and removes it from its list. Then it redisplays the list. The selected items are no longer available.

This is possible because the script enables the `MultiEdit` property. In `MultiEdit` mode, the dialog box isn't destroyed, but hidden, and it can reappear anytime you use `Show`. In addition, in `MultiEdit` mode, the dialog box returns additional information: The internal key name of the selected items is appended to the list information and returned. With this key, you can remove list entries using `RemoveItem`.

```
' 6-13.VBS

set fs = CreateObject("Scripting.FileSystemObject")
set lview = CreateObject("listview.tool")
```

```
set folder = fs.GetFolder("C:\")
lview.width = 600
lview.height = 400
lview.AddHeader "File name", 50
lview.AddHeader "Size", 20, 1
lview.AddHeader "Type", 30

' read files into ListView:
for each file in folder.files
    lview.AddItem file.name
    lview.AddSubitem 1, AlignNumber(file.size)
    lview.AddSubitem 2, file.type
next

' enable MultiEdit feature
lview.MultiEdit = true

' show ListView Form until user hits Cancel:
do
    set result = lview.Show("Files on Drive C:\")

    ' did the user select something?
    if result.Count=0 then
        ' no, exit
        exit do
    end if

    ' split result:
    details = Split(result.Item(1), vbCrLf)

    ' now the information is contained in an array
    msg = "You selected: " & details(0) & vbCr
    msg = msg & "File Size is " & ltrim(details(1)) & " Bytes." _
& vbCr
    msg = msg & "File Type is " & details(2) & vbCr
    msg = msg & "Internal ListView item key is: " & details(3)

    MsgBox msg, vbInformation

    lview.removeItem details(3)
loop

MsgBox "Done!"

function AlignNumber(number)
    size = len(CStr(number))
    AlignNumber = Space(20-size) & number
end function
```

Sorting lists without dialog boxes

The great sorting capabilities that the ListView offers can be used separately, too. This way, you can easily sort any kind of list (see Figure 6-13). You don't need to display the ListView dialog box.

Whenever you query the files in a folder, Windows returns them in the order they were originally saved. They are not sorted. The following script demonstrates how to build a file list and then have it sorted in the background by your ListView:

```
' 6-14.VBS

set fs = CreateObject("Scripting.FileSystemObject")
set lview = CreateObject("listview.tool")

' open sample folder:
set folder = fs.GetFolder("C:\")

' design some column headers
lview.AddHeader "File name", 50
lview.AddHeader "Type", 30

' read files into ListView:
for each file in folder.files
    lview.AddItem file.name
    lview.AddSubitem 1, file.type
next

' Sorting:
' sort for type, then for name
' use reverse order in script:
lview.Sort 0     ' sort column 0 (name)
lview.Sort 1     ' sort column 1 (type)

' read sorted result without displaying any dialog box:
set result = lview.ReadResult

' convert collection to strings:
list = ""
for each entry in result
    entry = Split(entry, vbCrLf)
    list = list & entry(0) & vbTab & entry(1) & vbCr
next

MsgBox list
```

The sorting capabilities are so powerful you can even sort for multiple columns: In the example, the script first sorts column 0 (file name), then column 1 (file type). The result is a sorted list that lists the files sorted by type and within the types sorted by name.

```
VBScript                                              ×

MSDOS.---           --- File
SYSTEM.1ST          1ST File
cd.ocx     ActiveX Control
typelib2.ocx        ActiveX Control
typelib3.ocx        ActiveX Control
arcldr.exe          Application
arcsetup.exe        Application
VIDEOROM.BIN        BIN File
cursor.bmp          Bitmap Image
db pics.bmp         Bitmap Image
hand.bmp            Bitmap Image
boot.ini   Configuration Settings
SUHDLOG.DAT         DAT File
SIPOBJ.DBG          DBG File
AUTOEXEC.DOS        DOS File
BOOTSECT.DOS        DOS File
CONFIG.DOS          DOS File
compare.htm         Microsoft HTML Document 5.0
docu.htm Microsoft HTML Document 5.0
doku.htm Microsoft HTML Document 5.0
temp.html           Microsoft HTML Document 5.0
TYPELIB.HTM         Microsoft HTML Document 5.0
COMMAND.COM         MS-DOS Application
ntdetect.com        MS-DOS Application
AUTOEXEC.BAT        MS-DOS Batch File
BOOTLOG.PRV         PRV File
CONFIG.SYS          System file
IO.SYS     System file
LOGO.SYS            System file
MSDOS.SYS           System file
NTBOOTDD.SYS        System file
ntldr      System file
PAGEFILE.SYS        System file
HARDWARE.TAG        TAG File
SOFTWARE.TAG        TAG File
BOOTLOG.TXT         Text Document
code.txt   Text Document
coded.txt Text Document
debug9x.log         Text Document
decoded.txt         Text Docum

                  ┌──────────┐
                  │    OK    │
                  └──────────┘
```

Figure 6-13: Using ListView to sort arbitrary lists.

You need commands to specify the number of list categories and another one to actually store values in your list.

Diving into documentation and source code

To get your personal copy of the ListView.tool owner's manual, launch script 5-12.VBS and have it auto-document listview.ocx. Search for listview.ocx first to find out its exact path name.

The documentation file is contained on the companion CD: info\documentation\listview\.

The source code is somewhat lengthy, but well-documented. It's not so much the code but rather the ListView object model that makes it a little hard to understand. In addition, I was forced to include some API calls. Visual Basic 5 (and VBCCE, too) are buggy when it comes to sizing column headers. For some unknown reason, VB always adds some extra space to your width values, so it's almost impossible to size the columns neatly this way.

The source code shows a workaround: It uses the internal SendMessage function of Windows to send resizing messages directly to the ListView elements.

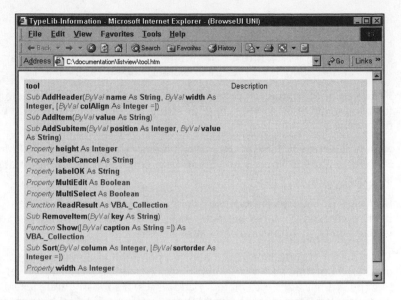

Figure 6-14: Easily auto-document any COM object — even your own!

Successfully Dealing with API Functions

You now know how to successfully deal with API functions. It's a good time to review some of the basic technologies the previous examples have employed. You don't have to go through this, but you might find it helpful once you start changing the example code to suit your own needs.

On the following pages, I'll show you how to feed text strings to API functions and get results back safely. I'll also clarify the ANSI/UNICODE issue, which will help with writing code that runs both on Windows 95/98 and on Windows NT/2000.

String handling — undocumented Visual Basic commands

Chapter 4 already revealed the basics about API calls. There's one more issue to solve, though, and it frequently drives Visual Basic programmers nuts. You guessed it — it's string handling.

Many API functions expect strings as arguments. The functions then store some value into the string so you can retrieve it afterwards.

The Icon Picker, for example, expects the address of a string in which you have stored the path to the icon library file. In return, the function writes the new icon file into the string if the user changes the file. So, all you need to do is provide a string to the function and read its contents afterwards.

In theory, at least. In everyday life, there are a lot more details to think about.

First of all, many API functions don't expect a string but rather a reference to a string: its memory address. Therefore, you need to declare this argument as `ByVal` and as `Long`. It's an address pointer, not a string.

Next, you need to make sure you reserve enough space for the data the function might want to store in your string. So, fill your string with empty data using `String`.

Now you are ready to pass the string's memory address to the API function. But wait a minute! There's no Visual Basic command that would tell you this address. Right?

But there is. You can always use `StrPtr`. `StrPtr` is an undocumented Visual Basic command. It works perfectly well, but it remains hidden because in the wrong hands, this function can cause trouble.

Secret

There's a lot of confusion about address pointers, and many programmers invest a lot of time and energy using complicated API functions or Byte arrays to copy string values into memory addresses. It's mostly unnecessary, and very slow too. Starting with Visual Basic 5, convenient (yet hidden) functions are built right into VB to handle most of these tasks for you. And because the VB CCE you're using is based on VB5, you can use these functions as well.

Whenever you deal with pointers yourself, you are no longer protected by the internal Visual Basic safety net. So, you need to make sure you are passing valid pointers to the places you intend to point to.

Dealing with ANSI and UNICODE

As if things weren't tricky enough, Microsoft is currently transforming its internal string mechanics from ANSI to UNICODE. ANSI strings store one character per byte. That's enough for some of us, but not enough for all the Chinese characters — let alone all the globally available characters. Therefore, as Microsoft expands worldwide, it migrates its Windows versions to UNICODE. Here, each character is represented by two bytes, allowing for 65,536 different characters.

What does this mean for us? Windows 9.x (and partially Windows NT) uses ANSI strings. Windows 2000 is all UNICODE, yet it still contains some ANSI support for backwards-compatibility.

The Icon Picker is again a good example. This function expects the file name to be ANSI on Windows 9.x/NT and UNICODE on Windows 2000. Because Visual Basic stores its strings in UNICODE anyway, your code will work perfectly well on Windows 2000 without any conversion. On all other Windows versions, however, you'll get strange results. The dialog box won't be able to find your icon files because it will misinterpret the UNICODE filename where it expects an ANSI string.

Fortunately, Visual Basic contains the appropriate conversion tools. Just use StrConv. It offers a rich set of conversion schemes and allows for easy UNICODE-ANSI-UNICODE roundtrips. In the Icon Picker example, the code first checks whether it's being run on a non-Windows 2000 system. If so, it converts the Visual Basic UNICODE strings to ANSI, feeds them to the API-function, and reconverts the result back to UNICODE so Visual Basic can handle it.

Cutting excess string space

Whenever you provide string space to an API function, you most likely reserve more space than you actually need — just in case. Before you can use the resulting strings in Visual Basic, you need to adjust string size, however.

Secret

API functions are closely related to C. They determine the size of a string by a terminating null character (vbNullChar). Visual Basic, in contrast, doesn't care about nulls. It stores the string length in two bytes right before the string data starts. So, you definitely need to cut off excess space before you can use the string content in Visual Basic.

This is easy — just have Visual Basic look for the first null character and cut off the rest:

```
stringvar = left(stringvar, Instr(stringvar, vbNullChar)-1)
```

Experimenting and getting source code for free

Always remember: Your Visual Basic Control Creation Edition is a full Visual Basic development environment! I strongly encourage you to search the Internet for source code examples. There are many great Web sites out there with tutorials and samples of various API techniques.

Just launch your VBCCE and choose Open Project from the File menu. Then load the sample project you downloaded from the Internet and experiment with it!

Undocumented

Your VBCCE is based on Visual Basic 5.0. Many examples already use Visual Basic 6.0, and you may get error messages when trying to open those projects. However, in most cases, you just need to open the .vbp file in your editor and remove the attributes that caused the error. A common problem is the line retained =. Completely remove this line, save the .vbp file, and reopen it. This way, you can open and use most Visual Basic 6 projects.

Summary

You have discovered how to wrap system dialog boxes in COM objects and call them from script. Using the `ListView` element, you created your own list box dialog box and found ways to have it sort arbitrary lists quickly and safely. Calling API functions leaves it to you to handle string pointers and string formats. You now know how to pass string address pointers and how to deal with ANSI/UNICODE conversion to write code that runs equally well on all Windows versions. As a result, you now have a whole armory of new commands that display virtually any dialog box you may ever need.

Part II

Conquering the File System

Chapter 7: Accessing the File System

Chapter 8: Advanced File System Tricks

Chapter 9: Mastering Links

Chapter 7

Accessing the File System

In This Chapter

▶ Access drives, folders, and individual files

▶ Peek into any file, and changing file contents at will

▶ Determine free space on drives, and overcome the 2GB bug

▶ Search the entire hard drive for outdated files or empty folders recursively

The Windows Scripting Host comes with a secret script extension, called `Scripting.FileSystemObject`. This object grants full access to the entire file system. In this chapter, you'll discover how to peek into files, copy, move, delete and create new files from scratch. In addition, I'll show you some workarounds to correctly deal with drive sizes greater than 2GB

Finding the Secret Backdoor to the File System

The file system is one of the most interesting areas of your computer. It's where all of your data is stored, and there are numerous tasks that scripts can handle for you, including reorganizing data, finding orphan files, doing backups, and more.

How do you get access to your files? Both the WSH and VBScript lack file system commands. There's no way to open files, delete data, or copy folders. However, this makes perfect sense because both WSH and VBScript are designed as platform-independent technologies. The file system, in contrast, is very special, and its technology can vary from operating system to operating system.

Still, your scripts have full access to your file system. Microsoft has placed all the necessary commands into a separate module. `scrrun.dll` is automatically registered as a `Scripting.FileSystemObject` COM component, and whenever you need file system support, just include a reference to this object in your scripts.

Accessing a drive

Where's the secret back door to your file system? Actually, there are many doors. One is to get access to any one of your drives using `GetDrive`:

```
' 7-1.VBS

' get access to file system commands:
set fs = CreateObject("Scripting.FileSystemObject")

set drivec = fs.GetDrive("C:\")
MsgBox TypeName(drivec)
emptyspace = drivec.AvailableSpace
MsgBox "Avaialable on C:\: " & _
FormatNumber(emptyspace/1024^2,1) & " MB"
```

This simple script accesses drive C:\ and returns a `Drive` object. The `Drive` object contains many useful properties and methods. The `AvailableSpace` property, for example, reports the available space on this drive (see Figure 7-1).

Figure 7-1: Accessing a drive and retrieving Volume information.

Undocumented

Actually, there are two very similar properties: `AvailableSpace` and `FreeSpace`. Whereas `FreeSpace` reports the physically unoccupied space on the particular drive, `AvailableSpace` reports the space available to a user. It takes into account other limitations, such as disk quotas. Both commands report a maximum of 2GB of space. This is an intrinsic limitation, and you will hear more about it a little later in the chapter. You will also discover methods to solve this limitation and report available space even on drives larger than 2GB.

It only takes a couple of additional lines to enumerate all files in the root folder of your drive:

```
' 7-2.VBS

' get access to file system commands:
set fs = CreateObject("Scripting.FileSystemObject")

set drivec = fs.GetDrive("C:\")
set root = drivec.RootFolder
for each file in root.files
    list = list & file.name & vbCr
next

MsgBox list
```

When dealing with the file system, you work with many different objects. In the example, the drive, the folder, and each individual file are represented by an individual object. Always remember to use Set whenever you retrieve an object reference and want to assign it to a variable.

Finding information about properties and methods

How did I know about all the methods and properties I used in the previous examples? I didn't. I looked them up, and you can, too. In fact, it's a good idea to first get together all the documentation you need to fully exploit the FileSystemObject. It's easy — you've already prepared the necessary tools in the previous chapters. Have a look at Table 7-1:

Table 7-1	Scripts You Can Use To Auto-Document COM Objects
Script	**Description**
3-12.VBS	Find out the particular syntax of a command. For example, enter GetDrive.
3-7.VBS	Auto-document all properties and methods of FileSystemObject: Enter the name of the object: scrrun.dll. Then enter the object you want to document: FileSystemObject.
3-10.VBS	Auto-document the Drive object or any other object: Just enter the name of the object: for example, Drive
5-12.VBS	Generate a fully color-coded reference to all the commands and objects. Enter the name of the COM object you want to document: scrrun.dll. Then open your documentation folder C:\documentation\scrrun and browse through the automatically generated documentation files. Open Drive.htm to discover the internal structure of the Drive object you just used.

Getting Details About Your Drives

All your drives are represented by the Drive object. How do you get one? You ask for it! One way is the GetDrive method, but there are others, too.

The drives method enumerates all drives available on your system:

```
' 7-3.VBS

' get access to file system commands:
set fs = CreateObject("Scripting.FileSystemObject")

' retrieve list of all available drives:
set drivecollection = fs.Drives
```

```
' enumerate drives
for each drive in drivecollection
    list = list & drive.path & vbCr
next

MsgBox list
```

Another "door" to the `Drive` object goes the opposite direction: Get a folder object and retrieve the `Drive` object of the drive the folder is stored in:

```
' 7-4.VBS

' get access to file system commands:
set fs = CreateObject("Scripting.FileSystemObject")

' get access to a folder
' get windows folder
set winfolder = fs.GetSpecialFolder(0)
MsgBox "Windows folder: " & winfolder.name

' get drive object:
set drive = winfolder.Drive
MsgBox "Windows is installed on Drive " & drive.DriveLetter
```

Closely examining the Drive object

There are many ways to retrieve a `Drive` object. What can you do once you have a reference to a `Drive` object, though?

Take a look at its internal structure (see Table 7-2):

Table 7-2   The Drive Object

Property/Method	Description
Property AvailableSpace	Get available space
Property DriveLetter As String	Drive letter
Property DriveType As DriveTypeConst	Drive type
Property FileSystem As String	Filesystem type
Property FreeSpace	Get drive free space
Property IsReady As Boolean	Check if disk is available
Property Path As String	Path
Property RootFolder As IFolder	Root folder
Property SerialNumber As Long	Serial number
Property ShareName As String	Share name
Property TotalSize	Get total drive size
Property VolumeName As String	Name of volume

Is the drive ready for action?

It's always a good idea to prevent errors whenever possible (see Figure 7-2). Drives can have removable media such as a ZIP drive or disk drive. Use isReady to find out whether a media is inserted before you start querying for any additional information:

```
' 7-5.VBS

set fs = CreateObject("Scripting.FileSystemObject")

' let's check drive A:
set drivea = fs.GetDrive("A:\")

' loop until drive is ready or user cancels:
do until drivea.isReady
    response = MsgBox("Please insert disk in drive A:!", vbOKCancel)
    if response = vbCancel then
        ' user wants to quit, maybe no disk at hand:
        MsgBox "Cancel accepted", vbExclamation
        WScript.Quit
    end if
loop

' let's label the drive:
volname = drivea.VolumeName
newname = InputBox("Assign a new Volume label to the disk:", _
.volname)
if newname = vbEmpty then
    ' user cancelled:
    MsgBox "Volume name remains unchanged."
else
    drivea.VolumeName = newname
    MsgBox "New Volume name assigned: " & newname
end if
```

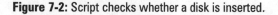

Figure 7-2: Script checks whether a disk is inserted.

isReady not only prevents access to drives with no media inserted. You can also, for example, write a shutdown script that closes Windows and uses isReady to make sure no media is left in the drives. With the help of the CD-ROM tray API commands in Chapter 4, you can even automatically open CD ROM trays if media is left in the drive before shutting down the computer. All the methods and properties you discover throughout this book are just building blocks, and the beauty of scripting is your freedom to use these building blocks in any way you want.

Changing a drive's volume name

`VolumeName` is a read/write property: You can both read the current volume label and assign new names. This is possible for all write-enabled drives, and you even get to see your new label for hard drives in the Explorer window.

The Volume label traditionally plays an important role with installation disks. By assigning volume labels to disks, your script can check whether the user inserted the correct disk.

Using a drive's serial number

Another important means of identification is the serial number. Each drive has an individual serial number, and you can ask for it by querying the `SerialNumber` property.

Undocumented

The serial number is assigned during media formatting. Because the serial number will also be copied whenever you duplicate disks, it's no good for copy protection schemes. However, a serial number of 0 indicates that the media wasn't fully formatted. "Pre-formatted" disks, for example, display a serial number of 0. Because it's dangerous to store valuable data on such disks without fully formatting them beforehand, you can use the Serial Number property to build additional security into your scripts. See the following example.

```
' 7-6.VBS

set fs = CreateObject("Scripting.FileSystemObject")
set drivea = fs.GetDrive("A:\")

' loop until drive is ready or user cancels:
do until drivea.isReady
    response = MsgBox("Please insert disk in drive A:!", vbOKCancel)
    if response = vbCancel then
        ' user wants to quit, maybe no disk at hand:
        MsgBox "Cancel accepted", vbExclamation
        WScript.Quit
    end if
loop

serno = drivea.SerialNumber
if serno = 0 then
    MsgBox "This disk was never fully formatted!"
else
    MsgBox "Disk serial number: " & serno
end if
```

Determining drive type and file system

There are many different drive types out there, and maybe you need to sort out read-only drives. How can you determine whether a drive is a CD-ROM drive?

Easy. `DriveType` **tells you the type of drive, and** `FileSystem` **reports the type of file system used on this drive (see Figure 7-3).**

Figure 7-3: Retrieve Volume Label and file system information.

```
' 7-7.VBS

set fs = CreateObject("Scripting.FileSystemObject")

' define array with clear text description
dt = Split("unknown;removable;fixed;remote;CD-ROM;RAM-Drive", ";")

' get list of drives
set drivecoll = fs.Drives

' enumerate all drives
for each drive in drivecoll
    ' check whether drive is ready:
    if drive.isReady then
        drivetype = drive.DriveType
        filesystem = drive.FileSystem
        label = drive.VolumeName
        letter = drive.DriveLetter
        msg = msg & "Drive " & letter & ": (" & label _
& ") " & dt(drivetype) & " (" & filesystem & ")" & vbCr
    else
        msg = msg & "Drive " & letter & ": is not ready." & vbCr
    end if
next
MsgBox msg, vbInformation
```

Finding out available space on drives

Data storage is always a scarce resource. Your scripts will need to check whether there is enough storage space available before starting a lengthy copy operation, and it's a good idea to let scripts warn you once available space drops below a certain threshold.

The `Drive` object offers three properties, including `AvailableSpace`, `FreeSpace`, and `TotalSize`. However, all three properties impose a serious limitation: They can only deal with drives up to a maximum size of 2GB. Or, in other words: Neither one will ever report more than 2GB.

Undocumented

The `FileSystemObject` uses old API functions to retrieve drive sizes. These old functions can't deal with drive sizes above 2GB.

```
' 7-8.VBS

set fs = CreateObject("Scripting.FileSystemObject")
set drive = fs.GetDrive("C:\")

avail = drive.AvailableSpace
free = drive.FreeSpace
total = drive.TotalSize

msg = "Statistics Drive C:\" & vbCr
msg = msg & "Available Space: " & fn(avail) & vbCr
msg = msg & "Free Space: " & fn(free) & vbCr
msg = msg & "Total Size: " & fn(total)

MsgBox msg

function fn(bytes)
    fn = FormatNumber(bytes/1024^2,2) & " MB"
end function
```

Undocumented

`AvailableSpace` and `FreeSpace` will only differ if you have set up disk quotas. Disk quotas limit the amount of space an individual user can use. This feature is implemented in Windows 2000.

Fixing the 2GB bug

There's really no reason why your scripts shouldn't report the true space even on today's larger disks. To overcome the 2GB limitation, all you need to do is use the correct and up-to-date API functions. Just wrap them in a COM object as outlined in Chapter 4. I have prepared a COM object for you that correctly reports drive sizes, demonstrating the use of API functions (see Figure 7-4).

CD

To view the internal mechanics, open `\components\filesys\filesys.vbp` in your Visual Basic CCE and compile the project. To just use the new methods, install the software package — `\install\filesys\setup.exe`.

```
' 7-9.VBS

set tool = CreateObject("filesystem.tool")

free = tool.FreeSpace("C:\")
total = tool.TotalSize("C:\")

msg = "Statistics Drive C:\" & vbCr
msg = msg & "Free Space: " & fn(free) & vbCr
msg = msg & "Total Size: " & fn(total)
```

```
MsgBox msg

function fn(bytes)
    fn = FormatNumber(bytes/1024^2,2) & " MB"
end function
```

Figure 7-4: Your new COM object can deal with drives larger than 2GB.

Calling file system APIs directly

The `filesystem.tool` COM object demonstrates some very important new techniques. Have a look:

```
Option Explicit

' old version
Private Declare Function GetDiskFreeSpace Lib "kernel32" _
Alias "GetDiskFreeSpaceA" (ByVal lpRootPathName As String, _
lpSectorsPerCluster As Long, lpBytesPerSector As Long, _
lpNumberOfFreeClusters As Long, lpTotalNumberOfClusters As _
Long) As Long

' new version without 2 GB limitation
' use Currency var type as "long integer"
Private Declare Function GetDiskFreeSpaceEx Lib "kernel32" _
Alias "GetDiskFreeSpaceExA" (ByVal lpRootPathName As String, _
lpFreeBytesAvailableToCaller As Currency, lpTotalNumberOfBytes _
As Currency, lpTotalNumberOfFreeBytes As Currency) As Long

' error code for undefined API functions:
Private Const errNoSuchFunction = 453

Private Sub GetSizes(ByVal DriveLetter As String, TotalBytes As
Double, FreeBytes As Double)
    Dim drvLetter As String
    Dim free As Currency
    Dim total As Currency
    Dim allfree As Currency
    Dim ok As Integer
    Dim lngSPC As Long   ' sectors per cluster
    Dim lngBPS As Long   ' bytes per sector
    Dim lngTC As Long    ' total number of clusters
    Dim lngFC As Long    ' free clusters

    TotalBytes = 0
    FreeBytes = 0
```

```
    ' was a valid drive letter specified?
    If Len(DriveLetter) = 0 Then
        Err.Raise vbObjectError + 512 + 20, _
"FileSystem Tool: Drive Size", _
"You did not specify a drive letter!"
        Exit Sub
    End If

    ' transform letter in drive specs:
    drvLetter = UCase(Left(DriveLetter, 1)) & ":\"

    ' valid drive letter?
    If Left(drvLetter, 1) < "A" Or Left(drvLetter, 1) > "Z" Then
        Err.Raise vbObjectError + 512 + 21, _
"FileSystem Tool: Drive Size", _
"The specified drive letter """ & DriveLetter _
& """ was invalid!"
        Exit Sub
    End If

    ' API call is undefined on older systems with 2 GB limitation
    ' so catch errors!
    On Error Resume Next
    ok = GetDiskFreeSpaceEx(drvLetter, free, total, allfree)

    ' is new API call supported?
    If Err.Number = errNoSuchFunction Then
        ' no. This system can only use 2 GB max drives anyway,
        ' so use older version
        ' first turn back on error handling:

        Err.Clear
        On Error GoTo 0

        ' find out space info
        ok = GetDiskFreeSpace(drvLetter, lngSPC, lngBPS, lngFC, lngTC)

        If ok Then
            ' calculate actual bytes:
            TotalBytes = CDbl(lngTC) * lngSPC * lngBPS
            FreeBytes = CDbl(lngFC) * lngSPC * lngBPS
        End If
    ElseIf Err.Number = 0 And ok Then
        ' reset error handling
        Err.Clear
        On Error GoTo 0

        ' adjust for Currency var type:
        TotalBytes = CDbl(total) * 10000
        FreeBytes = CDbl(free) * 10000
    Else
        Err.Raise vbObjectError + 512 + 22, "FileSystem Tool", "Failed
to retrieve drive size information"
    End If
End Sub
```

```
Public Function TotalSize(ByVal drive As String) As Double
    Dim total As Double
    Dim free As Double
    GetSizes drive, total, free
    TotalSize = total
End Function

Public Function FreeSpace(ByVal drive As String) As Double
    Dim total As Double
    Dim free As Double
    GetSizes drive, total, free
    FreeSpace = free
End Function
```

There are actually two completely different API functions that can retrieve space on a drive—the older GetDiskFreeSpace function and the new GetDiskFreeSpaceEx function. Both functions look at drives in completely different ways, but while GetDiskFreeSpace uses the older and more "mechanically" oriented cluster sizes to report free space, the new function returns the byte count already summed up.

Undocumented

The cluster-oriented approach of the older function is the true reason why it can't deal with drives larger than 2GB. There is a maximum of clusters and a maximum of bytes per cluster. Modern file systems have changed this way of organizing data.

There are two drawbacks when using GetDiskFreeSpaceEx. First, it's not available on all Windows systems. Older Windows versions still exclusively use the FAT file system with its 2GB limit. And because GetDiskFreeSpaceEx needs to report potentially large numbers, it uses the Long Integer variable type. This variable type isn't supported in Visual Basic.

To overcome both drawbacks, the code uses some handy tricks that can help with other API functions, too. First, it uses on error resume next to take error handling in its own hands. Then, it just checks whether calling GetDiskFreeSpaceEx raised the errNoSuchFunction error. If so, it falls back and uses the old GetDiskFreeSpace function, which is available on any Windows system.

There are numerous ways to deal with Long Integer variable types. Most programmers define user types and do a lot of calculation switching bits back and forth. In most cases, this is completely unnecessary. Visual Basic supports a variable type called Currency. Even though this variable type, as its name implies, originally was designed to deal with currencies, it stores its values internally as Long Integer.

Undocumented

The Currency variable type really is the missing Long Integer variable type. The only difference is the decimal point, which you can adjust by multiplying the variable appropriately.

Your code can therefore use Currency in API declarations whenever an API function expects a Long Integer. To retrieve the value, just multiply the variable by 10, 000 to adjust for the decimals. There's definitely no need for brain-mangling bit operations.

Accessing Folders

Folders are the containers your files are organized in. Similar to drives, there are many ways to get a hold of a folder object:

```
' 7-10.VBS

' accessing a folder directly:
set fs = CreateObject("Scripting.FileSystemObject")
set folder = fs.GetFolder("C:\")
MsgBox TypeName(folder)
```

It's easy to enumerate the subfolder of any given folder using a collection and subfolders:

```
' 7-11.VBS

set fs = CreateObject("Scripting.FileSystemObject")
set folder = fs.GetFolder("C:\")
set foldercollection = folder.subfolders
for each subfolder in foldercollection
    list = list & subfolder.name & vbCr
next

MsgBox list
```

You can even get direct access to any of the special folders:

```
' 7-12.VBS

set fs = CreateObject("Scripting.FileSystemObject")

for x=0 to 2
    set specialfolder = fs.GetSpecialFolder(x)
    MsgBox x & " = " & specialfolder.path
next
```

And there's also the old relationship between `Drive` object and `Folder` object:

```
' 7-13.VBS

set fs = CreateObject("Scripting.FileSystemObject")

' get Drive:
set drive = fs.GetDrive("C:\")
set rootfolder = drive.RootFolder

' get folder directly
set rootfolder2 = fs.GetFolder("C:\")
if rootfolder is rootfolder2 then
    MsgBox "both objects are identical"
else
    MsgBox "objects are different"
end if
```

As it turns out, it doesn't matter which route you take: In both cases, you end up with the same `Folder` object representing folder "C:\".

Examining the Folder object

Take a look at the `Folder` object (see Table 7-3). What can it do for you?

Table 7-3   The Folder Object

Property/Method	Description
Property Attributes As FileAttribute	Folder attributes
Sub Copy(ByVal Destination As String, [ByVal OverWriteFiles As BooleanTrue])	Copy this folder
Function CreateTextFile(ByVal FileName As String, [ByVal Overwrite As BooleanTrue], [ByVal Unicode As BooleanFalse]) As ITextStream	Create a file as a TextStream
Property DateCreated As Date	Date folder was created
Property DateLastAccessed As Date	Date folder was last accessed
Property DateLastModified As Date	Date folder was last modified
Sub Delete([ByVal Force As BooleanFalse])	Delete this folder
Property Drive As IDrive	Get drive that contains folder
Property Files As IFileCollection	Get files collection
Property IsRootFolder As Boolean	True if folder is root
Sub Move(ByVal Destination As String)	Move this folder
Property Name As String	Get name of folder
Property ParentFolder As IFolder	Get parent folder
Property Path As String	Path to folder
Property ShortName As String	Short name
Property ShortPath As String	Short path
Property Size	Sum of files and subfolders
Property SubFolders As IFolderCollection	Get folders collection
Property Type As String	Type description

Determining a folder's total size

The Folder object contains a very powerful (and somewhat slow) method called Size. It calculates the total size this folder occupies and includes any files and subfolders. This method can be extremely useful. The following script generates a handy list with all folders and their sizes. This list helps to identify where all your precious hard disk space went, and it can be the basis of some serious cleaning up:

```
' 7-14.VBS

set fs = CreateObject("Scripting.FileSystemObject")

' space to store information
dim folderspecs(10000,1)

' reset counter and define as global variable
counter = 0

' check all drives
set drivecollection = fs.Drives
for each drive in drivecollection
    ' is it a hard drive?
    if drive.DriveType = 2 then
        ' is it ready? It should...
        if drive.isReady then
            ' start recursive reporting
            response = MsgBox("Checking Drive " _
& drive.DriveLetter _
& vbCr & counter _
& " folders checked so far...", vbOkCancel)

            ' leave an exit to cancel prematurely so
            ' no user is trapped in length operations:
            if response = vbCancel then exit for

            CheckFolder(drive.RootFolder)
        end if
    end if
next

' sort result, larger folders first
MsgBox "Sorting results..."
SortInfo

' generate list
output = "C:\list.txt"
set outputfile = fs.CreateTextFile(output, true)
for x=0 to counter-1
    size = FormatNumber(folderspecs(x, 0)/1024^2,1)
    size = right(space(30) & size, 10) & " MB"& space(5)
    outputfile.WriteLine size & folderspecs(x,1)
next

outputfile.close
```

```
' launch report file:
set wshshell = CreateObject("WScript.Shell")
wshshell.run output


sub CheckFolder(folderobj)
    ' determine folder size

    ' important: always turn off error handling!
    on error resume next
    size = folderobj.size
    ' check for access violation errors
    if not err.Number=0 then
        size=-1
        err.clear
    end if

    ' turn error handling back on:
    on error goto 0

    ' add entry:
    folderspecs(counter,0) = size
    folderspecs(counter,1) = folderobj.path

    ' increment counter:
    counter = counter + 1

    ' check all subfolders
    ' this is the basis of recursive calling

    ' important! Always turn off error handling
    ' to handle access violation errors:
    on error resume next

    for each subfolder in folderobj.subfolders
        ' check each subfolder individually
        ' by calling myself
        CheckFolder subfolder
    next

    ' turn error handling back on:
    err.clear
    on error goto 0
end sub

Sub SortInfo
    for x = 0 to counter-1
        for y = x+1 to counter-2
            if folderspecs(x,0)<folderspecs(y,0) then
                ' wrong order? Switch!
                temp = folderspecs(x,0)
                folderspecs(x,0)=folderspecs(y,0)
                folderspecs(y,0)=temp
                temp = folderspecs(x,1)
                folderspecs(x,1)=folderspecs(y,1)
                folderspecs(y,1)=temp
```

```
            end if
        next
    next
end sub
```

Undocumented

Access to files and folders may be limited. On Windows NT/2000, you might not have the permissions, and even on regular Windows systems, files currently open may prevent the WSH from accessing these files. In either case, to prevent errors, turn off error handling before you access file or folder details. Always make sure to re-enable error handling as soon as possible. File operations can be dangerous and should never be done with error handling completely turned off.

This script uses recursive calling to search through all the folders and subfolders. Recursive calling is very powerful but also sometimes a bit confusing (see Figure 7-5).

```
list - Notepad                                                    _ □ ×
File   Edit   Format   Help
  1,046.0 MB    C:\                                                    ▲
    765.0 MB    D:\WINNT
    604.1 MB    C:\WINNT
    545.9 MB    D:\WINNT\system32
    450.6 MB    C:\WINNT\system32
    346.6 MB    D:\Program Files
    265.1 MB    D:\Documents and Settings
    256.4 MB    D:\WINNT\system32\dllcache
    254.5 MB    C:\pics
    227.4 MB    D:\Documents and Settings\tob
    224.9 MB    D:\Documents and Settings\tob\Desktop
    216.8 MB    C:\WINNT\system32\dllcache
    205.1 MB    D:\Program Files\Microsoft office
    194.6 MB    D:\Program Files\Microsoft office\office
    162.2 MB    D:\Documents and Settings\tob\Desktop\pic
    111.0 MB    D:\Program Files\Common Files
     95.7 MB    D:\Program Files\Common Files\Microsoft Shared
     94.7 MB    D:\Program Files\Microsoft office\office\1031
     76.7 MB    D:\WINNT\Fonts
     59.5 MB    D:\Documents and Settings\tob\Desktop\idgcd
     54.6 MB    D:\Documents and Settings\tob\Desktop\idgcd\install
     54.1 MB    D:\WINNT\Driver Cache\i386
     54.1 MB    D:\WINNT\Driver Cache
     50.0 MB    C:\WINNT\Driver Cache\i386                            ▼
```

Figure 7-5: List folders by size — script calculates total folder content size.

Recursive calling means that a script procedure calls itself again and again. `CheckFolder` checks the size of itself and of all subfolders. This is the prerequisite to be a suitable recursive procedure. Each subfolder will once again call `CheckFolder` for its subfolders, and eventually every folder on your system will be scanned.

Finding and deleting empty folders

Installations and uninstallations often leave many empty folders on your system. While it would be far too dangerous to allow any script to find and delete such folders automatically, it's very helpful to build a little detection script.

This next script finds any empty folder and asks whether you want to delete it. However, the script uses the `DateLastAccessed` property to only list those folders you didn't access for at least 30 days. In addition, it creates a log file, `C:\emptydelete.txt`, and carefully keeps track of any folders you deleted so you can restore empty folders that turn out to be needed for something after all.

Caution

Delete folders only if you feel confident with your system and its internal structure. The system needs some empty folders for internal purposes, and although Windows is smart enough to restore them, you better not mess with it. Deleting folders you did not explicitly create yourself should always be left to experts.

```
' 7-15.VBS

set fs = CreateObject("Scripting.FileSystemObject")
logfile = "C:\emptydelete.txt"
set logbook = fs.OpenTextFile(logfile, 8, true)

' check Drive C:\
set drive = fs.GetDrive("C:\")
CheckFolder drive.RootFolder
logbook.close

MsgBox "Done with checking!"

sub ReportEmptyFolder(folderobj)
    on error resume next
    lastaccessed = folderobj.DateLastAccessed
    on error goto 0
    response = MsgBox("Empty folder detected:" & vbCr _
& folderobj.path & vbCr & "Date last accessed:" _
& vbCr & lastaccessed & vbCr _
& "Do you want to delete this folder?", _
vbYesNoCancel + vbDefaultButton2)
    if response = vbYes then
        logbook.WriteLine now & vbTab & folderobj.path
        folderobj.delete
    elseif response=vbCancel then
        MsgBox "I quit!"
        WScript.Quit
    end if
end sub

sub CheckFolder(folderobj)
    on error resume next
    isEmptyFolder folderobj
    for each subfolder in folderobj.subfolders
        CheckFolder subfolder
    next
end sub

sub isEmptyFolder(folderobj)
    on error resume next
    if folderobj.Size=0 and err.Number=0 then
        ' are there subfolders in the folder?
        if folderobj.subfolders.Count=0 then
```

```
                     ' at least 30 days unused?
                     dla = folderobj.DateLastAccessed
                     if DateDiff("d", dla, date)>=30 then
               ReportEmptyFolder folderobj
         end if
         end if
 end if
 end sub
```

There are actually two ways of deleting folders. You can use the `Delete` method built into any folder object. This is how the script gets rid of empty folders. In addition, the `FileSystemObject` offers the `DeleteFolder` method. Here, you specify the path name of the folder you want to delete.

Creating new folders

Your script can easily add folders. The following script shows how to automatically create all folders in a given path:

```
' 7-16.VBS

set fs = CreateObject("Scripting.FileSystemObject")

' generate folders for this path:
generated = CreateFolders("C:\DOCU\TEST\SUBFOLDER\TEST.TXT")
MsgBox "I've created " & generated & " folders for you!"

function CreateFolders(path)
    count = 0        ' number of created folders
    start = 1        ' scan path beginning at pos 1

    ' search for "\"
    pos = Instr(start, path, "\")

    ' loop until no more "\"
    do until pos=0
        ' extract subpath to current "\"
        folderpath = left(path, pos-1)

        ' does this folder already exist?
        if not fs.FolderExists(folderpath) then
            ' no, increment counter:
            count = count + 1
            ' create folder:
            fs.CreateFolder folderpath
        end if

        ' move to next "\" and scan for more:
        start = pos+1
        pos = Instr(start, path, "\")
    loop
```

```
' return # of newly created folders
    CreateFolders = count
end function
```

This script automatically generates all necessary folders in the given path and reports back the number of folders it actually generated.

Organizing Files

Folders and files are handled very similarly. Each file is represented by a File object. Let's first look at the information provided by the File object (see Table 7-4):

Table 7-4   The File Object

Property/Method	Description
`Property Attributes As` `FileAttribute`	File attributes

`Sub Copy(ByVal Destination`
`As String, [ByVal OverWriteFiles`
`As BooleanTrue])`
	Copy this file

`Property DateCreated As Date`	Date file was created
`Property DateLastAccessed As Date`	Date file was last accessed
`Property DateLastModified As Date`	Date file was last modified
`Sub Delete([ByVal Force As` `BooleanFalse])`	Delete this file
`Property Drive As IDrive`	Get drive that contains file
`Sub Move(ByVal Destination` `As String)`	Move this file
`Property Name As String`	Get name of file

`Function OpenAsTextStream([ByVal`
`IOMode As IOModeForReading], [ByVal`
`Format As TristateTristateFalse])`
`As ITextStream`
	Open a file as a TextStream

`Property ParentFolder As IFolder`	Get folder that contains file
`Property Path As String`	Path to the file
`Property ShortName As String`	Short name
`Property ShortPath As String`	Short path
`Property Size`	File size
`Property Type As String`	Type description

Accessing files

Accessing individual files is very similar to accessing folders. You can ask for a specific file:

```
' 7-17.VBS

set fs = CreateObject("Scripting.FileSystemObject")

filename = "C:\AUTOEXEC.BAT"
if fs.FileExists(filename) then
set file = fs.GetFile(filename)
MsgBox filename & " is " & file.size & " bytes."
else
    MsgBox filename & " does not exist."
end if
```

Or you can enumerate all files in a folder using files:

```
' 7-18.VBS

set fs = CreateObject("Scripting.FileSystemObject")

' access folder:
set folder = fs.GetFolder("C:\")
for each file in folder.files
    list = list & file.name & ": " & file.Type & vbCr
next

MsgBox list
```

Secret

Keep in mind that access to a file may be restricted or impossible: If the file is already open and owned by another program, you may not be able to access it. Likewise, if you specify the wrong path, the file cannot be found. So it's a good idea to use FileExists to check whether the file really exists, and to turn off error handling for those parts of your script where you try to access properties of the File object. Never forget to turn error handling back on using on error goto 0!

Mastering File Attributes

File Attributes are just plain bits. They aren't really powerful by themselves. What makes them powerful is the fact that Windows reads the attributes before it starts file operations on the file — and acts accordingly!

For example, if the read-only file attribute is set, you can't save the file. Instead, whenever you choose Save from the File menu, the Save As dialog pops up and asks you to save your changes as a different file.

This is great news because you can take advantage of the file attributes to protect template files and keep track of file changes using the Archive attribute. All you need to do is find a way to read and change the file attributes. Here's a list (Table 7-5):

Table 7-5   File Attributes

Bit value	Description
1	Read Only
2	Hidden
4	System
8	Volume (Drive)
16	Directory (Folder)
32	Archive
64	Alias (Link)
128	Compressed (NT only)
2048	Compressed (Win2000 only)

Reading file and folder attributes

Unfortunately, these attributes are crunched into two bytes, and to retrieve the actual meaning, you need to do some bit checking:

```
' 7-19.VBS

set fs = CreateObject("Scripting.FileSystemObject")
' check attributes of file
set file = fs.GetFile("C:\MSDOS.SYS")
MsgBox CheckAttribs(file)

' check attributes of folder
set folder = fs.GetFolder("C:\")
MsgBox CheckAttribs(folder)


function CheckAttribs(obj)
    description = Split("read-only;hidden;System;Drive;" _
& "Folder;Archive;Link;128;256;512;1024;compressed" _
& ";4096;8192", ";")
    attribs = obj.Attributes
    for x=0 to 13
        if (attribs and 2^x) then
            msg = ucase(description(x) & ": set")
        else
            msg = description(x) & ": not set"
        end if
        CheckAttribs = CheckAttribs & msg & vbCr
    next
end function
```

Bit-checking is fairly simple: Use and compare the bit value with the number. If the result is larger than 0 (which is always interpreted as true), then you know the bit is set (see Figure 7-6).

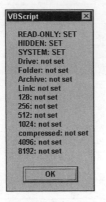

Figure 7-6: Convert Attribute bits into real text.

To check whether a file is write-protected, you can write:

```
' 7-20.VBS

set fs = CreateObject("Scripting.FileSystemObject")

filepath = "C:\MSDOS.SYS"
MsgBox "Is " & filepath & " write protected? " _
    & isWriteProtect(filepath)

function isWriteProtect(path)
    set fs = CreateObject("Scripting.FileSystemObject")
    if fs.FileExists(path) then
        isWriteProtect = CBool(fs.GetFile(path).Attributes and 1)
    else
        MsgBox path & "doesn't exist!", vbInformation
    end if
end function
```

Changing a file's attribute

The Attributes property is read/write, but it's a little tricky to change a file's attribute. Some of the attribute bits are read-only. Obviously, it would make no sense and cause immense confusion to set the Volume bit on a file.

Therefore, always set read/write bits only, and leave the rest alone.

The following example removes the read-only bit from MSDOS.SYS, opens the file in the editor, and allows you to change Windows 9.x Start options. Once you close the editor, the read-only bit is restored:

```
' 7-21.VBS

set fs = CreateObject("Scripting.FileSystemObject")
set wshshell = CreateObject("WScript.Shell")

filename = "C:\MSDOS.SYS"
set file = fs.GetFile(filename)

' remove read only bit:
file.Attributes = file.Attributes and not 14000 and not 1

' open file in editor:
wait = wshshell.run("notepad.exe " & filename,,true)

' restore write protect
file.Attributes = file.Attributes and not 14000 or 1
```

and not 14000 removes all write-protected bits. and not 1 deletes the write protection bit. or 1 sets this bit.

Secret

The Archive bit is a very special Attribute. It's managed by Windows. Whenever you save a file, Windows sets the files' Archive bit. You just need to clear this bit to check whether a file has changed over time. The Archive bit is used by Backup programs, and you'll see a little later in the chapter how scripts can also use the Archive bit to back up only those files that have changed since your last backup.

Changing File Content

You are not limited to organizing files and folders. You can also peek into files, create new files, and actually write data to files.

Peeking into files

The FileSystemObject offers a rich set of functions to manipulate text files. You are not limited to text files, though. Provided you know how to interpret the data, you can also open binaries or write binaries.

The following script opens a text file and displays its contents as a dialog box (see Figure 7-7):

```
' 7-22.VBS

set fs = CreateObject("Scripting.FileSystemObject")
filename = "C:\AUTOEXEC.BAT"

if fs.FileExists(filename) then
     set handle = fs.OpenTextFile(filename)
     content = handle.ReadAll
```

```
    handle.close
    MsgBox content
else
    MsgBox filename & " doesn't exist!"
end if
```

```
VBScript                                                    [x]
    mode con codepage prepare=((850) C:\WIN98\COMMAND\ega.cpi)
    mode con codepage select=850
    keyb gr,,C:\WIN98\COMMAND\keyboard.sys

                        [  OK  ]
```

Figure 7-7: Read in a text file and display contents as a dialog box.

Reading Registry entries

Using ReadAll will only work on rather small files. It just takes too much memory to read large files completely into a single variable.

A better approach is reading line by line. Now, however, you'll need to find ways to detect the end of the file.

The next example shows a couple of new techniques. First, the script launches regedit remotely using hidden options to create a text dump of the entire Registry. Then the script opens the text dump and retrieves information about all installed fonts.

As a result, you receive a list of installed fonts, their true file names, and a status report as to whether or not the file currently exists (see Figure 7-8).

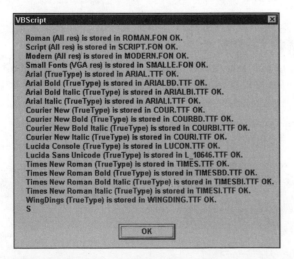

Figure 7-8: Finding out installed system fonts and checking for integrity.

Secret

`regedit` is the well-known Registry editor. This tool not only displays the content of your Windows Registry. It also can dump the entire Registry content to a file using the /E option. Since the WSH has only limited abilities to search the Registry, dumping the content and then searching it can be one way of retrieving information otherwise unreachable. The /S option prevents any dialog boxes from appearing. /S is short for "silent." Chapter 14 introduces methods to manage the Registry content directly.

```
' 7-23.VBS

set fs = CreateObject("Scripting.FileSystemObject")
set wshshell = CreateObject("WScript.Shell")

dump = "C:\dump.txt"

wait = wshshell.run("REGEDIT.EXE /S /E """ & dump & """",,true)

' re-enable error handling
on error goto 0

' font key:
key1 = "[HKEY_LOCAL_MACHINE\SOFTWARE\Microsoft" _
& "\Windows NT\CurrentVersion\Fonts]"
key2 = "[HKEY_LOCAL_MACHINE\SOFTWARE\Microsoft" _
& "\Windows\CurrentVersion\Fonts]"

' open dump file for reading
Const forReading = 1
Const useDefault = -2
set handle = fs.OpenTextFile(dump, forReading, false, useDefault)

' search entire dump until font section is reached
do until handle.atEndOfStream
    line = handle.ReadLine
    if found then
        ' end of font section reached?
        if not left(line,1)="""" then
            exit do
        else
            ' remove quotes:
            line = Replace(line, """", "")
            fontinfo = Split(line, "=")
            fontname = fontinfo(0)
            fontpath = fontinfo(1)
            msg = msg & fontname & " is stored in " & fontpath

            ' full path name available?
            if Instr(fontpath, "\")=0 then
                ' no, font stored in system folder:
                fontpath = "%windir%\fonts\" & fontpath
                fontpath = _
                    wshshell.ExpandEnvironmentStrings(fontpath)
            end if
```

```
                    if fs.FileExists(fontpath) then
                        msg = msg & " OK." & vbCr
                    else
                        msg = msg & " FILE MISSING!" & vbCr
                    end if
            end if
        ' font section reached?
        elseif Trim(ucase(line)) = Trim(ucase(key1)) or _
            Trim(ucase(line)) = Trim(ucase(key2))then
            ' yes!
            found = true
        end if
loop

handle.close

MsgBox msg
```

Take a close look at how this script gets access to the dump file! It uses `OpenTextFile` in conjunction with the option `useDefault`. This option is of utmost importance. System files are often stored either in UNICODE or in ANSI, depending on the Windows version you use. `OpenTextFile` by default interprets text files as ANSI. On Windows 2000 systems, the Registry dump would be unreadable this way.

By using `useDefault`, `OpenTextFile` interprets the text file content according to the system defaults. Always use `useDefault` when dealing with system files.

Note also how this script checks for two different Registry keys in order to run on both Windows 9.x and Windows NT/2000.

Reading script files

Although it might seem odd, your script file can read itself into memory, too. This is useful to embed additional information into your script file. Take a look at the next example: It uses Internet Explorer to display an HTML message and reads the HTML content as part of the script file (see Figure 7-9):

```
' 7-24.VBS

set window1 = OpenMessageWindow("DISPLAY1", 300, 100)
set window2 = OpenMessageWindow("DISPLAY2", 400, 200)

sub event_onQuit
    MsgBox "Hey! You closed my output window!", vbExclamation
    WScript.Quit
end sub

function OpenMessageWindow(title, width, height)
set ie = WScript.CreateObject("InternetExplorer.Application", _
"event_")
    ' read in script file line by line
```

```
        set fs = CreateObject("Scripting.FileSystemObject")
        set handle = fs.OpenTextFile(WScript.ScriptFullName)
        do until handle.atEndOfStream
            line = handle.ReadLine

            if line = "REM HTML START " & title then
                start = true
            elseif line = "REM HTML END" then
                start = false
            elseif start then
                html = html & mid(line,2) & vbCrLf
            end if
    loop
page = "JavaScript:'" & html & "'"
ie.navigate page

    ie.width = width
    ie.height = height

' turn off toolbars
ie.Toolbar = false

    ' turn off status bar
    ie.Statusbar = false

do
loop while ie.ReadyState<>4

ie.visible = true

' return reference to IE object:
        Set OpenMessageWindow = ie
end function

sub PrintNew(obj, text)
    obj.document.body.innerHTML = text
end sub

sub Print(obj, text)
    obj.document.body.insertAdjacentHTML "beforeEnd", text
end sub

REM HTML START DISPLAY1
'<head>
'<title>Welcome!</title>
'<style>
'    p    {font: 12pt Arial}
'</style>
'</head>
'<body scroll=no>
'<p>This is my HTML message!</p>
'</html>
REM HTML END
```

```
REM HTML START DISPLAY2
'<head>
'<title>Another message!</title>
'<style>
'    p    {font: 22pt Times New Roman; background: "#FF00FF"}
'</style>
'</head>
'<body scroll=no>
'<p>This is my second HTML message!</p>
'</html>
REM HTML END
```

Note

Internet Explorer and its methods are described in detail in Chapters 5 and 19.

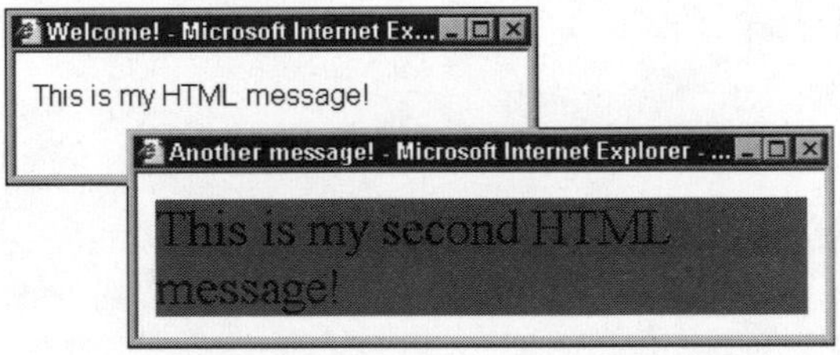

Figure 7-9: Embedding HTML in script files and displaying it as a dialog box.

Creating Files

There are two ways to create new files:

- New file from scratch: use `CreateTextFile`
- Create new file only if file doesn't exist yet: use `OpenTextFile`

In addition, you can use `OpenTextFile` to open an existing file for reading or appending.

Logging the use of your computer

For example, place a link to the following script into your `StartUp` program group. Every time the user logs on, the script adds an entry to a log file:

```
' 7-25.VBS

set fs = CreateObject("Scripting.FileSystemObject")
set network = CreateObject("WScript.Network")

logfile = "C:\user.txt"

' append to file and create file if it does not exist:
Const forAppending = 8
set handle = fs.OpenTextFile(logfile, forAppending, true)
handle.WriteLine now & vbTab & network.UserName
handle.close
```

Traditionally, it has been difficult to execute scripts when the user logs off. Even if you use Scheduled Tasks from your Control Panel, you won't find such an event. Windows 2000's Local Computer Policy snap-in, however, features both logon and logoff scripts, so it's easy to also log information once a user closes Windows. Your script can even automatically calculate how many hours the person was working if this is what you want to find out.

Renaming files

Automatically renaming files can be of tremendous use. Suppose you maintain a folder with graphics you like to use. Over time, hundreds and hundreds of files accumulate, and they all use their own naming scheme. It would be tremendous work to manually rename all these files. A script does the same thing in no time.

Place the script in the same folder you use to store the graphics files, then launch the script. All .bmp graphics files will be renamed using a template you specify. You can even call this script repeatedly whenever you have changed the folder content. The script will automatically fill in "holes" in the numbering scheme caused by deletions, and it will leave untouched file names that already use the naming template.

Don't rename files if you already made references to this file. For example, if you created link files that point to your files, renaming the files will obviously cause the links to break.

```
' 7-26.VBS

set fs = CreateObject("Scripting.FileSystemObject")


' naming template
template = "pix###"

' find out the folder this script is stored in
mename = WScript.ScriptFullName
mepath = left(mename, InstrRev(mename, "\"))

' access folder
set folder = fs.GetFolder(mepath)


' reduce template to fixed part
template1 = left(template, Instr(template, "#")-1)
' length of numbering scheme
template2 = len(template) - len(template1)
' start counter
counter = 0

' scan through files in folder
for each file in folder.files
```

```
' find out extension
ext = lcase(fs.GetExtensionName(file.name))

' is it a bmp graphics file?
if ext="bmp" then
    ' yes, already renamed?
    if not lcase(left(file.name, len(template1)))=lcase(template1)
then
        ' no, rename!
        do
            newfilename = template1 & right("000000" & counter,
template2) & ".bmp"
            counter = counter + 1
        loop while fs.FileExists(mepath & newfilename)
        file.name = newfilename
    end if
end if
next

MsgBox "Renaming complete!"
```

Summary

In this chapter, you first learned how to auto-document the objects and structures of the `Scripting.FileSystemObject` object, and then you put those methods and properties to work. By accessing drives, folders, and files, you easily retrieved all the information needed for daily maintenance scripts and for automatically reorganizing your data. You developed many useful tools to automatically rename graphics archives as well as to read (and change) file attributes. With the help of your own COM object, you can even overcome the 2GB bug, allowing your scripts to deal with drives of any size.

Chapter 8

Advanced File System Tricks

In This Chapter

▶ Use built-in `Copy` methods to copy files with the progress indicator and `Undo` functions

▶ Create your own `Backup` tool to quickly back up thousands of files

▶ Delete files to the Recycle Bin, emptying the Recycle Bin, and formatting drives

▶ Retrieve extended file version information and returning self-defined objects to your scripts

▶ Discover the secret `shell` view on the file system, calling context menu commands remotely, and displaying property pages

▶ Call undocumented Windows API functions and automatically resolve the UNICODE/ANSI conflict

---

You are not limited to the Scripting Host way of accessing the file system. In this chapter, you learn how to write your own file system script extensions and use the build-in Windows methods to copy and move files. You'll be able to delete files to the recycle bin, and discover the Windows shell objects which grant additional file management functions to your scripts.

Using Advanced File System Methods

In the previous chapter, you gained a good understanding of the file system and how to control folders and files by script. There's a lot more to it, though. Don't limit yourself to the methods the `Scripting.FileSystemObject` brings along. Find ways to access important API functions directly so you can use the Recycle Bin and file copy dialogs. Retrieve interesting advanced information about executables and `.dll` files, and discover the completely different approach the new Web view takes to manage the file system.

Kidnapping the shell's copy station

Although the `Scripting.FileSystemObject` provides you with all the methods necessary to toss around files and folders, the Windows shell doesn't use any of these. Instead, Windows uses its own set of commands, and for good reason.

The regular file transport commands are really very rudimentary. They are dependable, like a Volkswagen Beetle, but not very fancy. For example, deleting files or folders using `Delete` will immediately trash the data, without any chance of recovery (even if the operation was just an accident). There's no way the `Scripting.FileSystemObject` can delete files or folders to the recycler. There are no undo capabilities, either, and if more than just a couple of files are involved in your file operation, no dialog box reports the progress, keeping the user uninformed.

Undocumented

In addition, the `Scripting.FileSystemObject` copy and move commands are very picky. They act very differently depending on whether or not your file names end with "\" and can produce strange results if you don't stick exactly to the specifications.

So how does Windows do the trick? It uses its own file transportation methods, and you can, too.

Getting access to the Windows file services

The Windows file transportation department resides in `shell32.dll`. One single API function called `SHFileOperation` handles all the file operations done by the Windows shell. Depending on the flags you specify, this function can delete to the recycler, as well as copy or move large numbers of files while displaying a progress dialog box.

To access this functionality, all you need to do is wrap the function as a COM object. It's easy. Launch your Visual Basic CCE and enter the following code. Or even better — open the entire project file directly from the companion CD, using `\components\shellcopy\shellcopy.vbp`. If you don't like to compile the code yourself, install the prepared package — `\install\shellcopy\setup.exe`.

Understanding SHFileOperation

`SHFileOperation` is a rather easy API function: The only argument required is a structure called `shfileopstruct`. This structure contains the commands you want the shell to execute. First of all, you specify the kind of file operation: whether you want the shell to delete, copy, or move something. Next, you specify the list of files affected by your file operation. Finally, you are free to specify a set of flags, effectively fine-tuning your file operation. These flags determine whether dialog boxes will be shown and whether or not the user is able to undo the file operation by pressing [Strg]+[Z].

```
Option Explicit
```

```vb
Private Const FO_MOVE = &H1
Private Const FO_COPY = &H2
Private Const FO_DELETE = &H3
Private Const FO_RENAME = &H4

Private Const FOF_MULTIDESTFILES = &H1
Private Const FOF_CONFIRMMOUSE = &H2
Private Const FOF_SILENT = &H4
Private Const FOF_RENAMEONCOLLISION = &H8
Private Const FOF_NOCONFIRMATION = &H10
Private Const FOF_WANTMAPPINGHANDLE = &H20
Private Const FOF_ALLOWUNDO = &H40
Private Const FOF_FILESONLY = &H80
Private Const FOF_SIMPLEPROGRESS = &H100
Private Const FOF_NOCONFIRMMKDIR = &H200
Private Const FOF_NOERRORUI = &H400
Private Const FOF_NOCOPYSECURITYATTRIBS = &H800
Private Const FOF_NORECURSION = &H1000
Private Const FOF_NO_CONNECTED_ELEMENTS = &H2000
Private Const fof_wantnukewarning = &H4000

' command block
Private Type shfileopstruct
    hwnd        As Long        ' window handle
    wFunc       As Long        ' kind of file op
    pFrom       As String      ' list of source files
    pTo         As String      ' list of destination files
    fFlags      As Integer     ' flags
    fAborted    As Boolean
    hNameMaps   As Long
    sProgress   As String
End Type

' API call for shell file operation
Private Declare Function SHFileOperation Lib "shell32.dll" _
Alias "SHFileOperationA" (lpFileOp As shfileopstruct) As Long

Public Function FileOP(ByVal source As String, Optional ByVal _
dest As String = vbNullChar & vbNullChar, Optional ByVal _
method As Long = FO_COPY, Optional ByVal flag As _
Long = (FOF_NOCONFIRMATION Or FOF_NOCONFIRMMKDIR Or _
FOF_MULTIDESTFILES Or FOF_NOERRORUI)) As Long

Dim SHFileOP As shfileopstruct

    ' check whether source file list is valid
    If Len(source) = 0 Then
        Err.Raise vbObjectError + 1, "FileOP", _
           "You did not specify list of files"
        Exit Function
    End If

    ' make sure flags don't contain "dangerous" bits:
    flag = flag And Not 32

    ' tell file op struct what to do
```

```
    With SHFileOP
        .wFunc = method
        .pFrom = source & vbNullChar & vbNullChar
        .pTo = dest & vbNullChar & vbNullChar
        .fFlags = flag
    End With

    ' execute:
    FileOP = SHFileOperation(SHFileOP)
End Function
```

You could define a universal wrapper for `SHFileOperation` and leave it to your scripters to figure out and supply the flags for specific file operations. A much better approach is to define a couple of functions, each specializing in one of the many kinds of file operations available through `SHFileOperation`. This is how the sample COM object has done it. `Recycle`, for example, specifically deletes files or folders to the recycler, so there's no confusion about the flags and modes.

```
Public Function Recycle(ByVal source As String, Optional _
ByVal safe As Boolean = True) As Long

Dim SHFileOP As shfileopstruct

    With SHFileOP
        .wFunc = FO_DELETE
        .pFrom = source & vbNullChar & vbNullChar
        .pTo = vbNullChar & vbNullChar
        .fFlags = FOF_ALLOWUNDO Or FOF_NOCONFIRMATION
        If safe Then
            .fFlags = .fFlags Or fof_wantnukewarning
        End If
    End With

    ' execute:
    Recycle = SHFileOperation(SHFileOP)
End Function

Public Function Copy(ByVal source As String, ByVal dest As _
String, Optional ByVal safe As Boolean = False) As Long

Dim SHFileOP As shfileopstruct

    With SHFileOP
        .wFunc = FO_COPY
        .pFrom = source & vbNullChar & vbNullChar
        .pTo = dest & vbNullChar & vbNullChar
        .fFlags = FOF_ALLOWUNDO Or FOF_NOCONFIRMATION _
Or FOF_NOCONFIRMMKDIR
        If safe Then
            .fFlags = .fFlags Or FOF_RENAMEONCOLLISION
        End If
    End With

    ' execute:
```

```
        Copy = SHFileOperation(SHFileOP)
End Function

Public Function CopyMultiDest(ByVal source As String, ByVal _
dest As String, Optional ByVal safe As Boolean = False) As Long

Dim SHFileOP As shfileopstruct

    With SHFileOP
        .wFunc = FO_COPY
        .pFrom = source & vbNullChar & vbNullChar
        .pTo = dest & vbNullChar & vbNullChar
        .fFlags = FOF_ALLOWUNDO Or FOF_NOCONFIRMATION _
Or FOF_NOCONFIRMMKDIR Or FOF_MULTIDESTFILES
        If safe Then
            .fFlags = .fFlags Or FOF_RENAMEONCOLLISION
        End If
    End With

    ' execute:
    CopyMultiDest = SHFileOperation(SHFileOP)
End Function

Public Function Move(ByVal source As String, ByVal dest As _
String, Optional ByVal safe As Boolean = False) As Long

Dim SHFileOP As shfileopstruct

    With SHFileOP
        .wFunc = FO_MOVE
        .pFrom = source & vbNullChar & vbNullChar
        .pTo = dest & vbNullChar & vbNullChar
        .fFlags = FOF_ALLOWUNDO Or FOF_NOCONFIRMATION _
Or FOF_NOCONFIRMMKDIR
        If safe Then
            .fFlags = .fFlags Or FOF_RENAMEONCOLLISION
        End If
    End With

    ' execute:
    Move = SHFileOperation(SHFileOP)
End Function
```

Deleting Files to the Recycle Bin

Deleting files and folders without a safety net is risky. Windows offers such a safety net — the Recycle Bin stores deleted data for a while so you can easily retrieve accidentally deleted data.

With the help of your new COM object, your scripts can delete files to the Recycle Bin, too. The following script gets access to your temp folder and deletes any files that are older than two days:

```
' 8-1.VBS

' make sure you have installed the custom COM object
```

```
' as outlined in the book

set tool = CreateObject("shellcopy.tool")

' select all files in TEMP folder older than 2 days
set fs = CreateObject("Scripting.FileSystemObject")
set temp = fs.GetSpecialFolder(2)

for each file in temp.files
    if DateDiff("d",file.DateLastModified, date)>2 then
        list = list & file.path & chr(0)
    end if
next

' delete in Recycler
if len(list)>0 then
    MsgBox tool.Recycle(list)
end if
```

GetSpecialFolder returns the folder object of one of the Windows special
folders. Index 2 represents the temp folder where Windows stores temporary
files. The temp folder often contains a lot of outdated files no longer in use. To
make sure your script doesn't delete files still in use, it determines how old the
files are. DateDiff calculates the difference between the current date and the
date the files were created.

Recycle deletes files to the Recycle Bin. The important thing to notice is the
delimiter — Recycle expects each file name to be separated by a null string:
Chr(0). Figure 8-1 shows the progress dialog box that appears automatically
whenever the shell needs more than just a second to complete a file operation.

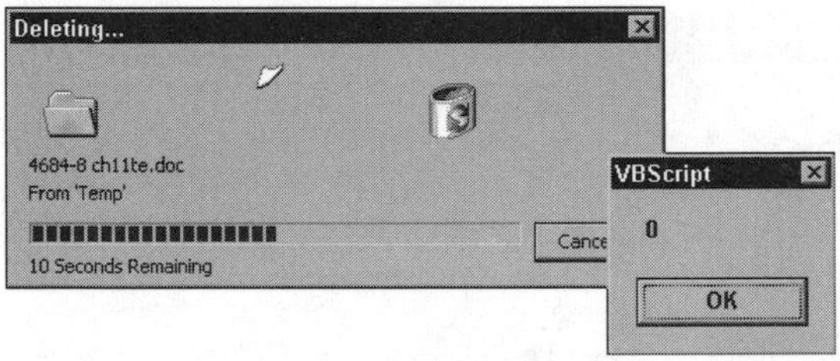

Figure 8-1: Use the shell to delete files to the Recycle Bin.

Secret

Always use fully qualified path names. If you don't, the files won't be deleted
to the Recycle Bin. Instead, Windows will delete them immediately.

On Windows 2000 systems, SHFileOperation supports additional flags.
One of them is fof_wantnukewarning, and Recycle uses this flag by
default. Whenever you try to delete a file from a drive without a Recycle
Bin (like a disk drive, for example), you receive a warning stating that
the file you are deleting will be permanently deleted. On other Windows
versions, you do not get such a warning.

Emptying the recycler

Now that you can delete files to the Recycle Bin, you might wonder how your scripts can actually flush the Recycle Bin and permanently delete its content. It's easy: Just use another API function called SHEmptyRecycleBin. Or even easier: Use the method EmptyRecycler I have prepared for you:

```
Option Explicit

Private Const SHERB_NOCONFIRMATION = &H1
Private Const SHERB_NOPROGRESSUI = &H2
Private Const SHERB_NOSOUND = &H4

Private Declare Function SHEmptyRecycleBin Lib "shell32.dll" _
Alias "SHEmptyRecycleBinA" (ByVal hwnd As Long, _
ByVal root As Long, ByVal flags As Long) As Long

Public Function EmptyRecycler(Optional ByVal _
flags As Long = SHERB_NOCONFIRMATION) As Long
    EmptyRecycler = SHEmptyRecycleBin(0, 0, flags)
End Function
```

The next script shows how to empty your Recycle Bin:

```
' 8-2.VBS

set tool = CreateObject("shellcopy.tool")
tool.EmptyRecycler
```

By default, EmptyRecycler doesn't show a confirmation dialog box. It does, however, show a progress indicator if your Recycle Bin contains more than just a handful of files.

To control the process in more detail, you are free to specify additional flags, as shown in Table 8-1.

Table 8-1   Additional Flags for Emptying the Recycler

Flag	Description
1	Don't show a confirmation dialog box (default)
2	Don't show a progress indicator
4	Don't play the empty recycler sound

Just pass the sum of the desired flags as an argument to EmptyRecycler.

Undocumented

Actually, SHEmptyRecycleBin allows you to empty individual Recycle Bins located on individual drives. In this example, the COM object doesn't use this feature, however, because on some Windows versions, deleting individual Recycle Bins messes up Registry values. This leads to strange behavior, preventing you from emptying your Recycle Bin.

Copying and Moving Files

Copying and moving files and folders is extremely easy—thanks to your new commands. They take care of most things. For example, if the destination folder doesn't yet exist, Windows automatically creates it. Use flag NOCONFIRMMKDIR to determine whether windows should ask for permission before automatically generating new folders. Use RENAMEONCOLLISION to have Windows rename destination files that already exist. With FILESONLY and NORECURSION, you can safeguard recursive file operations. Recursive file operations take place when you use wildcard characters, such as C:*.EXE, in your source file names. NOCOPYSECURITYATTRIBS is a new flag and only takes effect on Windows 2000 machines: It prevents Windows from copying the security attributes associated with a file.

Backing up valuable data

The next script demonstrates how powerful file copy can be. It's a full backup script, and all you need to do is specify the source folder and destination folder. The script determines which files need to be updated by checking whether the source files already exist in the backup set, and if they do, whether their content has changed since the last backup.

Secret

This script uses the Archive attribute to check whether a file's contents have changed. It clears the Archive attribute whenever it has copied a file. And it only copies files where the Archive attribute is set. Remember: Windows sets the Archive attribute automatically the moment you save a file.

If your backup includes more than just a few files, the copy method automatically displays a progress indicator, as shown in Figure 8-2, telling you what's going on. Note, however, that it may take some seconds to create the file list, and during this part, you don't see any dialog box.

```
' 8-3.VBS

' make sure you have installed the custom COM object
' as outlined in the book

set tool = CreateObject("shellcopy.tool")
set fs = CreateObject("Scripting.FileSystemObject")

' global variables:
source = "D:\SOURCES\"
dest = "C:\BACKUP\"

' list of files to be copied:
sourcelist = ""
' list of destination files:
destlist = ""
```

```
' counts checked files
counter1 = 0
' counts copied files
counter2 = 0

' check whether folder names are properly formatted:
if not right(source,1)="\" then source = source & "\"
if not right(dest,1)="\" then dest = dest & "\"

' select files to copy:
BackupFolder fs.GetFolder(source)

' copy files if any:
if counter2>0 then tool.CopyMultiDest sourcelist, destlist

' report
MsgBox "Backup done:" & vbCr & counter1 & " files checked." & vbCr &
counter2 & " files copied." & vbCr & counter1-counter2 & " files up-
to-date."


sub BackupFolder(folderobj)
    ' determine corresponding destination folder
    destfolder = dest & mid(folderobj.path, len(source)+1)

    ' create folder if missing
    ' this is not absolutely necessary as SHFileOperation creates
    ' folders automatically. Still, it's needed if you want to create
    ' empty folders in your backup set
    if not fs.FolderExists(destfolder) then
        fs.CreateFolder destfolder
    end if

    ' check all files in current folder
    for each file in folderobj.files
        ' determine corresponding destination file name
        destfilename = dest & mid(file.path, len(source)+1)
        ' increment file counter
        counter1 = counter1 + 1

        ' select file if it does not exist in backup or
        ' if original file has changed (archive attribute set):
        if (not fs.FileExists(destfilename)) or _
                ((file.Attributes and 32)=32) then
            ' increment file copy counter
            counter2 = counter2 + 1
            ' add file name to source list
            sourcelist = sourcelist & file.path & Chr(0)
            ' add destination file name to dest list
            destlist = destlist & destfilename & Chr(0)
            ' clear archive attribute
            file.Attributes = file.Attributes and not 14000 _
                and not 32
```

```
        end if
next

' do the same for any subfolders
' clear this part if you do not want recursive backups
for each subfolder in folderobj.subfolders
        BackupFolder subfolder
next
end sub
```

This script really is versatile, and it eliminates the hassle normally involved in backups. This script doesn't compress the backed up files. However, even commercial backup software doesn't squeeze files well, and if you are using Windows NT/2000, you can have the operating system compress your backup folder. Not compressing files is of great advantage: This backup method doesn't involve proprietary backup file sets.

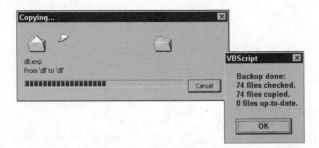

Figure 8-2: Back up entire folders (including subfolders) to any destination.

You can always access your backup files through the regular Explorer because your backed up files and folders remain regular files and folders. You don't need special software to retrieve backed up files. Even more important: Through the use of the Archive bit, your backup script is extremely efficient. It only copies true changes, so you don't need to wait forever for your backup to complete, and it returns a backup report, as shown in Figure 8-3.

If you wanted to use the same efficient strategy with commercial backup software, you'd have to do incremental backups. They're no fun, especially because you end up with various backup sets, and if you have some kind of emergency, you'll need to extract files from many different backup sets. But this is your solution — it's very basic, very easy, and very efficient.

Figure 8-3: Your backup script only copies files that have changed since the last backup.

Note

The script checks folders separately, and if a folder is missing in your backup set, it will be automatically created. This is somewhat redundant. The `SHFileOperation` function automatically creates any needed folders. However, it won't create empty folders. To include empty folders in your backup, you need to check for them yourself.

Copying files to multiple folders

The backup script demonstrates another technique, called `MultiDest` copying. The regular copy command copies a list of files to one common folder. This wouldn't work for your backup solution, because, after all, you want to be able to copy many different files from many different folders to many different destination folders.

Here comes `CopyMultiDest` to the rescue! It's actually just the Copy method using the special `MULTIDESTFILES` flag. With this flag enabled, `SHFileOperation` expects to receive two file lists: one containing the original (source) filenames and another one containing the destination filenames. So for each file, you define an entry in both lists.

Always note the difference. The regular copy method accepts a list of source files and a destination folder. The `CopyMultiDest` method accepts two filename lists.

Formatting Drives

Maybe one of these days you'll find it necessary to format a drive. But you're out of luck—Visual Basic is incapable of doing this.

So how does Windows pop up its Format Drive dialog box? It uses the undocumented `SHFormatDrive` API call—and you can, too! Either open the project from the companion CD (`\components\format\format.vbp`) or install the prepared package (`\install\format\setup.exe`).

```
Option Explicit

Private Declare Function SHFormatDrive Lib "shell32" _
(ByVal hwnd As Long, ByVal drive As Long, ByVal fmtID As _
Long, ByVal options As Long) As Long

Private Declare Function GetDriveType Lib "kernel32" _
Alias "GetDriveTypeA" (ByVal nDrive As String) As Long

Private Const SHFMT_ID_DEFAULT = &HFFFF
Private Const SHFMT_OPT_FULL = 1
Private Const SHFMT_OPT_QUICK = 0
Private Const SHFMT_OPT_SYSONLY = 2
Private Const SEM_FAILCRITICALERRORS = 1
```

```
Public Function format(ByVal driveletter As String, _
Optional quick As Boolean = True, _
Optional ByVal safe As Boolean = True)

Dim drive As String
    Dim driveindex As Long
    Dim mode As Long

    drive = Left(driveletter, 1) & ":\"
    driveindex = Asc(UCase(driveletter)) - Asc("A")
    If (Not safe) Or GetDriveType(drive) = 2 Then
        If quick Then
            mode = SHFMT_OPT_QUICK
        Else
            mode = SHFMT_OPT_FULL
        End If
        format = SHFormatDrive(0, driveindex, SHFMT_ID_DEFAULT, mode)
    Else
        Err.Raise vbObjectError + 1, "format()", "Drive " & drive _
& " is a fixed disk and cannot be formatted."
    End If
End Function
```

Format is straightforward to use: Just specify the drive letter of the drive you want to format. Windows pops up the Format Drive dialog box and pre-selects Quick Format. To overrun this default and pre-select a full format, use false as a second argument. Figure 8-4 shows the dialog box that pops up automatically if no disk is inserted into your drive.

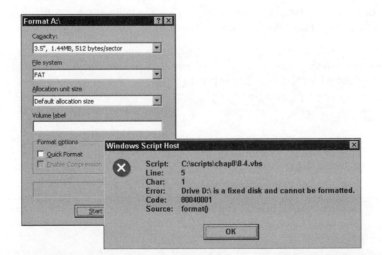

Figure 8-4: The script invokes the official format dialog box and reports missing disks.

Format has a built-in safety guard. Whenever you specify a fixed drive, such as a hard drive, the method will raise an error, and you'll receive a message similar to the one shown in Figure 8-5. You don't need to format hard drives very often, and doing so by accident can cost you a fortune. If you must format a hard drive, overrun the safety guard: Specify false as a third parameter. Note the use of GetDriveType: This API function reveals the type of a drive. It's analogous to the Scripting.FileSystemObjects' Drive object's DriveType property.

```
' 8-4.vbs

set tool = CreateObject("format.tool")
MsgBox tool.Format("A:\")
MsgBox tool.Format("D:\")
```

Secret

SHFormatDrive can only pop up the dialog box. So there's no way you can automatically launch the formatting process, right? Sure there is! Once the dialog box is open, you can use SendKeys to fill in the necessary key strokes. However, formatting drives without user interaction is potentially dangerous.

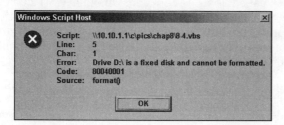

Figure 8-5: The script won't format fixed drives unless you explicitly ask for it.

Format returns a status letting you know if everything went well, as shown in Table 8-2.

Table 8-2	Format's Error Codes
Error Code	**Description**
0	All is OK.
-1	An Error occurred; drive may still be formattable.
-2	A user interrupted the last format.
-3	Drive media is not formattable.

Note, however, that your new Format method doesn't check for errors. whether a drive really exists. It concentrates only on formatting the drive you specify. However, with the methods of the Scripting. FileSystemObject, you can easily add error-checking. For example, use GetDrive to see whether a drive exists, and use isReady to check whether it contains media. It's completely up to you: Either do the error-checking inside of your scripts, or enhance the COM object code.

Secret On Windows 9.x machines, you can use `rundll32.exe` to launch `SHFormatDrive` directly. Choose Run from your Start menu and enter: `rundll32.exe shell32.dll, SHFormatDrive` [Enter]. Don't insert spaces before or after the comma. `Rundll32.exe` is only available on Win9.x. It calls the entry point of any `.dll` function and is used by the system. However, `rundll32.exe` doesn't allow you to specify any arguments. Calling `.dll` functions this way may crash the system if the `.dll` functions can't handle this.

Uncovering Extended File Version Information

The new Scripting Host has finally brought to you a way of determining a file's version number, called `GetFileVersion`. On older WSH 2.0 versions, `GetFileVersion` will raise an error, however, if the examined file doesn't contain version information. What's even more annoying is the fact that many more useful pieces of information are buried in most executable files. Why can you only retrieve the file version?

You can get much more! Just call the `GetFileVersionInfo` API function directly, and you will be able to retrieve information about debug, preview, and patched flags, determine the operating system a file was designed for (distinguishing DOS applications and true Windows applications), and more.

While we are at it, you will also see how to define objects yourself. The following COM object returns all the file information as an object. This object contains the information about a specific file and can be queried using various properties. It acts just like a `File` or `Drive` object, making it easy for you to structure information.

Accessing file version information

`Version.dll` delivers all the functions necessary to extract file version information. I've again prepared a working example: Load the project (`\components\version\version.vbp`) or install the software package (`\install\version\setup.exe`).

To be able to retrieve the information hassle-free, this time the COM object returns an information object to your script. Your basic COM module, therefore, just consists of one method, called `GetVersion`. This method creates a new object called `version`, initializes this object with the filename of the file you are interested in, and returns the object to your script:

```
Public Function GetVersion(ByVal filename As String) As version
    Set GetVersion = New version
    GetVersion.Init filename
End Function
```

All the mechanical parts are stored in the version object. Where did it come from? You provided it! Take a look at your Project window: In addition to the User Control, your project consists of a class module. This module defines your version object.

Secret

Class modules are really nothing new. They are just additional modules containing arbitrary code. In contrast to your User Control, class modules can be instantiated using the New operator. They act as separate black boxes, and most importantly of all, you can return class modules to your script — class modules are separate COM objects.

Take a look at the content of your class module. Here, you find all the API declarations involving version.dll. One very important method is called Init. It initializes the data structures of your object. After all, a plain vanilla version object won't do much good. Before you can use it, the version object needs to read in the version information of some file. This is done by Init.

The retrieved information is made accessible through properties. Each property first checks whether infoavailable is true — in essence, it checks whether or not you have initialized your object yet.

Another very important design concept is the use of global variables. The information Init retrieves must be globally available so the property procedures can access and return it. This is why the information structure VS_FIXEDFILEINFO is declared as Private, outside of any method or procedure. udtVerBufferG is therefore globally accessible from inside the version object.

Finding out file versions and copyright information

Thanks to your COM object's architecture, it's now extremely easy to retrieve all kinds of interesting file information (See Figure 8-6). Check out how easy it is to determine your Explorer's file version, among other information:

```
' 8-5.VBS

set version = CreateObject("file.versioninfo")

set wshshell = CreateObject("WScript.Shell")
windir = wshshell.ExpandEnvironmentStrings("%WINDIR%")

filename = "explorer.exe"
set obj = version.GetVersion(windir & "\" & filename)
if obj.isVer then
    msg = msg & "Version: " & obj.FileVersion & vbCr
    msg = msg & "Designed for: " & obj.OS & vbCr
    msg = msg & "Designed by: " & obj.CompanyName & vbCr
    msg = msg & "Description: " & obj.FileDescription & vbCr
    msg = msg & obj.LegalCopyright
end if

MsgBox "Information about " & filename & vbCr & msg
```

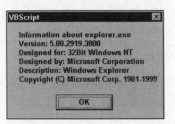

Figure 8-6: Retrieve extended version information for any file.

Figure 8-6 shows only part of the information your new tool makes available. Table 8-3 shows the complete list of information you are now able to retrieve:

Table 8-3   Custom Properties Your Tool Retrieves

Property	Description
CompanyName	Name of company that designed this file.
FileDescription	Description of what the file is supposed to do.
FileType	Type of file, e.g. Application, DLL, Driver, Font.
FileVersion	File version number..
InternalName	Name this file is referenced internally (independent of how you renamed the file).
isDebug	True: file contains debug code.
isPatch	True: file has been patched.
isPrerelease	True: file is a prerelease version.
isPrivate	True: file is for private use only.
isSpecial	True: some indicator for "special" build.
isVer	True: file contains version information.
LegalCopyright	Copyright information.
OriginalFileName	Original file name (in case someone renamed the file).
OS	Operating system this file was designed for.
ProductName	Name of the product this file belongs to.
ProductVersion	Version of the product this file is part of.
SubType	Additional file information, e.g. type of driver or type of font.

Searching for 16-Bit Windows files

Curious to see how many 16-bit applications are still floating around on your system? It's easy now:

```
' 8-6.VBS

set version = CreateObject("file.versioninfo")

set fs = CreateObject("Scripting.FileSystemObject")

' start with windows folder
set windir = fs.GetSpecialFolder(0)

list = ""
' recursively check all folders
' may take some time...
CheckFolder windir

MsgBox list

sub CheckFolder(folderobj)
    ' check any file with extension "com" or "exe"
    for each file in folderobj.files
        ext = lcase(fs.GetExtensionName(file.name))
        if ext="exe" or ext="com" then
            set obj = version.GetVersion(file.path)
            if obj.isVer then
                ' if 16bit then add to list
                if obj.OS = "16Bit Windows" then
                    list = list & file.path & vbCr
                end if
            end if
        end if
    next

    ' check all subfolders (recursive search)
    for each subfolder in folderobj.subfolders
        CheckFolder subfolder
    next
end sub
```

Figure 8-7 lists all files located in your Windows folder (or any of its subfolders) marked as "16bit."

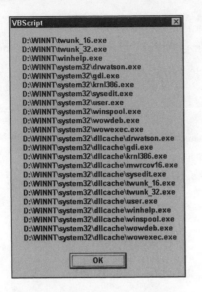

Figure 8-7: Identify all 16-bit applications running on your system.

Searching for DOS files

How can you retrieve a list of pure DOS executables? You could check the OS property for MS-DOS, but this wouldn't get you very far. DOS executables aren't team players most of the time—they selfishly use the entire computer for themselves, instead. They don't care much about other operating systems, and this is why most DOS executables don't even contain version information.

Just search for any file with a .com or .exe extension that doesn't contain valid version information: isVer returns false. You can safely assume that such executables are DOS executables.

Exploring Windows system files

Of course, you can—and should—combine the functions and methods you've created throughout this book. Remember the ListView control in Chapter 6? It allowed you to list information in columns and sort these columns any way you wanted. The List view control is the perfect companion for building a little tool that lets you explore core Windows files—with the help of the extended version information. Figure 8-8 demonstrates how much better your script can now display the results.

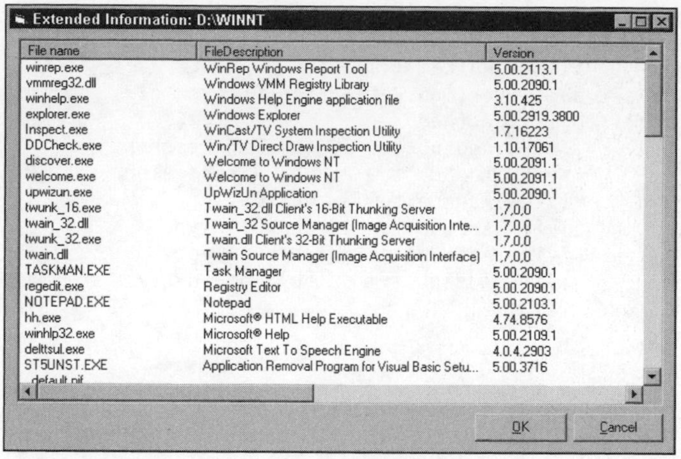

Figure 8-8: Windows tells you hidden details about its system files.

Note

For this example to run, you need to install both the version COM and the ListView COM: \install\listview\setup.exe.

```
' 8-7.VBS

set fs = CreateObject("Scripting.FileSystemObject")
set lview = CreateObject("listview.tool")
set version = CreateObject("file.versioninfo")
windir = fs.GetSpecialFolder(0).Path

CheckFolder windir
CheckFolder windir & "\system"
CheckFolder windir & "\fonts"




sub CheckFolder(name)
    set folder = fs.GetFolder(name)

    ' scale dialog box
    lview.width = 600
    lview.height = 400

    ' design some column headers

    lview.AddHeader "File name", 30
    lview.AddHeader "FileDescription", 50
    lview.AddHeader "Version", 30
    lview.AddHeader "Operating System", 30
    lview.AddHeader "File Type", 30
    lview.AddHeader "Subtype" , 30
    lview.AddHeader "CompanyName", 30
```

```
' read files into ListView:
for each file in folder.files
        lview.AddItem file.name
    set obj = version.GetVersion(file.path)
    if obj.isVer then
            lview.AddSubItem 1, obj.FileDescription
            lview.AddSubItem 2, obj.FileVersion
            lview.AddSubItem 3, obj.OS
            lview.AddSubItem 4, obj.FileType
            lview.AddSubItem 5, obj.SubType
            lview.AddSubItem 6, obj.CompanyName
    end if
next

' sort result
' 0 = first column
' 1 = second column...
lview.Sort 1, 1

    set result = lview.Show("Extended Information: " & name)
end sub
```

The script opens the Windows folder, the system folder, and the fonts folder. It also displays extended file information. File Description turns out to be a most valuable information source: It reveals the deeper meaning of many of the hidden and undocumented Windows executables and retrieves information about fonts (see Figure 8-9).

Tip

Just click on any of the column headers to sort the result. Click again to sort the opposite way.

File name	FileDescription	Version	Operating System	File Type
vga865.fon	VGA (640x480) res...	3.10	16Bit Windows	Font
vga863.fon	VGA (640x480) res...	3.10	16Bit Windows	Font
vga860.fon	VGA (640x480) res...	3.10	16Bit Windows	Font
vga850.fon	VGA (640x480) res...	3.10	16Bit Windows	Font
vgaoem.fon	VGA (640x480) res...	3.10	16Bit Windows	Font
vgasys.fon	VGA (640x480) res...	3.10	16Bit Windows	Font
vgafix.fon	VGA (640x480) res...	3.10	16Bit Windows	Font
symbole.fon	Symbol font 8,10,12...	3.10	16Bit Windows	Font
smalle.fon	Small fonts (VGA re...	3.10	16Bit Windows	Font
smallf.fon	Small fonts (8514/a...	3.10	16Bit Windows	Font
script.fon	Script font (all resol...	3.10	16Bit Windows	Font
roman.fon	Roman font (all reso...	3.10	16Bit Windows	Font
cga40woa.fon	Non-Windows appli...	3.10	16Bit Windows	Font
cga80woa.fon	Non-Windows appli...	3.10	16Bit Windows	Font
dosapp.fon	Non-Windows appli...	3.10	16Bit Windows	Font
ega40woa.fon	Non-Windows appli...	3.10	16Bit Windows	Font
ega80woa.fon	Non-Windows appli...	3.10	16Bit Windows	Font
app850.fon	Non-Windows appli...	3.10	16Bit Windows	Font
cga40850.fon	Non-Windows appli...	3.10	16Bit Windows	Font
cga80850.fon	Non-Windows appli...	3.10	16Bit Windows	Font
ega40850.fon	Non-Windows appli...	3.10	16Bit Windows	Font

Extended Information: D:\WINNT\fonts

OK   Cancel

Figure 8-9: You can sort columns and retrieve system information such as installed fonts.

Compressing (and decompressing) files

Microsoft has included a little hidden present for you. As part of the Visual Basic CCE, it ships the `vbskco32.dll` file. This file contains the function to compress files. The ability to decompress files is included with any Windows version — `lz32.dll` offers the necessary functions.

Being able to compress files is of great help. Just imagine you need to hand over data that doesn't fit on a disk. Compress the data, and chances are you will be able to squeeze your data on the disk.

Undocumented

Decompressing files is a standard Windows functionality. Many installation packages and font files come in compressed format. You can recognize such files by looking for underscores in the files' extensions. The creation of compressed files is not supported by Windows by default. However, because the VB CCE comes with the Application Wizard, and because this wizard produces compressed setup packages, the VB CCE includes the necessary compression functions. By taking advantage of `vbskco32.dll`, you are free to compress your own files and decompress them later.

Getting access to compression functions

I've prepared a compression wrapper for you. Again, it's a COM object. Either open the project and compile it yourself with `\components\compress\compress.vbp`, or just install the prepackaged setup file: `\install\compress\setup.exe`.

Note

If you decide to recompile the project, make sure the file `vbskco32.dll` is stored in your Windows system folder. If it's not, you need to specify the full path name in the `LcbCompressFile` declaration.

The COM object's name is `compress.files`. It provides you with the two methods — `CompressIt` and `ExpandIt`.

Squeezing files onto a disk

How do you store compressed files onto a disk? Just use the following script. Either drag files onto the script icon, or open the script directly. The script will now display a message similar to the one shown in Figure 8-10 and offer to place a reference to itself in your `SendTo` menu. From now on, you can right-click any file, choose Send to, and then choose Compress to Disk. The file will be compressed and stored on your drive A:\. Your script will keep you informed and pop up messages like the one shown in Figure 8-11.

Change the drive letter in the script if you'd like to use a different drive instead. Note that this script can only work if your Scripting Host is capable of drag-and-drop operations. Make sure you have upgraded to at least WSH 2.0, as outlined in the Preface.

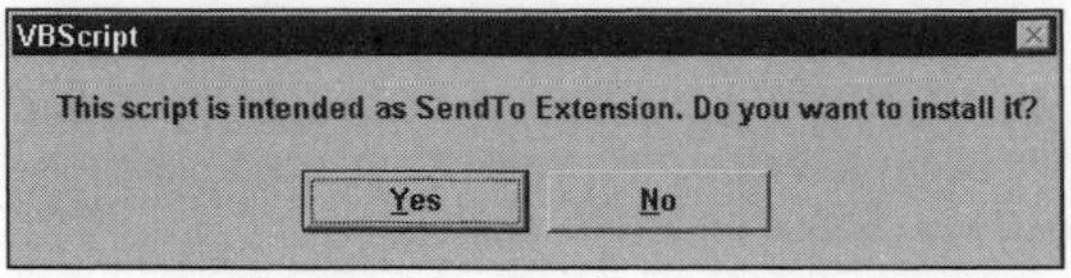

Figure 8-10: If you launch the script directly, it will install itself into the SendTo menu.

```
' 8-8.VBS

set args = WScript.Arguments

destination = "A:\"

if args.Count>0 then
    set tool = CreateObject("compress.files")
    counter = 0
    for each file in args
        filename = mid(file, InstrRev(file, "\")+1)
        destname = destination & filename & ".compress"
        MsgBox file & "->" & destname
        returnval = tool.CompressIt(file, destname)
        if returnval>=0 then counter = counter + 1
    next
    MsgBox "Compressed " & counter & " files."
else
    answer = MsgBox("This script is intended as SendTo Extension." _
& " Do you want to install it?", vbYesNo)
    if answer = vbYes then
        set wshshell = CreateObject("WScript.Shell")
        sendto = wshshell.SpecialFolders("SENDTO")
        set scut = wshshell.CreateShortcut(sendto _
& "\Compress to Disk.lnk")
        scut.TargetPath = WScript.ScriptFullName
        scut.IconLocation = "shell32.dll,1"
        scut.Save
        MsgBox "Installed."
    end if
end if
```

The script adds the .compress extension to your compressed files to indicate that they are no longer regular files and can't be opened directly.

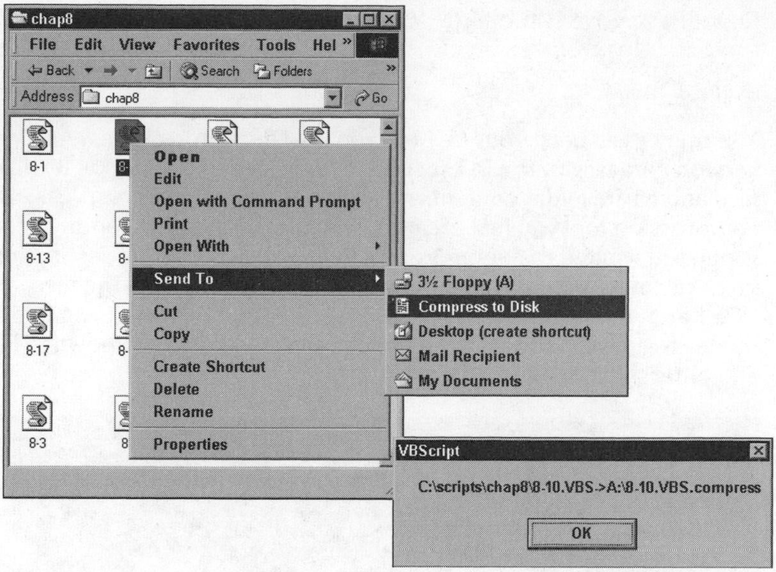

Figure 8-11: Your new context menu command compresses files to disk.

Decompressing compressed files

Decompressing works similarly. The next script decompresses any compressed files stored on a disk. The script prompts for a folder in which it stores the revitalized files.

```
' 8-9.VBS

set args = WScript.Arguments
set fs = CreateObject("Scripting.FileSystemObject")
set tool = CreateObject("compress.files")

destination = "A:\"

destfolder = InputBox("Where do you want to store " _
& "the files?",,"C:\TEMP")

if not right(destfolder,1)="\" then destfolder = destfolder & "\"

if not fs.FolderExists(destfolder) then
    fs.CreateFolder destfolder
end if

set folder = fs.GetFolder(destination)
for each file in folder.files
    if lcase(fs.GetExtensionName(file.name))="compress" then
        newfilename = destfolder & _
Replace(mid(file.path, 4), ".compress", "")
```

```
            tool.ExpandIt file.path, newfilename
      end if
next
MsgBox "Done."
```

Secret

You don't even need your COM wrapper to decompress files. Any Windows version comes with the DOS command-line tool expand.exe. It will decompress files and entire folder contents, provided the files were compressed using the compression tool you just created. Therefore, your new compression command is perfectly suited to compress distribution files. On your destination system, you don't need a Windows Scripting Host to decompress the files. A simple DOS batch file will do the job. However, expand.exe won't run in pure DOS mode. To see all options, open the command window as shown in Figure 8-12 and enter expand.exe /?.

```
D:\WINNT\system32\cmd.exe                                    _ □ ×
Microsoft Windows 2000 [Version 5.00.2128]
(C) Copyright 1985-1999 Microsoft Corp.

D:\WINNT\system32>expand /?
Microsoft (R) File Expansion Utility  Version 5.00.2090.1
Copyright (C) Microsoft Corp 1990-1999.  All rights reserved.

Expands one or more compressed files.

EXPAND [-r] Source Destination
EXPAND -r Source [Destination]
EXPAND -D Source.cab [-F:Files]
EXPAND Source.cab -F:Files Destination

   -r           Rename expanded files.
   -D           Display list of files in source.
   Source       Source file specification.  Wildcards may be used.
   -F:Files     Name of files to expand from a .CAB.
   Destination  Destination file ¦ path specification.
                Destination may be a directory.
                If Source is multiple files and -r is not specified,
                Destination must be a directory.

D:\WINNT\system32>_
```

Figure 8-12: Windows already contains the tools to decompress your files.

Some second thoughts about compression

The compression algorithms the previous functions use are not optimized. You get much better compression ratios using WinZIP or other commercial compression tools. Still, the built-in file compression functions come in handy, especially as you are now able to access compressed system files individually. The most important advantage is that compressed files can be decompressed solely with built-in Windows functions or with the help of expand.exe.

To find compressed system files, search for *.??_. This will list all files with an underscore at the end of their file extensions.

Secret

The system uses the third letter of a file's extension to indicate that it's compressed. In order to re-create the original file, you'll need to manually change the file extension and replace the underscore with the missing letter. There's no clue to which letter this could be—it's all up to your experience. From what you have learned so far, though, it's safe to assume that a .dl_ file extension expands to .dll, whereas a .tt_ extension expands to .ttf.

The Secret Shell View on the File System

So far, the `Scripting.FileSystemObject` has been your secret door into the Windows file system. It has provided you with all the methods and properties necessary to access and manipulate files and folders. There's another secret door, though, and it's almost undocumented.

An inside view of the shell.Application object

This second secret door is used by the shell and hides behind the `shell.Application` object. Let's check out how your scripts can benefit from `shell.Application`. Table 8-4 takes a look at all the internal methods and properties.

However, the `shell.Application` object will only be accessible if you have installed Internet Explorer 4 or use Windows 98/2000. For some unknown reason, `shell.Application` isn't accessible on Internet Explorer 5.

Table 8-4   Shell.Application Properties and Methods

Method/Property	Description
`Property Application As Object`	Get `Application` object
`Function BrowseForFolder (ByVal Hwnd As Long, ByVal Title As String, ByVal Options As Long, [ByVal RootFolder]) As Folder`	Browse the name space for a `Folder`
`Sub CascadeWindows`	Cascade Windows
`Sub ControlPanelItem (ByVal szDir As String)`	Run a `controlpanelItem`
`Sub EjectPC`	Undock a notebook PC
`Sub Explore(ByVal vDir)`	Explore a folder
`Sub FileRun`	Bring up the file run
`Sub FindComputer`	Find a computer
`Sub FindFiles`	Find files
`Sub Help`	Display shell help
`Sub MinimizeAll`	Minimize all windows

Continued

Table 8-4 *(continued)*

Method/Property	Description
`Function namespace (ByVal vDir) As Folder`	Get special folder from `ShellSpecialFolderConstants`
`Sub Open(ByVal vDir)`	Open a folder
`Property Parent As Object`	Get `Parent` object
`Sub RefreshMenu`	Refresh the menu
`Sub SetTime`	Bring up the Set time dialog box
`Sub ShutdownWindows`	Exit Windows
`Sub Suspend`	Suspend the PC
`Sub TileHorizontally`	Tile windows horizontally
`Sub TileVertically`	Tile windows vertically
`Sub TrayProperties`	Handle `Tray` properties
`Sub UndoMinimizeALL`	Undo Minimize All
`Function Windows As Object`	Collect open folder windows

Accessing folders the shell way

Always remember: The `Scripting.FileSystemObject` was created for programmers only. It's not an internal part of Windows, and so the shell must use its own set of file system commands. You are about to enter a completely new and different world. Any objects you encounter here are completely different from the `Scripting.FileSystemObject`, even if they share some names.

This is how the shell accesses a folder:

```
' 8-10.VBS

set shell = CreateObject("Shell.Application")
set folder = shell.namespace("C:\")
MsgBox "Object Type: " & TypeName(folder)
```

Your script retrieves a `folder` or `Folder2object`, depending on your system's shell version. Table 8-5 shows the methods and properties of this object.

Table 8-5   Shell.Application Folder Object

Method/Property	Description
`Property Application As Object`	Get `Application` object
`Sub CopyHere(ByVal vItem, [ByVal vOptions])`	Copy items to this folder
`Function GetDetailsOf (ByVal vItem, ByVal iColumn As Long) As String`	Get the details about an item
`Function Items As FolderItems`	Collec items in a folder
`Sub MoveHere(ByVal vItem, [ByVal vOptions])`	Move items to this folder
`Sub NewFolder(ByVal bName As String, [ByVal vOptions])`	Create a new sub-folder in this folder
`Property OfflineStatus As Long`	(new) Offline status of the server
`Property Parent As Object`	Get `Parent` object
`Property ParentFolder As Folder`	Get `Parent` object
`Function ParseName (ByVal bName As String) As FolderItem`	Parse the name to get an item
`Property Self As FolderItem`	(new) Folder's `FolderItem` interface
`Sub Synchronize`	(new) Synchronize all offline files
`Property Title As String`	Get the display name for the window

Undocumented

There are actually two objects — `Folder` and `Folder2`. The `Folder` object is used by Windows 98 and Internet Explorer 4. `Folder2` is a revised object introduced by Windows 2000. It contains additional methods and properties (marked as "new" in Table 8-3).

Finding out a folder's name

The shell.Application object really is the shell view of the file system, and the following script proves it:

```
' 8-11.VBS

set shell = CreateObject("Shell.Application")
set folder = shell.namespace("C:\")
MsgBox "Shell Name of folder C:\: " & vbCr & folder.Title
if TypeName(folder)="Folder2" then
     MsgBox "Real Name of folder C:\: " & vbCr & folder.self.Path
end if
```

The Folder object's Title property returns the folder name from the shell's view. Figure 8-13 proves that it's no plain path name. Instead, it's the name of the drive as it appears in the Explorer.

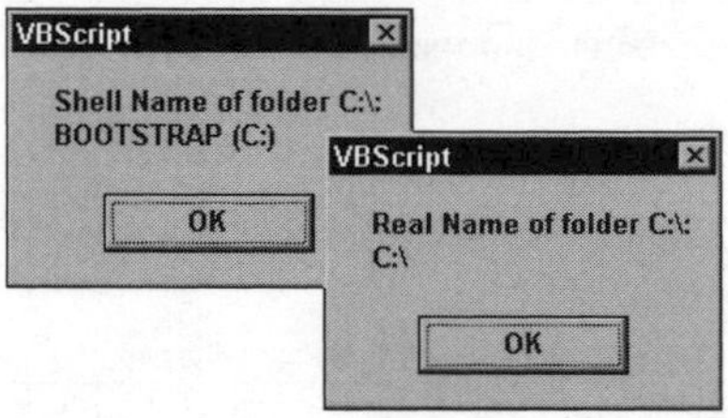

Figure 8-13: In the shell, files and folders may have special names.

To retrieve the true path name, the script uses the Folder2 object's Self property. This property is new and not available in Folder objects. You can use this property only on Windows 2000.

Reading folder contents

Every element stored in a folder is represented by a FolderItem object. In fact, you've already used the FolderItem object. The Folder2 object's Self property returns the FolderItem object representing the folder, and its path property reveals the folder's official path name. Table 8-6 shows how a FolderItem object is organized.

Table 8-6   The FolderItem Object

Method/Property	Description
Property Application As Object	Get Application object.
Function ExtendedProperty (ByVal bstrPropName As String)	(new) Access an extended property.

Method/Property	Description
`Property GetFolder As Object`	If the item is a folder, return folder object.
`Property GetLink As Object`	If the item is a link, return link object.
`Sub InvokeVerb ([ByVal vVerb])`	Execute a command on the item.
`Sub InvokeVerbEx([ByVal vVerb], [ByVal vArgs])`	(new) Extended version of `InvokeVerb`.
`Property IsBrowsable As Boolean`	Is the item browsable?
`Property IsFileSystem As Boolean`	Is the item a file system object?
`Property IsFolder As Boolean`	Is the item a folder?
`Property IsLink As Boolean`	Is the item a link?
`Property ModifyDate As Date`	Modification date?
`Property Name As String`	Get the display name for the item.
`Property Parent As Object`	Get the `Parent` object.
`Property Path As String`	Get the path name to the item.
`Property Size As Long`	Size.
`Property Type As String`	Type.
`Function Verbs As FolderItemVerbs`	Get the list of verbs for the object.

Undocumented

As with the `Folder` object, there are again two objects representing a folder content—the old `FolderItem` object and the revised `FolderItem2` object. With Windows 2000, you always get a `FolderItem2` object and can take advantage of the additional methods marked as "new."

You now know all the details to open a folder and list its content the way the shell does it:

```
' 8-12.VBS

set shell = CreateObject("Shell.Application")
set folder = shell.namespace("C:\")
for each folderitem in folder.items
    list = list & folderitem.name & vbTab & folderitem.size _
 & vbTab & folderitem.ModifyDate & vbCr
next

MsgBox list
```

Figure 8-14 shows a sample output. The columns may appear disarranged, and this is due to the proportional font used in the dialog box. You could easily output the information as an HTML table and get perfectly aligned columns.

This is all pretty neat, but where's the real advantage over the `Scripting.FileSystemObject` methods? Hang on.

list	72264	1/14/2000 12:43:22 AM
dump	21901200	1/14/2000 12:47:40 AM
BACKUP	0	1/14/2000 12:59:54 AM
pics	0	1/3/1997 2:19:34 AM
technet	0	2/16/1999 7:49:22 PM
inetpub	0	1/1/1997 12:22:22 AM

Figure 8-14: The shell can provide all kinds of detailed file information.

Retrieving secret file information

One advantage is the `GetDetailsOf` method provided by the `Folder` object. It returns interesting information about the files — have a look at the sample output shown in Figure 8-15.

```
' 8-13.VBS

set shell = CreateObject("Shell.Application")
set folder = shell.namespace("C:\")
for each folderitem in folder.items
    for x=-1 to 28
        description = folder.GetDetailsOf(0, x)
        if description<>"" then
            list = list & "(" & x & ")"& description & ": " _
& folder.GetDetailsOf(folderitem, x) & vbCr
        end if
    next
    list = list & vbCr
next

MsgBox list
```

Secret

On Windows 2000, `getDetailsOf` reveals much more information. Windows 9.x and NT limit themselves to the usual pieces of information found in the Explorer Details view. On Windows 2000, rightclick on any one of the column headers in Details view to see the advanced information directly.

`GetDetailsOf` actually leads a double life. Call it with its first argument set to 0, and it returns the description of the property. Call it with its first argument set to a `FolderItem` object, and it returns the actual information about this object. The second argument selects the kind of information you want to query.

```
(0)Name: fertig
(1)Size:
(2)Type: File Folder
(3)Modified: 12/23/1999 12:08 PM
(4)Attributes:
(5)Comment:
(6)Created: 12/23/1999 12:08 PM
(7)Accessed: 12/23/1999 12:00 AM
(8)Owner: Everyone
(10)Author:
(11)Title:
(12)Subject:
(13)Category:
(14)Pages:
(15)Copyright:
(16)Company Name:
(17)Module Description:
(18)Module Version:
(19)Product Name:
(20)Product Version:
(21)Sender Name:
(22)Recipient Name:
(23)Recipient Number:
(24)Csid:
(25)Tsid:
(26)Transmission Time:
(27)Caller Id:
(28)Routing:
```

Figure 8-15: `GetDetailsOf` reveals all kinds of detail object information.

On Windows 9.x and NT, use `index -1` to retrieve additional information, such as author name, about Microsoft Office files. Windows 2000 has integrated this information in its standard set of information.

Undocumented

Accessing special virtual Windows folders

You probably have noticed that Windows Explorer can do much more than just present regular folders. The Windows Explorer can display any kind of information source. The Control Panel, for example, is a completely virtual folder that doesn't exist anywhere on your hard drive. Still, it can be displayed as if it were a folder. Why?

It's all a matter of "namespace." The regular file system uses path names as unambiguous selectors. It's a namespace, and path names are the tools to select individual elements in this namespace. Control Panel, the Printer folder, and any of the other virtual folders use their own namespaces and their very own way of identifying objects. Windows keeps track of this with the use of PIDLs. PIDLs are unique identifiers not bound to any specific namespace.

Fortunately, you very seldom have to deal with PIDLs yourself. Take a look at the Folder Picker dialog box introduced in Chapter 6 if you must convert PIDLs to file names.

The `shell.Application` object hides the internal mechanics of virtual folders from you. Just access a virtual folder using `namespace`, and supply the index number of the virtual folder you want to see, as outlined in Table 8-7.

Table 8-7   Code Numbers Of Windows Special Folders

Constant	Description
0	Special Folder DESKTOP
2	Special Folder PROGRAMS
3	Special Folder CONTROLS
4	Special Folder PRINTERS
5	Special Folder PERSONAL
6	Special Folder FAVORITES
7	Special Folder STARTUP
8	Special Folder RECENT
9	Special Folder SENDTO
10	Special Folder BITBUCKET
11	Special Folder STARTMENU
16	Special Folder DESKTOPDIRECTORY
17	Special Folder DRIVES
18	Special Folder NETWORK
19	Special Folder NETHOOD
20	Special Folder FONTS
21	Special Folder TEMPLATES
22	Special Folder COMMON STARTMENU
23	Special Folder COMMON PROGRAMS
24	Special Folder COMMON STARTUP
25	Special Folder COMMON DESKTOPDIR
26	Special Folder APPDATA
27	Special Folder PRINTHOOD
28	Special Folder LOCAL APPDATA
29	Special Folder ALTSTARTUP
30	Special Folder COMMON ALTSTARTUP
31	Special Folder COMMON FAVORITES
32	Special Folder INTERNET CACHE
33	Special Folder COOKIES
34	Special Folder HISTORY

Constant	Description
35	Special Folder COMMON APPDATA
36	Special Folder WINDOWS
37	Special Folder SYSTEM
38	Special Folder PROGRAM FILES
39	Special Folder MYPICTURES
40	Special Folder PROFILE
41	Special Folder SYSTEMx86
48	Special Folder PROGRAM FILESx86

The following script shows how to enumerate the content of Control Panel:

```
' 8-14.VBS

set shell = CreateObject("Shell.Application")

' open Control Panel
set folder = shell.namespace(3)
for each folderitem in folder.items
    subfolder = false
    for x=0 to 1
        description = folder.GetDetailsOf(0, x)
        content = folder.GetDetailsOf(folderitem, x)
        if content="" and not subfolder then
            list = list & folderitem.name & " (Subfolder)" & vbCr
            subfolder = true
        elseif not subfolder then
            list = list & "(" & x & ")"& description _
& ": " & content & vbCr
        end if
next
    list = list & vbCr
next

MsgBox list
```

Here's an interesting point: GetDetailsOf reveals a completely different set of information about the folder items. It's all a matter of the namespace your folder lives in.

Translating between namespaces

Let's focus for a moment on the classic file system. There are two ways to access files and folders: Scripting.FileSystemObject uses the regular path names to identify objects, and shell.Application uses the shell's naming conventions to access objects.

Secret

The regular path names and the shell's naming convention are slightly different. You have seen that drive C in the shell is represented through the display name of the drive. Similarly, filenames in the shell are represented exactly the way the shell and the Explorer display them. If, for example, you have chosen to make file extensions invisible, files are accessed just by plain filenames. This imposes problems: Imagine two files of different type but with the same name — there's no longer any way to differentiate between them. Fortunately, the shell supplies you with the tools to uniquely identify objects and translate classic file paths to shell objects.

To access any file or folder, you use two methods — namespace and ParseName. namespace gives access to folders. It automatically translates the path name into whatever the shell uses as a descriptor for the folder. Once you have access to the folder, ParseName translates any filename to the shell's file-naming convention.

The only thing you need to do is split up a file path into a folder and true filename. Have a look:

```
' 8-15.VBS

set shell = CreateObject("Shell.Application")
filepath = "C:\MSDOS.SYS"
folder = left(filepath, InstrRev(filepath, "\"))
file = mid(filepath, InstrRev(filepath, "\")+1)

' get access to folder containing the file
set folderobj = shell.namespace(folder)
set folderitem = folderobj.ParseName(file)

' folderitem now represents your file

MsgBox folderItem.Name
```

The script gets access to the file and displays its name. Note that the name is displayed according to your shell settings: If your shell currently hides file extensions, the file extension will not be shown.

Undocumented

Always note the difference in the naming convention — ParseName translates a regular filename into the shell's naming convention. It's your secret back door inside the shell namespace. You can't supply ParseName with the name returned by the FolderItem object. If you do, ParseName might raise an error, because it can't find a file without its extension.

Calling a file's Property page

Why would you benefit from accessing files and folders through the shell? Because the shell can do some extra tricks the Scripting.FileSystemObject is unable to do. For example, you can call any context menu you like. To display the Properties page of any file, use this approach:

```
' 8-16.VBS

set shell = CreateObject("Shell.Application")
```

```
filepath = "C:\MSDOS.SYS"
folder = left(filepath, InstrRev(filepath, "\"))
file = mid(filepath, InstrRev(filepath, "\")+1)

' get access to folder containing the file
set folderobj = shell.namespace(folder)
set folderitem = folderobj.ParseName(file)

' folderitem now represents your file

folderItem.InvokeVerb("Properties")
MsgBox "Properties window open"
```

You will only see the Properties window if you supply the exact context menu command displayed in the file's context menu.

Secret

If the context menu command contains an underlined shortcut character, you need to place an ampersand (&) before this character. To call a context menu command called Properties, you would call `P&roperties`.

Since the dialog box is bound to your script process, it will disappear once your script is done. This is why the script displays a `MsgBox` dialog box, as shown in Figure 8-16: It keeps your script alive so the Properties window remains visible.

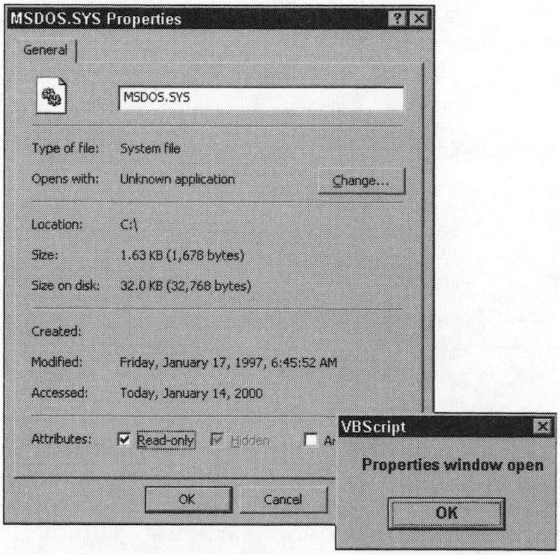

Figure 8-16: Your script has full control over Properties pages.

Note that opening the Properties page is only one example. You can call any context menu in any namespace. For example, you could list the modules of your Control Panel and offer to open the selected command panel module by calling its Open context menu.

Opening Properties windows as modal windows

Properties windows should remain open no matter what your script does. The only way to achieve this is to detach the dialog box from your script process. Although this may sound complicated, it's actually very easy. All you need to do is mimic the regular Windows behavior!

The following script opens an Internet Explorer window and keeps it invisible. It forces the window to navigate to the folder the file is contained in. A loop waits for the Internet Explorer to initialize itself. Then, the script accesses the folder object invisibly displayed in the Internet Explorer window or document.folder. It's the same kind of object your previous script accessed through namespace, only this time the object is handled by Internet Explorer, not your script.

```
' 8-17.VBS

ShowProperties "C:\MSDOS.SYS"
ShowProperties "C:\AUTOEXEC.BAT"

sub ShowProperties(filepath)
    set shell = CreateObject("Shell.Application")
    set ie = CreateObject("InternetExplorer.Application")

    folder = left(filepath, InstrRev(filepath, "\"))
    file = mid(filepath, InstrRev(filepath, "\")+1)

    ie.navigate folder

    do until ie.readyState=4
    loop

    set folderobj = ie.document.folder
    set folderitem = folderobj.ParseName(file)

    ' folderitem now represents your file
    folderItem.InvokeVerb("Properties")
end sub
```

The rest of the script is identical to the previous one, in that it gets hold of the file using ParseName and calls the Properties verb. The resulting dialog box opens and remains open.

Secret

Don't worry about invisible Internet Explorer! Windows automatically closes its process the moment you close the dialog box.

Accessing context menu Commands the smart way

InvokeVerb is a very powerful method once you know the exact name of the Context menu command you must call. Unfortunately, there are no true naming standards, and keyboard shortcut &-characters can be placed anywhere inside a verb name—not to mention localized Windows versions.

Don't worry about naming conventions! The standard Context menu commands are always accessible using standard Windows names, regardless of how those commands are named in the Context menu, as shown in Table 8-8.

Table 8-8	**[Context Menu Commands]**
Command	**Description**
Properties	Properties-Command
Open	Open-Command
OpenAs	Open As-Command
Print	Print-Command

To access other commands, you can retrieve the names of supported commands using the Verbs property, and receive the names as shown in Figure 8-17.

```
' 8-18.VBS

set shell = CreateObject("Shell.Application")

filepath = "C:\MSDOS.SYS"
folder = left(filepath, InstrRev(filepath, "\"))
file = mid(filepath, InstrRev(filepath, "\")+1)

set folderobj = shell.namespace(folder)
set folderitem = folderobj.ParseName(file)

set folderitemverbs = folderitem.Verbs
for each folderitemverb in folderitemverbs
     list = list & folderitemverb.name & vbCr
next

MsgBox list
```

Figure 8-17: Retrieve the available Context menu commands.

The folderitemverbs collection returns the actual names of each Context menu command. Each folderitemverb object is organized as outlined in Table 8-9. Not only can you retrieve the name, DoIt also executes the command.

Caution

On Windows 9.x, the `Verbs` method contains a serious bug. It doesn't return a `FolderItemVerbs` object but rather a useless `FolderItemVerb` object. You can't enumerate Context menu commands on Windows 9.x.

Table 8-9   Properties and Methods of FolderItemVerb Objects

Method/Property	Description
`Property Application As Object`	Get `Application` object
`Sub DoIt`	Execute the verb
`Property Name As String`	Get display name for item
`Property Parent As Object`	Get `Parent` object

Calling Properties pages using API calls

The `Shell.Application` object only delegates your requests to common API functions. To display property pages, the direct approach has some advantages. You can easily open drive or printer Property pages, not just file Property pages. Even more interesting, if the Property page consists of more than one tab, you can also select the Active tab.

As usual, you have the choice: Either open the source code (`\components \property\property.vbs`) and compile the project yourself, or install the prepared package (`\install\property\setup.exe`).

Opening Property pages is straightforward: Create a COM object and use this code:

```
' open properties

Private Type OSVERSIONINFO
    dwOSVersionInfoSize As Long
    dwMajorVersion As Long
    dwMinorVersion As Long
    dwBuildNumber As Long
    dwPlatformID As Long
    szCSDVersion As String * 128
End Type

Private Declare Function GetVersionEx Lib "kernel32" _
Alias "GetVersionExA" (ByRef lpVersionInformation _
As OSVERSIONINFO) As Long
Private Declare Function SHObjectProperties Lib "shell32.dll" _
Alias "#178" (ByVal hwnd As Long, ByVal uflags As Long, _
ByVal lpstrname As Long, ByVal lpcstrparams As Long) As Boolean

Public Function ShowProp(ByVal filename As String, _
Optional ByVal page As String) As Boolean

Dim file As String
```

```
    Dim pagenr As Long

    ' adjust to ANSI/UNICODE
    If Not isNT Then
        ' convert to ANSI
        filename = StrConv(filename, vbFromUnicode)
        page = StrConv(page, vbFromUnicode)
    End If

    If IsMissing(page) Then
        pagenr = 0
    Else
        pagenr = StrPtr(page)
    End If

    ShowProp = SHObjectProperties(0, 2, StrPtr(filename), pagenr)
    If ShowProp = False Then
        ' try printer dialog
        ShowProp = SHObjectProperties(0, 1, StrPtr(filename), pagenr)
    End If
End Function

Public Function isNT() As Boolean
    Dim osinfo As OSVERSIONINFO
    osinfo.dwOSVersionInfoSize = Len(osinfo)

    GetVersionEx osinfo

    If osinfo.dwPlatformID = 2 Then
        isNT = True
    Else
        isNT = False
    End If
End Function
```

SHObjectProperties **is an undocumented API function — the** declare **statement must use an Alias and the direct ordinal (#178) to access this feature. As always with undocumented functions, it expects string input to be UNICODE on NT and ANSI on Win9.x. Your COM object therefore needs to find out whether it's running on NT or not. On non-NT machines, it converts the strings to ANSI using the undocumented** StrConv **function.**

```
' 8-19.VBS

set tool = CreateObject("property.tool")
MsgBox tool.ShowProp("C:\")
MsgBox tool.ShowProp("C:\MSDOS.SYS")
' adjust printer name to some installed printer:
MsgBox tool.ShowProp("HP Laserjet")
```

SHObjectProperties **can display Property pages for file system objects and for printers. Use 2 as the second argument for file system objects and 1 for printer objects. The COM object automatically tries both methods, so you can use it for both files/folders and printer names. It returns true if the Property page was opened; otherwise, it returns false, and Figure 8-18 shows the result.**

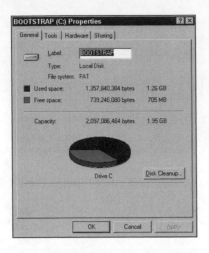

Figure 8-18: Open Property pages for drives, files, and printers using the API directly.

However, if you specify a file or folder that doesn't exist, you will always end up with a printer error message. If you don't like this, split the procedure in two and use individual methods for file system and printer objects.

Your new ShowProp method can do a trick no other method is capable of: You can preselect a tab on the Property page. Supply the name of the tab as a second argument. For example, to open the Shared tab for drive C:, use this command:

```
tool.ShowProp "C:\", "Sharing"
```

Note

SHObjectProperties displays modeless dialog boxes. They are visible only as long as your script is running. Here, there's no easy way to attach the dialog box to another process. However, if you use 4 as the second argument, SHObjectProperties displays modal dialog boxes for drives only. They halt your script so you can wait for the user to make some selection. You can use this trick only for drives. It won't work for files, folders, or printers.

Summary

In this chapter, you used many undocumented Windows API functions to create handy little script extensions, to copy and compress files, and even to create entire backup sets. These functions allow you to delete items to the Recycle Bin, empty the Recycle Bin, or format drives—all previously impossible for your scripts. You are now also able to retrieve extended file version information, finding out the purpose of internal Windows files. A new secret back door to the shell allows you to access folders and files the way the Windows Explorer does it, allowing you to call Context menu commands and display Properties windows. This chapter clarifies many of the advanced techniques and shows how COM objects can return information objects and how undocumented API functions can be called by any Windows version, automatically solving the UNICODE/ANSI conflict.

Chapter 9

Mastering Links

In This Chapter

▶ Learn more about the power of shortcut files

▶ Createand modify shortcut files by script

▶ Search for invalid links and duplicating keyboard shortcuts

▶ Change shortcut icons dynamically

▶ Preselect a shortcut's window size

▶ Use the hidden `Shell Link` object to resolve broken links

▶ Discover the undocumented link resolving mechanism and the new Windows 2000 Distributed Link Tracking Service

▶ Open a shortcut target's Properties page

▶ Mark a shortcut target file in the Explorer

Now that you know how to handle your file system, take a look at link files. In this chapter, you learn what link files are and how to use them to customize menus. You also learn how to create new link files from scratch and how to check existing link files for errors. Using secret API functions, you can even automatically repair broken link files.

Why Do I Need Links Anyway?

Links are small but extremely powerful files. They represent files, folders, and system objects located somewhere else. Links build the foundation of customizing Windows. Links make the Programs menu work. To see how important links really are, start a search for `*.LNK`.

Scripts can use links to place themselves in important places. You can add your script to the Start menu, place it into the Send To folder, or insert a reference into the Startup folder. In addition, scripts can use their link functions for maintenance. Scripts can search for links, check whether their destinations are still valid, and sort out any broken links.

More importantly, scripts can check the internal keyboard shortcuts and make sure there are no duplicate entries. Windows doesn't check for this, allowing you to assign multiple keyboard shortcuts to more than one link file, or even to override important built-in Windows shortcuts — resulting in erroneous behavior.

By using some undocumented Windows magic, you can even resolve broken links and mark files and folders.

Creating a new link file

The WScript.Shell object contains all the methods needed for managing links. The following example asks for a name and places a shortcut to the Windows editor right on your desktop:

```
' 9-1.VBS

set wshshell = CreateObject("WScript.Shell")
desktop = wshshell.SpecialFolders("desktop")

linkname = InputBox("What do you want to call your new link?", _
,"Windows Editor")

target = "notepad.exe"
linkname = desktop & "\" & linkname & ".lnk"

' create new shortcut object
set scut = wshshell.CreateShortcut(linkname)

' fill in information
scut.TargetPath = target

' save shortcut object
scut.Save

MsgBox "Done - new shortcut on your desktop!"
```

Take a look at your desktop. The script adds a new shortcut and, when you open it, launches the editor.

Examining the shortcut object

All this magic was done with the help of a shortcut object. A shortcut object represents the internal properties of a link file. CreateShortcut is your secret key to the shortcut object. It always returns a shortcut object. If you specified a link file that doesn't yet exist, the new shortcut object is empty. However, you can easily access the hidden properties of existing shortcuts. Just specify an existing shortcut file path.

Secret

`CreateShortcut` will fail if the specified file name doesn't carry the `.link` file extension. The resulting shortcut object is not the actual shortcut. It's just an information object stored somewhere in memory. To write the properties of the shortcut object back to the actual shortcut file, you must call the object's `Save` method.

Table 9-1 shows how shortcut objects are organized.

Table 9-1	The Shortcut Object
Property/Method	**Description**
`Property Arguments As String`	Additional command-line arguments you want to pass to the target file
`Property Description As String`	Optional descriptive information about what this shortcut is used for
`Property FullName As String`	Full path name of the link file (undocumented)
`Property Hotkey As String`	Keyboard shortcut
`Property IconLocation As String`	Display icon of the shortcut
`Property RelativePath As String`	Not fully supported (undocumented)
`Sub Save`	Saves the information to the shortcut
`Property TargetPath As String`	Path name of the shortcut target file
`Property WindowStyle As Long`	Type of window the shortcut should open
`Property WorkingDirectory As String`	Initial directory setting

Accessing Existing Link Files

`CreateShortcut` is somewhat misleading, as it doesn't create a shortcut file. It creates a shortcut object. You can easily manage existing link files using `CreateShortcut` and reveal their internal properties.

Searching for invalid links

The next script checks your entire Programs menu and reports any invalid links. Figure 9-1 shows the result.

Caution

For your convenience, the script offers to delete invalid links. Before you delete something, always think twice. Shortcut targets on network drives or targets to disk drives may not currently be available but may still be useful. Check the message dialog box carefully before you decide to clean up your Programs menu!

```
' 9-2.VBS

set wshshell = CreateObject("WScript.Shell")
set fs = CreateObject("Scripting.FileSystemObject")

' global variables
num_checked = 0
num_error = 0
num_deleted = 0

programs = wshshell.SpecialFolders("programs")
set folderobj = fs.GetFolder(programs)
CheckFolder folderobj

msg = "I have checked " & num_checked & " links." & vbCr
msg = msg & "I found " & num_error & " invalid links." & vbCr
msg = msg & "You asked me to delete " & num_deleted & " links"
MsgBox msg, vbInformation

sub CheckFolder(folderobj)
    for each file in folderobj.files
        ext = lcase(fs.GetExtensionName(file.name))
        if ext = "lnk" then
            num_checked = num_checked + 1
            set scut = wshshell.CreateShortcut(file.path)
            target = scut.TargetPath
            if not fs.FileExists(target) then
                num_error = num_error + 1
                msg = "Link """ & file.path & """ points to """ _
& target & """" & vbCr
                msg = msg & "The target no longer exists! Do " _
& "you want to delete the link?"
                response = MsgBox(msg, vbQuestion + vbYesNo _
+ vbDefaultButton2)
                if response = vbYes then
                    num_deleted = num_deleted + 1
                    file.delete
                end if
            end if
        end if
    next

    for each subfolder in folderobj.subfolders
        CheckFolder subfolder
    next
end sub
```

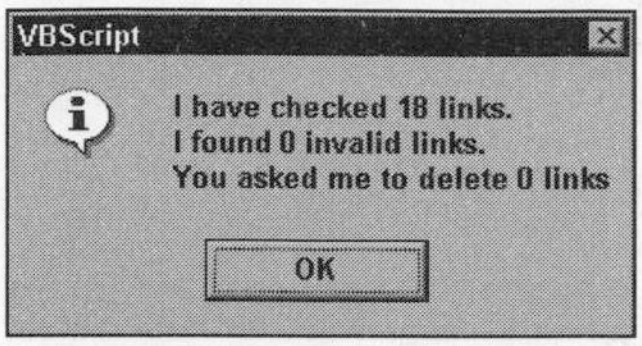

Figure 9-1: Check for invalid and outdated links in your Programs menu.

Finding (and eliminating) duplicate keyboard shortcuts

Keyboard shortcuts are extremely useful—after all, any shortcut file with a keyboard shortcut can be invoked just by pressing the keys you specify. Just right-click on a link file and choose Properties. Then enter your keyboard shortcut in the shortcut text field and click OK.

But, this doesn't always work!

Keyboard shortcuts can launch files only if the shortcut is located either on your desktop or inside the Programs menu. These are the only places Windows looks for keyboard shortcuts. It would just take much too long to check all link files anywhere in the file system.

Undocumented

One of the most annoying reasons for failure is duplicate shortcut keys. Windows doesn't make any effort to prevent you from assigning new keyboard shortcuts that are already in use by some other link file. Once you have multiple link files using the same key combination, it's up to Windows which file will be launched.

Even worse, it's possible to override Windows' internal shortcuts. If you assign [F1] to a link file, this key will no longer invoke Windows help.

It's very hard to resolve duplicate keyboard shortcuts because Windows can't list the shortcuts in use. You would have to open the Properties page of each and every link file manually to look for shortcuts. That's too much work. The following script creates a shortcut list automatically and presents the result as an HTML file similar to the one shown in Figure 9-2.

```
' 9-3.VBS

set wshshell = CreateObject("WScript.Shell")
set fs = CreateObject("Scripting.FileSystemObject")
startmenu = wshshell.SpecialFolders("startmenu")
desktop = wshshell.SpecialFolders("desktop")

outputfile = "C:\LINKLIST.HTM"
dim links(1000,1)
counter = 0
```

```
CheckFolder fs.GetFolder(desktop), false
CheckFolder fs.GetFolder(startmenu), true

for x=0 to counter-1
    for y=x+1 to counter-2
        if links(x,1)>links(y,1) then
            temp = links(x,1)
            links(x,1) = links(y,1)
            links(y,1) = temp
            temp = links(x,0)
            links(x,0) = links(y,0)
            links(y,0) = temp
        end if
    next
next

set output = fs.CreateTextFile(outputfile, true)
output.WriteLine "<html><body>"
output.WriteLine "<H3>List of Shortcut Hotkeys</H3>"
output.WriteLine "<p>" & counter & " hotkeys found.</p>"
output.WriteLine "<table border=1>"
for x= 0 to counter-1
    output.WriteLine "<tr><td>" & links(x,1) & "</td><td>" _
& links(x,0) & "</td></tr>"
next
output.WriteLine "</table></body></html>"
output.close

wshshell.run "iexplore.exe " & outputfile

sub CheckFolder(folderobj, subdirs)
    for each file in folderobj.files
        ext = lcase(fs.GetExtensionName(file.name))
        if ext = "lnk" then
            set scut = wshshell.CreateShortcut(file.path)
            hotkey = scut.HotKey
            if not (hotkey="" or hotkey="!") then
                links(counter,0) = file.path
                    links(counter,1) = hotkey
                    counter = counter + 1
            end if
        end if
    next

    if subdirs then
        for each subfolder in folderobj.subfolders
            CheckFolder subfolder, subdirs
        next
    end if
end sub
```

A bubble-like algorithm sorts the keyboard shortcuts, so duplicate entries are easy to recognize. Note that this script searches for links only on the desktop and inside the Start menu, as these are the only places where keyboard shortcuts work.

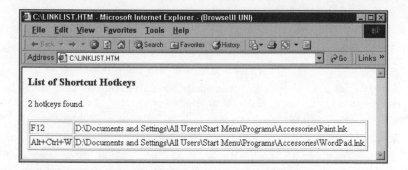

Figure 9-2: Build a list of keyboard shortcuts and find duplicate entries.

The script searches recursively only in the Start menu. Subfolders on the desktop won't be searched.

Undocumented

Undefined HotKey entries return either an empty string or "!". Some special characters such as "ö" will not be shown by the HotKey property. Instead, you only see the modifier keys. Take a look at the file's Properties page to see the actual shortcut key.

To eliminate duplicate shortcuts, just open the Properties page and delete the shortcut entry.

Changing a Shortcut Icon

By default, Windows uses the file that the `TargetPath` property points to as an icon resource. You don't need to accept this default. Just specify your own icon file as `IconLocation` property. This is especially useful if you plan to insert scripts into the Start menu or the Send To folder.

Where do you get icons to choose from? The Windows system folder is filled with icon resources you can use. Or, you can create your very own personal icons! It's all possible.

Borrowing system icons

System icons hide in files like `shell32.dll` or `moricons.dll`. To specify an icon, supply `IconLocation` with the filename and icon index: for example, `shell32.dll,2`.

How do you know which files to pick, though? Not every file is a good icon resource, but I've prepared many icon tools for you. You can get a head start by jumping to Chapter 22. Or use the following script—it uses the `ListView` control along with the Icon Picker dialog box, both of which you created in Chapter 6. Make sure you install both `\install\listview\setup.exe` and `\install\iconpick\setup.exe` from the companion CD before you launch `script 9-4.vbs`.

This script automatically changes the icon of any link file. Drag a link file onto the script icon.

Note

It may take some seconds for the script to search for available icons. Be patient, have cup of coffee, and relax. Your reward is a huge list of available icons. It will provide you with many more choices than the official dialog box could ever offer.

First, the script searches both your Windows folder and the system folder for files that contain at least three icons. This can take some seconds. Next, it displays all icon files as shown in Figure 9-3 so you can select one. The Icon Picker dialog box then displays the icons stored in the selected file. Figure 9-4 shows the result. Choose an icon, or choose Cancel to select a different icon file.

Icons available	Icon Library
shell32.dll	108
moricons.dll	107
compstui.dll	99
netshell.dll	62
progman.exe	49
mmsys.cpl	39
pifmgr.dll	38
cdplayer.exe	35
dsuiext.dll	34
inetcpl.cpl	34
stobject.dll	33
setupapi.dll	32
shdocvw.dll	31
msdtcprx.dll	28
msdxm.ocx	28
msihnd.dll	28
rasdlg.dll	27
ntbackup.exe	26
cscdll.dll	22
mshtml.dll	22
cryptui.dll	19
regwizc.dll	18

Figure 9-3: A ListView lists all the icon files available on your system.

```
' 9-4.VBS

set fs = CreateObject("Scripting.FileSystemObject")

' any arguments supplied?
set args = WScript.Arguments
if args.Count=0 then
    MsgBox "Drag a link file on my icon to see me at work!"
    WScript.Quit
elseif lcase(fs.GetExtensionName(args(0)))<>"lnk" then
```

```
        MsgBox "I only accept link files (shortcuts)!"
        WScript.Quit
end if

' access COM objects:
set iconpick = CreateObject("iconpicker.tool")
set lview = CreateObject("listview.tool")
set wshshell = CreateObject("WScript.Shell")

' find out icon library folders:
set windir = fs.GetSpecialFolder(0)
set sysdir = fs.GetSpecialFolder(1)

' initialize list view:
lview.width = 600
lview.height = 400
lview.AddHeader "Icons available", 30
lview.AddHeader "Icon Library", 70
lview.MultiEdit = true


' build list of available icons
PopulateList windir
PopulateList sysdir

' Sort by icon count:
lview.Sort 1, 1

do
    ' Select Icon Lib:
    set result = lview.Show("Extended Information: " & name)

    if result.Count>0 then
    ' extract library file name
    lib = Split(result(1), vbCrLf)
    libname = lib(0)
    else
        libname = ""
    end if

    ' library selected? good:
    if not libname="" then
        ' show icons in library:
        icon = iconpick.PickIcon(libname)
    end if
' loop until either icon is chosen or library
' selection was cancelled:
loop until libname = "" or not icon=""

' did user select an icon?
if not icon="" then
    ' yes: access selected shortcut:
    set scut = wshshell.CreateShortcut(args(0))
```

```
    ' change icon and save information
    scut.IconLocation = icon
    scut.Save
    MsgBox "Changed link file icon!"
else
    MsgBox "You did not specify an icon..."
end if

sub PopulateList(folderobj)
    ' search for icon files in entire folder
    for each file in folderobj.files
        ' how many icons are stored in file?
        iconcount = iconpick.CountIcons(file.path)
        if iconcount>2 then
            ' pad icon count with spaces so
' sorting as string works
            iconcount = right(space(10) & iconcount, 10)
            lview.AddItem file.name
                lview.AddSubItem 1, iconcount
        end if
    next
end sub
```

Figure 9-4: The Icon Picker dialog box lists the icons available.

Once you have selected an icon, the script changes the shortcut's IconLocation property to the selected icon. Figure 9-5 shows the final result: Your shortcut file has changed its icon!

Note

This script will only work if you have properly registered both the Listview tool and the icon picker tool. You can find convenient setup.exe packages for both tools on the companion CD. Should you receive "Can't create object" error messages, install both setup.exe files: \install\listview\setup.exe and \install\iconpick\setup.exe.

Depending on the number of files in your Windows and system folders, it may take up to a minute for the script to collect all icon files. Be a little patient! In Chapter 22, I present a way to conserve the list of icon files in a text file. This way, you can open the icon library list much more rapidly.

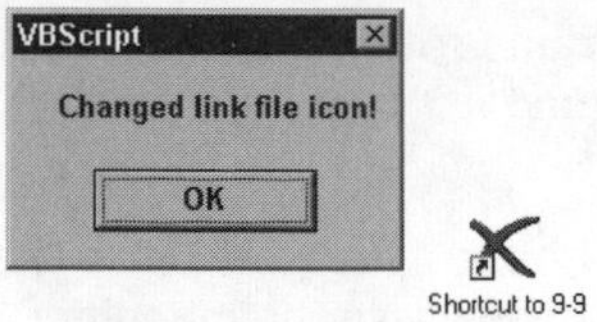

Figure 9-5: Your shortcut object has received a new icon.

Note also that the icon index depends on the Windows version you use. The Icon index is a simple counter that selects the icon based on its position inside the icon file. Microsoft changes the icon order frequently, so the same index number may select different icons on different Windows versions.

Undocumented

Aside from the icon index, there are fixed icon resource identifiers. They don't change with Windows versions, because they uniquely identify a specific icon. Resource identifiers are used just the way you use icon indices but are negative numbers. Unfortunately, there's no easy way to find out the resource identifier of an icon—you either know it or you don't.

Changing your program menu's icons

Your new link file icon-changer works perfectly well for any link file. Because your Program menu contains link files, it's an excellent way to spice up both your Start menu and Program menu.

Just drag any custom Start menu or Program menu entry onto your script. This is all you need to do to assign completely new icons to any entry.

Tip

You can only change link file icons this way. If you want to change the icons of built-in Start menu commands, such as Help or Run or folder icons, take a look at Chapter 22. Drag-and-drop doesn't work on Windows 95/NT systems without IE4 desktop update. But, you still can right-click on the Start button and choose Open. This way, you can access the Start menu and Program menu content directly. Just drag the link file out of the Explorer window onto your script icon. Don't drop the link file anywhere else or you will move the file out of the menus. [Strg]+[Z] reverts any accidental move.

Creating your own icons

You don't need to stick to system icons. A plain bitmap file can act as an icon, too. This is why you can use the built-in Windows paint program to create your own icons.

Launch Paint from the Accessories program group. If it's missing, install it from your Windows CD using the Add/Remove Programs module in the Control Panel.

First, you should resize the paint area. Choose Attributes from the Image menu, then limit the paint area to 32×32 pixels. Use the magnifier tool to magnify the drawing area.

Now, paint your icon! When you are finished, save your new icon. Be careful: To be recognized as an icon, you must save the file with the .ico file extension. Save your graphic as C:\test.ico!

Undocumented

On Windows 9.x, white automatically is converted to "transparent," so your icons behave like "real" icons. On Windows 2000, the white background is converted to black, so here your homemade icons aren't as useful.

Next, you can use your self-made icon file for your links:

```
' 9-5.VBS

set wshshell = CreateObject("WScript.Shell")
desktop = wshshell.SpecialFolders("desktop")
linkfile = desktop & "\My own icon!.lnk"

set scut = wshshell.CreateShortcut(linkfile)
scut.TargetPath = "notepad.exe"
scut.IconLocation = "C:\icon2.ico"
scut.Save

MsgBox "Link saved."
```

Inserting Scripts into Special Places

Links are a perfect tool to introduce your scripts into special places. For example, if you want your script to automatically change the Windows startup screen each time you launch Windows, place a shortcut to this script into your Startup folder. Windows will automatically launch your script on startup.

Cross-Reference

Read more about autostarting your scripts in Chapter 13.

Starting scripts automatically

How do you place your script's reference into the Startup program group? Easy. The next script demonstrates the technique:

```
' 9-6.VBS

set wshshell = CreateObject("WScript.Shell")
set fs = CreateObject("Scripting.FileSystemObject")

startup = wshshell.SpecialFolders("startup")
linkname = startup & "\mywelcome.lnk"
if not fs.FileExists(linkname) then
    set scut = wshshell.CreateShortcut(linkname)
    scut.Targetpath = WScript.ScriptFullName
    scut.Save
    MsgBox "I inserted myself into the Startup group!"
else
    ' do the stuff you want to be done at windows launch
    MsgBox "Hey, I'm the Scripting Host! Use me!"
end if
```

This script combines both the startup registration and the actual commands you want to be executed at Windows startup. The script checks whether it is registered in the Startup program group. If so, it executes its code. If not, it places a shortcut to itself into the startup group and displays a message similar to the one shown in Figure 9-6.

VBScript	☒
I inserted myself into the Startup group!	
OK	

Figure 9-6: Insert scripts into your Startup program group.

SpecialFolders("startup") reveals the path name to your Startup group, and WScript.ScriptFullName returns your script's path name.

Autostarting any script

Obviously, it's a waste of CPU power to check whether or not the script is already placed into the Startup group every time. For this reason, it's better to delegate the registration to a separate script.

Secret

If at all possible, don't place more than one script into your Startup group. Starting many scripts at the same time can cause trouble. While a script accesses a COM object, this COM object may not be accessible to other scripts. If you must autostart more than one script, place a "loader script" into your StartUp group and remove any other reference to scripts. This loader script will then use the WScript.Shell's Run method to subsequently call any needed scripts. Use the Run's third argument and provide true so that Run waits for each script to end before it calls the next.

Building your own installation scripts

Use the techniques just outlined to create your own script-install procedures. After all, these techniques do more than allow you to place script references into the Startup group. With the help of `Scripting.FileSystemObject`, you can easily create new folders that act as new program groups. Also, `SpecialFolders` ("programs") returns the path of your Program menu, so your installation script can create entirely new program groups and place your script references inside them. With your knowledge about link icons and the `IconLocation` property, you can even assign new and exciting icons to your program group items.

Using scripts as a Send To extension

Thanks to the built-in drag-and-drop capabilities, your scripts can act as extensions to the Send To Context menu. To be able to recognize the `SendTo's` arguments, your script only needs to query the Arguments collection. This allows you to create your own "Send to anywhere" commands. The script copies the files themselves. The built-in `SendTo` targets follow Windows' process — they will copy if the target is located on a different drive and will move if both source and target drive are the same.

The next script sends any file you drag onto it to any drive or folder you select. For this script to work, you need to register the `BrowseForFolder` extension first. Take a look at Chapter 6, or install the extension from the companion CD, using `\install\folderpicker\setup.exe`.

```
' 9-7

set args = WScript.Arguments
if args.Count=0 then
    MsgBox "You did not drag any file on me..."
    WScript.Quit
end if

' get access to browse dialog
set browse = CreateObject("folder.tools")
set fs = CreateObject("Scripting.FileSystemObject")

' select destination
' open "My Computer" to select drive/folder
destination = browse.BrowseForFolder(17, _
"Where do you want to copy the file(s)?")

' check whether destination is valid
```

```
if destination="" then
    MsgBox "You did not choose a valid destination for this
operation!"
    WScript.Quit
end if

' add "\" if missing:
if not right(destination,1)="\" then destination = destination & "\"

' is selected destination a valid drive/folder?
if not fs.FolderExists(destination) then
    MsgBox """" & destination & """ is no valid file system folder!"
else
    ' try to copy all selected files:
    for each filename in args
        ' does file exist?
        if fs.FileExists(filename) then
            ' overwrite condition?
            nameonly = mid(filename, InstrRev(filename, "\")+1)
            destname = destination & nameonly
            ' file already exist? Ask before overwriting anything:
            if fs.FileExists(destname) then
                result = MsgBox("File """ & destname _
& """ already exists! Overwrite?", _
vbYesNo + vbExclamation)
            else
                ' new file, always copy:
                result = vbYes
            end if

            if result = vbYes then
                ' copy file
                fs.CopyFile filename, destination
                msg = msg & filename & " -> " & destination _
& " copied..." & vbCr
            else
                msg = msg & filename & _
" already exists. Not copied..." & vbCr
            end if
        else
            msg = msg & filename & _
" is no valid file name, not copied..." _
& vbCr
end if
    next
    MsgBox msg, vbInformation
end if
```

This script works nicely, and with it, you can drag any file onto your script icon to copy it. The browser dialog box in Figure 9-7 makes it easy to select the destination folder. But how do you get it inside the Send To menu?

Figure 9-7: Send files anywhere with your new `SendTo` command.

Use the following script to drag the previous script onto its icon. This creates a link and saves it in the special Send To folder. From now on, to send a file anyplace, right-click it and choose Send To, and then choose Anywhere. Your new command will appear in the Send To Context menu. Figure 9-8 shows the result.

```
' 9-8.VBS

set args = WScript.Arguments
if args.Count=0 then
     MsgBox "You did not drag any file on me..."
     WScript.Quit
end if

set wshshell = CreateObject("WScript.Shell")
name = InputBox("How do you want to name your new command?", _
     , "Copy anywhere")
linkfile = wshshell.SpecialFolders("sendto") & "\" _
& name & ".lnk"

set scut = wshshell.CreateShortcut(linkfile)
scut.TargetPath = args(0)
scut.IconLocation = "shell32.dll,13"
scut.Save

MsgBox "Placed command in Send To Folder!"
```

Figure 9-8: Send files anywhere using your new script command extension.

Advanced Shortcut Tricks

There's still more to discover — passing arguments to link targets, using Internet links, and determining the window style a link will use, to mention just a few. Although none of these tricks are needed in everyday life, they may help you with some specific problems.

Providing optional arguments

Sometimes it's necessary to provide arguments for your link. For example, you might want to open folders using hidden Internet Explorer options. Assign these options to the shortcut object Arguments property. The following script places a link on your desktop. This link opens your private My Documents folder in two-pane Explorer view and limits the Explorer to this folder. Figure 9-9 shows how much better this special folder organizes your personal files and folders.

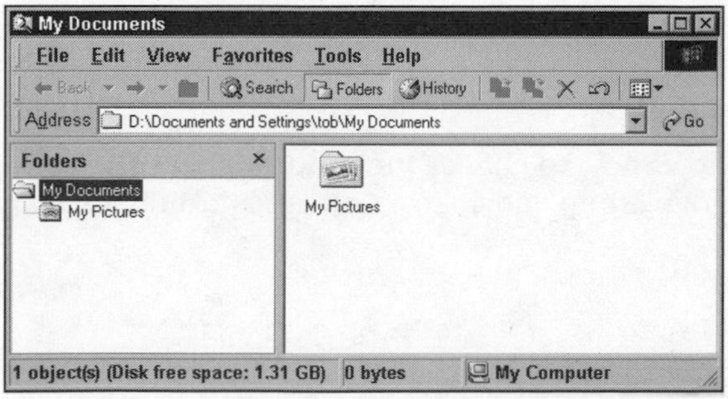

Figure 9-9: Special Internet Explorer options allow you to limit the tree view to special folders.

Undocumented

Never use additional arguments with the `TargetPath` property. The `Target Path` should point to the target file path only. Older WSH versions on Windows 9.x didn't care about this and allowed you to include arguments with `Target Path`. On Windows 2000, however, this will cause serious errors. Therefore, always place additional arguments into the `Arguments` property.

```
' 9-9.VBS

set wshshell = CreateObject("WScript.Shell")
desktop = wshshell.SpecialFolders("desktop")
personal = wshshell.SpecialFolders("MyDocuments")

set scut = wshshell.CreateShortcut(desktop & "\MyDocs.lnk")
scut.TargetPath = "explorer.exe"
scut.Arguments = "/e,/root," & personal
scut.IconLocation = "shell32.dll,20"
scut.Save

MsgBox "New link created on your desktop."
```

Selecting a new window size

Links can open the target file using different window styles. You can control whether the target file is opened in a minimized, normal, or maximized window. This is especially useful if you plan to launch shortcuts automatically using the StartUp program group. To prevent screen cluttering, it's best to open those shortcuts in minimized windows. This way, when you start Windows, the autostart applications will nicely align in the taskbar and leave your desktop untouched.

First, take a look at your options in Table 9-2:

Table 9-2	Window Styles Used With Shortcuts
Option	**Description**
1	Window is normal size.
3	Window is maximized.
7	Window is minimized — best for autostarts.

The next script shows how to change the window style. The script accesses your Startup program group and changes all autostart links to minimized windows:

```
' 9-10.VBS

set wshshell = CreateObject("WScript.Shell")
```

```
set fs = CreateObject("Scripting.FileSystemObject")
autostart = wshshell.SpecialFolders("startup")

set folder = fs.GetFolder(autostart)
for each file in folder.files
    ext = lcase(fs.GetExtensionName(file.name))
    if ext="lnk" then
        set scut = wshshell.CreateShortcut(file.path)
        scut.WindowStyle = 7
        scut.Save
        counter = counter + 1
    end if
next
MsgBox "Changed " & counter & " shortcuts to minimized style."
```

This script will only change shortcuts in your personal StartUp folder. On Windows NT/2000, you might find additional shortcuts in the special StartUp folder for all users. To access these shortcuts, use `SpecialFolders`("AllUsersStartup").

Undocumented

The window styles outlined in Table 9-2 are only a subset of all available window styles. The shortcut object limits you to three alternatives. If you provide different numbers, they will be converted to 1.

Accessing the shell link object

The shell again has its very own way of handling link files. To access a link file, use the following approach:

```
set wshshell = CreateObject("WScript.Shell")
desktop = wshshell.SpecialFolders("desktop")

' create dummy link the conventional way
linkfile = desktop & "\testlink.lnk"
set scut = wshshell.CreateShortcut(linkfile)
scut.TargetPath = "notepad.exe"
scut.Save

' access link via Shell
set linkobj = GetLink(linkfile)
MsgBox "I received object: " & TypeName(linkobj)


function GetLink(name)
set shell = CreateObject("Shell.Application")
    folder = left(name, InstrRev(name, "\"))
    file = mid(name, InstrRev(name, "\")+1)

    set folderobj = shell.NameSpace(folder)
    set folderitem = folderobj.ParseName(file)
    if folderitem.isLink then
        set GetLink = folderitem.GetLink
```

```
      else
            set GetLink = Nothing
      end if
end function
```

Why would you take the extra effort to access a link through the shell? One example is to resolve links. The shell offers many extra tricks that the WScript.Shell link methods can't provide. Let's take a look at the shell's link object first.

Examining the shell's link object

Table 9-3 shows how a shell link object is organized. Its official name is IshellLink:

Table 9-3   The Shell Link Object

Property/Method	Description
Property Arguments As String	Get the arguments for the link
Property Description As String	Get the description for the link
Function GetIconLocation (pbs As String) As Long	Get the IconLocation for the link
Property Hotkey As Long	Get the Hotkey for the link
Property Path As String	Get the target path of the link
Sub Resolve(ByVal fFlags As Long)	Tell the link to resolve itself
Sub Save([ByVal vWhere])	Tell the link to save the changes
Sub SetIconLocation (ByVal bs As String, ByVal iIcon As Long)	Set the IconLocation for the link
Property ShowCommand As Long	Get the Show Command for the link (the kind of window the link opens)
Property WorkingDirectory As String	Get the working directory for the link

Many methods correspond to the methods of the WScript.Shell shortcut object. But there's more—what about Resolve?

Resolving links

Links are fragile. Once you move the target file to another place—or yet worse, delete it—the link is helpless. In these situations, the shell tries to resolve the link. Resolving means the shell tries to track where the target file has been moved and adjusts the link's target appropriately. You can easily view this process by creating a new text file on your desktop and then right-clicking the file and choosing Create Shortcut. Then, delete the text file. The shortcut is still there, and once you open it, the shell displays a dialog box while it searches for the target.

Undocumented

Windows 2000 does a much better job in link resolving. The built-in Distributed Link Tracking (DLT) service keeps track of moved files and can easily determine the correct new position as long as the file still exists. In this case, you won't see any dialog boxes. Windows changes the link target silently in the background. In order to see the resolve dialog box, you must delete the target file.

Above, you saw how your scripts can browse through your links and check the target. So far, your scripts haven't been able to repair damaged links. They could only offer to delete them. A little later in this chapter, you learn additional methods that allow your scripts to resolve links the way the shell does.

Resolving is accomplished through the Resolve method. This is how you resolve a link:

```
' 9-12.VBS

set wshshell = CreateObject("WScript.Shell")
desktop = wshshell.SpecialFolders("desktop")

' change this line to the name of the link you want to resolve!
linkfile = desktop & "\testlink.lnk"
set linkobj = GetLink(linkfile)
linkobj.Resolve(4)

function GetLink(name)
set shell = CreateObject("Shell.Application")
    folder = left(name, InstrRev(name, "\"))
    file = mid(name, InstrRev(name, "\")+1)

    set folderobj = shell.NameSpace(folder)
    set folderitem = folderobj.ParseName(file)
    if folderitem.isLink then
        set GetLink = folderitem.GetLink
    else
        set GetLink = Nothing
    end if
end function
```

To test this script, change the link name to a test link you place on your desktop, and then remove the link's target file. The script expects a link named testlink to be on your desktop.

Unfortunately, the script is not very helpful, because if the link's target exists, it won't do a thing. If the link's target is missing, it won't resolve it. Instead, it complains about the missing link, as shown in Figure 9-10.

Secret

The dialog box shown during link resolving needs a parent window. Your script doesn't have a window, so the shell can't display its progress window; instead, it pops up its complaint. It won't resolve the link unless you either provide a window or turn off the progress dialog box.

> **Problem with Shortcut**
>
> The drive or network connection that the shortcut 'testlink.lnk' refers to is unavailable. Make sure that the disk is properly inserted or the network resource is available, and then try again.
>
> OK

Figure 9-10: So far, the Resolve method won't resolve your link.

To make your script work, you need to turn off the shell's user interface. This is done through flags. Table 9-4 presents the complete list of flags.

Table 9-4   Flags for Link Resolving

Flag	Description
1	NO_UI: don't show progress dialog box while resolving a link
2	ANY_MATCH: not used anymore
4	UPDATE: update the link's target property with the found alternative target
8	NOUPDATE: don't update the link
16	NOSEARCH: don't use the search heuristics
32	NOTRACK: don't use Windows 2000 object tracking (Win2000 only)
64	NOLINKINFO: don't use the net and volume relative info
128	INVOKE_MSI: If the link is part of an application, invoke the Windows Installer to (re)install the missing application part (Win2000 only).

Because you don't have a dialog box informing you about the newly found target, your script will need to take care of it. This script checks a link's target, resolves the link if the target is missing, and asks for your permission to change the target:

```vbs
' 9-13.VBS

' where's my desktop?
set wshshell = CreateObject("WScript.Shell")
desktop = wshshell.SpecialFolders("desktop")

' change this line to the name of the link you want to resolve!
linkfile = desktop & "\testlink.lnk"

' check target of this linkfile and resolve if necessary!
ResolveLink linkfile

sub ResolveLink(name)
set shell = CreateObject("Shell.Application")
    set fs = CreateObject("Scripting.FileSystemObject")

    ' split path in folder and file
    folder = left(name, InstrRev(name, "\"))
    file = mid(name, InstrRev(name, "\")+1)

    ' access file through shell:
    set folderobj = shell.NameSpace(folder)
    set folderitem = folderobj.ParseName(file)

    ' check whether it really is a shortcut:
    if folderitem.isLink then
        ' get link object
        set linkobj = folderitem.GetLink
        ' remember old target:
        oldtarget = linkobj.Path
        ' old target still valid?
        if fs.FileExists(oldtarget) then
            ' yes, nothing else to do: exit
            exit sub
        end if

        ' target invalid? Resolve!
        ' use flag 1 to disable user interface
        ' don't use update flag 4 yet! First ask if ok!
        linkobj.Resolve(1)

        ' read new target
        newtarget = linkobj.Path
        msg = "Link """ & name & """ points to """ _
& oldtarget & """" & vbCr
        msg = msg & "This target doesn't exist any longer. " & vbCr

        ' no new target found? Then get rid of this link!
        if oldtarget = newtarget then
            msg = msg & "Do you want to delete the link?"
            result = MsgBox(msg, vbYesNo + vbExclamation)
            if result = vbYes then
                fs.DeleteFile name
```

```
                  end if
            else
                  ' new target found!
                  msg = msg & "I've determined that """ & newtarget _
& """ resembles the lost target the best." & vbCr
                  msg = msg & "Do you want me to adjust the target?"
                  result = MsgBox(msg, vbYesNo + vbQuestion)

                  ' if user allowed update, call Save method to
                  ' activate new settings in link:
                  if result = vbYes then
                        linkobj.Save
                  end if
end if
      end if
end sub
```

Note how the script makes use of the Resolve flags. It uses flag 1 to turn off the dialog box. This is the only way to start the resolving process unless you provide a window for the dialog box (see the following section). Don't use flag 4 to update your shortcut.

If you do so, Windows will automatically change your link's target path and working directory. Because your script first wants to ask for permission, it doesn't use automatic update. After the user has given his or her okay in the dialog box, as shown in Figure 9-11, the script calls the link object Save method (if a new target was identified) or removes the link.

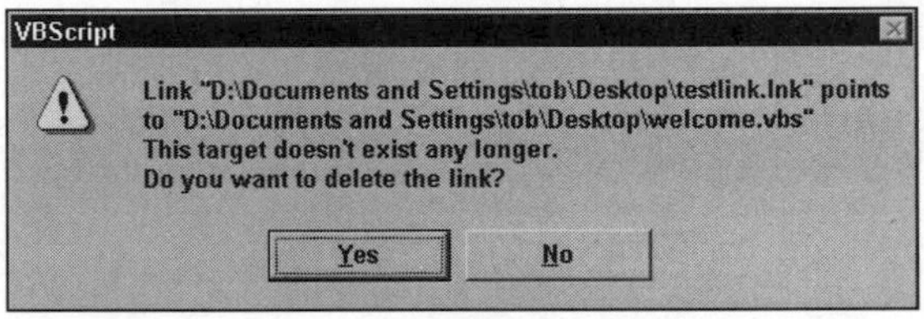

Figure 9-11: Your script uses its own user interface to present the results.

Background: How Windows resolves links

How does Windows resolve a link anyway? Let's have a look:

■ On Windows 2000, it first asks the Distributed Link Tracking Service. This service tracks all file movements and is a very quick and safe way of updating links. If you don't want to use DLTS, use Resolve with the NOTRACK flag.

- If DLTS doesn't find the file, or if you are using Windows 9.x or NT, Windows invokes its search heuristics. It looks in the target's last known directory to find a file with a different name but with the same attributes and file-creation time. If it isn't successful, it recursively searches subdirectories for a file with the target's name and creation date. If still not successful, it looks on the desktop and other local volumes. Search heuristics take a long time and are not very dependable. Whenever you use search heuristics to resolve a link, you must double-check the result manually. To avoid search heuristics, use the NOSEARCH flag.

- If both approaches fail, the system opens a dialog box and asks for your help. You now can manually choose the new target file. Most of the time, this is absolutely useless because the user won't know the new target destination either. The dialog box is only shown if you did not use the NO_UI flag. You will never see this dialog box with any of the scripts above.

Through the Resolve flags, you have tight control over the resolution process. For example, on Windows 2000 systems, you might want to automatically resolve with DLTS only, as search heuristics are not a dependable mechanism — specify NOSEARCH and NO_UI.

Using the official link resolving dialog box

The question still remains — why can't your scripts use the official Resolve dialog box? Things would become so much easier, and while the system searched for a link target, the user would see a progress indicator.

You can! Just provide a window the dialog box can access. This window doesn't need to be visible. The following script uses a hidden Internet Explorer window and can finally resolve links exactly the way the shell does it — see Figure 9-12.

```
' 9-14.VBS

set wshshell = CreateObject("WScript.Shell")
desktop = wshshell.SpecialFolders("desktop")

linkfile = desktop & "\testlink.lnk"
ResolveLink linkfile, 4+32


sub ResolveLink(filepath, flag)
    set ie = CreateObject("InternetExplorer.Application")

    ' split path in folder and file:
    folder = left(filepath, InstrRev(filepath, "\"))
    file = mid(filepath, InstrRev(filepath, "\")+1)

    ' navigate to folder and wait until it is displayed:
    ie.navigate folder
    'ie.visible = true
```

```
        do until ie.readyState=4
        loop

        ' access file:
        set folderobj = ie.document.folder
        set folderitem = folderobj.ParseName(file)

        ' is it really a link?
        if folderitem.isLink then
                set linkobj = folderitem.GetLink
                ' resolve:
                linkobj.Resolve(flag)
        end if
end sub
```

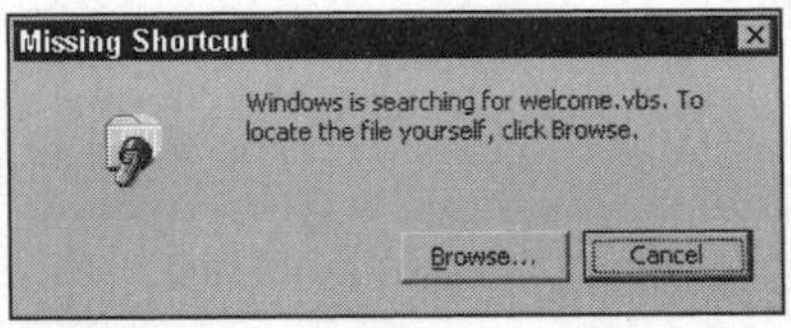

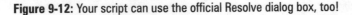

Figure 9-12: Your script can use the official Resolve dialog box, too!

This time, the shell displays its dialog box. The script uses two flags — 4 for automatic update and 32 to turn off link-tracking (on Windows 2000). If you don't turn link-tracking off, on Windows 2000, you will not see the dialog box. Link-tracking is highly efficient and works in a matter of milliseconds. In addition, if link-tracking identified the target, it won't ask for your permission to update the link. Link-tracking safely identifies the target. Search heuristics, in contrast, can only guess and always asks for confirmation. In real life, never turn off link-tracking, as it's the best way for resolving links.

You'll note that the results are similar. If Windows can't determine a new target, it offers to delete the shortcut as depicted in Figure 9-13. This message looks almost like your custom message shown in Figure 9-11.

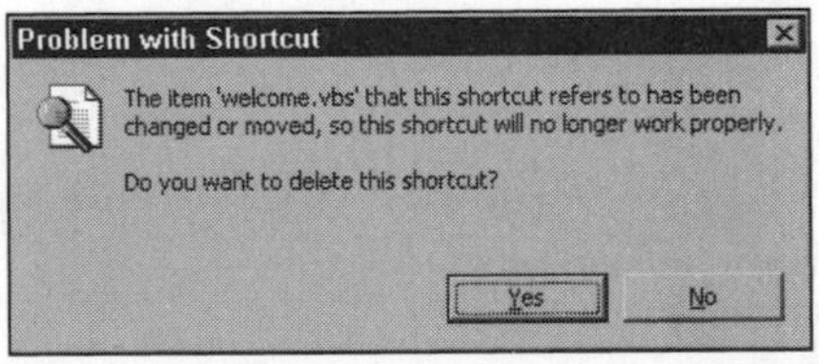

Figure 9-13: If the link can't be resolved, Windows offers to delete the link.

Secret

This script uses the Internet Explorer to access the link file. Because Internet Explorer has its own window, the dialog box can be made visible. The IE window, however, is hidden. If you wanted to, you could also make it visible using ie.visible=true. However, using a hidden IE window has some drawbacks you should know about. The system closely monitors the hidden IE application, and if you don't use it for a while, the system closes it down. This is why you should handle all IE requests within one procedure. Never split the action up. Otherwise, you might receive a "server application no longer available" error.

Designing Context menu extensions

With this new knowledge, you can now create many useful command extensions. For example, links traditionally have an annoying drawback— right-clicking a link and choosing Properties will always invoke the link's Properties page—there's no easy way to call the real target's Properties page.

The next script adds the missing command. It determines the link target and calls the target's Properties page:

```
' 9-15.VBS

set args = WScript.Arguments
if args.Count=0 then
    MsgBox "This script is intended as context menu command."
    WScript.Quit
end if

set wshshell = CreateObject("WScript.Shell")

if not lcase(right(args(0),3))="lnk" then
    MsgBox "You did not specify a link!"
    WScript.Quit
end if

set scut = wshshell.CreateShortcut(args(0))
filepath = scut.TargetPath

if filepath="" then
    MsgBox "Link points to virtual object. Can't display properties!"
    WScript.Quit
end if

' split path in folder and file:
folder = left(filepath, InstrRev(filepath, "\"))
file = mid(filepath, InstrRev(filepath, "\")+1)

set ie = CreateObject("InternetExplorer.Application")

if file="" then
```

```
        file = folder
        folder = "::{20D04FE0-3AEA-1069-A2D8-08002B30309D}"
end if


' navigate to folder and wait until it is displayed:
ie.navigate folder
'ie.visible = true
do until ie.readyState=4
loop

' access file:
set folderobj = ie.document.folder
set folderitem = folderobj.ParseName(file)
folderitem.InvokeVerb("Properties")
```

Note

Exchange "Properties" in the last script line with whatever your system calls the Properties command. Remember: Only Windows 2000 allows the use of generic command names.

This script won't work by itself. It expects the link file name as argument. You can drag a link file onto the script icon. Or better yet, you can integrate your new command into the link Context menu.

The next script provides a quick solution. Store your Properties script in a safe place, then drag it onto the following script's icon.

```
' 9-16.VBS

set args = WScript.Arguments
if args.Count>0 then
     set fs = CreateObject("Scripting.FileSystemObject")
     set wshshell = CreateObject("WScript.Shell")

     ext = lcase(fs.GetExtensionName(args(0)))
     if ext<>"vbs" then
          MsgBox "You did not drag a VBS script!"
          WScript.Quit
     end if

name = InputBox("How do you want to call your command?",, _
"True Properties")

     key = "HKCR\lnkfile\shell\" & name & "\"

     wshshell.RegWrite key, name
     wshshell.RegWrite key & "command\", _
"wscript.exe """ & args(0) & """ ""%L"""
else
     MsgBox "Please drag a VBS script on my icon!"
end if
```

Cross-Reference

Learn more about context menus and how to insert your own commands in Chapter 14

Understanding virtual folders

Your Properties script uses the Internet Explorer to get access to the target file and invoke its Properties page. This is necessary for the Properties dialog box to become attached to the system shell.

To access a file in Internet Explorer (or through other shell methods), you first need to navigate to the folder that the target file or folder resides in. Next, you can use `ParseName` to get access to the target file or folder.

This imposes a problem when trying to access a root drive. Where's the parent folder of drive C:\, and how do you get Internet Explorer to navigate to this parent folder?

The parent folder of all drives is My Computer. Because this is a virtual folder, you can't access it through a path name. Instead, you need to specify its internal identifier.

Undocumented

Explorer (and Internet Explorer) can navigate to any virtual folder. Specify two colons as the path name, followed by the Class-ID of the virtual folder you want to visit.

The script uses My Computer's internal Class-ID to navigate to the root of all drives once it detects that no filename was specified. This only happens if the target is a root drive.

Note also that some links don't return a `TargetPath` property value. `Target Path` is empty whenever a link points to some internal system component such as a printer. In these cases, your script can't display the Properties page and pops up a message.

Secret Class-IDs of virtual folders

Take a look at Table 9-5! It lists all the hidden Class-IDs of virtual folders your Explorer can navigate to. To try them out, open your Start menu and choose Run. Next, enter `explorer.exe`, a space, and two colons. Then enter the Class-ID. Don't forget the curly brackets. The Explorer promptly navigates to the virtual folder you specified.

For example, to open the Network Neighborhood, enter this command: `EXPLORER.EXE ::{208D2C60-3AEA-1069-A2D7-08002B30309D}`, as shown in Figure 9-14.

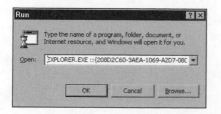

Figure 9-14: Open virtual folders using secret Explorer options.

Undocumented

Explorer can only navigate to those virtual folders that are accessible from your desktop. If you have deleted the Recycle Bin from your desktop, for example, you won't be able to use the Class-ID any more to navigate there.

Table 9-5   Class-IDs of Desktop Items

Class-ID	Virtual Folder
{208D2C60-3AEA-1069-A2D7-08002B30309D}	Network Neighborhood
{20D04FE0-3AEA-1069-A2D8-08002B30309D}	My Computer
{3DC7A020-0ACD-11CF-A9BB-00AA004AE837}	Internet
{450D8FBA-AD25-11D0-98A8-0800361B1103}	My Documents
{645FF040-5081-101B-9F08-00AA002F954E}	Recycle Bin

Selecting a link target

Here's another useful Context menu extension. Ever wondered where the file or folder to which a link points actually lives? The following script is the solution: It opens the containing folder and marks the drive, folder, or file your link points to.

Just insert this script into the link Context menu using the same helper script you used to insert the True Properties command: Save the following script in a safe place, drag it onto the helper script icon, and specify a name: for example, "Show Target."

```
' 9-17.VBS

set args = WScript.Arguments
if args.Count=0 then
    MsgBox "This script is intended as context menu command."
    WScript.Quit
end if

set wshshell = CreateObject("WScript.Shell")

if not lcase(right(args(0),3))="lnk" then
    MsgBox "You did not specify a link!"
    WScript.Quit
end if

set scut = wshshell.CreateShortcut(args(0))
filepath = scut.TargetPath

if filepath="" then
    MsgBox "Link points to virtual object. Can't mark!"
    WScript.Quit
end if
```

```
MarkFile filepath

sub MarkFile(filepath)
' split path in folder and file:
folder = left(filepath, InstrRev(filepath, "\"))
file = mid(filepath, InstrRev(filepath, "\")+1)

set ie = CreateObject("InternetExplorer.Application")

if file="" then
        file = folder
    folder = "::{20D04FE0-3AEA-1069-A2D8-08002B30309D}"
end if

' navigate to folder and wait until it is displayed:
ie.navigate folder
do until ie.readyState=4
loop

' access file:
set folderobj = ie.document.folder
set folderitem = folderobj.ParseName(file)

' mark file:
ie.document.selectItem folderitem, 1+4+8+16

' show IE window
ie.visible = true
end sub
```

This script uses yet another undocumented method: selectItem. This method is provided by the Internet Explorer shell view, accessible through ie.document. Table 9-6 provides a complete list of all properties and methods.

Table 9-6   The Internet Explorer WebView Object

Property/Method	Description
`Property Application As Object`	Get Application object
`Property FocusedItem As FolderItem`	The currently focused item in the folder
`Property Folder As Folder`	Get the folder being viewed
`Property Parent As Object`	Get Parent object
`Function PopupItemMenu (ByVal pfi As FolderItem, [ByVal vx], [ByVal vy]) As String`	Show Items menu and return command selected

Continued

Table 9-6 *(continued)*

Property/Method	Description
Property Script As Object	Return the scripting automation model
Function SelectedItems As FolderItems	The collection of Selected Items in folder
Sub SelectItem (pvfi, ByVal dwFlags As Long)	Select the item
Property ViewOptions As Long	Return the view options for showing a folder

SelectItem is by far the most useful method. The other methods can be used to determine which items are currently selected in the IE window.

SelectItem expects the FolderItem object that you want to mark. As second parameter, it asks for flags. Table 9-7 provides the list.

Table 9-7   WebView Item Selection Flags

Flag	Description
0	Remove selection
1	Select
3	Rename item
4	Remove all selections except for the current object
8	Move selected item into the visible part of the window
16	Give focus to selected item

Summary

You have discovered two ways of accessing shortcut files: the official WScript.Shell shortcut object and the hidden shell mechanism. The shell mechanism provides additional methods for resolving broken links.

Many sample scripts have demonstrated how to manage all of your shortcut files and search for broken links or duplicate keyboard shortcuts. You've even seen how to add new Context menu commands to your shortcut file Context menu for opening a target's Properties page or for marking the target file in the Explorer. As a side effect, you've seen how to open the Explorer with hidden options and using Class-IDs.

Part III

Starting and Controlling Other Software

Chapter 10: Launching Any Program By Script

Chapter 11: Controlling Running Software

Chapter 12: Gaining Full Control Over Any Window

Chapter 13: Starting Scripts Automatically

Chapter 10

Launching Any Program By Script

In This Chapter

▶ Learn how to launch any program by script

▶ Launch entire program groups

▶ Use hidden windows and other window styles

▶ Wait for programs and analyze their return values

▶ Build special maintenance scripts that check your hard drives

▶ Remote control programs and dialog boxes by sending keystrokes via `SendKeys`

▶ Bring windows to the foreground use secret API magic

▶ Directing keystrokes to the right window safely

▶ Enumerate all open windows and close down all running programs by script

▶ Execute DOS commands and read in their results

▶ Launch Control Panel applets and preselect their tabs

▶ Hook into modern software and borrow their internal methods for your own purposes

Scripts can control other programs. In this chapter, you learn how to launch external programs. You also discover ways to determine windows style, hide program windows, remote control other programs, and thus use scripts as a powerful macro language to control just about any task.

Launching Programs

Scripts replace the classical batch files. They are much easier to develop, yet are much more powerful. Batch files were commonly used to launch software. Your scripts can do this, too—and a lot more on top of it. In fact, scripts can act as software glue. They tie together programs and individual program functions to create completely new problem solvers.

Scripts can exploit other software in three ways:

- **Launching directly:** The `WScript.Shell` object sports the `Run` method. This method launches any program as if you had launched it manually. `Run` can launch programs both synchronously and asynchronously, so your script can wait for the program to complete and read its return value, or it can launch programs consecutively.

- **Using DOS:** Even DOS commands can be executed. Your script just needs to launch the command line interpreter and feed it the DOS commands.

- **Accessing Specialties:** Most modern software packages contain an interface called `IDispatch`. Your script can access those software packages using `CreateObject` and borrow their internal functions for its own purposes. For example, if you have installed Microsoft Office, your script can borrow its spell-checker and check any file you want.

Secret

In most respects, scripts are far superior to classical batch files. However, scripts need the Scripting Host in the background. You can't run scripts outside of Windows. Beginning with Windows 2000, Microsoft has chosen scripts to be the new official "batch" files. Here, you can assign scripts to the logon or logoff process, eliminating the need for batch files altogether.

Launching programs directly

To launch other software, all you need are a few scripting lines. Have a look:

```
' 10-1.VBS

set wshshell = CreateObject("WScript.Shell")
wshshell.Run "notepad.exe"
```

This little script launches your editor. Pretty straightforward, no?

Undocumented

Always supply the fully qualified path name whenever the file isn't stored in one of the folders included by the path environment variable. Notepad is stored inside the Windows folder, so you don't need a path. Other software might reside in its own folder. In this case, a path name is mandatory.

There's one little peculiarity about `Run`, and it's that it chokes on spaces. Whenever a path name you supply contains spaces, `Run` won't execute it. Instead, it interprets the space as delimiter and views the rest as argument.

Secret

To work around this "space" problem, always delimit your path name in quotes. Use double quotes inside strings. To launch the software `C:\my software\test.exe`, use `wshshell.Run """C:\my software\test.exe"""`.

Here are some more neat tricks:

- **Does the file exist?** To make sure your `Run` command doesn't raise an error, first check whether the file you want to launch really exists. Use the `FileExists` method provided by the `Scripting.FileSystemObject`.

- Run doesn't only launch executables. You can easily provide a regular filename. In this case, Run will automatically launch the program that is associated with this file type and load the document. However, if no program is associated with the file type, you'll get a nasty error message.

- Open documents with your program of choice—you can specify arguments and determine which program should open a specific file. For example, to open an HTML file with a browser other than Internet Explorer, use the browser executable path in quotes, a space, and then the document path in quotes.

- For environment variables, Run automatically converts environment variables you might have defined in your Login script. To call a program inside your Windows folder, use %WINDIR%: for example, wshshell.Run "%WINDIR%\explorer.exe".

Launching an entire program group

Computer users would rather delegate work to their computers. Why do things manually if your computer can take care of it? One approach to make life easier is the Startup Group. Any program shortcut you copy into this special program group is launched automatically whenever you log on to Windows.

This sounds like a great idea, but unfortunately most of us do a lot of different things with our computers. Autostarting programs make sense only if you use these programs every day. Otherwise, they can become very annoying.

A completely different approach is to use custom program groups. You can create individual program groups for any major task you do with your computer. For example, you can create a group called "grafx" and copy all the program shortcuts in it that you usually use to create and modify artwork. Do the same for all the other tasks, such as Internet, music, word processing, and whatever else you can think of.

Now you only need a quick way of launching entire program groups. The following script will do the job.

This script uses the BrowseForFolder dialog box you created in Chapter 6. Make sure you compiled or installed the project: \install\folderpicker\ setup.exe. The Browse dialog box isn't really necessary, but it makes things a lot more convenient.

```
' 10-2.VBS

set browse = CreateObject("folder.tools")
set fs = CreateObject("Scripting.FileSystemObject")
set wshshell = CreateObject("WScript.Shell")

' which prg group do you want to launch?
entry  = browse.BrowseForFolder(2, _
"Which group or program do you want to launch?", &h4001)
```

```
' did user cancel dialog?
if entry = "" then
    MsgBox "Cancel accepted.", vbInformation
    WScript.Quit
end if

' find out whether use has selected group or individual program
if fs.FileExists(entry) then
    ' a single program
    Launch entry, 1
elseif fs.FolderExists(entry) then
    ' a group
    set folder = fs.GetFolder(entry)

    ' folder empty?
    if folder.files.count=0 then
        MsgBox "The group """ & fs.GetBaseName(folder) _
& """ is empty. This script won't " _
& "execute files in subfolders."
        WScript.Quit
    end if

    list = "Do you really want to launch these programs?" _
& vbCr & vbCr
    for each file in folder.files
        list = list & fs.GetBaseName(file.name) & vbCr
    next
    if MsgBox(list, vbYesNo + vbQuestion)=vbYes then
        for each file in folder.files
            Launch file.path, 2
        next
    end if
else
    MsgBox """" & entry & """ is missing!"
end if


sub Launch(path, flag)
    on error resume next
    wshshell.Run """" & path & """", flag
    on error goto 0
end sub
```

Tip

Drag your script icon onto the Start button to insert a reference into your
Start menu. Next, right-click the new Start menu entry and choose Properties.
Now you can assign a shortcut key to quickly invoke your new program
launcher. Your script can launch both individual files and entire groups.

The script allows you to select both program groups and individual files. If
you select a group, the script lists all the programs it is going to start and asks
for your permission (see Figure 10-1). It launches the programs in minimized
windows so multiple program windows won't clutter your desktop. If you
select an individual program, the script will launch it directly and as a normal
window.

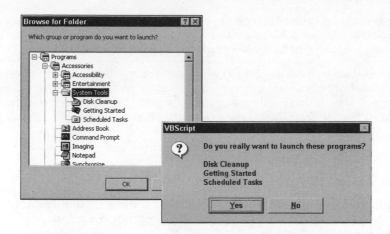

Figure 10-1: The script lists all programs you are about to launch and asks for permission.

Determining window size

The Run method can even determine the kind of window the launched program will get. Specify the window style as second argument. Table 10-1 summarizes your options.

Table 10-1   Window Sizes Relevant to the Run Method

Code	Description
0	No window at all.
1	Normal window.
2	Minimized window.
3	Maximized window.
4	Same window as last time the program was called.
5	Same as 4, window gets focus.
6	Minimized window, next window gets focus.
7	Minimized window, active window remains active.
8	Normal window, active window remains active.
9	Normal window gets focus.

In everyday life, options 1 through 3 cover all you need.

Option 0 is special: It launches the program without a window. The program remains hidden. This can be extremely useful when launching DOS commands or service programs you want to hide from the user. However, calling a program without a window may be dangerous: You no longer receive error messages, and you have no way of closing the program manually.

Tip

Use Option 0 (hidden window) with care: During development, always use a different option so you can see whether your program behaves the way you expect. Use option 0 only with programs that close themselves automatically after they are done. Never use option 0 with programs that might require user interaction.

Waiting for a program to finish

So far, the Run method will launch the files and immediately return control to your script. You can launch a whole series of programs, and they will all be executed at the same time.

This approach is not always best. You might want to know the result of some program, or call programs consecutively. Let's do it!

Just specify true as third parameter, and the Run method will wait for the program to complete. In addition, it now returns the program's return value so you can check whether the program did its job or encountered problems.

This example demonstrates the general concept: The editor is launched, and the script waits until you close it. The second MsgBox statement executes after you close the editor window.

```
' 10-3.VBS

set wshshell = CreateObject("WScript.Shell")
MsgBox "Please enter something, then close the editor!"
result = wshshell.Run("notepad",,true)
MsgBox "Thank you!"
```

Run reads the return value and passes it to your script. Whether this return value makes any sense or not is completely up to the program you launched. Each program is free to return any value. The next script demonstrates how useful the return value can be. It launches the ScanDisk disk checker utility. This utility is available on Win9.x only:

```
' 10-4.VBS

set wshshell = CreateObject("WScript.Shell")

returncodes = Split("ok;detected error and corrected it;" _
& "DSKMAINT.DLL missing;out of memory;couldn't" _
& " correct disk error;couldn't check a drive;check " _
& "interrupted;disk error prevented further checking", ";")

result = wshshell.run( _
"scandskw.exe /allfixeddisks /silent /noninteractive",, true)
```

```
' mask unused bits
result = result and not 65528

MsgBox "Result: " & result & ": " & returncodes(result)
```

The script uses a couple of secret options to start ScanDisk automatically and without user intervention. You can expand the script to include many other disk maintenance utilities, too. For example, after checking a drive using ScanDisk, you can defrag the drive using defrag.exe. Because the script executes one program after the other, the maintenance tools won't run into each other, and you can call your maintenance script at night to do the lengthy maintenance work.

Calling disk tools silently

Disk tools are useless for remote action if they require user input — after all, you want your script to run unattended. This is why most disk tools can be preconfigured. Both SCANDSKW.EXE and DEFRAG.EXE work this way.

To preconfigure a disk tool, choose Run from your Start menu and call the disk tool with the option /sageset:number. Replace "number" with any number: for example, SCANDSKW.EXE /SAGESET:1. The disk tool won't start. Instead, a configuration dialog box appears, and you can choose exactly which options you want your script to use.

To call the disk tool with those preconfigured details, have your script launch the tool with the /sagerun:number option: for example, SCANDSKW.EXE /SAGERUN:1. It's the only option you need. Automatically, the tool starts and uses the configuration details you previously specified.

Undocumented

SAGE stands for "System AGEnt," the Windows 9.x service that calls programs automatically at intervals. So, the /sage... options actually belong to the System Agent, allowing it to call tools without user intervention. Your scripts can take advantage of this.

Remote Controlling Running Programs

Many programs do their job without any user intervention, which is good. But what if you need to press some keys to make the program work? What if the program pops up annoying dialog boxes?

Relax! The Scripting Host 2.0 has the answer: SendKeys. This handy method sends keystrokes to the active window so you can boss it around any way you please. SendKeys makes it easy to remote control any program.

Getting to know SendKeys

The WScript.Shell object provides SendKeys. It can send individual keys as well as key combinations to any window.

SendKeys is new and will only work with WSH 2.0. Make sure you have updated your Scripting Host as outlined in the Preface.

Here's a little taste:

```
' 10-5.VBS

set wshshell = CreateObject("WScript.Shell")
wshshell.Run "notepad.exe"

' wait a second
WScript.Sleep 1000

' write something to the window:
wshshell.SendKeys "It's me!"

' wait another second
WScript.Sleep 1000

' close the window
wshshell.SendKeys "%{F4}"
```

This script opens the editor, waits a second, outputs some text, and closes the window using the key combination [Alt]+[F4]. Because you "entered" text into the editor, it will ask whether you want to save your changes, as shown in Figure 10-2. A little later in the chapter, you see how easy it is to extend this script to take care of this dialog box as well.

One disadvantage of SendKeys is the fact that it sends the keystrokes "blindly" to the foreground window. If the editor doesn't pop up quickly enough or hides behind other windows, the example will fail. A little later in the chapter, you discover ways to work around this problem.

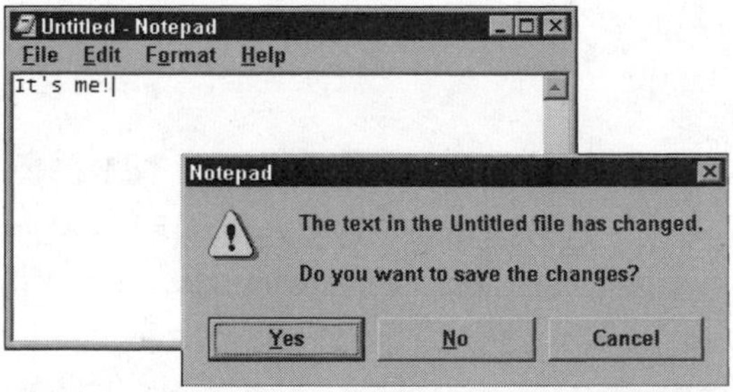

Figure 10-2: The script remotely inserts text and tries to close the window.

Sending keys and key combinations

SendKeys uses the special codes outlined in Table 10-2 to "press" any of the special keys.

Table 10-2   SendKeys Key Codes

Key	Code
BACKSPACE	{BACKSPACE}, {BS}, or {BKSP}
BREAK	{BREAK}
CAPS LOCK	{CAPSLOCK}
DEL or DELETE	{DELETE} or {DEL}
DOWN ARROW	{DOWN}
END	{END}
ENTER	{ENTER} or ~
ESC	{ESC}
F1	{F1}
F10	{F10}
F11	{F11}
F12	{F12}
F13	{F13}
F14	{F14}
F15	{F15}
F16	{F16}
F2	{F2}
F3	{F3}
F4	{F4}
F5	{F5}
F6	{F6}
F7	{F7}
F8	{F8}
F9	{F9}
HELP	{HELP}
HOME	{HOME}
INS or INSERT	{INSERT} or {INS}
LEFT ARROW	{LEFT}
NUM LOCK	{NUMLOCK}

Continued

Table 10-2   *(continued)*

Key	Code
PAGE DOWN	{PGDN}
PAGE UP	{PGUP}
PRINT SCREEN	{PRTSC}
RIGHT ARROW	{RIGHT}
SCROLL LOCK	{SCROLLLOCK}
TAB	{TAB}
UP ARROW	{UP}
[Shift] (modifier key)	+
[Ctrl] (modifier key)	^
[Alt] (modifier key)	%

The SendKeys string "%{F4}" represents the key combination [Alt]+[F4]. It closes the active window.

You can even send keys repeatedly. To send 30 spaces, use {SPACE 30}.

Directing keys to the right window

Sending keystrokes to a window is extremely versatile but also dangerous. SendKeys "blindly" sends keystrokes to the currently active window. If the user has clicked another window, or if the window you wanted to control didn't receive the focus in the first place, your keys may be transmitted to the completely wrong window, causing unexpected behavior.

To fight this, Microsoft invented the AppActivate method. This method brings any window you wish to the foreground—at least in theory.

AppActivate is provided by the WScript.Shell object and expects the name of the window you want to give the focus to. Specify the name exactly as it appears in the window's title bar.

Undocumented

You don't need to specify the full window name. Specifying only part of it switches to the next window title that matches the caption.

As an example, the following script opens two windows and switches back and forth five times. But what is this? After the first cycle, window switching doesn't work anymore! Instead, the windows just nervously flash their command buttons in the task bar. They won't jump to the foreground.

```
' 10-6.VBS

set wshshell = CreateObject("WScript.Shell")
windir = wshshell.ExpandEnvironmentStrings("%WINDIR%")

wshshell.Run " explorer exe " & windir
wshshell.Run "notepad.exe " & windir & "\win.ini"

for x = 1 to 5
    ' wait a second
    WScript.Sleep 1000
    ' activate window 1
    wshshell.AppActivate windir
    ' wait another second
    WScript.Sleep 1000
    ' activate window 2
    wshshell.AppActivate "WIN"
next
```

Secret

Beginning with Windows 98, Microsoft has built new code into the window subsystem. A window can only receive the focus if the calling application currently owns it. Your script owns the focus when you call it and can therefore control the focus. However, once your script has given away the focus, it can't do any focus switching anymore. Instead, the windows will only flash their buttons. This also explains why sometimes even the VBScript MsgBox dialog box remains hidden behind other windows.

This is extremely bad news. AppActivate is rendered useless, and your scripts have no safe way of determining which window currently gets the focus.

Telling windows to switch focus no matter what

There's an easy solution to the problem, although this solution is absolutely undocumented. Through secret Windows APIs, you can disable the focus lock. If you do, your scripts can happily change focus to any window. No more flashing window buttons!

To be able to crack the focus lock, you'll need some more details. Actually, Windows uses a parameter called ForegroundLockTimeout. This parameter defines a time period that defaults to 200 seconds. If a program receives the focus and is idle for this time period, Windows allows other programs to steal the focus. This mechanism is intended to prevent programs from jumping in the foreground while you are working with some other window.

Your scripts have no simple way of retrieving the focus once they have given it away using AppActivate. However, your scripts can set the Foreground LockTimeout value to 0. This effectively turns off the focus lock, and AppActivate works no matter who currently owns the focus.

How do you change the focus timeout value? You need to define a custom COM object! This one does the job. It also includes a function to find out the name of the currently active window.

```
Option Explicit

Private Const SPI_GETFOREGROUNDLOCKTIMEOUT = &H2000
Private Const SPI_SETFOREGROUNDLOCKTIMEOUT = &H2001

Private Declare Function SystemParametersInfo Lib "user32" _
Alias "SystemParametersInfoA" (ByVal uAction As Long, _
ByVal uParam As Long, ByVal lpvParam As Any, _
ByVal fuWinINI As Long) As Long
Private Declare Function GetActiveWindow Lib "user32" () _
As Long
Private Declare Function GetWindowText Lib "user32" _
Alias "GetWindowTextA" (ByVal hwnd As Long, ByVal _
lpString As String, ByVal cch As Long) As Long


Public Sub SetActivation(ByVal millisecs As Long)
    SystemParametersInfo SPI_SETFOREGROUNDLOCKTIMEOUT, 0, millisecs, 0
End Sub

Public Function GetActivation() As Long
    SystemParametersInfo SPI_GETFOREGROUNDLOCKTIMEOUT, 0,
VarPtr(GetActivation), 0
End Function

Public Function GetActiveWindowName() As String
    Dim result As Long
    Dim windName As String

    windName = Space(260)
    result = GetWindowText(GetActiveWindow, windName, 260)
    GetActiveWindowName = Left(windName, result)
End Function
```

CD

Load the complete project into your VB CCE and compile it yourself, using \components\appactivate\appactivate.vbp. Or just install the prepared software package: \install\appactivate\setup.exe.

Now your window switching works perfectly smoothly:

```
' 10-7.VBS

set wshshell = CreateObject("WScript.Shell")
set apptool = CreateObject("app.activate")

windir = wshshell.ExpandEnvironmentStrings("%WINDIR%")

wshshell.Run windir
wshshell.Run "notepad.exe " & windir & "\win.ini"
```

```
' turn off focus lock and remember timeout value
timeout = apptool.GetActivation
apptool.SetActivation 0

for x = 1 to 5
    ' wait a second
    WScript.Sleep 1000
    ' activate window 1
    wshshell.AppActivate windir
    ' wait another second
    WScript.Sleep 1000
    ' activate window 2
    wshshell.AppActivate "WIN"
next

' restore timeout value
apptool.SetActivation timeout
```

This is the ultimate prerequisite to use SendKeys safely. From now on, you can choose the window you want to output keystrokes to.

Finding out whether a window exists

There might be another concern: What if the window you want to switch to doesn't exist? How do you know it opened correctly? How do you determine whether or not the user has closed the window in the meantime? AppActivate tells you! If you use it as function, it will return true or false. A false means no such window was found!

In addition, the new GetActiveWindowName method reports the name of the currently active window.

Undocumented

Actually, GetActiveWindowName doesn't report the name of the "active" window. Instead, it returns the name of the foreground window. This window doesn't necessarily have to have the focus. SendKeys always sends to the window in the foreground window. Turning off focus timeout was needed only to put arbitrary windows to the foreground. SendKeys doesn't care about the focus.

Safely directing keystrokes to the window of your choice

So, this is what a safe SendKeys wrapper might look like. It sends keys to the window you specify and won't send them to any other window.

Note

It is only through this wrapper that you can use SendKeys in real-life scenarios. Without it, it's much too dangerous to send out keystrokes without knowing who receives them.

```
' 10-8.VBS

set wshshell = CreateObject("WScript.Shell")
set apptool = CreateObject("app.activate")

timeout = 0

EnableSwitching

' now you are all set to safely use SendKeys!

' launch Editor
wshshell.run "notepad.exe"
' wait 1 second
WScript.Sleep 1000
' determine name of editor:
editname = apptool.GetActiveWindowName
if instr(editname, "Notepad")=0 then
    ' didn't start!
    MsgBox "I tried to start the Editor. Instead, """ & editname _
& """ is the active window. I quit."
    WScript.Quit
end if

' list drive C:\ to editor
set fs = CreateObject("Scripting.FileSystemObject")
set folder = fs.GetFolder("C:\")
for each file in folder.files
    SendKeys file.name & "{ENTER}", editname
next

DisableSwitching

MsgBox "Done!"

sub SendKeys(keys, windowname)
    ' check whether output window is active
    windname = lcase(apptool.GetActiveWindowName)

    ' wrong window, switch:
    if not lcase(windowname)=left(windname, len(windowname)) then
    ok = wshshell.AppActivate(windowname)
        if not ok then
            MsgBox "Window """ & windowname & """ is missing!"
            DisableSwitching
            WScript.Quit
        end if
    end if
    wshshell.SendKeys keys, true
    Wscript.Sleep 100
end sub
```

```
sub EnableSwitching
    timeout = apptool.GetActivation
    apptool.SetActivation 0
end sub

sub DisableSwitching
    apptool.SetActivation timeout
end sub
```

The script reads the folder's contents and sends it to your editor window, as shown by Figure 10-3.

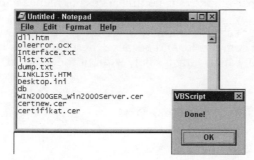

Figure 10-3: SendKeys now safely inserts a complete folder listing into your editor window.

This script solves many problems. EnableSwitching turns off the focus lock so your script can switch to any window. GetActiveWindowName automatically retrieves the name of the currently active window. This has a double use: After launching the editor, your new output window, the script can safely determine the window title, so you don't have to guess any longer or hard-code a name into your script.

Secondly, the new SendKeys procedure can use GetActiveWindowName to find out whether or not the right window is in the foreground. If it's not, it uses AppActivate to switch to the window, and listens to AppActivate's return value. If it's false, the script knows that the user has closed the window, and stops. Try it out! Try switching the window while the script outputs the file list — you'll find it won't work! The script switches back immediately. Try closing the output window. The script detects the missing window and quits. No more danger of keystrokes getting into the wrong hands!

Your self-defined SendKeys procedure internally calls the official SendKeys method. It does two surprising things. First, it calls SendKeys with a second parameter: true. This lets SendKeys wait until the destination window receives the keystrokes. Next, it delays the script for 100 milliseconds. Why? Your script is too fast for SendKeys, and without delay, some keystrokes would get lost.

When remote controlling software, you might have to send keystrokes to many different windows. Maybe you are calling menu commands that pop up dialog boxes you need to fill out. Always remember to supply the correct window name. Use the dialog box title name to send keystrokes to this window instead of the application window.

Remote controlling menus and the Start menu

The most important use of SendKeys is getting access to menus and kicking dialog boxes out of the way. SendKeys can do anything you can do with the mouse. For example, your scripts can easily open and access the Start menu, calling any of the official commands. And because these shortcuts don't relate to any window, you can use them safely without the wrapper.

```
' 10-9.VBS

set wshshell = CreateObject("WScript.Shell")

' open Start Menu
wshshell.SendKeys "^{ESC}"

' call Shutdown
wshshell.SendKeys "{UP}{ENTER}"

' you could continue and completely shutting down windows
' or use any other option offered by the Shutdown screen
```

Why did the script use {UP}{ENTER} to invoke the Shutdown command? Wouldn't it be easier to call it through its key combination? No. Key combinations only work if they are unique. If you had inserted a custom Start menu entry whose name started with the same letter as the system command, the key combination would no longer work. In the Start menu, it's much safer to use {UP} to move to the system command you require. Still, you might need to adjust the script if you have disabled some of the official Start menu commands.

There are many hidden, yet useful, system keyboard commands you may want to use:

- [Alt]+[Tab] switches back and forth between two windows.

- [F10] activates the menu bar.

- [Shift]+[F10] activates the context menu of the currently selected item.

- [Alt]+[Space] opens the Windows' system menu.

- [Alt]+[F4] closes the active window.

When calling menu or command shortcuts, always use lowercase letters. If you send [Alt]+[F] ("%F"), the program might interpret your keys as [Alt]+[Shift]+[F], invoking a completely different function than you intended.

Shutting down all running programs

After some work, the desktop is often cluttered with numerous open windows, and it takes several clicks to close them all manually. Isn't there a way to automate this? How convenient it would be to define a keystroke that closes all open windows!

Listing all running programs

You can do this. However, first you need to invent some method to enumerate the names of all open windows. Load the complete project from the CD: \components\windowlist\windowlist.vbp. Or install the prepared package: \install\windowlist\setup.exe.

```
Option Explicit

Public WindowList As String

Public Const GW_OWNER = 4
Public Const GWL_EXSTYLE = (-20)
Public Const WS_EX_TOOLWINDOW = &H80
Public Const WS_EX_APPWINDOW = &H40000


Declare Function EnumWindows Lib "user32" (ByVal lpEnumFunc As _
Long, ByVal lParam As Long) As Long
Declare Function IsWindowVisible Lib "user32" (ByVal hwnd As Long) _
As Long
Declare Function GetWindowText Lib "user32" Alias _
"GetWindowTextA" (ByVal hwnd As Long, ByVal lpString As _
String, ByVal cch As Long) As Long
Declare Function GetParent Lib "user32" (ByVal hwnd As Long) As Long
Declare Function GetWindow Lib "user32" (ByVal hwnd As Long, _
ByVal wCmd As Long) As Long
Declare Function GetWindowLong Lib "user32" Alias _
"GetWindowLongA" (ByVal hwnd As Long, ByVal nIndex _
As Long) As Long

Private Function EnumWindowsCallBack(ByVal hwnd As Long, _
ByVal lParam As Long) As Long

Dim lReturn     As Long
    Dim lExStyle     As Long
    Dim bNoOwner     As Boolean
    Dim sWindowText As String

    If IsWindowVisible(hwnd) Then
        If GetParent(hwnd) = 0 Then
            bNoOwner = (GetWindow(hwnd, GW_OWNER) = 0)
            lExStyle = GetWindowLong(hwnd, GWL_EXSTYLE)

            If (((lExStyle And WS_EX_TOOLWINDOW) = 0) And bNoOwner) _
Or ((lExStyle And WS_EX_APPWINDOW) _
```

```
                     And Not bNoOwner) Then

sWindowText = Space$(256)
                    lReturn = GetWindowText(hwnd, sWindowText, _
Len(sWindowText))
                    If lReturn Then
                        WindowList = WindowList & Left$(sWindowText, _
lReturn) & vbCrLf
                    End If
                End If
            End If
        End If
    End If
    EnumWindowsCallBack = True
End Function

Public Function EnumWin() As String
    Dim hwnd As Long
    WindowList = ""
    Call EnumWindows(AddressOf EnumWindowsCallBack, hwnd)
    If Len(WindowList) > 1 Then
        WindowList = Left(WindowList, Len(WindowList) - 2)
    End If
    EnumWin = WindowList
End Function
```

To achieve your goal, you need to dive deeply into the Windows API mechanics. First of all, you can't write this code in the code segment of your COM User Control. It wouldn't work. Instead, you need to create a separate code module: In the VB CCE Project window, right-click your project and choose Add and Module.

Undocumented

This code uses callback functions. Callback functions are self-defined functions that are passed to some Windows API function. The API function then calls your callback function many times, mostly in conjunction with some enumeration process. To be able to pass a VisualBasic function such as Callback, you need to pass its memory address. Fortunately, VisualBasic sports the AddressOf operator. However, this operator won't work in User Controls. You need to use it in separate code modules.

EnumWin is the main function you need to call to get a list of all the running windows. The real work is done by EnumWindows, a secret API function. It asks for the name of some callback function and then calls this function for every window currently defined.

Your callback function EnumWindowsCallback has the job of dealing with any window passed by EnumWindows. So, the Windows API function just enumerates the windows but leaves it to your callback function to figure out whether you find the particular window interesting or not.

Cross-Reference

Chapter 12 reveals all the details about the many system windows and how to track them down.

This is hard work. Windows consists of hundreds, if not thousands, of windows, even if you can see only a handful. Take a look at your task bar: A separate window displays each button, including the start button, and you obviously don't want to enumerate all of these internal windows.

This is why your callback function does a lot of filtering. First of all, it sorts out invisible windows. Next, it sorts out any window that is part of a parent window, eliminating child windows. Finally, it filters out any windows that are neither application nor toolbox windows, and it also rejects windows that are owned by another window. The results are the true main windows you see on your screen.

Your code works all right, but how can your scripts access it? Define this little function in the User Control part of your COM object:

```
Public Function ListWindows() As String
    ListWindows = EnumWin
End Function
```

Now you are all set. The next script enumerates all currently running window titles, and Figure 10-4 shows a sample result:

```
' 10-10.VBS

set tool = CreateObject("Window.List")
MsgBox tool.ListWindows
```

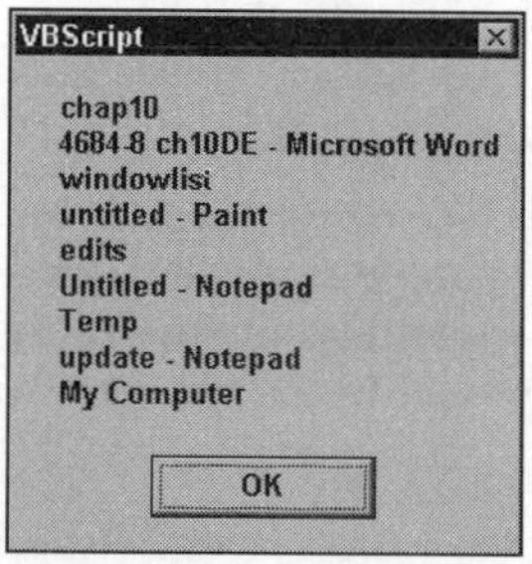

Figure 10-4: Automatically find out names of all open windows.

Sending a "close" command to running programs

Now it's easy to `AppActivate` each window in the list and tell it to close down:

```
' 10-11.VBS

set wshshell = CreateObject("WScript.Shell")
set apptool = CreateObject("app.activate")
set tool = CreateObject("Window.List")

timeout = 0
```

```
list = tool.ListWindows
list = Split(list, vbCrLf)

EnableSwitching
for each window in list
    ok = wshshell.AppActivate(window)
    if ok then
        wshshell.SendKeys("%{F4}")
    else
        MsgBox "Can't switch to """ & window & """!"
    end if
next
DisableSwitching
wshshell.Popup "Done closing windows.", 1

sub EnableSwitching
    timeout = apptool.GetActivation
    apptool.SetActivation 0
end sub

sub DisableSwitching
    apptool.SetActivation timeout
end sub
```

Note

You could easily filter the window names returned by ListWindows to include only special windows. For example, use Scripting.FileSystem Object FileExists and FolderExists to see whether a window title represents a file or folder, and close just the Explorer windows.

Closing down specific applications

Your script works all right at this point, but it's not very selective. It closes down any window visible on screen. Maybe you are a programmer and work with a lot of editor windows. Every once in a while, you would like to hit a key and close all editor windows. But, is it possible to just shut down the editor windows and nothing else?

Yes! However, it requires even more API artistry. Unfortunately, Windows 9.x and Windows NT/2000 use a completely different approach in finding out the executable name behind a window.

I have designed a little variation of the COM object you created above. It not only returns the window names but also the path names of the executables running the window. The COM object works both on NT and 9.x because it incorporates both ways of retrieving the .exe name. Because space is scarce, I decided not to print the listing. You'll find the complete source code on the CD: \components\windowlist2\winlist2.vbp. To be able to use the object, either compile the project yourself or install the prepared package: \install\windowlist2\setup.exe.

Take a look what your new object does (Figure 10-5 gives a quick preview):

```
' 10-12.VBS

set tool = CreateObject("window.list2")
MsgBox tool.ListWindows
```

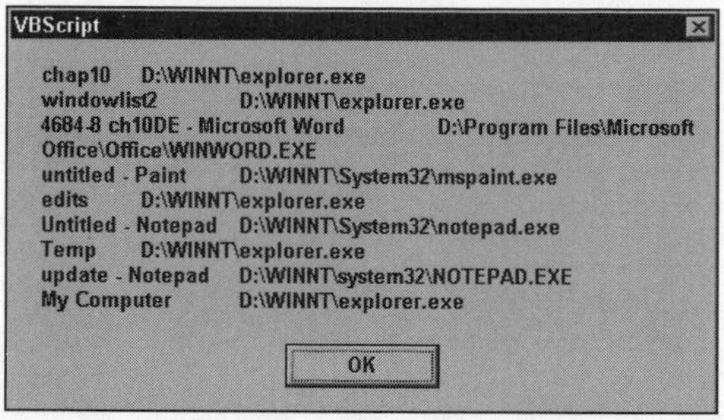

Figure 10-5: Find out the executable names working inside the open windows.

This time, the method lists both the window name and the executable path. It uses a vbTab as delimiter. Now it's easy to create a more selective close-down script. The following script closes down the editor only—all other windows remain intact. It's just a slightly enhanced version of the previous script and demonstrates how to separate window name and executable path using Split.

```
' 10-13.VBS

' specify which program you want to close down:
closedown = "notepad.exe"

set wshshell = CreateObject("WScript.Shell")
set apptool = CreateObject("app.activate")
set tool = CreateObject("Window.List2")

timeout = 0

list = tool.ListWIndows
list = Split(list, vbCrLf)

EnableSwitching
for each windowinfo in list
    infofield = Split(windowinfo, vbTab)
    window = infofield(0)
    exec = lcase(infofield(1))
    exec = mid(exec, InstrRev(exec,"\")+1)
    if exec = closedown then
        ok = wshshell.AppActivate(window)
        if ok then
            wshshell.SendKeys("%{F4}")
        else
```

```
                  MsgBox "Can't switch to """ & window & """!"
            end if
        end if
next

DisableSwitching
wshshell.Popup "Done closing windows.", 1

sub EnableSwitching
    timeout = apptool.GetActivation
    apptool.SetActivation 0
end sub

sub DisableSwitching
    apptool.SetActivation timeout
end sub
```

Executing DOS Commands

DOS commands may be outdated, but they are still there. And for some tasks, DOS commands are still a reasonable alternative. I'll leave it up to you to choose which DOS commands may be useful. In this part, I focus on how to call DOS commands, and how to retrieve their results.

Feeding DOS commands to the interpreter

DOS commands are not separate program files. Don't confuse them with DOS programs. You can launch DOS programs the same way you launch Windows programs, using the Run method. But how do you launch a DOS command like DIR? There's no DIR.EXE or DIR.COM your script could call.

All the internal DOS commands are part of COMMAND.COM, the DOS command interpreter. You just need to feed the commands you want to execute to this interpreter, and they will be executed. Easy.

You don't even have to know the exact location of COMMAND.COM. The environment variable %COMSPEC% reveals its internal name.

Secret

On Windows NT/2000, the DOS command interpreter is still there. Here, it's called CMD.EXE. You don't need to worry about the name, because %COMSPEC% always contains the path name to the DOS interpreter no matter where it's stored and no matter what it's called.

So, to list the directory of drive C:\, use the following script:

```
' 10-14.VBS

set wshshell = CreateObject("WScript.Shell")
wshshell.Run "%COMSPEC% /k dir c:\"
```

Maybe you wonder what the /k option does. It's the flag that makes the interpreter execute the following command. Without this option, you'd just get an empty DOS box.

/k isn't the only possible flag. It's useful only if you want to open a DOS window and keep it open. Most of the time, this is not what you want. Your scripts just want to launch a DOS command without any spectacular window, and most importantly, without user intervention. To close the DOS window once your command is finished, use /c instead of /k.

Reading in the DOS command results

If you used /c in the example above, you won't have much fun. The DOS interpreter would open the DOS window, execute the DIR command, and close the window within a matter of seconds. You need a way to transfer the result into your scripts. Take a look at the following script — it shows how to store the result and read it into your script (see Figure 10-6):

```
' 10-15.VBS

set wshshell = CreateObject("WScript.Shell")
set fs = CreateObject("Scripting.FileSystemObject")

outputfile = "C:\TEMP.TXT"
command = "%COMSPEC% /c dir c:\ > " & outputfile

' wait for the command to finish
result = wshshell.Run(command,,true)

' read in result
set file = fs.OpenTextFile(outputfile)
text = file.ReadAll
file.close

wshshell.Popup text
```

Tip

During this process, the DOS window may flash up. This may be a little annoying, and you can keep it hidden by using 0 as window style (use 0 as second parameter for Run). It wouldn't be very wise, though. DOS may direct questions or error messages at you, and if you hide the DOS window, you'd never know and wonder why your script appears to hang. Hide windows only if you must, and only once you have tested your DOS command many times and are convinced that it doesn't require user interaction.

How did your script get access to the DOS command's output? Easy: You redirected the output into a text file. This is what the > operator did. In addition, the Run method used synchronous calling (third parameter is set to true), so your script waits for the DOS command to complete the output file. Next, it can access the output file and read in whatever the DOS command has left behind.

```
Windows Script Host                                    [X]

     Volume in drive C is BOOTSTRAP
     Volume Serial Number is 1915-1700

     Directory of c:\

     12/23/1999  12:08p    <DIR>        fertig
     12/23/1999  07:06p    <DIR>        OPLIMIT
     01/11/2000  12:59a    <DIR>        bilder
     01/12/2000  05:01p    <DIR>        idgpic
     01/13/2000  05:15p           1,128 coded.txt
     05/12/1999  04:08p    <DIR>        Eigene Dateien
     05/12/1999  03:52p    <DIR>        Programme
     01/13/2000  06:25a           1,126 decoded.txt
     02/14/1999  11:39a               0 t3vvqtlp.2
     02/14/1999  11:44a    <DIR>        FOUND.000
     01/13/2000  05:13p           4,450 temp.html
     01/11/2000  01:21a    <DIR>        WINNT
     01/11/2000  01:26a    <DIR>        Dokumente und Einstellungen
     01/12/2000  03:21p           5,200 SIPOBJ.DBG
     01/13/2000  07:04a             423 OBJECT.TXT
     01/13/2000  06:56p           3,832 docu.txt
     01/13/2000  06:52p             276 doku_IWebCollection.txt
```

Figure 10-6: Read in the results of DOS commands.

Secret

DOS and Windows are two completely different worlds. DOS uses the old ASCII text code, while Windows sticks to its ANSI text code. You won't notice the difference until you read special characters. All character codes above 128 are handled differently by these two schemes, and when reading in DOS results, special characters may look garbled. You can, however, use Replace and replace all special characters with the ANSI equivalent.

Feeding answer files to DOS commands

Some DOS commands won't work without user interaction. They require the user to press Y or some other key before they take action. How can you automate that?

You already know the answer! Just provide an answer file. Answer files are plain text files, and each line represents the answer to one question. This means you can redirect input to DOS commands in exactly the same way you redirected output. Use < this time.

For example, to format the disk drive on Windows 9.x, you can use this script:

```
' 10-16.VBS

if FormatDisk("Disk1") then
     MsgBox "Done formatting!"
else
     MsgBox "You interrupted the formatting process..."
end if

function FormatDisk(name)
     set wshshell = CreateObject("WScript.Shell")
     set fs = CreateObject("Scripting.FileSystemObject")
```

```
       ' exchange with different drive letter if necessary:
       set drive = fs.GetDrive("A:")
       do until drive.isReady or result=vbCancel
           result = MsgBox("Please insert disk to be formatted " _
& " in drive A:\. Caution: disk will be completely" _
& " erased!", vbOkCancel)
       loop
       if result = vbCancel then
           FormatDisk = false
           exit function
       end if

       ' prepare answers
       answerfile = "c:\answers.txt"
       set answers = fs.CreateTextFile(answerfile, true)
       answers.WriteLine                    ' ENTER
answers.WriteLine left(name,11)        ' Disk name
       answers.WriteLine "N"                ' N: no more disks
       answers.close

       ' execute DOS command and feed answers

       ' replace 1 with 0 to hide DOS window
       result = wshshell.Run("%COMSPEC% /C FORMAT A: < " _
& answerfile,1,true)
       FormatDisk = true
end function
```

Again, it's a little risky to let the DOS command run in a hidden window. What if the disk contains a media error, or someone takes it out of the drive? You'd never see any DOS error messages, so the safe approach is to leave the DOS window visible.

Launching Control Panel Items

Ever wondered where all the Control Panel items live? They are individual files, and you can bring up any Control Panel item directly. A script can prompt the user to change some setting and have the appropriate item pop up right away.

Control Panel items have something in common with DOS commands. They are not executables, so you can't launch them directly. Instead, you have to feed them to a special DLL function.

Where do Control Panel items live?

Control Panel items are individual files. Commonly, they share the CPL file extension, but DLL files can act as Control Panel items, too. Let's do a little search! Search for *.CPL and see what you get!

Each of the files the search function finds contains one or more Control Panel items. How do you call them?

Executing Control Panel items

Windows contains a special API function called `Control_RunDLL`. This function executes CPL files. Fortunately, you don't need to access this API function directly. There's a shortcut. It's called `CONTROL.EXE`. This program "wraps" the API function for you and sends the CPL file to `shell32.dll`.

Try it out! Choose Run from your Start menu and enter this command: `CONTROL main.cpl`. It works: The main Control Panel module appears. Because `CONTROL.EXE` is an executable, you now know all that's needed to call any Control Panel applet via script.

But there's more. Close the mouse dialog box and enter this command: `CONTROL main.cpl,@1`. Don't insert spaces before or after the comma. This time, the keyboard dialog box pops up. `Main.cpl` contains more than one Control Panel applet, and you can choose the one you need.

Undocumented

Always close Control Panel applets before you try to open another one. Windows may not be able to open the new one as long as the old one is still visible.

You can even preselect individual tabs. `CONTROL main.cpl,@1,1` opens the keyboard dialog box and selects the second tab (tabs start with index 0).

Next, check out the other `.cpl` files your search has listed. Note that not every Control Panel applet supports tab preselection, though. You'll find many useful shortcuts to important system dialog boxes. For example, try `CONTROL sysdm.cpl,,2`. The result may vary, depending on your Windows version (see Figure 10-7).

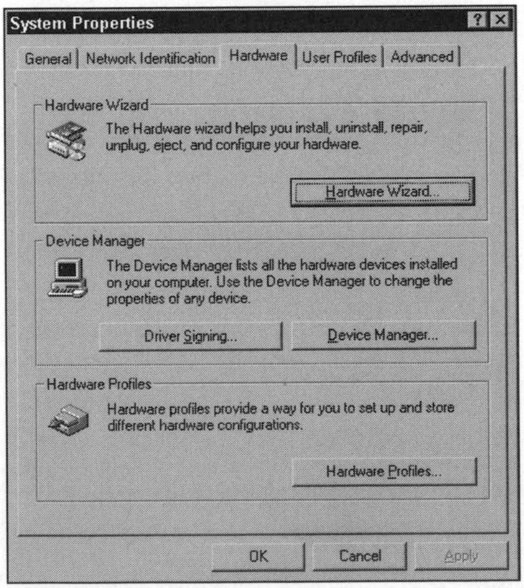

Figure 10-7: Open Control Panel applets and preselect a tab.

```
' 10-17.VBS

set wshshell = CreateObject("WScript.Shell")
wshshell.Run "CONTROL.EXE sysdm.cpl,,2"
```

Secret

You can't call CONTROL.EXE synchronously; in other words, you can't make your script wait for the Control Panel dialog box to be closed again. Remember: CONTROL.EXE passes control to shell32.dll only. It will exit immediately after it has fed the CPL file to the API function.

Accessing Software Through CreateObject

Actually, you have launched and controlled external software throughout this book. Each and every call to CreateObject has accessed some external software and borrowed some of its functionality. So far, however, you have worked with simple "in-process" COM objects most of the time.

Most modern software packages use a modular design. They store their special functionality in separate COM modules. This makes it much easier for the software vendor to design add-ons and re-use functions already provided by some component.

There are also pirates waiting to exploit this vast amount of software power, too — your scripts! Accidentally, the modular design allows your own scripts to also access any special function a software package may have to offer — even if the software vendor would have much rather kept these functions to its own components.

The only way software vendors can prevent third-party users from exploiting their software is to not document the methods and properties. Without a name and arguments list, you won't be able to call any external function.

Secret

Actually, a software vendor would just have to get rid of the IDispatch interface to prevent script access, and, in fact, simple software packages often lack this interface. IDispatch is the secret back door through which scripts can access the internal components. However, macro languages become increasingly important for any software vendor. Any software that wants to be compatible with VisualBasic for Applications or any other late-bound script language needs IDispatch and involuntarily gives your scripts access to all of its functions

Fortunately, most software packages come with a hidden TypeLibrary, and you have already found many ways to peek into these information files. They provide you with all the information needed.

Remote controlling Microsoft Word

Take a look at MS Word (WinWord). It comes as part of Microsoft Office, and because it's one of the leading office software suites, you'll find it installed on many computers.

How do you access its internal methods? First, you need to find out its TypeLibrary. Most likely, the TypeLibrary is stored in the same folder as the executable. So search for Winword.exe and write down the folder name.

Next, use the following helper script. It checks all files in the folder you specify and returns a list of all files that contain TypeLibrary information. You get a result similar to the one shown in Figure 10-8.

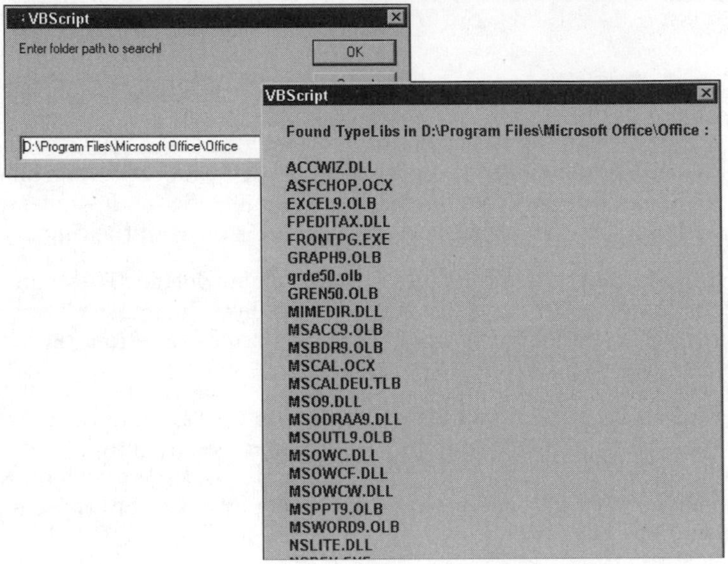

![VBScript dialog windows showing folder search input "D:\Program Files\Microsoft Office\Office" and a results window listing found TypeLibs: ACCWIZ.DLL, ASFCHOP.OCX, EXCEL9.OLB, FPEDITAX.DLL, FRONTPG.EXE, GRAPH9.OLB, grde50.olb, GREN50.OLB, MIMEDIR.DLL, MSACC9.OLB, MSBDR9.OLB, MSCAL.OCX, MSCALDEU.TLB, MSO9.DLL, MSODRAA9.DLL, MSOUTL9.OLB, MSOWC.DLL, MSOWCF.DLL, MSOWCW.DLL, MSPPT9.OLB, MSWORD9.OLB, NSLITE.DLL]

Figure 10-8: Automatically search a folder for TypeLibrary information.

Note To use this and the subsequent scripts, you need to install the TypeLibrary helper tools if you haven't done so already: \install\typelib\setup.exe.

```
' 10-18.VBS

searchfolder = inputBox("Enter folder path to search!")

set tool = CreateObject("typelib.decoder")
set fs = CreateObject("Scripting.FileSystemObject")

if not fs.FolderExists(searchfolder) then
    MsgBox """" & searchfolder & """ does not exist!"
    WScript.Quit
end if

set folder = fs.GetFolder(searchfolder)

list = "Found TypeLibs in " & searchfolder & " :" & vbCr & vbCr

for each file in folder.files
```

```
    if tool.isTypeLib(file.path) then
        list = list & file.name & vbCr
    end if
next

MsgBox list
```

The list of filenames gives a good clue which file is responsible for your executable. Microsoft Word 2000, for example, stores its TypeLibrary in a file called MSWORD9.OLB.

To view all the internal methods, launch script 5-12 and provide it with the full path name of the file. It will extract all the TypeLibrary information into your documentation folder (see Chapter 5 for details) and will offer to open the folder for you.

In the Word subfolder, you now find a vast number of information files (see Figure 10-9). You might even feel slightly overwhelmed. In a minute, though, you know exactly where to start your search.

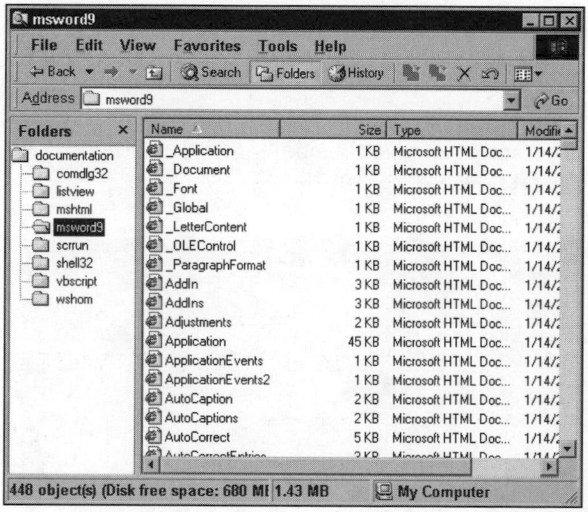

Figure 10-9: Add the WinWord documentation to your documentation folder.

Accessing the Word spell-checker

To access software through IDispatch, you need to know its ProgID. In Chapter 3, you created a list of all available ProgIDs. To access MS Word, for example, use Word.Application:

```
' 10-19.VBS
set word = CreateObject("Word.Application")
MsgBox TypeName(word)
```

These lines establish a connection to your object and return the name of the object you received. It's Application. Switch back to your documentation folder and search for a file called Application. There it is — open Application.htm.

A search for "spelling" quickly brings GetSpellingSuggestions to your attention. All right! So how do you check the spelling of some words? Here's an example:

```
' 10-20.VBS
set word = CreateObject("Word.Application")
word.documents.Add

checkword = InputBox("Enter a word, and I check the spelling!")

set suggestions = word.GetSpellingSuggestions(checkword)
if suggestions.Count = 0 then
    MsgBox "I have no alternatives for you..."
else
    list = "I've some suggestions for """ & checkword & """:" & vbCr
    for each suggestion in suggestions
        list = list & suggestion & vbCr
    next
    MsgBox list
end if

word.Quit
```

It really works: Your script checks the spelling with the help of WinWord and gives spelling suggestions (see Figure 10-10).

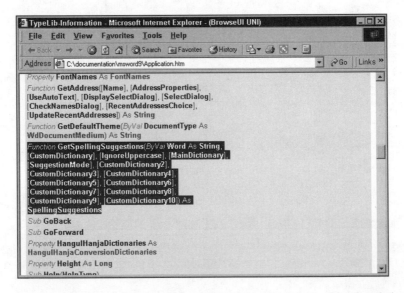

Figure 10-10: Your self-made documentation contains all the method descriptions needed.

Secret

To be able to use the methods of your WinWord object, you need to initialize it. `Word.documents.Add` adds a blank new document. Without a document, Word won't allow you to use its methods because it thinks you are a software pirate. Fool WinWord in thinking your requests come from some document macro. Don't forget to close WinWord after use: Even if WinWord remains invisible, it's still there and will otherwise clutter your memory space.

A whole new universe . . .

At this point, you probably have a good feeling for the millions of new and exciting functions your scripts can use. You can even get detailed information about all the methods and properties your documentation has revealed. Visit `msdn.microsoft.com/library` to take a look into the huge MS technical library. It contains the complete MS Office reference for free. And search the entire Internet for method names you find interesting! Chances are great you will find many useful examples and comments on tricks and other undocumented implications.

Finally, don't forget that TypeLibraries and `IDispatch` are general concepts. They not only apply to MS Office. Check out your favorite drawing program like Corel Draw, and you will discover all kinds of handy graphics functions and converting algorithms. It's a whole new universe, and with this knowledge, your scripts can finally act as software glue — picking out the best and most powerful functions from existing software packages to create your very own (and very free) personal software solutions.

Summary

This chapter is full of powerful new methods and tricks that you can use to exploit the special capabilities of external programs. First, you learned how to run external programs and safely send keystrokes to control them. You found a dependable way to switch any window to the foreground, and you also found that running many programs consecutively builds the basis for maintenance tools and true batch file replacements.

New script extensions allow you to determine the names of all open windows and close them all down at once. You can now launch DOS commands and Control Panel applets. Most importantly, you know how to hook into modern software and use its internal functionality for your own purposes.

Chapter 11

Controlling Running Software

In This Chapter

▶ Learn how ProcessIDs identify running tasks

▶ Close any running program entirely by script

▶ Find out the individual module names within a program

▶ Find out the Windows version you are currently running

▶ Enumerate all running processes

▶ Monitor running programs and find out when they are closed

In this chapter, you gain many new methods to control running processes. Among the most important enhancements are your new ability to determine whether a specific program is running and methods to end programs anytime.

Controlling Software Through ProcessIDs

ProcessIDs are internal handles to all running processes. Whenever you use the Run method introduced in the last chapter, you actually work with ProcessIDs. However, Run hides the ProcessIDs from you. This may be convenient at the beginning, but soon it becomes a major obstacle.

Knowing the ProcessID is very useful. It allows you to detect whether a program is (still) running. It allows you to switch to a specific program window, and you can remotely shut down an application, too.

Accessing ProcessIDs directly

Because the Run method won't tell you the ProcessID of software it launches, you are much better off designing your own Run method. This way, you are free to return any information you find valuable, including the ProcessID. I have designed a COM object for you that offers not only an advanced Run method, but also a small armada of helper functions. They allow you to examine the state of an application and to close it down any time.

Full source code is provided on the companion CD, at `\components\ process\process.vbp`. Make sure you either compile it or install the COM object using the prepared package: `install\process\setup.exe`.

This is all you need to launch a program, retrieve its ProcessID, and close it down any time you please:

```
' 11-1.VBS

set tool = CreateObject("process.id")

procID = tool.Run("NOTEPAD.EXE")
MsgBox "I have started the editor and will close it in a second!" _
& " This is possible because I know its ProcessID: " _
& procID, vbSystemModal

tool.EndProcess procID

MsgBox "The editor is gone!"
```

The Run method launches the program asynchronously and returns the ProcessID. With its help, you can now closely monitor your application. EndProcess shuts down the application.

Closing applications under all circumstances

EndProcess is your "nice" way of closing down programs. EndProcess merely whispers "please shut down" to your program. It can't guarantee that the program really closes down. Your program may open a Save As dialog box instead and wait indefinitely for you to answer it.

So, now that you know the ProcessID, it's up to you what the program does. KillProcess is your deadly weapon. It kills the program no matter what (see Figure 11-1).

Undocumented

Use KillProcess with care! Killing a process will guarantee that it closes down. However, the program has no time to save any unsaved changes. Even worse, if the program has opened external DLLs, killing a process won't allow the process to decrement the DLL counter. The DLL may therefore stay in memory although it's not in use anymore. Use KillProcess only if you must.

The next script demonstrates how to use KillProcess. The script first tries to close down the program the "nice" way. It uses a new second argument, specifying a time interval (in milliseconds). If the program doesn't close down within this time frame, EndProcess returns false, indicating the failure.

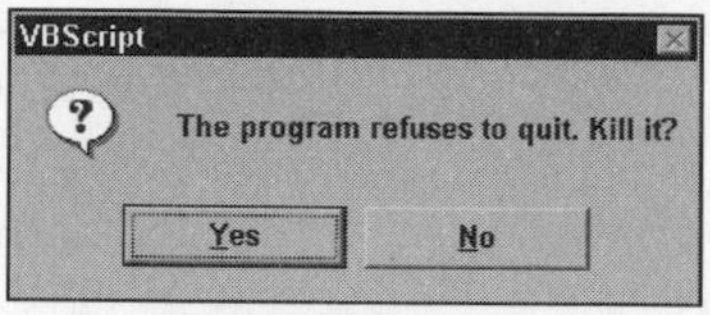

Figure 11-1: Your script can close programs even if they refuse to quit.

Your script informs you and asks for permission to close the program the hard way, as shown by Figure 11-1. If you agree, KillProcess will terminate the program for sure.

```
' 11-2.VBS

set proc = CreateObject("process.id")

pid = proc.Run("NOTEPAD.EXE")
MsgBox "I started the editor and will close it down in a second", _
    vbSystemModal

if not proc.EndProcess(pid, 5000) then
    answer = MsgBox("The program refuses to quit. Kill it?", _
vbYesNo + vbQuestion)
    if answer = vbYes then
        proc.KillProcess(pid)
    end if
end if
```

To test this script, once the editor appears, type in some characters. Then click OK. The script will leave you five seconds to answer the Save As dialog box. If the window is still open after this time period, the script gets nervous and asks whether you want to kill the program. If you agree, it closes the editor using KillProcess. The Save As dialog box disappears, and all unsaved information is lost.

Closely monitoring a program

The official Run method allows you to launch a program and wait for it to finish. This can be of great help, but it halts your script while the external program is executed. What if the external program doesn't respond? What if it takes a long time to execute? Because your script has passed all control to the external program, it's helpless and can't interrupt the running program.

A much better approach would be some message indicating whether or not a program is still running. This way, it would be up to your script to decide whether or not the external program should be interrupted. In fact, the following script illustrates the general concept of running external software with a timeout. In addition, your new methods could also determine the amount of time a program or tool needs to complete some task.

The next script launches the editor and grants you 10 seconds to enter something. Once the time is up, the script closes the editor (see Figure 11-2).

```
' 11-3.VBS

set tool = CreateObject("process.id")

MsgBox "You have 10 seconds to enter something..."
pid = tool.Run("NOTEPAD.EXE")

' wait for program to exit - check every second
do
    WScript.Sleep 1000      ' sleep 1 sec
    counter = counter + 1
' exit after 10 secs or once program closed down
loop while counter<10 and tool.isTaskRunning(pid)

' check whether program is still running
if tool.isTaskRunning(pid) then
    tool.EndProcess(pid)
    MsgBox "Time's up!", vbSystemModal
end if
```

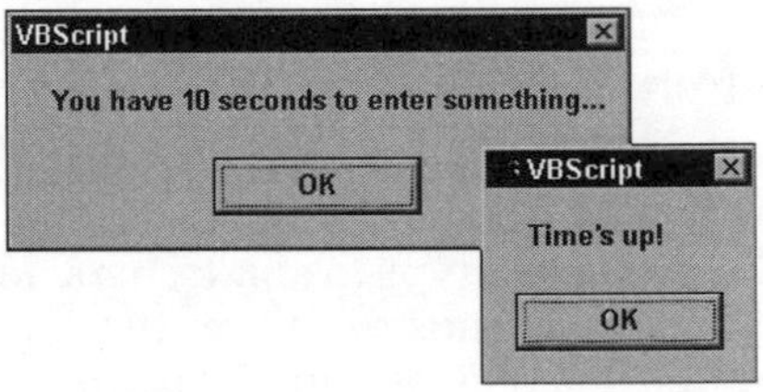

![VBScript dialog boxes: "You have 10 seconds to enter something..." with OK button, and "Time's up!" with OK button]

Figure 11-2: Monitor a program and enforce time-outs.

It's up to you to close the program using `EndProcess` or to resort to `KillProcess`. `KillProcess` closes the program for sure but leaves no time to save unsaved changes. You've already seen an example that uses both `EndProcess` and `KillProcess` in combination.

Running programs synchronously

Your new custom `Run` method offers the same options the official `Run` method provides. For example, you can launch a program and have your script wait for it to end. `WaitForTask` does the job. This method waits until the process you specified ends:

```
' 11-4.VBS

set tool = CreateObject("process.id")
pid = tool.Run("NOTEPAD.EXE")
WScript.Sleep 1000
MsgBox "I'll continue after you closed the editor", vbSystemModal
tool.WaitForTask pid
MsgBox "You closed the editor!"
```

In contrast to the official Run method, after you launch the program, your script remains in control. It can do other things; for example, it can open dialog boxes and provide the user with instructions. Once your script is done, it can convert the asynchronous mode to synchronous mode by calling WaitForTask.

Controlling window style

The official Run method was able to control the window style a program was launched in. Your new custom Run method can do that, too. It accepts the same window style parameter as second argument. So, to launch software in a minimized window, specify 7 as window style. Your custom Run method supports the same set of window styles the official Run method supports, with one exception — the hidden windows (style 0) are not supported.

Note

ScanDisk is only supported on Win9.x. It won't work on Windows NT/2000.

```
' 11-5.VBS

set tool = CreateObject("process.id")

' launch ScanDisk in a hidden window
' ScanDisk only works on Win95/98!
pid = tool.Run("SCANDSKW.EXE /allfixeddisks /silent " _
& "/noninteractive", 7)

' check every 60 seconds to see whether program is still running
ok = false
do
    WScript.Sleep 1000
    counter = counter + 1
    if tool.isTaskRunning(pid) and counter>60 then
        response = MsgBox("Program is still running. " _
& "Do you want to close it down?", vbYesNo)
        if response = vbNo then
            ' reset counter
            counter = 0
        end if
    end if
loop until counter>60 or tool.isTaskRunning(pid)=false

' still running?
if tool.isTaskRunning(pid) then
```

```
        tool.EndProcess(pid)
end if

MsgBox "Done!"
```

Closing external programs

So far, your `EndProcess` and `KillProcess` methods are only able to close programs you launch. Use `EndProgram` and `KillProgram` to end or kill any window. Instead of a `ProcessID`, this time you specify the exact window name. The methods require you to specify the window title exactly as it appears in the window title bar.

Secret

Explorer windows are different: They are run by a central Explorer instance and can't be closed down using your new methods. To close down Explorer windows, use the SendKeys alternative described above.

```
' 11-6.VBS

' closes down window "Document1 - Microsoft Word"
set tool = CreateObject("process.id")
tool.EndProgram("Document1 - Microsoft Word")
```

The method returns true if the window can be closed. You can even specify a timeout and leave the window some time to display its Save As dialog box. The next script closes down the same window and waits for a maximum of 10 seconds. If the window isn't closed within this time frame, the method returns false. Your script can then use `KillProgram` to kill the program forcefully.

```
' 11-7.VBS

' closes down window "Document1 - Microsoft Word"
set tool = CreateObject("process.id")
windowname = "Document1 - Microsoft Word"
closed = tool.EndProgram(windowname, 10000)
if not closed then
    result = MsgBox("Window didn't close - use the force?", vbYesNo)
    if result = vbYes then
        tool.KillProgram(windowname)
    end if
else
    MsgBox "Window has been closed."
end if
```

Splitting Programs into Modules

Programs are not monolithic blocks. Instead, they consist of a number of participating modules. Maybe you have tried to copy a program file to another computer just to discover that it won't run. No wonder: Most programs require a lot of collaborating staff in the background, and only installing a software with its install utility will copy those files to your computer.

It's easy to break up a running program into all of its modules. First, you need to get access to the program's `ProcessID`. Next, you can find out which modules are connected to this process.

All of the dirty work is done by another COM object I have designed for you. Either use it as is, or take a look at its design! It's very interesting because Windows NT uses a completely different set of APIs inside `psapi.dll`. Windows 9.x uses a much more advanced technique hidden in `kernel32.dll`, which is not available to Windows NT. Windows 2000 includes both techniques.

Secret

It's not trivial to examine running tasks. After all, in a multitasking environment, you never know when a task quits. So, during examination, the running tasks may vary. With Windows 95, Microsoft has introduced a new "snapshot" technique: It takes a system snapshot and allows you to examine this snapshot no matter what your tasks do in the meantime. This approach worked so well that Microsoft built it into Windows 2000, too. On Windows NT, in contrast, you need to browse through the actual running tasks. The COM object I designed includes both techniques. It works on all Windows versions.

Make sure you either compile the COM object yourself, using `\components\ spy\spy.vbp`, or install the prepared software package: `\install\spy\ setup.exe`.

Which Windows version is running?

As outlined above, it depends on the Windows version you are running which approach to take. So, the first task is to find out which version you are using. As a service, the COM object makes these methods publicly available, so you can use them for all kinds of purposes (see Figure 11-3):

```
' 11-8.VBS

set tool = CreateObject("module.spy")
if tool.isNTKernel then
     MsgBox "You are running on NT Kernel!"
else
     MsgBox "You are running Windows 95/98!"
end if

if tool.isModernWin then
     MsgBox "You are running Win9x or Windows 2000!"
else
     MsgBox "You are running Windows NT"
end if
```

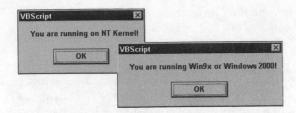

Figure 11-3: Find out which Windows version currently is running.

Enumerating running processes

Ever wondered which processes are currently running on your machine? The next script has the answer, and you'll get a result similar to the one shown in Figure 11-4:

```
' 11-9.VBS

set tool = CreateObject("module.spy")
list = tool.ListProcesses
MsgBox "Currently running:" & vbCr & vbCr & list
```

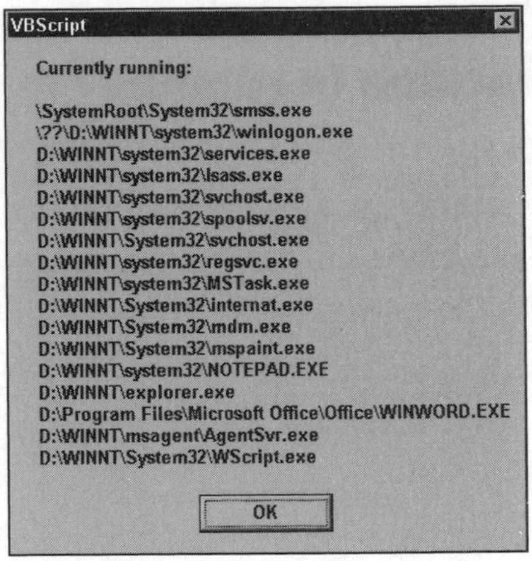

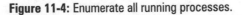

Figure 11-4: Enumerate all running processes.

Now it's easy to find out whether or not a specific program is currently running:

```
' 11-10.VBS

set tool = CreateObject("module.spy")
list = tool.ListProcesses
if Instr(1, list, "\notepad.exe", 1)=0 then
```

```
        MsgBox "Notepad editor is NOT running."
else
        MsgBox "Notepad editor IS running."
end if
```

Secret

Note the use of `Instr`. The script uses it with all possible options and asks for a textual comparison (forth argument set to 1). This is necessary in order to use case-independent comparison.

You can even check how many instances of some program are currently running (see Figure 11-5):

```
' 11-11.VBS

set tool = CreateObject("module.spy")
list = tool.ListProcesses
start = 1
do
        pos = Instr(start, list, "\notepad.exe", 1)
        if pos>0 then
                prgcount = prgcount + 1
                start = pos+1
        end if
loop until pos=0

MsgBox "Notepad editor currently runs " & prgcount & " times."
```

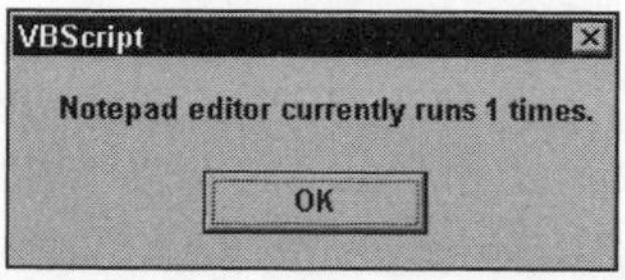

![VBScript dialog box reading "Notepad editor currently runs 1 times." with an OK button]

Figure 11-5: Determine how many instances of a specific program are running at the same time.

Listing program modules

To find out the internal modules a program consists of, use `ModuleList`. The following example opens an editor window and uses the resulting ProcessID to enumerate its modules. Figure 11-6 shows a sample result.

```
' 11-12.VBS

set proc = CreateObject("process.id")
set spy = CreateObject("module.spy")

' start editor
pid = proc.Run("NOTEPAD.EXE")

' wait for Program to be launched
```

```
WScript.Sleep 1000

' let's see all internal modules:
modules = spy.ModuleList(pid)
MsgBox modules

' close editor window
proc.EndProcess pid
```

Note

You can enumerate modules even if you haven't started the program yourself. Use `ModuleListFromName` to specify any window name.

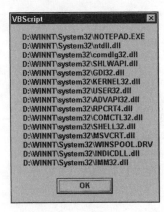

Figure 11-6: Listing the internal modules in use by Notepad Editor

To list the modules "behind" any window, use this technique:

```
' 11-13.VBS

set wshshell = CreateObject("WScript.Shell")
set spy = CreateObject("module.spy")

' open window folder
windir = wshshell.ExpandEnvironmentStrings("%WINDIR%")
wshshell.Run "explorer.exe " & windir

' wait for window to initialize
WScript.Sleep 1000

' let's see all internal modules:
modules = spy.ModuleListFromName(windir)
MsgBox "EXPLORER uses these modules:" & vbCr & vbCr & modules
```

Tip

You can examine any window this way. For example, open a Control Panel applet and specify its name. The following script enumerates any window.

```
' 11-14.VBS

set spy = CreateObject("module.spy")

' let's see all internal modules:
winname = InputBox("Please specify the window title!")
modules = spy.ModuleListFromName(winname)
MsgBox winname & " uses these modules:" & vbCr & vbCr & modules
```

Summary

Your new custom Run method provides you with the ProcessIDs. The ProcessID allows you all kinds of neat tricks. You now have complete control over any program and can close it down, using force if necessary. You can break down a program into its basic modules and find out which programs are currently running. These new methods are your prerequisite to fully remote-controlling external programs.

Chapter 12

Gaining Full Control Over Any Window

In This Chapter

▶ Access any window directly using its handle

▶ Retrieve any window's class name for safe identification

▶ Bring a window safely into the foreground

▶ Make windows invisible and change window style dynamically

▶ Flash a window's title bar

▶ Capture window content and save it to disk

▶ Explore window internals and walking window hierarchies

Window handles are the key to manipulating any window. In this chapter, you learn many new methods for solving common problems. Among the many new solutions, your scripts will be able to switch windows to the foreground and capture entire window contents.

Full Control Over Any Window

Windows are all over the place—they resemble universe containers for your programs and play an important role in reserving space. Surprisingly enough, the Scripting Host doesn't offer any window support at all. Microsoft didn't include any methods to control the size of windows, move them around, or bring them into the foreground.

Fortunately, the Windows API contains numerous functions to remote control any window. To access these features, all you need to do is open the COM project I have designed for you: \components\winmanager\winmanager.vbp. Even easier, you can install the prepared software package: \install\winmanager\setup.exe.

Accessing any window

The first step into the window world is accessing individual windows. Windows administers individual windows similar to processes. Each window has its individual ID, the window handle. It's just a number. You have numerous ways to find out the window handle of any window.

Accessing a window by name

If you know the name of the window you want to access, use `GetWindow-Handle`. The following example asks you for a window name. Type in any window name, but take care to type in the window name exactly as it appears in the window's title bar. The script returns the window class (see Figure 12-1).

```
' 12-1.VBS

set tool = CreateObject("window.manager")

winname = InputBox("Please enter the window name as it appears in" _
    & " its title bar!")

handle = tool.GetWindowHandle(winname)
if handle=0 then
    MsgBox "Couldn't find a window named """ & winname & """"
else
    classname = tool.GetWindowClassName(handle)
    msg = "Window """ & winname & """ ID " & handle & vbCr
    msg = msg & "is of class """ & classname & """"
    MsgBox msg
end if
```

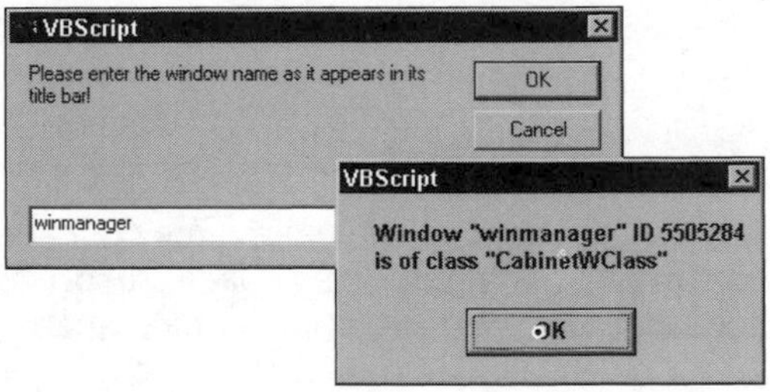

Figure 12-1: Script returns window handle and class name.

It worked. Your script will retrieve the window handle and the window class, as shown in Figure 12-1.

Secret

In addition to the window handle, Windows groups each window by kind. Each application can assign a class name to its windows. On Windows 2000, for example, each Explorer window carries the "CabinetWClass" class tag. Your script can find out the class of any window. You'll see a little later in the chapter how the class name can help identify the right window.

Accessing window by class name

Accessing a window by name is not very safe. For example, the application might display the document name in its title bar, so the window name depends on the kind of document opened by the application.

Class names can help. Let's assume you want to get access to a Notepad editor window. Each Notepad window uses "notepad" as class name. The class name never changes, no matter which document the editor has loaded. The next script finds out if an editor window is open and displays its name:

```
' 12-2.VBS

set tool = CreateObject("window.manager")

handle = tool.GetWindowHandleFromClass("notepad")
if handle = 0 then
    MsgBox "Currently, no editor window open!"
else
    MsgBox "Notepad title: " & tool.GetWindowName(handle)
end if
```

Caution

Class is a reserved VBScript key word. Don't use it as a variable name. I did, and I regretted it.

Accessing a window by class name and title

To safely identify a window, you can even provide both pieces of information. Retrieve the handle by window name and class name. This way, you won't get a window of unexpected type just because it may share the same name.

Use `GetWindowHandle` and supply the class name as second argument.

Accessing the foreground window

The foreground window is especially important. It's the window that receives the keyboard and mouse events, and your `SendKeys` method sends keystrokes to this window.

Finding out the foreground window is especially useful. For example, you can automatically "hook" to a program window your script launched:

```
' 12-3.VBS

set tool = CreateObject("window.manager")
set wshshell = CreateObject("WScript.Shell")

' launch editor
wshshell.Run "notepad.exe"

' wait until window really is in foreground
do
    handle = tool.GetForegroundWindowHandle
    ' find out window class
    classname = lcase(tool.GetWindowClassName(handle))
    ' is right window in foreground?
```

```
if not classname = "notepad" then
          ' wait 1 sec
WScript.Sleep 1000
counter = counter + 1
' waited 5 secs, ask what's going on!
if counter>5 then
              MsgBox classname
              response = MsgBox("Please click notepad to" _
                & " foreground!", vbOkCancel)
              if response = vbCancel then WScript.Quit
              counter=0
          end if
    else
        ok = true
    end if
loop until ok

MsgBox "Notepad in foreground: Handle " & handle
```

Note

When comparing the class name, always use `lcase` to convert it to lowercase letters and compare it to lowercase names. This way, the class name becomes case-insensitive. Wondering which class name a specific window uses? Check out the scripts above to retrieve the class name. Class names never change, and once you know the class name of your application, you are set forever.

The script demonstrates a solution to a common problem. Sometimes, the window you launch from your script doesn't jump into the foreground. Instead, it just nervously flashes its button in the task bar. The reason for this odd behavior was already explained in Chapter 10. The script works around it by checking the foreground window class and asking the user to manually bring the window to the foreground. It's not very elegant, but since you don't know the window handle of your launched window, you can't get around it. There are better ways, though—read on!

Accessing a launched window

There's a better solution! Just use the custom `Run` command you developed in the previous chapter! It returns the ProcessID, and with the help of the ProcessID, you can retrieve the associated window handle. As a side effect, you now have a safe way to determine when the window has initialized itself.

```
' 12-4.VBS

set proc = CreateObject("process.id")
set win = CreateObject("window.manager")

procID = proc.Run("notepad.exe")
if procID=0 then
    MsgBox "Error launching the program..."
    WScript.Quit
end if

' wait for the program to initialize
do
    handle = win.GetWindowFromProcess(procID)
```

```
        ' wait if window isn't on screen yet
        if handle=0 then
        counter = counter + 1
            WScript.Sleep 200
            ' wait 10 secs max
            if counter>50 then
                MsgBox "Your software didn't launch!"
                WScript.Quit
            end if
        end if
loop while handle=0

MsgBox "Editor launched: ID " & handle, vbSystemModal
MsgBox "Bury it under some window so I can bring it up-front!", _
 vbSystemModal

' bring window to front
win.ActivateWindow handle
```

This script does a number of surprising things. First, it uses your custom Run method to retrieve the ProcessID of the program you launched. Next, it loops and waits for GetWindowFromProcess to return the window handle. The moment GetWindowFromProcess returns a valid handle (non-zero), your script knows the program is visible on-screen. It outputs the window handle, as shown by Figure 12-2.

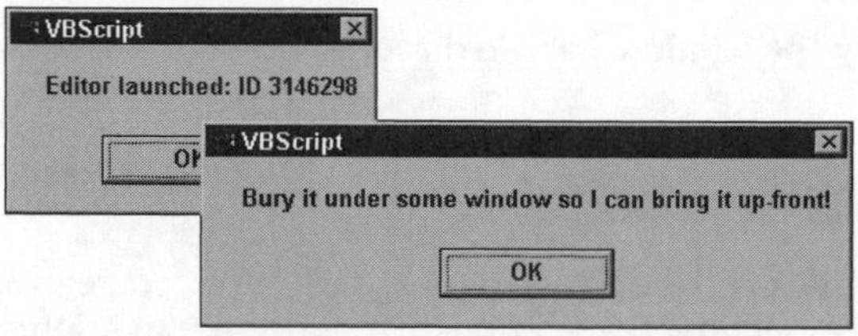

Figure 12-2: Check whether or not a program launched, retrieve its window handle, and bring it to the front.

GetWindowFromProcess is a complicated method. It must enumerate all running windows to find the one with the specified ProcessID. This is why the loop uses a delay of 200 milliseconds between the checks. Without the delay, the loop would eat up way too much CPU power.

Bringing a window to the foreground

The script can do even more. It also demonstrates how to safely bring a window up-front. Once the script asks you to bury the editor window, click some other window so that the editor gets covered. The dialog box will still be visible because of the vbSystemModal option. Click OK. The script uses ActivateWindow in conjunction with the window handle to bring your editor window in front. From now on, you can make sure a program window really is visible.

Secret

`ActivateWindow` works on all Windows versions because internally it temporarily turns off focus lock. Without this step, your script wouldn't be able to send windows in front. Read more about focus lock in Chapter 10.

Closing a window

Knowing the window handle, you can also close the window. `QuitWindow` acts as if you sent [Alt]+[F4] to the window. It's up to the window to decide whether it first wants to pop up some dialog box. `QuitWindow` expects the window name as argument.

Secret

If you must close down a window, don't tamper with it. Instead, use `Get-ProcessIDFromWindow` to retrieve the ProcessID, then use `EndProcess` or `KillProcess` as outlined in the previous chapter.

```
' 12-5.VBS

set tool = CreateObject("window.manager")

MsgBox "I am going to close the foreground window!", vbSystemModal
handle = tool.GetForegroundWindowHandle
name = tool.GetWindowName(handle)
if MsgBox("Do you want to quit """ & name & """?", vbYesNo)=vbYes then
    tool.QuitWindow(name)
end if
```

You can also specify the window handle directly: Use `QuitWindowHandle`.

Making Windows Invisible

Window handling isn't dynamic with the Scripting Host. You can choose the window style when launching the window through the `Run` method. You can't change the window style later on, though. This is too bad.

It would be very helpful to run a program as hidden and pop up its window once a certain timeout is reached—just to make sure the program is still running smoothly. But how?

Your script loses control over the window the moment it launches the external program, but you still have its handle. This handle is the key to dynamic changes.

Finding out the current window style

The window style is just a number. It represents the window size and mode. Table 12-1 lists all available window styles:

Table 12-1   Window Styles

Window Style	Description
0	Hidden
1	Maximized
2	Minimized, next window in order activated
3	Normal size
4	Activates window
5	Activates as maximized
6	Activates as minimized
7	Minimized, not activated
8	Shows window in current mode, not activated
9	Shows window in most recent mode, not activated
10	Shows window as normal window

Many of the options sound similar. They aren't. For example, if you minimize a window using window style 2, the window will float around with its title bar still visible. To minimize a window to the task bar, use window style 7.

It's easy to find out the current window style of any window. The script asks you to click a window, then it reports the current window style, as shown in Figure 12-3.

```
' 12-6.VBS

set tool = CreateObject("window.manager")
MsgBox "Click the window of choice, then click OK!", vbSystemModal
handle = tool.GetForegroundWindowHandle
msg = """" & tool.GetWindowName(handle) & """" uses window mode "
msg = msg & tool.GetShowCommand(handle)
MsgBox msg, vbSystemModal
```

Figure 12-3: Find out the current window style of any window.

Changing window style dynamically

You can change window style any time. To check out the various window styles available, use the next script to enter a new window style. It then applies the new style to the foreground window. Click Cancel to stop the experiment.

```
' 12-7.VBS

set tool = CreateObject("window.manager")
MsgBox "Click the window of choice, then click OK!", vbSystemModal
handle = tool.GetForegroundWindowHandle
originalstyle = tool.GetShowCommand(handle)
do
     oldstyle = tool.GetShowCommand(handle)
     style = InputBox("Current window style: " & oldstyle _
& vbCr & "Please enter new style (0-10):")
     if style = vbEmpty then
          exit do
elseif not isNumeric(style) then
          MsgBox "Please enter a number!"
     elseif Fix(style)<0 or Fix(style)>10 then
          MsgBox "Please enter a number between 0 and 10!"
     else
          tool.SetShowCommand handle, style
     end if
loop
tool.SetShowCommand handle, originalstyle

MsgBox "Done."
```

Now it's easy to hide a window. Here's how:

```
' 12-8.VBS

set win = CreateObject("window.manager")
set proc = CreateObject("process.id")

' launch editor
procID = proc.Run("NOTEPAD.EXE")

' make sure program launched
do
handle = win.GetWindowFromProcess(procID)
if handle = 0 then
     WScript.Sleep 200
     counter = counter + 1
     if counter>10 then
          MsgBox "Program didn't start"
          WScript.Quit
     end if
end if
loop while handle=0

win.SetShowCommand handle, 0
```

```
MsgBox "Notepad now is invisible.", vbSystemModal
win.SetShowCommand handle, 10
win.ActivateWindow handle
MsgBox "Now it's visible again!"
```

Secret

Use ActivateWindow to make sure the window really gets the focus. If you don't, the window may be buried behind other windows.

Changing Window Size and Moving Windows

There's no way for your script to determine the window size. Not yet. Through your window handle, you can not only resize a window but also move the window around on-screen.

Finding out current window dimensions

Wondering how big a window is? Find out!

```
' 12-9.VBS

set tool = CreateObject("window.manager")
MsgBox "Click the window of choice, then click OK!", vbSystemModal
handle = tool.GetForegroundWindowHandle
MsgBox "Current Window Size:" & vbCr _
& tool.GetWindowCoordinates(handle)
```

The script returns the window coordinates as left, top, right, and bottom (see Figure 12-4).

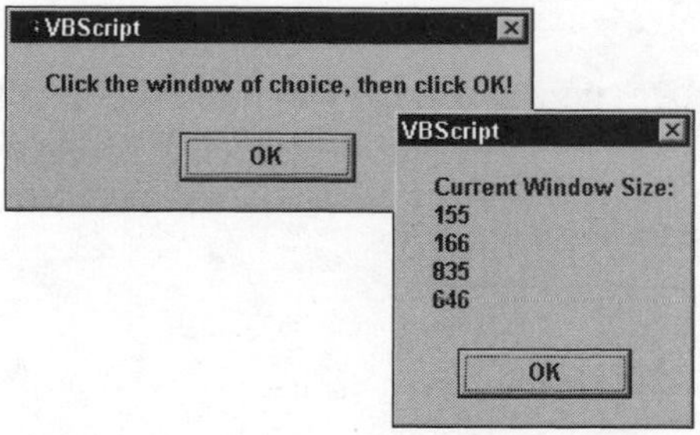

Figure 12-4: The script reports the window's size.

Secret

Wait a minute! The coordinates may be off. This is perfectly normal, because the window coordinates apply to the restored window mode only. If your window is minimized or maximized, you'll still get the window coordinates for restored (normal) mode. This makes sense—a minimized or maximized window has no real "size." With the previous methods, you can find out whether the window is in normal mode, and if not, you can easily switch to normal mode and use individual window sizes.

Changing window size

The opposite way works well, too: You can re-size any window any time.
Here's the solution:

```
' 12-10.VBS

set win = CreateObject("window.manager")
set proc = CreateObject("process.id")

' launch editor
procID = proc.Run("NOTEPAD.EXE")

' make sure program launched
do
handle = win.GetWindowFromProcess(procID)
if handle = 0 then
    WScript.Sleep 200
    counter = counter + 1
    if counter>10 then
        MsgBox "Program didn't start"
        WScript.Quit
    end if
end if
loop while handle=0

' reset window to (100,150) - (500,400)
win.SetWindowCoordinates handle, 100, 150, 500, 400
MsgBox "New coordinates: " & vbCr & win.GetWindowCoordinates(handle)

' reset window to (-40,30), width 300, height 400
win.SetWindowCoordinates2 handle, -40, 30, 300, 400
MsgBox "New coordinates: " & vbCr & win.GetWindowCoordinates(handle)
```

Secret

Use negative numbers to move the window off-screen to the left. In turn, you
can use this script to move any "lost" window into the visible desktop area.
`SetWindowCoordinates2` automatically calculates the width and height
into the appropriate screen coordinates.

Moving windows around

To make transitions smoothly, you can even move windows around. Just make
sure the window is in normal mode. Obviously, a minimized or maximized
window can't move.

```
' 12-11.VBS

set win = CreateObject("window.manager")
MsgBox "Click the window of choice, then click OK!", vbSystemModal
handle = win.GetForegroundWindowHandle

' switch to normal mode
style = win.GetShowCommand(handle)
if style<>1 then win.SetShowCommand handle, 1
```

```
' find out current x and y (left upper corner)
coordinates = Split(win.GetWindowCoordinates(handle), vbCr)

startx = coordinates(0)
starty = coordinates(1)

' move window diagonally
for i = 1 to 100
    call win.WindowMove(handle, startx + i, starty + i)
next

' move back, one dimension only

for i = 1 to 100
    call win.WindowMove(handle, startx + 100 - i)
next

for i = 1 to 100
    call win.WindowMove(handle, , starty + 100 - i)
next
```

If you omit either the x or y coordinate, `WindowMove` will replace the missing value with the current window position.

Resizing windows

Changing the window size works very similar: Use WindowSize!

```
' 12-12.VBS

set win = CreateObject("window.manager")
MsgBox "Click the window of choice, then click OK!", vbSystemModal
handle = win.GetForegroundWindowHandle

' switch to normal mode
style = win.GetShowCommand(handle)
if style<>1 then win.SetShowCommand handle, 1

' find out current size
coordinates = Split(win.GetWindowCoordinates(handle), vbCr)
width = coordinates(2) - coordinates(0)
height = coordinates(3) - coordinates(1)

for x = 1 to 200
    win.WindowSize handle, width+x, height+x
next

for x = 1 to 200
    win.WindowSize handle, width+200-x
next

for x = 1 to 200
    win.WindowSize handle, , height+200-x
next
```

Again, if you omit either width or height, WindowSize will replace the missing argument with the current width or height.

Flashing a Window Title Bar

Whenever Windows wants to catch your attention, it flashes the window title bar. You can do the same, too!

Secret

There are actually two API functions in charge. FlashWindow "manually" changes the title bar state from "selected" to "non-selected" and vice versa. To flash a window using FlashWindow, you need to call this function repeatedly. Windows 98 and Windows 2000 offer a better solution — FlashWindowEx flashes a windows title bar for as long as you want.

Flashing title bars manually

Use FlashWindowManually to flash a window title bar the old way. You'll soon discover that this approach isn't very handy. Your script needs to call the function, and, depending on the processor load, flashing won't work smoothly:

```
' 12-13.VBS

set tool = CreateObject("window.manager")
MsgBox "Click the window of choice, then click OK!", vbSystemModal

' flash foreground window
handle = tool.GetForegroundWindowHandle

for x=1 to 10
    state = not tool.FlashWindowManually(handle, state)
    WScript.Sleep 500
next

' revert to normal
tool.FlashWindowManually handle, false
```

Flashing title bars automatically

A much better approach is automatic flashing. This time, Windows takes care of all the flashing. You just tell Windows to start and stop the flashing:

```
' 12-14.VBS

set tool = CreateObject("window.manager")
MsgBox "Click the window of choice, then click OK!", vbSystemModal

' flash foreground window
handle = tool.GetForegroundWindowHandle

tool.StartFlash handle, 200
```

```
MsgBox "Click OK to stop flashing!", vbSystemModal

tool.StopFlash handle
```

Note

This new and convenient flashing method only works on Windows 98/Windows 2000.

`StartFlash` even allows you to provide the flashing interval. The script uses a flashing interval of 200 milliseconds, but you can adjust flashing to any time interval you like.

As a default, `StartFlash` flashes the window until you call `StopFlash`. There are alternatives. Specify your own flags as third argument (see Table 12-2):

Table 12-2	Flags Controlling Caption Flashing
Flag	**Description**
1	Flash caption only
2	Flash tray button only
1+2 = 3	Flash caption and tray button (default)
4	Flash continuously until StopFlash is called or counter reaches 0
8	Interrupt timer once window becomes active window
4+8 = 12	Flash until window becomes active window

There's even a fourth (optional) argument: a counter. It's set to −1 by default: flash until `StopFlash` is called. By setting the counter to a positive number, Windows will flash the window only for as many times as specified.

```
' 12-15.VBS

set tool = CreateObject("window.manager")
MsgBox "Click the window of choice, then click OK!", vbSystemModal

' flash foreground window
handle = tool.GetForegroundWindowHandle

' flash tray button only, use 600 ms frequency,
' flash 10 times
tool.StartFlash handle, 600, 2, 10
```

Manipulating Window Buttons

Whenever a new window is created, the creating process can specify all kinds of window details. It can specify whether or not the window is going to be resizable and if there should be Maximize buttons in its title bar.

Your scripts don't have this freedom. The Run method won't allow you to specify these details. Again, here comes the window handle to the rescue.

Disabling minimize and maximize

From now on, it's up to your script whether a certain window can be minimized or maximized. Have a look. Figure 12-5 shows a Notepad window without Minimize and Maximize buttons.

```
' 12-16.VBS

set tool = CreateObject("window.manager")
MsgBox "Click the window of choice, then click OK!", vbSystemModal

' use foreground window as guinea pig
handle = tool.GetForegroundWindowHandle

call tool.MinimizeButton(handle, false)
call tool.MaximizeButton(handle, false)
MsgBox "I have disabled minimize and maximize buttons!", vbSystemModal
call tool.MinimizeButton(handle, true)
call tool.MaximizeButton(handle, true)
```

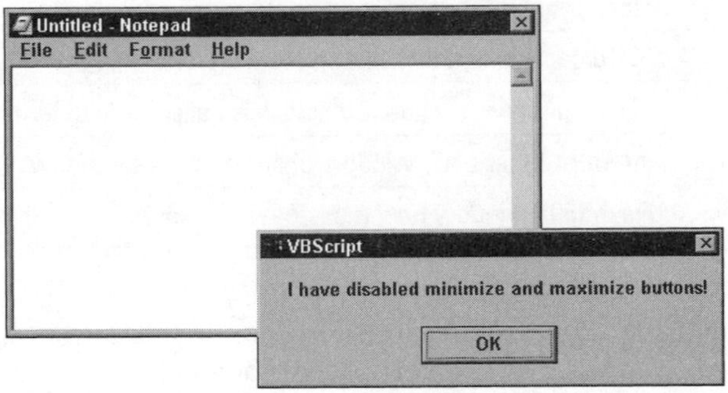

Figure 12-5: Notice how the script has disabled Minimize and Maximize buttons in the title bar.

Caution

It's up to the application whether it will hide the buttons completely or just gray them out. Likewise, it's up to the application whether or not the buttons will re-appear. If they stay hidden, click the window title bar. This causes the title bar to refresh, and the buttons are reverted to normal. Disabling the buttons also disables the corresponding context menu commands.

Disabling the window system menu

Are you familiar with the window system menu? It hides behind the little icon at the far-left position in the title bar. Whenever you click this icon, the main window menu pops up.

You can disable this menu if needed. As a side effect, the icon will disappear, too.

```
' 12-17.VBS

set tool = CreateObject("window.manager")
MsgBox "Click the window of choice, then click OK!", vbSystemModal

' use foreground window as guinea pig
handle = tool.GetForegroundWindowHandle

call tool.SysMenu(handle, false)
MsgBox "I have disabled the window system menu!", vbSystemModal
call tool.SysMenu(handle, true)
```

Secret

Disabling the window system menu also disables the window context menu. Right-clicking a window button in the task bar will no longer open a menu. As with the previous methods, to get back the system menu, you might have to manually click the window title bar.

Disabling window resizing

The window frame controls window size. Change the window frame to disable window resizing.

```
' 12-18.VBS

set tool = CreateObject("window.manager")
MsgBox "Click the window of choice, then click OK!", vbSystemModal

' use foreground window as guinea pig
handle = tool.GetForegroundWindowHandle

call tool.ThickFrame(handle, false)
MsgBox "You can't resize the window anymore!", vbSystemModal
call tool.ThickFrame(handle, true)
```

Hiding and Cascading All Windows

So far, you have always needed to call the API functions yourself. Some selected window functions are generally accessible, though. The `Shell.Application` object contains the necessary methods. They help you to keep a clean desktop.

Minimizing all open windows

Do you want to take a look at your desktop, but as usual numerous windows cover it? Or do you want to start a program and catch the user's attention, but there are too many open windows and things get confusing?

Do something about it! `MinimizeAll` minimizes all windows, and `UndoMinimizeAll` restores the windows after you are done:

```
' 12-19.VBS

set shell = CreateObject("Shell.Application")
shell.MinimizeAll
MsgBox "I've minimized all windows!"
shell.UndoMinimizeAll
MsgBox "They are back...", vbSystemModal
```

MinimizeAll is very important to catch the user's attention. If your script is supposed to interact with the user, then call `MinimizeAll` first to get rid of any other window. Restore the windows using `UndoMinimizeAll` after you are done.

Undocumented

There are some hidden keyboard shortcuts that do the same. You can invoke `MinimizeAll` by pressing [Win]+[M]. `UndoMinimizeAll` is accessed through [Win]+[Shift]+[M]. `MinimizeAll` minimizes only regular windows. Dialog boxes remain visible, so it's an excellent way of finding "lost" dialog boxes. On Windows 98/2000, there's another shortcut: [Alt]+[D] minimizes all windows, including dialog boxes. The same keyboard shortcut restores the windows.

Cascading and tiling windows

Right-click the clock at the right side of your task bar! A context menu pops up, and, among other things, you can organize your open windows: Tile them or cascade them.

Caution

Any one of these commands will resize your windows! Don't use the tile option if more than just a few windows are open. Otherwise, the windows will become very small. In general, all of these methods have a tendency to mess up your neatly arranged window sizes.

The same is available to your script. Use the `Shell.Application` methods `TileHorizontally`, `TileVertically`, or `CascadeWindows`.

Exploring Window Internals and Child Windows

You now have a very good understanding of window mechanics. It's time to enter one of the most undocumented, yet most exciting, parts of Windows: Explore system windows, find out how windows are interconnected, and turn the entire window architecture upside down!

This is not just fun. It gives you an excellent understanding of how core Windows parts like the Start menu and the task bar really work.

Accessing system windows

Before you can enter the hidden world of Windows internal windows, you need to find the secret back door. How can you access a system window like the task bar's Start button? You don't know its name or class, so you can't use any of the previous methods.

You don't need to! Just use the point-and-click approach! `GetWindow-HandleFromCursor` automatically retrieves the window handle from the window the cursor is pointing to. In order for you to have enough time to point to the right window, the method has a built-in delay.

The next script lets you analyze any window. Point at the Start menu button, for example:

```
' 12-20.VBS

set tool = CreateObject("window.manager")

MsgBox "Point at the window you are interested in!" _
     & " I'll grab the window 5 seconds after you clicked OK!", _
     vbSystemModal

handle = tool.GetWindowHandleFromCursor(5)
coords = tool.GetWindowCoordinates(handle)

msg = "Grabbed Window ID " & handle & vbCr
msg = msg & "Window Name: " & tool.GetWindowName(handle) & vbCr
msg = msg & "Class Name: " & tool.GetWindowClassName(handle) & vbCr
msg = msg & "Coordinates: " & vbCr & tool.GetWindowCoordinates(handle)

MsgBox msg
```

Figure 12-6 shows the class name of the Start button. What can you do with your new knowledge? You are now in charge! For example, move the Start button. Point to the Start button and see how the script moves it to the right:

```
' 12-21.VBS

set tool = CreateObject("window.manager")

MsgBox "Point at your Start Menu Button!" _
     & " I'll grab the window 5 seconds after you clicked OK!", _
     vbSystemModal

handle = tool.GetWindowHandleFromCursor(5)
coords = tool.GetWindowCoordinates(handle)

msg = "Grabbed Window ID " & handle & vbCr
```

```
msg = msg & "Window Name: " & tool.GetWindowName(handle) & vbCr
msg = msg & "Class Name: " & tool.GetWindowClassName(handle) & vbCr
msg = msg & "Coordinates: " & vbCr & tool.GetWindowCoordinates(handle)

info = Split(coords, vbCr)
xpos = info(0)
MsgBox msg
MsgBox "Moving the Start Menu Button..."
for x=1 to 400
     tool.WindowMove handle, xpos + x
next
MsgBox "The button still works! Want to reset it?"
tool.WindowMove handle, xpos
```

VBScript

Point at your Start Menu Button! I'll grab the window 5 seconds after you clicked OK!

OK

VBScript

Grabbed Window ID 5112094
Window Name:
Class Name: Button
Coordinates:
0
0
56
22

OK

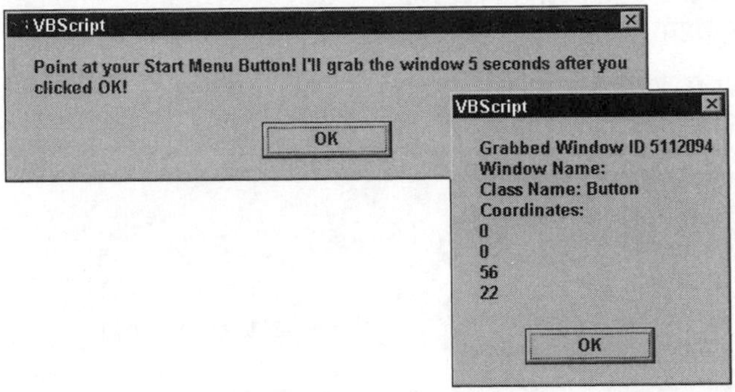

Figure 12-6: Analyzing any window by pointing at it

Wow — the system really is modular. Even the very core components are just regular windows and behave as any window you created.

Think about your new power: You can hide the Start button or move it off-screen. However, how can you access the button (or any other system window) without first having to point at it? The Start button does not have a unique name, and its class is not unique, either.

Finding window parents

Windows are organized hierarchically. After all, someone must have created the window. The creator is the window parent. Use GetParentHandle to find the parent window!

The next script allows you to point at some window. This is the starting point. From here, you can climb the hierarchy and discover the entire window chain. Start your experiment by pointing at the Start menu button!

```
' 12-22.VBS

set tool = CreateObject("window.manager")
```

```
MsgBox "Point at the window you are interested in!" _
     & " I'll grab the window 5 seconds after you clicked OK!", _
     vbSystemModal

handle = tool.GetWindowHandleFromCursor(5)
do
     MsgBox CreateInfo(handle)
     handle = tool.GetParentHandle(handle)
loop until handle = 0

MsgBox "You have reached the top of the window chain!"


function CreateInfo(handle)
coords = tool.GetWindowCoordinates(handle)

msg = "Grabbed Window ID " & handle & vbCr
msg = msg & "Window Name: " & tool.GetWindowName(handle) & vbCr
msg = msg & "Class Name: " & tool.GetWindowClassName(handle) _
& vbCr
msg = msg & "Coordinates: " & vbCr _
& tool.GetWindowCoordinates(handle)
     CreateInfo = msg
end function
```

As it turns out, the Start button is a direct child of the tray bar, and the tray bar has a unique class name: Shell_TrayWnd. You use this inside knowledge a little later in the chapter to access the Start button directly.

Finding child windows

The opposite way is possible, too: You can browse the window chain from top to bottom. Let's see how Shell_TrayWnd is organized:

```
' 12-23.VBS

set tool = CreateObject("window.manager")

handle = tool.GetWindowHandleFromClass("Shell_TrayWnd")
do
     MsgBox CreateInfo(handle)
     handle = tool.GetChildHandle(handle)
loop until handle = 0

MsgBox "You have reached the bottom of the window chain!"


function CreateInfo(handle)
coords = tool.GetWindowCoordinates(handle)

msg = "Grabbed Window ID " & handle & vbCr
msg = msg & "Window Name: " & tool.GetWindowName(handle) & vbCr
msg = msg & "Class Name: " & tool.GetWindowClassName(handle) _
& vbCr
```

```
msg = msg & "Coordinates: " & vbCr _
& tool.GetWindowCoordinates(handle)
    CreateInfo = msg
end function
```

Hiding the Start menu button

The taskbar only has one child — the Start button. So, now you know how to access the button directly, and you can do different things with it. Like hide it, for example. Figure 12-7 shows the result.

```
' 12-24.VBS

set tool = CreateObject("window.manager")
handle = tool.GetWindowHandleFromClass("Shell_TrayWnd")
buttonhandle = tool.GetChildHandle(handle)

style = tool.GetShowCommand(buttonhandle)
tool.SetShowCommand buttonhandle, 0
MsgBox "Start button is invisible!", vbSystemModal
tool.SetShowCommand buttonhandle, style
```

Figure 12-7: Your script can make the Start button invisible.

Enumerating child windows

Actually, GetChildHandle isn't telling you the truth. You probably have already assumed that the Start menu button isn't the only window owned by the task bar.

GetChildHandle uses the API function GetWindow with GW_CHILD as argument. This function returns only the child window at the top of the window staple. This happens to be the Start button. Moving it around in the previous example has shown that it's located above all other tray windows. To find out all child windows, you need a different approach.

To see all child windows, you need to enumerate them using a callback function. I've done the work for you, so have a look at the window kindergarten hidden inside your task bar (see Figure 12-8):

```
' 12-25.VBS
```

```
set tool = CreateObject("window.manager")
handle = tool.GetWindowHandleFromClass("Shell_TrayWnd")
list = tool.EnumChildWindows(handle)
MsgBox list

' split up in individual handles
info = Split(list, vbCr)
for each window in info
     info2 = Split(window, vbTab)
     handle = info2(0)
     MsgBox CreateInfo(handle)
next

function CreateInfo(handle)
coords = tool.GetWindowCoordinates(handle)

msg = "Grabbed Window ID " & handle & vbCr
msg = msg & "Window Name: " & tool.GetWindowName(handle) & vbCr
msg = msg & "Class Name: " & tool.GetWindowClassName(handle) _
& vbCr
msg = msg & "Coordinates: " & vbCr _
& tool.GetWindowCoordinates(handle)
     CreateInfo = msg
end function
```

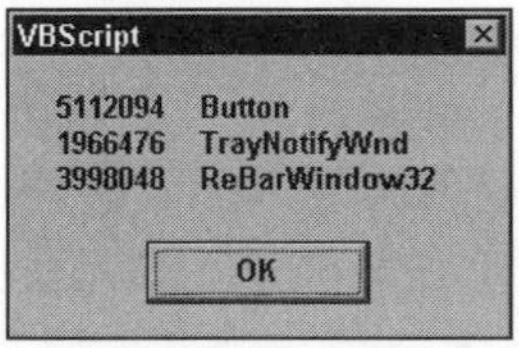

VBScript

5112094	Button
1966476	TrayNotifyWnd
3998048	ReBarWindow32

OK

Figure 12-8: Enumerate all child windows in the task bar area.

Browsing through system windows

Class names and window handles aren't very intuitive. I've designed a
little tool for you to visually browse through the windows (see Figure 12-9).
It makes exploring a lot more fun. Just make sure you installed the COM
object first: \install\treeview\setup.exe. Full source code is included:
\components\treeview\tvtool.vbp. Make sure you have also installed
the window.manager COM object: \install\winmanager\setup.exe.

An Explorer-like tree view control lists all open windows. Click a node in the
tree view to see a snapshot of this window region in the right pane. You can
even copy the selected window bitmap to the clipboard: Click Copy.

```
' 12-26.VBS

set tool = CreateObject("window.manager")
set tree = CreateObject("treeview.tool")

' enumerate all windows: use 0 as window handle
handle = 0
```

```
EnumerateWindow handle, ""

' show dialog
MsgBox tree.ShowDialog


' recursively search all child windows
sub EnumerateWindow(handle, root)
    ' don't list minimized windows:
    sc = tool.GetShowCommand(handle)
    minimized = (sc=0) or (sc=2) or (sc=6) or (sc=7)

    ' don't list invisible windows
    ' do list if handle is zero!
    if (tool.WindowVisible(handle) and not minimized) _
or handle=0 then
        name = tool.GetWindowName(handle)
        if name = "" then name = "(none)"
        classname = tool.GetWindowClassName(handle)
        if handle=0 then
            classname = "Root"
            name = ""
        end if

        ' add new node in TreeView
        newroot = tree.AddNode(classname & ": " _
& name, handle, root)

        if handle = 0 then
            tree.ExpandNode newroot
        end if

        ' enumerate child windows...
        list = tool.EnumChildWindows(handle)
        ' split up in individual handles
        info = Split(list, vbCr)
        for each window in info
            info2 = Split(window, vbTab)
            handle = info2(0)
            ' ...and call procedure recursively!
            EnumerateWindow handle, newroot
        next
    end if
end sub
```

Undocumented

Use 0 as handle to enumerate all available windows. `EnumChildWindows` will enumerate all top-level windows when you specify 0 as handle.

This tool makes window exploration easy! There are just a couple of details to note:

■ Is the window covered? The tool lists all visible windows, but it can't guarantee that the window region is really visible. If some other window is covering part or your entire window, you'll get garbled images. This is by design. Your tool can only copy the display memory bound by the window you selected. It can't do anything about other windows in the way.

- The Tree View tool has a built-in ToolTip capability. Whenever the name of a node is too long to fit entirely into the control, the ToolTip appears. Just wait for it to go away or use the cursor keys to navigate through your tree. The tool returns the window handle of the selected window.

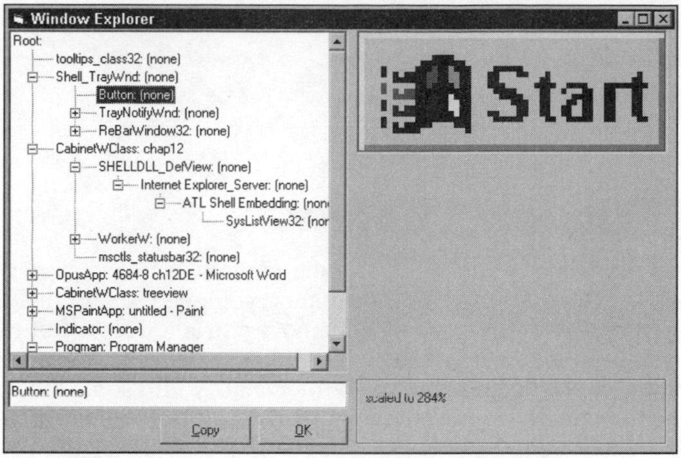

Figure 12-9: Explore any window and get a thumbnail preview.

Hiding the desktop

Maybe you have noticed an odd entry in your Window Explorer: Progman: Program Manager. Although you are running 32-bit Windows, the good old Program Manager is still there!

In contrast to Windows 3.11, now it represents the entire desktop. Check it out: The following script hides your entire desktop:

```
' 12-27.VBS

set tool = CreateObject("window.manager")
handle = tool.GetWindowHandle("Program Manager", "Progman")
oldstyle = tool.GetShowCommand(handle)
tool.SetShowCommand handle, 0
MsgBox "Hiding the desktop!"
tool.SetShowCommand handle, oldstyle
```

Changing desktop View mode

If you browse through its child windows, you'll discover the child object SysListView32. This object is really an Explorer window. It represents all the icons on your desktop.

Normal Explorer windows offer you many different view options. The desktop, however, always displays its content as Large Icons. Always? Not if you try the next script. Since you now know the window handle, it's easy to set the View mode manually:

```
' 12-28.VBS

set tool = CreateObject("window.manager")
handle = tool.GetWindowHandle("Program Manager", "Progman")
handle = tool.GetChildHandle(handle)
handle = tool.GetChildHandle(handle)

for x = 1 to 4
    tool.ViewMode handle, x
    MsgBox "Desktop now in View mode " & x
next
```

Capturing Window Content

Windows share one common fact — their content is stored somewhere in display memory. To capture the content, you need to find the display memory and copy it into your own memory storage. This is not enough, though. To be able to display the captured memory, copy it to the clipboard, or store it as a file, you need to wrap the memory into some kind of container. You need to convert the raw memory snapshot into an OLE picture.

I have designed a COM object that does all of this for you. This object is the foundation for capturing any screen area or window. To use the following scripts, make sure you have installed the COM object: \install\capture\ setup.exe. Full source code is provided on your CD: \components\capture\ capture.vbp.

Capturing the entire screen

Capturing the screen is very easy: `GetForegroundWindowHandle` retrieves the window handle of the window in the foreground, and `CaptureWindow` converts the display memory into an OLE picture.

Your COM object now can easily copy it to the clipboard or use `SavePicture` to save it as a file.

```
' 12-29.VBS

set tool = CreateObject("OLE.bitmap")
set wshshell = CreateObject("WScript.Shell")

' capture screen to file:
filename = "C:\myshot.jpg"
tool.CaptureScreenToFile filename

' display (works only if graphics software is available)
MsgBox "I'll now try to show the screenshot to you...", vbSystemModal
wshshell.Run filename
```

You want to copy the screen shot to the clipboard to insert it into other programs directly? Go ahead: `CaptureScreenToClip` does the job.

Capturing the active window

Capturing the active window works similarly. Use `CaptureActive-WindowToClip` and `CaptureActiveWindowToFile`. Internally, this time the method uses the `GetForegroundWindow` API function to retrieve the active window's handle.

Capturing any window

Using a window handle, you can capture any window or any child window inside of some window. If you know the window handle already, use `CaptureWindowToClip` or `CaptureWindowToFile`. If you don't know the window handle, you can point at the window you want to capture: Use `CaptureCursorToClip` or `CaptureCursorToFile`:

```
' 12-30.VBS

set tool = CreateObject("OLE.bitmap")
set wshshell = CreateObject("WScript.Shell")

' capture screen to file:
filename = "C:\myshot.jpg"
delay = 5

MsgBox delay & " secs after you clicked OK, I'll capture!" & vbCr _
     & "Please point at the window!", vbSystemModal
tool.CaptureCursorToFile delay, filename


' display (works only if graphics software is available)
MsgBox "I'll now try to show the screenshot to you...", vbSystemModal
wshshell.Run filename
```

The script displays a dialog box. Click OK. Now you have five seconds to point at the window you want to capture. For example, click the Start menu button and point at the Start menu.

Provided you have installed graphics software that is capable of displaying .bmp files, the script presents the captured shot to you.

Displaying a window preview

The COM object contains a little tool for you — `ShowWindow` pops up a dialog box and displays a preview of any window, as shown in Figure 12-10.

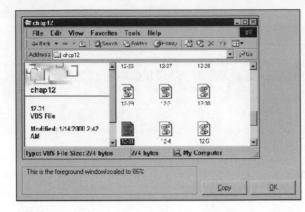

Figure 12-10: Preview any window and capture the window to the clipboard.

```
' 12-31.VBS

set tool = CreateObject("OLE.bitmap")
set win = CreateObject("window.manager")

' get foreground window handle
handle = win.GetForegroundWindowHandle

' display preview (and allow to capture)
tool.ShowWindow handle, "This is the foreground window!"
```

Summary

In this chapter, you learn how to access windows directly using their handles. Self-defined COM objects provide numerous ways to find out window handles, and using the handles, it becomes possible to hide windows or change window style dynamically. Your scripts now can even resize and move any window on-screen.

Additional tools let you browse through window hierarchies and dive into the many hidden and undocumented system windows. Knowing these, you can hide the entire desktop or move the Start button around.

Even better, another COM object lets you capture any window handle and convert the display memory into an OLE picture object that you can save to file or copy to the clipboard.

Chapter 13

Starting Scripts Automatically

In This Chapter

▶ Launch scripts automatically when a user logs on — or even before anybody logs on

▶ Start scripts invisibly from inside your Registry

▶ Use the system agent to launch service scripts in intervals

▶ Insert scripts as context menu extensions into any context menu

▶ Find out about the hidden system variables used inside context menus

▶ Copy file names to the clipboard

Scripts can be launched in a variety of ways. In this chapter, you learn how to launch scripts automatically and how to introduce your own scripts into any context menu and use it as a Windows command extension.

Starting Scripts the Smart Way

What if you want your script to launch automatically — say, every Wednesday afternoon — to search for outdated files? What if you want to use scripts to find out details about a drive? Launching scripts manually is no real alternative.

Fortunately, Windows allows you to run scripts automatically, launch scripts with keystrokes, and even insert your scripts into context menus of any file type.

Launching scripts at logon

The easiest way to launch a script is to place a shortcut into the StartUp program group. The following script helps you do this.

```
' 13-1.VBS

set args = WScript.Arguments
if args.Count=0 then
    MsgBox "Please drag a vbs script file on my icon." _
```

```
             & " I'll place it into the Startup group!"
      WScript.Quit
end if

set fs = CreateObject("Scripting.FileSystemObject")
set wshshell = CreateObject("WScript.Shell")

scriptfile = args(0)
if not lcase(fs.GetExtensionName(scriptfile))="vbs" then
      MsgBox "I only accept vbs script files!"
      WScript.Quit
end if

startup = wshshell.SpecialFolders("Startup")
name = InputBox("Under which name should I place the script " _
      & """" & fs.GetBaseName(scriptfile) & """" into the StartUp-" _
      & "Group?", "autostart script")

set scut = wshshell.CreateShortcut(startup & "\" & name & ".lnk")
scut.TargetPath = scriptfile
scut.Save

MsgBox "Script has been successfully linked to your StartUp group!"
```

Drag a script file onto this script icon and specify a name, as shown in Figure 13-1. The script automatically inserts a shortcut to your script into the StartUp program group, and the next time you log on to Windows, your script will be executed.

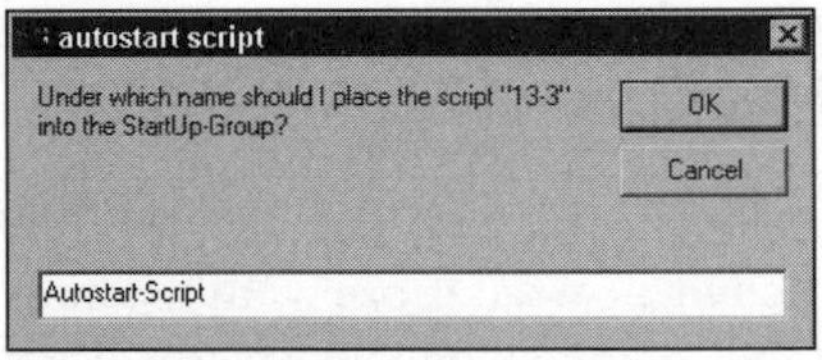

![autostart script dialog box with text "Under which name should I place the script "13-3" into the StartUp-Group?" and buttons OK and Cancel, with input field containing "Autostart-Script"]

Figure 13-1: Insert scripts into the StartUp group and specify a name.

Secret

To launch the script, no matter which user logs on, place the shortcut into the common StartUp group (instead of your personal StartUp group). Replace Startup with AllUsersStartUp. The common StartUp group is available on Windows 98, NT, and 2000.

Hiding script launch

The StartUp group is visible to the user. Maybe you'd rather launch your script from a hidden place. The Registry provides such a place: It's the Run key. To place your script into the Run key, use the following script:

```
' 13-2.VBS

set args = WScript.Arguments
if args.Count=0 then
    MsgBox "Please drag a vbs script file on my icon." _
        & " I'll place it into the Startup group!"
    WScript.Quit
end if

set fs = CreateObject("Scripting.FileSystemObject")
set wshshell = CreateObject("WScript.Shell")

scriptfile = args(0)
if not lcase(fs.GetExtensionName(scriptfile))="vbs" then
    MsgBox "I only accept vbs script files!"
    WScript.Quit
end if

key = "HKLM\Software\Microsoft\Windows\CurrentVersion\Run\"
' use this key on Windows NT/2000:
'key = "HKLM\Software\Microsoft\Windows NT\CurrentVersion\Run\"

wshshell.RegWrite key & "myscript", scriptfile
MsgBox "Script has been successfully added to the Run key!"
```

Note

Windows 9.x and Windows NT/2000 use different keys. Note the comment in the script file and use the appropriate key.

The key used by the script applies to all users. It's part of HKEY_LOCAL_ MACHINE, so it's a user-independent setting. If you want to launch your script for individual users only, replace HKLM with HKCU (currently logged-on user) or HKU\username\.

Caution

The script can only add one script file to the Run key because it always uses the subkey named myscript. Any time you add a new script file, the old entry will be replaced. You could work around this behavior and assign different subkey names, but this wouldn't make much sense. Although there is no limitation on how many script files you can launch automatically, you should always stick to one file only. Running more than one script at the same time can cause trouble when both scripts try to access a COM object at the same time. If you must launch more than one script, use a "launch" script only and launch your scripts from inside this script, using synchronous calling as outlined in Chapter 10.

To get rid of Registry-controlled script launching, start the Registry Editor, choose Run from your Start menu, and enter REGEDIT. Then, use the Edit menu to search for the key Run and delete the subkey your script added. Figure 13-2 shows the Registry Editor. Or, let a script do the work:

```
' 13-3.VBS

set wshshell = CreateObject("WScript.Shell")
key = "HKLM\Software\Microsoft\Windows\CurrentVersion\Run\"
```

```
' use this key on Windows NT/2000:
'key = "HKLM\Software\Microsoft\Windows NT\CurrentVersion\Run\"

wshshell.RegDelete key & "myscript"
MsgBox "Deleted script entry from Registry."
```

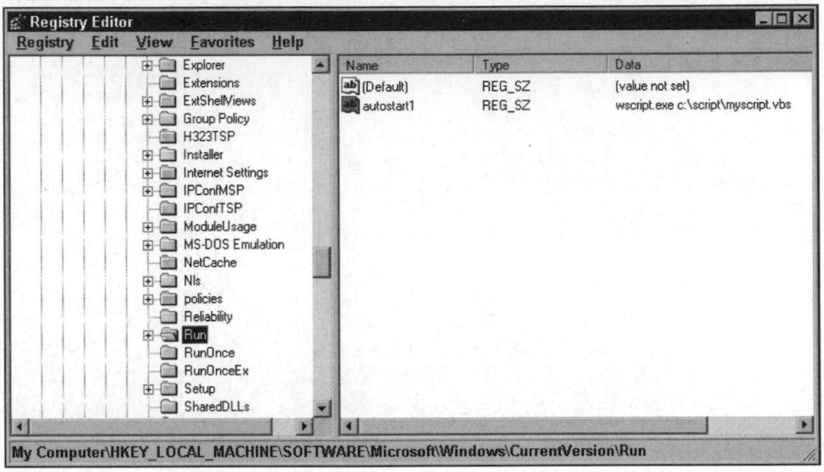

Figure 13-2: Launch scripts from inside the Registry using the Run key.

Launching scripts before logon

You can even launch scripts before anybody logs on. For example, in a company setting, computers may be switched on automatically in the morning. Your script can accomplish boring maintenance work before people actually start working on the machines.

However, this only works on Windows 9.x. There isn't any NT security available for this, so even though nobody has logged on, your script can do whatever it pleases. On Windows NT/2000, you can't run scripts prior to logging on.

To launch scripts prior to logon, use the previous scripts but use a different key. Instead of Run, use the RunServices key!

Launching scripts in intervals

Microsoft has developed a flexible system to launch software automatically in intervals. This system is called System Agent or Scheduled Tasks. It may not be available on your system. For Windows 95, it comes separately with the Plus! pack. On Windows 98 and 2000, it's already included. Open My Computer on the desktop, and you see the icon Scheduled Tasks. On Windows 2000, open Scheduled Tasks in the Control Panel.

The dialog boxes will look similar to the one shown in Figure 13-3 (the wizard works slightly different on different Windows versions).

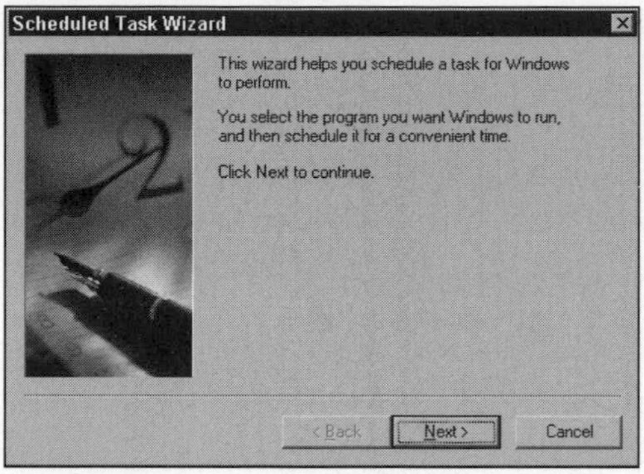

Figure 13-3: The Scheduled Task Wizard helps schedule your scripts for automatic launch.

The task scheduler can launch any program, including your scripts. It's the perfect solution for any maintenance or backup script. Just supply the script name.

Secret Even without the task scheduler, you can make your scripts check in regular intervals. Just use a loop and delay the loop for as long as you want the interval to last. For example, a `WScript.Sleep 10*60*1000` delays the loop for 10 minutes, instructing the script to check every 10 minutes for disk space, Internet connections, or whatever you want to monitor. However, you have no way of stopping your script except by opening the task list and killing `wscript.exe` manually.

Inserting Scripts into Context Menus

Windows is object-oriented: Whenever you right-click an object, a context menu appears and offers the most fundamental commands this object has to offer.

Did you know that context menu entries are fully programmable? You can easily insert your own commands and use scripts as context menu extensions!

For example, let's assume you want a command to find out the size of some folder or drive. This is what your command would look like:

```
' 13-4.VBS

set fs = CreateObject("Scripting.FileSystemObject")
set args = WScript.Arguments
if args.Count=0 then
    MsgBox "Please drag a file, folder or drive on my icon!"
```

```
        WScript.Quit
end if

' args(0) now contains the file/folder/drive name
' find out which type it is
if fs.FileExists(args(0)) then
     set object = fs.GetFile(args(0))
elseif fs.FolderExists(args(0)) then
     set object = fs.GetFolder(args(0))
else
     MsgBox "You did not drag a file/folder/drive - can't find out" _
          & " size!"
     WScript.Quit
end if

MsgBox """" & args(0) & """ size: " & _
FormatSize(object.size), vbInformation

function FormatSize(bytes)
     if bytes<1024^2 then
          FormatSize = FormatNumber(bytes/1024,1) & " KB"
     else
          FormatSize = FormatNumber(bytes/1024^2,1) & " MB"
     end if
end function
```

It works: Dragging a file or folder onto your script icon reports its size, as shown in Figure 13-4. For folders, the `Scripting.FileSystemObject` correctly calculates the cumulative size of all files and subfolders stored in the folder.

Figure 13-4: Your script determines sizes of files, folders, and drives — even on the network.

Inserting new commands into the folder context menu

How do you place your script into the folder context menu? All you need is some background information on context menu mechanics. It's not complicated.

In the Registry, each registered file type gets its own key in the HKEY_ CLASSES_ROOT branch. This key is named after the file type extension, so your script files would use the .vbs key.

The (Standard) value of this key points to another key, the main program entry. This is where context menus are defined.

The shell subkey organizes context menu entries. Under this key, you find separate keys for each context menu command, and another subkey called command contains the actual command to be executed.

Confusing? Not really! The next script inserts any script into the context menu of your folders (and drives):

```
' 13-5.VBS

set wshshell = CreateObject("WScript.Shell")

' find out the script file you want to use as command extension
set args = WScript.Arguments
if args.Count=0 then
    MsgBox "Please drag a vbs script file onto my script icon!"
    WScript.Quit
end if

' did I receive a vbs file?
if not lcase(Mid(args(0), InstrRev(args(0), ".")))=".vbs" then
    MsgBox "I only accept vbs script files!"
    WScript.Quit
end if

' insert this key as new context menu command:
name = InputBox("How do you want to call your new command?", _
,"Show size")

' start with this key. Folders don't have a file type so
' you can use this key right away:
key1 = "HKCR\Folder\shell\"

' insert command name
wshshell.RegWrite key1 & name & "\", name

' insert command
wshshell.RegWrite key1 & name & "\command\", _
"wscript.exe " & """" & args(0) & """" & " ""%L"""

MsgBox "New command installed successfully!"
```

Drag your size script onto this script icon. The script asks for a name (see Figure 13-5). Automatically, it then generates the appropriate Registry entries. The next time you right-click a folder or drive, the context menu shows your new command, and when you test it, Windows calculates the size (see Figure 13-6). Note that Windows actually recalculates the size of any file, so it may take some seconds on large drives.

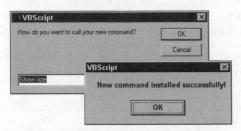

Figure 13-5: Insert any script into the folder context menu.

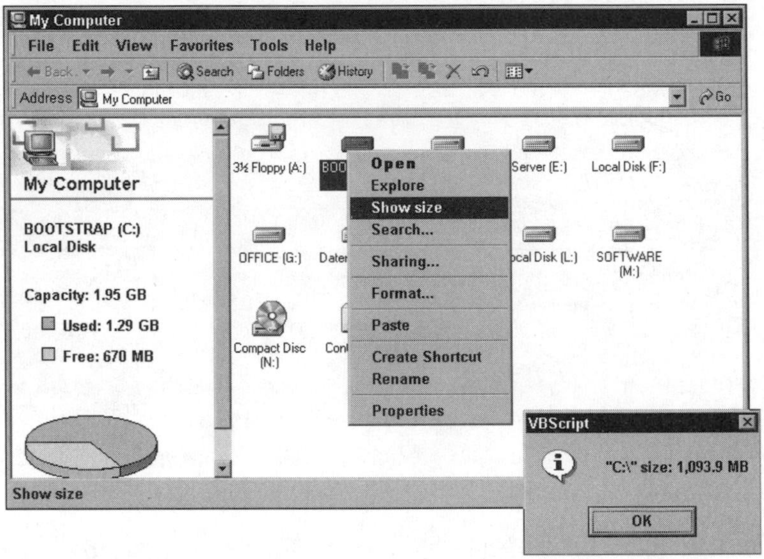

Figure 13-6: Your new context menu command in action as it calculates the drive size

Insider knowledge about context menus

Remember some key points in order for your extensions to work:

■ Never run a script directly. The context menu wants to execute something, and .vbs files can't be executed directly. Always use `wscript.exe` as executable and specify the script name as argument.

■ Enclose the script name in quotes. This is why the script uses `""""`, which resolves to a single quote. If you don't use quotes, you'll get in trouble once your script path name contains spaces.

■ Append a `%L` to your command string. `%L` is an internal variable and delivers the (long) path name of the object your user clicked. This is how your script finds out which folder it should examine. Don't use the standard variable `%1`. `%1` delivers the same information but not as long file name. Instead, `%1` interprets spaces as delimiters and is used for command line arguments only.

- To qualify as a context menu extension, your script needs a "receiver" to read in the name of the object the user has clicked. Since the object name is passed as command line argument, your script only needs to query WScript.Arguments and take the first argument as object name.

- Use & in your context menu name to define keyboard shortcuts.

Cross-Reference

For an in-depth look at the context menu system, see Chapter 16.

The best way to get rid of context menu entries is to open the Registry Editor and manually surf to the key. Delete the subkey your script created in the shell subkey. In Chapter 15, you get all the methods necessary to enumerate and automatically delete Registry entries.

Secret

Not all context menu commands are defined this way. There are other context menus derived from the ShellEx subkey. These commands are "handlers" that are tightly integrated into the shell. The context menu commands that an object displays most of the time are combinations. For example, drives combine the context menu commands defined in the keys drive and folder. Folders combine context menu commands defined in the keys directory and folder, so drives and folders share the context menu commands defined in folder. Regular files, in contrast, combine the commands defined in their own key with those defined in *. Whenever you hold down [Shift] while right-clicking a file, you also see the context menu commands defined in Unknown. Files not associated with any program always resort to the context menu commands defined in Unknown.

Inserting new commands into any file's context menu

In the previous example, your destination — the drives and folders — didn't have a file type. This is why the script jumped to the folder subkey right away. You can replace folder in the example above with any one of the keys listed in Table 13-1 to change the destination of your script.

Table 13-1	Registry Keys Representing Important Context Menus
Key	**Description**
Drive	Command appears for drives only.
Directory	Command appears for folders only.
*	Command appears for all files.
Unknown	Command appears for unknown files or when you hold down [Shift] while opening a file context menu.

But what if you want to insert your command into a specific context menu — say, the context menu of your .vbs script files?

In this case, you need to find out the file type main key. The next script shows how to do this:

```
' 13-6.VBS

set wshshell = CreateObject("WScript.Shell")

' find out the script file you want to use as command extension
set args = WScript.Arguments
if args.Count=0 then
    MsgBox "Please drag a vbs script file onto my script icon!"
    WScript.Quit
end if

' did I receive a vbs file?
if not lcase(Mid(args(0), InstrRev(args(0), ".")))=".vbs" then
    MsgBox "I only accept vbs script files!"
    WScript.Quit
end if

' which file type do you want to append?
filetype = InputBox("Please enter the file extension for the " _
    & "file type you want to add a context menu command to!", _
    , ".vbs")
if not left(filetype,1)="." then filetype = "." & filetype


' find out whether this key exists
on error resume next
prgkey = wshshell.RegRead("HKCR\" & filetype & "\")

' file type unknown!
if not err.number=0 then
    MsgBox "File Type """ & filetype & """ is unknown!"
    WScript.Quit
end if
on error goto 0

' insert this key as new context menu command:
name = InputBox("How do you want to call your new command?", _
    ,"Show size")

' start with this key
key1 = "HKCR\" & prgkey & "\shell\"

' insert command name
wshshell.RegWrite key1 & name & "\", name

' insert command
wshshell.RegWrite key1 & name & "\command\", _
    "wscript.exe " & """" & args(0) & """" & " ""%L"""

MsgBox "New command installed successfully!"
```

Copying the filename to the clipboard

Here's another suggestion for a useful context menu add-on: This script places the object name handed by %L into the clipboard. It uses a special COM object to access the clipboard, so make sure you have installed \install\clipboard\setup.exe from your CD! Full source code is provided: \components\clipboard\clipboard.vbp.

```
' 13-7.VBS

set wshshell = CreateObject("WScript.Shell")

set args = WScript.Arguments
if args.Count=0 then
    MsgBox "Please drag a file onto my script icon!"
    WScript.Quit
end if

set tool = CreateObject("Clip.board")
tool.SetClipBoardText args(0)
wshshell.Popup "Pasted information into clipboard", 1, _
"Info", vbInformation
```

Modify script 13-5.VBS to place it into the * subkey so it appears in the context menus of all files. All you need to do is replace "folder" with *. After you have copied a filename to the clipboard, use [Strg]+[V] to insert it any place.

Summary

In this chapter, you gained a good overview of how to start script files. Besides the manual launch, Windows offers many alternatives to call scripts automatically.

One of the most fascinating possibilities is using simple script files as context menu extensions. You learned how to enable your scripts to "receive" the context menu object name and how to place scripts in any context menu.

Part IV

Accessing the Operating System

Chapter 14: Getting Access to the Registry

Chapter 15: Registry Tweaks

Chapter 16: Getting System Information

Chapter 17: Working with Events

Chapter 18: Developing Unix-like Commands

Chapter 14

Getting Access to the Registry

In This Chapter

▶ Find out why the Registry is so important and how to back up its contents

▶ Find out how the Registry organizes the internal Windows settings into different branches

▶ Use script commands to read and write to the Registry, and learn how to safely exchange the registered owner information

▶ Store your own values into the Registry and delete Registry information you no longer need

▶ Enumerate entire Registry branches and list all entries hidden inside a key

The Windows Registry is the ultimate place to control Windows at a very granular level. Learn how to access and manipulate the Registry by script, and use a custom COM control to add Registry methods not found in the standard `WScript.Shell` object.

Getting to Know the Registry

The Registry is an incredible source of power — it's here that Windows stores all its internal settings. You can control many Registry settings through system dialog boxes, but many more Windows options are hidden and available only through direct Registry access.

Let's take a look at the Registry's anatomy first. Then, I'll show you how to back up your Registry. Once you know the Registry better, it's safe to use scripts to manipulate Registry entries and create your own dialog boxes for any Windows option missing in the official dialog boxes.

Where does the Registry live?

The Registry actually is a database. It's merely data storage, and it's organized differently for Windows 9.x and Windows NT/2000.

Registry on Windows 9.x

On Windows 9.x systems, the Registry consists of two files — USER.DAT and SYSTEM.DAT. They are stored in the Windows folder and marked as hidden. SYSTEM.DAT contains all common settings, and USER.DAT contains user-related information.

Secret

If you have set up your Windows 9.x to support multiple user profiles, the Registry still uses the central SYSTEM.DAT. For the user information, it uses individual USER.DAT files stored in the profiles subfolder.

Registry on Windows NT/2000

Windows NT/2000 organizes the Registry differently. Here, only users with Administrator or Power User membership have access to the files. The common machine-related information is stored in the subfolder SYSTEM32\CONFIG and consists of these files:

DEFAULT

SAM

SECURITY

SOFTWARE

SYSTEM

The user-related information is stored in a file called NTUSER.DAT. These files are stored individually in a subfolder called PROFILES/username/.

Accessing Registry content

You don't need to care much about the physical location of your Registry data. All Windows versions come with a special Registry Editor. Just choose Run from your Start menu and enter REGEDIT.

Caution

Don't change any Registry settings yet. The Registry Editor has direct access to the Registry, and any changes will be written to your "live" Registry immediately, without a way to undo the changes. You may easily crash your entire system or render it useless once you restart.

The Registry Editor makes the Registry data visible and uses an Explorer-like two-pane view. In the left column, you see the Registry keys. In the right pane, you see the actual data contained in the selected key.

Table 14-1 shows how the Registry splits up information into a number of main keys, the "handles."

These handles and their subkeys act like file system folders and share the same icon, too. View Registry keys as information folders, and view the data in the right pane as information files.

Table 14-1   Main Windows Registry Keys

Main Key	Description
HKEY_LOCAL_MACHINE	Hardware information and information that applies to all users.
HKEY_CURRENT_USER	User information for the currently logged-on user. It is actually a shortcut to HKEY_USERS\username\.
HKEY_USERS	Access to all user information (accesses all available NTUSER.DAT). On Windows 9.x, you only see your own user account. .default represents the default user account, which is used as long as nobody has logged on.
HKEY_CLASSES_ROOT	Shortcut to HKEY_CLASSES_ROOT\Software\Classes. Contains information about registered file types and COM objects.
HKEY_CURRENT_CONFIG	Mostly a shortcut into HKEY_LOCAL_MACHINE\System\Current Control Set.
HKEY_DYN_DATA	Dynamic performance data only available on Windows 9.x.

The right pane splits information up into a name and a value. The name represents an entry while the value represents its content. To stick to the file system analogy, view the name as filename and the value as file content. Each key has at least one name entry: (Standard).

Backing up the Registry

Before you start experimenting with the Registry, you should make sure to create a backup. It's your only safety net. If something goes wrong or you accidentally delete the wrong item, you can always restore your backup. Without a backup, you would be lost and would most likely need to reinstall your complete system.

Secret

Backing up the Registry is generally a good idea. Many Windows problems occur during software- or hardware-modification. With the help of a current Registry backup, you can undo those errors and revitalize your system in a matter of seconds. A Registry backup, therefore, is one of the most important safeguards you can take advantage of.

Backing up on Windows 95

On your Windows CD, you'll find the folder ERD. Copy it to your hard drive, then launch ERU.EXE. It will create a complete backup of important system files, including the Registry. Don't use disks to store the backup—they are too small and won't save the Registry. Instead, store the backup somewhere on your hard drive.

To restore the Registry, you must start your computer in DOS mode. Hold down [F8] while Windows 95 starts and choose Command Prompt Only from the hidden boot menu. Then, navigate to the folder in which you stored your backup using the CD.

Secret

You can't call your backup set from outside the backup folder. You need to change the current directory to the backup directory.

In your backup folder, call ERD [Enter]. The backup will be restored.

Backing up on Windows 98

Windows 98 automatically backs up the Registry every day and maintains the last five copies. You can find them in the SYSBCKUP folder inside your Windows folder.

To restore a backup, start your computer in DOS mode and call SCANREG /RESTORE. Windows checks the current Registry and then offers to restore one of the five last backup sets.

Secret

The Registry will constantly grow in size because deleted entries aren't really deleted. They are just marked as "bad." To re-create your Registry from scratch and discard any unused data, start your computer in DOS mode and use SCANREG /FIX.

Backing up on Windows NT

On Windows NT, you can use the RDISK.EXE utility to create a rudimentary emergency backup disk. It doesn't contain the complete Registry and will only restore the most important keys.

To create a full Registry backup, use the backup software provided with Windows NT. Make sure to select the option Backup Local Registry to include the Registry files.

Caution

You must restore a Registry on the same system that you created the backup. Restoring it on a system with different hardware won't work.

The easiest way to recover from Registry problems is the Last Known Good configuration. If you select this option during boot time, Windows NT will automatically use the last Registry that worked without errors.

Backing up on Windows 2000

Windows 2000 comes with a sophisticated backup program. It allows you to back up files, folders, and the system-relevant parts. The system backup includes the Registry.

Windows 2000 also includes a Last Known Good configuration you can use to quickly solve Registry problems. In addition, Windows 2000 sports many other recovery options organized in its boot menu. Press [F8] while Windows 2000 offers its boot menu option on-screen.

Exporting parts of the Registry

Complete Registry backups are necessary, but you don't need to back up the entire Registry every time you make changes. A much easier way is to export part of the Registry. To do this, you select the branch you want to save in the left Registry Editor pane. Then, you call Export Registry from the Registry menu.

Now, you can export the selected branch or all of the Registry to a REG file. REG files are plain text files — you can open them in any text editor to view the saved settings.

To restore the saved branch, all you need to do is open the REG file. Its content will be merged into the Registry.

Secret

REG files can only add entries. So, if you have made a backup and then added keys to the Registry, merging the backup won't remove the added keys. It will only restore the backed-up entries.

You can even restore REG files automatically You call REGEDIT /S regfilename, for example, by script.

Re-creating a Registry from scratch

On Windows 9.x, you have another option to restore the Registry. If you have exported the entire Registry as REG file, you can rebuild the Registry using this file. In DOS mode, enter REGEDIT /C regfilename.

Caution

Recreating a Registry only works if the REG file really contains the entire backup. The /C option doesn't merge information. Instead, the Registry will be created based entirely on the information stored in the REG file. Also, on old Windows 95 systems, due to an error in REGEDIT.EXE, the creation process fails.

The re-creation process can take many hours. It doesn't have to be that slow, though. If you launch SMARTDRV beforehand, the re-creation process only takes minutes. SMARTDRV activates the old DOS-compliant hard drive cache. Without this cache, file operations in pure DOS mode are incredibly slow.

Reading and Writing to the Registry

How can you access Registry values by script? The WScript.Shell object offers the methods needed, which are RegRead and RegWrite.

Reading the Registered Owner

When you installed Windows, the installer prompted you for your name and organization. This information is stored inside your Registry, and if you want to change these entries, all that's needed is a little change to your Registry.

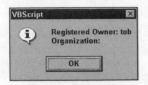

Figure 14-1: Read the Registered Owner information.

Let's first see how to retrieve the information:

```
' 14-1.VBS

set wshshell = CreateObject("WScript.Shell")

key = "HKLM\Software\Microsoft\Windows\CurrentVersion\"
' use this key for Win NT/2000
' key = "HKLM\Software\Microsoft\Windows NT\CurrentVersion\"

owner = ReadKey(key & "RegisteredOwner")
org = ReadKey(key & "RegisteredOrganization")

msg = "Registered Owner: " & owner & vbCr
msg = msg & "Organization: " & org

MsgBox msg, vbInformation

function ReadKey(key)
     on error resume next
     ReadKey = wshshell.RegRead(key)
     if not err.number=0 then
         MsgBox "Couldn't open key """ & key & """: " _
& err.description
         WScript.Quit
     end if
end function
```

The script wraps the RegRead method as ReadKey function. Why? Because RegRead raises an error if the key you are trying to access is missing or not accessible. To prevent this, the function turns off error handling and checks for errors.

Secret

Windows 9.x and Windows NT/2000 use different Registries. Although the Registries are not compatible, they have a very similar architecture. In the example, replace Windows with Windows NT to adjust the script to Windows NT/2000. You can also use the Windows version-checking methods from the previous chapters to adjust the keys automatically.

Changing Registry information

Now that you know where Windows stores the registration info, how can you change the information? Use RegWrite.

```
' 14-2.VBS

set wshshell = CreateObject("WScript.Shell")

key = "HKLM\Software\Microsoft\Windows\CurrentVersion\"
' use this key for Win NT/2000
' key = "HKLM\Software\Microsoft\Windows NT\CurrentVersion\"

ownerkey = key & "RegisteredOwner"
orgkey = key & "RegisteredOrganization"
owner = ReadKey(ownerkey)
org = ReadKey(orgkey)

newowner = InputBox("Change owner information!",,owner)
if newowner = vbEmpty then WScript.Quit
wshshell.RegWrite ownerkey, newowner

neworg = InputBox("Change organization information!",,org)
if neworg = vbEmpty then WScript.Quit
wshshell.RegWrite orgkey, neworg

MsgBox "Changed information"

function ReadKey(key)
     on error resume next
     ReadKey = wshshell.RegRead(key)
     if not err.number=0 then
         MsgBox "Couldn't open key """ & key & """: " _
& err.description
         WScript.Quit
     end if
end function
```

This time, an InputBox dialog box presents you with the current Registry values and allows you to change the information. Right-click My Computer on the desktop and choose Properties to verify that your changes really take effect.

Tricks and tips around Registry edits

RegRead and RegWrite are both pretty straightforward. However, there are some details you should know:

- If the key you supply ends with a \, then RegRead reads the keys (Standard) value, and RegWrite writes the (Standard) value.

- If the key you supply doesn't end with a \, then RegRead uses the last part of your key as entry name. For example, HKCR\.vbs would try to access the entry .vbs. This would fail because .vbs is a subkey. You would have to access it through HKCR\.vbs\.

- In general, it's best to stick to the file system analogy. If your key ends with a \, it represents a "folder" (key). If it doesn't end with a \, it represents a "file" (an entry in the right Registry Editor pane).

As a default, `RegWrite` creates new entries as String Value. If you want to create entries of different type, add the desired type according to Table 14-2.

Table 14-2   Registry Variable Types

Entry Type	Description
REG_SZ	String Value
REG_EXPAND_SZ	String Value
REG_DWORD	Integer Value
REG_BINARY	Integer Value

To write a `DWORD` entry to the Registry, use the following syntax: `wshshell.RegWrite key, value, REG_DWORD"`.

Deleting Registry values

You can even delete Registry information using `RegDelete`. For example, you could store your own data in the Registry and delete it on request:

```
' 14-3.VBS

set wshshell = CreateObject("WScript.Shell")

mykey = "HKCU\Software\mystorage\counter"

' read counter
counter = ReadKey(mykey)

' use information
msg = "You have launched this script " & counter & " times. Reset?"
answer = MsgBox(msg, vbYesNo)
if answer=vbYes then
    wshshell.RegDelete mykey
else
    ' increment counter
    counter = counter + 1
    ' update
    wshshell.RegWrite mykey, counter, "REG_DWORD"
end if

function ReadKey(key)
    on error resume next
    ReadKey = wshshell.RegRead(key)
    if not err.number=0 then
        ReadKey = 0
```

```
        err.clear
    end if
end function
```

This script uses the Registry as a global data store and maintains a counter. Each time you launch the script, it increments the counter and tells you how often you have run it. Once you choose to reset, it deletes the counter and starts over again.

 Tip Use the key `"HKCU\Software\"` as the base for your own information keys if you want to store them on a per-user basis. Use the key `"HKLM\Software\"` if you want to store common information. If you changed the script to `"HKLM\Software\..."`, it would count script usage no matter which user launched the script. In all cases, you need the proper permissions to modify the Registry.

Note the changes in `ReadKey` — if the key doesn't exist, the function returns 0, indicating that there is no counter. Note also that deleting the key doesn't remove all of your entries, only the counter entry. Your key `"HKLM\Software\mystorage\"` remains in the Registry and has to be deleted separately.

Creating Advanced Registry Tools

The built-in Registry methods the `WScript.Shell` object offers are a good start, but they are by no means complete. Originally, Microsoft added these methods only so scripts would be able to store their private data in the Registry. In order to manage the Registry professionally, you need more.

For example, `RegRead` and `RegWrite` can't deal with binary data. Although `RegWrite` supports the data type `"REG_BINARY"`, it can only write one byte of data — often not enough. Nor are there any methods for enumerating keys, so in order to read a key, you need to know its exact location and name.

This is why I have re-programmed the Registry methods. On the one side, I have expanded the official Registry methods you already know. Additionally, I have included many more methods that help enumerate keys and develop Windows version-independent Registry tools.

To use those new methods, all you need to do is install the new COM object. It's located on your CD: `\install\registry\setup.exe`. Full source code is provided at `\components\registry\registry.vbp`.

Enumerating subkeys

Here's an example: This script enumerates all keys in `HKEY_CURRENT_ROOT` using the new method `RegEnum` — Figure 14-2 shows a lot of subkeys. They won't all fit into the dialog box.

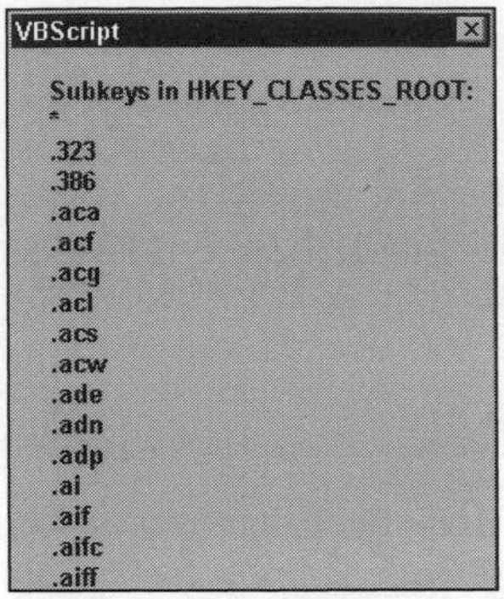

Figure 14-2: Enumerate all subkeys in a branch.

```
' 14-4.VBS

set regaddon = CreateObject("regtool.tob")
set collection = regaddon.RegEnum("HKCR\")

for each subkey in collection
     list = list & subkey & vbCr
next

MsgBox "Subkeys in HKEY_CLASSES_ROOT:" & vbCr & list
```

The method actually returns a `Collection` object. To view the subkey names, the script converts the collection into a string.

Listing subkey entries

You can even enumerate the values stored inside a key (see Figure 14-3). Again, you use `RegEnum`. Provide the key name, but don't put a \ at the end. Here's an example:

```
' 14-5.VBS

set regaddon = CreateObject("regtool.tob")
set collection = regaddon.RegEnum("HKCU\Control Panel\Colors")

for each subkey in collection
     list = list & subkey & vbCr
next

MsgBox "Entries in HKCU\Control Panel\Colors:" & vbCr & list
```

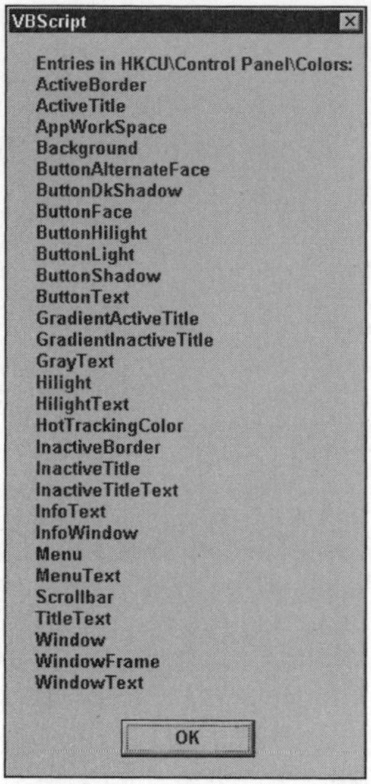

```
VBScript                                  X
   Entries in HKCU\Control Panel\Colors:
   ActiveBorder
   ActiveTitle
   AppWorkSpace
   Background
   ButtonAlternateFace
   ButtonDkShadow
   ButtonFace
   ButtonHilight
   ButtonLight
   ButtonShadow
   ButtonText
   GradientActiveTitle
   GradientInactiveTitle
   GrayText
   Hilight
   HilightText
   HotTrackingColor
   InactiveBorder
   InactiveTitle
   InactiveTitleText
   InfoText
   InfoWindow
   Menu
   MenuText
   Scrollbar
   TitleText
   Window
   WindowFrame
   WindowText

                  OK
```

Figure 14-3: Enumerate all values inside a key.

Version-independent Windows settings

Note that, previously, Windows 9.x and Windows NT/2000 used different keys to store their internal settings. This was bad, because your scripts would have had to be adjusted depending on which Windows version they were supposed to run.

Not any longer. The Registry toolkit supports a couple of extra main branches. Aside from HKLM, HKCU, and HKCR, you can also specify WINUSER and WINMACHINE. WINUSER directs you to HKEY_CURRENT_USER\Software\ Microsoft\Windows (NT)\CurrentVersion\, and WINMACHINE represents the same key in HKEY_LOCAL_MACHINE.

Now it's easy to write true version-independent scripts. For example, to retrieve the registered owner, two lines will suffice. The result is shown in Figure 14-4.

```
' 14-6.VBS

set tool = CreateObject("regtool.tob")
MsgBox "Registered Owner: " _
& tool.RegRead("WINMACHINE\RegisteredOwner")
```

Note how `WINMACHINE` automatically selects the right internal key, no matter which Windows version you are running.

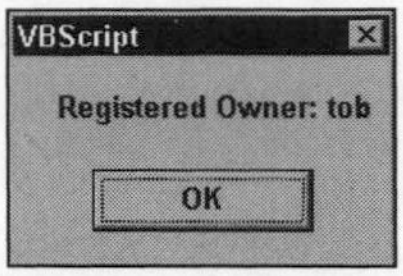

VBScript ✕
Registered Owner: tob
OK

Figure 14-4: Read keys using generic key names for Windows 9.x/NT.

Writing Registry scripts for specific Windows versions

Windows 9.x and Windows NT/2000 are really two different worlds. They share a lot of techniques, but not all features are available on all systems. Therefore, there's a definite need to find out the type of operating system so you can quit a script automatically if it's not suited for the Windows version running.

This function is already included. Use `GetWinVer` to find out whether or not your system is Windows 9.x or Windows NT/2000. Figure 14-5 shows a sample result.

```
' 14-7.VBS

set tool = CreateObject("regtool.tob")
MsgBox "You're running " & tool.GetWinVer
```

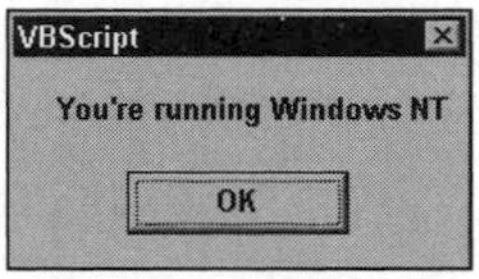

VBScript ✕
You're running Windows NT
OK

Figure 14-5: Determine which Windows version is running your script.

 Note

`GetWinVer` determines the Platform ID. It cares only about the Windows kernel. You'll get Windows NT for both Windows NT and Windows 2000. To find out the version number and additional version information, take a look at Chapter 10.

Finding out the variable type

Registry values can be stored in many different variable types. The built-in Registry methods can't retrieve the variable type. But you can, and Figure 14-6 shows an example:

```
' 14-8.VBS
```

```
set tool = CreateObject("regtool.tob")
dummy = tool.RegRead("HKCR\vbsfile\", regtype)
MsgBox "The Variable Type is: " & regtype
```

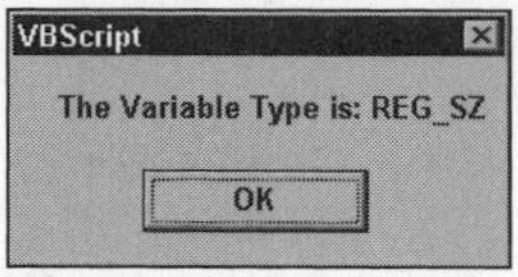

Figure 14-6: Find out the exact variable type of stored Registry values.

Reading binary data

The regular `RegRead` method is capable of reading binary data. However, the binary data is returned as variable array. To make things simpler and to restrict your set of Registry methods to strings as data carriers, your new `RegRead` method reads binary data as a string value. Have a look at Figure 14-7.

```
' 14-9.VBS

set tool = CreateObject("regtool.tob")
idno = tool.RegRead("WINMACHINE\DigitalProductID")
MsgBox "Your windows product ID: " & vbCr & idno
```

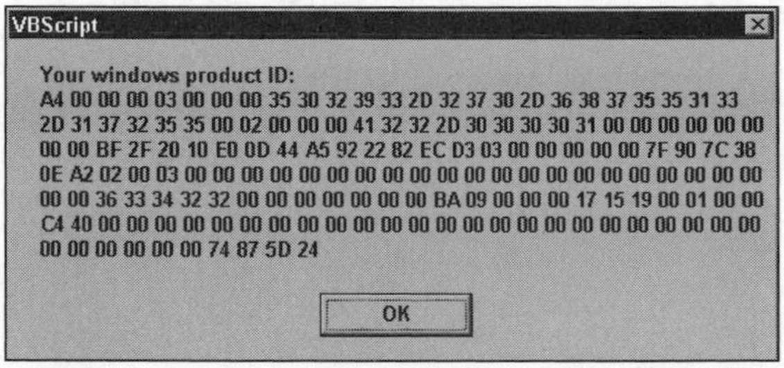

Figure 14-7: Read in binary data.

Writing binary data

The regular `RegWrite` method can't write binary data at all. It's restricted to writing a single byte only. Your new `RegWrite` method can do more: Write as many bytes of data as you want. Again, `RegWrite` handles binary data as a string, so supply your binary data as hexadecimal string values, and separate each byte with a space character:

```
' 14-10.VBS

set tool = CreateObject("regtool.tob")
tool.RegWrite "HKCU\Software\mykey", _
"48 65 6C 6C 6F 20 57 6F 72 6C 64 21", "REG_BINARY"
```

A look into the Registry Editor reveals that your data has been saved as binary (see Figure 14-8).

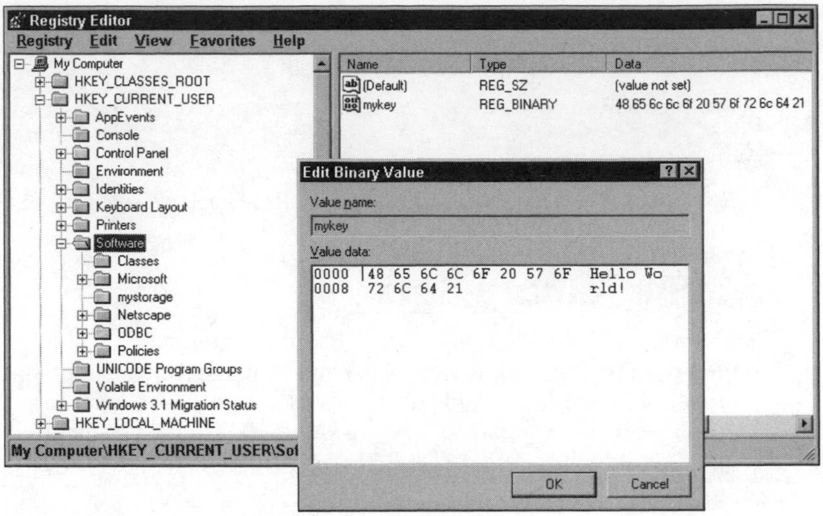

Figure 14-8: Easily write binary data to the Registry.

Deleting Registry keys and values

To balance it out, your Registry kit also includes its own `RegDelete` method. It works just like the official `RegDelete`. To delete your binary test value from the previous example, use this script:

```
' 14-11.VBS

set tool = CreateObject("regtool.tob")
tool.RegDelete "HKCU\Software\mykey"
```

Secret

You can't delete a key that doesn't exist. You can, however, delete a value that doesn't exist, without raising an error. Note that you can't delete a key that contains subkeys. Delete the subkeys first.

Finding out if a key exists

Trying to read a key that doesn't exist will raise an error. You don't need to guess anymore, and you don't need to switch off error handling, either. Just use the new `KeyExists` method:

```
' 14-12.VBS

set tool = CreateObject("regtool.tob")
if tool.KeyExists("HKCR\.doc\") then
    MsgBox "DOC files are registered on your system"
```

```
else
    MsgBox "DOC files are not registered on your system"
end if
```

Additional things to remember . . .

Always remember: There are keys in the Registry acting as "folders," and there are values storing the actual data, the "files." Whenever you want to access a key, make sure to write a \ at the end of your key path. Whenever you want to access a value, append the value name to the key name and don't write a \ at the end.

To read and write the (Standard) value of a key, just supply the key name and do write a \ at the end.

Summary

In this chapter, you learned the Registry basics: namely, to protect, read, write, and delete the data stored in the Registry. This fundamental knowledge already enables you to store your own data inside the Registry and to change system values at will. Much more importantly, this knowledge is the foundation for all the system tweaks I am going to introduce to you in the next chapter.

In addition, a complete Registry toolkit offers you all the methods needed to professionally manage your Registry. You are now able to enumerate subkeys and handle binary data and determine whether a specific key really exists in your Registry.

Chapter 15

Registry Tweaks

In This Chapter

▶ Search for undocumented Registry functions and control those settings via script

▶ Activate your new Registry settings without restarting the system

▶ Control the Windows Icon Cache

▶ Search the Registry for key names and values

▶ Change names of system icons and find out how system icons are placed on the desktop and into the My Computer namespace

▶ Change system icons

▶ Control and manipulate Windows settings through API calls

▶ Manage Active Window Tracking and new cool Windows features entirely by script

▶ Activate and configure screen savers from code

Registry manipulations are the key to many undocumented Windows tweaks. In this chapter, you not only learn how to implement those tweaks but also how to make Windows recognize your changes without the need to restart the system.

The Registry: Zillions of Undocumented Features

Windows contains a lot more functions than are accessible through official dialog boxes. Many of the Windows settings are available only through direct Registry manipulation. Fortunately, with the new Registry methods introduced in the previous chapter, you no longer need to fiddle around inside the Registry manually. Instead, you can design your own custom tools.

Note

Many of the following scripts take advantage of the new methods provided by your custom Registry COM object. Make sure you have installed it: \install\registry\setup.exe.

You might be thinking, wait a minute! Designing new dialog boxes is all right, but where do you get information about the actual Registry settings that your new dialog boxes should control? Especially because the Registry is heavily undocumented, it may seem like a mystery. But luckily, there are a number of ways. On the following pages, I show you how to use snapshot comparisons and how to use secret tools to uncover hidden Registry settings.

Comparing Registry snapshots

If you want your script to mimic some setting controlled by an official dialog box, you can always compare the Registry:

1. Start the Registry Editor, Choose Run in your Start menu, and then enter REGEDIT. Next, export the entire Registry to a text file, choose Export Registry File from your Registry menu, and then store the entire Registry in a file called C:\before (see Figure 15-1). Make sure to choose All to export the entire Registry.

2. Now, invoke the change you want to control by script. Call the dialog box, set your new value, and click Apply.

3. Repeat Step 1 and call the export file c:\after.

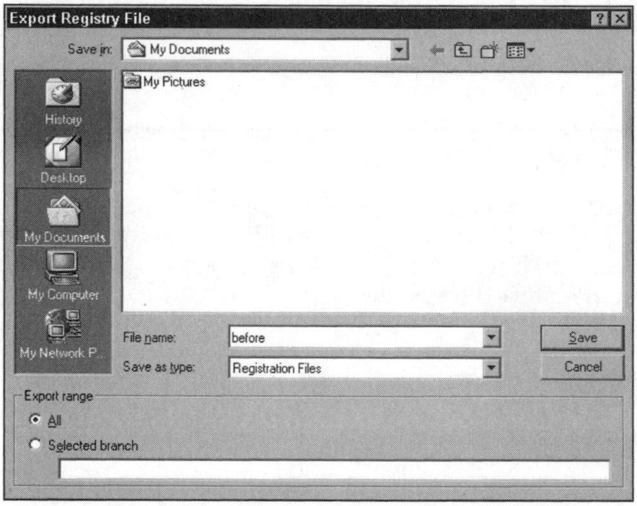

Figure 15-1: Export the entire Registry to create a snapshot.

You now have two text files — before.reg and after.reg. To find out the changes made by the official dialog box, you need to compare them (see Figure 15-2).

Secret

On each Windows 98 CD, there's a little hidden tool called `WINDIFF.EXE`, which is part of the MS Resource Kit Sampler. It compares two files and highlights the differences, and it works on all Windows versions. Copy `WINDIFF.EXE` and `GUTILS.DLL` to your Windows folder. Now you can invoke `WINDIFF` by choosing Run in your Start menu: `WINDIFF` [Enter]. `WINDIFF` is copyrighted material. Make sure it is legal for you to use `WINDIFF`.

After you have created your snapshots, launch `WINDIFF`, choose File, and then choose Compare Files. Enter the first file name: `c:\before.reg`. Then, enter the second file: `c:\after.reg`.

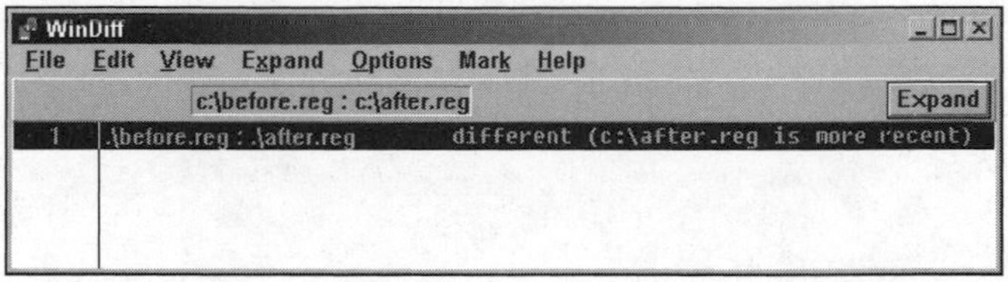

Figure 15-2: Compare both Registry snapshots to see the changes.

`WINDIFF` compares both files and determines which one is newer. This doesn't help too much yet. Next, click the red line to select it, then click on Expand in the right upper corner.

Now, `WINDIFF` compares the snapshots. This can take a while, especially on Windows NT/2000. Just be a little patient. As a result, `WINDIFF` displays the contents of your snapshots and marks in color the parts that have changed. Press [F8] to jump from change to change (see Figure 15-3).

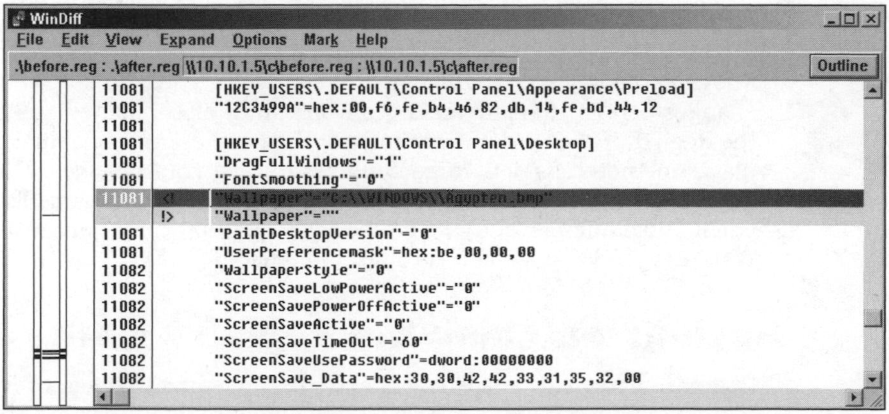

Figure 15-3: `WINDIFF` has detected where the desktop wallpaper setting is stored.

If you can't get a hold of `WINDIFF.EXE`, you can use your word processor, too. WinWord, for example, offers a version comparison feature. Specify both files to have WinWord find the differences. Note, however, that it may take up to an hour for WinWord to process large export files.

A much more convenient way is the shareware TechFacts 95. You get it at `www.winutils.com/diagnost.htm`. It generates a Registry snapshot and compares it to a previous snapshot in a matter of seconds (see Figure 15-4).

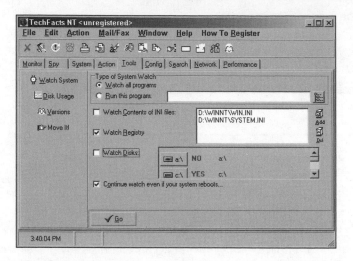

Figure 15-4: TechFacts generates snapshots of Registry and folders.

Once you know the differences, most of the time, the secret keys are obvious. Don't let Windows fool you—any MRU entries can be safely ignored. MRU stands for Most Recently Used, and these keys store your recent input settings.

Secret

Knowing the Registry keys is only the first step. The next step is making changes happen. Registry changes won't show effect immediately. After all, the Registry is just a database and not the main control of a nuclear power plant. You need a way to force Windows to read your changes. The brute force approach is restarting Windows. That's not very elegant. This is why you'll find a number of useful methods throughout this chapter to have Windows read in your new settings immediately.

Spying: Watching the Registry work

Comparing Registry snapshots is extremely useful, but it can't reveal undocumented features. After all, undocumented features are hidden and not accessible through regular dialog boxes. Your snapshot approach can only show Registry settings you can already invoke somehow.

There's another excellent tool available on the Internet, and it's absolutely free. It's called RegMon. Surf to www.sysinternals.com to grab the latest version.

RegMon shows, in real-time, any changes made to your Registry. You can actually watch dialog boxes and software write changes to the Registry.

Secret

You may be surprised how much Registry access is going on every single second. If RegMon constantly reports Registry access even though you are doing nothing special, it's a clue that some background programs are querying the Registry. That's bad because it interferes with your spying plans. Close down all software until the Registry access stops. The most annoying type of software are the "performance meters" in the tray area— anti-virus software and MS Office's FindFast indexing service. On Windows 9.x, you can always press [Ctrl]+[Alt]+[Del] to invoke the task list and manually close down any program you suspect is causing the trouble.

Although it's fascinating to watch RegMon list all the Registry access occurring while you open programs or dialog boxes, it won't help you much. And it's information overkill! To find the truly interesting and undocumented Registry keys, use a different approach.

In the Events menu, choose Filter. Use "*" for both Process and Path Include, and select Log Reads and Log Errors only. Then click Apply (see Figure 15-5).

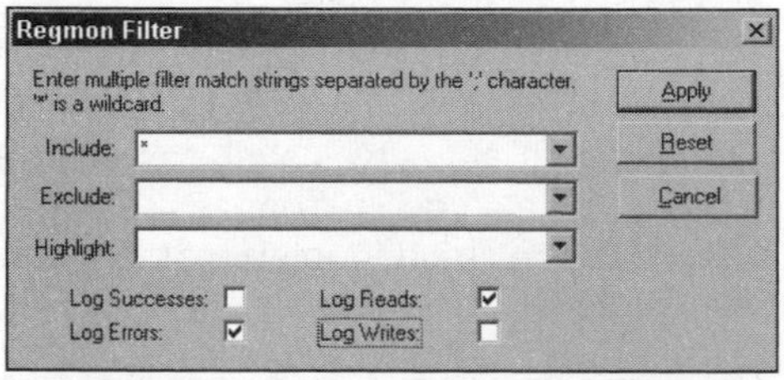

Figure 15-5: Filter the results and display only undocumented missing entries.

Now, RegMon lists only Registry keys that aren't there but are queried by someone. This is your highway to Undocumented City. Try it out.

Open your Start menu and choose Settings. RegMon lists a number of keys Windows can't find. One is Max Cached Icons; another one is Shell Small Icon Size (both are undocumented); see Figure 15-6.

Tip

Sysinternals.com offers many more useful spying tools. Get yourself filemon, and see file changes happen in real-time. Or pick portmon to spy on your communication ports. All of these tools run on any Windows version and are extremely small in size.

Registry Monitor - Systems Internals: http://www.sysinternals.com

#	Ti...	Process	Path
1	5.4...	csrss.exe	HKLM\SYSTEM\ControlSet001\Control\Nls\Locale\0000002A
2	5.4...	csrss.exe	HKLM\SYSTEM\ControlSet001\Control\Nls\Locale\Alternate Sorts\0000002A
3	5.4...	csrss.exe	HKLM\System\CurrentControlSet\Control\Nls\Codepage\42
4	5.4...	csrss.exe	HKLM\SYSTEM\ControlSet001\Control\Nls\Locale\0000002A
5	5.4...	csrss.exe	HKLM\SYSTEM\ControlSet001\Control\Nls\Locale\Alternate Sorts\0000002A
6	5.4...	csrss.exe	HKLM\System\CurrentControlSet\Control\Nls\Codepage\42
7	5.4...	csrss.exe	HKLM\SYSTEM\ControlSet001\Control\Nls\Locale\0000002A
8	5.4...	csrss.exe	HKLM\SYSTEM\ControlSet001\Control\Nls\Locale\Alternate Sorts\0000002A
9	5.4...	csrss.exe	HKLM\System\CurrentControlSet\Control\Nls\Codepage\42
10	5.4...	csrss.exe	HKLM\SYSTEM\ControlSet001\Control\Nls\Locale\0000002A
11	5.4...	csrss.exe	HKLM\SYSTEM\ControlSet001\Control\Nls\Locale\Alternate Sorts\0000002A
12	5.4...	csrss.exe	HKLM\System\CurrentControlSet\Control\Nls\Codepage\42
13	8.3...	csrss.exe	HKLM\SYSTEM\ControlSet001\Control\Nls\Locale\0000002A
14	8.3...	csrss.exe	HKLM\SYSTEM\ControlSet001\Control\Nls\Locale\Alternate Sorts\0000002A
15	8.3...	csrss.exe	HKLM\System\CurrentControlSet\Control\Nls\Codepage\42
16	8.5...	csrss.exe	HKLM\SYSTEM\ControlSet001\Control\Nls\Locale\0000002A
17	8.5...	csrss.exe	HKLM\SYSTEM\ControlSet001\Control\Nls\Locale\Alternate Sorts\0000002A
18	8.5...	csrss.exe	HKLM\System\CurrentControlSet\Control\Nls\Codepage\42
19	8.5...	csrss.exe	HKLM\SYSTEM\ControlSet001\Control\Nls\Locale\0000002A
20	8.5...	csrss.exe	HKLM\SYSTEM\ControlSet001\Control\Nls\Locale\Alternate Sorts\0000002A
21	8.5...	csrss.exe	HKLM\System\CurrentControlSet\Control\Nls\Codepage\42
22	9.0...	explorer.exe	HKLM\SOFTWARE\MICROSOFT\Windows\CURRENTVERSION\Explorer\Max Cached Icons
23	9.0...	explorer.exe	HKCU\Control Panel\Desktop\WindowMetrics\Shell Small Icon Size

Figure 15-6: RegMon reports undocumented secret Registry keys.

Writing a script to access undocumented features

Let's pick out the key HKCU\Control Panel\Desktop\WindowMetrics\ Shell Small Icon Size. Its name already gives a clue as what this setting controls. The official dialog box only lets you customize the large icon size, and there's no control to customize the small icon size. Small icons are used in dialog boxes and inside the Explorer's tree pane.

If you want to play it safe, the next thing you should do is surf to an Internet search site like www.altavista.com. Search for the last part of your Registry path, such as Shell Small Icon Size. Chances are you'll get a lot of information provided by other Windows researchers.

Note

Install the custom Registry component first: \install\regtool\setup.exe. Full source code is provided at \components\regtool\regtool.vbp.

Now develop an interface to control the feature:

```
' 15-1.VBS

set tool = CreateObject("regtool.tob")

key = "HKCU\Control Panel\Desktop\WindowMetrics\Shell Small Icon Size"
if tool.keyExists(key) then
    keyval = tool.RegRead(key, keytype)
    msg = "Current setting: " & keyval & " (type: " & keytype & ")"
else
```

```
        keyval = 0
        msg = "Current setting: key does not exist!"
end if

msg = msg & vbCr & vbCr & "Specify a new setting, or leave " _
& "blank to delete key!"

' set value
newval = InputBox(msg,,keyval)

if newval = vbEmpty then
     WScript.Quit
elseif newval = "" then
     answer = MsgBox("Do you really want to delete the key?", _
vbYesNo + vbCritial)
     if answer = vbYes then
          on error resume next
          tool.RegDelete key
          on error goto 0
          MsgBox "Deleted."
     end if
else
     tool.RegWrite key, newval
     MsgBox "Written."
end if

' make changes happen
tool.RefreshWindowMetrics
```

This script is your universal Registry interface. Just replace the variable key with whatever key you want to control. The script first queries the key to find out if it exists and then returns its actual value and type. Next, it allows you to change the value (see Figure 15-7).

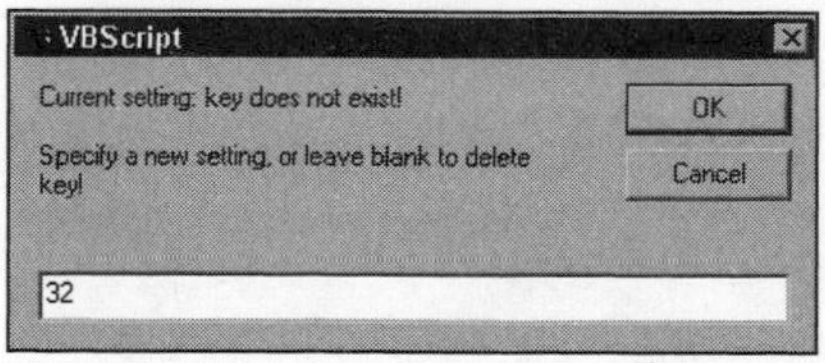

![VBScript dialog box titled "VBScript" showing "Current setting: key does not exist!" and "Specify a new setting, or leave blank to delete key!" with OK and Cancel buttons and an input field containing "32"]

Figure 15-7: Enter a new value for your undocumented Registry setting.

Undocumented

There are three key value data types stored in the Registry. They are REG_SZ (text), REG_DWORD (integer), and REG_BINARY (hexadecimal data of arbitrary length). The script defaults to REG_SZ if the key did not previously exist. If you change an existing key, the script automatically uses the previous data type to write your new value. But, you won't need to worry about data types too much.

If you change the value to 32, for example, and click OK, the script will write it into the Registry and report success. Nothing has changed, yet. Once you click OK again, though, suddenly all the small icons use your new value as size, and this includes the small icons in the tray area, the tree pane of your Explorer, and any icons in detail view (see Figure 15-8).

Note

Changing the small icon size in the middle of the game may cause garbled images. Close any Explorer window and reopen it to see the new icons in their full glory. Note, however, that some dialog boxes can't expand, and if you increase the small icon size, the dialog box controls look a little strange—to say the least.

You have successfully created a new control for an undocumented Windows feature you discovered.

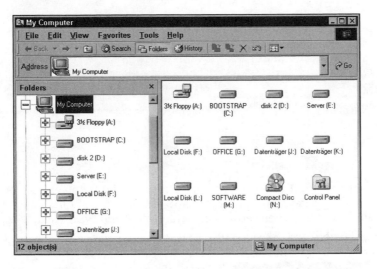

Figure 15-8: Suddenly, Explorer uses your new size for all of its small icons.

Forcing Windows to recognize your new settings

You've seen that setting the new value isn't enough. You need to force Windows to read your new value. Usually, you need to restart Windows (or close down explorer.exe in the task list). The script uses a more elegant way—its method RefreshWindowMetrics causes Windows to reread all settings in the WindowMetric subkey of the Registry.

And there's another thing to notice. Dealing with undocumented features is your responsibility—don't expect Microsoft to support you. For example, changing any Windows setting through the official dialog box will also reset the small icon sizes. To change the small icon size back to normal, delete your new key. To do this, restart your script and enter a blank value. The script then asks if you want to delete the key. Click Yes and OK. Now, your icons will revert back to normal.

Max Cached Icons key

There is another undocumented key that is very useful too. Windows caches all icons for speed—the negative side of this is that the icons are garbled once the icon cache gets out of sync. If you work with a lot of icons, it makes perfect sense to enlarge the icon cache. Specify the number of icons you want to cache in the Max Cached Icons key and restart Windows.

A quick way to restore a damaged icon cache is `FlushIconCache`, another important method provided by your new Registry control:

```
' 15-2.VBS

set tool = CreateObject("regtool.tob")
tool.FlushIconCache
```

Searching for interesting Registry keys

Another approach to learning about undocumented Registry keys (and value names) is to search for them. Just specify a search word like "desktop" and see what you get.

The Registry Editor supports searching. However, the built-in search function is targeted at finding specific keys quickly. You always get one key at a time and need to press [F3] manually to continue the search. Also, because the Registry Editor searches all branches, you will find the same keys multiple times. Remember: Some main Registry branches are just shortcuts to other branches.

Secret

Another caveat is the fact that Registry Editor starts its search at the currently selected position. In order to search the complete Registry, you must make sure that the topmost key in the left pane is selected. Otherwise, you are going to miss a lot of entries.

For research purposes, the following scripts do a better job. They search for keys, value names, and values, respectively. They also limit the search to the two main branches—`HKEY_LOCAL_MACHINE` and `HKEY_CURRENT_USER`. As a drawback, your scripts are a lot slower than the Registry Editor and may take some time to complete the search.

Note

All of the search scripts above may take some minutes to execute, depending on the size of your Registry. Get a cup of coffee and take a break.

Searching for key names

The following script searches for key names that contain the search word specified in `searchfor`. It outputs the result as a `MsgBox` dialog box, which obviously isn't the best solution: Everything beyond 1,000 characters is lost. Save the result to a file or display it as an HTML file.

```
' 15-3.VBS

set tool = CreateObject("regtool.tob")
```

```
searchfor = "Desktop"
list = ""

SearchBranch "HKEY_LOCAL_MACHINE\"
SearchBranch "HKEY_CURRENT_USER\"

MsgBox list

sub SearchBranch(key)
    on error resume next
    set subkeys = tool.RegEnum(key)
    for each subkey in subkeys
        if Instr(lcase(subkey), lcase(searchfor))>0 then
            list = list & key & subkey & "\" & vbCr
        end if
    next

    for each subkey in subkeys
        SearchBranch key & subkey & "\"
    next
end sub
```

For example, Figure 15-9 displays the results of a search for "desktop."

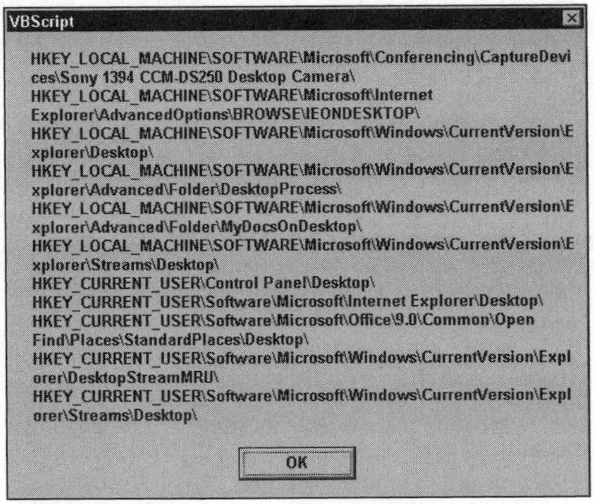

Figure 15-9: Find all Registry keys that contain the word "desktop."

Searching for value names

With a slight variation, the script can search for value names. The following example lists all value names that contain vbs.

```
' 15-4.VBS

set tool = CreateObject("regtool.tob")
```

```
searchfor = "vbs"
list = ""

SearchBranch "HKEY_LOCAL_MACHINE\"
SearchBranch "HKEY_CURRENT_USER\"

MsgBox list

sub SearchBranch(key)
    on error resume next

    ' enumerate values
    set subvalues = tool.RegEnum(left(key, len(key)-1))
    for each valuename in subvalues
        if Instr(lcase(valuename), lcase(searchfor))>0 then
            list = list & key & valuename & vbCr
        end if
    next
    set subkeys = tool.RegEnum(key)
    for each subkey in subkeys
        SearchBranch key & subkey & "\"
    next
end sub
```

Searching for values

Another modification allows your script to search for the actual Registry values that match your `searchfor` search criteria. This script searches for Registry entries containing ".scr".

```
' 15-5.VBS

set tool = CreateObject("regtool.tob")

searchfor = ".scr"
list = ""

SearchBranch "HKEY_LOCAL_MACHINE\"
SearchBranch "HKEY_CURRENT_USER\"

MsgBox list

sub SearchBranch(key)
    on error resume next

    ' enumerate values
    set subvalues = tool.RegEnum(left(key, len(key)-1))
    for each valuename in subvalues
        ' retrieve value
        valcontent = tool.RegRead(key & valuename)
        if Instr(lcase(valcontent), lcase(searchfor))>0 then
            list = list & key & valuename & "=" & valcontent & vbCr
        end if
    next
    set subkeys = tool.RegEnum(key)
```

```
        for each subkey in subkeys
            SearchBranch key & subkey & "\"
        next
end sub
```

Controlling program settings

Most of your programs store their internal settings in the Registry, too. You'll find those settings either in HKEY_CURRENT_USER\Software \CompanyName\Product (for individual users) or HKEY_LOCAL_MACHINE \Software\CompanyName\Product (for machine-wide settings). Replace CompanyName and Product with the appropriate values of your software.

It may be extremely useful to control these settings. For example, maybe you want to launch your favorite game with different options for the input device or network. Identify the settings first, using the snapshot technique described previously. Then, write a script that sets the appropriate settings and launches your game. This way, you can write a number of launcher scripts that all launch your game, but also automatically set the settings you like. And, because your program will be launched after you made the changes, the program will recognize your changes.

Protecting program settings

You can do even more. Imagine yourself in a teaching environment — your students love to play around with all the program options, but once your lesson is over, you need to spend another half an hour resetting all the program options to the default.

You don't have to! Start the Registry Editor REGEDIT.EXE and identify the branch in the Registry that stores your program settings. Export this branch: Registry - Export Registry File. The entire branch is saved as a REG file.

You can now reset all program settings to the default by simply opening the REG file and re-importing the values. Or leave this work to a script. Use the WScript.Shell Run method to read in your REG file automatically: for example, as part of the StartUp group at each Windows logon:

```
set wshshell = CreateObject("WScript.Shell")
wshshell.Run "REGEDIT.EXE /S """ & regfile & """"
```

Undocumented

The /S option gets rid of the annoying "Are you sure..." message. REGEDIT silently reads in the REG file, and no curious student will ever get a clue why all the settings are reset to normal each time he or she logs in.

Managing System Icons on the Desktop

The desktop is your private storage area. Here, you can put any files you need for quick access. In addition, Windows places some of its own icons on your desktop. These system icons work differently. Often, you can't rename these icons, and there might be no way of deleting them, either.

With the help of the Registry, though, you will be able to control your entire desktop. You can kick off any system icons you don't want, change their names, and even place new system icons on your desktop.

Changing the name of the Recycle Bin

On every desktop, you'll find a Recycle Bin. You can't disable it, and you can't rename it. Right? Sure you can. The next script allows you to rename the Recycle Bin to whatever you like (see Figure 15-10).

```
' 15-6.VBS

set wshshell = CreateObject("WScript.Shell")
machinekey = "HKLM\SOFTWARE\Classes\CLSID\{645FF040-5081-101B-" _
& "9F08-00AA002F954E}\"

' use this key for Windows 2000
'userkey = "HKCU\Software\Microsoft\Windows\CurrentVersion\" _
'     & "Explorer\CLSID\{645FF040-5081-101B-9F08-00AA002F954E}\"

userkey = "HKCU\Software\Classes\CLSID\{645FF040-5081-101B-" _
     & "9F08-00AA002F954E}\"

on error resume next
oldname2 = wshshell.RegRead(machinekey)
oldname1 = wshshell.RegRead(userkey)
if oldname1="" then oldname1="(undefined)"
on error goto 0

msg = "Your Recycle Bin is named """ & oldname2 & """" & vbCr
msg = msg & "It's current user setting is """ & oldname1 & """" & vbCr
msg = msg & "Do you want to change its name?"

response = MsgBox(msg, vbYesNo + vbQuestion)
if response = vbYes then
    name = InputBox("Please enter the new name!")
    if name = "" then
        if oldname1="" then
            WScript.Quit
        else
            response = MsgBox("Do you want to delete the " _
& "user setting?", vbYesNo + vbQuestion)
            if response = vbYes then
                wshshell.RegWrite userkey, ""
            end if
        end if
    else
        wshshell.RegWrite userkey, name
        MsgBox "Name has changed. Refresh your desktop!"
    end if
end if
```

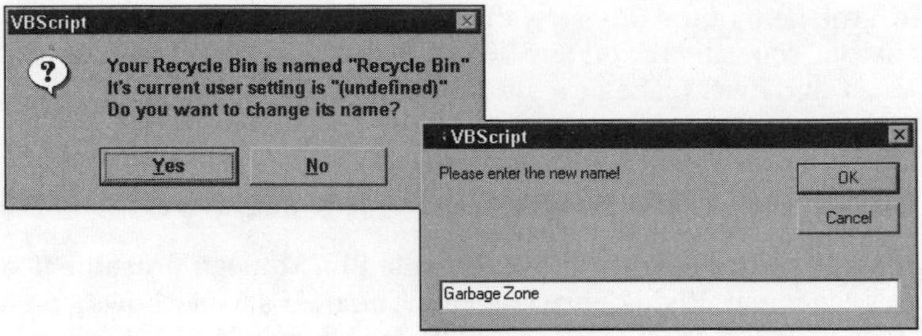

Figure 15-10: Rename your Recycle Bin.

Click your desktop and press [F5] to refresh the desktop. Immediately, your icon name changes.

Tip

To delete your user-defined name, choose to rename the icon and then click Cancel.

System components carry a unique name tag, the Class ID. On all Windows versions, the Recycle Bin uses the Class ID {645FF040-5081-101B-9F08-00AA002F954E}.

The basic information applies to all users and is stored in `HKEY_LOCAL_ MACHINE\Software\Classes\CLSID\{645FF040-5081-101B-9F08- 00AA002F954E}` **or its alias:** `HKEY_CLASSES_ROOT\CLSID\{645FF040- 5081-101B-9F08-00AA002F954E}`.

In addition, there may be a user-specific setting stored in the `HKEY_ CURRENT_USER` branch. If there is, the Recycle Bin uses a different name on a per-user basis.

The script reads both keys and reveals the standard name and a username if one is specified. You then have the opportunity to specify a new username.

Undocumented

There's a lot confusion about where Windows stores the user settings, and some versions, such as Windows 95, don't recognize user settings at all. In this case, change the script and use `machinekey` as `userkey`, too. On Windows 98, user settings are stored in `HKCU\Software\Classes`, so it's the exact mirror image of the machine settings: `HKLM\Software\Classes`. On Windows 2000, in contrast, user settings are stored as part of the Explorer settings. The appropriate key is marked in the preceding script. Change the user key if you run Windows 2000. It is unclear whether this new location is a bug or a feature.

More secrets about desktop items

Maybe you wonder where the system desktop items came from in the first place. They are not regular icons, and even more surprising, on some systems, you can delete system icons from the desktop, and on others, you can't.

The secret is a key named NameSpace. It's stored here: HKEY_LOCAL
_MACHINE\SOFTWARE\Microsoft\Windows\CurrentVersion\Explorer
\Desktop\NameSpace. In it, Windows defines all system icons visible on
the desktop (see Figure 15-11). The next script takes advantage of this
insider knowledge and lists all system desktop items:

```
' 15-7.VBS

set tool = CreateObject("regtool.tob")

key1 = "HKEY_LOCAL_MACHINE\SOFTWARE\Microsoft\Windows\" _
& "CurrentVersion\Explorer\Desktop\NameSpace\"
key2 = "HKCR\CLSID\"

set desktopitems = tool.RegEnum(key1)

list = "System icons currently installed on desktop:" & vbCr & vbCr

for each icon in desktopitems
    if not left(icon,1) = "{" then
        icon = "{" & icon & "}"
    end if
    name = tool.RegRead(key2 & icon & "\")
    if name = "" then name = "(unknown name)"
    list = list & name & " (Class ID: " & icon & ")" & vbCr
next

MsgBox list, vbInformation
```

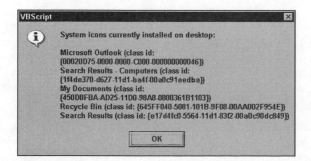

Figure 15-11: List all system icons that are visible on your desktop.

The key doesn't list all system icons: My Computer and Network Neighborhood
are not included. Many other items are included, though, and you also get their
Class IDs.

Secret

The NameSpace key lists only optional system icons. My Computer and
Network Neighborhood are not optional. They are always part of the
system and can't be disabled — at least not through NameSpace.

Hiding the Recycle Bin

All optional system icons can be hidden — just delete the icon entry in the `NameSpace` key. The next script hides the Recycle Bin and is also able to restore it:

```
' 15-8.VBS

set tool = CreateObject("regtool.tob")

key1 = "HKEY_LOCAL_MACHINE\SOFTWARE\Microsoft\Windows\" _
& "CurrentVersion\Explorer\Desktop\NameSpace\"
recycler = "{645FF040-5081-101B-9F08-00AA002F954E}\"

' check whether recycle bin is already hidden
if tool.KeyExists(key1 & recycler) then
    ' recycle bin is currently visible
    msg = "Do you want to hide the recycle bin?"
    response = MsgBox(msg, vbYesNo + vbQuestion)
    if response = vbYes then
        tool.RegDelete key1 & recycler
    end if
else
    ' recycle bin is hidden
    msg = "Do you want to restore the recycle bin icon?"
    response = MsgBox(msg, vbYesNo + vbQuestion)
    if response = vbYes then
        tool.RegWrite key1 & recycler, "Recycle Bin"
    end if
end if
```

Note that again you need to refresh your desktop by pressing [F5] to see the results. Read on to find the missing scripting method to refresh the desktop automatically.

The Secret dual-store

The main information store for all desktop objects is located in the `HKEY_LOCAL_MACHINE` branch of the Registry. This setting applies to all users. It's used as default. In addition, Windows may store different settings in the `HKEY_CURRENT_USER` branch. These settings override the default system settings and apply to the current user only.

So, if you want to hide the Recycle Bin only from some users, first delete it from the `HKEY_LOCAL_MACHINE` key, as shown in the previous example. Then, change the preceding script and replace `HKEY_LOCAL_MACHINE` with `HKEY_CURRENT_USER`. Now you can control the Recycle Bin individually for every user.

This "dual world" is a relatively new technique introduced by Windows 98. Here, only a limited number of settings can be specified in the user branch. Windows 2000 fully exploits the feature and allows you to store any object setting on a per-user basis.

Secret

The registry key HKEY_CLASSES_ROOT used to be just a shortcut to HKEY_ LOCAL_MACHINE\Software\Classes\CLSID. Not anymore. In Windows 2000, HKEY_CLASSES_ROOT reads both the HKEY_LOCAL_MACHINE user-independent setting and the HKEY_CURRENT_USER user-specific setting. If it finds user-specific settings, they override the machine-wide settings. As a rule of thumb, use HKEY_CURRENT_ROOT if you want to get the currently active settings, and read the HKEY_LOCAL_MACHINE and HKEY_CURRENT_USER keys directly if you want to receive the machine-default or user-specific settings.

Refreshing the desktop automatically

Your scripts can manipulate the Registry in any way they want. They can't force Windows to recognize the changes, though. This is why you had to refresh the desktop manually in the previous examples.

Obviously, this is not a perfect solution. This is why I have developed another COM object. It provides various methods to force Windows to recognize Registry changes. Make sure you install the new component (\install\regupdate\setup.exe). Full source code is provided at \components\regupdate\regupdate.vbp.

To force Windows to read in the desktop-related Registry keys, you need a way to refresh the desktop through API calls. Here's how:

```
Option Explicit

Const SHCNF_IDLIST = &H0
Const SHCNE_ALLEVENTS = &H7FFFFFFF

Private Declare Function SHGetSpecialFolderLocationD Lib _
"shell32.dll" Alias "SHGetSpecialFolderLocation" _
(ByVal hwndOwner As Long, ByVal nFolder As Long, _
ByRef ppidl As Long) As Long

Private Declare Function SHChangeNotify Lib "shell32.dll" _
(ByVal wEventID As Long, ByVal uFlags As Long, ByVal _
dwItem1 As Long, ByVal dwItem2 As Long) As Long

Private Declare Function GetDesktopWindow Lib "User32" () As Long

Public Sub RefreshDesktop()
    Dim lpil As Long

    Call SHGetSpecialFolderLocationD(GetDesktopWindow, 0, lpil)
    Call SHChangeNotify(SHCNE_ALLEVENTS, SHCNF_IDLIST, lpil, 0)
    Call SHChangeNotify(&H800, SHCNF_IDLIST Or &H1000, lpil, 0)
    Call SHChangeNotify(&H8000000, SHCNF_IDLIST, 0, 0)
End Sub
```

The script first retrieves the System ID for the desktop. Next, it sends notification messages to the desktop to inform it about changes. This is enough to trick the desktop into refreshing itself.

You now can complete the preceding scripts. Include one more line at the beginning:

```
set refresh = CreateObject("registry.update")
```

And include one line at the end of your script:

```
refresh.RefreshDesktop
```

This is all you need. From now on, your scripts change the Recycle Bin immediately, and there's no need anymore for manual refreshing.

Finding and restoring system icons

How do you find system icons you can use on your desktop? It's simple. Each system icon is really a COM object, so it's listed in the HKCR\CLSID\ key. Unfortunately, hundreds of COM objects are registered. So how do you find the ones that are eligible as desktop icons? Use a little trick. COM objects designed as desktop icons have a subkey called ShellFolder. Now it's easy to retrieve a list of all system icons available (see Figure 15-12):

Note

Make sure you have installed the COM object: (\install\registry\ setup.exe).

```
' 15-9.VBS

set tool = CreateObject("regtool.tob")
set wshshell = CreateObject("WScript.Shell")

key = "HKCR\CLSID\"

' enumerate all registered COM objects
set result = tool.RegEnum(key)

list = "Desktop COM objects:" & vbCr & vbCr

for each comobject in result
    ' find object with ShellFolder subkey
    subkey = key & comobject & "\ShellFolder\"
    if tool.KeyExists(subkey) then
        name = ""
        on error resume next
        name = tool.RegRead(key & comobject & "\")
        on error goto 0
        if name = "" then name = "(unknown)"
        list = list & comobject & ": " & name & vbCr
    end if
next

wshshell.Popup list
```

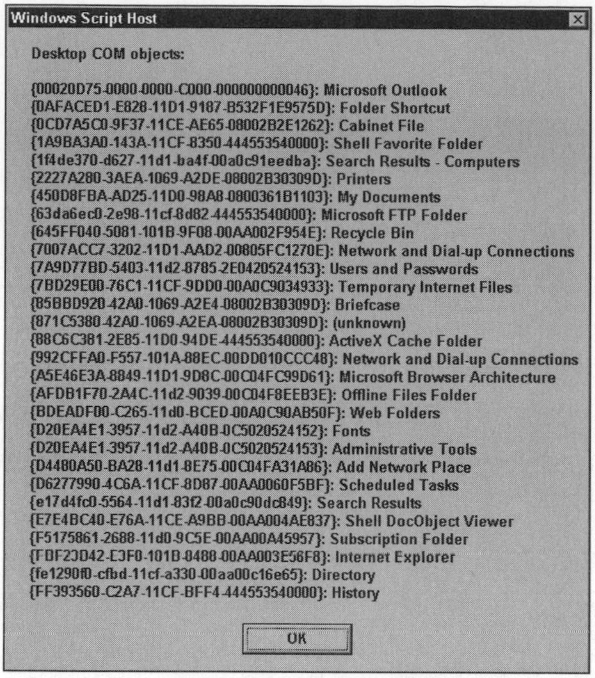

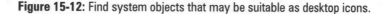

Figure 15-12: Find system objects that may be suitable as desktop icons.

With only a slight modification, you can use this script to restore any of the system desktop icons — and add system icons not available before (see Figure 15-13):

```
' 15-10.VBS

set tool = CreateObject("regtool.tob")
set refresh = CreateObject("registry.update")
set wshshell = CreateObject("WScript.Shell")

key = "HKCR\CLSID\"
key1 = "HKEY_LOCAL_MACHINE\SOFTWARE\Microsoft\Windows\" _
    & "CurrentVersion\Explorer\Desktop\NameSpace\"

' enumerate all registered COM objects
set result = tool.RegEnum(key)

list = "Desktop COM objects:" & vbCr & vbCr

for each comobject in result
    ' find object with ShellFolder subkey
    subkey = key & comobject & "\ShellFolder\"
    if tool.KeyExists(subkey) then
        on error resume next
```

```
name = ""
tip = ""
name = tool.RegRead(key & comobject & "\")
tip = tool.RegRead(key & comobject & "\InfoTip")
on error goto 0
if not (name = "" and tip = "") then
      if name = "" then name = "unknown"
      msg = "Found system icon: " & name & vbCr
      if not tip="" then
            msg = msg & "Additional info: " & tip & vbCr
      end if
if tool.KeyExists(key1 & comobject & "\") then
            ' icon already visible
            msg = msg & "The icon is already visible. Do" _
                  & " you want to hide it?"
            answer = MsgBox(msg, vbYesNoCancel + vbQuestion)
            if answer = vbYes then
                  tool.RegDelete key1 & comobject & "\"
                  refresh.RefreshDesktop
            end if
      else
            ' icon is currently hidden
            msg = msg & "The icon is currently hidden." _
                  & " Do you want to make it visible?"
            answer = MsgBox(msg, vbYesNoCancel + vbQuestion)
            if answer = vbYes then
                  tool.RegWrite key1 & comobject & "\", name
                  refresh.RefreshDesktop
            end if
      end if
      if answer = vbCancel then WScript.Quit
end if
   end if
next
```

Not all symbols really do work on your desktop. A small minority won't open
or will display error messages. Just launch your script again, and you can
kick those system icons back off-screen.

VBScript

? Found system icon: Shell Favorite Folder
The icon is currently hidden. Do you want to make it visible?

[Yes]   [No]   [Cancel]

Figure 15-13: Add and remove system icons from your desktop.

Caution

On Windows 2000, the `NameSpace` key contains some system icons with
no obvious use. `Search Results`, for example, doesn't show an icon.
Still, this object is very important. It's responsible for displaying search
results inside Explorer windows. Disabling this system "icon" will disable
the built-in search capabilities of your Explorer. As a general rule, don't
disable anything you can't see on your desktop.

Adding commands to system context menus

Strangely, some of your new desktop icons can be easily removed by just dragging them onto your Recycle Bin or choosing delete from the context menu, whereas others just won't go away. What's going on? And why do system icons have a `ShellFolder` subkey, anyway?

The `ShellFolder` subkey contains one very important value, and that is `Attributes`. This value controls the context menu, and it's this setting that determines whether or not a system icon can be deleted manually, among other things.

```vbscript
' 15-11.VBS

set tool = CreateObject("regtool.tob")
set refresh = CreateObject("registry.update")

key1 = "HKEY_LOCAL_MACHINE\SOFTWARE\Microsoft\Windows\" _
& "CurrentVersion\Explorer\Desktop\NameSpace\"

' get all visible system desktop icons
set result = tool.RegEnum(key1)

for each icon in result
    name = ""
    on error resume next
    name = tool.RegRead(key1 & icon & "\")
    if name = "" then name = "(unknown)"
    on error goto 0

    msg = "Found System Icon: " & name & vbCr
    msg = msg & "Do you want to change its context menu?"
    answer = MsgBox(msg, vBYesNo + vbQuestion)
    if answer = vbYes then
        on error resume next
        attrib = tool.RegRead("HKCR\CLSID\" & icon _
& "\ShellFolder\Attributes")
        if err.number=0 then
            attrib1 = CInt("&H" & left(attrib,2))
        else
            attrib1 = 0
        end if

        if (attrib1 and 16)=0 then
            mode = "NOT "
        else
            mode = ""
        end if

        msg = "RENAME is currently " & mode & "enabled. " _
            & "Do you want to enable it?"
        answer = MsgBox(msg, vbYesNo + vbQuestion)
        if answer = vbYes then
            attrib1 = attrib1 or 16
        else
```

```
                attrib1 = attrib1 and not 16
        end if


        if (attrib1 and 32)=0 then
                mode = "NOT "
        else
                mode = ""
        end if

        msg = "DELETE is currently " & mode & "enabled. " _
                & "Do you want to enable it?"
        answer = MsgBox(msg, vbYesNo + vbQuestion)
        if answer = vbYes then
                attrib1 = attrib1 or 32
                on error resume next
                removmsg = ""
                key2 = key1 & icon & "\Removal Message"
                removmsg = tool.RegRead(key2)
                on error goto 0
                msg = "Please enter a removal message!"
                newmsg = InputBox(msg,,removmsg)
                tool.RegWrite key2, newmsg
        else
                attrib1 = attrib1 and not 32
        end if

        if (attrib1 and 64)=0 then
                mode = "NOT "
        else
                mode = ""
        end if

        msg = "PROPERTIES is currently " & mode & "enabled. " _
                & "Do you want to enable it?"
        answer = MsgBox(msg, vbYesNo + vbQuestion)
        if answer = vbYes then
                attrib1 = attrib1 or 64
        else
                attrib1 = attrib1 and not 64
        end if

        newattrib = right("00" & hex(attrib1), 2) & mid(attrib, 3)
        tool.RegWrite "HKCR\CLSID\" & icon _
                & "\ShellFolder\Attributes", newattrib, "REG_BINARY"


        refresh.RefreshDesktop
    end if
next
```

Now, you can supply any system desktop icon with its own Delete or Rename context menu command and leave it up to your users whether or not they want to customize their desktops (see Figure 15-14). Script 15-10.VBS helps you to get back any system icon you might have deleted.

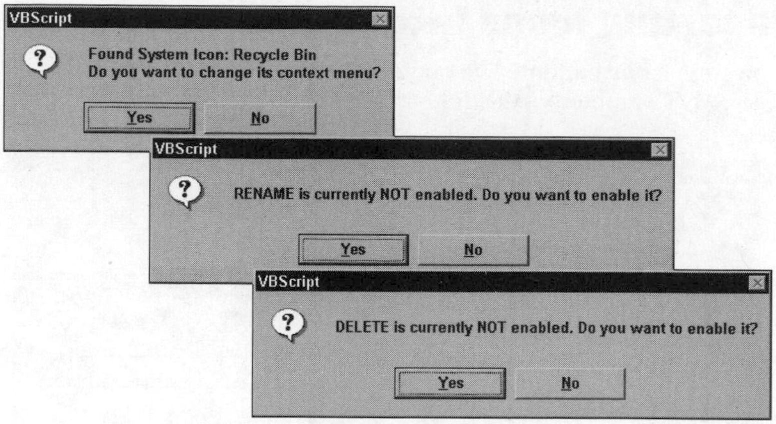

Figure 15-14: Add a `Rename` command to your Recycle Bin context menu.

Defining a removal message

Deleting system icons from the desktop is a one-way street for most users, because they can't get system icons back once they are deleted. The restoration script `15-9.VBS` isn't available to everyone.

That's why it's a good idea to warn users before they permanently delete system icons. Windows sports a built-in warning mechanism exclusively for system icons (see Figure 15-15). If you have tried the preceding script and enabled the delete command, the script has asked you for a removal message. This message is embedded into the system icon warning message whenever the user chooses the `Delete` command.

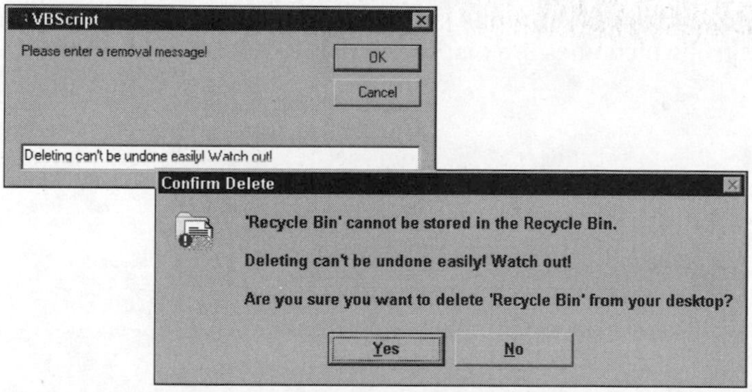

Figure 15-15: Define your own removal message.

Secret

The warning message only appears if your recycle bin generally issues warning messages. Right-click your Recycle Bin and choose Properties to enable the warning message. If the warning message is disabled, system icons will be deleted immediately without any further comments.

Inserting icons into your Explorer

System icons not only live on your desktop. Some of them also exist inside the My Computer virtual folder (see Figure 15-16).

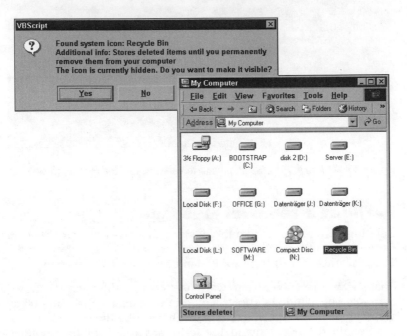

Figure 15-16: Add additional system icons like the Recycle Bin into My Computer.

Here, Windows uses the exact same technique: Again, a `NameSpace` key controls which system icons appear in My Computer. Use the next script to control which ones are displayed:

```
' 15-12.VBS

set tool = CreateObject("regtool.tob")
set refresh = CreateObject("registry.update")
set wshshell = CreateObject("WScript.Shell")

key = "HKCR\CLSID\"
key1 = "HKEY_LOCAL_MACHINE\SOFTWARE\Microsoft\Windows\" _
    & "CurrentVersion\Explorer\MyComputer\NameSpace\"

' enumerate all registered COM objects
set result = tool.RegEnum(key)

list = "Desktop COM objects:" & vbCr & vbCr

for each comobject in result
```

```
' find object with ShellFolder subkey
subkey = key & comobject & "\ShellFolder\"
if tool.KeyExists(subkey) then
    on error resume next
    name = ""
    tip = ""
    name = tool.RegRead(key & comobject & "\")
    tip = tool.RegRead(key & comobject & "\InfoTip")
    on error goto 0
    if not (name = "" and tip = "") then
        if name = "" then name = "unknown"
        msg = "Found system icon: " & name & vbCr
        if not tip="" then
            msg = msg & "Additional info: " & tip & vbCr
        end if
        if tool.KeyExists(key1 & comobject & "\") then
            ' icon already visible
            msg = msg & "The icon is already visible. Do" _
                & " you want to hide it?"
            answer = MsgBox(msg, vbYesNoCancel + vbQuestion)
            if answer = vbYes then
                tool.RegDelete key1 & comobject & "\"
                refresh.RefreshDesktop
            end if
        else
            ' icon is currently hidden
            msg = msg & "The icon is currently hidden." _
                & " Do you want to make it visible?"
            answer = MsgBox(msg, vbYesNoCancel + vbQuestion)
            if answer = vbYes then
                tool.RegWrite key1 & comobject & "\", name
                refresh.RefreshDesktop
            end if
        end if
        if answer = vbCancel then WScript.Quit
    end if
end if
next
```

Tip

Why waste space on your desktop? Delete the Recycle Bin from your desktop using script 15-11.VBS and transfer it into your MyComputer NameSpace. Here, it's still around in case you need to access the Recycle Bin properties.

Controlling Windows Settings Through API

You don't need to access the Registry directly to find out about specific Windows settings or to change their values. The Windows API contains many useful functions to change Windows settings directly, and among them are a vast number of functions not accessible through any official dialog box.

Retrieving Windows settings

The `SystemParametersInfo` API function can both read and write Windows settings. I have designed a COM object that makes it easy for your scripts to take advantage of this and a number of additional API functions to control Windows settings directly.

Note

Before you try to run any of the script examples, make sure you have installed the COM object (`\install\regupdate\setup.exe`). Full source code is provided at `\components\regupdate\regupdate.vbp`.

You can use the following script framework to ask for any of the Windows properties listed in Table 15-1:

```
' 15-13.VBS

set reghelper = CreateObject("registry.update")

returntype = "boolean"
retval = reghelper.GetASetting(settingID, returntype)
```

Full window drag: Retrieving Boolean values

For example, to find out whether or not Windows currently uses full window drag (moves windows as full windows instead of ghosted outline), look up the appropriate Property ID in Table 15-1. The table reveals that this property carries the ID 38. It's a Boolean return value(see Figure 15-17). This is all you need to know to customize the script framework from above:

```
' 15-14.VBS

set reghelper = CreateObject("registry.update")

boolvar = reghelper.GetASetting(38, "boolean")
if boolvar then
    MsgBox "Full window drag is currently enabled."
else
    MsgBox "Full window drag is NOT enabled."
end if
```

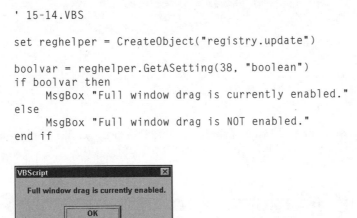

Figure 15-17: Find out whether full window drag is currently enabled on your system.

Flash count: Returning long-integer values

Windows uses different ways of returning the requested information. In the previous example, the answer was a Boolean variable — either true or false. Other properties return long-integer numbers. For example, on Windows 98 and 2000, you can find out how many times the operating system flashes a window button if it can't switch the window to the foreground. This information is a dword integer. Use the appropriate variable type to store the return value:

```
' 15-15.VBS

set reghelper = CreateObject("registry.update")

dwordvar = reghelper.GetASetting(&H2004, "long")
MsgBox "Flash count: " & dwordvar
```

Desktop work area: Retrieving long-integer arrays

Some information is returned as an array. For example, you can find out the current work area on-screen. The work area is the current resolution minus any space occupied by the task bar(s). Windows returns this information as an array of four long-integer numbers:

```
' 15-16.VBS

set reghelper = CreateObject("registry.update")

coords = reghelper.GetASetting(48, "array4")
MsgBox "Work area result: " & vbCr & coords

' Split up coordinates
carray = Split(coords, vbCr)
msg = "Work area (" & carray(0) & "," & carray(1) _
    & ") x (" & carray(2) & "," & carray(3) & ")"
MsgBox msg
```

GetASetting doesn't return the array. Instead, it converts the array members to strings and returns one string, using vbCr as delimiter. You can output the result directly, or you can re-convert the result into an array using Split. The example shows both alternatives.

Caution

Working with dynamic arrays is not trivial. The API function used internally by GetASetting expects the array to be big enough to store its return values. It's completely up to you to specify the right array size. If you size the array too small, chances are your script will crash because the API function will write results into memory that you do not own. To play it safe, just stick to the information provided in Table 15-1. You can also always use an extra-large array that will hold the information for sure: for example, "array100."

Desktop wallpaper: Reading text strings

There's one last variable type, and that's text strings. On Windows 2000, you can easily find out the current desktop wallpaper file. Here's how to retrieve a string value:

```
' 15-17.VBS

set reghelper = CreateObject("registry.update")

wallpaper = reghelper.GetASetting(115, "string260")
MsgBox "Current wallpaper: " & vbCr & wallpaper
```

In this case, your script grants the API function a maximum of 260 characters of storage space. The resulting string will be automatically truncated to the real character count. 260 is the maximum file path length, so it's a good value to use as maximum.

Gaining full access to all Windows settings

I've provided the four prototypes of scripts you will run into. Table 15-1 lists all information your scripts can request. It also specifies property ID and return value type, so you can adjust the sample scripts to whichever information you need to request.

Table 15-1   Property-IDs to change Windows Settings

Property ID	Return Type	Description
&H1000	Boolean	True: Active Window Tracking enabled. Windows activates the window the mouse is over. Applies to Win98/2000 only.
&H100C	Boolean	True: Windows activated through Active Window Tracking will be brought to the foreground.
&H2002	long	Time in milliseconds specifying the Active Window Tracking delay.
&H1002	Boolean	True: Menus will be animated. Applies to Win98/2000 only.
&H1012	Boolean	True: Menus will use fade effect. False: Menus will use slide effect.
		Applies to Windows 2000 only. Valid only when menu animation is generally turned on.
&H1004	Boolean	True: Combo box content will slide open. Applies to Windows 98/2000.
&H1006	Boolean	True: Scrolling effect for list boxes enabled. Applies to Win98/2000.
&H1008	Boolean	True: Window title bars use color gradient. Applies to Win98/2000.

Property ID	Return Type	Description
&H100A	Boolean	True: Menu access keys are always underlined. Applies to Win98/2000.
&H100E	Boolean	True: Hot tracking is enabled. The mouse selects items it points to.
&H101A	Boolean	True: Cursor shadow enabled.
&H2004	long	Number of times Windows flashes a window button if it can't switch the window to the foreground immediately.
&H2000	long	Amount of time, in milliseconds, following user input during which the system doesn't allow other windows to switch in the foreground.
&H1016	Boolean	True: Tooltip animation is turned on.
&H1018	Boolean	True: Tooltips fade; false: Tooltips slide in.
&H103E	Boolean	True: Animation effects for the UI are generally enabled.
1	Boolean	True: System beep enabled.
5	long	Border size of windows.
10	long	Keyboard speed; determines how rapidly the keyboard repeats keystrokes. 0 (30 repetitions per second) to 31 (2.5 repetitions per second).
13	long	Horizontal spacing of icons.
14	long	Number of idle seconds after which the screen saver is turned on.
16	Boolean	True: Screen saver is generally enabled.
22	long	Keyboard delay: 0 (approx. 250 ms) to 3 (approx. 1 sec) keyboard delay before keys will be automatically repeated.
24	long	Vertical spacing of icons.
25	Boolean	True: Icon titles will wrap.
27	Boolean	True: Menus are left-aligned; false: menus are right-aligned.
38	Boolean	True: Full window drag enabled.
48	array4	Returns the current work area as top x, y, bottom x, y.
68	Boolean	True: User relies on the keyboards. Software shows keyboard shortcuts which otherwise may be hidden.

Continued

Table 15-1	*(continued)*	
Property ID	*Return Type*	*Description*
74	Boolean	True: Font smoothing enabled. Available on Windows 95 only in conjunction with Plus!-Pack.
79	long	Timeout value after which screen saver enters low-power mode.
83	Boolean	True: Low-power mode of screen saver is enabled.
92	Boolean	True: Windows 95 + Plus!-Pack.
94	long	Enables mouse trails. 0 or 1: feature disabled; positive value: number of trailing mouse images (max. 10).
95	Boolean	True: Mouse automatically is moved over the dialog default button.
98	long	Width in pixels of the mouse hover rectangle.
100	long	Height in pixels of the mouse hover rectangle.
102	long	Time in milliseconds that the mouse must be over an object for Windows to select it.
104	long	Number of lines scrolled with each rotation of a mouse wheel.
106	long	Time, in milliseconds, used as menu show delay. This delay affects opening windows, showing tooltips, and selecting icons.
112	long	Speed of mouse: 1 (slowest) to 20 (fastest).
114	Boolean	True: Screen saver is currently running.
115	String	Name of current desktop wallpaper.
&2006	long	Width of selection caret used as input cursor in text boxes.

Changing Windows settings

Your scripts can also change Windows settings.

Secret

Setting new values doesn't necessarily mean you see the results immediately. Whether you set values manually using the Registry Editor or through the use of SystemParametersInfo, in either case the changes will only be reflected once you force Windows to reread the Registry settings. I have provided the necessary methods to make the changes happen, and they are documented where appropriate.

To make changes easy, the `registry.update` component already includes the appropriate method, which is `ChangeSetting`. Supply the setting ID you want to change and supply two parameters with the new values. Optionally, you can control whether the setting should be stored permanently or used temporarily. By default, `ChangeSetting` changes the values permanently. If you specify 0 as fourth argument, the settings will not be stored in your user profile and will be used only temporarily.

Secret

`ChangeSetting` doesn't use the same Setting IDs as `GetASetting`. As a rule of thumb, add 1 to the `GetASetting` Setting ID provided in Table 15-1 to get the ID for changing the setting. For example, to control whether menus will align to the left or right, look up the Setting ID in Table 15-1. (In this case, it's 27.) The ID for setting this value, therefore, is 28, and below you'll find an example of how to change menu alignment using this ID. There are only very few exceptions to this rule. Still, `ChangeSetting` accepts two values. Which one should be used for the new value? Either. Try out both ways or take a look at the many examples provided below.

```
' 15-18.VBS

set tool = CreateObject("registry.update")

' current menu alignment
status = tool.GetASetting(27, "boolean")
if status then
     msg = "Menus are currently right aligned. Change?"
else
     msg = "Menus are currently left aligned. Change?"
end if

answer = MsgBox(msg, vbYesNo + vbQuestion)
if answer = vbYes then
     call tool.ChangeSetting(28, not status, 0)
     MsgBox "Done."
end if
```

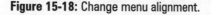

Figure 15-18: Change menu alignment.

Changing icon spacing

You can arrange icons on your desktop manually, or you can let Windows take care of icon arrangements. You control this feature by right-clicking the desktop: Choose Arrange Icons and Enable Automatically.

To change icon spacing, use the following script:

```
' 15-19.VBS

set tool = CreateObject("registry.update")

' read in old values:
sx = tool.GetASetting(13, "long")
sy = tool.GetASetting(24, "long")

msg = "Your current icon spacing is " & sx & " x " & sy & vbCr
msg = msg & "Do you want to change this?"

answer = MsgBox(msg, vbYesNo + vbQuestion)
if answer = vbYes then
    newsx = Ask("Your new horizontal icon spacing", sx)
    newsy = Ask("Your new vertical icon spacing", sy)
    Call tool.ChangeSetting(13, newsx, 0, 1)
    Call tool.ChangeSetting(24, newsy, 0, 1)

    ' Make changes happen:
    tool.RefreshWindowMetrics

    MsgBox "Setting has changed!"
end if

function Ask(question, default)
    Ask = InputBox(question,,default)
    if ask = vbEmpty then WScript.Quit
    if not isNumeric(ask) then
        MsgBox "You did not enter a number!", vbCritical
        WScript.Quit
    end if
    Ask = CInt(Ask)
end function
```

Your script now can change icon spacing in a range much greater than usually allowed by the official dialog box.

Secret

To make your changes happen, the script uses the new method RefreshWindowMetrics. This method sends a message to all open windows (including the desktop), informing it of changes in the Window Metrics section of the Registry. Broadcast messages like this one should be sent using asynchronous messaging. SendMessageTimeout sends the message but doesn't wait forever if a window doesn't respond.

Managing Active Window Tracking

Active Window Tracking is a new feature, available for Windows 98 and 2000. Turned on, it activates windows by merely pointing at them. You can completely control this feature through script. Aside from enabling and disabling the feature altogether, you can also determine whether or not the selected window jumps to the foreground, and how long you need to point at a window to select it (see Figure 15-19).

The next script shows how to implement user controls to manage this feature. It demonstrates both the use of `GetASetting` (according to the information found in Table 15-1) and `ChangeSetting`.

```
' 15-20.VBS

set tool = CreateObject("registry.update")

' current state
state = tool.GetASetting(&H1000, "boolean")
if state then
    msg = "Active Window Tracking is currently enabled. Do you" _
        & " want to disable it?"
    response = MsgBox(msg, vbYesNo + vbQuestion)
    if response = vbYes then
        tool.ChangeSetting &H1001, 0, false, 1
    else
        AskDetails
    end if
else
    msg = "Active Window Tracking is currently disabled." _
        & " Do you want to enable it?"
    response = MsgBox(msg, vbYesNo + vbQuestion)
    if response = vbYes then
        tool.ChangeSetting &H1001, 0, true, 1
        AskDetails
    end if
end if

sub AskDetails
    msg = "Should the active window jump to the foreground?"
    response = MsgBox(msg, vbYesNo + vbQuestion)
    if response = vbYes then
        tool.ChangeSetting &H100D, 0, true, 1
    else
        tool.ChangeSetting &H100D, 0, false, 1
    end if

    oldtimeout = tool.GetASetting(&H2002, "long")
    msg = "Specify time (in milliseconds) for activation timeout!"
    timeout = Ask(msg, oldtimeout)
    tool.ChangeSetting &H2003, 0, timeout, 1
end sub


function Ask(question, default)
    Ask = InputBox(question,,default)
    if ask = vbEmpty then WScript.Quit
    if not isNumeric(ask) then
        MsgBox "You did not enter a number!", vbCritical
        WScript.Quit
    end if
    Ask = CInt(Ask)
end function
```

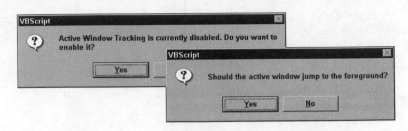

Figure 15-19: Manage Active Window Tracking.

Changing window borders

By default, Windows uses a 1-pixel window frame around each window. The window frame doesn't have to be this size, though. It's easy to enlarge it:

```
' 15-21.VBS

set tool = CreateObject("registry.update")

' current status of beep
status = tool.GetASetting(5, "long")
msg = "Current window border size: " & status & vbCr
msg = msg & "Do you want to change the setting?"

answer = MsgBox(msg, vbYesNo + vbQuestion)
if answer = vbYes then
     newsize = Ask("New window border size",status)
     call tool.ChangeSetting(6, newsize, 0)
     MsgBox "Done."
end if

function Ask(question, default)
     Ask = InputBox(question,,default)
     if ask = vbEmpty then WScript.Quit
     if not isNumeric(ask) then
          MsgBox "You did not enter a number!", vbCritical
          WScript.Quit
     end if
     Ask = CInt(Ask)
end function
```

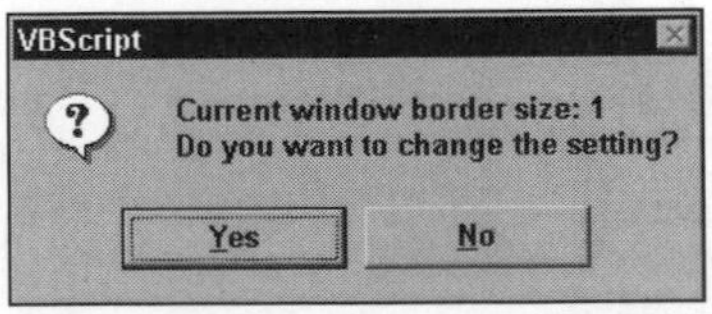

Figure 15-20: Expand window frames and color-code the active window.

Changing window colors

Why would anybody change the window frame size? There are a couple of good reasons. For example, you may find it easier to hit the frame with your mouse pointer. Another good reason is to better mark the active window. Specify different colors for active and inactive window frames.

The next script shows you how to change window frame colors:

```
' 15-22.VBS

set tool = CreateObject("registry.update")

oldactive = tool.GetSystemColor(10)
oldinactive = tool.GetSystemColor(11)

' change colors
tool.SetSystemColor 10, &H00FF00
tool.SetSystemColor 11, &HFF0000

msg = "Changed window frame colors. You can only see the colors if " _
& "you have expanded the window frame to more than 1 pixel " _
& "width. Do you want to keep the new colors?"
answer = MsgBox(msg, vbYesNo + vbQuestion)
if answer = vbNo then
    tool.SetSystemColor 10, oldactive
    tool.SetSystemColor 11, oldinactive
    MsgBox "Old color values restored."
end if
```

Changing window colors is discussed in more depth later. I've provided this example only to demonstrate how window border enlargement can be used to display colored window frames. Changing window colors (and other system colors) uses a different technique. It's not done by `SystemParametersInfo`.

Controlling the system beep

On systems without a sound card, Windows uses the internal speaker to beep whenever something exciting happens. Systems with sound cards installed use the sound schemes instead.

To control the internal speaker, use this script:

```
' 15-23.VBS

set tool = CreateObject("registry.update")

' current status of beep
status = tool.GetASetting(1, "boolean")
if status then
    msg = "System Beep is enabled. Do you want to disable it?"
else
```

```
        msg = "System Beep is disabled. Do you want to enable it?"
end if

answer = MsgBox(msg, vbYesNo + vbQuestion)
if answer = vbYes then
    call tool.ChangeSetting(2, not status, 0)
    MsgBox "Done."
end if
```

Using Icon Title Wrap

Long icon names are truncated automatically so they won't interfere with neighbor icons. However, you can specify whether or not Windows uses a wrapping technique to continue the icon title in the next line.

```
' 15-24.VBS

set tool = CreateObject("registry.update")

' current status of beep
status = tool.GetASetting(25, "boolean")
if status then
    msg = "Icon Title Wrap is enabled. Do you want to disable it?"
else
    msg = "Icon Title Wrap is disabled. Do you want to enable it?"
end if

answer = MsgBox(msg, vbYesNo + vbQuestion)
if answer = vbYes then
    call tool.ChangeSetting(26, not status, 0)
    MsgBox "Done."
end if
```

Controlling Screen Savers

Screen savers are special executables carrying the *.scr file extension. They are stored in the Windows system folder. Your scripts can change many internal screen saver settings and even launch screen savers.

Launching screen savers

Launching screen savers is easy—just use the WScript.Shell Run method and specify the screen saver name:

```
' 15-25.VBS

set wshshell = CreateObject("WScript.Shell")
wshshell.Run """%windir%\system32\sspipes.scr"""
```

Note

Change the script and supply a screen saver name that is currently installed on your system. Search for *.scr to see all currently installed screen savers.

This way, you can access any screen saver located anywhere on your system. Maybe you would much rather activate the current screen saver. Just query the Registry:

```
' 15-26.VBS

set wshshell = CreateObject("WScript.Shell")

' retrieve screen saver
on error resume next
exepath = ""
exepath = wshshell.RegRead("HKCU\Control Panel\Desktop\SCRNSAVE.EXE")
on error goto 0

if exepath="" or lcase(exepath) = "(none)" then
    MsgBox "No screen saver specified."
else
    wshshell.Run """" & exepath & """"
end if
```

This time, the script automatically starts the currently selected screen saver.

All the other screen-saver-related information is stored at the same location: HKCU\Control Panel\Desktop\. Either access this information directly or use the API functions.

Temporarily disabling screen savers

Maybe your script wants to make sure the screen saver is disabled. This may be necessary for maintenance scripts that check the hard disk's integrity using tools like ScanDisk. During ScanDisk and Defrag operations, no other software may change the hard disk's contents, but advanced screen savers do.

How can you make sure no screen saver jumps in front and messes up your maintenance work efforts? Tell Windows:

```
' 15-27.VBS

set tool = CreateObject("registry.update")

' current status of screen saver
status = tool.GetASetting(16, "boolean")
if status then
    ' temporarily disable screen saver
    call tool.ChangeSetting(17, false, 0)
end if

MsgBox "Your screen saver is now disabled for sure. You could now" _
    & " safely run your disk tools. Check your screen saver " _
```

```
            & "property page to see that the screen saver really is " _
            & "disabled. Click OK to return to previous state."

' restore previous state
call tool.ChangeSetting(17, status, 0)

MsgBox "Previous screen saver state restored."
```

Setting screen saver timeout

You can also change the screen saver timeout. Here's an example:

```
' 15-28.VBS

set tool = CreateObject("registry.update")

' current timeout
timeout = tool.GetASetting(14, "long")

' set new timeout
newtimeout = Ask("Specify new timeout in seconds!", timeout)
call tool.ChangeSetting(15, newtimeout, 0)

' activate screen saver
active = tool.GetASetting(16, "boolean")

if not active then
    answer = MsgBox("Do you want to enable your screen saver?", _
        vbYesNo + vbQuestion)
    if answer=vbYes then call tool.ChangeSetting(17, true, 0)
end if

function Ask(question, default)
    Ask = InputBox(question,,default)
    if ask = vbEmpty then WScript.Quit
    if not isNumeric(ask) then
        MsgBox "You did not enter a number!", vbCritical
        WScript.Quit
    end if
    Ask = CInt(Ask)
end function
```

If no screen saver is currently selected, Windows returns an "active" screen-saver status. Your only way to determine whether or not a screen saver is specified is querying the SCRRUN.EXE key as outlined in the previous script.

Secret

The official dialog box lets you specify a screen saver timeout in units of minutes only. This is why the minimum is fixed to 60 seconds. Your script can set a screen-saver timeout up to the second, although this rarely makes sense. For example, specifying a timeout of 1 would start the screen saver all the time — useful only for sabotage purposes. Specifying a timeout value below 1 disables the screen saver.

Finding out if a screen saver runs

Your script can even find out whether a screen saver is currently running. Have a look:

```
' 15-29.VBS

set tool = CreateObject("registry.update")

' screen saver running?
' check for 2 minutes
for x=1 to 60
    scr = tool.GetASetting(114, "boolean")
    if scr then
        MsgBox "Screen Saver kicked in!"
        exit for
    end if
    ' wait 2 sec
    WScript.Sleep 2000
next
```

Provided your screen saver kicks in within two minutes, the script will display a message the moment the screen saver is activated.

Fooling Windows and disabling CTRL+ALT+DEL

What seemed like a funny curiosity in the previous example does have real-world significance. Your script can also set the state of the screen saver. Setting the screen saver state doesn't actually start the screen saver (see Figure 15-21). It just fools Windows into thinking a screen saver is running.

On Windows 9.x, this has many consequences. For example, while a screen saver is running, you can't use CTRL+ALT+DEL to get to the task list and close down programs. So to disable this key combination, use the following script:

```
' 15-30.VBS

set tool = CreateObject("registry.update")

' make windows think a screen saver was running
call tool.ChangeSetting(97, true, 0)

MsgBox "CTRL+ALT+DEL disabled on Windows 95/98!"

' revert to normal
call tool.ChangeSetting(97, false, 0)
```

Changing screen saver settings

How can you configure the active screen saver? It's fairly easy: Each screen saver executable contains its own set of dialog boxes to configure the internal screen saver settings. However, it's not easy to get to these dialog boxes.

Secret

If you run a screen saver directly, it will display its configuration settings. To activate the screen saver, use the secret option /S. Unfortunately, in the Windows Registry, scr files are registered to use the /S option by default. This is why you can't supply options to the screen saver using the WScript.Shell Run method.

There is a secret way to supply options to screen savers. Instead of using the WScript.Shell Run method, use the Run method you developed in Chapter 11 instead. The difference is: The WScript.Shell Run method looks up the file path and starts the associated program. This is why this method can launch documents, too. Your own Run method launches the software directly.

Note

Make sure you have installed your COM extension: (process). See Chapter 11 for more details.

```
' 15-31.VBS

set proc = CreateObject("process.id")
set wshshell = CreateObject("WScript.Shell")

' retrieve screen saver
on error resume next
exepath = ""
exepath = wshshell.RegRead("HKCU\Control Panel\Desktop\SCRNSAVE.EXE")
on error goto 0

if exepath="" or lcase(exepath)="(none)" then
    MsgBox "No screen saver specified."
else
proc.Run """" & exepath & """"
end if.
```

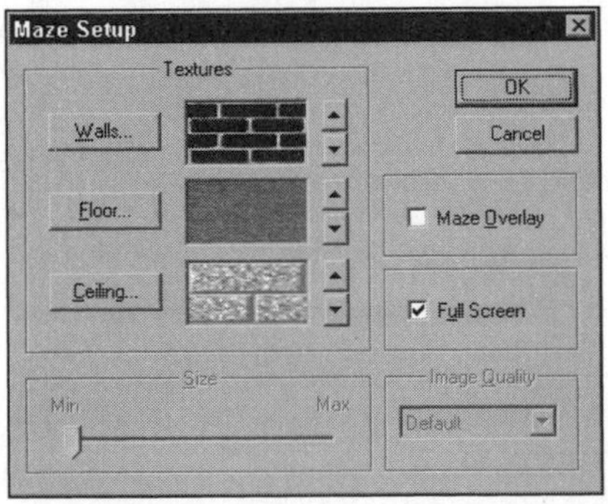

![Maze Setup dialog box with Textures section containing Walls, Floor, and Ceiling buttons, OK and Cancel buttons, Maze Overlay and Full Screen checkboxes, Size slider, and Image Quality dropdown.]

Figure 15-21: Invoke the property dialog box of the current screen saver.

This script displays the screen saver settings if a screen saver was specified. To prove the option theory, you just need to replace one line. Change

```
proc.Run """" & exepath & """"
```

with

```
proc.Run """" & exepath & """ /S"
```

Now, your script runs the screen saver. This is the default for scr files.

Installing new screen savers

You can even change the current screen saver or install one if none is specified. Under normal conditions, you'd use the Control Panel to install new screen savers. But did you know that you can access the Control Panel functions directly, too?

Here's an example. It mimics the screen saver Install context menu command:

```
' 15-32.VBS

set wshshell = CreateObject("WScript.Shell")

name = InputBox("Please enter path of screen saver!",,"logon.scr")
if name = vbEmpty then WScript.Quit

command = "rundll32.exe desk.cpl,InstallScreenSaver """ & name _
    & """"

wshshell.Run command
```

The script invokes the screen saver dialog box and preselects the screen saver you specified. If you did not specify a valid scr file, no screen saver will be specified.

Controlling low-power screen saver features

Windows allows the screen saver to enter a special power-saving mode when the screen saver runs for a specific time. Here's how to control the power-saving feature:

```
' 15-34.VBS

set tool = CreateObject("registry.update")

' current status
powersave = tool.GetASetting(83, "boolean")

if powersave then
msg = "Power Save Mode currently enabled. Disable?"
else
    msg = "Power Save Mode currently disabled. Enable?"
end if

answer = MsgBox(msg, vbYesNo + vbQuestion)
```

```
if answer = vbYes then
    powersave = not powersave
    call tool.ChangeSetting(85, Abs(CInt(status)), 0)
end if

if powersave then
    timeout = tool.GetASetting(79, "long")
    msg = "Current timeout is " & timeout & " seconds. Change?"
    answer = MsgBox(msg, vbYesNo + vbQuestion)
    if answer = vbYes then
        newtimeout = Ask("Specify new timeout in seconds!", timeout)
        call tool.ChangeSetting(81, newtimeout, 0)
    end if
end if

MsgBox "Done."

function Ask(question, default)
    Ask = InputBox(question,,default)
    if ask = vbEmpty then WScript.Quit
    if not isNumeric(ask) then
        MsgBox "You did not enter a number!", vbCritical
        WScript.Quit
    end if
    Ask = CInt(Ask)
end function
```

Secret

Your script can change the power-off timeouts up to the second. The official dialog box, in contrast, offers only selected timeout values. If you choose a timeout value not listed in the official drop-down list, the list will show a blank entry. To activate power-off features right away, set the power-off timeout temporarily to 1 second, wait 2 seconds using `WScript.Sleep 2000`, and reset the original value.

Powering off devices

The power-saving features include two phases of power saving: a low-power phase and a power-off phase. The previous script controlled the low-power phase. To manage the power-off phase, use the values in Table 15-2 instead:

Table 15-2   Property IDs for Power-Saving Features

ID	Description
84	Determines if `PowerOff` is active
86	Sets `PowerOff` activation
80	Determines `PowerOff` timeout
82	Sets `PowerOff` timeout

Animations and Visual Effects

Windows uses an ever-increasing number of visual effects, and Windows 2000, as the latest Windows family member, tops all of this by fading menus and cursor shadows.

Fortunately, it's up to you which effects you find useful and which effects you prefer to turn off. After all, visual effects eat up CPU power, although no serious impact is noticeable.

Turning off visual effects altogether

Windows 2000 uses so many visual effects that Microsoft decided to implement a way to disable them altogether. Note that the next example works only on Windows 2000. On all other Windows versions, you need to disable the visual effects individually, as shown later.

```
' 15-35.VBS

set tool = CreateObject("registry.update")

status = tool.GetASetting(&H103E, "boolean")
if status then
     msg = "Visual effects enabled. Do you want to disable them?"
else
     msg = "Visual effects disabled. Do you want to enable them?"
end if

answer = MsgBox(msg, vbYesNo + vbQuestion)
if answer = vbYes then
     call tool.ChangeSetting(&H103F, 0, not status)
     MsgBox "Done."
end if
```

Overview: Visual effects built into Windows

Table 15-3 lists all the visual effects built into Windows. The table also reveals which effects are available on which Windows version.

Table 15-3   Visual Effects Used to Enhance the User Interface

Effect	Description
ComboBox	Win98/2000: Combo boxes slide open.
Cursor Shadow	Win2000: Cursor drops a shadow.
Gradient Captions	Win98/2000: Window captions use a smooth color gradient instead of solid color.

Continued

Table 15-3 *(continued)*	
Effect	**Description**
Hot Tracking	Win98/2000: Window is selected merely by pointing at it. More about this feature has already been discussed above.
List Box	Win98/2000: List boxes use a sliding animation.
Menu Animation	Win98/2000: Menus use sliding or fading animation.
Menu Underlines	Win98/2000: Menus show keyboard shortcut underlines only if menu is selected. Works only in selected applications. Older applications show menu underlines all the time.
Selection Fade	Win2000: Selected menu item remains on-screen briefly while fading out after the menu is closed.
Tooltip Animation	Win2000: Enables tooltips to slide in or fade in.
Full Window Drag	Win95Plus/98/2000: Windows are moved completely with content.
Font Smoothing	Win95Plus/98/2000: Text characters are smoothened by using anti-aliasing techniques. Works only if all graphics cards use more than 256 colors.

Combo box animation

Combo box animation lets combo box contents slide out smoothly. However, you can always enable rapidly appearing combo boxes using this script:

```
' 15-36.VBS

set tool = CreateObject("registry.update")

status = tool.GetASetting(&H1004, "boolean")
if status then
    msg = "Combo Box animation enabled. Disable?"
else
    msg = "Combo Box animation disabled. Enable?"
end if

answer = MsgBox(msg, vbYesNo + vbQuestion)
if answer = vbYes then
    call tool.ChangeSetting(&H1005, 0, not status)
    MsgBox "Done."
end if
```

Cursor shadow

Windows 2000 uses a cursor shadow by default. The cursor appears to be above the desktop, and it's easier to recognize than the cursor arrow. If you prefer the old-fashioned cursor style, disable the shadow:

```
' 15-37.VBS

set tool = CreateObject("registry.update")

status = tool.GetASetting(&H101A, "boolean")
if status then
    msg = "Cursor shadow animation enabled. Disable?"
else
    msg = "Cursor shadow animation disabled. Enable?"
end if

answer = MsgBox(msg, vbYesNo + vbQuestion)
if answer = vbYes then
    call tool.ChangeSetting(&H101B, 0, not status)
    MsgBox "Done."
end if
```

Gradient captions

Windows 98 and 2000 use color-gradients in the window title bar so that colors are blended from one color to another (see Figure 15-22). If you don't like this, you don't have to live with it.

```
' 15-38.VBS

set tool = CreateObject("registry.update")

status = tool.GetASetting(&H1008, "boolean")
if status then
    msg = "Gradient captions enabled. Disable?"
else
    msg = "Gradient captions disabled. Enable?"
end if

answer = MsgBox(msg, vbYesNo + vbQuestion)
if answer = vbYes then
    call tool.ChangeSetting(&H1009, 0, not status)
    MsgBox "Done."
end if
```

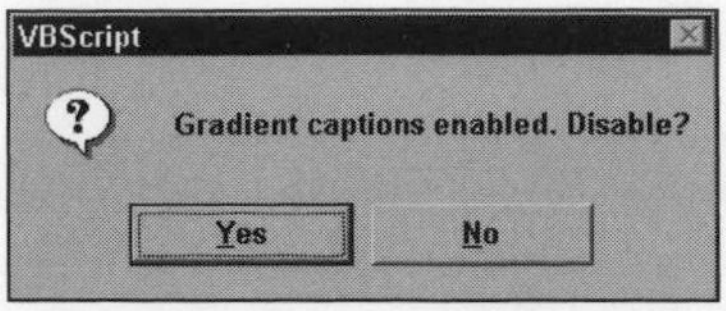

Figure 15-22: Enable or disable color gradient captions.

List box animation

List box animation lets the content slide down while you scroll. Again, this feature is optional, and the following script allows you to turn it off:

```
' 15-39.VBS

set tool = CreateObject("registry.update")

status = tool.GetASetting(&H1006, "boolean")
if status then
      msg = "List Box animation enabled. Disable?"
else
      msg = "List Box animation disabled. Enable?"
end if

answer = MsgBox(msg, vbYesNo + vbQuestion)
if answer = vbYes then
      call tool.ChangeSetting(&H1007, 0, not status)
      MsgBox "Done."
end if
```

Menu animation

Menu animations were first introduced by Windows 98 and expanded by Windows 2000. While this feature is turned on, menus elegantly slide into view. Beginning with Windows 2000, you have the choice between two animation styles — sliding animations and fading animations. The script not only controls the animation but also lets you choose between animation styles. Those styles will only show effect if you are using Windows 2000, though.

```
' 15-40.VBS

set tool = CreateObject("registry.update")

status = tool.GetASetting(&H1002, "boolean")
if status then
      msg = "Menu animation enabled. Disable?"
else
      msg = "Menu animation disabled. Enable?"
end if
```

```
answer = MsgBox(msg, vbYesNo + vbQuestion)
if answer = vbYes then
     status = not status
     call tool.ChangeSetting(&H1003, 0, status)
end if

if status then
     anim = tool.GetASetting(&H1012, "boolean")
     if anim then
          animtype = "fading"
     else
          animtype = "sliding"
     end if

     msg = "On Windows 2000, you may choose between animation styles."
     msg = msg & vbCr & "Currently, your system uses " _
          & animtype & " animation." & vbCr
     msg = msg & "Do you want to switch?"
     answer = MsgBox(msg, vbYesNo + vbQuestion)
     if answer = vbYes then
          call tool.ChangeSetting(&H1013, 0, not anim)
     end if
end if

MsgBox "Done."
```

Menu underlines

Menus indicate keyboard shortcuts by underlining the key in the menu name.
If you don't use keyboard shortcuts often, you might find it better to disable
such shortcuts. If you do use them often, keyboard shortcuts will only appear
once the menu is selected: for example, by pressing [F10].

Secret

The menu underline feature depends on the software you are running. Older
software doesn't care about this feature and shows keyboard shortcuts no
matter what.

```
' 15-41.VBS

set tool = CreateObject("registry.update")

status = tool.GetASetting(&H100A, "boolean")
if status then
     msg = "Menu Underline always shown. Enable?"
else
     msg = "Menu Underline only shown when menu active. Disable?" end
if

answer = MsgBox(msg, vbYesNo + vbQuestion)
if answer = vbYes then
     call tool.ChangeSetting(&H100B, 0, not status)
     MsgBox "Done."
end if
```

Menu show delay

Windows uses an internal counter to delay the opening of menus. This is important for menus to remain open even if you accidentally point to some other object. Here's how you control the delay:

```
' 15-42.VBS

set tool = CreateObject("registry.update")

delay = tool.GetASetting(106, "long")
msg = "Enter new menu delay in milliseconds!"
newdelay = Ask(msg, delay)
call tool.ChangeSetting(107, newdelay, 0)
MsgBox "Done."

function Ask(question, default)
    Ask = InputBox(question,,default)
    if ask = vbEmpty then WScript.Quit
    if not isNumeric(ask) then
        MsgBox "You did not enter a number!", vbCritical
        WScript.Quit
    end if
    Ask = CLng(Ask)
end function
```

Choosing a delay of 100 milliseconds will produce rapidly opening menus, at the price of rapidly closing menus the moment your mouse leaves the menu. On the other hand, a delay of 65,500 milliseconds turns off automatic menu opening. To open submenus, you now have to click the menu item. 400 milliseconds is the default value.

Secret

Menu show delay serves a dual purpose on Windows 98 machines. If you have configured Explorer to select icons by pointing at them (instead of clicking), the menu show delay determines how long you have to point at the object before it will be selected. Obviously, specifying a menu show delay of more than 1,000 milliseconds (one second) will generate a conflict. On Windows 2000, this problem has been resolved, and object selection doesn't interfere anymore with menu show delay. Ironically, on Windows 98, changes are reflected for object selection immediately, whereas you need to restart `explorer.exe` or Windows to activate the menu delay.

Specifying mouse hover timeout

On Windows 2000, Microsoft has finally divided menu show delay and mouse hovering delay. Mouse hovering delay determines how long you have to point at some object to get it selected. Mouse hovering can be enabled and disabled using the Explorer settings. Here's how to set and change the mouse hovering delay:

```
' 15-43.VBS

set tool = CreateObject("registry.update")
```

```
delay = tool.GetASetting(102, "long")
msg = "Enter new mouse hover delay in milliseconds!"
newdelay = Ask(msg, delay)
call tool.ChangeSetting(103, newdelay, 0)
MsgBox "Done."

function Ask(question, default)
     Ask = InputBox(question,,default)
     if ask = vbEmpty then WScript.Quit
     if not isNumeric(ask) then
          MsgBox "You did not enter a number!", vbCritical
          WScript.Quit
     end if
     Ask = CLng(Ask)
end function
```

Secret

Mouse hovering works only if the window the object is contained in is the active window. For example, if you can't select desktop icons by pointing at them, click the desktop first. This way, it becomes the active window, and mouse hovering works fine.

Selection fade

With Windows 2000, whenever you select a menu command, it will remain visible for a small period of time after the menu has already closed, and then it will fade out. This effect is called Selection Fade and is supposed to underline which menu command you have chosen. Turn it on or off as you like:

```
' 15-44.VBS

set tool = CreateObject("registry.update")

status = tool.GetASetting(&H1014, "boolean")
if status then
     msg = "Selection Fade enabled. Disable?"
else
     msg = "Selection Fade disabled. Enable?" end if

answer = MsgBox(msg, vbYesNo + vbQuestion)
if answer = vbYes then
     call tool.ChangeSetting(&H1015, 0, not status)
     MsgBox "Done."
end if
```

Tooltip animation

Tooltips are little information windows. If you point your mouse at some object, chances are a tooltip will display additional information about this object.

Secret

Whether or not tooltips appear for desktop items is controlled by your folder options. Click the View tab and select the Tooltip option to enable the desktop item Tooltips.

Tooltips can be animated (see script 15-46.VBS). They support the same general animation techniques as menus. On Windows 98, tooltip animation slides in the tip windows. On Windows 2000, you have the choice between sliding and fading animation:

```
' 15-46.VBS

set tool = CreateObject("registry.update")

status = tool.GetASetting(&H1016, "boolean")
if status then
    msg = "Tooltip animation enabled. Disable?"
else
    msg = "Tooltip animation disabled. Enable?"
end if

answer = MsgBox(msg, vbYesNo + vbQuestion)
if answer = vbYes then
    status = not status
    call tool.ChangeSetting(&H1017, 0, status)
end if

if status then
    anim = tool.GetASetting(&H1018, "boolean")
    if anim then
        animtype = "fading"
    else
        animtype = "sliding"
    end if

    msg = "On Windows 2000, you may choose between animation styles."
    msg = msg & vbCr & "Currently, your system uses " _
        & animtype & " animation." & vbCr
    msg = msg & "Do you want to switch?"
    answer = MsgBox(msg, vbYesNo + vbQuestion)
    if answer = vbYes then
        call tool.ChangeSetting(&H1019, 0, not anim)
    end if
end if

MsgBox "Done."
```

Changing the text of tooltips

You can change the tooltip description, too. The description is stored in a value called InfoTip. The next script searches all registered COM objects for this value and allows you to change the description (see Figure 15-23).

Note

This script changes the default machine-wide settings. Your new tooltip descriptions apply to all users. Per-user settings are possible only on Windows 2000. Here, store the new description in the HKEY_CURRENT _USER branch.

```
' 15-47.VBS

set tool = CreateObject("regtool.tob")
set refresh = CreateObject("registry.update")

' get access to registered COM objects
set comobjects = tool.RegEnum("HKCR\CLSID\")
for each comobject in comobjects
     key = "HKCR\CLSID\" & comobject & "\"

     if tool.KeyExists(key & "InfoTip") then
          name = ""
          tip = ""
          on error resume next
          name = tool.RegRead(key)
          tip = tool.RegRead(key & "InfoTip")
          if name = "" then name = "(unknown)"
          on error goto 0
          msg = "Found COM object: " & name & vbCr
          msg = msg & "Tooltip Text: " & tip & vbCr
          msg = msg & "Do you want to change the description?"
          answer = MsgBox(msg, vbYesNoCancel + vbQuestion)
          if answer = vbCancel then
               WScript.Quit
          elseif answer = vbYes then
               msg = "Please enter new description!"
               newname = InputBox(msg,,tip)
               if newname = vbEmpty then
                    WScript.Quit
               else
                    tool.RegWrite key & "InfoTip", newname
                    MsgBox "Changed description"
                    refresh.RefreshDesktop
               end if
          end if
     end if
next
```

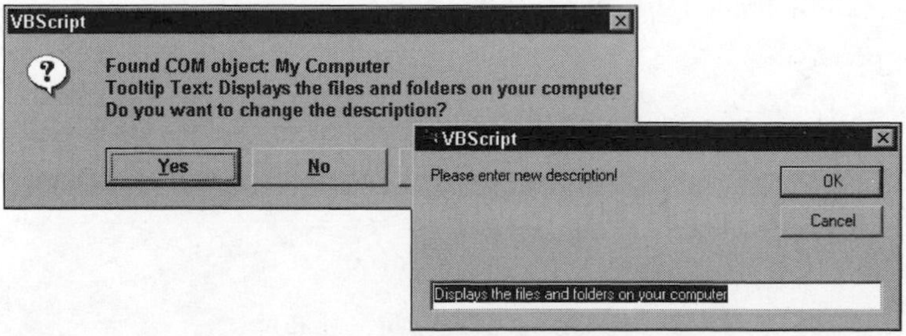

Figure 15-23: Change tooltips and specify the text yourself.

Full window drag

On slow computers, it takes too much CPU power to refresh the window contents while you move them. This is why older Windows versions use ghosted window borders during drag operations. Beginning with Windows 95 Plus!, Windows also supports full window drag. It's enabled by default on Windows 98 and 2000. You can manually control this setting:

```
' 15-48.VBS

set tool = CreateObject("registry.update")

status = tool.GetASetting(38, "boolean")
if status then
    msg = "Full Window Drag enabled. Disable?"
else
    msg = "Full Window Drag disabled. Enable?"
end if

answer = MsgBox(msg, vbYesNo + vbQuestion)
if answer = vbYes then
    call tool.ChangeSetting(37, Abs(CInt(not status)), 0)
    MsgBox "Done."
end if
```

Font smoothing

Font smoothing was introduced with Windows 95 Plus! and is a standard feature in Windows 98 and 2000. Font smoothing uses an optical trick to produce crispy text, through a technique called anti-aliasing. It smoothes out jaggy characters by inserting additional pixels of different shades.

Secret

Font smoothing needs a considerable amount of extra colors to "fill in" the jaggy character outlines. Therefore, to use this feature, your graphics adapter needs to support more than 256 colors. On multi-display systems, font smoothing is disabled automatically the moment one of the graphics adapters uses 256 colors or less. This is because font smoothing is a system-wide setting and cannot be limited to individual displays.

```
' 15-49.VBS

set tool = CreateObject("registry.update")

status = tool.GetASetting(74, "boolean")
if status then
    msg = "Font smoothing enabled. Disable?"
else
    msg = "Font smoothing disabled. Enable?"
end if

answer = MsgBox(msg, vbYesNo + vbQuestion)
if answer = vbYes then
    call tool.ChangeSetting(75, Abs(CInt(not status)), 0)
    MsgBox "Done."
end if
```

Setting blinking text cursor width

On Windows 2000, you can change the size of the blinking text input cursor. By default, this cursor uses a 1-pixel width. If you prefer a block cursor, specify a width of 10 (see Figure 15-24):

```
' 15-50.VBS

set tool = CreateObject("registry.update")

caret = tool.GetASetting(&H2006, "long")
newcaret = Ask("Specify new caret width!", caret)
call tool.ChangeSetting(&H2007, 0, newcaret)
MsgBox "New caret width enabled. This only applies to Win2000!"

function Ask(question, default)
    Ask = InputBox(question,,default)
    if ask = vbEmpty then WScript.Quit
    if not isNumeric(ask) then
        MsgBox "You did not enter a number!", vbCritical
        WScript.Quit
    end if
    Ask = CInt(Ask)
end function
```

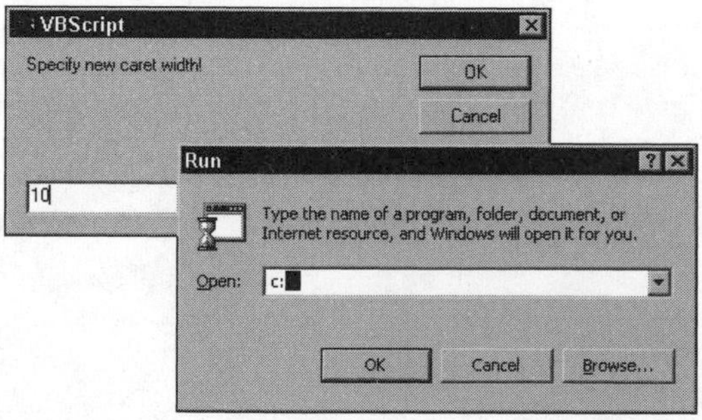

Figure 15-24: Change the cursor width and get an old-style block cursor.

Specifying a new desktop wallpaper

Your script can even change the desktop wallpaper. Drag any .bmp file onto the following script icon to install it as new desktop wallpaper:

```
' 15-51.VBS

set args = WScript.Arguments
if args.Count=0 then
    MsgBox "Please drag bmp files on my icon!"
    WScript.Quit
end if

if not lcase(right(args(0),3))="bmp" then
```

```
        MsgBox "I only accept bmp files!"
        WScript.Quit
end if

set tool = CreateObject("registry.update")
call tool.ChangeSetting(20, 0, args(0))
MsgBox "New wallpaper enabled!"
```

Changing the wallpaper mode

There's no direct API function to set the wallpaper mode. Changing wallpaper with the help of the previous script will change the wallpaper *file* only. It won't change the wallpaper style, and so your wallpaper may appear only as a small picture centered on-screen.

However, you can combine your new wallpaper command with your Registry methods, by setting the wallpaper mode directly inside of the Registry and then calling your wallpaper method to update the setting.

To make things a little more complex, Windows stores the wallpaper mode in two different settings. `TileWallpaper` determines whether the wallpaper is tiled or displayed as a single image. `WallpaperMode` determines whether the image is displayed in original size or stretched to fit the screen.

The following script converts the wallpaper settings to a single number between 0 and 2.

Secret

Changing the wallpaper style directly won't do a thing to your display. In order to make the change happen, you need to reset the wallpaper using the API call. Because the script wants to change the wallpaper style only, it first retrieves the current wallpaper using `GetWallpaper`, changes wallpaper style, and then resets the wallpaper to the same wallpaper currently enabled. This way, only wallpaper style is changed.

```
' 15-52.VBS

set tool = CreateObject("registry.update")
set wshshell = CreateObject("WScript.Shell")

' get current wallpaper settings
wallpaper = GetWallpaper
mode = GetWallpaperMode

if wallpaper = "" then
    MsgBox "Sorry, currently no wallpaper specified!"
    WScript.Quit
end if

' cycle through modes
for x= 0 to 2
    SetWallpaperMode x
    SetWallpaper wallpaper
    MsgBox "Wallpaper Mode " & x, vbSystemModal
next
```

```
' restore old settings:
SetWallpaperMode mode
SetWallpaper wallpaper

function SetWallpaper(newpaper)
     call tool.ChangeSetting(20, 0, newpaper)
end function

function GetWallpaper
     key = "HKCU\Control Panel\Desktop\Wallpaper"

     on error resume next
     GetWallpaper = wshshell.RegRead(key)
end function

sub SetWallpaperMode(mode)
     key1 = "HKCU\Control Panel\Desktop\WallpaperStyle"
     key2 = "HKCU\Control Panel\Desktop\TileWallpaper"

     on error resume next
     select case mode
         case 0:      ' original size, no tiling
         wshshell.RegWrite key1, 0
         wshshell.RegWrite key2, 0
         case 1:       ' center on screen:
         wshshell.RegWrite key1, 0
         wshshell.RegWrite key2, 1
         case 2:        ' stretch
         wshshell.RegWrite key1, 2
         wshshell.RegWrite key2, 0
         case else
         MsgBox "Specify wallpaper mode 0-2!"
         WScript.Quit
     end select
end sub

function GetWallpaperMode
     key1 = "HKCU\Control Panel\Desktop\WallpaperStyle"
     key2 = "HKCU\Control Panel\Desktop\TileWallpaper"

     on error resume next
     mode1 = wshshell.RegRead(key1)
     mode2 = wshshell.RegRead(key2)
     on error goto 0

     if mode1=0 and mode2=0 then
         GetWallpaperMode =  0
     elseif mode1=0 and mode2=1 then
         GetWallpaperMode = 1
     elseif mode1=2 and mode2=0 then
         GetWallpaperMode = 2
     else
         MsgBox "Unknown wallpaper mode: " & mode1 & "/" & mode2
     end if
end function
```

Enabling "Snap-To-Button"

Did you know that Windows 2000 can help you deal with dialog boxes? Instead of navigating to the buttons and dragging the mouse pointer over your entire desktop to get there, have Windows place the mouse cursor over any dialog box's default button.

This feature is called `SnapToDefButton`. The next script can enable (and disable) the feature. It's disabled by default:

```
' 15-53.VBS

set tool = CreateObject("registry.update")

status = tool.GetASetting(95, "boolean")
if status then
    msg = "Snap-To-Default enabled. Disable?"
else
    msg = "Snap-To-Default disabled. Enable?"
end if

answer = MsgBox(msg, vbYesNo + vbQuestion)
if answer = vbYes then
    call tool.ChangeSetting(96, Abs(CInt(not status)), 0)
    MsgBox "Done."
end if
```

Undocumented

Microsoft states that the snapping feature is available on Windows 98, NT4, and Windows 2000. However, on my test systems, it worked only with Windows 2000. You can check it out on your system by using the previous script to enable the feature, and then run the script again. If it still reports a disabled state, the feature isn't supported on your system. Internally, Windows stores the setting in `HKCU\Sontrol Panel\ Mouse\SnapToDefaultButton`.

More Undocumented Registry Tweaks

Of course, this book can only cover a fraction of the undocumented Registry settings available. Therefore, this chapter focuses on how to find out undocumented settings for yourself, and how to create scripts controlling these features.

There are two more concepts I'd like to share with you. First, you learn how the Registry manages the shortcut arrow. Next, you discover some new Registry tweaks available only on Windows 2000. Take them as templates for your own experiments and findings.

Getting rid of shortcut arrows

Shortcut arrows appear in the lower-left corner of shortcut icons. Actually, the shortcut arrow is an overlay icon placed on top of the regular icon. So, you can both disable and change the overlay icon.

Shortcut arrows are controlled by a Registry value called isShortcut. Any file that carries this internal tag displays the shortcut arrow overlay.

To get rid of it, you need to do two things. First, delete the isShortcut value. Next, have Windows update its internal icon cache. The next script demonstrates an easy solution: It allows you to turn the shortcut overlay on and off.

Note

The script uses the Registry extension discussed in the previous chapter. Make sure you have installed the COM object — \install\registry\setup.exe.

```
' 15-54.VBS

set reg = CreateObject("regtool.tob")

key = "HKCR\lnkfile\isShortcut"
if reg.KeyExists(key) then
    msg = "Shortcut arrows visible. Do you want to hide arrows?"
    answer = MsgBox(msg, vbYesNo + vbQuestion)
    if answer = vbYes then
        reg.RegDelete(key)
        call reg.FlushIconCache
        MsgBox "Done."
    end if
else
    msg = "Shortcut arrows invisible. Do you want to enable arrows?"
    answer = MsgBox(msg, vbYesNo + vbQuestion)
    if answer = vbYes then
        reg.RegWrite key, ""
        call reg.FlushIconCache
        MsgBox "Done."
    end if
end if
```

Note that the Registry extension already includes the necessary method, called FlushIconCache, for refreshing the icon cache. This method temporarily changes icon size, so there may be some screen flicker.

Secret

This script manages regular Windows shortcuts only. DOS shortcuts remain untouched. If you want to manage DOS shortcuts, change the Registry key: Replace lnkfile with piffile. That's all.

Shortcut arrows for any files

The shortcut arrow overlay is so versatile you can use it for any file type. Although this rarely makes sense, it's still an interesting feature. The next script asks for the file extension you want to control. You then have the opportunity to turn the shortcut overlay on or off.

```
' 15-55.VBS

set reg = CreateObject("regtool.tob")

ext = InputBox("Please enter the file extension you want " _
    & "to control!",,".doc")
if ext = vbEmpty then WScript.Quit
```

```
if not left(ext,1)="." then ext = "." & ext
key = "HKCR\" & ext & "\"
if not reg.KeyExists(key) then
    MsgBox "the file type you specified is not registered."
    WScript.Quit
end if

mainkey = "HKCR\" & reg.RegRead(key) & "\"
if not reg.KeyExists(mainkey) then
    MsgBox "the file type you specified isn't properly registered!"
    WScript.Quit
end if

scutkey = mainkey & "isShortcut"
if reg.KeyExists(scutkey) then
    msg = "Shortcut arrows visible. Do you want to hide arrows?"
    answer = MsgBox(msg, vbYesNo + vbQuestion)
    if answer = vbYes then
        reg.RegDelete(scutkey)
        call reg.FlushIconCache
        MsgBox "Done."
    end if
else
    msg = "Shortcut arrows invisible. Do you want to enable arrows?"
    answer = MsgBox(msg, vbYesNo + vbQuestion)
    if answer = vbYes then
        reg.RegWrite scutkey, ""
        call reg.FlushIconCache
        MsgBox "Done."
    end if
end if
```

Changing the shortcut arrow

You don't need to disable shortcut arrows altogether just because you don't like their looks. In fact, disabling shortcut arrows generally isn't a good idea: Shortcuts look exactly like original files, and it becomes hard to distinguish between them.

A better way is to replace the shortcut arrow with some other overlay icon. Obviously, you should choose an icon that is mostly transparent so the file icon won't be covered too much. Have a look at Chapter 22 for a selection of useful icons.

```
' 15-56.VBS

set reg = CreateObject("regtool.tob")

' changing the Shortcut arrow
reg.RegWrite "HKLM\Software\Microsoft\Windows\CurrentVersion\" _
    & "explorer\Shell Icons\29", "shell32.dll,30"
```

```
' updating the Cache
reg.FlushIconCache
```

Secret

Are you wondering why the script doesn't use the Windows version-independent setting WINMACHINE instead of HKLM...? You don't need to! Custom icon settings are stored in the Windows branch of the Registry no matter which Windows version you are using.

The example replaces the shortcut arrow with another overlay icon provided by shell32.dll. You can use any other icon library instead. Chapter 22 has the details. Table 15-4 lists useful overlay icons you may find on your system:

Table 15-4	**Icon Resources Suitable as Link Overlay**
Icon	**File**
✳	cdfview.dll,0
▽	cdfview.dll,1
●	mmsys.cpl,24
☆	msrating.dll,4
❗	progman.exe,38

New icons for all system icons

Actually, the preceding script can change any system icon, not just shortcut arrows. To access other icons, replace the index number (29 for shortcut arrows) with the index number of the icon you want to change, and supply an alternate icon resource.

Secret

There's an easy trick to retrieve the icon index for any system icon: Just right-click any shortcut file, click the Change Icon button, and delete the name of the icon file. Then, press enter. Now, Windows shows its standard shell32.dll icon file. This file contains all the system icons, and you can count the icons to get their index numbers. For example, to change the folder icon, use index number 3.

Sizing the Cool Switch window

Do you know about the Cool Switch window? Hold down [Alt] and press [Tab]. As long as there are at least two open windows, a small window appears in the center of your screen, and you can quickly switch to another running application by pressing [Tab] a couple of times until the application is selected.

This is not too exciting. The real news is that Windows 2000 employs some secret Registry keys, and these keys control the size of the window. You can specify column and row numbers. Note, however, that this setting is supported only by Windows 2000:

```
' 15-57.VBS

set wshshell = CreateObject("WScript.Shell")

key = "HKCU\Control Panel\Desktop\"

on error resume next
columns = wshshell.RegRead(key & "CoolSwitchColumns")
rows = wshshell.RegRead(key & "CoolSwitchRows")
on error goto 0

if columns=0 then columns = 7
if rows =0 then rows = 3

newcolumns = Ask("Specify number of columns!", columns)
newrows = Ask("Specify number of rows!", rows)

wshshell.RegWrite key & "CoolSwitchColumns", newcolumns
wshshell.RegWrite key & "CoolSwitchRows", newrows

MsgBox "Settings changed. You need to restart your system!"

function Ask(question, default)
    Ask = InputBox(question,,default)
    if ask = vbEmpty then WScript.Quit
    if not isNumeric(ask) then
        MsgBox "You did not enter a number!", vbCritical
        WScript.Quit
    end if
    Ask = CInt(Ask)
end function
```

Summary

There are countless undocumented settings inside the Windows Registry, and you now know how to identify them and create your own dialog boxes to manage them. You also saw that changes may not take place immediately and that you need to force Windows to recognize your new settings. The example scripts provided numerous ways for you to update the Icon Cache, refresh the Desktop, and invoke system settings through the API.

Chapter 16

Getting System Information

In This Chapter

▶ Determine the location of Windows special folders such as Desktop and My Documents

▶ Delete your Documents menu to ensure privacy

▶ Delete references to document types you don't work with anyway

▶ Find out important networking details such as username and computer name

▶ Retrieve memory statistics and determine current work load, physical memory, and virtual memory management details

▶ Detect wheel mouse, sound card, and boot mode

▶ Retrieve current video resolution and change resolution and video refresh rate on-the-fly

▶ List all installed fonts and create your personal font sampler page

▶ Analyze your processor type and Windows version

▶ Find out if specific DLL functions are available on your system

S cript developers need information. This chapter provides methods to retrieve all kinds of information about your system, your configuration, and your installation folders.

Finding Out Important Path Information

Where does Windows live? The true name of the Windows folder may vary from system to system, and so do the names of all the other special folders Windows uses.

For your scripts, it's extremely important to know the special Windows folder locations. Maybe you want to insert your script into the StartUp program group to start it automatically at logon. Or maybe you need access to the RecentDocs folder to delete references you don't need.

The following sections demonstrate how to retrieve the path names of all your special Windows folders.

Retrieving special folder path names

The `WScript.Shell` object is your solution. It offers the `SpecialFoders` method. This method returns the actual path name of any special Windows folder (see Figure 16-1). Here's how to retrieve the path to your program groups (the groups you see when you open Programs in the Start menu):

```
' 16-1.VBS

set wshshell = CreateObject("WScript.Shell")

path = wshshell.SpecialFolders("Programs")
MsgBox "The path to your private Programs folder:" & vbCr & path
```

Figure 16-1: Retrieve path names of special Windows folders.

Secret

On Windows 98, NT, and 2000, there may be individual user profiles. This is why these Windows versions divide many user settings into private settings and common settings that apply to all users. To retrieve the location of the program groups for all users, just replace `"Programs"` with `"AllUsersPrograms"`.

See how you can take advantage of this:

```
' 16-2.VBS

set wshshell = CreateObject("WScript.Shell")
set fs = CreateObject("Scripting.FileSystemObject")

path = wshshell.SpecialFolders("Programs")
for each folder in fs.GetFolder(path).subfolders
    list = list & folder.name & vbCr
next

MsgBox "List of your private program groups:" & vbCr & list
```

Table 16-1 lists all the special folder names you can use with `SpecialFolders`:

Table 16-1   Key Names for Windows Folders

Name	Description
AllUsersDesktop	Desktop items for all users
AllUsersStartMenu	Start menu custom items for all users
AllUsersPrograms	Program groups for all users
AllUsersStartup	Auto-starting shortcuts for all users
Desktop	Desktop items for current user
Favorites	Favorites items for current user
Fonts	Installed system fonts
MyDocuments	Private document folder for current user
NetHood	Custom items for Network Neighborhood virtual folder
PrintHood	Custom items for Printers virtual folder
Programs	Program groups for current user
Recent	List of recently used documents for current user
SendTo	SendTo items
StartMenu	Start menu custom items for current user
Startup	Auto-starting shortcuts for current user
Templates	Template files for New menu items

The "AllUsers..." settings apply to common objects only. On Windows 95, they are unavailable, and if you don't use multiple user profiles, chances are these folders are empty.

Cleaning up your Documents menu

The Documents menu inside your Start menu stores the most recently used 15 files for easy access. Unfortunately, Windows doesn't care about the file types, so the Documents menu records just any file you happen to open. Therefore, important files can get kicked out of this menu easily by other not-so-important files. Furthermore, the Documents menu becomes unwieldy and confusing if it contains a lot of unwanted files.

You can do something about it. Clean your menu up! Have a script go through all the shortcuts, determine their targets, and delete any reference that points to a file type you are not interested in!

```
' 16-3.VBS

set wshshell = CreateObject("WScript.Shell")
set fs = CreateObject("Scripting.FileSystemObject")

' find out location of special folder
recent = wshshell.SpecialFolders("Recent")

' access folder
set folder = fs.GetFolder(recent)

' go through all shortcuts
for each file in folder.files
    ' get extension type
    ext = lcase(fs.GetExtensionName(file.name))
    ' is it a shortcut? It should be!
    if ext="lnk" then
        ' open shortcut
        set scut = wshshell.CreateShortcut(file.path)
        ' find target
        target = scut.TargetPath

        ' target still valid?
        if not fs.FileExists(target) then
            ' no, delete
            file.delete
        else
            ' does target reference "important" file type?
            ext = lcase(fs.GetExtensionName(target))
            select case ext
                ' add extensions for all file references
                ' you want to keep:
                case "doc"
                case "bmp"
                case "vbp"
                case else
                    ' points to something else, delete
                    file.delete
            end select
        end if
    end if
next

wshshell.Popup "Cleaned Documents Menu!", 2
```

Take a look at your Documents menu, then launch the script. When you
recheck your Documents menu, you'll see that the script has deleted all
references to file types you did not specify in your script. Now, the
Documents menu only contains references to files you really work
with. It looks much cleaner and has gained room for new references.

Secret

When you call the script for the first time, it may take some seconds to complete the cleaning process. This is due to a Windows bug — the Documents menu stores only the most recent 15 documents. Internally, whenever the limit is reached, Windows deletes old entries to make room for new entries. This works perfectly well and happens inside the Registry. Outside, in your RECENT folder, Windows often leaves behind unused shortcuts. Over time, hundreds of shortcuts may be left behind in your RECENT folder, and it's a good idea to clean them up.

Use your new script whenever you find your Documents menu crammed with entries. Even better, you can launch your script automatically at Windows logon so that you always start with a clean Documents menu. See Chapter 13 for details.

Cleaning the Documents menu automatically

If you want your script to clean up the Documents menu automatically at given intervals, you can use this script instead:

```
' 16-4.VBS

set wshshell = CreateObject("WScript.Shell")
set fs = CreateObject("Scripting.FileSystemObject")
recent = wshshell.SpecialFolders("Recent")
set folder = fs.GetFolder(recent)

do
for each file in folder.files
        ext = lcase(fs.GetExtensionName(file.name))
        if ext="lnk" then
            set scut = wshshell.CreateShortcut(file.path)
            target = scut.TargetPath

            if not fs.FileExists(target) then
                file.delete
            else
                ext = lcase(fs.GetExtensionName(target))
                select case ext
                    case "doc"
                    case "bmp"
                    case "vbp"
                    case else
                            file.delete
                end select
            end if
        end if
next
' sleep for a minute
    WScript.Sleep 1000*60
loop
```

Caution

This script runs forever. It cleans your Documents menu, and then it sleeps for a minute and cleans again. You have no way of stopping this script except by calling the Task List and closing down WScript.exe manually. If you run scripts this way, always make sure you include a "sleep phase" so your script won't eat up all your CPU power. In Chapter 17, you also get a new way of inserting a "script icon" into the tray area. With this tray icon, you can stop scripts anytime.

Check it out: Open a file with a file type not listed in your script. Then, check your Documents menu: It contains a reference to this file. Now, wait a minute and check again. The document reference is gone. Your script has silently done its job in the background.

Finding the Windows folder

SpecialFolders gives access to any special folder, but it can't return the Windows folder name. What now?

Actually, you have two choices. Windows always stores the Windows folder in an environment variable called %WINDIR%. Use ExpandEnvironmentStrings to retrieve the path name. Or you can use the Scripting.FileSystemObject method called GetSpecialFolder. This method returns a folder object you can use to access the folder content directly.

Where does Windows live?

Here's how to retrieve the Windows folder path name (see Figure 16-2):

```
' 16-5.VBS

set wshshell = CreateObject("WScript.Shell")
windir = wshshell.ExpandEnvironmentStrings("%WINDIR%")
MsgBox "Windows Folder: " & windir
```

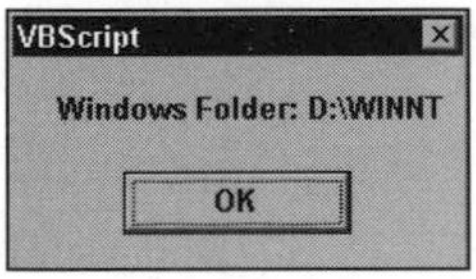

```
VBScript                    [X]

Windows Folder: D:\WINNT

        [    OK    ]
```

Figure 16-2: Find out your current Windows folder.

ExpandEnvironmentStrings can retrieve other environment variables, too. For example, to find out the name of your DOS command interpreter, use this script:

```
' 16-6.VBS

set wshshell = CreateObject("WScript.Shell")
compath = wshshell.ExpandEnvironmentStrings("%COMSPEC%")
MsgBox "DOS Interpreter: " & compath
```

Accessing the Windows folder directly

If you need to get access to the Windows folder contents anyway, get the folder handle directly:

```
' 16-7.VBS

set fs = CreateObject("Scripting.FileSystemObject")
set windir = fs.GetSpecialFolder(0)
MsgBox "Windows Folder: " & windir.Path
for each subfolder in windir.subfolders
     list = list & subfolder.name & vbCr
next
MsgBox "Windows folder subfolders: " & vbCr & list
```

GetSpecialFolder can retrieve other special folders, too, as shown in Table 16-2.

Table 16-2   Key Codes for Windows Folders

Index	Description
0	Windows Folder
1	System Folder
2	Temp Folder

Reading Network Information

The WScript.Network object provides a basic set of networking methods and properties. You can use them to find out the current username, and to remotely install network printers.

Inside view: WScript.Network

Table 16-3 provides a complete list of all the properties and methods provided by WScript.Network.

Table 16-3   WScript.Network Properties and Methods

Property/Method	Description
`Sub AddPrinterConnection(ByVal bstrLocalName As String, ByVal bstrRemoteName As String, [pvarUpdateProfile], [pvarUserName], [pvarPassword])`	Maps the remote printer to a local resource name
`Property ComputerName As String`	Retrieves the computer network name
`Function EnumNetworkDrives As IWshCollection`	Lists all current network connections
`Function EnumPrinterConnections As IWshCollection`	Lists all current network printer connections
`Sub MapNetworkDrive(ByVal bstrLocalName As String, ByVal bstrRemoteName As String, [pvarUpdateProfile], [pvarUserName], [pvarPassword])`	Maps the network drive to a local resource
`Sub RemoveNetworkDrive(ByVal bstrName As String, [pvarForce], [pvarUpdateProfile])`	Removes a mapped network drive
`Sub RemovePrinterConnection(ByVal bstrName As String, [pvarForce], [pvarUpdateProfile])`	Removes a network printer
`Sub SetDefaultPrinter(ByVal bstrName As String)`	Sets the default printer
`Property UserDomain As String`	Retrieves the current user domain
`Property UserName As String`	Retrieves the current username
`Property UserProfile As String`	Retrieves the current user profile

Listing current username

To find out the name of the currently logged on user (see Figure 16-3), use the following script:

```
' 16-8.VBS

set wshnet = CreateObject("WScript.Network")

user = wshnet.UserName
domain = wshnet.UserDomain
computer = wshnet.ComputerName
```

```
msg = "This computer is called """ & computer & """" & vbCr
msg = msg & "You are logged on as """ & user & """" & vbCr
msg = msg & "Your domain is """ & domain & """" & vbCr

MsgBox msg, vbInformation
```

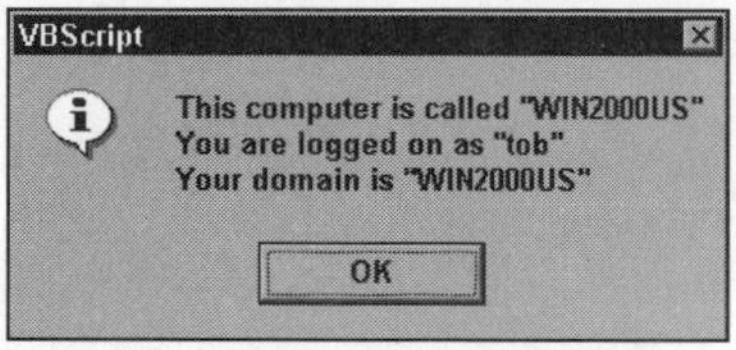

Figure 16-3: Determine logon name and domain name.

Managing Memory Consumption

Memory is valuable, so it's a good idea to find out the current memory situation before scripts start extensive tasks. Controlling your system's memory statistics, you can also find out if your system has enough RAM installed or if it would benefit from some additional RAM (see Figure 16-4).

Unfortunately, the WSH has no access to the memory statistics. You do. Just install the memory COM object I have prepared (\install\memory\ setup.exe). Full source code is provided at \components\memory\ memory.vbp.

Retrieving memory statistics

Table 16-4 describes what you can do with the new memory COM object:

Table 16-4   New Methods to Check Memory Status

Method	Description
`Function GetMemory As String`	Current memory status as Text string report
`Function Mem_load As Long`	Current memory load in percent
`Function Mem_page_avail As Long`	Memory available in current page file
`Function Mem_page_total As Long`	Memory reserved in current page file
`Function Mem_phys_avail As Long`	True RAM memory available
`Function Mem_phys_total As Long`	True total RAM memory installed
`Function Mem_virt_avail As Long`	Maximum virtual memory available
`Function Mem_virt_total As Long`	Total virtual memory available

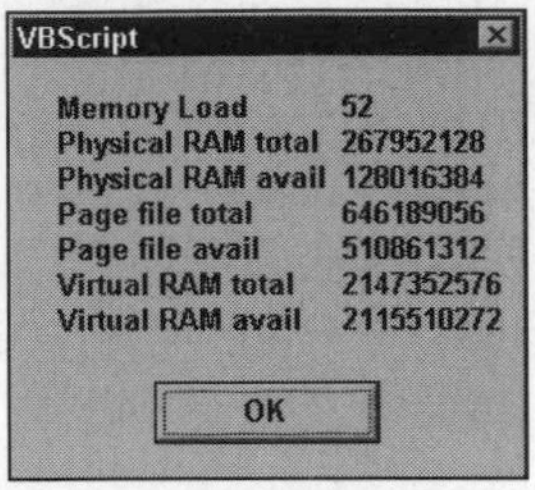

Figure 16-4: Check memory consumption and work load.

If you just need a general overview, use the convenient `GetMemory` method:

```
' 16-9.VBS

set tool = CreateObject("memory.stats")
MsgBox tool.GetMemory
```

Running in physical memory only

If you don't want to start a script under low memory conditions, check for the current memory load. For example, you can start your script if memory load is below 80 percent:

```
' 16-10.VBS

set tool = CreateObject("memory.stats")

if tool.Mem_load<80 then
    MsgBox "Memory load below 80% - I do the job!"
else
    MsgBox "Memory load critical. Try again later!"
    WScript.Quit
end if
```

Likewise, you can use `Mem_phys_avail` to check whether there is any "real" memory left. If this method returns 0, you know for sure that your system needs to resort to the slow paging memory.

Checking memory installed and memory consumed

You can also use your new methods to find out how much RAM is installed in your system. This script is smart enough to issue a recommendation whether or not your system will benefit from additional RAM (see Figure 16-5).

However, to get valid answers, you should launch your standard set of applications before you start the script so you have realistic memory conditions to test:

```
' 16-11.VBS

set tool = CreateObject("memory.stats")
ram = tool.Mem_phys_total
avail = tool.Mem_phys_avail
needed = tool.Mem_page_total - tool.Mem_page_avail

msg = "Your System has " & MB(ram) & " RAM installed." & vbCr
if avail=0 then
     msg = msg & "This is not enough! Your system currently " _
           & " borrows " & MB(needed) & " from the file system."
else
     msg = msg & "Currently, your system doesn't need additional" _
           & " memory. In fact, " & MB(avail) & " RAM is currently" _
           & " unused!"
end if

MsgBox msg, vbInformation

function MB(bytes)
     MB = FormatNumber(bytes/1024^2,1) & " MB"
end function
```

> **VBScript** ✕
>
> (i) Your System has 255.5 MB RAM installed.
> Currently, your system doesn't need additional memory. In fact,
> 122.7 MB RAM is currently unused!
>
> [OK]

Figure 16-5: Automatically test whether your system needs additional RAM.

Secret

Windows uses different types of RAM. If the physical ("real") RAM is used up, it accesses the virtual RAM. This RAM is stored on the hard drive. Using virtual RAM slows down the system enormously, but it's the only way to keep the system running once your physical RAM is exploited. The page file is the "external" RAM that Windows uses on your hard drive. The virtual RAM setting shows the maximum size the page file can use.

Getting Miscellaneous Windows Settings

GetSystemMetrics is an extremely versatile API function. Obviously, it is responsible for system metrics and places a focus on window sizes. But this function can retrieve a lot of additional information.

I have wrapped this and a couple of other functions into a COM object. Make sure you have installed \install\miscinfo\setup.exe. Source code is provided at \components\miscinfo\miscinfo.vbp.

Querying system metrics

Whenever you need to know the exact size of some graphical window element, you can count on MetricsInformation. Just pass the index number of the property you are interested in, and it will return the value. For example, the next script finds out the current icon size (see Figure 16-6):

```
' 16-12.VBS

set tool = CreateObject("misc.information")
x = tool.MetricsInformation(13)
y = tool.MetricsInformation(14)
MsgBox "Icon size: " & x & " x " & y & " pixels."
```

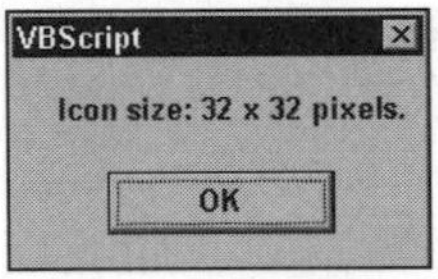

VBScript

Icon size: 32 x 32 pixels.

OK

Figure 16-6: Determine current icon size.

Table 16-5 lists all the properties and index values available:

Table 16-5	Index Numbers Referring to System Information
Index	**Description**
0,1	Width and height of primary display adapter
2	Size of horizontal scroll bar
3	Size of vertical scroll bar
4	Height of window caption
5,6	Width and height of window borders
7,8	Frame sizes for fixed-sized windows
9	Height of thumb box on vertical scroll bars
10	Width of thumb box on horizontal scroll bars
11,12	Width and height of icons
13,14	Width and height of cursor
15	Height of single-line menus

Index	Description
16,17	Width and height of client area of a full-sized window on primary monitor
18	Height of kanji window
19	True if mouse is present
20	Height of arrow bitmap on vertical scroll bars
21	Width of arrow bitmap on horizontal scroll bars
22	True if debug version of USER.EXE is installed
23	True if mouse buttons are swapped
24-27	Reserved
28,29	Minimum width and height of a window
30,31	Width and height of buttons in window caption or title bar
32,33	Width and height of window frame
34,35	Minimum width and height a window can scaled to
36,37	Rectangle defining the area in which a double-click must occur to be recognized as a double-click
38,39	Horizontal and vertical icon spacing
40	True if menus align to the right
41	True if pen Windows extension is installed
42	True if double-byte character set USER.EXE is installed
43	Number of mouse buttons
44	True if security is present
45,46	Frame sizes for 3D window frames
47,48	Width and height of grid cell minimized windows are arranged in
49,50	Recommended width and height of small icons
51	Height of small captions
52,53	Width and height of small caption buttons
54,55	Width and height of menu bar buttons
56	Specifies how Windows minimizes windows
57,58	Width and height of a default minimized window
59,60	Maximum width and height a scalable window can expand to
61,62	Width and height of default maximized window on primary monitor
63	True if network is present

Continued

Table 16-5	(continued)
Index	**Description**
64-66	Reserved
67	Boot mode 0: Normal boot 1: Fail-safe boot 2: Fail-safe boot with network
68,69	Rectangle defining the area a mouse must leave before a drag operation takes place
70	True if user requires applications to display information visually (handicapped features)
71,72	Width and height of menu check marks
73	True if CPU is slow (low-end)
74	True if system is enabled for Hebrew and Arabic languages
75	Win98/Win NT4/2000: true if mouse wheel is present
76,77	Win98/2000: coordinates for left and top of virtual screen
78,79	Win98,2000: width and height of virtual screen. Virtual screen is the bounding rectangle of all display adapters.
80	Win98/2000: number of display monitors
81	Win98/2000: true if all displays use same color format
82	Win2000: true if Input Method Manager is enabled
&H1000	WinNT4SP4/2000: true if associated with Terminal Server Session

Identifying slow computers

Table 16-5 doesn't limit itself to pure metrics information. There are a couple of jewels buried under the window and icon sizes. For example, you can easily find out if Microsoft considers your system to be slow:

```
' 16-13.VBS

set tool = CreateObject("misc.information")
slow = CBool(tool.MetricsInformation(73))

if slow then
    MsgBox "Your machine is slow!"
else
    MsgBox "Your machine is fast!"
end if
```

Secret

Some properties represent integers, while other properties resemble Boolean true/false pairs. In any way, `MetricsInformation` returns integers. Any 0-value represents false; any value other than 0 indicates true. You don't need to worry about this conversion too much, though. Use `CBool` to convert the result to Boolean automatically where appropriate.

Detecting mouse/wheel information

You can even query the type of your mouse (see Figure 16-7). Let's see if you use a mouse wheel, and let's count mouse buttons, too:

```
' 16-14.VBS

set tool = CreateObject("misc.information")
mouse = CBool(tool.MetricsInformation(19))
swapped = CBool(tool.MetricsInformation(23))
buttons = tool.MetricsInformation(43)
wheel = CBool(tool.MetricsInformation(75))

if not mouse then
    MsgBox "Sorry, no mouse present!"
else
    msg = "Your mouse has " & buttons & " buttons and "
    if not wheel then msg = msg & "no "
    msg = msg & "wheel. The mouse buttons are "
    if not swapped then msg = msg & "not "
    msg = msg & "swapped."
    MsgBox msg
end if
```

```
VBScript                                          [X]
Your mouse has 3 buttons and wheel. The mouse buttons are not
swapped.

                    [   OK   ]
```

Figure 16-7: Identify the type of mouse currently in use.

Is a network present?

Check out how easy it is to find out about a network:

```
' 16-15.VBS

set tool = CreateObject("misc.information")
network = CBool(tool.MetricsInformation(63))

if network then
```

```
        MsgBox "Network is present!"
else
        MsgBox "NO Network present!"
end if
```

Controlling boot mode

You can even find out if Windows started as usual or used its Safe mode to boot up:

```
' 16-16.VBS

set tool = CreateObject("misc.information")
boot = tool.MetricsInformation(64)

select case boot
    case 0
        MsgBox "Normal boot"
    case 1
        MsgBox "Safe mode"
    case 2
        MsgBox "Safe mode with network"
    case else
        MsgBox "Unknown result"
end select
```

Managing Screen Resolution and Refresh Rate

Screen resolution and refresh rate are very important system settings. Flickering screens and red eyes aren't necessary evils if your system uses the best settings available. To control screen resolution and find out the best refresh rate, I have developed another COM object that provides full scripting access to all necessary API functions.

Make sure you have installed the COM object \install\screen\setup.exe. Full source code is provided at \components\screen\screen.vbp.

Finding out all available screen resolutions

Available screen resolutions depend on both your graphics adapter and your display monitor. Use EnumModes to list all available modes (see Figure 16-8):

```
' 16-17.VBS

set tool = CreateObject("screen.tool")
set wshshell = CreateObject("WScript.Shell")
wshshell.Popup tool.EnumModes
```

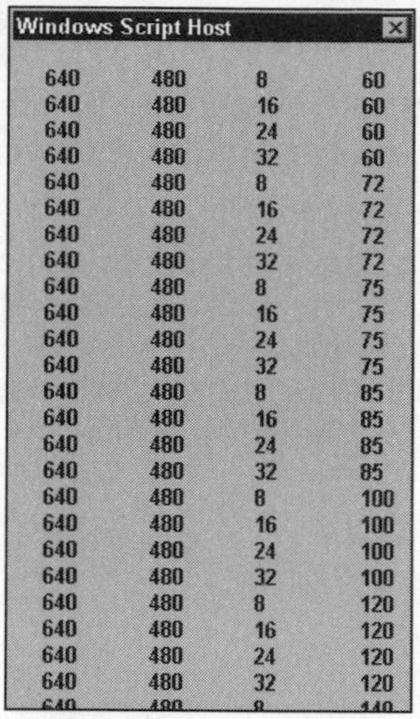

Figure 16-8: Determine all possible video resolutions.

The result is probably a huge dialog box. It contains all available display
modi, listing resolution, color depth, and display frequency.

Secret

Color depth determines how many colors can be displayed simultaneously.
The number of colors is determined by 2^color depth. The best trade-off
between memory consumption and color quality is a color depth of 16.
Display frequency determines how many pictures will be drawn per second.
On classical tube monitors, make sure the display frequency is above 70Hz.

Determining the current video settings

You can also find out your current settings (see Figure 16-9). Use
GetDisplaySettings and provide four arguments. The method returns
resolution, color depth, and frequency:

```
' 16-18.VBS

set tool = CreateObject("screen.tool")
tool.GetDisplaySettings xres, yres, color, frequ
MsgBox "Current resolution: " & xres & " x " & yres & vbCr _
    & "Colors: " & 2^color & vbCr & "Frequency: " _
    & frequ & "Hz."
```

Figure 16-9: Retrieve current video settings.

Finding out the best frequency setting

Generally, the higher your display frequency, the better the picture quality. The next script reveals which frequencies are available at a given screen resolution.

Caution

The highest frequency is not the best choice under all circumstances. If your graphics adapter (actually, it's RAMDAC) is driven to its limits, pictures won't be as crisp anymore. In addition, your display monitor needs to support the frequency. If, for any reason, your display monitor shows distortions or begins to whistle, change back the frequency immediately! If you don't, your display can be seriously damaged.

```
' 16-19.VBS

set tool = CreateObject("screen.tool")
MsgBox tool.GetFrequency(1024, 768)
```

The script returns all available frequencies (and color depths) for the given resolution.

Changing display frequency

You can even change the display frequency entirely by script. Use `ChangeFrequency` and specify the new frequency. Optionally, you can specify 0 as second argument to change the frequency temporarily. Windows won't store it in your user profile, so the next time you start Windows, it will use the old frequency:

```
' 16-20.VBS

set tool = CreateObject("screen.tool")
if tool.ChangeFrequency(75) then
    MsgBox "Changed display frequency to 75 Hz."
else
    MsgBox "Couldn't change frequency. Check available settings!"
end if
```

The method returns true if the change was successful. On some systems, a restart may be required to enable the new settings.

Changing screen resolution

If you need to, your script can change the resolution and control all display settings. Use `ChangeDisplay` and supply the new x- and y-resolution. Optionally, you can specify the color depth, and if you specify 0 as fourth argument, the setting will be temporary. Use `ResetDisplay` to change back from your temporary setting to the original setting.

The next script changes display mode temporarily to 640 × 480 and then returns it back to the original display settings:

```
' 16-21.VBS

set tool = CreateObject("screen.tool")

if tool.ChangeDisplay(640,480,,0) then
    MsgBox "Changed display resolution to 640x480"
    tool.ResetDisplay
else
    MsgBox "Couldn't change resolution. Check available settings!"
end if
```

Enumerating System Fonts

It's hard for your scripts to find out about all available system fonts because there is no such function. Your script would have to read the Registry and determine the installed fonts. This is time-consuming and absolutely not necessary.

Visual Basic can enumerate installed system fonts with ease, so a much better approach is to wrap the Visual Basic command so that your Visual Basic scripts can access it too. Just install the COM object `\install\ miscinfo\setup.exe`.

```
' 16-22.VBS

set tool = CreateObject("misc.information")
MsgBox tool.EnumFonts
```

Creating a font sample page

What can you do with your font list? A lot of things! For example, you now can easily create font sample pages and print them out (see Figure 16-10). The next time you want to design an invitation or a flyer, you can pick the best fonts out of your sample list.

```
' 16-23.VBS

set tools = CreateObject("misc.information")
set ie = WScript.CreateObject("InternetExplorer.Application", "ie_")

msg = "Build a font sample page. Please insert sample text!"
title = "Font Sample Page"
```

```
default = "ABCDEFGŽŸ‡abcdefg½‼◆12345!""§$%ß"
template = InputBox(msg, title, default)
standardformat = "<font style=""{12pt " _
        & "Arial}"">"

fontliste = Split(tools.EnumFonts, vbCr)

OpenIE 500,400,"Font Sample Page"

for each font in fontliste
    AddToIE font
next

MsgBox "Done. Right click on font list to print or save!", _
vbSystemModal

sub AddToIE(fontname)
    size= 15
    format = "<font style=""{font: " & size _
        & "pt " & fontname & "}"">"
    html = ""
    html = html + standardformat _
        + "Font name: "  + fontname _
        + "</font><BR>"
    html = html + format + template _
        + "</FONT><HR>"
    ie.document.body.insertAdjacentHTML _
        "beforeEnd", html
end sub

sub OpenIE(width, height, title)
    ie.height =height
    ie.width =width
    ie.toolbar = 0
    ie.statusbar = 0
    page = "JavaScript:'<TITLE>" + title _
        + "</TITLE>'"
    ie.navigate(page)
    do while (ie.ReadyState<>4)
    loop
    ie.visible = true
end sub

sub ie_onquit
    MsgBox "You cancelled!", _
        vbExclamation
    WScript.Quit
end sub
```

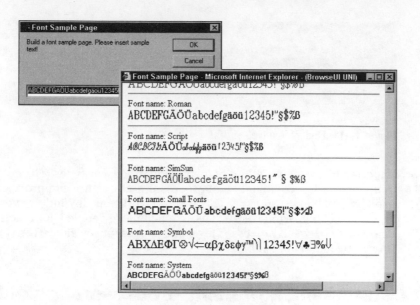

Figure 16-10: Automatically create a font sample page.

Analyzing your processor

Your script can even get extended information about your processor. The API function `GetSystemInfo` reveals processor type and the number of processors.

Determining your processor type

The next script demonstrates different methods to find out your exact processor type (see Figure 16-11):

```
' 16-24.VBS

set tool = CreateObject("misc.information")

proc1 = tool.GetProcessorType
proc2 = tool.GetProcessor

msg = "Old way of retrieving Processor:" & vbCr & proc1 & vbCr
msg = msg & "New way of retrieving Processor:" & vbCr & proc2

MsgBox msg
```

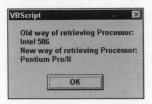

Figure 16-11: Find out the type of CPU.

Secret

Windows uses a new method of identifying processor types. The common denominator is a combination of processor architecture and processor type used by `GetProcessorType`. This method works on all Windows versions. Windows NT and Windows 2000 use a much more detailed approach and distinguish between processor level and processor revision. This approach is used by `GetProcessor`.

Determining how many processors are onboard

On Windows NT/2000, you can use mainboards with up to 32 CPUs working in parallel (depending on the Windows version). If you are lucky enough to own such a system, you can every morning double-check if all the CPUs are still there:

```
' 16-25.VBS

set tool = CreateObject("misc.information")
MsgBox "Number of CPUs in this system: " & tool.GetProcessorNumber
```

Dealing with Windows Versions

There are lots of different Windows versions out there, and fortunately your scripts will run on all 32-bit Windows versions without any adjustments.

However, this only applies to the script mechanics. Of course, Windows 9.x, NT, and 2000 all offer different features, and maybe your script can only do its job on specific Windows versions.

But how can you safely identify the current Windows version? `GetVersionEx` has the answer for you! This API function reads out Windows version, build number, and more. I have wrapped the function for you. Just make sure you have installed the COM object `\install\osversion\setup.exe`. As always, source code is included at `\components\osversion\osversion.vbp`.

Getting an overview: Windows version details

If you just need a general overview, use the `OSVersion` method. It returns all kinds of Windows version information, ready for display (see Figure 16-12):

```
' 16-26.VBS

set tool = CreateObject("os.version")
MsgBox tool.OSVersion
```

```
VBScript                    [X]

    Major version       5
    Minor version       0
    Build      2128
    Platform ID         2

           OK
```

Figure 16-12: Retrieve Windows version and Platform ID.

Secret

The Platform ID identifies the Windows Kernel. Windows NT and Windows 2000 return a Platform ID of 2, while Windows 9.x returns 1. To distinguish the Windows versions, use the major version. A platform ID of 2 and a major version of 4 identifies Windows NT 4.0. A platform ID of 1 and a major version of >4 identifies Windows 98. The minor version reveals additional information. A Platform ID of 1 and a major version of 4 applies to both Windows 95 and some Windows 98 versions. To check for Windows 95, make sure the minor version equals 0. The Build identifies the version within a specific Windows version.

Determining Windows version

You don't need to calculate the Windows version yourself. Use the `WinKind` method instead:

```
' 16-27.VBS

set tool = CreateObject("os.version")
MsgBox tool.WinKind
```

This method returns the exact Windows type (see Figure 16-13). If you are interested in finding out whether you are running on an NT basis or not, use `WinType`. This method reveals the type of platform.

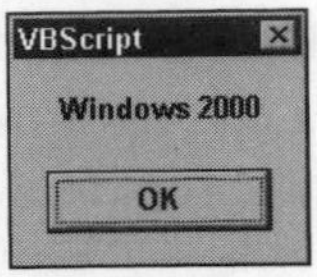

Figure 16-13: `WinType` and `WinKind` finding out your current Windows type

Extracting individual version information

You can also retrieve individual version information. Here's an example:

```
' 16-28.VBS

set tool = CreateObject("os.version")
MsgBox "Windows-Version: " & tool.WinVer
MsgBox "Platform ID: " & tool.Platform
MsgBox "Build: " & tool.Build
```

Determining system support for specific functions

Knowing the Windows version does not necessarily mean you know whether or not your system supports a specific feature. Microsoft has published so many service packs and add-ons that things have become a little confusing.

If you know the version of the system file the feature requires, you can use the file version tool introduced in Chapter 7 to check whether your system meets the requirements.

If you know the feature is contained in some DLL function call, you can check whether the DLL on your system supports the function. Have a look:

```
' 16-29.VBS

set tool = CreateObject("os.version")
MsgBox tool.DLLExists("kernel32", "GetVersionExA")
MsgBox tool.DLLExists("kernel32", "GetVersionExW")
```

This script tests whether `kernel32.dll` contains the DLL functions `GetVersionExA` and `GetVersionExW`. Remember: `GetVersionExA` represents the ANSI version and is generally available on any Windows version. `GetVersionExW` represents the (wide) UNICODE version and is available only on Windows NT/2000.

Secret

When checking for a function name, make sure you use the correct one. DLL function names are case-sensitive, and most functions are available as "A" and "W" versions. Don't check for `GetVersionEx` because this function doesn't exist. Check for `GetVersionExA` or `GetVersionExW`. See Chapter 5 for additional details and ways to list all functions stored in DLLs.

Finding DLLs that contain specific functions

As a programmer, you might have the opposite problem: You might know the name of some DLL function, but you don't know which DLL contains this function.

There are numerous ways to search for DLL functions and retrieve the hosting DLL name (this topic is covered extensively in Chapter 5). However, the approach used by DLLExists can be easily expanded to search for DLL functions. I've included it into the COM object, and to search for a DLL function, you can use the method FindFunction:

```
' 16-30.VBS

set tool = CreateObject("os.version")
MsgBox tool.FindFunction("GetVersionExA")
```

It may take some seconds for the script to execute. After all, it has to query numerous DLL files.

Secret

Internally, the COM object uses LoadLibraryEx both for DLLExists and FindFunction. LoadLibraryEx has one important advantage over LoadLibrary, and that's that it accepts additional options that load the DLL without actually executing the DLLMain part. Because you are querying the DLL only, you don't want the DLL mechanics to start. Note that LoadLibraryEx doesn't support 16-bit DLLs, so if the function in question is part of a 16-bit DLL, you won't find it. Use the alternate methods described in Chapter 5 instead.

Figure 16-14: Find out which DLL contains the "GetVersionExA" function — or any other you might require.

Summary

In this chapter, you discovered numerous ways to find out system information. You now can read memory statistics, and you can detect device types and video resolutions. The automatic font sampler generator shows vividly how this information can be used in everyday tasks. Methods to find out the current Windows version and support for specific DLL functions are an important prerequisite to select systems with certain features only.

Even more importantly, your new tools allow you to change critical system settings. You can optimize video refresh and dynamically change screen resolution.

Chapter 17

Working with Events

In This Chapter

▶ Learn about events and how your scripts can receive them

▶ Control Internet Explorer through events

▶ Create your own COM objects and fire events yourself

▶ Use the VB timer control to add timer capabilities to your scripts

▶ Stop scripts after a predetermined timeout kicks in

▶ Show icons in the tray area as long as your script runs, and cancel scripts with the tray icon

▶ Create modeless dialog boxes and indicate progress while your script is at work

E vents provide a way for programs to communicate with each other. Your scripts can use events, too. In this chapter, learn how to listen to events and how to raise events yourself. With this knowledge, you can place your own icons into the tray area of the task bar and turn modal dialog boxes into modeless dialog boxes.

What's So Thrilling About Events?

In a multi-tasking environment, there's an important challenge—how can programs communicate with one another? The answer is events.

Events work like alarm bells. Whenever something special happens, an event is raised. The event itself is just a message. Your program (or script) can happily ignore the event, and most scripts do.

Programs (and scripts) need a special "event sink" to receive events. The event sink listens to events fired by someone else. Once an event is received, your script can react to it.

The special aspect of events is the fact that they work asynchronously. Your script can receive the event any time, no matter what it is currently doing for you. Events, therefore, can interrupt your script at any time.

Receiving events

Where do events come from? And how can your scripts listen to events? First of all, events always come from "the outside." For example, Internet Explorer uses a whole set of events to indicate special states. Once someone closes an Internet Explorer window, for example, it raises an onQuit event (see Figure 17-1).

Your script can receive such events only if it is currently using the program that issued the event. Your script can, for example, create an instance of Internet Explorer to display results and listen to its onQuit event to make sure it won't send data to a window that doesn't exist anymore:

```
' 17-1.VBS

set ie = WScript.CreateObject("InternetExplorer.Application", _
    "event_")

ie.visible = true
MsgBox "Close the IE window to see what happens!", vbSystemModal
MsgBox "Script ends now."

sub event_onQuit
    MsgBox "Hey! You are about to close the window!", _
        vbSystemModal
end sub
```

Figure 17-1: Your script responds to an IE onQuit event.

The script opens an Internet Explorer window. But look what happens when you close the window. Closing the window raises an onQuit event. Because your script has established an event sink, it's able to listen to events that Internet Explorer raises. The procedure event_onQuit is executed and then displays a message right before the window closes down.

However, your script can respond to the event only as long as it's still running. If you click the dialog box's OK button twice, the script ends. It no longer exists and can no longer listen to events. If you close the IE window, no message appears.

Implementing an event sink

Implementing an event sink is easy — just use the WScript.Shell method and CreateObject instead of VBScript CreateObject. Supply an event sink name as second argument.

Next, define a procedure and name it appropriately. In the preceding example, the procedure is called event_onQuit. event_ is the name of the event sink, and onQuit is the name of the event this procedure is attached to.

Using events

How do you know the event names a given object supports? You ask for them! In Chapter 3, you learned methods to decode the TypeLibrary of any object. The following script uses the methods developed in my typelib COM object to retrieve the events the object supports.

Make sure you have installed the typelib COM object
\install\typelib\setup.exe.

```
' 17-2.VBS

set tool = CreateObject("typelib.decoder")
set wshshell = CreateObject("WScript.Shell")

set result = tool.EnumInterface("shdocvw.dll", "InternetExplorer", 2)
for each eventname in result
     list = list & eventname & vbCr
next

wshshell.popup "Events supported by Internet Explorer:" & vbCr & _
     vbCr & list
```

EnumInterface queries the TypeLibrary stored in shdocvw.dll. In Chapter 3, you created a list revealing the TypeLibrary filenames of any COM object found on your computer.

EnumInterfaces lists only the events. You can use this method to query any information category, as shown in Table 17-1.

Table 17-1	Information Categories Stored in TypeLibraries
Code	**Description**
1	Classes
2	Events
4	Constants

Continued

Table 17-1	(continued)
Code	**Description**
8	Declarations
16	AppObject
32	Records
64	Intrinsic Aliases
128	Unions
239	All (default)

Try it! Use the script and replace code 2 with code 1. Now, the script returns the properties and methods supported by Internet Explorer. Code 4 lists a combination of both properties/methods and events — so you can even add together code numbers to search for multiple categories at once.

The `InternetExplorer` object supports many different events. Your script can take advantage of any one of them:

```
' 17-3.VBS

set ie = WScript.CreateObject("InternetExplorer.Application", _
    "event_")

ie.visible = true
MsgBox "I am hiding the window!", vbSystemModal
ie.visible = false
MsgBox "Closing IE..."
ie.quit
MsgBox "Script ends."

sub event_onQuit
    MsgBox "Hey! You are about to close the window!", _
        vbSystemModal
end sub

sub event_OnVisible(mode)
    MsgBox "Changed visibility to " & mode
end sub
```

Secret

All IE events are procedures (defined as sub). Internet Explorer raises the event but doesn't ask you for permission. Your script can only respond to the message; it can't cancel the pending operation. This is not always the case. Some objects define events as functions, allowing your script to return a value. In most cases, returning false cancels the pending operation. Note also that the `OnVisible` event supplies an argument.

Defining Your Own Events

Although scripts can't raise events, your COM objects can. This is good news, because this way your own COM objects can catch your script's attention anytime.

Creating a timer control

Visual Basic includes a timer control, which can be programmed to some interval. And, it raises timer events automatically.

You can easily add timer capabilities to your scripts. Just create a COM object that includes a timer control and translate the timer event to a public event your script can receive.

First, add a timer control to your COM object: In the Toolbar window, double-click the timer control icon. Next, add some code to make your timer control accessible from the outside.

Note

Make sure you follow the instructions and compile the new COM object as `timer.event`. The best way is to open the complete source project from the CD at `\components\timer\timer.vbp`. Too lazy to compile the object yourself? Then install the prepared package: `\install\timer\setup.exe`.

```
Option Explicit

Public Event TimerFired()

Public Sub EnableTimer()
    Timer1.Enabled = True
End Sub

Public Sub DisableTimer()
    Timer1.Enabled = False
End Sub

Public Sub HandleEvents()
    DoEvents
end sub

Public Sub SetTimer(ByVal interval As Long)
    Timer1.interval = interval
End Sub

Private Sub Timer1_Timer()
    RaiseEvent TimerFired
End Sub
```

`EnableTimer`, `DisableTimer`, and `SetTimer` all set properties for the timer control (which by default is named Timer1). The interesting part is the event-handling. Whenever the timer fires, it raises a timer event. This event is a private event. The event will happen only inside your COM object. To receive the event, your code uses the `Timer1_Timer` procedure.

Because you want to pass the event on to your script, you need to raise a public event yourself. The code defines a public event called `TimerFired`. Whenever the internal timer event is received by the `Timer1_Timer` procedure, it raises the public event `TimerFired`.

Now, your scripts can use the new timer capabilities. Here's an easy test:

```
' 17-4.VBS

set tool = WScript.CreateObject("timer.event", "timer_")


' set timer to 2 sec interval
tool.SetTimer 2000

' enable timer
tool.EnableTimer

MsgBox "Timer is enabled!"

sub timer_TimerFired
    MsgBox "Timer has fired!"
end sub
```

This script sets the timer interval to two seconds (2,000 milliseconds). Then, the script enables the timer and displays a message, as shown in Figure 17-2. From now on, every two seconds, a timer event is generated. It launches the `timer_TimerFired` procedure. Note that while this procedure is busy displaying its message, no further events will be recognized. Also, once the script ends, there will be no more timer messages.

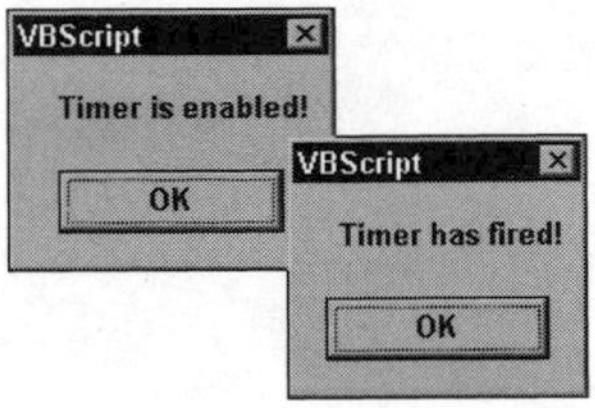

Figure 17-2: Enhance your script with a timer control.

Creating a debugging timer

Timer events can be used for all kinds of things. One of them is implementing a script timeout. The following script implements an emergency break — if the script runs for more than 20 seconds, a dialog box appears and asks whether you want to interrupt it (see Figure 17-3).

```
' 17-5.VBS

set tool = WScript.CreateObject("timer.event", "timer_")
' set script timeout to 20 seconds
```

```
tool.SetTimer 20000
tool.EnableTimer

' simulate a script error
do
     ' check for events
     tool.HandleEvents
loop


' your timeout procedure
sub timer_TimerFired
     msg = "Your script is still running. Do you want to quit?"
     response = MsgBox(msg, vbYesNo + vbQuestion + vbDefaultButton2)
     if response = vbYes then WScript.Quit
end sub
```

Secret

Sometimes, your script is too busy to respond to events. Loops are optimized internally, and while your script executes a loop, it won't pay attention to events. This is why the script places a call to `HandleEvents` inside the loop. `HandleEvents` calls the `DoEvents` command, allowing events to be executed.

Figure 17-3: The timer event asks for confirmation if a script runs for more than 20 seconds.

You may wonder why I used a timer control instead of the `//T` option. It's true that calling a script with `WSCRIPT.EXE //T:secs` establishes a timeout after which the scripting host discards the script. If you call a script with the line below, it will end after 10 seconds no matter what:

```
wscript.exe //T:10 myscript.vbs
```

However, the timer control can do much more. It allows your script to react to the pending timeout. For one thing, you can do clean-up work, which is impossible with the `//T:` approach. In Chapter 20, you'll learn a lot about Internet controls. Imagine that you automate some Internet download process and want to make sure it doesn't loop forever. If you establish a timeout using `//T:secs`, the script will be interrupted after the number of seconds you specify. The Internet connection will remain active, though, and if you dial into the Internet, your phone line will remain busy.

Not so with the timer control. Once the timer event fires, you have all the time in the world to respond to it and close down the Internet connection properly.

Showing icons in the tray area

Thanks to events, you can now solve one of the big limitations of scripts. Because scripts don't have their own windows, they run invisibly. This is bad because you have neither a clue whether the script is still running nor an easy way to interrupt a script when you need to.

This is why I have developed yet another COM object. It allows you to place an icon into the taskbar tray area (see Figure 17-4). The icon is visible while the script is running, and if you click the icon, you can interrupt the script at any time. Placing the mouse pointer over the icon shows a tool tip telling you when the script was started.

Make sure you have installed the COM object \install\tray\setup.exe. Full source code is provided at \components\tray\tray.vbp.

```
' 17-6.VBS

' enable quit on demand:
set tool = WScript.CreateObject("tray.icon", "event_")
call tool.QuitOnDemand

' do some dummy stuff...
for x = 1 to 1000
    for y = 1 to 10000000
    tool.HandleEvents
    test = left("teststring",1) + mid("testing", 3, 2)
    next
next

' disable icon in tray area
call tool.Quit

' called whenever someone asks the script to quit
sub event_QuitNow
    WScript.Quit
end sub
```

The moment the script is launched, a new icon appears in the tray area. The script then executes some extensive loops so that you have a chance to prematurely quit it.

Now point at the new icon. A tooltip reveals when the script was started. Clicking the icon invokes a dialog box, which asks whether you want to cancel the script. If you choose Yes, the event_QuitNow procedure is executed. WScript.Quit quits the script immediately.

Caution

Make sure your script calls the Quit method before it stops. If you don't, the script icon will remain in the tray area.

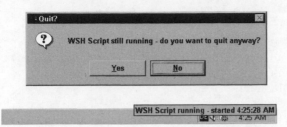

Figure 17-4: Control your scripts through icons in the tray area.

QuitOnDemand **can do a lot of additional tricks. It supports up to four optional parameters, as shown in Table 17-2.**

```
QuitOnDemand message, icon file, icon index, tooltip text
```

Table 17-2   Parameters Supplied to QuitOnDemand

Parameter	Description
message	Message you want to display when the tray icon is clicked
icon file	File that contains the icon you want to display in the tray: for example, shell32.dll
icon index	Index of icon in the icon file
tooltip text	Message you want to display in the tray icon tooltip window

Replace QuitOnDemand **with the following command to see the differences:**

```
call tool.QuitOnDemand("Wanna quit?", "shell32.dll", 3, "Hey!")
```

This time, the script displays a folder icon and uses the messages you supplied.

Tray icons under the hood

Let's take a look at how the magic works:

```
Option Explicit

Public Event QuitNow()

Private Type NOTIFYICONDATA
    cbSize As Long
    hwnd As Long
    uId As Long
    uFlags As Long
```

```
        uCallBackMessage As Long
        hIcon As Long
        szTip As String * 64
End Type

Private Const NIM_ADD = &H0
Private Const NIM_MODIFY = &H1
Private Const NIM_DELETE = &H2
Private Const NIF_MESSAGE = &H1
Private Const NIF_ICON = &H2
Private Const NIF_TIP = &H4
Private Const WM_MOUSEMOVE = &H200

Private Type GUID
    Data1    As Long
    Data2    As Integer
    Data3    As Integer
    Data4(7) As Byte
End Type

Private Type PicBmp
    Size As Long
    Type As Long
    hBmp As Long
    hPal As Long
    Reserved As Long
End Type


Private Declare Function OleCreatePictureIndirect Lib _
"olepro32.dll" (PicDesc As PicBmp, RefIID As GUID, _
ByVal fPictureOwnsHandle As Long, IPic As IPicture) As Long
Private Declare Function Shell_NotifyIcon Lib "shell32" _
Alias "Shell_NotifyIconA" (ByVal dwMessage As Long, _
pnid As NOTIFYICONDATA) As Boolean
Private Declare Function ExtractIconEx Lib "shell32.dll" _
Alias "ExtractIconExA" (ByVal lpszFile As String, _
ByVal nIconIndex As Long, phiconLarge As Long, phiconSmall _
As Long, ByVal nIcons As Long) As Long
Private Declare Function DrawIconEx Lib "User32" (ByVal hdc As _
Long, ByVal xLeft As Long, ByVal yTop As Long, ByVal hIcon _
As Long, ByVal cxWidth As Long, ByVal cyWidth As Long, _
ByVal istepIfAniCur As Long, ByVal hbrFlickerFreeDraw As _
Long, ByVal diFlags As Long) As Long
Private Declare Function DestroyIcon Lib "User32" (ByVal _
hIcon As Long) As Long

Private nid As NOTIFYICONDATA
Private msg
Private busy As Boolean
Private init As Boolean

Public Sub FireEvent()
    If busy Then Exit Sub
```

```
        busy = True
        If MsgBox(msg, vbDefaultButton2 + vbYesNo + vbQuestion _
+ vbSystemModal, "Quit?") = vbYes Then
            RaiseEvent QuitNow
            Quit
        End If
        busy = False
End Sub

Public Sub HandleEvents()
    DoEvents
End Sub

Public Sub QuitOnDemand(Optional ByVal message As String = _
"WSH Script still running - do you want to quit anyway?", _
Optional ByVal name As String = "shell32.dll", Optional _
ByVal index As Long = 21, Optional ByVal tooltip As _
String = "WSH Script running")

    init = True
    msg = message
    SetIconInternal name, index

    Set Form1.parent = Me
    nid.cbSize = Len(nid)
    nid.hwnd = Form1.hwnd
    nid.uId = vbNull
    nid.uFlags = NIF_ICON Or NIF_TIP Or NIF_MESSAGE
    nid.uCallBackMessage = WM_MOUSEMOVE
    nid.hIcon = Form1.icon
    nid.szTip = tooltip & " - started " & Time & vbNullChar
    Shell_NotifyIcon NIM_ADD, nid
End Sub

Public Sub Quit()
    If init Then
        Shell_NotifyIcon NIM_DELETE, nid
        init = False
    End If
End Sub

Public Sub SetIconInternal(ByVal name As String, ByVal index As Long)
    Dim handle As Long
    Dim Size As Long
    Dim iconnumber As Long

    iconnumber = ExtractIconEx(name, -1, 0, 0, 0)

    If iconnumber >= index Then
        Call ExtractIconEx(name, index, 0, handle, 1)
        Size = 16
        Form1.icon = CreateBitmapIcon(handle)
        Form1.Refresh
```

```
        End If
End Sub

Public Function CreateBitmapIcon(ByVal hBmp As Long) As Picture
    Dim ok As Long
    Dim Pic As PicBmp
    Dim IPic As IPicture
    Dim IID_IDispatch As GUID

    With IID_IDispatch
        .Data1 = &H20400
        .Data4(0) = &HC0
        .Data4(7) = &H46
    End With

    With Pic
        .Size = Len(Pic)
        .Type = vbPicTypeIcon
        .hBmp = hBmp
        .hPal = 0
    End With

    ok = OleCreatePictureIndirect(Pic, IID_IDispatch, 1, IPic)
    Set CreateBitmapIcon = IPic
End Function
```

Shell_NotifyIcon is the API function responsible for tray icons. It uses a
NOTIFYICONDATA structure to pass the arguments necessary to display the
icon.

Because your COM object is invisible and doesn't participate in window message
exchange, the code uses an additional form as event receiver for the tray icon.
The NOTIFYICONDATA structure is filled with the forms window handle and the
form icon. Instead of using complicated event callback procedures, the code
asks NOTIFYICONDATA to use the official MouseMove event in case someone
moves the mouse over the tray icon.

Changing form icons dynamically

One issue remains — how is it possible to display a custom icon in the tray
area? How can you assign an icon to the form? SetIconInternal uses
ExtractIconEx to extract the bitmap handle of any icon stored in any icon
resource file. However, you'll only get the raw handle. You can't assign the
icon handle to the form directly.

Converting bitmap handles to OLE pictures

First, you need to convert the icon handle into an OLE picture object of the
subtype icon. This is done by CreateBitmapIcon. This method accepts any
handle to bitmap data and returns a valid OLE picture of type vbPicTypeIcon.
Now it's easy to assign this picture to the icon property of the form.

Responding to tray icon events

Let's take a look at how the form handles the mouse events:

```
Public parent As Object

Private Const WM_LBUTTONDOWN = &H201
Private Const WM_LBUTTONUP = &H202
Private Const WM_LBUTTONDBLCLK = &H203
Private Const WM_RBUTTONDOWN = &H204
Private Const WM_RBUTTONUP = &H205
Private Const WM_RBUTTONDBLCLK = &H206

Private Sub Form_MouseMove(Button As Integer, Shift As Integer, X As
Single, Y As Single)
    Dim msg As Long
    msg = X / Screen.TwipsPerPixelX

    Select Case msg
        Case WM_LBUTTONDOWN
            parent.FireEvent
        Case WM_LBUTTONUP
        Case WM_LBUTTONDBLCLK
        Case WM_RBUTTONDOWN
        Case WM_RBUTTONUP
        Case WM_RBUTTONDBLCLK
    End Select
End Sub
```

Whenever the mouse moves over the tray icon, a MouseMove event is raised.
The form responds to WM_LBUTTONDOWN only and calls the procedure Fire
Event. Because this procedure is defined in your COM object, it uses the
parent variable. Your code has initialized this variable with a reference to
itself: me.

```
Public Sub FireEvent()
    If busy Then Exit Sub
    busy = True
    If MsgBox(msg, vbDefaultButton2 + vbYesNo + vbQuestion _
+ vbSystemModal, "Quit?") - vbYes Then
        RaiseEvent QuitNow
        Quit
    End If
    busy = False
End Sub
```

FireEvents first checks if it is currently processing a quit request. If it is, the
public busy variable is true, and the procedure exists. If not, the procedure
asks whether you want to quit your script. If you choose Yes, it raises the
public event QuitNow and removes the icon from the tray area.

Your script doesn't know about any of this. However, once it receives the
QuitNow event, it calls the WScript.Quit method and quits.

In order for your script to quit, your script needs to listen to the `QuitNow` event and act accordingly. As outlined above, you should call `HandleEvents` regularly inside of loops. If you don't, the `QuitNow` event may not be processed until the loop has finished.

Creating Modeless Windows

Modeless windows are windows that work independently from your script. They are visible and serve as output area, but your script can still do whatever it likes. In contrast, modal windows take over control. While a modal window is active, your script stops and waits for the window to be closed.

Unfortunately, the ActiveX COM objects that your free Visual Basic CCE creates can only deal with modal windows. This is because your COM objects are single-threaded. Only one part of your script-COM object-architecture can be executed at one time.

Events change this concept completely. You have seen that events can trigger action anytime anywhere. So even though a modal window has drawn all attention to itself, if you can manage to raise an event and pass it to the calling script, it regains control while the modal window is still visible.

Output status information to a modal window

Let's turn a boring modal window into an exciting modeless window your script can use to output status information (see Figure 17-5).

I've prepared a little COM object that does the trick.

Load the complete project from the CD (\components\modeless\modeless.vbp). Or install the component for immediate action (\install\modeless\setup.exe).

```
Option Explicit

Public Event WakeUp()
Public Event QuitNow()

Public Sub WriteDialog(ByVal text As String)
    Form1.Label1.Caption = text
End Sub

Public Sub ShowDialog()
    Set Form1.parentobj = Me
    Form1.enableEvent = True
    Form1.Show vbModal
End Sub

Public Sub CloseDialog()
    Form1.Quit
```

```
End Sub

Public Sub FireEvent()
    RaiseEvent WakeUp
End Sub

Public Sub FireQuitEvent()
    RaiseEvent QuitNow
End Sub

Public Sub HandleEvent()
    DoEvents
End Sub
```

There are two public events — `WakeUp` and `QuitNow`. They are fired by `Fire Event` and `FireQuitEvent`. `ShowDialog` displays the modal dialog box. Here's the inside of the form:

```
Public enableEvent As Boolean
Public parentobj As Object

Private Sub Command1_Click()
    parentobj.FireQuitEvent
End Sub

Private Sub Form_Resize()
    If Me.Visible And enableEvent Then
        parentobj.FireEvent
        enableEvent = False
    End If
End Sub

Public Sub Quit()
    Me.Hide
End Sub
```

How do you get the form to fire the `WakeUp` event the moment it is displayed? Use the forms `Resize` procedure. This procedure is called anytime a form is resized, and the `Show` method also invokes this procedure.

To make sure the form fires only once, the `Resize` procedure blocks the event firing mechanism using `enableEvent`: Once the event is fired the first time, it sets `enableEvent` to false and prohibits any further event firing.

Figure 17-5: Output status information to modeless windows while your script is at work.

Your User Control is the only place where you can fire public events. This is why ShowDialog has stored a reference to the UserObject (Me) in the public form variable parentobj. The form can now call UserObject procedures.

Now, let's take a look at how you can control your modeless window:

```
' 17-7.VBS

set fs = CreateObject("Scripting.FileSystemObject")
' create COM reference and catch events:
set tool = WScript.CreateObject("modeless.dialog", "event_")

list = ""
quit = false

tool.WriteDialog "Starting..."
' enter MODAL mode, window takes over
tool.ShowDialog
' this part is continued after the window has been closed
MsgBox list

sub event_WakeUp
    ' this event is fired once the modal window becomes visible
    ' this event is the key and lets your script regain control
    ' while the modal window is still visible and thinks its in
    ' charge

    ' recursively search all folders
    ShowFiles fs.GetFolder("C:\")

    ' IMPORTANT: use a MsgBox statement!
    ' it reassigns the window handle to the correct thread
    MsgBox "Close Down"

    ' close the modal dialog window
    tool.CloseDialog
end sub

sub event_QuitNow
    ' this event is fired once someone clicks the Cancel button
    ' quit is set to true. Inside of ShowFiles, quit is queried
    ' and if it's true, the procedure exits immediately
    quit = true
end sub

sub ShowFiles(dirobj)
    ' did someone hit Cancel? Then quit!
    if quit then exit sub

    ' search all files in current folder
    for each file in dirobj.files
        ' write status information to modal window
```

```
        tool.WriteDialog dirobj.path & vbCr & dirobj.files.count _
& " files..." & vbCr & file.name

        ' add files to list
        list = list & file.path & vbCr

        ' IMPORTANT: call HandleEvent frequently to allow your COM
        ' object to get some CPU cycles to respond to mouse action
        ' If you don't, you can't click the Cancel button because
        ' the COM object is completely busy
        tool.HandleEvent

        ' again, did someone hit Cancel? Leave loop immediately!
        if quit then exit sub
    next

    ' recursively search all subfolders
    for each subfolder in dirobj.subfolders
        ShowFiles subfolder
    next
end sub
```

Pretty impressive, huh? You've just gained a new way of letting people know your script is still alive. Without the new pseudo-modeless window, listing all files would leave the script user wondering what's going on. Use the window whenever a script takes a long time to execute. Not only do you get a great way of providing feedback, your window also allows the user to cancel action.

There are various properties to set for the form so it appears correctly. The easiest way is to load the project \components\modeless\modeless.vbp. Make sure your form uses AutoRedraw. In my example, the form doesn't use a caption and is automatically centered in the middle of the screen.

Some words of caution

Converting a modal window into a modeless window is not a trivial thing. Your events kick the threads around, and VisualBasic wonders what's going on. However, the preceding technique is completely safe. If you change the code, though, always make sure no abandoned threads are left behind. Open your task manager window and search for WScript.exe after your script is done.

Abandoned threads occur when your script doesn't clean up after itself. Suppose you have displayed a modal window using ShowDialog. From this point on, the modal window is officially in charge. Your COM object secretly passes back control to your script using the WakeUp event. Now your script is back in charge, although the modal window still thinks it's the only one there.

If your script would simply close down now using WScript.Quit, you would leave an abandoned thread behind. WScript.Quit should close down the modal window, but because your script sneaked back into control, it is closed, and the original Wscript session remains active.

So, it's important to pass back control to the modal window once your script is done and to let it close gracefully. In the example above, it's important to issue a MsgBox statement just before you close down the modal window. This way, your WakeUp event procedure is back in charge and can be closed normally. If you don't issue this statement, your script won't find its way back to where it started.

Secret

Use the WScript.Shell Popup method if you want to close the mandatory message box automatically. Set wshshell = CreateObject("WScript. Shell"). Replace MsgBox "Close Down" with wshshell.Popup "Close Down", 1.

Using progress bars to spice up dialog boxes

You are probably wondering what this new technique can do for you. There are tremendous possibilities, and because the file-search dialog box from above is a very useful example, I have spiced it up a bit to demonstrate how easy it now is to create professional dialog boxes.

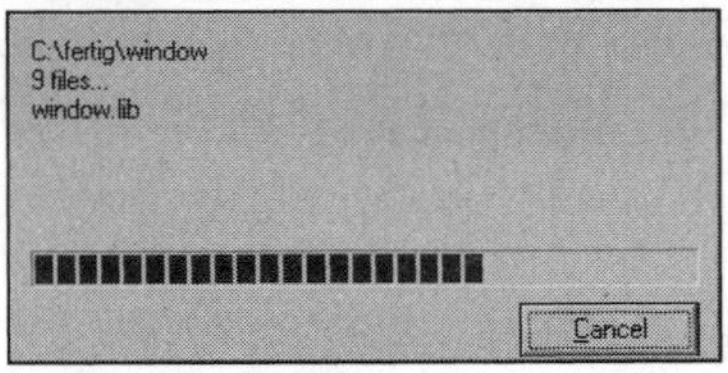

C:\fertig\window
9 files...
window.lib

[|||||||||||||||||||||||||]   [Cancel]

Figure 17-6: Display modeless progress bars to indicate script progress.

My COM object actually contains two forms, and the second form features a progress bar.

Secret

The progress bar is part of COMCTL32.OCX, a user control provided by Microsoft. Make sure you include this file in your distribution if you plan to give away your own progress bar controls.

To use the progress bar display, use ShowProgressDialog instead of ShowDialog. To set the progress bar, use SetProgress. Make sure you specify a value between 0 and 100:

```
' 17-8.VBS

set fs = CreateObject("Scripting.FileSystemObject")
set tool = WScript.CreateObject("modeless.dialog", "event_")
```

```
list = ""
quit = false

tool.WriteDialog "Starting..."

' this time, use progress bar dialog
tool.ShowProgressDialog

MsgBox list

sub event_WakeUp
    ShowFiles fs.GetFolder("C:\")
    MsgBox "Close Down"
    tool.CloseDialog
end sub

sub event_QuitNow
    quit = true
end sub

sub ShowFiles(dirobj)
    if quit then exit sub

    counter = 0
    filecount = dirobj.files.count
    for each file in dirobj.files
        counter = counter + 1
        tool.WriteDialog dirobj.path & vbCr & filecount _
            & " files..." & vbCr & file.name

        ' calculate percent done
        percent = Fix(counter * 100/filecount)
        ' set progress bar accordingly
        tool.SetProgress percent

        list = list & file.path & vbCr
        tool.HandleEvent
        if quit then exit sub
    next
    for each subfolder in dirobj.subfolders
        ShowFiles subfolder
    next
end sub
```

Tip

The progress bar is perfect for well-defined operations. Searching a folder is well-defined: You know the number of files in the folder, and you know the number of files you have already found. From here, it's easy to calculate the percentage using a formula such as `actual value * 100 / end value`. You can't use the progress bar for operations without a clearly defined scope.

Summary

Events are great. Although they are not absolutely necessary and you can completely ignore them, exploring events provides you with a whole new world of opportunities. This chapter provided some highly unusual examples: for instance, the concept of events allowing your scripts to continue execution although a modal window is visible.

Events solve many other problems, too: From now on, you can display icons in the tray area to indicate that your script is running (and still feeling well). Through the tray icon, you can communicate with your script and, for example, cancel execution.

As a side effect, the COM objects discussed in this chapter show some rather interesting techniques — you learned how to extract icons from system resources and how to convert those extracted icons into OLE pictures. These OLE pictures then can be used freely with Visual Basic.

Chapter 18

Developing Unix-like Commands

In This Chapter

▶ Use scripts in DOS boxes and let them behave as if they were DOS commands

▶ Control the DOS Input and Output streams

▶ Use piping and feeding with the results of other commands in your scripts to further process or filter them

▶ Make sure your scripts are launched inside a DOS box

Scripts can act like DOS or UNIX commands. In this chapter, learn how to hook a script into the DOS Input and Output streams. Also discover how scripts read in arguments and support piping.

Developing Your Own Command-Line Macros

DOS and UNIX have one thing in common—they use a command box, and you must enter commands instead of clicking fancy icons with the mouse. Various extensions provide a graphical user interface to both UNIX and DOS, and Windows 9.x to some extent "wraps" DOS commands and offers easy-to-use icons and menus.

Still, many computer professionals prefer the command-line style for administering systems. The Scripting Host allows you to append the set of commands available and generate your own.

Creating a new command

Scripts need a way to read input and write output to the DOS box in order to become "real" commands. The new WSH 2.0 is able to do that. It can link itself into the DOS Input and Output streams and access them as `TextStream` objects. In essence, scripts control input and output to the DOS box the same way they control input and output to files.

Take a look at the following example. It accesses the DOS Input and Output streams and echos back whatever you type in. Use exit to quit the script.

```
' 18-1.VBS

set inputstream = WScript.StdIn
```

```
set outputstream = WScript.StdOut

do
     data = inputStream.ReadLine
     if data = "exit" then
WScript.Quit
     else
          outputstream.WriteLine UCASE(data)
     end if
loop
```

If you try to launch this script, you'll receive an error message (see Figure 18-1). The scripting host complains about an invalid handle. What's going on?

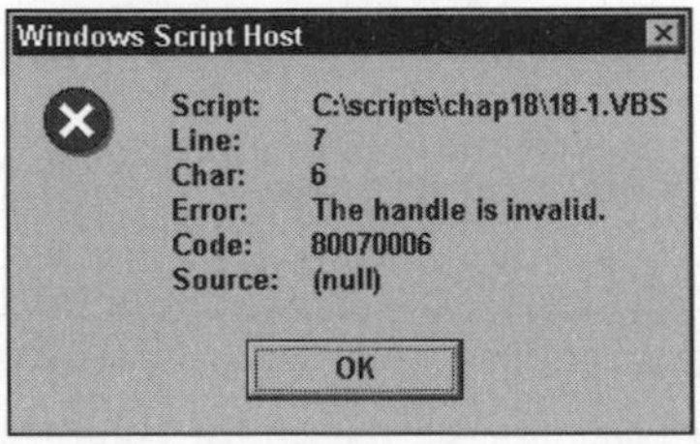

Figure 18-1: You can't access DOS streams from outside a DOS box.

Secret

Launching scripts, by default, executes the scripts in the Windows environment. WSCRIPT.EXE takes care of the script, and because WSCRIPT.EXE is not a DOS box, there are no Input and Output streams the script can link into.

For your script to work, you must execute it inside a DOS box. Either launch the script manually via CSCRIPT.EXE or right-click the script icon and choose Open With Command Prompt.

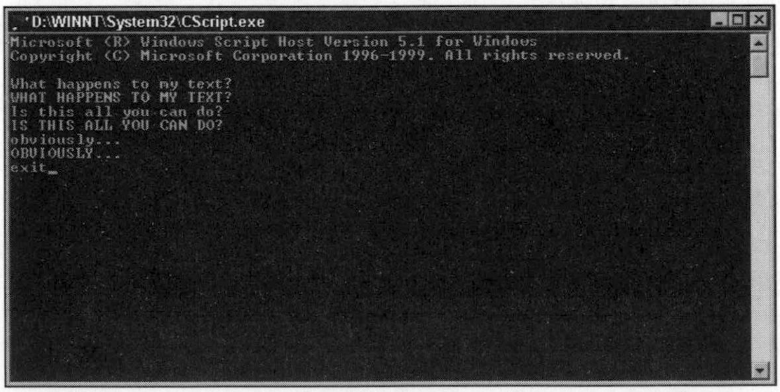

Figure 18-2: The script processes entered text.

Now, the script works perfectly well. You can type in characters, and the script will return them in uppercase. Exit closes the script.

Calling scripts like DOS commands

On previous Windows versions, calling a script from the command line isn't fun. You need to append CSCRIPT.EXE and specify the full path name to your script. For example, if you have stored your previous script as C:\18-1.VBS, you'd have to call it this way:

```
CSCRIPT.EXE C:\18-1.VBS
```

Obviously, this isn't practical, and luckily, Windows 2000 is much more advanced. Here, .vbs files are included in the search path and work like executables. Provided you have stored your script in a folder that is part of the search path (the Windows folder, for example), you can call your script directly. You don't even need to specify the file extension:

```
18-1 [Enter]
```

However, again Windows defaults to WSCRIPT.EXE, and although the script is launched, you will get the error message complaining about invalid handles.

Secret

You can choose whether WSCRIPT.EXE or CSCRIPT.EXE will execute scripts by default. WSCRIPT.EXE //H:CScript changes the default to CSCRIPT.EXE, and WSCRIPT.EXE //H:WScript changes the setting back to WSCRIPT.EXE.

So if you want to use scripts as commands, you can change the default script engine to CSCRIPT.EXE and get away with it:

```
WSCRIPT.EXE //H:CScript
```

Now, at least on Windows 2000, you can call your scripts exactly the way you'd call any DOS command or executable file. However, now all scripts are launched by CSCRIPT.EXE, even the ones you launch by clicking the script icon on the Windows desktop.

Detecting whether a script runs in a DOS box

To solve this problem, and to prevent error messages regarding invalid handles, your script will need a way to determine whether it's hosted by WSCRIPT.EXE or CSCRIPT.EXE. Knowing this, it can relaunch itself in the appropriate hosting environment. This way, your script always gains access to the DOS handles, and you aren't forced to change the default script host.

It's easy. The WSH provides two important properties. FullName returns the full name of the current script host. Your script just needs to extract the filename to find out whether it's CSCRIPT.EXE or some other host.

If it's not CSCRIPT.EXE, your script can use the WScript.Shell method Run to relaunch itself using CSCRIPT.EXE. ScriptFullName reveals the script's own full path name.

Here's the solution:

```
' 18-2.VBS

' which engine runs this script?
engine = lcase(mid(WScript.FullName,
InstrRev(WScript.FullName,"\")+1))
if not engine="cscript.exe" then
    ' re-launch script using cscript.exe
    set wshshell = CreateObject("WScript.Shell")
    wshshell.run "CSCRIPT.EXE """ & WScript.ScriptFullName & """"
    WScript.Quit
end if
MsgBox "I run as DOS-Box!"
```

The stub shown in Figure 18-3 is all you need to make sure the script is run by CSCRIPT.EXE.

Figure 18-3: Automatically make sure your script is executed by CSCRIPT.EXE.

However, it's only a partial victory. Because your script is now launched by WSCRIPT.EXE first and relaunched by CSCRIPT.EXE, it will always use a new and private DOS window. This solution works great for individual scripts that run stand-alone, but it's no solution if you want to mix DOS commands and your own commands. Here, your only choice is to temporarily change the default host.

Changing the default host

The next script could be your first real command extension (see Figure 18-4). Save it as DOS.VBS in your Windows folder. From now on, it's easy to switch default hosts. Call the script DOS.VBS without arguments. It switches hosts and reports the active host. Or use DOS "on" or DOS "off" as argument. DOS on activates CSCRIPT.EXE, and DOS off activates WSCRIPT.EXE as default host. From now on, right before you start working with your script commands, enter DOS on. Once you are finished, enter DOS off.

Note

Again, remember that only Windows 2000 allows you to call your script directly. Place your script into the Windows folder so you don't need to specify its full path name. On all other Windows systems, you need to append CSCRIPT.EXE and provide the full path to your script.

```
' DOS.VBS

set wshshell = CreateObject("WScript.Shell")

' which engine runs this script?
engine = lcase(mid(WScript.FullName,
InstrRev(WScript.FullName,"\")+1))

set args = WScript.Arguments

if args.Count = 0 then
    ' no arguments
    if engine = "wscript.exe" then
        wshshell.run "WSCRIPT.EXE //H:CScript"
    else
        wshshell.run "WSCRIPT.EXE //H:WScript"
    end if
else
    if args(0) = "on" then
        wshshell.run "WSCRIPT.EXE //H:CScript"
    else
        wshshell.run "WSCRIPT.EXE //H:WScript"
    end if
end if
```

Undocumented

Scripts won't work well as command extensions on systems other than Windows 2000. On Windows 9.x and NT, you need to call the script using a script engine and the full script path name. That's not very practical.

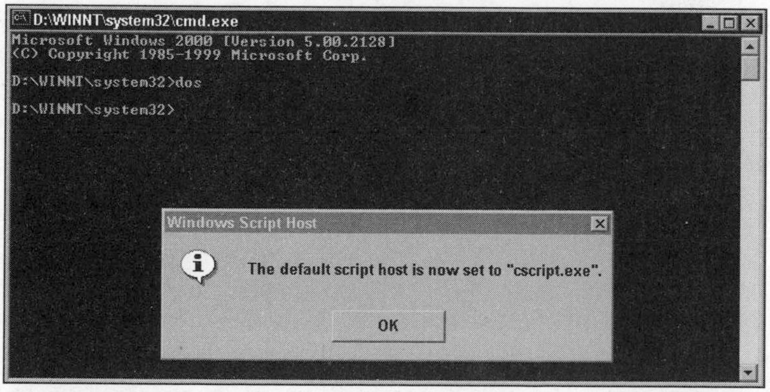

Figure 18-4: Your new "DOS" command controls which script engine executes your scripts.

Automatically changing default hosts

Here's another solution. The next script changes the default host to CSCRIPT. EXE, then launches a command box and waits. Once you are done with your command-line work and close the box, the script wakes up again and changes the default host back to WSCRIPT.EXE:

```
' 18-3.VBS

set wshshell = CreateObject("WScript.Shell")

' set cscript.exe as standard
wshshell.run "WSCRIPT.EXE //H:CScript"

' launch command window and wait
ok = wshshell.run("""%comspec%""",,true)

' change back to default
wshshell.run "WSCRIPT.EXE //H:WScript"
```

Whenever you need to do command-line work, make sure to open the command box with this script. This way, you can always be sure that your scripts are executed inside the box.

Using piping: Feeding results to your commands

Script commands support piping. Piping is a simple means of cascading commands. For example, the DIR DOS command lists folder contents. However, most folders contain many more files than fit on one screen page. So in order to read the entire listing, you can "feed" it to another command called more. This command stops output once a screen is full until you enter a key:

```
DIR | MORE
```

Developing pipe commands

Your scripts can easily participate in piping. For example, the next script creates your own more command.

Caution

Don't launch this script directly! If you do, your keyboard is interpreted as Input stream, and because there's no defined end to keyboard input, you'll stumble into an endless loop. Close the DOS window if this happens to you.

```
' NEWMORE.VBS

engine = lcase(mid(WScript.FullName, _
InstrRev(WScript.FullName,"\")+1))
if not engine = "cscript.exe" then
MsgBox "Launch with CSCRIPT.EXE!"
```

```
WScript.Quit
end if

set inputstream = WScript.StdIn
set outputstream = WScript.StdOut

do
     counter = counter + 1
     if outputstream.atEndOfStream then exit do
     outputstream.WriteLine inputstream.ReadLine
     if counter > 20 then
          MsgBox "Click OK to continue!"
          counter = 0
     end if
loop

outputstream.WriteLine "That's it!"
```

And this is how you invoke it:

```
DIR | CSCRIPT.EXE %WINDIR%\NEWMORE.VBS
```

To play it safe, you should issue the DIR command first without piping it to your script. Make sure the DIR command executes without asking questions. If DIRCMD is set to some option, DIR may pause after 25 lines and ask you to press a key. Set DIRCMD to nothing:

```
SET DIRCMD= [Enter]
```

Caution

If the DOS command feeds results to your script too fast, the script asks the DOS command to hold on a second. To continue feeding, you need to press a key. So if the script appears to hang, press a key. Usually, this behavior is an indication that your system is too slow and can't process your script at the usual speed. If it happens to you, piping is pretty much useless.

Every 20 lines, a dialog box asks you to click OK.

Secret

Although Windows 2000 does a good job launching script files as executables, piping only works if you specify CSCRIPT.EXE as script host in your command line. You can't use DIR | NEWMORE or else you'll get an invalid handle error. The reason is because the pipe gets lost the way Windows launches script files. By explicitly specifying CSCRIPT.EXE, the pipe is attached to CSCRIPT.EXE and passed on to the script. It's bad news, but it's the truth.

Writing filters through piping

There are more useful examples of how piping can help you. For example, the next script is a piping extension that finds filenames for you:

```
' MYFILTER.VBS

engine = lcase(mid(WScript.FullName, _
InstrRev(WScript.FullName,"\")+1))
```

```
if not engine = "cscript.exe" then
MsgBox "Launch with CSCRIPT.EXE!"
WScript.Quit
end if


search = lcase(InputBox("Enter File name or part of it!"))

set inputstream = WScript.StdIn
set outputstream = WScript.StdOut

do until inputstream.atEndOfStream
    line = inputstream.ReadLine
    if Instr(lcase(line), search)>0 then
        outputstream.WriteLine "FOUND: " & line
    end if
loop

outputstream.WriteLine "Done."
```

Feed it with a recursive DOS DIR **search, and it filters out anything you ask for:**

```
DIR C:\ /S | CSCRIPT.EXE %WINDIR%\MYFILTER.VBS
```

You can even redirect the result into a file:

```
DIR C:\ /S | CSCRIPT.EXE %WINDIR%\MYFILTER.VBS > C:\RESULT.TXT
```

Summary

Scripts can act as command-line commands and participate in both DOS streams and piping. However, the use is limited: Only Windows 2000 allows you to specify script names directly. On all other systems, you must use CSCRIPT.EXE and provide the full script path.

Also, DOS Input and Output handles are valid only if you launch your script from inside a DOS box. You have discovered a number of solutions to make sure scripts are launched this way.

Still, there are many useful scenarios in which DOS scripts come in handy. Among the most fascinating uses are interpreter-like solutions: You can use the DOS box as a platform for your script and input commands and output the results.

Part V

Accessing Hidden Components

Chapter 19: Using the WebBrowser Control

Chapter 20: Internet and Communications

Chapter 21: Fax, Printer, Scanner, and Graphics

Chapter 22: Fun, Tricks, and Multimedia

Chapter 23: Using Databases

Chapter 24: Managing Windows NT/2000 Server

Using the WebBrowser Control

In This Chapter

▶ Discover the versatile `WebBrowser` control, and create your own dialog boxes using plain HTML templates

▶ Enumerate and access DHTML elements

▶ Link script procedures to DHTML buttons using `GetRef`, and bypass Internet Explorer security dialogs

▶ Control your `WebBrowser` form window through HTML commands

▶ Validate HTML form input, and color-code missing form fields

▶ Let your COM object respond to events fired by the `WebBrowser` control, and disable the context menu this way

▶ Use radio buttons and determine which radio button was selected

▶ Customize your HTML dialog container, change caption text, and disable sizing

The `WebBrowser` control is the heart of Internet Explorer. It can display HTML documents and is a very versatile design element you can incorporate into your own dialog boxes. In this chapter, learn how to use the `WebBrowser` control to create fully configurable HTML-based custom dialog boxes and transfer the results back into your scripts.

The WebBrowser Control: Mastering Real-World Tasks

Microsoft has stuffed all kinds of controls into Windows, and while most s of them are busy working for the operating system, your scripts can access those components, too.

One of the most versatile controls is the `WebBrowser` control. It works inside of any Internet Explorer window, and because Microsoft keeps expanding the role HTML plays, you'll see this control in many Windows 2000 system dialog boxes, too.

The `WebBrowser` control is actually a miniature Web browser. It contains everything necessary to load and display HTML content.

Secret

Actually, Internet Explorer is just a wrapping around the `WebBrowser` control. The Internet Explorer application provides the toolbars and other gadgets helpful to navigate the Web, but the true power comes from the `WebBrowser` control embedded in Internet Explorer.

The `WebBrowser` control is by no means limited to displaying Web pages. In Chapter 5, I showed you how to use Internet Explorer as a versatile Scripting Host output window. Now it's time to take a close look at the real heart of Internet Explorer. The `WebBrowser` control is the perfect foundation for truly customizable dialog boxes. It makes much more sense to use the `WebBrowser` control directly instead of accessing it through Internet Explorer and paying the price for all of the overhead involved.

Creating custom dialog boxes

There's a definite need for custom dialog boxes. The built-in set of dialog boxes accessible to the Scripting Host is very limited, and it's impractical to create COM objects for any custom dialog box you may need.

A much more versatile approach are HTML dialog boxes. You can create them with your favorite HTML editor in a matter of minutes, and it's easy to design these dialog boxes just as you can design a Web page.

All you need is a way to display your HTML dialog boxes. Displaying is easy — just feed the HTML template to the `WebBrowser` control. In addition, you'll need some extra tricks to be able to retrieve the results typed into your dialog box.

I've designed a COM object that uses the `WebBrowser` control and includes many fascinating tricks for interacting with the user. Install the COM object `\install\webdialog\setup.exe`. Full source code is provided at `\components\webdialog\webdialog.vbp`.

Designing your form: Creating an HTML template

The first thing needed is an HTML template. This template defines the elements of your dialog box. Here's a simple example. Type it into your favorite text editor and save it as `TEMPLATE.HTM` in the same folder you are going to use for the sample scripts:

```
<html>
<head>
<style>
p       {font: 12pt Arial}
</style>
</head>
<body bgcolor = "#CCCCCC" scroll="no">

<p>Your name: <input type="text" name="namefield"></p>
<input type="button" name="help" value="Help">

</body>
</html>
```

Next, open the template file. Internet Explorer displays the form, and you can check whether everything looks the way you planned.

Displaying the template dialog box

Now you are ready to display the form template with your new custom dialog COM object (see Figure 19-1).

Make sure the following sample script is stored in the same folder you stored your HTML template!

```
' 19-1.VBS

set tool = CreateObject("Web.dialog")

' current path
myname = WScript.ScriptFullName
cp = left(myname, InstrRev(myname, "\"))

' template
template = cp & "template.htm"

' size dialog
tool.Width = 400
tool.Height = 300
tool.Title = "My Form"
tool.SetIcon "shell32.dll", 3
tool.Resizable = true

' display dialog and return object reference
set webcontrol = tool.ShowDialog(template)
MsgBox TypeName(webcontrol)
```

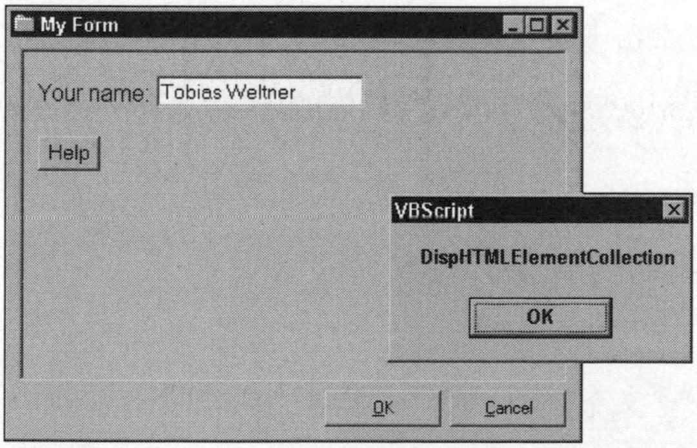

Figure 19-1: Use an HTML template to design your own dialog box.

The script creates a dialog box and displays your HTML template. Once you click OK, the COM object returns a reference to the element collection. You'll need this reference in a minute. First, take a look at your options in Table 19-1.

Table 19-1   Properties and Methods to Control the WebBrowser Dialog Box

Method/Property	Description
`Property CancelButton As String`	Caption name of Cancel button.
`Function DisplayDialog As Object`	Shows dialog box and returns element collection.
`Property Height As Long`	Height of dialog box in pixels.
`Function LoadDialog(ByVal template As String) As Object`	Loads dialog template and returns element collection.
`Property OKButton As String`	Caption name of OK button.
`Property Resizable As Boolean`	True: Dialog box is resizable.
`Sub SetIcon(ByVal iconlib As String, ByVal index As Long)`	Sets the dialog box icon. Supply name of icon file and icon index.
`Sub ShowButtons(ByVal mode As Boolean)`	True: Dialog box displays OK and Cancel buttons.
`Function ShowDialog(ByVal template As String) As Object`	Combines `LoadDialog` and `ShowDialog`: Loads a template file, displays the dialog box, and returns element collection.
`Property Title As String`	Title of dialog box.
`Property Width As Long`	Width of dialog box in pixels.

Getting access to template elements

Displaying your HTML template alone won't be enough. You need a way to access the elements in your HTML template in order to query their values. After all, you want to know what the user has entered into your form (see Figure 19-2).

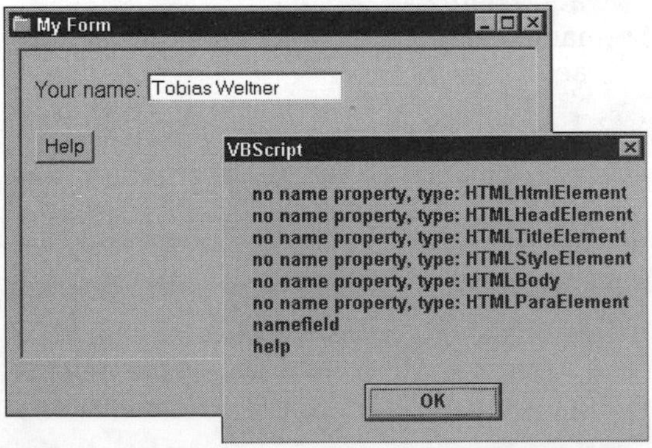

Figure 19-2: Examine the elements accessible in your HTML template.

The COM object returns a reference to the element collection. This collection contains references to all the elements you placed onto your HTML page. Let's check out how to read this collection:

```
' 19-2.VBS

set tool = CreateObject("Web.dialog")

' current path
myname = WScript.ScriptFullName
cp = left(myname, InstrRev(myname, "\"))

' template
template = cp & "template.htm"

' size dialog
tool.Resizable = true
tool.Width = 400
tool.Height = 300
tool.Title = "My Form"
tool.SetIcon "shell32.dll", 3

' display dialog and return object reference
set webcontrol = tool.ShowDialog(template)

' read all named elements
for each element in webcontrol
    on error resume next
    elname = element.name
    if not err.number=0 then
        ' element has no name tag!
        elname = "no name property, type: " & TypeName(element)
    end if
    on error goto 0
    list = list & elname & vbCr
next

MsgBox list
```

This time, once you click OK, the script returns a list of all the elements inside your HTML template. There are a lot of unnamed control elements, but you also see all the named elements. Named elements are elements you assigned a NAME= tag.

Now it's easy to retrieve the results someone has entered into your form:

```
' 19-3.VBS

set tool = CreateObject("Web.dialog")

' current path
myname = WScript.ScriptFullName
cp = left(myname, InstrRev(myname, "\"))
```

```
' template
template = cp & "template.htm"

' size dialog
tool.Resizable = true
tool.Width = 400
tool.Height = 300
tool.Title = "My Form"
tool.SetIcon "shell32.dll", 3

' display dialog and return object reference
set webcontrol = tool.ShowDialog(template)

' read input
if TypeName(webcontrol)="Nothing" then
    MsgBox "You cancelled!"
else
    MsgBox "You entered: " & webcontrol.namefield.value
end if
```

Tip

Expand your HTML template to ask for more than one piece of information. It's completely up to you how complex you want your dialog window to get!

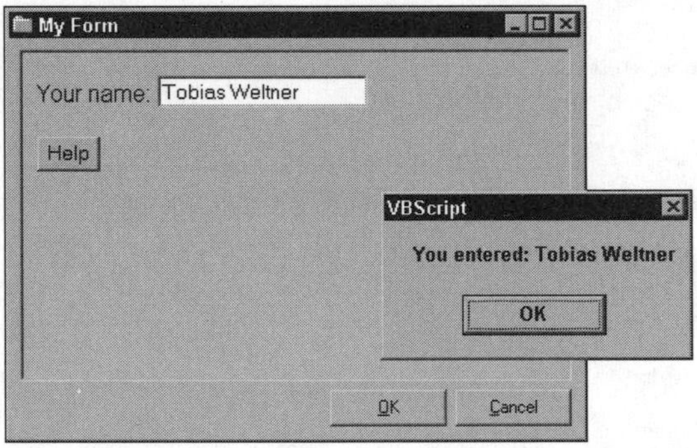

Figure 19-3: It works — your script retrieves the input.

Designing dialog box templates

The most obvious advantage of HTML dialog boxes is their versatility. You can change the design of your dialog box templates without having to change the COM object in any way, and you don't need any complicated subclassing techniques to dynamically add or remove form elements. There's only one thing you need to ensure, and that's to supply a NAME= tag for each input element you want to query. Without the NAME= property, your script can't access the element's value.

Also take a look at the BODY tag. This tag defines the background color and turns off the vertical scroll bar.

The STYLE section uses a style sheet to change the font the P element uses. Style sheets are a great way to globally assign formatting information to your form elements.

Revealing implementation details

Before I show you more tricks you can do with your new HTML dialog box tool, here are some implementation details. If you don't care how the COM object does its work, skip this part!

The Resizable property is one of the most remarkable features: This property controls whether or not your form window is resizable. This may not seem to be a big deal, but actually it is. You can't change properties like this one during run-time. The window frame—which determines whether the form is resizable or not—needs to be defined at design-time.

There are ways to overcome this limitation, but they are very complex. The COM object uses a much simpler approach. It actually uses two forms—one is resizable, and the other one isn't. The Resizable property sets a global reference to one of the two forms, and all other properties and methods use this reference. This is why you should use the Resizable property before you use any of the other properties and methods.

Generally, your dialog box is centered onscreen. Again, there are many complex ways to center a form, but they are completely unnecessary. The form contains a property called StartUpPosition, and this property just needs to be set to CenterScreen. That's all there is to it.

The VBScript has some interesting parts, too! It uses ScriptFullName to retrieve its own file path and extracts the pure path information. This way, the script "knows" the folder name it is stored in. This folder is appended to the template filename, and as a result, you don't need to fiddle around with template file paths. Just make sure the template file is stored in the same folder you stored your script in.

Advanced WebBrowser Tricks

Let's take a quick look at the architecture of your HTML dialog boxes. Three components are involved. Your script is part one. It launches the COM object, which in turn displays the WebBrowser control. This is part two. Part three is your HTML template, shown inside the WebBrowser control.

To get the most out of this architecture, you need ways to communicate between these components. Communication requires handles to the participating objects, and in the preceding examples, you saw how this works.

CreateObject returns a handle to the COM object so your script can call its internal methods. ShowDialog in turn again returns a handle. To be exact, it returns an element collection, and this element collection contains the handles of all the elements inside your HTML template. Both your script and your COM object can access any single HTML element in your template, and the example used this handle to retrieve the value entered into the text field.

Calling script procedures through your HTML template

Maybe you noticed the Help button on the sample form. It was of no use — clicking the button didn't do a thing.

Not yet, anyway. Test your new knowledge about inter-component communications and hook up a script procedure to this button (see Figure 19-4).

Your script needs to access the button. That's easy, because your script knows the element's reference so it can access all properties. How can your script ask the button to execute a script procedure? Your script needs to get a reference to the script procedure and pass it to the `onclick` event of the button. Sounds complicated, but it isn't!

```
' 19-4.VBS

set tool = CreateObject("Web.dialog")

' current path
myname = WScript.ScriptFullName
cp = left(myname, InstrRev(myname, "\"))

' template
template = cp & "template.htm"

' size dialog
tool.Width = 400
tool.Height = 300
tool.Title = "My Form"

' load template first! This way, you get a handle
' to the HTML elements without displaying the form yet
set webcontrol = tool.LoadDialog(template)

' configure the dialog
' hook up a script procedure to the help button
webcontrol.help.onclick = GetRef("showhelp")

' now display the dialog. Note that the help button now
' invokes the showhelp procedure!
set webcontrol = tool.DisplayDialog

' read input
if TypeName(webcontrol)="Nothing" then
    MsgBox "You cancelled!"
```

```
else
MsgBox "You entered: " & webcontrol.namefield.value
end if

sub ShowHelp
    MsgBox "Please enter your full name!"
end sub
```

Now it works! Every time you click the Help button, a help message appears. This help message comes from your script. The help button remotely invokes the ShowHelp procedure defined in your script. You now can call any script procedure while the dialog box is still visible. Imagine the possibilities — not only can you supply Help buttons for any input field, you can also update form elements through a database, or you can check the form contents before you allow the user to quit the form.

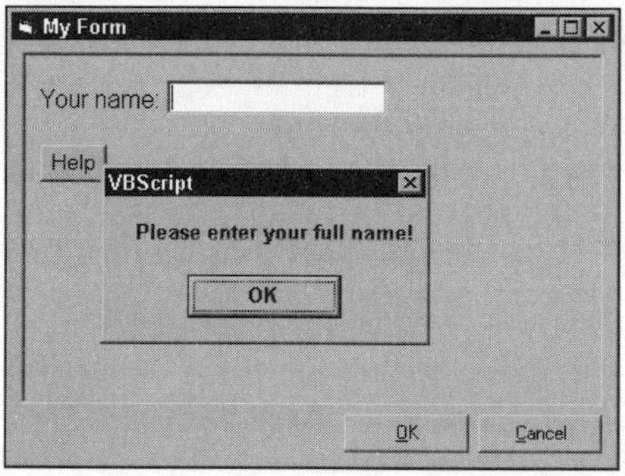

Figure 19-4: The Help button invokes the help procedure of your own script.

The magic behind this is GetRef. This method returns a reference to the script procedure, which in turn can be attached to the button onClick event.

Communication between the HTML template and the COM object

So far, your script has communicated with both the COM object and the HTML template elements. Is there a way your HTML template can communicate with the COM object, too?

The COM object hosts your HTML template, and it can be nice to include buttons in your template that control the COM object. For example, you can include a button that closes the dialog box. But how?

Your HTML document needs a reference to your COM object. This is why the COM object tries to insert such a reference into your HTML document. hookquit tries to assign the reference to a variable called parentobj. However, this fails because there is no such variable inside your HTML document.

But, you can change your HTML template. Open it inside a text editor and add a script block. Then save it as `TEMPLATE2.HTM`: (see Figure 19-5)

```
<html>
<head>
<style>
p    {font: 12pt Arial}
</style>
</head>
<body bgcolor = "#CCCCCC" scroll="no">

<script language="VBScript">
set parentobj = Nothing
sub Quit
    if not TypeName(parentobj)="Nothing" then
        parentobj.Quit false
    end if
end sub

sub Leave
    if not TypeName(parentobj)="Nothing" then
        parentobj.Quit true
    end if
end sub
</script>


<p>Your name: <input type="text" name="namefield"></p>
<input type="button" name="help" value="Help">
<input type="button" name="quit" value="Quit!" onclick="Quit()">
<input type="button" name="leave" value="Done!" onclick="Leave()">

</body>
</html>
```

Now try your script again: Exchange `TEMPLATE.HTM` inside the script with `TEMPLATE2.HTM`, or use script `19-4-2.VBS`. The form has changed, and there are two more buttons — Quit and Done. Quit does exactly what your Form window Cancel button does, and Done mimics the OK button.

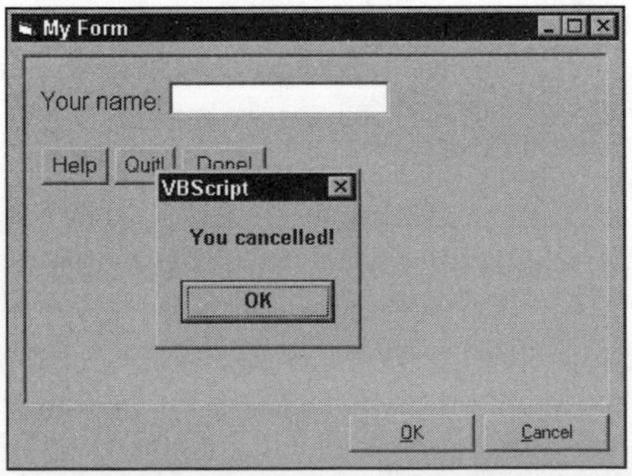

Figure 19-5: You new template features a Quit button that closes the form.

Take a look at the new script block. It defines an object reference called parentobj and sets it to Nothing. Then, it defines two procedures — Quit and Leave. These call the Quit method defined in the parentobj object. But what is the parentobj object anyway?

To make things work, your COM object inserts a reference to its own Form object into the HTML document parentobj variable. This happens inside hookquit.

Parentobj now points to the form object of your COM object, and inside the form, there's now a Quit procedure. Your HTML document now can remotely access your form object's internal procedures (see Figure 19-6).

Tip

You can expand this concept easily. Your HTML document now can access any internal method your COM object provides.

Because now that your HTML document can handle the OK and Cancel operations remotely, your dialog box no longer needs to provide its own buttons. Remove them.

```
' 19-5.VBS

set tool = CreateObject("Web.dialog")

' current path
myname = WScript.ScriptFullName
cp = left(myname, InstrRev(myname, "\"))

' template
template = cp & "template2.htm"

' size dialog
tool.Width = 400
tool.Height = 300
tool.Title = "My Form"

' remove buttons
tool.ShowButtons false

' load template first! This way, you get a handle
' to the HTML elements without displaying the form yet
set webcontrol = tool.LoadDialog(template)

' configure the dialog
' hook up a script procedure to the help button
webcontrol.help.onclick = GetRef("showhelp")

' now display the dialog. Note that the help button now
' invokes the showhelp procedure!
set webcontrol = tool.DisplayDialog

' read input
if TypeName(webcontrol)="Nothing" then
```

```
      MsgBox "You cancelled!"
else
MsgBox "You entered: " & webcontrol.namefield.value
end if

sub ShowHelp
      MsgBox "Please enter your full name!"
end sub
```

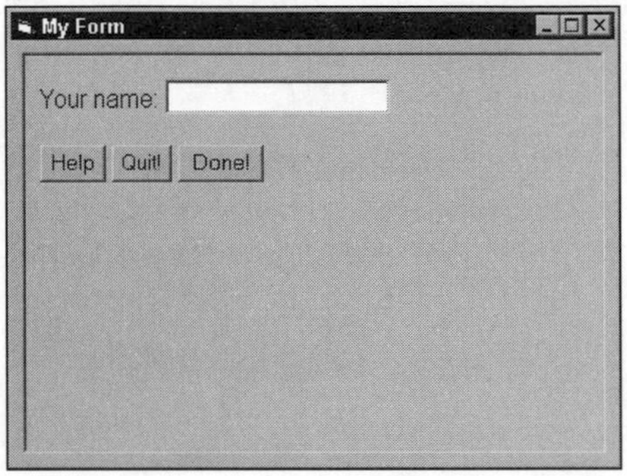

Figure 19-6: Get rid of the standard buttons and use your own template to control the form.

Now, you are absolutely free in your design. Your input elements can access the COM object methods and hook them to their own events. Your own OK and Cancel buttons can use DHTML script to check the input before allowing the form to close.

Automatically closing the form on RETURN

For example, the next HTML template accesses the document's onkeypress event. It checks for the character codes 13 (RETURN) and 27 (ESC) and calls the COM object methods to either send the input or cancel the dialog box.

As a result, the keys [Esc] and [Enter] now are connected to the Cancel and OK buttons. Once you finish your input with [Enter], the form is automatically closed, and you don't need to grab the mouse and click OK. Save this template as TEMPLATE3.HTM and change your scripts accordingly. You can also use script 19-5-2.VBS on the CD.

```
<html>
<head>
<style>
p    {font: 12pt Arial}
</style>
</head>
<body bgcolor = "#CCCCCC" scroll="no">
```

```
<script language="VBScript">
set parentobj = Nothing
'done = false
sub Quit
    if not TypeName(parentobj)="Nothing" then
        parentobj.Quit false
    end if
end sub

sub Leave
    if not TypeName(parentobj)="Nothing" then
        parentobj.Quit true
    end if
end sub

sub document_onkeypress()
    ' this procedure is executed anytime a key is pressed
    ' retrieve key code of key pressed
    keycode = window.event.keyCode
    ' is it RETURN? Leave!
    if keycode = 13 then
        Leave
    ' is it ESC? Quit!
    elseif keycode = 27 then
        Quit
    end if
end sub

</script>


<p>Your name->: <input type="text" name="namefield"></p>
<input type="button" name="help" value="Help">
<input type="button" name="quit" value="Quit!" onclick="Quit()">
<input type="button" name="leave" value="Done!" onclick="Leave()">

</body>
</html>
```

Hooking COM procedures to individual elements

The previous template responds to [Esc] and [Return] no matter which
element is currently selected. Maybe you don't like this idea. You can also
hook the keyboard checker to specific input elements. Save this template as
TEMPLATE4.HTM and change your scripts accordingly, or use script 19-5-
3.VBS.

```
<html>
<head>
<style>
p     {font: 12pt Arial}
</style>
```

```
<script language = "VBScript">
sub focusit
    document.all.namefield.focus()
end sub
</script>


</head>
<body bgcolor = "#CCCCCC" scroll="no" onload="call
window.setTimeOut('focusit()', 100)">


<p>Your name->: <input type="text" name="namefield"
onkeypress="checkkeyboard()"></p>
<input type="button" name="help" value="Help">
<input type="button" name="quit" value="Quit!" onclick="Quit()">
<input type="button" name="leave" value="Done!" onclick="Leave()">

<script language="VBScript">
set parentobj = Nothing

sub Quit
    if not TypeName(parentobj)="Nothing" then
        parentobj.Quit false
    end if
end sub

sub Leave
    if not TypeName(parentobj)="Nothing" then
        parentobj.Quit true
    end if
end sub

sub checkkeyboard()
    keycode = window.event.keyCode
    if keycode = 13 then
        Leave
    elseif keycode = 27 then
        Quit
    end if
end sub

</script>
</body>
</html>
```

This time, the [Esc] and [Enter] keys are recognized only inside your text box element. The script inside the template has placed the keyboard check into a regular procedure called `checkkeyboard`. This procedure is then hooked to the `keypress` event of the text box.

The script demonstrates another nice advantage — your text box element receives the focus automatically, and you no longer have to click the element before entering text. Now, your dialog box is ready, and you can type in text immediately. And [Enter] sends the input to your script. Your HTML dialog box is just as convenient to use as the built-in `InputBox` method.

Secret

Assigning the input focus to an element in regular Web pages is easy. Just call the focus method of the element that you want to receive the focus. However, this won't work in the preceding example. The focus() method can switch focus to the element only once it is visible onscreen. This is why the script calls the focus method in the BODY tag onload property. This still isn't enough. Even though the document is loaded when onload is executed, it takes some extra time for the elements to be fully programmable. This is why the script doesn't call the focusit procedure directly. Instead, it uses the timer built into the window object and calls it with a 100-millisecond delay. Note also that the focusit procedure needs to be defined in the HEAD section. It needs to be defined before the WebBrowser control parses the BODY tag. If you want another element to receive the focus, just change the element name in the focusit procedure.

Checking for valid form entries

Using your own OK and Cancel buttons instead of the buttons the COM object provides has many advantages. For example, you can double-check the user input before you allow the form window to close. Save this template as TEMPLATE5.HTM and change your scripts accordingly, or use script 19-5-4.VBS (see Figure 19-7).

```
<html>
<head>
<style>
p      {font: 12pt Arial}
</style>

<script language = "VBScript">
sub focusit
    document.all.namefield.focus()
end sub
</script>

</head>
<body bgcolor = "#CCCCCC" scroll="no" onload="call
window.setTimeOut('focusit()', 1000)">


<p>Your name->: <input type="text" name="namefield"
onkeypress="checkkeyboard()"></p>
<input type="button" name="help" value="Help">
<input type="button" name="quit" value="Quit!" onclick="Quit()">
<input type="button" name="leave" value="Done!" onclick="Leave()">
<input type="button" name="focus" value="Focus!" onclick="focusit()">

<script language="VBScript">
set parentobj = Nothing

sub Quit
```

```
        if not TypeName(parentobj)="Nothing" then
            parentobj.Quit false
        end if
    end sub

    sub Leave
        if document.all.namefield.value="" then
            document.all.namefield.style.background = "#FF0000"
            MsgBox "You did not fill out the form!"
            document.all.namefield.style.background = "#FFFFFF"
            document.all.namefield.focus
        elseif not TypeName(parentobj)="Nothing" then
            parentobj.Quit true
        end if
    end sub
    sub checkkeyboard()
        keycode = window.event.keyCode
        if keycode = 13 then
            Leave
        elseif keycode = 27 then
            Quit
        end if
    end sub

    </script>
    </body>
    </html>
```

The Leave procedure now checks whether the user has entered text at all. If the text field is empty, the script flashes the text box background color and displays a message. As long as the text box is empty, the Cancel button is the only way to close the form window.

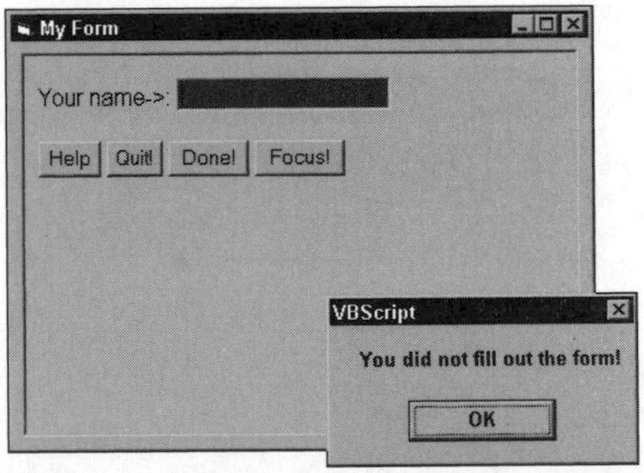

Figure 19-7: Automatically focus and check the input.

Use this as a foundation for your own checks. You can check more than one field. You can check the content and make sure the user has entered the type of data you expect. You can even disable the OK button for as long as the user input contains errors.

Responding to WebBrowser control events

So far, your COM object displays any HTML file you provide. But how can you access the events raised by the `WebBrowser` control?

Use the WithEvents statement. The COM object defines a variable called `htmldoc` of type `HTMLDocument` as `WithEvents`. The deeper meaning behind this is that the variable `htmldoc` now can host a reference to an HTML document and can also handle any events the HTML page may raise.

Then, the `LoadDialog` procedure assigns the handle to the `WebBrowser` control document to this variable. From now on, your COM object can respond to events raised by the HTML document.

And it does. The function `htmldoc_oncontextmenu` is called anytime a user tries to open a context menu. Because you don't want an Internet Explorer-style context menu to appear on your dialog box, the function always returns false, effectively disabling context menus.

Note

The `oncontextmenu` event is supported only on IE5.

Reading Groups of Radio Buttons

HTML forms can consist of more than just text boxes. Radio buttons work like the radio buttons on your old car stereo — only one selection in a group can be chosen at any time. Radio buttons are perfect for offering mutually exclusive options. However, how do you create Radio button groups, and even more important, how can your script read the selected option?

Creating a group of radio buttons

Radio buttons are plain `INPUT` elements of type "radio." Their name property groups them together (see Figure 19-8).

Secret

Radio buttons work mutually exclusively only when you group them together. Grouping takes place by assigning the same name to all radio button elements in this group.

Here's an example file. Save it as `TEMPLATE6.HTM`.

```
<html>
<head>
<style>
p    {font: 12pt Arial}
.mystyle {font: 10pt Arial; font-weight: bold}
</style>
</head>

<body bgcolor = "#CCCCCC" scroll="no">
```

```
<fieldset><legend class="mystyle">Choose an Option!</legend>
<p><input type="radio" value="Option 1" checked name="R1">Option 1<br>
  <input type="radio" name="R1" value="Option 2">Option 2<br>
  <input type="radio" name="R1" value="Option 3">Option 3<br></p>
</fieldset>

</body>
</html>
```

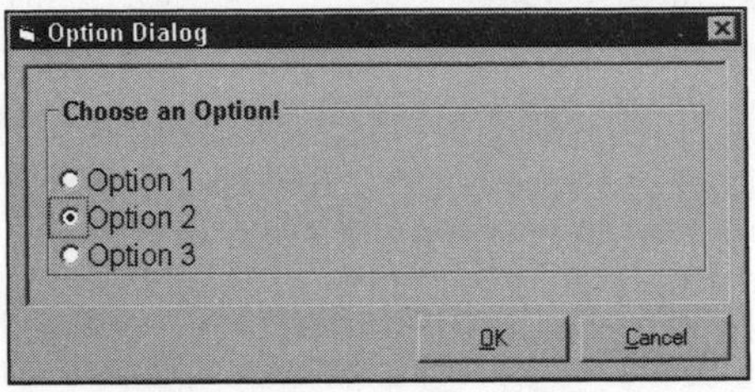

Figure 19-8: Use fixed-sized dialog boxes and display any kind of form element you like.

To display this template, use the following script:

```
' 19-6.VBS

set tool = CreateObject("Web.dialog")

' current path
myname = WScript.ScriptFullName
cp = left(myname, InstrRev(myname, "\"))

' template
template = cp & "template6.htm"

' size dialog
tool.Resizable =false
tool.Width = 400
tool.Height = 200
tool.Title = "Option Dialog"

set webcontrol = tool.ShowDialog(template)

' read input
MsgBox "Done!"
```

The dialog box form displays nicely, but your script can't read the selected option. If you try to access the webcontrol.r1.value option, you get an error (see Figure 19-9).

Secret

Whenever you group an input field by naming all elements the same, it's treated as an array. You can't access individual elements of a group directly. Instead, you need to determine the size of the array (the number of elements in the group) and pick the one you are interested in.

Because there are three elements called r1, you need to treat r1 as an object array. Actually, in your template, there is no element called r1, but there are three elements called r1(0), r1(1), and r1(2). This is how you can read any group of input elements and determine the value of the checked one:

```
' read input
if TypeName(webcontrol)="Nothing" then
    MsgBox "You cancelled!"
else
for x=0 to (webcontrol.r1.length)-1
        if webcontrol.r1(x).checked then
            optionval = webcontrol.r1(x).value
    end if
next
MsgBox "You chose: " & optionval
end if
```

Option Dialog

Choose an Option!

- Option 1
- Option 2
- Option 3

OK

VBScript

You chose: Option 2

OK

Figure 19-9: Now you can read in the results from the options dialog box group.

Append this code to your script, and you are all set. Here's the complete script:

```
' 19-7.VBS

set tool = CreateObject("Web.dialog")

' current path
myname = WScript.ScriptFullName
cp = left(myname, InstrRev(myname, "\"))

' template
template = cp & "template6.htm"

' size dialog
tool.Resizable =false
tool.Width = 400
```

```
tool.Height = 200
tool.Title = "Option Dialog"

set webcontrol = tool.ShowDialog(template)

' read input
if TypeName(webcontrol)="Nothing" then
     MsgBox "You cancelled!"
else
     for x=0 to (webcontrol.r1.length)-1
          if webcontrol.r1(x).checked then
               optionval = webcontrol.r1(x).value
          end if
     next
     MsgBox "You chose: " & optionval
end if
```

Secret

Because the Web is based mainly on JavaScript, the HTML object model returns the number of elements in the group using the length property instead of the VBScript Count property. Still, your VBScript can use this property even though it doesn't follow VBScript naming conventions. A loop checks all elements in the group and returns the value of the element marked as checked.

You need to deal with element arrays only when you read form content from within a Web page using script statements. If you submit a form to some Web server, you don't need to care much. Submitting a form sends only the checked elements, so there won't be more than one r1 element, and you can access its value directly.

Summary

The WebBrowser control is a real gem. This chapter has shown you some of what it can do for you. The COM object I developed serves as a general-purpose dialog box container, and you have seen many examples on how to create your own dialog boxes using plain HTML templates.

This is a great foundation for teamwork. You can let a graphic designer create the dialog box design while you provide the COM object to host it.

Through advanced event handling, your COM container can be controlled entirely by your HTML template. You can even close the form window from inside your HTML script code.

Chapter 20

Internet and Communications

In This Chapter

▶ Connect and disconnect to the Internet by script automatically

▶ Establish FTP connections and retrieve FTP directory listings

▶ Download Web pages and FTP files automatically

▶ Upload FTP files from your local hard disk to your Web server

▶ Synchronize your local Web site with a remote Web server automatically

▶ Resolve IP addresses and host names using WinSock

In this chapter, learn how to add new scripting features that allow your scripts to automatically connect and disconnect to the Internet. Your scripts will even be able to resolve host names and transfer files between your local computer and Web servers using the built-in FTP capabilities.

Accessing the Internet

Wouldn't it be great to be able to connect to the Internet using scripts? This way, you could automatically retrieve information in regular intervals or upload files to your Web server.

Unfortunately, the Scripting Host offers next to no Internet support. This is surprising because Windows does contain all the functions necessary to connect, disconnect, and download files. Windows even contains all the functions necessary to do FTP file transfer. FTP file transfer is a method to send data across a TCP/IP network like the Internet. You can both download and upload any file you want.

In this chapter, you get all the scripting extensions necessary for full Internet access — a tremendously useful toolbox that you would have to pay a lot of money for if you bought it from third-party vendors.

Creating a universal Internet script extension

The script extension is just a COM object, and again it's created using the free Visual Basic CCE. You find the complete source code here: `\components\ internet\internet.vbp`. Take a look at it and change it any way you please.

To use the script extension, make sure you install the COM object `\install\internet\setup.exe`.

Connecting to the Internet

Regular scripts can connect to the Internet without any script extension (see Figure 20-1). All you need to do is supply a valid http address:

```
' 20-1.VBS

set wshshell = CreateObject("WScript.Shell")
wshshell.Run "http://www.altavista.com/"
```

However, this simple approach has a major limitation—the script can't establish the Internet connection itself but relies on your settings instead. If you dial into the Internet using a modem connection, you'll most likely end up with a dialog box asking for permission to dial. Even worse: Your script has no way of disconnecting the Internet connection once it is established. There's way too much manual work left for you.

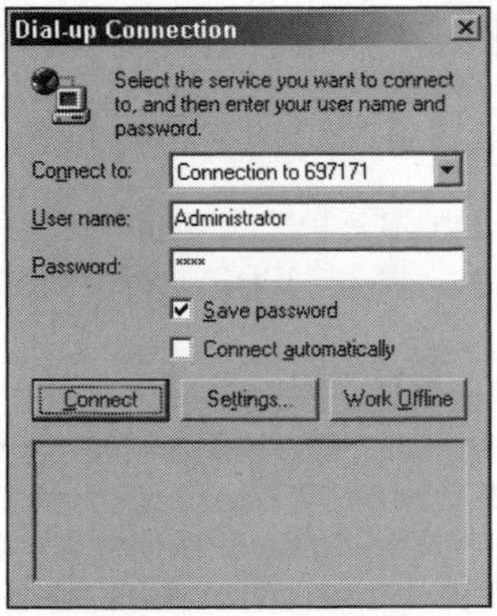

Figure 20-1: You need a way to bypass the connect dialog box and connect automatically.

So how can you connect to the Internet automatically, and how can you disconnect once your script is done?

Use your new script extension. The following script connects automatically and offers to disconnect at any time:

```
' 20-2.VBS

set tool = CreateObject("internet.communication")
set wshshell = CreateObject("WScript.Shell")

' automatically connect
if tool.ConnectInternet then
    wshshell.Run "http://www.altavista.com/"
    MsgBox "Click OK to close connection!", vbSystemModal
    if tool.DisconnectInternet then
        MsgBox "Connection closed."
    else
        MsgBox "Connection couldn't be closed down! " _
            & "It may be closed already!"
    end if
else
    MsgBox "Unable to connect to Internet. Is your modem turned on?"
end if
```

Closing the connection once the Web page is loaded

The previous script left it up to you to close the connection. You might want to close the connection yourself once the Web page is completely loaded. Try this:

```
' 20-3.VBS

set tool = CreateObject("internet.communication")
set ie = CreateObject("InternetExplorer.Application")

url = "www.altavista.com/"

' automatically connect
if tool.ConnectInternet then
    ie.navigate url
    do
    loop until ie.ReadyState=4
    ie.visible = true
    if not tool.DisconnectInternet then
        MsgBox "Warning: Connection could not be closed!"
    end if
else
    MsgBox "Unable to connect to Internet. Is your modem turned on?"
end if
```

This script connects to the Internet, loads a page, and disconnects immediately.

Secret

Use the InternetExplorer object to get much more granular control over the Internet. In the previous example, the script queried the ReadyState property. It returns 4 once the document is fully loaded.

Using FTP to download and upload files

FTP is the file transfer protocol. You can use it to download files from FTP servers and upload files to your own Web server. However, you need tools to get access to the FTP commands. That's bad because most tools don't support scripts, and they are expensive.

Fortunately, Windows already contains all the functions necessary to do FTP. Your script extension has wrapped them and made them accessible to your scripts. In this part, you gain complete control over Internet file handling.

General rules for accessing FTP

To do FTP, your script always follows the same set of steps:

1. Establish a connection to the Internet using `ConnectInternet`.

2. Establish a handle to the FTP server using `ConnectFTP`.

3. Call methods to manage the FTP server by supplying the handle to the FTP server you connected to.

4. Close the FTP server handle using `CloseHandle`.

5. Disconnect from the Internet using `DisconnectInternet`.

Let's take a look at some real-world examples.

Accessing an FTP server

You can access FTP servers anonymously. If you do, you can only connect to public servers, and most likely you are limited to downloading files only. On the other hand, you can authenticate yourself using a username and password and log on to the server as a specific user. Provided you have access to the server and the appropriate permissions, you'll now be able to do all kinds of stuff: for example, upload new files to your Web server or delete unnecessary files.

Use `ConnectFTP` to get access to any FTP server. If you just specify the FTP server name, the COM tool will connect you anonymously. If you specify an additional username and password, the tool tries to log on using your credentials. The result is always a handle. This handle is 0 if the connection request fails, and it's a number other than 0 if it succeeds. Use the handle to issue FTP commands to your server.

Retrieving an FTP directory listing

The first step should be a directory listing. Which files and folders are available on the FTP server you connected to? Have a look! The next script connects to the public server `ftp.microsoft.com` and retrieves the directory listing (see Figure 20-2):

```
' 20-4.VBS

set tool = CreateObject("internet.communication")

ftpdir = "ftp.microsoft.com"

' automatically connect
if tool.ConnectInternet then
    ' open FTP server
    handle = tool.ConnectFTP(ftpdir)
    dirlist = tool.Dir(handle)

    ' close connection
    tool.CloseHandle handle
    tool.DisconnectInternet

    ' display FTP directory
    MsgBox dirlist, vbInformation
else
    MsgBox "Unable to connect to Internet. Is your modem turned on?"
end if
```

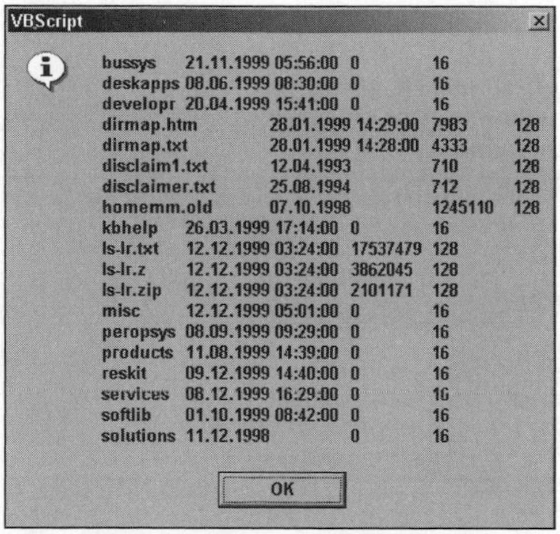

Figure 20-2: Retrieve information about FTP directory contents.

Trapping connect errors

You can further enhance your scripts by trapping errors in case the FTP connection can't be established. Use a mechanism like this:

```
    ' open FTP server
```

```
on error resume next
handle = tool.ConnectFTP(ftpdir)
if handle=0 then
     MsgBox "Connection failed!"
     WScript.Quit
end if
on error goto 0
```

Script 20-4.VBS returns information about files and folders according to the scheme outlined in Table 20-1.

Table 20-1   Information Retrieved from an FTP Server

Information	Description
File or Folder Name	Name of file or folder
File Date	Time stamp: When was the file written to the server?
File Size	Size of file in bytes
Attributes	File or folder attributes

The attributes listed in Table 20-2 give you additional information about the file or folder.

Table 20-2   File Attributes on FTP Servers

Attribute	Description
1	Write-protected
2	Hidden
4	System file
16	Folder
32	Shortcut
128	Compressed

You can either manually convert the information inside your script or leave this work to your script extension. Use FriendlyDir instead of Dir to retrieve a pre-formatted FTP directory listing (see Figure 20-3).

```
VBScript                                                         x

 (i)   /bussys           0 KB      DIR    21.11.1999 05:56:00
       /deskapps         0 KB      DIR    08.06.1999 08:30:00
       /developr         0 KB      DIR    20.04.1999 15:41:00
       dirmap.htm        7 KB      RW---K 28.01.1999 14:29:00
       dirmap.txt        4 KB      RW---K 28.01.1999 14:28:00
       Disclaim1.txt     0 KB      RW---K 12.04.1993
       disclaimer.txt    0 KB      RW---K 25.08.1994
       HOMEMM.old     1215 KB      RW---K 07.10.1998
       /KBHelp           0 KB      DIR    26.03.1999 17:14:00
       ls-lR.txt     17126 KB      RW---K 12.12.1999 03:24:00
       ls-lR.Z        3771 KB      RW---K 12.12.1999 03:24:00
       LS-LR.ZIP      2051 KB      RW---K 12.12.1999 03:24:00
       /MISC             0 KB      DIR    12.12.1999 05:01:00
       /peropsys         0 KB      DIR    08.09.1999 09:29:00
       /Products         0 KB      DIR    11.08.1999 14:39:00
       /ResKit           0 KB      DIR    09.12.1999 14:40:00
       /Services         0 KB      DIR    08.12.1999 16:29:00
       /Softlib          0 KB      DIR    01.10.1999 08:42:00
       /solutions        0 KB      DIR    11.12.1998

                        ┌──────────┐
                        │    OK    │
                        └──────────┘
```

Figure 20-3: FriendlyDir formats the directory listing.

Listing subfolders

The Dir method lists the current FTP directory by default. The current directory is the one you connected to. You can list any FTP directory, though. Just specify the relative or fully qualified folder name as second argument.

Secret

Relative filenames are relative to the current folder. Fully qualified filenames always work no matter which folder is selected as the current folder. They start with the FTP root folder and always begin with a "/" character.

However, there's a downside to this approach: Dir can't deal with spaces, and if you specify an invalid folder path, Dir returns an error protocol instead of the folder listing.

So don't use the second argument to select an FTP folder. Instead, change the current folder to the folder you want to list using ChDir. Then, use Dir to list this current folder.

Still, the second argument isn't worthless. Use it as a wildcard to select files. First, choose the folder you want to list using ChDir. Then, use Dir and specify the search filter using its second parameter.

The following script lists a subfolder called code and displays its content. Then, it uses *.VBS as filter to display VBS script files only (see Figure 20-4). Instead of Dir, it uses FriendlyDir to format the listing and make it more readable:

```
' 20-5.VBS

set tool = CreateObject("internet.communication")

ftpdir = "10.10.1.98"
```

```
' automatically connect
if tool.ConnectInternet then
    ' open FTP server
    handle = tool.ConnectFTP(ftpdir)
    ok = tool.ChDir(handle, "/code")
    if ok then
        MsgBox tool.Dir(handle)
        MsgBox tool.Dir(handle, "*.VBS")
    else
        MsgBox "ChDir failed: no such folder!"
    end if

    ' close connection
    tool.CloseHandle handle
    tool.DisconnectInternet
else
    MsgBox "Unable to connect to Internet. Is your modem turned on?"
end if
```

Secret

The script uses an IP address instead of a domain name. Obviously, you need to change this information to match a valid server. Using IP addresses instead of domain names can be useful in your company's intranet or between locally connected development environments.

VBScript			
20-1.VBS	2/20/1997 3:23:00 PM	103	128
20-10.VBS	2/20/1997 3:26:00 PM	262	128
20-11.VBS	2/20/1997 3:27:00 PM	276	128
20-2.VBS	2/20/1997 3:24:00 PM	515	128
20-3.VBS	2/20/1997 3:24:00 PM	461	128
20-4.VBS	2/20/1997 3:24:00 PM	457	128
20-5.VBS	12/13/1999 9:36:00 AM	528	128
20-6.VBS	2/20/1997 3:25:00 PM	760	128
20-7.VBS	2/20/1997 3:25:00 PM	780	128
20-8.VBS	2/20/1997 3:26:00 PM	4989	128
20-9.VBS	2/20/1997 3:26:00 PM	180	128

OK

Figure 20-4: Filter FTP listings using wildcards like *.

Receiving extended error information

Both Dir and FriendlyDir return extended error information if the FTP server is unable to provide the requested directory listing. Most likely, you either specified a folder that doesn't exist or you don't have the necessary permissions. The error message clarifies the issue and helps to identify the cause (see Figure 20-5).

VBScript

(i) 200 Type set to A.
     200 PORT command successful.
     150 Opening ASCII mode data connection for /bin/ls.
     550 testing: The system cannot find the file specified.

     [OK]

Figure 20-5: You'll receive error information if the FTP listing isn't accessible.

Downloading FTP files

To download FTP files from a server, use GetFile and provide the handle to your FTP server. The next example retrieves the file DISCLAIMER.TXT from the Microsoft server. The connection will be closed the moment the file is transferred to your disk, and the script opens the file after a successful download:

```
' 20-6.VBS

set tool = CreateObject("internet.communication")

ftpdir = "ftp.microsoft.com"
ftpfile = "disclaimer.txt"
newfile = "C:\msdisc.txt"

' automatically connect
if tool.ConnectInternet then

    ' open FTP server
    handle = tool.ConnectFTP(ftpdir)
    ok = tool.GetFile(handle, ftpfile, newfile)

    ' close connection
    tool.CloseHandle handle
    tool.DisconnectInternet

    ' process results locally:
    if ok then
        MsgBox "File has been downloaded and saved as """ _
            & newfile & """"
        ' open file:
        set wshshell = CreateObject("WScript.Shell")
        wshshell.Run """" & newfile & """"
    else
        MsgBox "Download error: " & tool.GetLastError
    end if

else
    MsgBox "Unable to connect to Internet. Is your modem turned on?"
end if
```

Secret

Although your script closes down the Internet connection as soon as no further data transfers are required, the script still is not foolproof. What if the server is so busy that the download takes hours to complete? Use a timeout. You can't use a general script timeout, though, because it would shut down your script without closing the Internet connection. Instead, use the timer control introduced in Chapter 17.

Uploading FTP files

Uploading files requires special permissions, so in most cases you need to log on to the FTP server with special credentials. The following script uploads the file C:\MYFILE.HTM to a sample server called ftp.wininfo.de. Exchange server names and upload filenames and credentials, with the appropriate names and credentials you want to use.

```
' 20-7.VBS

set tool = CreateObject("internet.communication")

ftpdir = "ftp.wininfo.de"
uploadfile = "C:\mypage.htm"
ftpname = "mypage.htm"
username = "itsme"
password = "secret"

' automatically connect
if tool.ConnectInternet then

    ' open FTP server
    handle = tool.ConnectFTP(ftpdir, username, password)
    ok = tool.PutFile(handle, uploadfile, ftpname)

    ' close connection
    tool.CloseHandle handle
    if MsgBox("Close Internet Connection?", vBYesNo) = vbYes then
        tool.DisconnectInternet
    end if

    ' process results locally:
    if ok then
        MsgBox "File has been uploaded and saved as """ _
            & ftpname & """"
    else
        MsgBox "Upload error: " & tool.GetLastError
    end if
else
    MsgBox "Unable to connect to Internet. Is your modem turned on?"
end if
```

Secret

FTP is your file transport department. Not only can you manage FTP services, you can also upload new HTML files to your Web server. Just make sure that your FTP base directory equals your Web server base directory or that your Web server base directory is accessible via FTP, and upload HTML files to your Web server. The moment those files are uploaded, you can view them as regular Web pages.

Synchronizing local folders and Web folders

Most Web-site developers develop on their local machines. Once a Web site is finished, it must be transferred to the real Web server. This is no big deal, because countless FTP tools allow you to upload files and folders.

However, most of these tools can only transport data. It's impossible to synchronize local folders and Web folders. Synchronizing means you only transfer files that have changed. That's important!

Imagine you have uploaded your Web site and made minor changes later on to your local copy. With the regular tools, you would have to upload your entire site again. If you can synchronize the folders, only the true changes have to be uploaded — and this saves tremendous time and costs.

Your scripts can easily do the job. You now have methods to retrieve a Web folder directory listing, and your script can compare this directory listing to your local folder. By comparing file size and file time, the script can identify changes and selectively upload only the new or changed files (see Figure 20-6).

Tip

This script works so well that I use it to completely manage my own Web site. I maintain a local copy of my Web Site and make changes only to the local copy. Whenever I have changed something, I launch my script. It automatically takes care of updating any necessary files and minimizes online time. I've "hard-coded" all the necessary connection information into my script so I don't have to enter anything to invoke the update process.

```
ftploq - Notepad                                           _|□|x|
File  Edit  Format  Help
12:44:18 AM      CONNECT automatically to Internet
12:44:18 AM      ACCESS GRANTED to FTP Server 10.10.1.1
12:44:18 AM      FILE ADDED /20-1.VBS
12:44:19 AM      FILE ADDED /20-10.VBS
12:44:19 AM      FILE ADDED /20-11.VBS
12:44:19 AM      FILE ADDED /20-2.VBS
12:44:19 AM      FILE ADDED /20-3.VBS
12:44:19 AM      FILE ADDED /20-4.VBS
12:44:20 AM      FILE ADDED /20-5.VBS
12:44:20 AM      FILE ADDED /20-6.VBS
12:44:20 AM      FILE ADDED /20-7.VBS
12:44:20 AM      FILE ADDED /20-8.VBS
12:44:20 AM      FILE ADDED /20-9.VBS
12:44:20 AM      CLOSED FTP connection
12:44:22 AM      4 secs online, 8.9 KB transferred, 2.24 KB/s.
```

Figure 20-6: Automatically upload entire local Web sites.

```
' 20-8.VBS

set args = WScript.Arguments
if args.Count=0 then
    dirname = InputBox("Please enter local folder path")
else
    dirname = args(0)
end if

set fs = CreateObject("Scripting.FileSystemObject")
set tool = CreateObject("internet.communication")

' does specified local folder exist?
if not fs.FolderExists(dirname) then
    ' no, quit!
    MsgBox "Folder """ & dirname & """ not found!"
    WScript.Quit
end if

' ask details about destination FTP server
ftpdir = InputBox("Please enter base FTP directory")
username = InputBox("Please enter user name")
password = InputBox("Please enter password")


' find out subfolder
if right(ftpdir,1)="/" then ftpdir = left(ftpdir, len(ftpdir)-1)

pos = Instr(ftpdir, "/")
if pos = 0 then
    subfolderpath = ""
else
    subfolderpath = mid(ftpdir, pos)
end if

' log results here:
logfile = "C:\ftplog.txt"

' count transfer volume:
transfer = 0

' create log file:
set reportfile = fs.CreateTextFile(logfile, true)


' ### now start synchronizing ###

' automatically connect
if tool.ConnectInternet then
    ' log start
    starttime = time
    Report "CONNECT automatically to Internet"
```

```
' open FTP server
on error resume next
handle = tool.ConnectFTP(ftpdir, username, password)

if not err.number=0 then
    Report "Error accessing server: " & tool.GetLastError
    Reportfile.close
    Showreport
    WScript.Quit
end if

Report "ACCESS GRANTED to FTP Server " & ftpdir

' synchronize folder
Synchronize dirname, subfolderpath

' close connection
tool.CloseHandle handle
Report "CLOSED FTP connection"

if MsgBox("Close Internet Connection?", vBYesNo) = vbYes then
    tool.DisconnectInternet
    Report "DISCONNECT Internet Connection"
end if

' calculate statistics
duration = DateDiff("s", starttime, time)
transferKB = FormatNumber(transfer/1024,1)
speed = FormatNumber((transfer/duration)/1024,2)
Report duration & " secs online, " & transferKB _
& " KB transferred, " & speed & " KB/s."
else
    MsgBox "Unable to connect to Internet. Is your modem turned on?"
    Report "Error: Unable to establish Internet connection"
end if

reportfile.close
ShowReport

sub Synchronize(local, web)
    ' access local folder
    set folder = fs.GetFolder(local)

    ' create dictionary to store the file names of web folder
    set dict = CreateObject("Scripting.Dictionary")
    ' compare case-insensitive
    dict.CompareMode = 1

    ' get current web folder dir listing
    ' first, change current directory using absolute path name
    ' next, get current directory listing
    tool.ChDir handle, "/" & web
    dirraw = tool.Dir(handle)
```

```
' split into individual lines
dirlist = Split(dirraw, vbCrLf)

' process each file
for each entry in dirlist
     ' split info details per line
     entryinfo = Split(entry, vbTab)
     ' check whether entry is a file:
     if (Fix(entryinfo(3)) and 16)=0 then
          ' if so, add to dict filename, modifydate
          dict.Add entryinfo(0), entryinfo(1)
     end if
next
if web = "" then
     fill = ""
else
     fill = "/"
end if

' check each file in local folder
for each file in folder.files
     ' exists on web server?
     if dict.Exists(file.name) then
          ' yes, check modify date
          timestamp = dict.Item(file.name)
          filetime = GetFileTime(file)
          if CDate(timestamp)<filetime then
               ' older, replace
               ok = tool.PutFile(handle, file.path, file.name)
               if ok then
                    Report "FILE UPDATE " & web & file.name
                    transfer = transfer + file.size
               else
                    Report "Update failed for " & web _
                         & file.name & ": " & tool.GetLastError
               end if
          else
               Report "FILE UNCHANGED " & web & file.name _
                    & " (up-to-date)"
          end if
     else
          ' file missing on web server
          ok = tool.PutFile(handle, file.path, file.name)
          if ok then
               Report "FILE ADDED " & web & "/" & file.name
               transfer = transfer + file.size
          else
               Report "Couldn't create " & web & file.name _
                    & ": " & tool.GetLastError
          end if
     end if
next
```

```
            ' recursively synchronize all subfolders
            for each subdir in folder.subfolders
                foldername = subdir.name
                if web = "" then
                    webfolder = foldername
                else
                    webfolder = web & "/" & foldername
                end if

                ' attempt to create subfolder on web server
                on error resume next
                ok = tool.MakeDir(handle, "/" & webfolder)
                on error goto 0
                if ok then
                    Report "CREATED DIR " & webfolder
                else
                    Report "OPENED DIR " & webfolder
                end if
                Synchronize subdir.path, webfolder
            next
        end sub

function GetFileTime(fileobj)
        ' get file time and return dummy file time if unavailable
        on error resume next
        GetFileTime = fileobj.DateLastModified
        if not err.number=0 then
            GetFileTime = CDate("1/1/80")
            err.clear
        end if
end function

sub Report(text)
        ' write to report
        reportfile.WriteLine time & vbTab & text
end sub

sub ShowReport
        set wshshell = CreateObject("WScript.Shell")
        wshshell.run """" & logfile & """"
end sub
```

Secret

The Dir method does have one major limitation. If you provide an FTP path, you can't use blanks. That's bad, but fortunately, there's a work-around. Change the current FTP folder to the folder you want to list—ChDir. Then, call Dir without a folder path to list the current folder. Wildcards are the reason behind the Dir limitation. Dir supports wildcards and interprets blanks as end-of-line.

The script recursively searches all subfolders in the folder you supplied and compares the files with the files on your FTP server. Outdated or missing files are uploaded and the script will create any necessary folders, as well as reconstruct the entire folder hierarchy on your Web server. The entire process is documented, and at the end you receive a detailed log report including all action taken, the overall online time, data transferred, and transfer rate (see Figure 20-7).

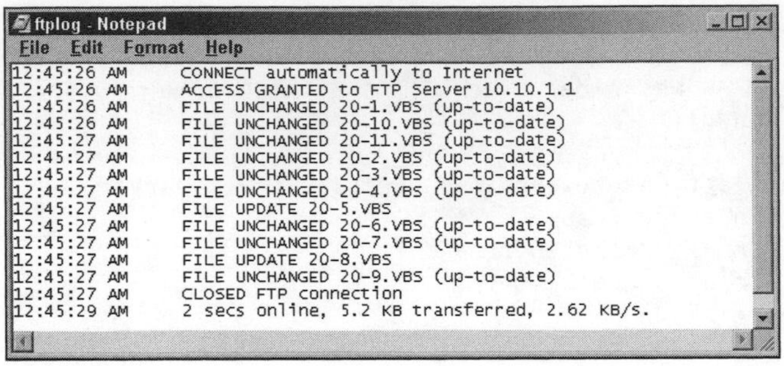

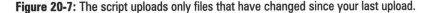

Figure 20-7: The script uploads only files that have changed since your last upload.

To successfully use this script, you should keep an eye on the following aspects:

■ Make sure the time on your local system and on your Web server is synchronized. The script relies on the time stamp. If the script updates files every time, use the `Dir` method described previously to check the time stamp of the files on your FTP server. Most likely, your FTP server is "ahead" in terms of time relative to your local system. Adjust the time on either system. Note, however, that existing files won't change their time stamps. You need to change files and save them again in order to write new time stamps.

■ Make sure you have the appropriate permissions. Most likely, you need to enable write access on your FTP server before you can upload any files. If you are using an MS Internet Information Server, use the IIS Management Console, select your FTP Service, right-click it, and choose Properties. Then, select the Base Directory and enable write access.

■ If the report shows failures to create files, make sure there's enough storage space left on your FTP server.

■ The script copies the content of the local folder you specified into the base FTP folder you provided. If you want the root folder to be created on your FTP server, then store the folder in another folder and specify this parent folder.

■ When developing Web sites, make sure to use relative path names instead of absolute path names wherever possible. You should try to avoid absolute path names at all. If you don't, you might need to do a lot of adjustments for your Web site to match the different IP addresses or domain names used by the "real" Web server.

Drag a folder onto your script icon to synchronize it with your FTP server.

Miscellaneous Internet Methods

Your Internet script extension contains some additional methods.
The following sections outline some useful ones.

Determining Internet connection type

`ConnectionState` reveals the kind of Internet connection your computer
currently uses (see Figure 20-8):

```
' 20-9.VBS

set tool = CreateObject("Internet.communication")
types = Split(",Modem,Network,Proxy,Modem busy", ",")
MsgBox "Connection type: " _
& types(tool.ConnectionState and not &HFFF8)
```

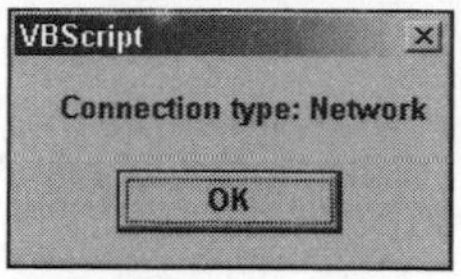

```
VBScript                    [x]

Connection type: Network

        [   OK   ]
```

Figure 20-8: Find out how your system is connected to the Internet.

Determining host names

Suppose you know the IP address of some Internet server and would like
to know the host name. Then use `HostByAddress`.

Secret

The host name isn't the same as the domain name. Instead, the host name is
the name of the server hosting the Web site. It may be identical to the domain
name you use to surf to the site, but chances are it is completely different.

```
' 20-10.VBS

set tool = CreateObject("Internet.communication")
ip = InputBox("Please enter IP-Address!")
tool.WinsockInit
tool.ConnectInternet
hostname = tool.HostByAddress(ip)
tool.WinsockQuit
tool.DisconnectInternet
MsgBox "Host name: " & hostname
```

This script uses a Winsock function. To be able to do that, it needs to initialize WinSock first: `WinsockInit`. Don't forget to close down your WinSock session: `WinsockQuit`.

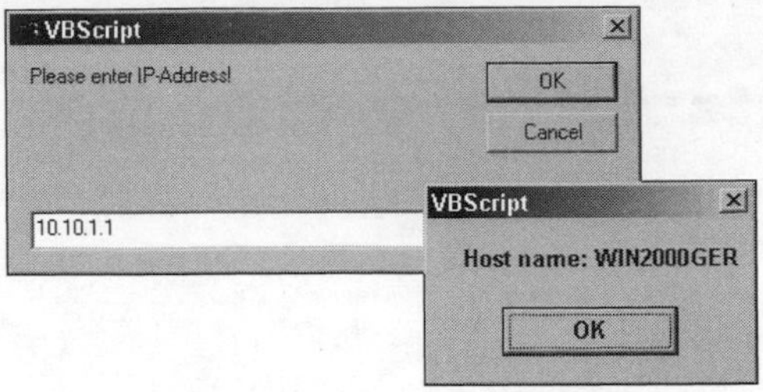

Figure 20-9: IP address resolving works in local networks, too.

Determining IP address

Maybe you know some domain name and would like to know the IP address. `HostByName` does the job:

```
' 20-11.VBS

set tool = CreateObject("Internet.communication")
dn = InputBox("Please enter domain name!",,"www.microsoft.com")
tool.WinsockInit
tool.ConnectInternet
ipadd = tool.HostByName(dn)
tool.WinsockQuit
tool.DisconnectInternet
MsgBox "IP-Address: " & ipadd
```

Secret

Both methods work for local networks, too. Instead of an Internet domain name, use the local machine name to retrieve its IP address (see Figure 20-10).

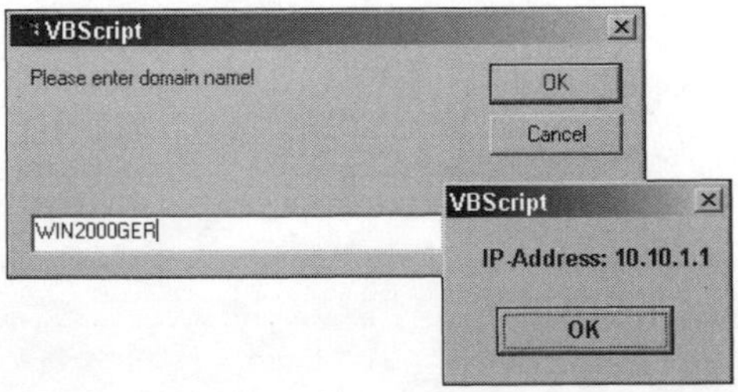

Figure 20-10: The other way around: resolving host names

Script Extension Internet Methods

Your new Internet script extension contains so many useful new methods, you'll need a way to keep track. Table 20-3 and Table 20-4 document both FTP and WinSock methods provided by your new COM object.

Table 20-3	FTP Methods
Method **Description**	
Function ConnectInternet ([ByVal mode As BooleanTrue]) As Boolean	Dials into the Internet
Function DisconnectInternet As Boolean	Disconnects Internet connection
Function OpenInternet As Long	Initializes Internet commands, returns handle
Function Connect(ByVal handle As Long, ByVal url As String, [ByVal user As String], [ByVal password As String]) As Long	Connects to FTP server, returns handle to server (ConnectInternet required)
Function ConnectFTP(ByVal ftppath As String, [ByVal user As String], [ByVal password As String]) As Long	Connects to FTP server, calls ConnectInternet internally
Sub CloseInternet	Closes Internet connection established by ConnectFTP
Sub CloseHandle(ByVal handle As Long)	Closes handle returned by OpenInternet and Connect
Function DeleteFile(ByVal connect As Long, ByVal name As String) As Boolean	Deletes FTP file; supply handle to FTP server retrieved by Connect or ConnectFTP
Function Dir(ByVal connect As Long, [ByVal path As String"*.*"]) ConnectFTP	Lists current directory listing; supply handle to FTP server retrieved by Connect or
Function FriendlyDir(ByVal connect As Long, [ByVal path As String]) As String	Same as DIR, formatted output
Function ChDir(ByVal connect As Long, ByVal dirname As String) As Boolean	Changes current FTP folder; supply handle to FTP server retrieved by Connect or ConnectFTP

Continued

Table 20-3 *(continued)*

Method	Description

`Function MakeDir`
`(ByVal connect As Long,`
`ByVal path As String) As Boolean`
	Creates new FTP folder; supply handle to FTP server retrieved by `Connect` or `ConnectFTP`

`Function RemoveDir`
`(ByVal connection`
`As Long, ByVal dirname`
`As Long) As Boolean`
	Deletes FTP folder; supply handle to FTP server retrieved by `Connect` or `ConnectFTP`

`Function PutFile(ByVal connect`
`As Long, ByVal source As String,`
`ByVal Dest As String) As Boolean`
	Uploads file to FTP server; supply handle to FTP server retrieved by `Connect` or `ConnectFTP`

`Function GetFile(ByVal connect`
`As Long, ByVal source As String,`
`ByVal Dest As String) As Boolean`
	Downloads file from FTP server; supply handle to FTP server retrieved by `Connect` or `ConnectFTP`

`Function RenameFile`
`(ByVal connection As Long,`
`ByVal oldName As String,`
`ByVal NewName As String)`
`As Boolean`
	Renames file; supply handle to FTP server retrieved by `Connect` or `ConnectFTP`

`Function GetExtendedError` `As String`	Reads extended error information of last error
`Function GetLastError As String`	Reads description of last error
`Function GetLastErrorNumber` `As Long`	Returns last error number

`Function Translate`
`(ByVal errnr As Long)`
`As String`
	Translates error number into clear text

Table 20-4 WinSock Methods

Method	Description
`Sub WinsockInit`	Initializes WinSock
`Sub WinsockQuit`	Closes WinSock session
`Function ConnectionState As Long`	Retrieves current connection type

Method	Description
`Function HostByAddress (ByVal sAddress As String) As String`	Returns host name, supplies IP address
`Function HostByName (ByVal Host As String) As String`	Returns IP address, supplies host name

Summary

This chapter is extremely useful for anyone who needs to transfer data. The Internet methods work in intranets, too.

Amazingly, Windows already contains all the functions necessary to do complete FTP file transfer. You don't need extra expensive tools. In fact, once you get accustomed to the new script methods, you can adjust the sample scripts to serve almost any purpose. The synchronization script has already proven to be far more functional than most commercially available products. Again, scripting has one advantage no commercial product can beat—it allows you to make changes and append the source in any way you please.

Chapter 21

Fax, Printer, Scanner, and Graphics

In This Chapter

▶ Discover Kodak Imaging and how you can control its functions by script

▶ Check your TWAIN scanner support, select picture sources, and scan images

▶ Automate scanning and scan in hundreds of images using batch automation

▶ Print any image and create your own scan-print-photocopy tool

▶ Scale printouts to fit the page

▶ Load, print, and save any picture file

▶ Rotate, scale, and zoom pictures, and create button faces from scanned images automatically

▶ Generate comprehensive thumbnail preview pages and organize your picture archives

▶ Convert the graphics format and choose compression and color depth

▶ Reveal compression settings and size information for any picture file, and repair picture file types automatically

---

All Windows versions come with a secret add-on called Kodak Imaging. It's fully scriptable, and in this chapter, you' learn how to use it to scan images from a TWAIN scanner and to print or save the images.

Say "Hi" to Kodak Imaging

Microsoft has included a tremendously useful tool in all 32-bit Windows versions, and it's called the Kodak Imaging tool (see Figure 21-1). This little tool hides in the Accessories program group (if it's missing, you can just install it from your Windows CD by using the Control Panel Software module and choosing the Windows Setup tab).

The Imaging tool is part of the base services offered by Windows. Just as WordPad gives you out-of-the-box access to WinWord documents, Imaging allows you to view graphics files, fax messages, and scan in pictures from any TWAIN-compatible flatbed scanner.

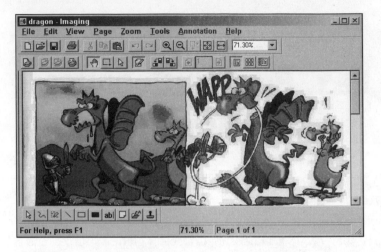

Figure 21-1: Kodak Imaging is a multi-purpose image viewing utility included with Windows.

At first sight, the Imaging tool doesn't seem to be special, but it is. It's fully scriptable. And it provides your scripts with new methods to read in pictures from any TWAIN picture source, as well as to print them out.

A closer look

Internally, the Imaging tool consists of a number of COM objects, as shown in Table 21-1.

Table 21-1	Components of Kodak Imaging
COM Object	*Description*
IMGADMIN.OCX	Administration tool
IMGEDIT.OCX	Display and print images, add notations
IMGSCAN.OCX	TWAIN-compatible scanner support
IMGTHUMB.OCX	Thumbnail view

Secret

Some Windows versions come with a very detailed help file that provides all the information necessary to script the components (see Figure 21-2). Search for IMGOCXD.HLP. Even if you don't find IMGOCXD.HLP on your system, you still can retrieve all the methods and properties available. Just use script 5-12 and enter the filenames listed above.

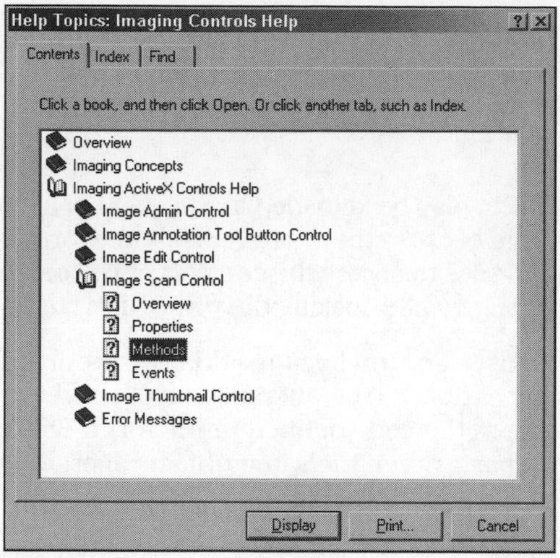

Figure 21-2: Kodak Imaging provides a full documentation.

Getting access to the control

You can't script the Kodak tools directly. Instead, you need to either embed them into a Web page or use them as controls inside a custom COM object. As you might suspect, I have created a sample COM object. It basically wraps the controls and provides public methods and properties your script can access. Install \install\scan\setup.exe (full source code is provided at \components\scan\scan.vbp).

Watch out because there are many different versions of Kodak Imaging around. If your source code won't compile and instead complains about illegal methods, then you need to replace the Imaging controls on the form with the controls installed on your system.

To do so, delete the controls from the form and then right-click the tool bar. Choose Components, and in the dialog box, click Browse. Now, search for the files listed in Table 21-1 and add them to your toolbar. At last, add those controls back to your form. Now you're done.

But there's an even easier way. You can install the pre-built COM object without recompiling it.

A word of caution

Take a look at the COM object source code. It's not complicated—the Imaging tool handles the difficult parts. Still, you need to be aware of some very important design rules.

The COM object places the Imaging controls on a separate form. This is done so you can display the edit control as a dialog box. However, there's a strict rule — always place the code managing the controls into the same object that hosts the controls. If you don't, you may experience protection faults and blue screens.

The reason is simple. The form may be unloaded in the event of an error. The controls aren't there anymore because they "lived" inside the form. If some other part of your COM object still tries to access the controls, it will send data to a memory address that's no longer valid, making the protection fault necessary.

Still, you need code in the User Control because this is the only place you can make internal functions accessible to the outside world. However, the code in the User Control only "wraps" the code defined in the form. This is okay. Just make sure all the complex parts are in the same object together with the Imaging controls they refer to.

Finding out if TWAIN support is available

Kodak Imaging requires that TWAIN software be installed on your system (see Figure 21-3). Most scanners and a lot of other imaging sources come with TWAIN drivers. To make sure, use your new COM object and find out:

![VBScript dialog box reading "TWAIN support is installed. Check out your scan sources!" with an OK button.]

Figure 21-3: Find out whether you have TWAIN support.

```
' 21-1.VBS

set tool = CreateObject("twain.manager")
ok = tool.ScannerAvailable
if ok then
    MsgBox "TWAIN support is installed. Check out your scan sources!"
    tool.SelectScanner
else
    MsgBox "No TWAIN support detected. Get a " _
        & "TWAIN-compliant Scanner!", vbExclamation
end if
```

If TWAIN support is detected, the script calls SelectScanner. This invokes a built-in dialog box that lists all TWAIN-compliant imaging sources available. If no TWAIN support was detected, you can't proceed. Get a TWAIN-compliant imaging device first.

Secret

Although many different imaging devices can be controlled via TWAIN, the Kodak Imaging tool specializes in scanners. You may or may not be able to use a digital camera or other devices. Non-compliant devices generate benign error messages.

Scanning Pictures

With the help of your new COM component, your scripts can now scan pages. There are many useful real-world tasks you can now master. For example, you can create your own little photocopy machine, or you can batch-scan a whole series of pictures without having to click too many buttons.

Saving scanned pictures to disk

The next script shows how to scan a picture and save it to disk. The script is pretty straightforward because it leaves the difficult stuff to the Imaging tool:

```
' 21-2.VBS

set tool = CreateObject("twain.manager")

' check whether twain support is available
if not tool.ScannerAvailable then
     MsgBox "No TWAIN support!", vbCritical
     WScript.Quit
end if

' fill in information
filename = "C:\mypic.jpg"

' scan and save as bmp graphic
tool.FileType = 3
' 1: TIFF (default)
' 2: AWD (Win 98 Fax format)
' 3: BMP

' tell control how to store
tool.PageOption = 6
' 0: create new picture. Error if picture already exists
' 1: create new picture. Ask if picture already exists (default)
' 2: append to existing picture
' 3: insert into existing picture at position specified by page
' 4: overwrite existing picture. If picture doesn't exist, error
' 5: overwrite existing picture, ask for permission. Error if
'          picture doesn't yet exist
' 6: always overwrite

' tell control how to scan
tool.ScanTo = 1
' 0: display image only (default)
' 1: display and write to disk
' 2: write to disk
' 3: write to disk using template and display
' 4: write to disk using template
' 5: fax image (fax software must be installed)

' show scanner setup?
tool.ShowSetup = true
```

```
' show quality dialog?
tool.ShowScanPreferences

' ok, scan page
tool.ScanPage(filename)

' now, display the scanned page in your favorite drawing program
set wshshell = CreateObject("WScript.Shell")
wshshell.run """" & filename & """"
```

This script scans in a page and displays it in your favorite drawing program. Run launches the file you scanned and then passes it to the program associated with its file type. If there's no program associated, Run fails.

Secret

The dialog boxes all come from your TWAIN scanner driver. They may look different on your system. Most scan dialog boxes feature a preview function. You can select part of the pre-scanned image and scan only the selected area. Note, however, that sometimes dialog boxes may be hidden behind other unnecessary windows, so it's a good idea to close them. The reason for this odd behavior is obvious — you are calling another process, and beginning with Windows 98, Microsoft doesn't allow external processes to focus their own windows as they please. But you've already seen how you can work around this issue. All you need to do is to decrease the focus lock time to zero.

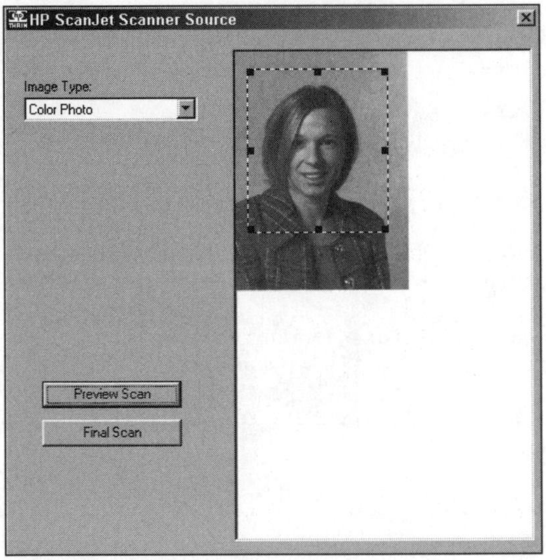

Figure 21-4: The scanner dialog box may look different and is provided by your TWAIN driver.

Automated scanning

The previous script displays all kinds of scan dialog boxes. Scan dialog boxes give you very detailed control over the scan quality, but you might want to automate scanning. First try to scan with the built-in defaults and see if it works (see Figure 21-5):

```
' 21-3.VBS

set tool = CreateObject("twain.manager")

' check whether twain support is available
if not tool.ScannerAvailable then
    MsgBox "No TWAIN support!", vbCritical
    WScript.Quit
end if

filename = "C:\mypic.jpg"
tool.FileType = 3
tool.PageOption = 6
tool.ScanTo = 1
tool.ShowSetup = false
tool.ScanPage(filename)
set wshshell = CreateObject("WScript.Shell")
wshshell.run """" & filename & """"
```

Undocumented

You may not be pleased with the default values. However, there's no way to set color options and other scan quality related issues remotely. You have two choices. One, you can display the official scan dialog box once, using ShowSetup = true. For all subsequent scans, you should turn the dialog off. Your scanner will now use the settings you chose in the dialog box for as long as your script runs. Or two, you can use SendKeys to automate any dialog box. Refer to Chapter 10 to find out how to switch to dialog boxes and send keystrokes.

Figure 21-5: The script can open the scanned picture only if you have drawing software installed.

Scanning large numbers of pictures

Perhaps you want to scan in a whole lot of pictures. For example, you might want to digitize some paperwork or put your family photo gallery onto your Web site. Scripts are the perfect solution. In addition, the Imaging tool supports template scanning. Template scanning means the tool automatically creates filenames with serial numbers.

Tip

Get yourself a document feeder. This way, scanning is truly automated, and you don't even need to place the pictures on your scanner anymore.

The next script scans as many pictures as you like and assigns unique filenames:

```
' 21-4.VBS

set tool = CreateObject("twain.manager")

' check whether twain support is available
if not tool.ScannerAvailable then
     MsgBox "No TWAIN support!", vbCritical
     WScript.Quit
end if

filename = "C:\pics\pic"
' bmp
tool.FileType = 3
' overwrite
tool.PageOption = 6
' template scan
tool.ScanTo = 4
' show setup for first picture scan
tool.ShowSetup = true
do
tool.ScanPage(filename)
' don't show setup for rest of scans
tool.ShowSetup = false

msg = "Scan completed! Scan another picture?"
answer = MsgBox(msg, vbYesNo + vbQuestion)
loop until answer = vbNo

MsgBox "Done."
```

The script invokes the scanning user interface only once: This way, you can specify the scan options. Your scanner uses these settings for all subsequent scans. Note that this time the script doesn't specify a filename. Instead, it provides a filename template. The Imaging tool stores all pictures in the folder C:\pics and uses pic as template. The individual files are called pic00000.jpg, pic00001.jpg, etc.

Note

Make sure the folder you want to store the pictures in really exists. If it's missing, the script will complain.

Scanning pictures with the preview function

The Imaging components can do much more than just scanning. If you want to, you can use the edit control to display scanned images and use the thumb control to show thumbnail previews of scanned pictures. However, these features are a different story.

The COM component demonstrates how to link a scan control to the edit control. This allows for actually viewing the scan as it takes place (see Figure 21-6). Make sure you have set ShowSetup to false because otherwise the official scan dialog box will cover your own scanning preview.

```
' 21-5.VBS

set tool = CreateObject("twain.manager")

' check whether twain support is available
if not tool.ScannerAvailable then
    MsgBox "No TWAIN support!", vbCritical
    WScript.Quit
end if

filename = "C:\mypic.jpg"
tool.FileType = 3
tool.PageOption = 6
tool.ScanTo = 1
tool.ShowSetup = false
tool.Width = 600
tool.Height = 400
tool.ScanPageUI(filename)
set wshshell = CreateObject("WScript.Shell")
wshshell.run """" & filename & """"
```

The preview window closes automatically after scanning is complete. If you want, you can easily change the COM source code to provide an additional Close button.

Figure 21-6: Watch the scan happen: The custom dialog box shows the scan in real-time.

Because we are talking about scripts, and scripts are all about automation, your dialog box needs to close without user interaction.

You can set the size of your preview window to anything you like. Use the Width and Height properties.

Printing Scanned Images

Scanning pictures is a cool feature, but it's only partially useful if you can't print your scanned images. Fortunately, the Imaging control provides printing capabilities, too.

Your personal photocopy machine

Save your trips to the copy shop. Instead, tie together your scanner and your printer, and create your own photocopy machine. If you own a color printer, you can even copy in full-color. If you install some fax software, you can print to the faxmodem and get a "real" fax machine.

```
' 21-6.VBS

set tool = CreateObject("twain.manager")

' check whether twain support is available
if not tool.ScannerAvailable then
     MsgBox "No TWAIN support!", vbCritical
     WScript.Quit
end if

filename = "C:\mypic.jpg"
tool.FileType = 3
tool.PageOption = 6
tool.ScanTo = 1
tool.ShowSetup = true
tool.Width = 600
tool.Height = 400
tool.ScanPageUI(filename)
tool.PrintImage
```

This is all you need. PrintImage prints the scanned image to your default printer and scales the picture to fit the page. If you want to select printer options first, use PrintImageUI instead. This displays the usual printer dialog box (see Figure 21-7). The printer dialog box has a special Option button that allows you to choose between different scale modes (see Figure 21-8).

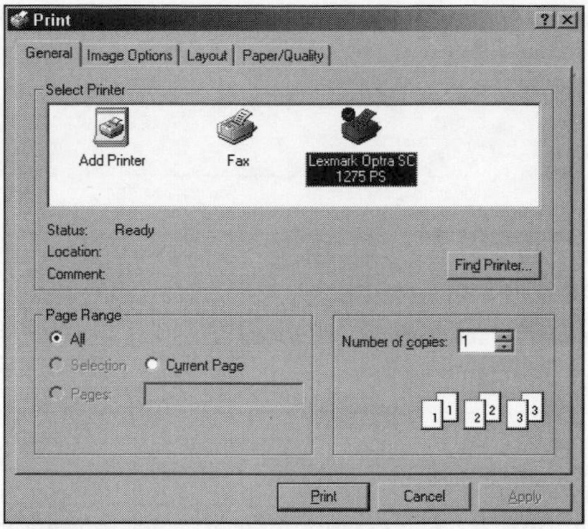

Figure 21-7: Use the official print dialog box to print your images.

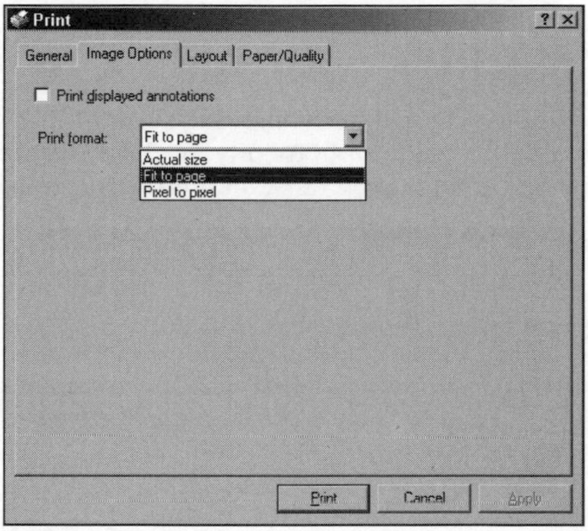

Figure 21-8: Your print dialog box may look different: You can always expand the image full-page.

You can specify the scale modes with `PrintImage`, too. Use the values shown in Table 21-2.

Table 21-2	Printer Options
Value	**Description**
0	Print image 1:1 (image appears smaller than original because printer pixels are smaller than display pixels)
1	Print image in original size
2	Fit to page (default)

Tip   The `PrintImage` and `PrintImageU` methods work completely independently from the scanning methods. You can use both methods to print any graphics file. For example, to print a .jpg graphic as a full-screen graphic, use `PrintImage 2, "mypic.jpg"`. To print it using the print dialog box, write `PrintImageUI "mypic.jpg"`.

A photocopy machine with editing functions

Maybe you'd like to edit the scanned image before you print it. It's easy to add image-editing capabilities to your photocopy machine. Just load the picture into your favorite graphics program, edit it, save the changes, and print it out. Here's an example:

```
' 21-7.VBS

set tool = CreateObject("twain.manager")

' check whether twain support is available
if not tool.ScannerAvailable then
    MsgBox "No TWAIN support!", vbCritical
    WScript.Quit
end if

filename = "C:\mypic.jpg"
tool.FileType = 3
tool.PageOption = 6
tool.ScanTo = 1
tool.ShowSetup = false
tool.Width = 600
tool.Height = 400
tool.ScanPageUI(filename)

' load image for editing
set wshshell = CreateObject("WScript.Shell")
MsgBox "Edit image and save it, then close program!", vbSystemModal
ret = wshshell.run(filename,,true)

tool.PrintImageUI
```

Managing Pictures

Aside from scanning, the Imaging tools provide great help when it comes to managing pictures. For example, you can open and save pictures and use the Imaging capabilities even if you don't own a scanner. Just use the open and save methods to open existing pictures, print them out, or change image attributes.

Loading and printing pictures

The print methods can work with almost any graphics file, not just the ones you scanned in. Even if you don't have TWAIN support at all, you can still use these parts to enhance your scripts with printing capabilities.

Take a look at the next script. It allows you to open a graphics file and print it out:

```
' 21-8.VBS

set tool = CreateObject("twain.manager")
result = tool.OpenFile
if not result="" then
     tool.PrintImageUI
else
     MsgBox "You cancelled."
end if
```

The Open dialog box (see Figure 21-9) shows all the graphics file types the Imaging tool can read. Almost any major graphics format is supported.

Figure 21-9: Use the official Open dialog box to load images from your hard drive.

Printing pictures without a dialog box

The `Open` dialog box is convenient only if you need to select specific pictures. What if you need to print out all the graphics files stored in some folder? Supply the filename directly to the `PrintImage` method and have your script print out all the pictures:

```
' 21-9.VBS

set tool = CreateObject("twain.manager")
set fs = CreateObject("Scripting.FileSystemObject")

picdir = "C:\pics"

set folder = fs.GetFolder(picdir)
for each file in folder.files
    ' try to print picture, use original size
    on error resume next
    tool.PrintImage file.path, 1
    on error goto 0
next
```

The beauty of this script is its versatility. It accepts a broad range of graphics formats, and you don't need to supply any hints or options. Thanks to `OnErrorResumeNext`, graphics files unsuitable for the Imaging control are silently rejected.

Converting Graphics Files

The Imaging tool has even more to offer. Its `Edit` control not only displays graphics, it also offers limited support for Image conversion and editing.

Note

Kodak Imaging can read almost any kind of graphic, but it can write only as a `TIFF` or `BMP` file. The following scripts, beginning with `21-10.VBS`, load and change graphic files. Because they save the changes into the original file, this only works if you open either `TIFF` or `BMP` files. Use the `SaveAs` method introduced later to open arbitrary file types and to save them in one of the two legal formats.

Rotating pictures

To load and save pictures independently from scanning them, use `Image` and `Save`. `Image` loads a file, and `Save` saves it, including any changes you have applied to the graphic in the meantime.

One of the most common image manipulation tasks is rotating something. You can rotate graphics in 90-degree steps to either side. Use `RotateLeft` and `RotateRight`.

The next script rotates a picture to the left. Load it into your favorite drawing program to see the results.

Caution

This script changes the original graphic file. Later, you learn methods to save the result of your image manipulation as a separate file. For now, use graphics that aren't valuable to you. For example, use the previous scripts to scan some pages to play with.

```
' 21-10.VBS

set tool = CreateObject("twain.manager")
set wshshell = CreateObject("WScript.Shell")

filename = "c:\mypic.jpg"

wshshell.Run """" & filename & """"
tool.Image = filename
tool.RotateLeft
tool.Save

wshshell.Run """" & filename & """"

MsgBox "Done!", vbSystemModal
```

You can further enhance your script by checking whether the specified file really exists. Use the `Scripting.FileSystemObject` method and the `FileExists` method like this:

```
set fs = CreateObject("Scripting.FileSystemObject")
if not fs.FileExists(filename) then
    MsgBox "File " & filename & " does not exist!"
    WScript.Quit
end if
```

Scaling pictures

You can scale your pictures, too. Use a zoom factor, or scale pictures to a certain width or height. Scaling works only between 2 percent and 6,500 percent. If you get out of this range, you'll receive an error.

This is how you "zoom" a picture to 50 percent of its original size:

```
' 21-11.VBS

set tool = CreateObject("twain.manager")
set wshshell = CreateObject("WScript.Shell")

filename = "c:\mypic.jpg"

wshshell.Run """" & filename & """"
tool.Image = filename
tool.Zoom 50
tool.Save

wshshell.Run """" & filename & """"
```

You can enlarge pictures, too. However, this will cause jagged images and reduce overall quality.

There are a couple more methods to scale graphics. `ScaleToPixelWidth` scales a picture to a certain width, and `ScaleToPixelHeight` **scales to a** certain height. `ScaleToMax` **scales a picture to a certain width or height,** whichever is lower. It requires two arguments for maximum width and height.

Creating buttons and icons

Are you a Web designer always in need of new button faces? Then create "real-world" buttons and icons. Drop a book cover or photograph on your scanner, and create a button graphic on the fly (see Figure 21-10).

```
' 21-12.VBS

set tool = CreateObject("twain.manager")
set wshshell = CreateObject("WScript.Shell")

' twain support?
if not tool.ScannerAvailable then
    MsgBox "No TWAIN support!", vbCritical
    WScript.Quit
end if

' ask for file to save scan in
filename = InputBox("Please enter file name!")
if not lcase(right(filename,3))="bmp" then
    MsgBox "Specify a BMP file!"
    WScript.Quit
end if

' set scan options:
tool.FileType = 3
tool.PageOption = 6
tool.ScanTo = 1
tool.ShowSetup = true
tool.Width = 600
tool.Height = 400
tool.ScanPage(filename)

' allow for editing:
response = MsgBox("Do you want to edit your scan?", vbYesNo)
if response = vbYes then
    MsgBox "Save and close program to continue. Now click OK!"

    ' open file in associated program:
    retval = wshshell.run("""" & filename & """",,true)

    ' IMPORTANT: re-set file name so changes will be reflected
    tool.Image = filename
end if

' ask for new dimensions
```

```
maxX = Ask("maximum width of button?","32")
maxY = Ask("maximum height of button?","32")

tool.ScaleToMax maxX, maxY

' save changes
tool.Save

' open file:
wshshell.Run """" & filename & """"
MsgBox "Button created."


' ask for numeric input
function Ask(question, default)
     Ask = InputBox(question,,default)
     if Ask=vbEmpty or not isNumeric(Ask) then
          MsgBox "Invalid size."
          WScript.Quit
     end if
end function
```

Undocumented

Unfortunately, the Image control uses a very strange BMP file format. Although files can be opened with most graphics software, you can't use these pictures as Windows icons.

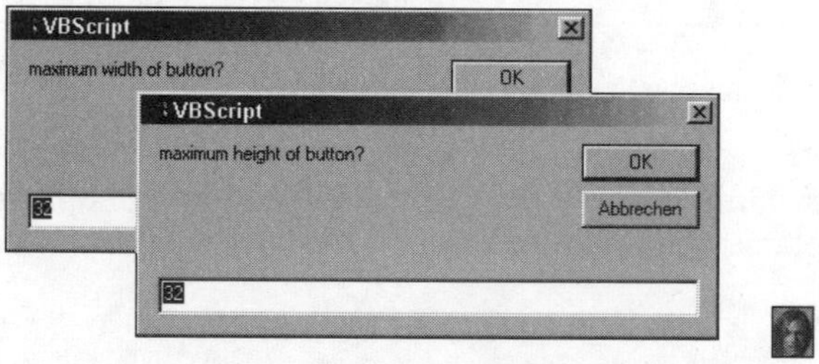

Figure 21-10: Automatically convert a scan to a button face.

The resulting file is rather large. This is normal for BMP files, as this file format stores the bitmap without compression. As a general rule, convert all of your artwork to either GIF or JPG files before you publish it on a Web site. There are plenty of tools out there to do the conversion.

Generating thumbnails and preview pages

The next script is very special. It takes advantage of the many graphics formats the Imaging tool can read. The script searches an entire folder for any type of graphic, creates a thumbnail of it, and composes an impressive preview page. This preview page can then be printed out (see Figure 21-11).

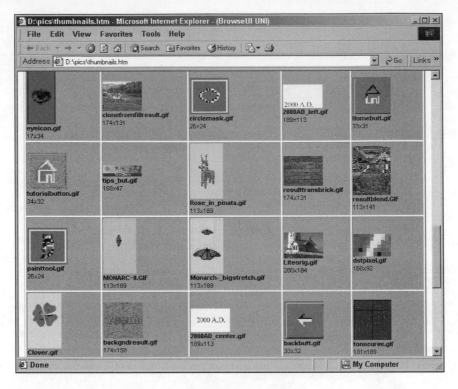

Figure 21-11: Create impressive thumbnail preview pages.

Note

Change the folder name in `picfolder` to the folder that contains the picture files. The script places the thumbnail file called `thumbnails.htm` in the same folder.

```
' 21-13.VBS

set tool = CreateObject("twain.manager")
set fs = CreateObject("Scripting.FileSystemObject")
counter = 0
maxrow = 5
maxX = 70
maxY = 100
picfolder = "C:\pics"
listing = picfolder & "\thumbnails.htm"
set html = fs.CreateTextFile(listing, true)

set folder = fs.GetFolder(picfolder)

InitDoc

for each file in folder.files
    on error resume next
```

```
        tool.Image = file.path
        on error goto 0
        if err.number = 0 and Instr(file.name, "thumb")=0 then
            thumbname = folder.path & "\" & fs.GetBaseName(file.name) &
"_thumb.jpg"
            width = tool.ImageWidth
            height = tool.ImageHeight
            tool.ScaleToMax maxX, maxY
            tool.SaveAs thumbname, 3, 5, 1, 0, true
            AddToDoc "<b>" & file.name & "</b><BR>" & width & "x" &
height, thumbname
        else
            err.clear
        end if
next

CloseDoc

MsgBox "Done!"

sub InitDoc
    html.WriteLine "<html><style>td {font: 8pt Arial; background:
""#AAAAAA""}</style><body><table border=2><tr>"
end sub
sub CloseDoc
    html.WriteLine "</tr></table></body></html>"
    html.close
end sub

sub AddToDoc(filename, thumbname)
    counter = counter + 1
    if counter > maxrow then
        counter = 1
        html.WriteLine "</tr><tr>"
    end if
    html.WriteLine "<td><img src=""" & thumbname & """><br>" &
filename & "</td>"
end sub
```

Tip

This script generates BMP preview thumbnails. They are decompressed and
take considerable space. You can easily expand the script and let it delete all
the thumbnails once the preview page is printed.

Obviously, you wouldn't want the script to convert your original files into
thumbnails. So, your script needs a way to save the thumbnail as a new file.
SaveAs does the job, and more. SaveAs can convert picture formats, too.

Converting picture quality and color formats

SaveAs not only saves the current picture to a new file, it can also convert files
(see Table 21-3). For example, you can change a color picture to grayscale.

SaveAs **uses this syntax:**

SaveAs name, filetype, pagetype, compressiontype, compressioninfo, safezoom

Table 21-3   SaveAs Options and Parameters

Argument	*Description*
name	name of file to save
filetype	1: TIFF
	2: AWD (Windows 98 only)
	3: BMP
pagetype	1: b/w
	2: gray4 (TIFF)
	3: gray8 (TIFF)
	4: palettized4
	5: palettized8
	6: RGB24 (TIFF)
	7: BGR24 (BMP)
compressiontype	BMP and AWD: always 1
	TIFF:
	1: no compression
	2: Group3(1D)
	3: Group3(Modified Huffman)
	4: PackBits
	5: Group4(2D)
	6: JPEG
	7: Reserved
	8: not applicable
	9: LZW
compressioninfo	0: no compression/default compression
	1: EOL
	2: Packed Lines
	4: Prefixed EOL
	8: Compressed LTR

Argument	Description
	16: Expand LTR
	32: Negate
	64: JPEG high compression/high quality
	128: JPEG: high compression/medium quality
	256: JPEG: high compression/low quality
	512: JPEG: medium compression/high quality
	1024: JPEG: medium compression/medium quality
	2048: JPEG: medium compression/low quality
	4096: JPEG: low compression/high quality
	8192: JPEG: low compression/medium quality
	16384: JPEG: low compression/low quality
`safezoom`	true: save image at current zoom level

Saving scanned pictures with compression

Even if your scanner doesn't allow your script to set color options, you can always scan in the highest quality available and determine the color depth when you save the picture. To be able to do that, you don't specify a filename to scan in. Instead, use a `ScanTo` value of 0: display only.

Once the image is scanned, you can save it using the advanced `SaveAs` options. For example, the next script scans in a picture and saves it as both a decompressed `BMP` file and a compressed `TIFF` file using `JPEG` compression at highest compression/highest quality. The script then reveals the difference in file size. The compressed image may very well take up only 10 percent of the space required by the decompressed file (see Figure 21-12). The exact savings vary and depend on the type of picture you scanned.

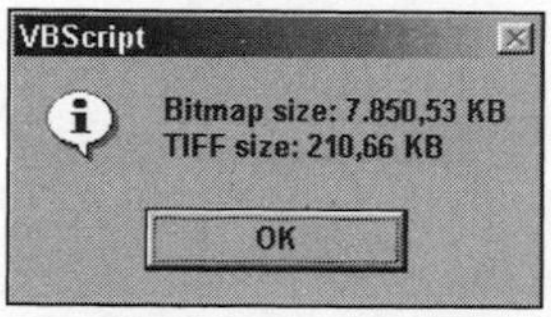

Figure 21-12: Saving images with compression saves a lot of room.

Secret

Maybe you're wondering about the terminology. How come a TIFF file can save images using JPEG compression? What about JPG files? TIFF files using JPEG compression remain TIFF files. They are not JPEG files. They just use the same type of compression, which is especially effective for photographs. Unfortunately, you can't change a TIFF file to JPEG just by using JPEG compression.

```
' 21-14.VBS

set tool = CreateObject("twain.manager")

' check whether twain support is available
if not tool.ScannerAvailable then
    MsgBox "No TWAIN support!", vbCritical
    WScript.Quit
end if

' tell control how to scan
tool.ScanTo = 0

' show scanner setup?
tool.ShowSetup = false
tool.ScanPageUI
' save as uncompressed bitmap
tool.SaveAs "c:\testpic.jpg", 3, 6, 1, 0
' save as highest quality lowest size jpeg
tool.SaveAs "c:\testpic.tif", 1, 6, 6, 64

' determine size differences
set fs = CreateObject("Scripting.FileSystemObject")
set file1 = fs.GetFile("c:\testpic.jpg")
set file2 = fs.GetFile("c:\testpic.tif")
msg = "Bitmap size: " & FormatNumber(file1.size/1024,2) & " KB" & vbCr
msg = msg & "TIFF size: " & FormatNumber(file2.size/1024,2) & " KB"
MsgBox msg, vbInformation
```

Choosing the right compression options

Choosing valid compression parameters isn't always easy. You are dealing with the most fundamental settings, and without some knowledge about graphic file formats, you'll quickly run into "invalid compression type" errors. For example, a gray8 page type doesn't support JPEG compression, and a Palettized4 page type is valid only if the image already contains a Palettized4 image.

So what? Try it out. There's one basic rule: Only TIFF files support compression at all. So always choose 1 as FileType. The rest is up to you and trial-and-error.

There's a smart way, too. Use the method GetImageInfo to retrieve compression settings of TIFF files that already exist (see Figure 21-13). Here's an example:

```
' 21-15.VBS

filetype = Split(",TIFF,AWD,BMP,PCX,DCX,JPG,XIF,GIF,WIFF", ",")
pagetype = Split(",BW,GRAY4,GRAY8,PALETTIZED4," _
& "PALETTIZED8,RGB24,BGR24", ",")
compressiontype = Split(",NO COMPRESSION,GROUP3(1D),GROUP3" _
& "(MODIFIED HUFFMAN),PACKBITS,GROUP4(2D),JPEG,RESERVED," _
& "GROUP3(2D),LZW", ",")
compressioninfo = Split("EOL,PACKED LINES,PREFIXED EOL," _
& "COMPRESSED LTR,EXPAND LTR,NEGATE,JPEG " _
& "HIGHCOMPRESS/HIGHQUAL,JPEG HIGHCOMPRESS/MEDIUMQUAL," _
& "JPEG HIGHCOMPRESS/LOWQUAL,JPEG MEDIUMCOMPRESS/HIGHQUAL," _
& "JPEG MEDIUMCOMPRESS/MEDIUMQUAL,JPEG " _
& "MEDIUMCOMPRESS/LOWQUAL,JPEG LOWCOMPRESS/HIGHQUAL," _
& "JPEG LOWCOMPRESS/MEDIUMQUAL,JPEG LOWCOMPRESS/LOWQUAL", ",")

set tool = CreateObject("twain.manager")

' select file:
filename = tool.OpenFile
if filename = "" then
    MsgBox "You didn't select a file!"
    WScript.Quit
end if

' get image size:
size = tool.ImageWidth & " x " & tool.ImageHeight & " pixels" & vbCr

' get compression info:
info = tool.GetImageInfo
infodetail = Split(info, vbCr)

' create report:
msg = filename & vbCr & size
param = infodetail(0)
msg = msg & "File type: " & filetype(param) & " (" _
& param & ")" & vbCr

param = infodetail(1)
msg = msg & "Page type: " & pagetype(param) & " (" _
& param & ")" & vbCr

param = infodetail(2)
msg = msg & "Compression: " & compressiontype(param) _
    & " (" & param & ")" & vbCr

msg = msg & "Compression Details:" & vbCr
if infodetail(3)=0 then
    msg = msg & "NO COMPRESSION (0)"
```

```
else
for x= 0 to 14
        if (infodetail(3) and 2^x)>0 then
            msg = msg & compressioninfo(x) _
                & " (" & 2^x & ")" & vbCr
        end if
next
end if

MsgBox msg, vbInformation
```

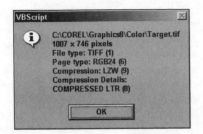

Figure 21-13: Determine detail information about images.

Repairing pictures with damaged file type info

Sometimes when you download pictures or receive them via e-mail, the file type extension gets lost. This can easily happen, because the file type information is just an add-on to the filename. This has tremendous consequences: You are unable to open the picture and have no way to correct the problem.

You can mimic this disaster on your own system by entering the Explorer options (folder options) and make the file extensions visible. Then, search for a picture file and rename it. Omit the file type extension and press [Enter]. Windows complains and warns that this file may not work any longer. Go ahead and try to open the file: It won't work anymore. Because there's no file type information anymore, Windows doesn't know which program to start. And because picture files are binary data, you don't know the file type, either. The picture has become useless.

But it won't be useless for long. The Imaging tool doesn't care about file type extensions. Instead, it opens the file and looks at the kind of data (see Figure 21-14). This is your perfect solution to repair lost file type extensions. Just drag any kind of file onto the script icon, and the script will tell you whether it's a picture type it can read and whether the file type extension needs repair.

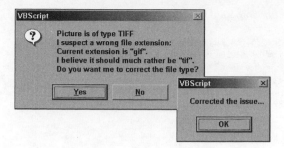

Figure 21-14: Correct wrong or missing picture file type extensions automatically.

```
' 21-16.VBS

filetype = Split(",TIFF,AWD,BMP,PCX,DCX,JPG,XIF,GIF,WIFF", ",")
fileext = Split(",tif,awd,bmp,pcx,dcx,jpg,xif,gif,wif", ",")

set args = WScript.Arguments
if args.Count=0 then
    MsgBox "Please drag a picture file on my icon!"
    WScript.Quit
end if

set tool = CreateObject("twain.manager")
set fs = CreateObject("Scripting.FileSystemObject")

' load picture if possible
on error resume next
tool.Image = args(0)
if not err.number=0 then
    MsgBox "Sorry! This is either no picture file, or I" _
        & " don't recognize it!"
    WScript.Quit
end if
on error goto 0

' get compression info:
info = tool.GetImageInfo
infodetail = Split(info, vbCr)
pictype = infodetail(0)
msg = "Picture is of type " & filetype(pictype) & vbCr

' get files current extension:
ext = lcase(fs.GetExtensionName(args(0)))

' is it correct?
if not ext = fileext(pictype) then
    msg = msg & "I suspect a wrong file extension:" & vbCr
    msg = msg & "Current extension is """ & ext & """." & vbCr
    msg = msg & "I believe it should much rather be """ _
        & fileext(pictype) & """." & vbCr
```

```
        msg = msg & "Do you want me to correct the file type?"

        answer = MsgBox(msg, vbYesNo + vbQuestion)
        if answer = vbYes then
                set file = fs.GetFile(args(0))
                name = fs.GetBaseName(args(0))
                file.name = name & "." & fileext(pictype)
                MsgBox "Corrected the issue..."
        else
                MsgBox "I'll leave file untouched..."
        end if
else
        msg = msg & "File extension is correct!"
        MsgBox msg, vbInformation
end if
```

Summary

Kodak Imaging is unbelievable—this innocent little tool can provide many extra functions for your scripts. While the Image tool itself is rather boring, your scripts can take the imaging functions to the max. Print or scan huge numbers of images as batch automation. Scan images and create your own color photocopy machine. Zoom, rotate, change format—you name it.

Another interesting aspect of Kodak Imaging is that it can actually read the internal format and size of image files. This information comes in handy when you want to create scripts that organize your graphics archive and delete pictures of low quality or small size.

The only serious limitation to Kodak Imaging is that it can save images as TIF and BMP only. There are countless tools out there, though, that convert from TIF to JPG or GIF, so you'll easily find a work-around.

Chapter 22

Fun, Tricks, and Multimedia

In This Chapter

▶ Extract icons from files

▶ Create a list of all icons available on your system

▶ Change individual folder icons and spice up your boring yellow folder symbols

▶ Open and close the CD-ROM tray, access multiple CD-ROM drives, and query the CD-ROM's capabilities

▶ Play audio CDs, WAV sounds, MIDI files, and AVI movies

▶ Record CD tracks to WAV files and control position and duration by the millisecond automatically

This chapter is all about fun. You learn to find system icons and change any folder, file, or Windows icon to something you like better. Access multimedia devices, play sounds, and even record your favorite audio CD as a WAV file. Truly amazing things happen inside the custom COM objects that provide the new functionality. In the source code, you find valuable information otherwise undocumented.

Extracting Icons from Files

Icons are fun. They act as visual clues, making it much easier to find important information. Drive icons indicate drive type, and file icons characterize file type. However, Windows keeps icons to itself and doesn't allow for much customization.

In this chapter, you learn how icons work and how you can extract icons from any icon resource. You discover how to save extracted icons as new icon files and change them any way you want. You also get numerous new methods to assign your new icons to any system icon you like.

Here's our task list:

1. Create a list of all the hidden icons available on your system.

2. Create a dialog box that allows you to select icon files from the list.

3. Create a dialog box that allows you to select icons from an icon file.

4. Create various scripts that assign the selected icon to folders, system icons, and links.

To get access to icon files, make sure you have installed the `iconhandler` COM object `\install\iconhandler\setup.exe`. Full source code can be found at `\components\iconhandler\iconhandler.vbp`.

Creating a list of available icons

In Chapter 9, you learned how to assign new icons to shortcuts, but it took a long time to scan the system folder for available icons. Because you are going to deal with icons a lot in this chapter, there's a better approach. You should create a list of available icons once—and then reuse it as often as you like. You can always update this list manually or by relaunching the following script.

This script may take a long time to search for the icons. Grab a cup of coffee. While you relax , think about the time you're saving. Because the script creates a reusable list of available icon resources, you'll never wait this long again. Instead, once the list is generated, you can load it into a dialog box and pick your icon immediately.

The script searches all local hard drives and creates a list of files that contain more than two icons:

```
' 22-1.VBS

set tool = CreateObject("icon.handler")
set fs = CreateObject("Scripting.FileSystemObject")
set wshshell = CreateObject("WScript.Shell")

iconlist = "C:\iconlist.txt"

' open icon list file
set list = fs.CreateTextFile(iconlist, true)

' search all local hard drives
for each drive in fs.Drives
    if drive.isReady and drive.DriveType=2 then
        SearchFolder drive.RootFolder
    end if
next

' close file
```

```
list.close

wshshell.run """" & iconlist & """"


sub SearchFolder(folderobj)
    ' don't search recycle bin
    if lcase(folderobj.name) = "recycled" then exit sub
    if lcase(folderobj.name) = "dllcache" then exit sub

    ' search for icons and create list
    for each file in folderobj.files
        ' number of icons stored in file:
        iconcount = tool.GetIconNumber(file.path)

        if iconcount>2 then
            list.WriteLine iconcount & vbTab & file.path
        end if
    next
    for each subfolder in folderobj.subfolders
        SearchFolder subfolder
    next
end sub
```

Tip You can interrupt the invisible script at any time. On Windows 9.x, press [Ctrl]+[Alt]+[Del], select WSCRIPT.EXE in the task list, and click End Task. On Windows NT/2000, select the Task Manager, select the Processes tab, and select WSCRIPT.EXE. Then, click End Process.

You don't want the script to work invisibly for too long? Perhaps you'd rather see what it does and have a way to interrupt the search (see Figure 22-1). In Chapter 8, I provided a method to create a modeless dialog box.

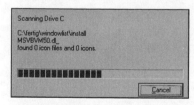

Figure 22-1: Watch while your script searches for icons on all hard drives.

The next script searches for system icons and displays its progress. It also offers a Cancel button to interrupt the search at any time. Just make sure you have installed the modeless dialog COM object \install\modeless\ setup.exe.

```
' 22-2.VBS

set tool = CreateObject("icon.handler")
```

```
set fs = CreateObject("Scripting.FileSystemObject")
set wshshell = CreateObject("WScript.Shell")
set dlg = WScript.CreateObject("modeless.dialog", "event_")

' define variables:
iconlist = "C:\iconlist.txt"
list = ""
quit = false
iconfilecount = 0
icons = 0

' open icon list file
set list = fs.CreateTextFile(iconlist, true)

' show modal window
' everything else is handled by event_WakeUp
dlg.ShowProgressDialog

' close file
list.close

wshshell.run """" & iconlist & """"

sub event_WakeUp
    ' will be executed the moment your modal dialog becomes visible
    ' search all local hard drives
    for each drive in fs.Drives
        if quit then
            ' make sure to display this message!
            ' otherwise your script won't find back to the
            ' starting process!
            wshshell.Popup "Interrupted search...", 1
            dlg.CloseDialog
            exit sub
        end if
        if drive.isReady and drive.DriveType=2 then
            SearchFolder drive.RootFolder
        end if
    next

' make sure to display this message!
' otherwise your script won't find back to the
' starting process!

    wshshell.Popup "Done!", 1
    dlg.CloseDialog
end sub

sub event_QuitNow
    quit = true
end sub
```

```
sub SearchFolder(folderobj)
    ' don't search recycle bin
    if lcase(folderobj.name) = "recycled" then exit sub
    if lcase(folderobj.name) = "dllcache" then exit sub

    ' search for icons and create list
    counter = 0
    filecount = folderobj.files.count
    drv = folderobj.Drive.Driveletter

    for each file in folderobj.files
        if quit then exit sub

        counter = counter +1
        percent = Fix(counter * 100/filecount)

        dlg.WriteDialog "Scanning Drive " & drv & vbCr _
            & vbCr & folderobj.path & vbCr & file.name _
            & vbCr & "found " & iconfilecount _
            & " icon files and " & icons & " icons."
        dlg.SetProgress percent

        dlg.HandleEvent
        ' number of icons stored in file:
        iconcount = tool.GetIconNumber(file.path)

        if iconcount>2 then
            iconfilecount = iconfilecount + 1
            icons = icons + iconcount
            list.WriteLine iconcount & vbTab & file.path
        end if
    next
    for each subfolder in folderobj.subfolders
        if quit then exit sub
        SearchFolder subfolder
    next
end sub
```

Review Chapter 8 to understand how modeless dialog boxes work. It's crucial to follow the design rules outlined in this chapter.

Selecting a file from your icon list

You now have a complete list of all icons available on your system. What can you do with it? Display it as a ListView dialog box. This way, you can select icon files from your list.

Note

Make sure you have installed the ListView COM object \install\listview\ setup.exe.

```
' 22-3.VBS

set tool = CreateObject("listview.tool")
set icontool = CreateObject("icon.handler")
set fs = CreateObject("Scripting.FileSystemObject")

tool.AddHeader "File name", 80
tool.AddHeader "Icon #", 30
tool.AddHeader "Path name", 60

' read in results from icon list
iconlist = "C:\iconlist.txt"
set list = fs.OpenTextFile(iconlist)
do until list.atEndOfStream
     line = list.ReadLine
     infos = Split(line, vbTab)
     ' insert spaces so numbers are sorted correctly:

     pos = InstrRev(infos(1), "\")
     tool.AddItem mid(infos(1), pos+1)
     tool.AddSubItem 1, right(space(10) & infos(0), 3)
     tool.AddSubItem 2, left(infos(1), pos-1)
loop

tool.Sort 1, 1
tool.MultiEdit = true

' repeat until icon selected or cancel
do
     set result = tool.Show("Select Icon File!")
     if result.Count>0 then
          ' we have an icon file!
          fileinfo = Split(result(1), vbCrLf)
          iconfile = fileinfo(2) & "/" & fileinfo(0)
          selectedicon = icontool.PickIcon(iconfile)
          if not selectedicon = "" then
               done = true
          end if
     else
          done = true
     end if
loop until done

if selectedicon = "" then
     MsgBox "You didn't select an icon!"
else
     MsgBox "You selected this icon:" & vbCr & selectedicon
end if
```

This script opens your icon list and displays the content as ListView (see Figure 22-2). It sorts the icon files by icon number, showing the icon files with the most icons at the top. You can sort the ListView by clicking the column headers.

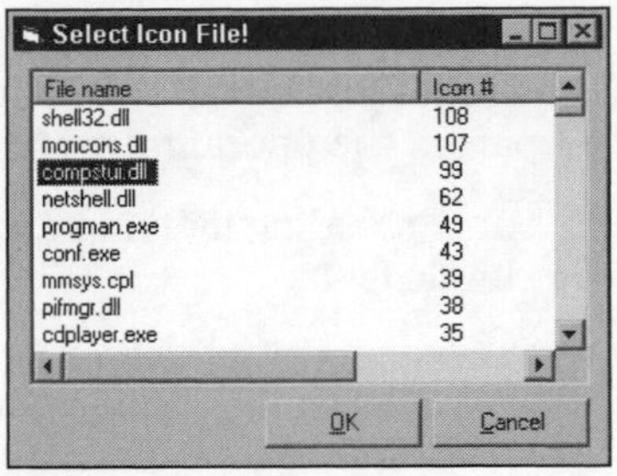

Figure 22-2: Select from hundreds of icon files.

Once you select an icon file, the script opens the official icon selection dialog box and presents the icons stored in the file (see Figure 22-3). If you like an icon, select it and click OK. The script reports the name and icon index of the icon you selected. If you don't find any icon appealing, click Cancel. The icon file list reappears, and you can select another file.

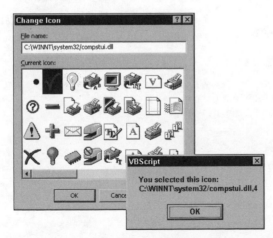

Figure 22-3: Use the undocumented Change Icon dialog box to look into the icon files.

You now have your basic tools ready for action — you can quickly display a list of all icons available, and you can also provide a way to pick an icon. But what can you do with the icon information the script delivers?

Changing Folder Icons

Windows 98 has silently introduced a completely new feature—regular folders can change their icons on an individual basis. You can assign new icons to any one folder (see Figure 22-4).

Secret

Actually, this new feature is part of the Internet Explorer 4 Desktop Update. It's available for free on Windows 95 and NT—just install the update. On Windows 98 and 2000, the features are part of the operating system.

All the new and fancy folder enhancements, including individual icons, Web view, and folder shortcuts, rely on two simple facts:

■ There must be a hidden DESKTOP.INI file inside the folder, which specifies the Class IDs of the COM components providing the new features.

■ The folder must have a system attribute. In addition, some other features require it to have a read-only flag, too. In essence, Microsoft recycled the folder attributes to serve a completely new purpose.

Fiddling around with folder DESKTOP.INI files is not the focus of this book, although it's very interesting. Instead, the next script fully automates the process of assigning individual icons to individual folders. It first lets you select a new icon and then incorporates it into the DESKTP.INI. It also manages the folder attributes and can even refresh the desktop automatically, so the changes become visible.

Just drag a folder onto your new script icon and see what happens.

```
' 22-4.VBS

set tool = CreateObject("listview.tool")
set icontool = CreateObject("icon.handler")
set fs = CreateObject("Scripting.FileSystemObject")


' was a folder dragged on the script icon?
set args = WScript.Arguments
if args.Count=0 then
     ' no, ask for it
     folder = InputBox("Please enter path of folder!")
else
     ' yes, use argument
     folder = args(0)
end if

' valid folder?
if not fs.FolderExists(folder) then
     MsgBox "Folder """ & folder & """ not found!"
     WScript.Quit
end if
```

```
' prepare ListView
tool.AddHeader "File name", 80
tool.AddHeader "Icon #", 30
tool.AddHeader "Path name", 60

' read in results from icon list
iconlist = "C:\iconlist.txt"
set list = fs.OpenTextFile(iconlist)
do until list.atEndOfStream
    line = list.ReadLine
    infos = Split(line, vbTab)
    ' insert spaces so numbers are sorted correctly:

    pos = InstrRev(infos(1), "\")
    tool.AddItem mid(infos(1), pos+1)
    tool.AddSubItem 1, right(space(10) & infos(0), 3)
    tool.AddSubItem 2, left(infos(1), pos-1)
loop

' sort by number of icons, descending order
tool.Sort 1, 1

' listview can be opened repeatedly
tool.MultiEdit = true

' repeat until icon selected or cancel
do
    set result = tool.Show("Select Icon File!")
    if result.Count>0 then
        ' we have an icon file!
        fileinfo = Split(result(1), vbCrLf)
        iconfile = fileinfo(2) & "/" & fileinfo(0)
        selectedicon = icontool.PickIcon(iconfile)
        if not selectedicon = "" then
            done = true
        end if
    else
        done = true
    end if
loop until done

if selectedicon = "" then
    ' check whether folder is already customized
    set tempfldr = fs.GetFolder(folder)
    ' is system attribut set?
    if (tempfldr.Attributes and 4)>0 then
        msg = "Do you want to get back default icon?"
        answer = MsgBox(msg, vbYesNo)
        if answer=vbYes then
            CleanUp tempfldr
        end if
    end if
else
```

```
        ' set new folder icon
        NewFolderIcon folder, selectedicon
end if


sub NewFolderIcon(pfad, icon)
        ' parts(0) stores existing desktop.ini content
        ' before icon definition, part(1) after icon
        ' definition
        dim parts(1)
        startpart = 0
        desktopini = pfad & "\desktop.ini"

        ' is there a desktop.ini already?
        if fs.FileExists(desktopini) then
                ' read file
                set tempfile = fs.OpenTextFile(desktopini)
                do until tempfile.atEndOfStream
                        line = tempfile.ReadLine
                        if lcase(left(line, 8)) = _
                                "iconfile" then
                                skip = true
                        elseif lcase(left(line, 9)) = _
                                "iconindex" then
                                skip=true
                        elseif lcase(left(line, 17)) = _
                                "[.shellclassinfo]" then
                                skip = true
                        else
                                skip = false
                        end if
                        if not skip then parts(startpart) = _
                                parts(startpart)+line & vbCrLf
                        if lcase(left(line, _
                                17))="[.shellclassinfo]" then
                                startpart=1
                        end if
                loop
                tempfile.close
                ' remove desktop.ini protection attributes
                set tempfile = fs.GetFile(desktopini)
                tempfile.Attributes = tempfile.Attributes and _
                        not 216 and not 7
        end if

        ' create new desktop.ini
        set tempdat = fs.CreateTextFile(desktopini, true)
        iconinfo = Split(icon, ",")
        icon1 = Trim(iconinfo(0))
        icon2 = Fix(iconinfo(1))

        ' write old desktop.ini part 1
        tempdat.WriteLine parts(0)
```

```
        ' write new icon info
        tempdat.WriteLine "[.ShellClassInfo]"
        tempdat.WriteLine "IconFile=" & icon1
        tempdat.WriteLine "IconIndex=" & icon2
        ' write old desktop.ini part 2
        tempdat.WriteLine parts(1)

        tempdat.Close

        ' set system attribute
        set folderobj = fs.GetFolder(pfad)
        folderobj.Attributes = _
            folderobj.Attributes and not 216 or 4

        ' hide desktop.ini
        set tempdatei = fs.GetFile(desktopini)
        tempdatei.Attributes = _
            tempdatei.Attributes and not 216 or 2

        ' refresh desktop to show changes
        Refresh folderobj
    end sub

    sub CleanUp(obj)
        desktopini = obj.path & "\desktop.ini"
        if fs.FileExists(desktopini) then
            ' read in old desktop.ini and
            ' remove icon information
            set tempfile = fs.OpenTextFile(desktopini)

            do until tempfile.atEndOfStream
                line = tempfile.ReadLine & space(20)
                if lcase(left(line, 8)) = _
                    "iconfile" then
                    skip = true
                elseif lcase(left(line, 9)) = _
                    "iconindex" then
                    skip = true
                elseif trim(line)="" then
                    skip = true
                elseif lcase(left(line, 17)) = _
                    "[.shellclassinfo]" then
                    flag = true
                else
                    if flag=true and left(line, _
                        1)="[" then
                        gesamt = Replace(gesamt, _
                            "[.shellclassinfo]", "",,,1)
                    end if
                    flag = false
                    gesamt = gesamt & trim(line) & vbCrLf

                    content = true
```

```
                end if
          loop
          tempfile.close
          set tempfile = fs.GetFile(desktopini)
          tempfile.Attributes = tempfile.Attributes and _
                not 216 and not 7

          if content then
                set tempfile = fs.CreateTextFile _
                      (desktopini, true)
                tempfile.Write gesamt
                tempfile.close
                set tempfile = fs.GetFile(desktopini)
                tempfile.Attributes = _
                      tempfile.Attributes and not 216 or 2
          else
                fs.Deletefile desktopini, true
                tempfldr.Attributes = _
                      tempfldr.Attributes and not 4and _
                      not 216
          end if
     end if
     Refresh tempfldr
end sub

sub Refresh(obj)
     ' delete system attribute
     atts = obj.Attributes and not 216
     obj.Attributes = atts and not 4
     ' refresh desktop
     icontool.RefreshDesktop
     ' set system attribut
     obj.Attributes = atts
     ' refresh again
     icontool.RefreshDesktop
end sub
```

If you want to get rid of customized folder icons, drag the folder onto your script icon and click Cancel. The script asks whether you want to exclude the icon information from your current DESKTOP.INI. If you agree, the icon returns back to the default.

Secret

This script can only change true folders. On your desktop, there may be additional icons that look like folders but are something different. My Documents, for example, is just a COM object defined in the Desktop NameSpace **Registry key.** Windows 2000 introduces folder shortcuts, too. They look exactly like folders but are shortcuts. Right-click a folder and choose Properties to make sure it really is a folder.

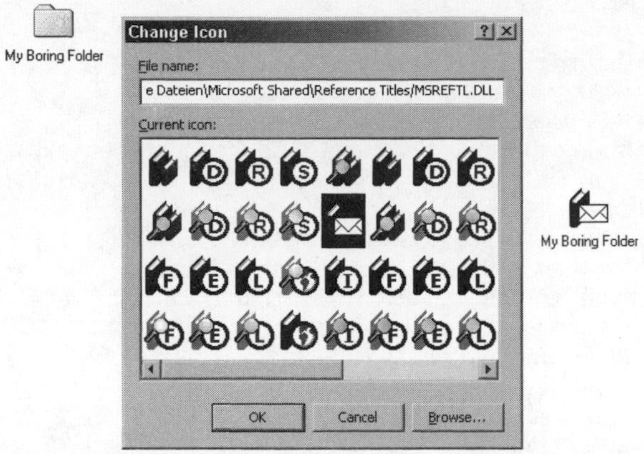

Figure 22-4: Change boring folder icons and replace them with icons you like.

Hiding folders

Changing individual folder icons not only helps to organize your data better. You can also use this technique to hide folders with sensitive data. Just assign a misleading icon to the folder. For example, choose shell32.dll as icon file and select the generic DOS program icon to your folder. Then, rename your folder to something like DOSCNFG.EXE. Now, your folder looks like some techbit DOS executable. But you can open the folder as usual.

Changing system icons

Windows uses private icons, too. All the system icons you see on your desktop — Network Neighborhood, My Computer, My Documents — and all the icons in your Start menu are actually private Window icons. You can change them, too.

Secret

All Windows icons are stored inside shell32.dll. You can use this icon file to select the system icon you want to change.

The next script opens shell32.dll and displays the icons inside it. Select the system icon you want to change, then select a replacement icon. The script automatically updates the system icon in the Registry and updates the icon cache. The new icon appears instantaneously.

```
' 22-5.VBS

set tool = CreateObject("listview.tool")
set icontool = CreateObject("icon.handler")
set fs = CreateObject("Scripting.FileSystemObject")
set wshshell = CreateObject("WScript.Shell")
```

```
' ask for system icon to change
msg = "Please select the system icon you want to change!"
MsgBox msg, vbInformation + vbSystemModal

' registry key for custom icons
key = "HKLM\Software\Microsoft\Windows\CurrentVersion\explorer\Shell
Icons\"

iconfile = icontool.PickIcon("shell32.dll")
if iconfile = "" then
    answer = MsgBox("You did not select an icon! Do you " _
        & "want to restore ALL default icons?", _
        vbYesNo + vbQuestion)
    if answer = vbYes then
        on error resume next
        wshshell.RegDelete key
        icontool.FlushIconCache
    end if
    WScript.Quit
else
    index = mid(iconfile, Instr(iconfile, ",")+1)
end if

' prepare ListView
tool.AddHeader "File name", 80
tool.AddHeader "Icon #", 30
tool.AddHeader "Path name", 60

' read in results from icon list
iconlist = "C:\iconlist.txt"
set list = fs.OpenTextFile(iconlist)
do until list.atEndOfStream
    line = list.ReadLine
    infos = Split(line, vbTab)
    ' insert spaces so numbers are sorted correctly:

    pos = InstrRev(infos(1), "\")
    tool.AddItem mid(infos(1), pos+1)
    tool.AddSubItem 1, right(space(10) & infos(0), 3)
    tool.AddSubItem 2, left(infos(1), pos-1)
loop

' sort by number of icons, descending order
tool.Sort 1, 1

' listview can be opened repeatedly
tool.MultiEdit = true

' repeat until icon selected or cancel
do
    set result = tool.Show("Select Icon File!")
    if result.Count>0 then
        ' we have an icon file!
```

```
                    fileinfo = Split(result(1), vbCrLf)
                    iconfile = fileinfo(2) & "/" & fileinfo(0)
                    selectedicon = icontool.PickIcon(iconfile)
                    if not selectedicon = "" then
                            done = true
                    end if
            else
                    done = true
            end if
    loop until done

    if selectedicon = "" then
            msg = "Do you want to restore the system icon you selected?"
            answer = MsgBox(msg, vbQuestion + vbYesNo + vbSystemModal)
            if answer = vbYes then
                    wshshell.RegDelete key & index
                    icontool.FlushIconCache
            end if
    else
            ' set new system icon
            wshshell.RegWrite key & index, selectedicon
            icontool.FlushIconCache
    end if
```

Secret

System icon changes normally require Windows to restart for them to become visible. Not so with this script. It makes changes visible immediately. `FlushIconCache` forces Windows to re-create its internal icon cache.

Changing a system icon

To change, for example, all folder icons, launch your script and then select the official folder icon in `shell32.dll`. Next, choose the icon file you want to use as a replacement. Select an icon and click OK. All the folder icons will change.

Restoring a system icon

To restore a system icon, launch your script and select the icon. To get back normal folder icons, select the official folder icon in `shell32.dll`. Then, don't select an icon file — click Cancel. The script asks if you want to revert to normal. Click Yes. The original icon will be restored.

Restoring all system icons

If you want to get rid of all custom icons, launch your script and click Cancel. The script asks whether you want to revert to normal. Click Yes. All system icons will be restored.

Tip

Almost all the icons in `shell32.dll` serve a special purpose. For example, many of the icons are used inside your Start menu. You can change those icons, too.

Extracting icons to files

So far, you have taken advantage of all the icons available on your system. You don't own these icons, though. This means that you can't change icons manually, or even be sure that the icons will be there forever. If your favorite icon is part of software that you decide to uninstall, your icon reference will get lost.

This is why it makes sense to extract icons to individual icon files. Your icon toolkit can do this. However, it can only extract icons as .bmp pictures. This is OK—on Windows 9.x, you just need to rename the .bmp file and assign .ico as file type. Now you can use the bitmap picture as an icon. However, on Windows 2000, this doesn't work as well anymore. Transparency information gets lost, and your icons always display a black background. The professional alternative is your Icon editors. You can get them free or as shareware from a number of places.

Tip

You can insert your own icons into your icon list. Just open the text file and add your icon information. This way, you can select your icons with all of the preceding scripts.

The next script shows the simple solution. It allows you to select an icon file and pick an icon. Then, the icon is extracted and saved as an .ico file. The script tries to launch the icon so you can make changes to it. If no program is associated with .ico files, you get an error.

In this case, open the new .ico file manually. The Open As dialog box appears. Just choose MS Paint as the new default program. It can display and edit your extracted icons. Make sure to save your images with the .ico file extension.

```
' 22-6.VBS

set tool = CreateObject("listview.tool")
set icontool = CreateObject("icon.handler")
set fs = CreateObject("Scripting.FileSystemObject")
set wshshell = CreateObject("WScript.Shell")

filename = "c:\testicon.ico"

' prepare ListView
tool.AddHeader "File name", 80
tool.AddHeader "Icon #", 30
tool.AddHeader "Path name", 60

' read in results from icon list
iconlist = "C:\iconlist.txt"
set list = fs.OpenTextFile(iconlist)
do until list.atEndOfStream
    line = list.ReadLine
    infos = Split(line, vbTab)
    ' insert spaces so numbers are sorted correctly:
```

```
            pos = InstrRev(infos(1), "\")
            tool.AddItem mid(infos(1), pos+1)
            tool.AddSubItem 1, right(space(10) & infos(0), 3)
            tool.AddSubItem 2, left(infos(1), pos-1)
loop

' sort by number of icons, descending order
tool.Sort 1, 1

' listview can be opened repeatedly
tool.MultiEdit = true

' repeat until icon selected or cancel
do
     set result = tool.Show("Select Icon File!")
     if result.Count>0 then
         ' we have an icon file!
         fileinfo = Split(result(1), vbCrLf)
         iconfile = fileinfo(2) & "/" & fileinfo(0)
         selectedicon = icontool.PickIcon(iconfile)
         if not selectedicon = "" then
             done = true
         end if
     else
         done = true
     end if
loop until done

if selectedicon = "" then
     MsgBox "You did not select an icon!"
else
     ' extract icon
     iconinfo = Split(selectedicon, ",")
     icontool.LoadIcon iconinfo(0), iconinfo(1)
     icontool.IconToFile filename
     wshshell.Run """" & filename & """"
end if
```

Searching for customized DESKTOP.INI folders

Now that you can extract icons to files, it's easy to write scripts to search for customized DESKTOP.INI folders. The next script searches your hard drive for any folder that has a system attribute and a DESKTOP.INI file (see Figure 22-5).

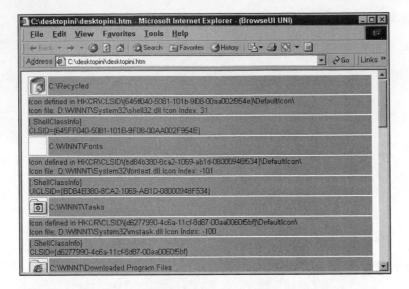

Figure 22-5: Find all customized folders and peek into `DESKTOP.INI`.

The script retrieves the icon, which can be specified either in the `DESKTOP.INI` file or inside the Windows Registry. It creates a list and displays icon and `DESKTOP.INI` content information.

```
' 22-7.VBS

set tool = CreateObject("listview.tool")
set icontool = CreateObject("icon.handler")
set fs = CreateObject("Scripting.FileSystemObject")
set wshshell = CreateObject("WScript.Shell")

mydir = "C:\desktopini\"
logbook = mydir & "desktopini.htm"
counter = 0

on error resume next
fs.CreateFolder mydir
on error goto 0

set list = fs.CreateTextFile(logbook, true)
list.WriteLine "<html><head><style>td {font: 10pt Arial;
background:""#AAAAAA""}</style></head><body><table>"
set windir = fs.GetSpecialFolder(0)
SearchFolder fs.GetFolder("C:\")
list.WriteLine "</table></body></html>"
wshshell.run "iexplore.exe """ & logbook & """"


sub SearchFolder(folderobj)
```

```
        for each subfolder in folderobj.subfolders
            CheckFolder subfolder
        next
        for each subfolder in folderobj.subfolders
            SearchFolder subfolder
        next
    end sub


    sub CheckFolder(subfolder)
        if fs.FileExists(subfolder.path & "\desktop.ini") _
            and (subfolder.Attributes and 4)>0 then
            set tempfile = fs.OpenTextFile(subfolder.path _
                & "\desktop.ini")
            iconfile=""
            iconindex=0
            deskini=""
            source=""
            do until tempfile.atEndOfStream
                line = tempfile.ReadLine
                testline = lcase(Replace(line, " ", ""))
                if watchout then
                    if left(testline, 9)="iconfile=" then
                        iconfile = mid(line, Instr(line, "=")+1)
                        source = "desktop.ini"
                    elseif left(testline, 10)="iconindex=" then
                        iconindex = mid(line, Instr(line, "=")+1)
                    end if
                    pos = instr(testline, "clsid=")
                    if pos>0 then
                        pos = instr(testline, "{")
                        classid = mid(testline, pos)
                        if iconfile = "" then
                            on error resume next
                            key = "HKCR\CLSID\" & classid _
                                & "\DefaultIcon\"
                            iconfile=""
                            iconfile = wshshell.RegRead(key)
                            on error goto 0
                            if not err.number=0 then
                                err.clear
                            else
                                iconfile = _
            wshshell.ExpandEnvironmentStrings(iconfile)

                                pos = Instr(iconfile, ",")
                                if pos=0 then
                                    iconindex = 0
                                else
                                    iconindex = mid(iconfile, _
                                        pos+1)
                                    iconfile = left(iconfile, _
                                        pos-1)
```

```
                                        end if
                                source = key
                        end if
                end if
            end if
        end if
        if testline = "[.shellclassinfo]" then
            watchout=true
        elseif left(testline, 1)="[" then
            watchout = false
        end if
        deskini = deskini & line & "<BR>"
    loop
    tempfile.close
    if not iconfile="" then
        counter = counter + 1
        icontool.LoadIcon iconfile, iconindex
        picname = mydir & "pic" & counter & ".jpg"
        icontool.IconToFile picname

        list.WriteLine "<tr><td><img src=""" & picname & """"
    else
        list.WriteLine "<tr><td>"
    end if
    list.WriteLine "</td><td>" & subfolder.path & "</td></tr>"
    list.WriteLine "<tr><td colspan=2>Icon defined in " _
        & source & "<br>Icon file: " & iconfile _
        & " Icon Index: " & iconindex & "</td></tr>"
    list.WriteLine "<tr><td colspan=2>" & deskini _
        & "</td></tr>"
    end if
end sub
```

Accessing Multimedia Devices

Multimedia refers to any kind of media—sound, video, pictures, and more.
Windows has standardized the way you can talk to multimedia devices with
the Media Control Interface (MCI). MCI takes the hassle out of programming
multimedia devices. Whether you want to remote control your CD-ROM or a
VCR, you always use the same set of commands.

In fact, controlling multimedia devices requires only one API function, and
that's mciSendString. This function sends text commands to any multimedia device and can also query settings. I have created a simple COM
object that "wraps" the function and also provides error information. This
is the entire code necessary:

```
Private Declare Function mciSendString Lib "winmm.dll" _
Alias "mciSendStringA" (ByVal lpstrCommand As String, _
ByVal lpstrReturnString As String, ByVal wReturnLength _
As Integer, ByVal hCallback As Integer) As Long
```

```
Private Declare Function mciGetErrorString Lib "winmm.dll" _
Alias "mciGetErrorStringA" (ByVal errorno As Long, ByVal _
buffer As String, ByVal length As Long) As Long

Function SendMCIString(ByVal command As String, _
Optional ByRef errormsg As Variant) As String
    Dim retval As Long
    Dim errmsg As String * 260

    ' send command text
    retval = mciSendString(command, 0, 0, 0)
    ' any errors?
    If Not retval = 0 Then
        ' yes, get clear text description
        mciGetErrorString retval, errmsg, Len(errmsg)
        SendMCIString = False
        errormsg = Left(errmsg, InStr(errmsg, Chr(0)) - 1)
    Else
        ' no, command executed
        SendMCIString = True
        errormsg = "ok"
    End If
End Function

Function QueryMCIString(ByVal command As String, _
ByRef result As Variant) As Boolean
    Dim output As String * 260
    Dim pos As Long

    ' send command text and provide buffer for results
    retval = mciSendString(command, output, Len(output), 0)
    ' any errors?
    If Not retval = 0 Then
        ' yes, get clear text description
        mciGetErrorString retval, errmsg, Len(errmsg)
        QueryMCIString = False
        result = Left(errmsg, InStr(errmsg, Chr(0)) - 1)
    Else
        ' no, return result
        QueryMCIString = True
        pos = InStr(output, Chr(0))
        If pos < 2 Then
            result = ""
        Else
            result = Left(output, pos - 1)
        End If
    End If
End Function
```

Either open this and compile it yourself using \components\mci\mci.vbp,
or install the COM object right away with \install\mci\setup.exe.

Opening and closing CD trays

In Chapter 4, you learned how to open and close CD-ROM trays. However, with that technique, you can only control your "default" CD-ROM drive. If you use more than one CD-ROM, you have no way of choosing which one to control.

Let's take a look at how you can specifically address a multimedia device such as your CD-ROM. Before you can do something with a device, you need to open it first. The Open command loads the device drivers into memory (if they aren't loaded already). CD-ROM drives are referred to as cdaudio. This is how you control the CD-ROM tray of the default drive:

```
' 22-8.VBS

set tool = CreateObject("mci.manager")
MCI "open cdaudio"
MCI "set cdaudio door open wait"
MsgBox "CD Tray Open!"
MCI "set cdaudio door closed wait"
MsgBox "CD Tray Closed!"
MCI "close cdaudio"

sub MCI(command)
    if not tool.SendMCIString(command, errormsg) then
        msg = "command: " & command & vbCr & "Error: " _
            & errormsg & vbCr & "Continue?"
        answer = MsgBox(msg, vbYesNo + vbCritical + vbSystemModal)
        if answer = vbNo then WScript.Quit
    end if
end sub
```

You can never be sure whether your CD tray will really open and close. Whether or not it supports this action is up to your CD-ROM drive type. So let's find out whether your CD-ROM supports what you want it to do:

```
' 22-9.VBS

set tool = CreateObject("mci.manager")

MCI "Open cdaudio"
caneject = ReadMCI("capability cdaudio can eject")
MCI "Close cdaudio"

if caneject then
    MsgBox "Your CD-ROM can open the tray automatically!"
else
    MsgBox "Your CD-ROM doesn't support tray mechanics!"
end if

sub MCI(command)
    if not tool.SendMCIString(command, errormsg) then
        msg = "command: " & command & vbCr & "Error: " _
```

```
                          & errormsg & vbCr & "Continue?"
            answer = MsgBox(msg, vbYesNo + vbCritical + vbSystemModal)
            if answer = vbNo then WScript.Quit
      end if
end sub

function ReadMCI(command)
      if not tool.QueryMCIString(command, result) then
            msg = "command: " & command & vbCr & "Error: " _
                  & result & vbCr & "Continue?"
            answer = MsgBox(msg, vbYesNo + vbCritical + vbSystemModal)
            if answer = vbNo then WScript.Quit
      else
            ReadMCI = CBool(result)
end if
end function
```

`ReadMCI` and `QueryMCIString` send commands to the MCI and return a value. In this example, the value is converted to Boolean using `CBool` because the answer to your question is either true or false. In other circumstances, you may ask for the number of tracks on an audio CD. Obviously, you don't convert those values to Boolean.

Figure 22-6: Find out whether your multimedia device supports specific functions.

Addressing a specific CD-ROM drive

So far, you have accessed the "standard" CD-ROM directly. If you want to address a drive specifically, use a different approach — open the drive, specify the type of multimedia device this drive represents, and assign a name to this device. Now you can address multiple CD-ROM drives simultaneously:

```
' 22-10.VBS

set tool = CreateObject("mci.manager")

OpenTray "D:"
MsgBox "CD Tray Open!"
CloseTray "D:"
MCI "set cdaudio door closed wait"
MsgBox "CD Tray Closed!"

sub OpenTray(driveletter)
MCI "open " & driveletter & " type cdaudio alias mydrive"
```

```
MCI "set mydrive door open wait"
MCI "close mydrive"
end sub

sub CloseTray(driveletter)
MCI "open " & driveletter & " type cdaudio alias mydrive"
MCI "set mydrive door closed wait"
MCI "close mydrive"
end sub

sub MCI(command)
     if not tool.SendMCIString(command, errormsg) then
          msg = "command: " & command & vbCr & "Error: " _
               & errormsg & vbCr & "Continue?"
          answer = MsgBox(msg, vbYesNo + vbCritical + vbSystemModal)
          if answer = vbNo then WScript.Quit
     end if
end sub
```

Caution

Because you are now free to access any drive, you can easily pick the wrong one. If it's not a multimedia device (for example, your hard drive), you'll get an error.

Determining what your CD-ROM is currently doing

You can easily get a detailed status report of what your CD-ROM is currently doing. Have a look:

```
' 22-11.VBS

set tool = CreateObject("mci.manager")

MCI "open cdaudio"
MsgBox ReadMCI("status cdaudio mode")
MCI "Close cdaudio"

sub MCI(command)
     if not tool.SendMCIString(command, errormsg) then
          msg = "command: " & command & vbCr & "Error: " _
               & errormsg & vbCr & "Continue?"
          answer = MsgBox(msg, vbYesNo + vbCritical + vbSystemModal)
          if answer = vbNo then WScript.Quit
     end if
end sub

function ReadMCI(command)
     if not tool.QueryMCIString(command, result) then
          msg = "command: " & command & vbCr & "Error: " _
               & result & vbCr & "Continue?"
          answer = MsgBox(msg, vbYesNo + vbCritical + vbSystemModal)
          if answer = vbNo then WScript.Quit
     else
          ' don't convert to boolean this time!!
```

```
            ReadMCI = result
        end if
end function
```

Tip

Call this script more than once. Then, check out what it tells you when the CD-ROM tray is open or when you are playing back an audio CD. "Mode" always returns the current status of your multimedia device (see Figure 22-7).

Figure 22-7: Check the state of your multimedia device.

Finding out if an audio CD is inserted

Your CD-ROM is a multimedia device only because it supports audio CDs. Data CDs don't count as multimedia, and as long as a data CD is inserted, you can't do much good with MCI. So, one of the first things to find out is whether a media is inserted and whether this media is an audio CD (see Figure 22-8):

```
' 22-12.VBS

set tool = CreateObject("mci.manager")

MCI "Open cdaudio"
do
media = CBool(ReadMCI("status cdaudio media present"))
if not media then
    MCI "set cdaudio door open"
    result = MsgBox("Insert CD-ROM!", vbOkCancel)
    ok = false
else
    ' check whether media is Audio CD!
    cdtype = lcase(ReadMCI("status cdaudio type track 1"))
    if cdtype = "audio" then
        ok = true
    else
    MCI "set cdaudio door open"
        result = MsgBox("Insert AUDIO CD-ROM!", vbOkCancel)
        ok = false
    end if
end if

if result = vbCancel then WScript.Quit
loop until ok

MCI "Close cdaudio"
MsgBox "CD-AUDIO is inserted!"

sub MCI(command)
```

```
      if not tool.SendMCIString(command, errormsg) then
          msg = "command: " & command & vbCr & "Error: " _
              & errormsg & vbCr & "Continue?"
          answer = MsgBox(msg, vbYesNo + vbCritical + vbSystemModal)
          if answer = vbNo then WScript.Quit
      end if
end sub

function ReadMCI(command)
      if not tool.QueryMCIString(command, result) then
          msg = "command: " & command & vbCr & "Error: " _
              & result & vbCr & "Continue?"
          answer = MsgBox(msg, vbYesNo + vbCritical + vbSystemModal)
          if answer = vbNo then WScript.Quit
      else
          ' don't convert to boolean this time!!
          ReadMCI = result
      end if
end function
```

This script makes sure you insert an audio CD-ROM. It will open the CD tray if either no media is present or the media is not of type "Audio."

Tip

Remember, whenever you insert an audio CD, Windows will automatically launch the CD Player as long as it's installed and you didn't disable automatic playback.

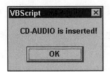

Figure 22-8: Check whether a CD-ROM media is inserted and whether it's an audio CD.

Querying audio CD parameters

Once an audio CD is inserted, your script can query the audio CD data. This is your prerequisite to remote-control the audio CD, which we cover in just a moment. First, let's take a closer look at the media you have inserted.

Note

To keep the following examples short, I didn't use the code mentioned previously to make sure you inserted an audio CD—I just assumed you did. If you didn't, you'll receive an error.

Determining the number of tracks

First, let's see how many tracks are stored on the audio CD and how long they are (see Figure 22-9):

```
' 22-13.VBS

set tool = CreateObject("mci.manager")
```

```
MCI "open cdaudio"
tracks = ReadMCI("status cdaudio number of tracks")
msg = "Your CD contains " & tracks & " tracks!" & vbCr

' set time format to m:s time format
MCI "Set cdaudio time format msf"

for x = 1 to tracks
    tracktype = ReadMCI("status cdaudio type track " & x)
    tracklength = ReadMCI("status cdaudio length track " & x)
    msg = msg & "Track " & x & " (" & tracktype & "): length " _
        & tracklength & vbCr
next

MCI "Close cdaudio"

MsgBox msg, vbInformation

sub MCI(command)
    if not tool.SendMCIString(command, errormsg) then
        msg = "command: " & command & vbCr & "Error: " _
            & errormsg & vbCr & "Continue?"
        answer - MsgBox(msg, vbYesNo + vbCritical + vbSystemModal)
        if answer = vbNo then WScript.Quit
    end if
end sub

function ReadMCI(command)
    if not tool.QueryMCIString(command, result) then
        msg = "command: " & command & vbCr & "Error: " _
            & result & vbCr & "Continue?"
        answer = MsgBox(msg, vbYesNo + vbCritical + vbSystemModal)
        if answer = vbNo then WScript.Quit
    else
        ' don't convert to boolean this time!!
        ReadMCI = result
    end if
end function
```

Secret

The script uses msf, which stands for minutes-seconds-frames. You can also use milliseconds and get the length of audio tracks up to 1/1000 of a second. Other multimedia devices use other time scales, and set ... time format allows you to choose the one you want to use.

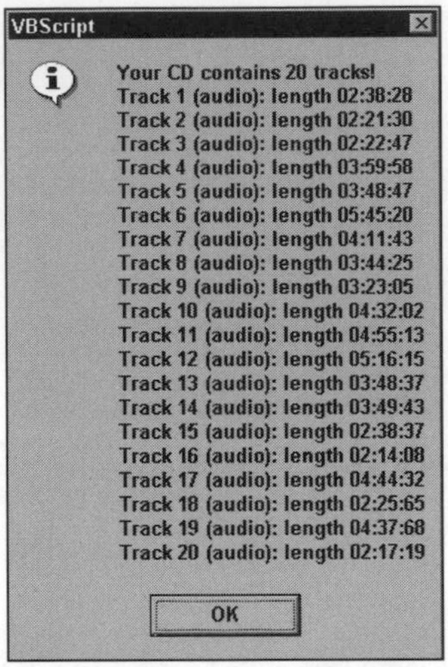

Figure 22-9: Find out more about the tracks on your audio CD.

Remote Controlling Audio Playback

You now know how to access multimedia devices. Although I am dealing primarily with your CD-ROM drive, the following examples demonstrate the general concept. You can easily apply those examples to different multimedia devices like VCRs, video-disc players, and the like.

Controlling position

The most important thing your script should control is setting the current position on the audio CD. Seek sets the current position according to the time format. The next script starts playing track 1 for 10 seconds:

```
' 22-14.VBS

set tool = CreateObject("mci.manager")

MCI "open cdaudio"
MCI "Set cdaudio time format tmsf"
' jump to track 5
MCI "Seek cdaudio to 5"
' play track
MCI "Play cdaudio"
' wait 10 secs
WScript.Sleep 10000
' stop
MCI "Stop cdaudio"
MCI "Close cdaudio"
```

```
MsgBox "Time's up!"

sub MCI(command)
     if not tool.SendMCIString(command, errormsg) then
          msg = "command: " & command & vbCr & "Error: " _
               & errormsg & vbCr & "Continue?"
          answer = MsgBox(msg, vbYesNo + vbCritical + vbSystemModal)
          if answer = vbNo then WScript.Quit
     end if
end sub
```

Changing time format from tracks to milliseconds

If you change the time format, you can control position in terms of milliseconds, too. For example, to play from absolute time position 10.0 seconds to 18.550 seconds, use this approach:

```
' 22-15.VBS

set tool = CreateObject("mci.manager")

MCI "open cdaudio"
MCI "Set cdaudio time format milliseconds"
MCI "Seek cdaudio to 10000"
MCI "Play cdaudio"
WScript.Sleep 8550
MCI "Stop cdaudio"
MCI "Close cdaudio"
MsgBox "Time's up!"

sub MCI(command)
     if not tool.SendMCIString(command, errormsg) then
          msg = "command: " & command & vbCr & "Error: " _
               & errormsg & vbCr & "Continue?"
          answer = MsgBox(msg, vbYesNo + vbCritical + vbSystemModal)
          if answer = vbNo then WScript.Quit
     end if
end sub
```

Another much easier approach uses from and to:

```
' 22-16.VBS

set tool = CreateObject("mci.manager")

MCI "open cdaudio"
MCI "Set cdaudio time format milliseconds"
MCI "Play cdaudio from 10000 to 18850 wait"
MCI "Close cdaudio"
MsgBox "Time's up!"
```

```
sub MCI(command)
    if not tool.SendMCIString(command, errormsg) then
        msg = "command: " & command & vbCr & "Error: " _
            & errormsg & vbCr & "Continue?"
        answer = MsgBox(msg, vbYesNo + vbCritical + vbSystemModal)
        if answer = vbNo then WScript.Quit
    end if
end sub
```

Here, the play command specifies both start and end positions. You don't need to delay your script anymore. The additional wait parameter halts script execution until the specified part is completely played back. Note that if you change the time format back to tmsf, you can just as easily determine the tracks your CD-ROM should play back.

Secret

Use the wait parameter with any MCI command to turn it into a modal command. Normally, your script just "sends" commands to the multimedia device and immediately continues to execute. Using wait, your script waits for the command to be completely executed before it continues with other things.

Dealing with Wave Audio, MIDI Files, and Miscellaneous Multimedia Types

You already know most of what you need to control other multimedia devices — they all work the same. Have a look:

Table 22-1   Generic Multimedia Commands

Type of Command	Description
Open	Opens the multimedia device/multimedia file
Close	Closes the multimedia device/multimedia file
Play, Pause, Seek, Stop	Controls playback
Status	Queries information
Set	Sets parameters
Capability	Determines device capabilities

These are the types of multimedia devices MCI supports:

Table 22-2   Multimedia Device Types

Device type	Description
cdaudio	CD-ROM drive
dat	Digital-audio tape player
digitalvideo	Digital video in a window
overlay	Overlay device (analog video, e.g. a TV card)
scanner	Image scanner
sequencer	MIDI sound file
vcr	Video tape recorder
videodisc	Video disk player
waveaudio	WAV sound samples
avivideo	AVI video file

Not all devices may be supported on your system. Each device requires at least one driver. If you have installed the Registry COM component from Chapter 14, you can list the installed drivers (see Figure 22-10):

```
' 22-17.VBS

set tool = CreateObject("regtool.tob")
key = "WINMACHINE\MCI"

if tool.KeyExists(key & "\") then
    set entries = tool.RegEnum(key)
    for each entry in entries
        list = list & entry & "=" _
            & tool.RegRead(key & "\" & entry) & vbCr
    next
else
    set fs = CreateObject("Scripting.FileSystemObject")
    set winfolder = fs.GetSpecialFolder(0)
    set systemini = fs.OpenTextFile(winfolder.path & "\system.ini")
    do until systemini.atEndOfStream
        line = systemini.ReadLine
        if lcase(left(line, 5))="[mci]" then
            watchout = true
        elseif left(line, 1)="[" then
            watchout = false
        elseif watchout then
            list = list & line & vbCr
        end if
```

```
        loop
        systemini.close
end if

MsgBox list, vbInformation
```

Secret

On older Windows systems, the MCI drivers are specified in SYSTEM.INI, a separate configuration file inside the Windows folder. More recent Windows versions store MCI information in the Registry. The script first looks in the Registry, and if it can't find the information, it searches the SYSTEM.INI file. Note also that the device names above are just recommendations. You can use any name as driver name. You can even change existing driver names to something else, although this is a bad idea — now, standard MCI scripts won't find the device names anymore.

Figure 22-10: Enumerate all MCI multimedia drivers installed on your system.

Playing back MIDI files

MIDI files are extremely small files. They only contain the tunes, not the space-consuming wave sampler. To play back a MIDI file, your sound card needs to be able to "synthesize" the wave samples for the instruments the MIDI file specifies.

First, check out if you own some MIDI files. Do a search on *.MID and see what you get. Once you find a MIDI file, you can use the following script to play it back:

```
' 22-18.VBS

set tool = CreateObject("mci.manager")

' exchange with your own MIDI file:
media = "C:\WINNT\Media\canyon.mid"

MCI "open " & media & " type sequencer alias canyon"
MCI "Play canyon wait"
MCI "Close canyon"

sub MCI(command)
    if not tool.SendMCIString(command, errormsg) then
        msg = "command: " & command & vbCr & "Error: " _
```

```
                            & errormsg & vbCr & "Continue?"
                answer = MsgBox(msg, vbYesNo + vbCritical + vbSystemModal)
                if answer = vbNo then WScript.Quit
        end if
end sub
```

If you don't include the wait parameter in your Play command, you won't hear any sound. Without wait, your script continues immediately and closes down the playback within milliseconds.

If you'd rather have an option to cancel playback, use something like this:

```
' 22-19.VBS

set tool = CreateObject("mci.manager")
set wshshell = CreateObject("WScript.Shell")

' exchange with your own MIDI file:
media = "C:\WINNT\Media\canyon.mid"

MCI "open " & media & " type sequencer alias canyon"
MCI "set canyon time format milliseconds"
length = Fix(CLng(ReadMCI("status canyon length"))/1000)

MCI "Play canyon"
msg = "Song plays for " & length & " secs. Click OK to interrupt!"
wshshell.Popup msg, length
MCI "Close canyon"

function ReadMCI(command)
    if not tool.QueryMCIString(command, result) then
        msg = "command: " & command & vbCr & "Error: " _
            & result & vbCr & "Continue?"
        answer = MsgBox(msg, vbYesNo + vbCritical + vbSystemModal)
        if answer = vbNo then WScript.Quit
    else
        ' don't convert to boolean this time!!
        ReadMCI = result
    end if
end function

sub MCI(command)
    if not tool.SendMCIString(command, errormsg) then
        msg = "command: " & command & vbCr & "Error: " _
            & errormsg & vbCr & "Continue?"
        answer = MsgBox(msg, vbYesNo + vbCritical + vbSystemModal)
        if answer = vbNo then WScript.Quit
    end if
end sub
```

Secret

The dialog box disappears automatically once the song has played. The script simply queries the length of the song, calculates the seconds, and uses the WScript.Shell Popup method to automatically close the dialog box once time is up.

Playing back WAV audio files

WAV audio files work exactly as MIDI files except that they are of type `waveaudio`. So if you'd rather specify a WAV file, replace sequencer with `waveaudio`.

Showing AVI movie files

Do a quick search and check whether any `AVI` files are available on your system. `AVI` files are digital movies, and because they too are considered multimedia, MCI can play them:

```
' 22-20.VBS

set tool = CreateObject("mci.manager")

' exchange with your own AVI file:
media = "C:\WINNT\clock.avi"

MCI "open " & media & " type avivideo alias movie"
MCI "play movie wait"
MCI "close movie"

sub MCI(command)
      if not tool.SendMCIString(command, errormsg) then
            msg = "command: " & command & vbCr & "Error: " _
                  & errormsg & vbCr & "Continue?"
            answer = MsgBox(msg, vbYesNo + vbCritical + vbSystemModal)
            if answer = vbNo then WScript.Quit
      end if
end sub
```

The script plays back the video in a default window. You can play back your movie full-screen, too. Just exchange the play command:

```
MCI "play movie fullscreen wait"
```

Figure 22-11: Play back AVI movie files.

Playing in slow motion

You can even control the playback speed and play back your video in slow motion or much faster than normal. Your script needs to set the playback speed before it calls the play command:

```
MCI "set movie speed 4000"
```

Secret

For AVI files, a speed setting of 1000 is the default in most cases. Setting the speed to 4000 plays the video at four times the normal speed.

Invoking secret fine-tuning options

The MCI AVI driver supports many more settings. For example, you can zoom your video. To display the settings dialog box, use this line:

```
MCI "configure movie"
```

Note

The settings you specify will be permanent and will apply to future sessions too.

Changing window style

Your script doesn't need to accept the default window as video output. You can provide your very own window and play the video inside a dialog box, or you can provide alternate window styles to disable the standard buttons in the video window title bar.

A simple example is included in the MCI COM object. This is how you display AVI movies inside your own dialog boxes:

```
set tool = CreateObject("mci.manager")

' exchange with your own AVI file:
media = "C:\WINNT\clock.avi"

tool.PlayInWindow media
```

Secret

Internally, the COM object uses the same MCI string commands. To hook the video to a special window handle, use `"window mymovie handle xyz"`.

Actually, you can display AVI videos in any window, and the next script kidnaps an editor window to display the video:

```
' 22-21.VBS

set wintool = CreateObject("window.manager")
set tool = CreateObject("mci.manager")
set wshshell = CreateObject("WScript.Shell")

wshshell.run "NOTEPAD.EXE"
WScript.Sleep 2000
handle = wintool.GetForegroundWindowHandle

' exchange with your own AVI file:
```

```
media = "C:\WINNT\clock.avi"

MCI "open " & media & " type avivideo alias movie"
MCI "window movie handle " & handle
MCI "play movie wait"
MCI "close movie"

sub MCI(command)
    if not tool.SendMCIString(command, errormsg) then
        msg = "command: " & command & vbCr & "Error: " _
            & errormsg & vbCr & "Continue?"
        answer = MsgBox(msg, vbYesNo + vbCritical + vbSystemModal)
        if answer = vbNo then WScript.Quit
    end if
end sub
```

Automatically recording CD tracks to WAV audio

The true power of scripting lies in the combination of different multimedia devices. For example, if you want to record a track of your favorite audio CD as a WAV audio file, the following script does the job for you.

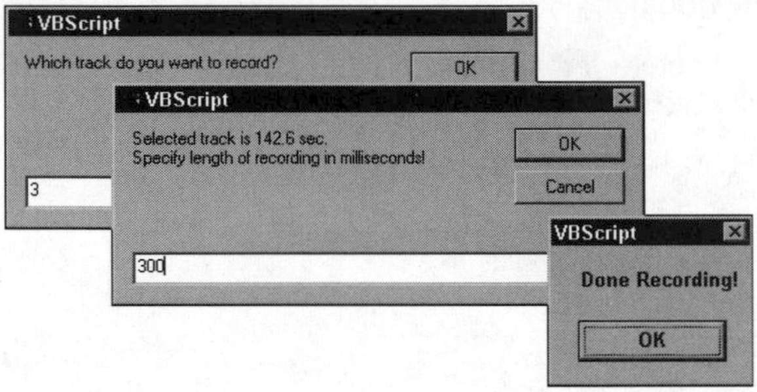

Figure 22-12: Record CD tracks to WAV files.

```
' 22-22.VBS

set tool = CreateObject("mci.manager")
set fs = CreateObject("Scripting.FileSystemObject")

track = Ask("Which track do you want to record?","1")
RecordToWave track, "D:\song.wav"
MsgBox "Done Recording!"

sub RecordToWave(track, name)
    if fs.FileExists(name) then
        msg = "File exists. Overwrite?"
        answer = MsgBox(msg, vbYesNo + vbQuestion)
        if answer = vbYes then
```

```
                fs.DeleteFile name, true
                counter = 0
                do until not fs.FileExists(name)
                    counter = counter + 1
                    if counter>10 then
                        MsgBox "Can't delete " & name
                        WScript.quit
                    end if
                    WScript.Sleep 1000
                loop
            else
                MsgBox "Can't save."
                WScript.Quit
            end if
        end if
        MCI "open cdaudio"
        MCI "set cdaudio time format tmsf"
        MCI "status cdaudio position track " & track
        MCI "set cdaudio time format milliseconds"

        call tool.QueryMCIString("status cdaudio length track " _
            & track & " wait", result)
        song = CLng(result)
        msg = "Selected track is " & FormatNumber(song/1000,1) _
            & " sec." & vbCr
        msg = msg & "Specify length of recording in milliseconds!"
        limit = Ask(msg,song)

        MCI "open new type waveaudio alias capture"
        MCI "set cdaudio time format tmsf"
        MCI "play cdaudio from " & track & " to " & track+1
        MCI "record capture"
        WScript.Sleep limit
        MCI "save capture " & name
        MCI "stop cdaudio"
        MCI "close cdaudio"
    end sub

sub MCI(command)
    if not tool.SendMCIString(command, errormsg) then
        msg = command & vbCr & errormsg & vbCr & "Continue?"
        response = MsgBox(msg, vbYesNo + vbCritical)
        if response = vbNo then WScript.Quit
    end if
end sub

function Ask(question, default)
    Ask = InputBox(question,,default)
    if Ask=vbEmpty or not isNumeric(Ask) then
        MsgBox "Invalid entry."
        WScript.Quit
    end if
    Ask = Fix(Ask)
end function
```

`RecordToWave` records a track of your audio CD and stores it as a WAV file. You can even specify if it should record the entire track or just part of it — up to the millisecond (see Figure 22-13).

Caution

WAV audio produces very large files in a very short period of time. Record only a couple of seconds at first and check the resulting file sizes to get accustomed to the demands.

Note that the Save command can only work if the file specified doesn't already exist. Save cannot replace files. Your script must therefore delete the file if it exists before a new recording can take place. If in doubt, delete the file manually before you launch the script.

Tip

MCI uses your system default values when storing WAV audio data. It also uses your system default sound input levels. Double-click the speaker symbol in your taskbar's tray area and select the recording panel to adjust the input levels and input sources.

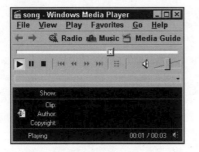

Figure 22-13: The resulting WAV file is exactly the length you specified.

Summary

In the first part of this chapter, you learned how Windows organizes its icons. Your scripts are now able to enumerate icon files, extract icons, and assign icons to system objects.

In the second part, you learned about the uniform multimedia interface MCI. You have seen how easy it is to control the most different multimedia devices with the exact same set of commands. Your scripts can now play audio and video files and even record CD-ROM audio tracks to your hard drive.

Chapter 23

Using Databases

In This Chapter

▶ Learn about ADO and MDAC, the standard interfaces to any database

▶ Check your ADO and MDAC versions, and update your system with the help of free downloads

▶ Access the sample database using a DSN-free connection

▶ Read and write to any database using scripts and SQL

▶ Deal with recordsets, count records, delete records, and retrieve information about table fields and variable types

▶ Eliminate the "single quote" problem and work around reserved SQL characters

▶ Create completely new database tables and delete old ones

▶ Learn all about the Index Server, and use Boolean operators to quickly find the documents you are looking for

▶ Do full text searches and queries in natural language

▶ Limit search scope to specific folders using the hidden `ixsso.Util` object

Microsoft has made database access easy. By using MDAC (Microsoft Database Access Components), your scripts can connect themselves to any kind of database and read information using SQL statements. Your scripts can even store information and change database structures. In this chapter, you learn how to add powerful database capabilities to your scripts.

Accessing Databases

Imagine what you could do if your scripts were able to "talk" to databases. You could create your own little address book, retrieve invoice information, or store user names.

Fortunately, Microsoft has created a standard interface to access any kind of database, including simple text databases as well as full-scale SQL servers or Oracle database servers.

Checking ADO version

This interface is called ActiveX Data Objects (ADO). Many products silently install ADO on your system, so let's check whether ADO is working on your system and whether it's up-to-date (see Figure 23-1).

```
' 23-1.VBS

set fs = CreateObject("Scripting.FileSystemObject")
set wshshell = CreateObject("WScript.Shell")

msg = "ADO status:" & vbCr & vbCr

' check whether Connection is accessible
on error resume next
set dummy = CreateObject("ADODB.Connection")
if not err.number = 0 then
    MsgBox msg & "ADODB.Connection isn't working!"
    WScript.Quit
else
    msg = msg & "ADODB.Connection is operational." & vbCr
end if
on error goto 0

' retrieve files
on error resume next
clsid = wshshell.RegRead("HKCR\ADODB.Connection\CLSID\")
exec = wshshell.RegRead("HKCR\CLSID\" & clsid & "\InProcServer32\")
path = Left(exec, InstrRev(exec, "\")-1)
path = Left(path, InstrRev(path, "\")-1) & "\Ole DB\"

if not err.number=0 then
    MsgBox msg & "Error retrieving file version information!"
    WScript.Quit
end if
on error goto 0

' check for ADO components
filename = "msdadc.dll"
if fs.FileExists(path & filename) then
    filever = fs.GetFileVersion(path &filename)
    msg = msg & filename & " exists: Version " & filever & vbCr
else
    msg = msg & filename & " is missing." & vbCr
end if

filename = "oledb32.dll"
if fs.FileExists(path & filename) then
    filever = fs.GetFileVersion(path &filename)
    msg = msg & filename & " exists: Version " & filever & vbCr
else
    msg = msg & filename & " is missing." & vbCr
```

```
end if
```

```
MsgBox msg, vbInformation
```

This script makes some assumptions. If your ADODB.Connection is operational, but neither file is found, you should search for the files manually.

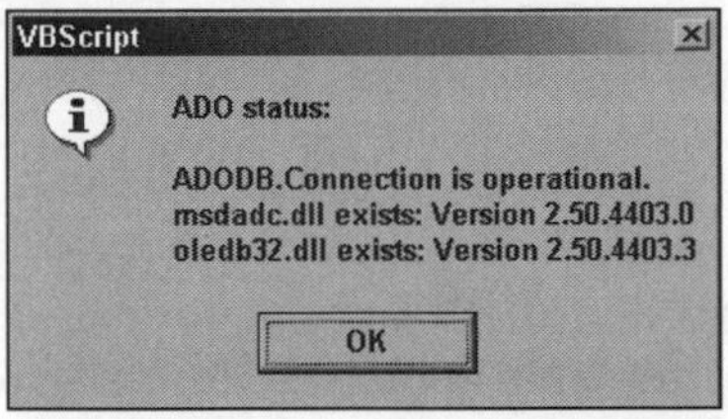

```
VBScript                              ×

  ( i )    ADO status:

          ADODB.Connection is operational.
          msdadc.dll exists: Version 2.50.4403.0
          oledb32.dll exists: Version 2.50.4403.3

                 [    OK    ]
```

Figure 23-1: Check whether ADO is operational and which MDAC version you have.

Use Table 23-1 to calculate the interface version your system currently uses.

Table 23-1   Information to Determine ADO Version Installed

ADODB.Connection	MSDADC.DLL	OLEDB32.DLL	Version
not operational	missing	missing	no MDAC (Microsoft Data Access Components) installed
operational	1.50.3506.0	missing	MDAC 1.5c
operational	2.0.3002.4	2.0.1706.0	MDAC 2.0
operational	2.0.3002.23	2.0.1706.0	MDAC 2.0 SP1/SP2
operational	2.10.3513.0	2.10.3513.0	MDAC 2.1.0.3513.2 (SQL)
operational	2.10.3711.2	2.10.3711.2	MDAC 2.1.1.3711.6 (Internet Explorer 5)
operational	2.10.3711.2	2.10.3711.9	MDAC 2.1.1.3711.11
operational	2.50.4403.0	2.50.4403.3	MDAC 2.5 (Windows 2000)

Do I need to upgrade or install anything?

Here's the good news. If your script reports ADODB.Connection operational, you are ready for action. Out of curiosity, you could check your MDAC version, but even if it's MDAC 1.5, you are fine.

And here's more good news. If MDAC is missing on your system, you can install it for free. Microsoft offers the complete software kit for downloading. But, you guessed it, there's some not-so-good news, too. Download addresses change frequently, and Microsoft download addresses change even more frequently. Start your search here: `www.microsoft.com/data/ado/default.htm`. Downloads are also available at `www.microsoft.com/data/download.htm`. Look for MDAC version 2.1 or later. The download is huge, though; more than 6MB are waiting for you.

Caution

Never touch a running system. If your system supports `ADODB.Connection`, then think twice before deciding to upgrade. There are minor inconsistencies between the MDAC versions, and installing a higher version on a system with applications that use a lower version might very well crash those applications. So, here's an easy rule—install MDAC only if it's not yet installed or if you specifically need a new feature only available in the update. Remember: Once you have upgraded to a higher MDAC version, you can't go back. You can't even uninstall MDAC. It's a one-way street.

Do install the MDAC update if any of the following example scripts raise a "Can't create Object" error. It's a rather common problem: On some systems, MDAC was installed at some time but parts of it became damaged or were uninstalled. Those systems can access `ADODB.Connection`, but they fail the moment you try to open a database.

Getting Access to a Database

First of all, you need a database to access. ADO is able to store data as plain text files in case you have no database at hand. On the companion CD, you find a sample MS Access database. You should use this database for all of your experiments if you don't have a database of your own. As it turns out, your scripts can change and even add tables to the sample database.

Opening and querying a database

To use a database, your script needs to open it first. There are many ways to open a database. Most often you will see the DSN approach: Using the Control Panel and its 32-bit ODBC Data Source module, you define a System DSN and store all the details about your database in the DSN. Then, your scripts just refer to the DSN name tag, and ADO reads the connection details from your DSN definition (see Figure 23-2).

However, the DSN approach has some major drawbacks. It requires you to set up the DSN first. You need to go through many dialog boxes. Not so good. A much easier way bypasses the DSN. Here, the script provides the connection details manually. Using this approach, you can distribute your database file and your scripts, and your users can access the data base information right away. No further setup is required.

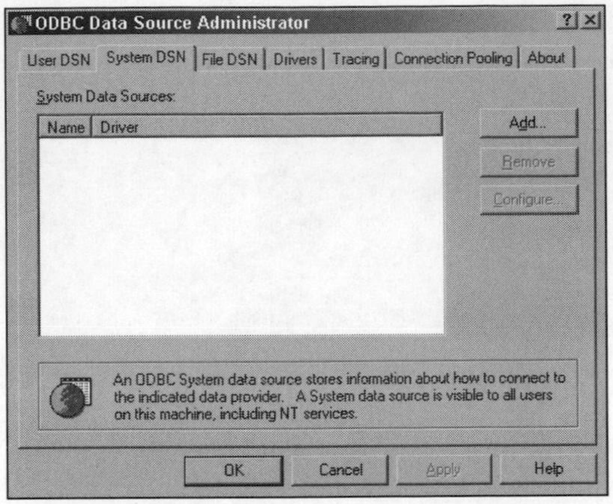

Undocumented

Figure 23-2: Don't use fixed DSNs, or you will lose a lot of flexibility.

Try it out. Along with the scripts of this chapter, you will find a sample database (`sample.mdb`). Copy the entire folder onto your hard drive and get rid of the write-protection attributes. You can then immediately start working with this database and even create your very own table design.

All files on a CD have a write-protection attribute. If you copy CD-ROM files to your local hard drive, they keep this attribute, and you can't change the files. Therefore, whenever you copy data from a CD ROM, you must remove the attribute: Right-click the files and choose Properties. Then, clear the write-protection attribute and click OK.

Now, without any further hassle, launch the script `23-2.VBS`. It will access the database and retrieve the sample information: my name and my e-mail address (see Figure 23-3).

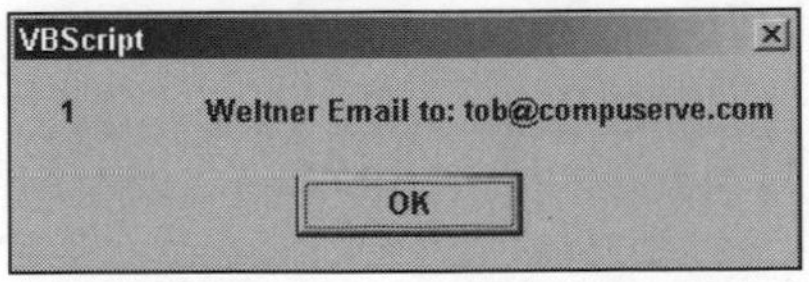

Figure 23-3: Retrieve database information without even owning a database.

Note

Next, launch the script `23-5.VBS`. Now you can enter a name and an e-mail address and add them to the sample database. To double-check, launch `23-2.VBS` again. It worked: The new entry appears (see Figure 23-4).

You can't add entries if you don't remove the write-protection attribute or if you launch the scripts directly from the CD-ROM.

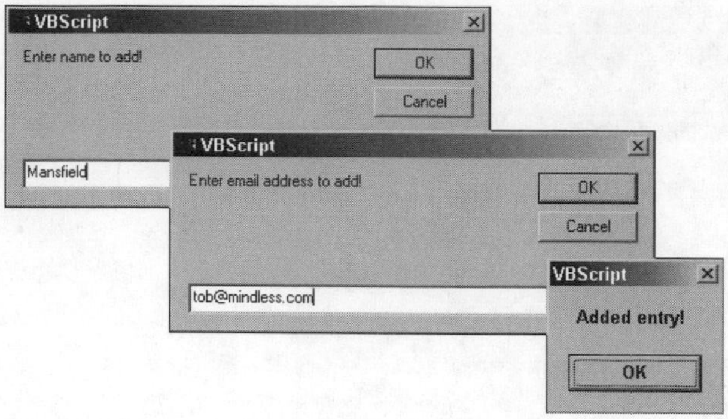

Figure 23-4: Add new entries to the sample database.

Reading database contents

Take a look at how 23-2.VBS retrieves the database information:

```
' 23-2.VBS
' determine current folder
myname = WScript.ScriptFullName
mypath = Left(myname, InstrRev(myname, "\"))

' open database
set db = CreateObject("ADODB.Connection")
db.Open("DRIVER={Microsoft Access Driver (*.mdb)}; DBQ=" _
& mypath & "SAMPLE.MDB")

' use SQL to select information
sql = "select * from info"
set rs = db.Execute(sql)

' read resulting record set
do until rs.EOF
    list = list & rs("id") & vbTab & rs("name") _
        & " Email to: " & rs("email") & vbCr
    rs.MoveNext
loop

' output information
MsgBox list
```

First, the script determines the current folder. Because you are not going to use a static DSN, your script must tell ADO the location of your database. In this case, the database is stored in the same folder with the script. Therefore, the script needs to find out the folder name it is stored in.

Next, it opens the database. It first gets a vanilla instance of the ADODB. Connection object and calls its open method to open the real database. Instead of a DSN, it provides the connection details directly, and DRIVER= specifies the database driver. DBQ= specifies the location of the database file.

Figure 23-5: Your scripts can actually read and write the database.

How do you get information from your database? You ask for it. Databases use the SQL database query language. To select all data in a specific table, use `SELECT * FROM tablename`. Because there's only one table stored in the sample database and this table is named info, you use `SELECT * FROM INFO`. `Execute` executes your SQL statement and returns the results as `recordset`.

The script now loops through the `recordset` until the end is reached and EOF is true. It can read the contents of each `recordset`. `RS("name")` retrieves the information of the "name" field of the current record. Alternatively, you can specify the field index. `RS(1)` would also retrieve the name field value because the name field happens to be the field number 1 (field count starts at 0, and field 0 in the sample table is called "id").

Caution

Always make sure your loop uses `MoveNext` to move on to the next table record. If you don't, your loop will constantly read the same record set, and you'll never reach the end of the table.

Finding out design information

So far, your script has had a great advantage in that it knows the names of the table fields and can access them directly. What if you don't know how many fields a table contains or what the table fields are called?

Find out (see Figure 23-6). Here's how:

```
' 23-3.VBS

' determine current folder
myname = WScript.ScriptFullName
mypath = Left(myname, InstrRev(myname, "\"))

' open database
set db = CreateObject("ADODB.Connection")
db.Open("DRIVER={Microsoft Access Driver (*.mdb)}; DBQ=" _
& mypath & "SAMPLE.MDB")

' use SQL to select information
sql = "select * from info"
set rs = db.Execute(sql)

' find out number of fields
fields = rs.fields.count
```

```
' find out field names
redim fieldnames(fields-1)
for x=0 to fields-1
    fieldnames(x) = rs.fields(x).name
next

' output information
msg = "Table contains " & fields & " fields:" & vbCr
for x = 0 to fields-1
    msg = msg & fieldnames(x) & vbCr
next

' output information
MsgBox msg
```

Figure 23-6: Read the names of all the fields available in the sample table.

Now you can create a script that reads information from any kind of table:

```
' 23-4.VBS

' determine current folder
myname = WScript.ScriptFullName
mypath = Left(myname, InstrRev(myname, "\"))

' open database
set db = CreateObject("ADODB.Connection")
db.Open("DRIVER={Microsoft Access Driver (*.mdb)}; DBQ=" _
& mypath & "SAMPLE.MDB")

' use SQL to select information
sql = "select * from info"
set rs = db.Execute(sql)

do until rs.EOF
    for x = 0 to rs.fields.count-1
        list = list & rs(x) & vbTab
    next
    list = list & vbCr
    rs.MoveNext
loop

' output information
MsgBox list
```

Adding new data to your database table

Next, let's examine how write.vbs manages to insert new data sets into your table:

```
' 23-5.VBS

' find out current folder
myname = WScript.ScriptFullName
mypath = Left(myname, InstrRev(myname, "\"))

' ask for new data
name = InputBox("Enter name to add!")
email = InputBox("Enter email address to add!")

' access database
set db = CreateObject("ADODB.Connection")
db.Open("DRIVER={Microsoft Access Driver (*.mdb)}; DBQ=" _
& mypath & "SAMPLE.MDB")

' use SQL to insert new data
sql = "insert into info (name, email) values ('" _
& name & "', '" & email & "')"

' uncomment next line to see SQL statement!
' MsgBox sql

' execute sql statement
set rs = db.Execute(sql)
MsgBox "Added entry!"
```

It's fairly easy: The script uses the same basic architecture. Instead of SELECT, it uses the INSERT INTO statement.

Caution

SQL uses single quotes to delimit text information. If you enter single quotes in your data text, they interfere with the single quotes the SQL statement uses. Try it out. Launch write.vbs and include single quotes. You'll get an ODBC error.

Solving the single quote problem

Obviously, you can't expect your users to avoid single quotes. You don't need to, either. Just convert single quotes to two single quotes. Two single quotes are recognized as data single quotes just as Visual Basic recognizes two quotes as a single quote inside of a text string.

So, after you ask for the information to save in your database, use a command like this:

```
datatext = Replace(datatext, "'", "''")
```

To pinpoint the issue: Replace a single quote with two single quotes.

Autonumber fields

Why didn't the `write.vbs` script add a number for the id column even though the new data set still received an id number?

When I designed the info table, I assigned the info field a variable type of "AutoNumber." This value is an automatic counter. It will issue a unique number to each new dataset. It's a good idea to use `AutoNumber` fields because they're your only way to uniquely identify data sets.

Retrieving variable fields

You can retrieve the variable types of your table fields, too (see Figure 23-7):

```
' 23-6.VBS

' determine current folder
myname = WScript.ScriptFullName
mypath = Left(myname, InstrRev(myname, "\"))

' open database
set db = CreateObject("ADODB.Connection")
db.Open("DRIVER={Microsoft Access Driver (*.mdb)}; DBQ=" _
& mypath & "SAMPLE.MDB")

' use SQL to select information
sql = "select * from info"
set rs = db.Execute(sql)

' find out number of fields
fields = rs.fields.count

' find out field names
redim fieldnames(fields-1)
for x=0 to fields-1
    fieldnames(x) = rs.fields(x).name & " Type: " & rs.fields(x).type
next

' output information
msg = "Table contains " & fields & " fields:" & vbCr
for x = 0 to fields-1
    msg = msg & fieldnames(x) & vbCr
next

' output information
MsgBox msg
```

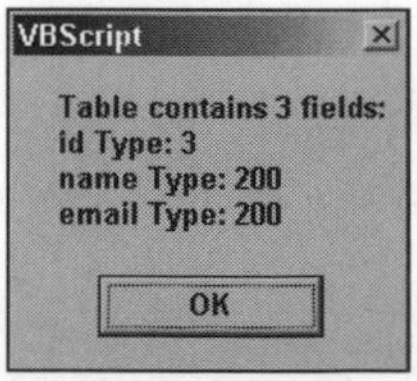

```
VBScript                    [x]

  Table contains 3 fields:
  id Type: 3
  name Type: 200
  email Type: 200

        [    OK    ]
```

Figure 23-7: Determine the variable type of database fields.

Table 23-2 shows which numeric values correspond to the variable type that can be stored in the field.

Table 23-2	Database Variable Types
Variable Type	**Description**
8, 12, 129, 130, 200, 201, 202, 203	Text strings
7, 133, 134, 135	Date
11	Boolean
9, 10, 13, 128, 132, 204, 205	Special
All else	Numeric

You need the variable type when trying to insert new data via INSERT INTO: String information must be enclosed in single quotes, date information must be converted via Cdate, and Boolean values must be converted using CBool.

Counting the number of records

SELECT not only retrieves database data, it also supports some commands to sum columns and count datasets. To count all recordsets, use this approach:

```
' 23-7.VBS

' determine current folder
myname = WScript.ScriptFullName
mypath = Left(myname, InstrRev(myname, "\"))

' open database
set db = CreateObject("ADODB.Connection")
db.Open("DRIVER={Microsoft Access Driver (*.mdb)}; DBQ=" _
& mypath & "SAMPLE.MDB")

' use SQL to count records
sql = "select count(*) as counter from info"
set rs = db.Execute(sql)

MsgBox "Table contains " & rs("counter") & " records."
```

Deleting records

SQL can also delete records. To delete a record, you need a unique way of identifying it. This is where the AutoNumber ID column comes into play. Each record gets a unique id number, and with this number you can delete individual records:

```
' 23-8.VBS

' determine current folder
myname = WScript.ScriptFullName
mypath = Left(myname, InstrRev(myname, "\"))

' open database
set db = CreateObject("ADODB.Connection")
db.Open("DRIVER={Microsoft Access Driver (*.mdb)}; DBQ=" _
& mypath & "SAMPLE.MDB")

' use SQL to select information
sql = "select * from info"
set rs = db.Execute(sql)

do until rs.EOF
    for x = 0 to rs.fields.count-1
        list = list & rs(x) & vbTab
    next
    list = list & vbCr
    rs.MoveNext
loop

' output information
delrec = InputBox(list & vbCr _
& "Enter ID of record you want to delete!")
if delrec = vbEmpty then WScript.Quit
sql = "DELETE FROM info WHERE id = " & delrec
db.Execute sql
MsgBox "Record deleted."
```

Undocumented

The AutoNumber counter is incremented each time you add a new record. Deleting records won't decrement the counter. So, when you add your next record, it won't get the id previously assigned to the deleted record. It always gets a unique id number.

Creating new database tables

SQL can even add completely new tables to your database. This way, you can use the sample database as the foundation for your own projects. The next script adds a table named `newtable` and defines the following fields:

id	AutoNumber
Name	String 200
Street	String 200
City	String 200

```
' 23-9.VBS

' determine current folder
myname = WScript.ScriptFullName
mypath = Left(myname, InstrRev(myname, "\"))

' open database
set db = CreateObject("ADODB.Connection")
db.Open("DRIVER={Microsoft Access Driver (*.mdb)}; DBQ=" _
& mypath & "SAMPLE.MDB")

' use SQL to select information
sql = "CREATE TABLE newtable (id COUNTER, Name TEXT(200), " _
& "Street TEXT(200), City TEXT(200))"
set rs = db.Execute(sql)

MsgBox "Table added!"
```

Adjust the sample scripts to add data to this table as you like.

Deleting tables

Now you just need a way to delete a table. The next script uses the SQL DROP statement to delete the newly added table:

```
' 23-10.VBS

' determine current folder
myname = WScript.ScriptFullName
mypath = Left(myname, InstrRev(myname, "\"))

' open database
set db = CreateObject("ADODB.Connection")
db.Open("DRIVER={Microsoft Access Driver (*.mdb)}; DBQ=" _
& mypath & "SAMPLE.MDB")

' use SQL to delete table
sql = "DROP TABLE newtable"
set rs = db.Execute(sql)

MsgBox "Table deleted!"
```

Note

There's a lot more to databases than that. You can access recordsets directly, use different cursor types to move back and forth in your record sets, and retrieve newly assigned AutoNumber values. Using SQL Server (or any other database server), you can call stored procedures and create SQL macros. All of this information deserves its own book, although I've provided all the scripting tools you need to access databases. If you find this interesting, I recommend you get yourself a SQL book, such as Microsoft SQL Server 7 Secrets or Microsoft Access 2000 Developer's Guide, both from IDG Books Worldwide.

Controlling the Index Server

Information management is a hot topic these days. There are millions of documents floating around, and it's not easy to keep your head straight in a world of information overkill.

Fortunately, there are easy solutions to this problem. Many years ago, Microsoft developed a tool called Index Server. The Index Server was targeted at the Internet, and its sole purpose was to automatically index a Web site so visitors could search for pages with particular content. Although the Index Server worked well, it was long considered to be some kind of experimental product. Microsoft wouldn't support it, and it was not an official part of the MS Internet Information Server.

Finally, the Index Server has evolved as a true commercial product. Its internal design has changed considerably, and what's even more important, the Index Server now is a standard part of Windows 2000.

This has enormous consequences. The Index Server no longer is just another Web service. It can index any kind of data store, and Windows 2000 uses the Index Server to index its entire local file system.

Windows 2000 hides the Index Server, though. You can do full text searches and be amazed at the speed, but there's no obvious way to control the Index Server. In fact, the built-in search uses only a small fraction of the Index Server's capabilities.

Despite this, you can access the Index Server through ADO directly and think of it as a database. Much of what you have just learned will fall right into place when applied to the Index Server.

Note

The following applies to Windows 2000 only. However, if you use Windows NT 4 and the Internet Information Server with Option Pack >=4, you can use all of the following scripts to index your Web page. Just adjust the catalog names and embed the scripts in your ASP Web pages.

Activating local file system indexing

Let's get some terminology straight first. The Index Server is a background service. It can automatically and silently index entire drives (see Figure 23-8). It doesn't have to, though. You still have the option to do full text searches the old way and have Windows snoop through the files as it executes the search.

So, first you should check the state of your Index Server. This is easy: Just select Search from your Start menu and search for files and folders. Explorer launches and displays the search panel in the left part of its window.

If you take a closer look, you'll find a remark about the Index Server — click Search Options if the remark is missing. The remark reveals whether the Index Server is turned on or off, and whether the Index is up-to-date or not.

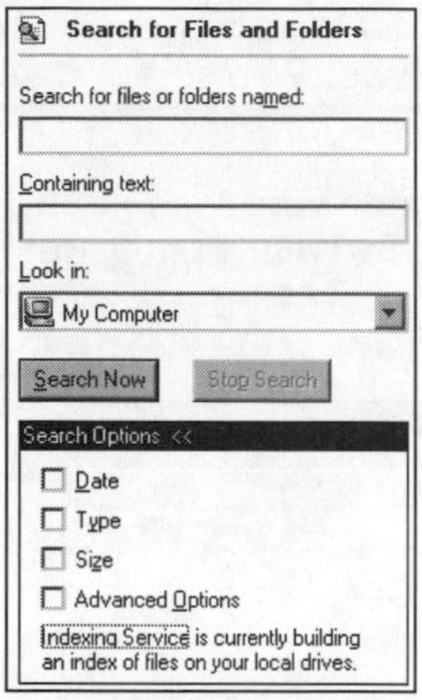

Figure 23-8: Activate the Windows 2000 Index Server.

Click Indexing Service to see more details. You now have the choice to turn indexing on or off (see Figure 23-9).

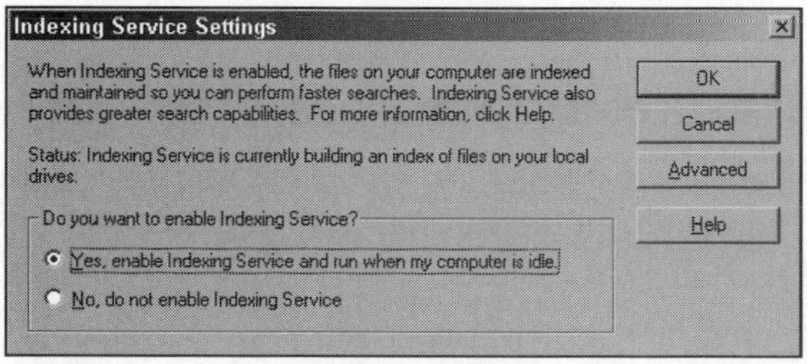

Figure 23-9: Turn on Indexing Service to index your entire local file system.

Turning the Index Server off may be necessary for special full text searches. While the Index Server is turned on, it only finds information stored in its index. If the index isn't up-to-date yet, if the file type you want to search isn't included in the indexing scheme, or if the file isn't stored in a folder included in the indexing scheme, you must turn off the Index Server to find the search text.

Click Advanced to gain even more control. You now see the catalogs your Index Server is working with. The window provides all the details and reveals whether a catalog is up-to-date and what the Index Server is currently doing (see Figure 23-10).

The Index Server doesn't update its catalogs immediately. Instead, it waits for the system to become idle. While you are busy working with your applications, the Index Server patiently waits in the background. This way, your work isn't slowed down.

Most likely, you'll see two catalogs: System and Web. System is the index of your local file system. Web is the index of your Web server if you have installed the Internet Information Server.

Undocumented

If the Web catalog is missing, you did not enable your Web Publishing functions. On Windows NT 4 with IIS, you find a Web catalog, but the local System catalog is missing.

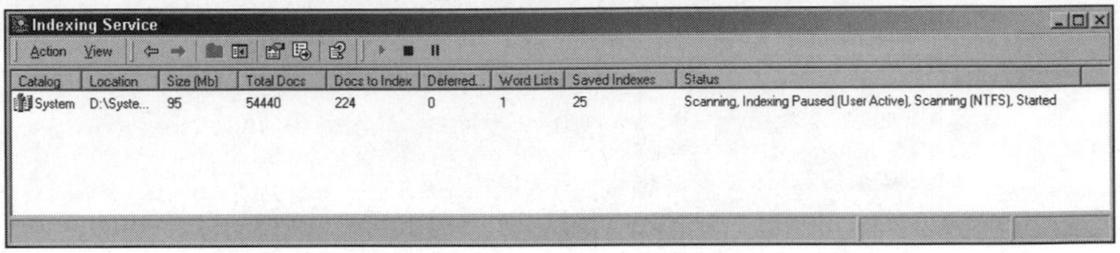

Catalog	Location	Size (Mb)	Total Docs	Docs to Index	Deferred...	Word Lists	Saved Indexes	Status
System	D:\Syste...	95	54440	224	0	1	25	Scanning, Indexing Paused (User Active), Scanning (NTFS), Started

Figure 23-10: See what your Index Server is currently doing.

Double-click a catalog to see which folders it includes.

In the toolbar, you find a button to make the hierarchical tree view visible.

Tip

Adding and removing folders from the index

Index catalogs for your local system and for your Web server are managed differently. The Web catalog should be managed with the Internet Information Server controls only. Your local index is managed by the Explorer.

To add a path to your catalog, open it as outlined above. Then point at an empty space in the window and right-click. Choose New and Folder. You can now explicitly add a folder path and specify whether this folder should be included in your index or not.

Undocumented

The folder you specify includes all of its subfolders. By default, the System catalog includes the root folders of all of your drives. This means that all data on your drives is automatically part of the index. In addition, there are some folder exclusions. The Index Server doesn't index the folders with all the personal settings.

Adding a new catalog

You can always add additional catalogs. This way, you can specify a specific catalog and search only for areas of your system defined in this catalog. However, adding additional catalogs generally isn't a good idea because it costs a lot of resources. The Index Server has to update each catalog individually, and there will be separate index files, taking many megabytes of extra space.

Secret

You don't need additional catalogs just because you would like to limit your search to specific folders. Instead, define the "scope" of your search and use the general System catalog for all of your searches.

Querying the Index Server

Now that you know the general architecture, let's search for some information. Check out the next script (see Figure 23-11): It lists the first 20 matches for documents that contain both "Microsoft" and "ADO:"

```
' 23-11.VBS

' Access Index Server
set index = CreateObject("ixsso.Query")

' Define search criteria
index.Query = "Microsoft and ADO"
' Define catalog to search
index.Catalog = "system"
' Select information to include in result set
index.Columns = "filename, size, hitcount, rank, path,
characterization"
' limit result to 20
index.MaxRecords = 20
' sort by rank (quality of result), descending order
index.SortBy = "rank[d]"
' allow optimization
index.AllowEnumeration = true

' Result is a record set
set rs = index.CreateRecordset("nonsequential")

' display file names
do until rs.EOF
    list = list & rs("filename") & vbCr
    rs.MoveNext
loop

MsgBox list
```

Query contains your search request. Here, you'll discover the first great difference from the old-fashioned full-text search. In this case, you can use Boolean operators such as and, or, and not to search for multiple key words.

MaxRecords limits the result set, and Columns specifies which columns to include in the result set.

Figure 23-11: Quickly find the first 20 documents matching "Microsoft" and "ADO."

Exploring information categories

Table 23-3 lists the information categories you can query.

Table 23-3	Index Server Information Categories
Column	**Description**
filename	Name of file
path	Path name
vpath	Virtual path name (used for Web access)
hitcount	Number of matches
rank	Relative hit count (0 to 100)
create	Time of file creation
write	Time of last file change
DocTitle	Title of document
DocSubject	Subject of document
DocPageCount	Number of pages
DocAuthor	Author name of document
DocKeywords	Keywords in document
DocComments	Comments in document
Characterization	Summary report of file content

The next script allows you to experiment with the advanced search capabilities. First, the script opens an input dialog box so you can type in your search criteria. It then lists the path names of the files in the result set:

```
' 23-12.VBS

do
    set index = CreateObject("ixsso.Query")
    index.MaxRecords = 20
    index.SortBy = "rank[d]"
    index.AllowEnumeration = true
    index.Catalog = "system"
    index.Columns = "filename, size, hitcount, rank, path," _
        & "characterization"
    criteria = InputBox("Search for:")
    if criteria=vbEmpty then exit do
    index.Query = criteria
    set rs = index.CreateRecordset("nonsequential")
    ' display file names
    list = ""
    do until rs.EOF
        list = list & rs("path") & vbCr
        rs.MoveNext
    loop
    MsgBox list

    if index.QueryTimedOut then
        MsgBox "Your query was too complex!"
    end if

    if index.QueryIncomplete then
        MsgBox "Search result is not complete!"
    end if

    if index.OutOfDate then
        MsgBox "Index is not up-to-date. Results may not " _
            & "be accurate."
    end if

loop
MsgBox "Done!"
```

Use the `QueryTimedOut`, `QueryInxcomplete`, and `OutOfDate` properties to check whether the index is current and whether your search has processed without errors.

Undocumented

The `ixsso.Query` object is non-recyclable. You can use it only for one query. Once you have issued your query using `CreateRecordset`, you can't use it for new searches. Instead, get a new instance and call `CreateObject` again.

Using Boolean operators

To combine multiple keywords, use Boolean operators. For example, to search for documents containing the words Microsoft and ADO but not MDAC, use this query:

```
Microsoft and ADO and not MDAC
```

Searching for phrases

You can even query in natural language. Use the $contents keyword:

```
$contents "How do I change screen resolution?"
```

Querying file properties

Use # in conjunction with one of the information categories listed in Table 23-3 and include file properties into your search. For example, to search for all WinWord documents starting with the letter "A," use this query:

```
#filename a*.doc
```

Or combine a natural language query with the selection of specific document types:

```
($contents "How do I change the screen resolution") and (#filename
*.htm or #filename *.hlp or #filename *.chm)
```

Use @ instead of # to compare file properties. For example, to list only .doc files greater that 10,000 bytes, write

```
#filename *.doc and @size>10000
```

Limiting searches to specific folders

Let's see how you can make real use of the Index Server. Let's assume you want to search the folder My Documents for WinWord and HTML documents only. You'd like to get a list of all the documents that match your key words.

How do you limit the scope of your search? You need another object, namely ixsso.Util. The following script does the job. It automatically limits the scope of the search to your personal My Documents folder and all of its subfolders.

```
' 23-13.VBS

set wshshell = CreateObject("WScript.Shell")
do
    set index = CreateObject("ixsso.Query")
    index.MaxRecords = 20
    index.SortBy = "rank[d]"
    index.AllowEnumeration = true
    index.Catalog = "system"
    index.Columns = "path, rank"
```

```
        criteria = InputBox("Search for:")
        if criteria=vbEmpty then exit do
        index.Query = criteria

        ' limit the scope
        set util = CreateObject("ixsso.Util")
        util.AddScopeToQuery index, _
            wshshell.SpecialFolders("MyDocuments"), "deep"
        set rs = index.CreateRecordset("nonsequential")
        ' display file names
        list = ""
        do until rs.EOF
            list = list & rs("path") & vbCr
            rs.MoveNext
        loop
        MsgBox list

        if index.QueryTimedOut then
            MsgBox "Your query was too complex!"
        end if

        if index.QueryIncomplete then
            MsgBox "Search result is not complete!"
        end if

        if index.OutOfDate then
            MsgBox "Index is not up-to-date. Results may " _
                & "not be accurate."
        end if

loop
MsgBox "Done!"
```

Creating your own search dialog box

Maybe you are fed up with the new search panel Microsoft has built into the Explorer. I personally liked the old search dialog box much better. What's even worse, the new search dialog box doesn't even support many of the advanced Index Server features.

This is why I have created a little COM object. Use it as a search dialog box or as a foundation for your own projects (see Figure 23-12). Install the COM object first (\install\index\setup.exe). Full source code is provided at \components\index\index.vbp.

```
' 23-14.VBS

set tool = CreateObject("index.search")
set wshshell = CreateObject("WScript.Shell")

selected = tool.ShowDialog
MsgBox "You selected: " & selected
```

```
MsgBox "You can re-open the search any time!"
selected = tool.ShowDialog
MsgBox "You can also clear the display!"
tool.DeleteDialog
selected = tool.ShowDialog
MsgBox "I now add scope to your search and only allow searches on
drive C: and your windows folder!"
tool.AddScope "C:\", "shallow"
tool.AddScope wshshell.ExpandEnvironmentStrings("%WINDIR%"), "shallow"
selected = tool.ShowDialog
MsgBox "Now I remove the scope again!"
tool.ClearScope
result = tool.ShowDialog
```

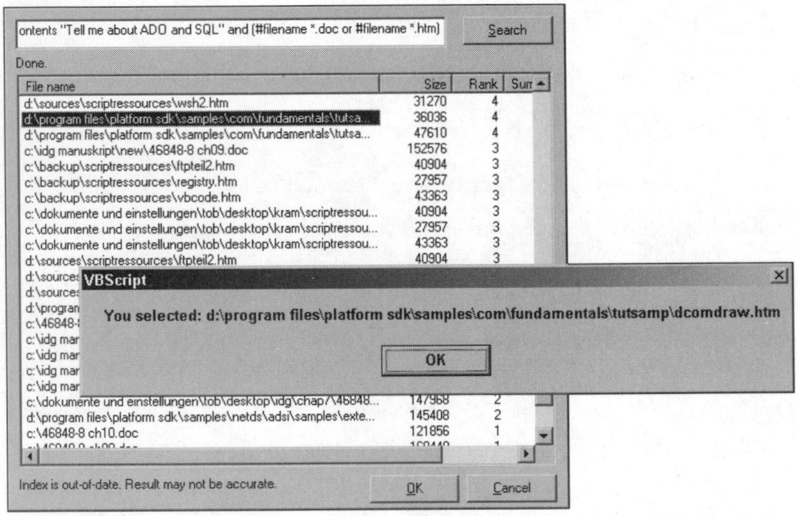

Figure 23-12: Create your own search dialog boxes and take advantage of powerful search options.

Fine-tuning Index Server

Your dialog box provides a summary column. In this column, the Index Server displays a short summary of the file. However, summaries are displayed only if the Index Server creates a summary in the first place. Summary creation is turned off by default for performance reasons.

To turn summary creation on, choose Search in the Start menu and search for Files and Folders. Then, click Index Server in the left column and choose Advanced. Click iconexpand.jpg to see the tree view.

Now, right-click the Indexing Service on Local Machine and choose Properties. Choose the Generate abstracts option and click OK (see Figure 23-13).

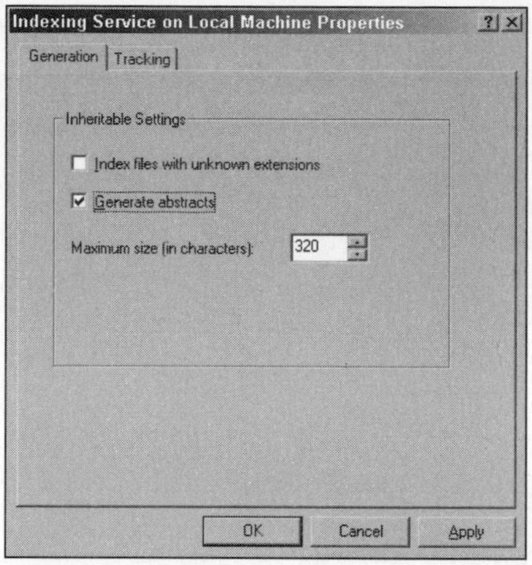

Figure 23-13: Turn on abstract generation if you want to use the "characterization" info column.

It takes a while for the Index Server to create summary information. You can always stop the Index Server and right-click the System catalog. Choose All Tasks and Empty Catalog to re-create it from scratch, and then restart the Index Server.

Secret

Summary

In this chapter, you saw how easy it is to use ADO to access any kind of database. Best of all, you can use a sample database and manage it completely by script — no additional software is required. You can read and write data to the database, and even create entirely new tables. Your scripts can now calculate invoices, create mass e-mail, and maintain your personal schedule.

Windows 2000 goes a step further. The Index Server acts like a database, but in reality it is a dynamic information store of all the data stored on your local drives. Scripts can easily take advantage of this powerful mechanism: Use Boolean search operators and even natural language queries to quickly find the information you need.

Chapter 24

Managing Windows NT/ 2000 Server

In This Chapter

▶ Manage Windows NT through the API — add/delete users, change permissions, and change group membership

▶ Find out about ADSI and how you get it

▶ Discover the ADSI object model, and change user account properties

▶ Manage services: start, stop, and pause them, even on remote systems

▶ Shut down your local machine or any remote computer

▶ Add secret Registry keys to automatically log onto Windows NT

Scripts are perfect for administering Windows NT/2000. Through API calls and the new ADSI (Active Directory Service Interface), your scripts can manage user accounts, file shares, printers, and services. In conjunction with the file system methods, you can easily transfer hundreds of user profiles in a matter of minutes. In this chapter, you learn how to use both the API and ADSI to manage all kinds of server-related tasks.

Managing Windows NT/2000 Security

Managing Windows NT/2000 can be annoying at times — it's just too much work to administer hundreds of user accounts manually. Isn't there some macro language that can automatically take care of routine work?

There is. VBScript and the Windows Scripting Host can help you administer Windows NT/2000, and Microsoft has made VBScript the official new automation language of Windows 2000. This shows you the new emphasis Microsoft puts on VBScript.

However, VBScript itself is only the framework. It doesn't provide any methods to access user accounts and change security settings. There are two ways to add these capabilities:

- Write your own COM objects. You've seen many COM objects throughout this book serve as scripting extensions, and Windows NT management functions provided by the API can easily " wrap" inside COM objects.

- Add ADSI to your system. ADSI is the new management standard introduced with Windows 2000. It's a general interface to standardize how scripts talk to different `namespaces`. You don't need Windows 2000 to take advantage of ADSI, though. ADSI is available separately, and it's free. All you need is to download the ADSI update.

Secret

The big ADSI advantage is its availability: You can find it on any Windows 2000 machine, and you can add it to other Windows versions. Also, ADSI is a general interface, and you can access Exchange mail accounts or the Active Directory. However, its drawback is speed: ADSI is much slower than direct API calls. Especially if you plan to batch-update large numbers of accounts, you should use the API approach.

Creating scripting extensions to manage user accounts

Table 24-1 lists some scripting extensions I've created to help you manage Windows NT/2000. However, these extensions are provided as *sample only*. In a professional production environment, review the source code to make sure it works as intended. Be extremely cautious if you decide to experiment with these extensions.

I've provided full source code so you can understand and expand the COM objects as you like. Make sure you have installed the COM objects `listset` in Table 24-1. They are needed for the API-based scripts.

Table 24-1   COM Objects Provided With This Book

COM Object	Description
`\install\ntuser\setup.exe`	Manage user accounts
`\install\ntservice\setup.exe`	Manage system services
`\install\ntshutdown\setup.exe`	Shutdown a system locally or remotely

Getting ready for ADSI

ADSI is exciting and much more suitable for scripting. It will be the new standard once Windows 2000 takes over, so it's a good idea to get accustomed with it. ADSI is free, and you can upgrade Windows NT 4 by going to `www.microsoft.com/adsi`.

Look for the suitable update for your system and download the package. It's comparably lightweight. Once you have updated your system to ADSI, you can immediately take advantage of all the ADSI sample scripts.

Managing User Accounts (the API Way)

Fiddling around manually with user accounts is very time-consuming and error-prone, at least in larger companies. Don't do it. You can forget most of the dialog boxes with your new scripting extensions and manage user accounts solely by script once you have installed the COM script extension as outlined previously.

Enumerating users

To find out which users are defined on a specific computer, use `EnumUsers`:

```
' 24-1.VBS

set tool = CreateObject("nt.user")

MsgBox tool.EnumUsers
MsgBox tool.EnumUsers("\\scenic")
```

You can query local users as well as user accounts on remote machines as long as you have the necessary permissions.

`EnumUsers` returns the information as `name`, `comment`, `usercomment`, and `full name`. Use `Split` to get to the individual information:

```
' 24-2.VBS

set tool = CreateObject("nt.user")

users = Split(tool.EnumUsers, vbCr)

for x=0 to UBound(users)-1
    infos = Split(users(x), vbTab)
    list = list & "Username: " & infos(0) & vbCr
    list = list & "Comment: " & infos(1) & vbCr & vbCr
next

MsgBox list, vbInformation
```

`EnumUsers` supports a second parameter that works as a filter:

Table 24-2   Filter Codes for Enumerating User Accounts

Filter	Description
1	Local user account data on a domain controller
2	Global user account data on a computer
4	Combination of all
8	Domain trust account data on a domain controller
16	Workstation or member server account data on a domain controller
32	Domain controller account data on a domain controller

The next script shows the differences. You can combine filter flags to include more than one group:

```
' 24-3.VBS

set tool = CreateObject("nt.user")

for i = 0 to 5
users = Split(tool.EnumUsers(,2^i), vbCrLf)

    list = "Enumerating using filter " & 2^i & vbCr
for x=0 to UBound(users)-1
        infos = Split(users(x), vbTab)
    list = list & "Username: " & infos(0) & vbCr
next
MsgBox list, vbInformation
next
```

Adding users

Your scripts can add users, too. Use `AddUser`:

```
' 24-4.VBS

set tool = CreateObject("nt.user")

if tool.AddUser("", "testaccount", "secret", _
5, "c:\users\test", "this is a test account") then
MsgBox "User account added!"
else
    MsgBox "Couldn't add user account: " & tool.GetLastError
end if
```

This is the complete syntax:

```
AddUser server, user, pwd, expires, homedir, comment, scriptdir
```

Table 24-3	AddUser Parameters
Argument	**Description**
server	Name of server or "" for local server
user	Name of user account
pwd	Password
expires	Days the password is valid
homedir	Home directory
comment	Comment describing the account purpose
scriptdir	Script directory

Deleting user accounts

DelUser deletes a user account. Note that deleting a user account can't be undone. Even if you re-create the account later, the new account gets new Security IDs and acts as a different account.

```
' 24-5.VBS

set tool = CreateObject("nt.user")

if tool.DelUser("", "testaccount") then
MsgBox "User account deleted!"
else
    MsgBox "Couldn't delete user account: " & tool.GetLastError
end if
```

Changing passwords

Your script can change user passwords, too. You have two options, one being to provide the old password as authentication. Or, if you are an administrator, you can use administrative override and skip the old password. This is especially useful if someone has forgotten his or her password or has left the company.

Execute script 24-4.VBS first to add a test user account, and then change the password:

```
' 24-6.VBS

set tool = CreateObject("nt.user")

if tool.ChangePassword("", "testaccount", _
"newpassword", "secret") then
MsgBox "Password has changed!"
else
```

```
      MsgBox "Couldn't change password: " & tool.GetLastError
end if
```

To use administrative override, you need administrator privilege. Skip the old password:

```
' 24-7.VBS

set tool = CreateObject("nt.user")

if tool.ChangePassword("", "testaccount", _
"newpassword") then
MsgBox "Password has changed!"
else
      MsgBox "Couldn't change password: " & tool.GetLastError
end if
```

Listing global groups

Your COM object can manage global groups, too. Local groups cannot be managed.

Note

Global groups are a feature of domains. On your local computer, you may not have access to global groups.

Take a look at your global groups:

```
' 24-8.VBS

set tool = CreateObject("nt.user")

MsgBox tool.EnumerateGroups
```

You can list the groups of individual servers, too:

```
' 24-9.VBS

set tool = CreateObject("nt.user")

MsgBox tool.EnumerateGroups("\\SCENIC")
```

You can even find out the groups a specific user belongs to:

```
' 24-10.VBS

set tool = CreateObject("nt.user")

MsgBox tool.EnumerateGroups("", "testaccount")
```

Maybe you want to list the users in a specific group. Here's how:

```
' 24-11.VBS

set tool = CreateObject("nt.user")

MsgBox tool.EnumGroupUsers("", "Power User")
```

Managing group membership

Your script can add users to groups and remove them from groups, too. This is how you make your test account a member of the domain administrators:

```
' 24-12.VBS

set tool = CreateObject("nt.user")

if  tool.AddUserToGroup("", "Power User", "testaccount") then
    MsgBox "User added to group!"
else
    MsgBox "Couldn't add user to group: " & tool.GetLastError
end if
```

To remove the account from the group, use this approach:

```
' 24-13.VBS

set tool = CreateObject("nt.user")

if  tool.DelUserFromGroup("", "Power User", "testaccount") then
    MsgBox "User removed from group!"
else
    MsgBox "Couldn't remove user from group: " & tool.GetLastError
end if
```

Finding the primary domain controller

Internally, the COM object uses a helper function to find the primary domain controller if you specify a domain name instead of a server name. You can use this method separately, too. Just replace the domain name in the sample script with a valid domain name:

```
' 24-14.VBS

set tool = CreateObject("nt.user")

MsgBox tool.GetPrimaryDCName("ASP")
```

Exploring the ADSI World

ADSI can access all kinds of namespaces. Namespaces refer to the way an application or service organizes its data. To access Windows NT security, ADSI uses the identifier WinNT:.

Let's check out what this namespace has to offer:

```
' 24-15.VBS

' get access to namespace
set namespace = GetObject("WinNT:")
```

```
' see what we get
for each object in namespace
    list = list & object.name & vbCr
next

MsgBox list
```

The `namespace` contains the names of all domains and workgroups currently online. You can dive into the hierarchy. For example, pick a listed domain and enumerate its content. Exchange the domain name in this example with a valid domain name. You can also use a computer name.

```
' 24-16.VBS

' get access to namespace
set namespace = GetObject("WinNT://ASP")

' see what we get
for each object in namespace
    list = list & object.name & vbCr
next

MsgBox list
```

Whoa: This time the script spits out all the user accounts and groups.

If you are interested in your local computer only, you can further enhance your scripts and have them use your computer name by default. Just use the `ComputerName` method provided by `WScript.Network`:

```
Set objNet = WScript.CreateObject("WScript.Network")
MsgBox objNet.ComputerName
```

Let's check out who is a member in a specific group:

```
' 24-17.VBS

Set net = WScript.CreateObject("WScript.Network")
local = net.ComputerName

' get access to namespace
set namespace = GetObject("WinNT://" & local & "/Power Users")

' see what we get
for each object in namespace
    list = list & object.name & vbCr
next

MsgBox list
```

This time, you get an error. You can't ask for user names this way.

Getting "real" error messages

Whenever ADSI raises an error, you won't get a clue what is going on. This is because ADSI raises OLE errors and doesn't support the VBScript-style `err.description` property. So, the first task is to find out why ADSI raises an error.

Fortunately, you don't need to invest much time: You've done it already. Remember? In Chapter 4, you developed a COM object that transforms OLE error numbers into clear text error messages. Just make sure you have installed the COM object: `\install\oleerr\setup.exe`. Now, you can find out the reason why ADSI complains:

```
' 24-18.VBS

Set net = WScript.CreateObject("WScript.Network")
local = net.ComputerName

' get access to namespace
set namespace = GetObject("WinNT://" & local & "/Power Users")

' see what we get
on error resume next
for each object in namespace
    list = list & object.name & vbCr
next

CheckError

MsgBox list

sub CheckError
    if not err.number=0 then
        ' an error occured
        set ole = CreateObject("ole.err")
        MsgBox ole.oleError(err.Number), vbCritical
        err.clear
    end if
end sub
```

You get an "Error not found" error: ADSI was unable to find what you requested. While `WinNT:` and domains are containers, groups are not. You can't enumerate their content and get away with it. Groups are single objects.

Is it a container?

The next script provides a method to check whether an object is a container or not:

```
' 24-19.VBS

Set net = WScript.CreateObject("WScript.Network")
local = net.ComputerName

list = WhatIsIt("WinNT://" & local)
list = list & WhatIsIt("WinNT://" & local & "/Power Users")
```

```
MsgBox list, vbInformation

function WhatIsIt(objname)
set obj = GetObject(objname)

if isContainer(obj) then
        WhatIsIt = objname & " is a container and of class " _
            & obj.class & vbCr
else
        WhatIsIt = objname & " is NO container and of class " _
            & obj.class & vbCr
end if
end function

function isContainer(obj)
    set classobj = GetObject(obj.Schema)
    isContainer = classobj.Container
end function
```

Enumerating group memberships

Groups are objects with their own properties and methods. Here are the methods:

Table 24-4   ADSI Group Methods

Method	Description
Description	Description of group
Members	Collection of members
IsMember	Tests whether a user is a member of this group
Add	Adds object to group
Remove	Removes object from group

So, this is how you enumerate the members of a group:

```
' 24-20.VBS

Set net = WScript.CreateObject("WScript.Network")
local = net.ComputerName

set group = GetObject("WinNT://" & local & "/Power Users")

' see what we get
for each member in group.Members
    list = list & member.name & vbCr
next

MsgBox list
```

Testing whether a user belongs to the group

Using IsMember, you can now ask the group whether a user is a member:

```
' 24-21.VBS

Set net = WScript.CreateObject("WScript.Network")
local = net.ComputerName

' get access to group
set group = GetObject("WinNT://" & local & "/Power Users")

' ask if user is member
if group.isMember("WinNT://" & local & "/Administrator") then
    MsgBox "User is group member!"
else
    MsgBox "User is no group member!"
end if
```

Creating a new user account

If you want to create new things, you need to hook yourself up to the parent container. For example, if you want to create a new user account in a domain, connect to the domain. Then, call the Create method and specify the class of object you want to create. Likewise, you can connect to a computer and create local accounts.

The following script adds a new account called testaccount so you can play around with group memberships and user rights:

```
' 24-22.VBS

Set net = WScript.CreateObject("WScript.Network")
local = net.ComputerName

set server = GetObject("WinNT://" & local)
set user = server.Create("User", "testaccount")
on error resume next
user.SetInfo
if err.number=0 then
    MsgBox "Account added."
else
    CheckError
end if

sub CheckError
    if not err.number=0 then
        ' an error occured
        set ole = CreateObject("ole.err")
        MsgBox ole.oleError(err.Number), vbCritical
        err.clear
    end if
end sub
```

You must call `SetInfo` to write your new object into the parent container. Without `SetInfo`, your new object is lost.

Note that Windows 2000 won't list new users in the user dialog box until you add them to at least one group.

Finding out all groups a user belongs to

Do you want to find out to which groups a specific user belongs? Use the `Groups` method. Most likely, however, your newly created account doesn't belong to any group yet, so the result will be an empty dialog box. I'll show you how to add and remove your `testaccount` to groups a little later in this chapter.

```
' 24-23.VBS

Set net = WScript.CreateObject("WScript.Network")
local = net.ComputerName

' get user
set user = GetObject("WinNT://" & local & "/testaccount")

list = "User is member of the following groups:" & vbCr

for each group in user.Groups
     list = list & group.name & vbCr
next

MsgBox list, vbInformation
```

Adding a user to the group

Use `Add` to add a user to a group:

```
' 24-24.VBS

Set net = WScript.CreateObject("WScript.Network")
local = net.ComputerName

' get access to group
set group = GetObject("WinNT://" & local & "/Power Users")

' add member
on error resume next
group.Add "WinNT://" & local & "/testaccount"
CheckError

sub CheckError
     if not err.number=0 then
           ' an error occured
```

```
            set ole = CreateObject("ole.err")
            MsgBox ole.oleError(err.Number), vbCritical
            err.clear
      else
            MsgBox "Done."
end if
end sub
```

Use script 24-23.VBS to check the new group membership.

Removing a user from a group

Use Remove to get rid of a user in a group:

```
' 24-25.VBS

Set net = WScript.CreateObject("WScript.Network")
local = net.ComputerName

' get access to group
set group = GetObject("WinNT://" & local & "/Power Users")

' remove member
on error resume next
group.Remove "WinNT://" & local & "/testaccount"
CheckError

sub CheckError
    if not err.number=0 then
          ' an error occured
          set ole = CreateObject("ole.err")
          MsgBox ole.oleError(err.Number), vbCritical
          err.clear
      else
          MsgBox "Done."
end if
end sub
```

Finding out secret group properties

Groups (and many other objects, too) support a rich set of properties. These properties control every aspect of the group behavior. Fortunately, you don't need huge reference works to search for the object properties. Use a script instead:

```
' 24-26.VBS

Set net = WScript.CreateObject("WScript.Network")
local = net.ComputerName

' get access to group
```

```
set group = GetObject("WinNT://" & local & "/Power Users")

' list properties
ListProperties group

sub ListProperties(obj)
    set ole = CreateObject("ole.err")
    on error resume next
    set classobj = GetObject(obj.Schema)
    for each prop in classobj.MandatoryProperties
        list = list & prop & " (mandatory)" & vbCr
    next

    for each prop in classobj.OptionalProperties
        list = list & prop & " (optional)" & vbCr
    next
    if err.number=0 then
        MsgBox list, vbInformation
    else
        MsgBox ole.OleError(err.number), vbExcamation
        err.clear
    end if
end sub
```

Querying group properties

Now that you know some Group properties, let's find out their values:

```
' 24-27.VBS

Set net = WScript.CreateObject("WScript.Network")
local = net.ComputerName

' get access to group
set group = GetObject("WinNT://" & local & "/Power Users")

on error resume next
MsgBox "Description: " & group.Description
MsgBox "groupType: " & group.groupType
CheckError

sub CheckError
    if not err.number=0 then
        ' an error occured
        set ole = CreateObject("ole.err")
        MsgBox ole.oleError(err.Number), vbCritical
        err.clear
    else
        MsgBox "Done."
end if
end sub
```

Group type is an integer value. Table 24-5 provides the real meaning.

Table 24-5	ADSI Group Type
Group Type	**Description**
2	Global group
4	Local group
8	Universal group
&H80000000	Security group (can be set with either group type)

Let's now enumerate all groups and find out the group type:

```
' 24-28.VBS

Set net = WScript.CreateObject("WScript.Network")
local = net.ComputerName

' get access to namespace
set groups = GetObject("WinNT://" & local)
groups.Filter = Array("Group")
' see what we get
for each group in groups
    grouptype = group.groupType
    if (grouptype and 2)>0 then
        typ = " (global group)"
    elseif (grouptype and 4)>0 then
        typ = " (local group)"
    elseif (grouptype and 8)>0 then
        typ = " (universal group)"
    end if

    if (grouptype and &H80000000)<>0 then
        sec = " (security group)"
    else
        sec = " (distribution group)"
    end if

    list = list & group.name & typ & sec & vbCr
next

MsgBox list
```

Secret

As a first step, the script has connected to a domain. Because it is interested only in objects of type "Group," it uses the Filter property to filter groups only. Filter always expects an array. You can filter for multiple object classes. Array("Group", "User") lists groups and users.

Setting user passwords

Use SetPassword to change an account password:

```
' 24-29.VBS

Set net = WScript.CreateObject("WScript.Network")
local = net.ComputerName

set user = GetObject("WinNT://" & local & "/testaccount")
set ole = CreateObject("ole.err")

on error resume next
user.SetPassword "secret"
if err.number=0 then
    MsgBox "Password changed."
else
    MsgBox "Couldn't change password: " _
        & ole.OleError(err.number)
end if
```

SetPassword is your administrative override—a brute force approach, because you don't need to know the old password. If you don't have administrator privileges and would like to change your own password, you can provide the old password as authentication:

```
' 24-30.VBS

Set net = WScript.CreateObject("WScript.Network")
local = net.ComputerName

set server = GetObject("WinNT://" & local)
set user = server.Create("User", "testaccount")
set ole = CreateObject("ole.err")

on error resume next
user.ChangePassword "secret", "newpassword"
if err.number=0 then
    MsgBox "Password changed."
else
    MsgBox "Couldn't change password: " _
        & ole.OleError(err.number)
end if
```

Changing user account information

User accounts contain properties, and you can change those properties:

```
' 24-31.VBS

set ole = CreateObject("ole.err")
```

```
Set net = WScript.CreateObject("WScript.Network")
local = net.ComputerName

set user = GetObject("WinNT://" & local & "/testaccount")

user.FullName = "My full name"
on error resume next
user.SetInfo
if err.number=0 then
     MsgBox "Done."
else
     MsgBox "Errors: " & ole.OleError(err.number)
end if
```

For a full list of properties, use this script:

```
' 24-32.VBS

Set net = WScript.CreateObject("WScript.Network")
local = net.ComputerName

' get access to group
set user = GetObject("WinNT://" & local & "/testaccount")

' list properties
ListProperties user

sub ListProperties(obj)
     set ole = CreateObject("ole.err")
     on error resume next
     set classobj = GetObject(obj.Schema)
     for each prop in classobj.MandatoryProperties
          list = list & prop & " (mandatory)" & vbCr
     next

     for each prop in classobj.OptionalProperties
          list = list & prop & " (optional)" & vbCr
     next
     if err.number=0 then
          MsgBox list, vbInformation
     else
          MsgBox ole.OleError(err.number), vbExcamation
          err.clear
     end if
end sub
```

Undocumented

Not all of the listed properties are really supported. If you try to read or write a property that isn't there, you get an "Error not found" error.

Forcing password changes

Do you want to force users (or an entire department, for that matter) to change their passwords? This is how you do it:

```
' 24-33.VBS

Set net = WScript.CreateObject("WScript.Network")
local = net.ComputerName

set user = GetObject("WinNT://" & local & "/testaccount")

user.Put "PasswordExpired", CLng(1)
user.SetInfo
```

That wasn't bad, was it?

Prohibiting password changes

Maybe it's the opposite way around, and you want to make sure a user can't change the password you assigned. This is the solution:

```
' 24-34.VBS

Set net = WScript.CreateObject("WScript.Network")
local = net.ComputerName

set user = GetObject("WinNT://" & local & "/testaccount")

flag = user.Get("UserFlags")
flag = flag or &H40
user.Put "UserFlags", flag
user.SetInfo
```

Table 24-6 lists all the kinds of flags you can use.

Table 24-6   User Account Properties

Flag	Description
1	Execute logon script.
2	Account disabled.
8	Home Directory required.
&H10	Lockout.
&H20	Password not required.
&H40	Password can't change.
&H80	Encrypted text password allowed.

Flag	Description
&H100	User has access to domain but not to trusted domains.
&H200	Normal account.
&H10000	Don't expire password.
&H40000	SmartCard required.

Disabling accounts

Use `AccountDisabled` to control whether an account is operational or not:

```
' 24-35.VBS

Set net = WScript.CreateObject("WScript.Network")
local = net.ComputerName

set user = GetObject("WinNT://" & local & "/testaccount")
user.AccountDisabled = true
user.SetInfo
```

Another way is to let an account expire. Use the following technique to create temporary accounts:

```
' 24-36.VBS

Set net = WScript.CreateObject("WScript.Network")
local = net.ComputerName

set user = GetObject("WinNT://" & local & "/testaccount")
user.AccountExpirationDate = "03/18/2001"
user.SetInfo
```

Secret

To enable an account forever, use an expiration date of "01/01/1970".

Unlocking accounts

The system can lock accounts — for example, if you try the wrong password too many times. To re-enable such an account, you need to unlock it:

```
' 24-37.VBS

Set net = WScript.CreateObject("WScript.Network")
local = net.ComputerName

set user = GetObject("WinNT://" & local & "/testaccount")
user.isAccountLocked = false
user.SetInfo
```

Managing Windows Services

Windows Services are programs that run silently in the background and provide some kind of service to the system. Hundreds of services are running at once, and it's critical to stable network operation that core services run smoothly.

Your scripts can manage services, query their status, and even start, stop, and pause services as needed. Again, you have two ways to approach this issue: Use the API or use ADSI.

Controlling services through the API

If you have installed the COM add-on (`ntservice`), you can browse for services right away. Use `GetServiceInfo`:

```
' 24-38.VBS

Const SERVICE_ACTIVE = 1
Const SERVICE_INACTIVE = 2
Const SERVICE_ACTIVEINACTIVE = 3

Const SERVICE_DRIVER = 15
Const SERVICE_WIN32 = 48

set tool = CreateObject("nt.services")
text = "Active drivers" & vbCr
MsgBox text & tool.GetServiceInfo(SERVICE_ACTIVE, SERVICE_DRIVER)
text = "Inactive drivers" & vbCr
MsgBox text & tool.GetServiceInfo(SERVICE_INACTIVE, SERVICE_DRIVER)
text = "Active Win32" & vbCr
MsgBox text & tool.GetServiceInfo(SERVICE_ACTIVE, SERVICE_WIN32)
text = "Inactive Win32" & vbCr
MsgBox text & tool.GetServiceInfo(SERVICE_INACTIVE, SERVICE_WIN32)

' Querying the status
MsgBox tool.ServiceStatus("Beep")
MsgBox tool.ServiceStatus("Netman")
MsgBox tool.ServiceStatus("Alerter")
```

Starting and stopping services

`ServicePause`, `ServiceStart`, and `ServiceStop` control individual services. Specify the server name as optional second argument.

Managing services through ADSI

ADSI manages services in the usual hierarchical way: Connect to the computer you want to monitor. Filter the object and list only objects of class `Service`. The `Status` property reveals the service state:

```
' 24-39.VBS
```

```
Set net = WScript.CreateObject("WScript.Network")
local = net.ComputerName

if not EnumServices(local, result) then
    MsgBox result, vbCritical
else
    MsgBox "Services:" & vbCr & result
end if

function EnumServices(server, result)
    states = Split(",Started,,Stop pend.,Running,,,Paused,Error", _
 ",")
    set winnt = GetObject("WinNT://" & server)
    winnt.Filter = Array("Service")

    on error resume next
    result = ""
    for each service in winnt
        result = result & service.Name & vbTab _
& States(service.Status) & vbCr
    next
    status = err.number
    on error goto 0

    if status=0 then
        EnumServices = true
    else
        set ole = CreateObject("ole.err")
        result = ole.OleError(status)
        EnumServices = false
    end if
end function
```

Managing individual services

Services are simple objects in the ADSI object model. You can connect directly if you know the name of the service:

```
' 24-40.VBS

Set net = WScript.CreateObject("WScript.Network")
local = net.ComputerName

set service = GetObject("WinNT://" & local & "/W3SVC")
MsgBox service.Name
MsgBox service.StartType
```

This script connects to the Web server service and determines the StartType (see Table 24-7). If there is no Web server service running on your system, the script generates an error.

Table 24-7	Service Start Types
StartType	**Description**
0	Service is started automatically during boot.
1	Service is started at OS initialization.
2	Service is started by the Service Control Manager.
3	Service is started on demand by the Service Control Manager.
4	Service is disabled.

You can change automatic service start: Assign a new value to the property and call SetInfo:

```
' 24-41.VBS

Set net = WScript.CreateObject("WScript.Network")
local = net.ComputerName

set service = GetObject("WinNT://" & local & "/W3SVC")
service.StartType = 3
service.SetInfo
```

You can also manually start and stop services. Use the Start, Stop, Pause, and Continue methods.

Controlling Network Shares

ADSI can even manage network shares. With your new freedom, you can use the Scripting.FileSystemObject to create new folders and add a network share using ADSI. This way, the new folder is accessible throughout your entire network.

Enumerating shared folders

Take a look at how ADSI enumerates shared folders. The key is to connect directly to the service responsible for sharing folders, in this case LanmanServer. The FileService service then provides a collection of all shared folders. It won't list hidden shares, though. Hidden shares are marked with a $.

```
'24-42.VBS

Set net = WScript.CreateObject("WScript.Network")
local = net.ComputerName
```

```
Set fs = GetObject("WinNT://" & local & "/LanmanServer")
If (fs.class = "FileService") then
    on error resume next
    For Each fish In fs
        desc = fish.Name
        if desc = "" then desc = "(no name)"
            list = list & desc & vbTab & fish.Path & vbCr
    next
end if
MsgBox list
```

Adding network shares

It's easy to add your own shares by using the `Create` method to add an object of type `FileShare` and by providing it with a unique name. The sample script uses the share name `Public`. Replace it with any name you wish, but make sure the name is unique. You can't use names that already serve as a share name.

```
' 24-43.VBS

Set net = WScript.CreateObject("WScript.Network")
local = net.ComputerName

foldername = "C:\testfolder"
set fs = CreateObject("Scripting.FileSystemObject")
if not fs.FolderExists(foldername) then
    fs.CreateFolder foldername
end if
Set cont = GetObject("WinNT://" & local & "/LanmanServer")
Set share = cont.Create("FileShare", "Public")
share.Path = foldername
share.SetInfo
MsgBox "folder is now shared"
```

Accessing shared folder properties

Provided you have assigned a name to your shared folder, you can access it directly through ADSI. This provides you with all the secret properties about the share.

```
' 24-44.VBS

Set net = WScript.CreateObject("WScript.Network")
local = net.ComputerName

Set share = GetObject("WinNT://" & local & "/LanmanServer/Public")
MsgBox share.Path
```

Use the following properties to get advanced information about your shares:

Table 24-8   Secret Properties

Property	Description
CurrentUserCount	Number of users currently working with the share (R)
Description	Description of folder purpose (R/W)
HostComputer	Path name of host (R/W)
Path	Path name of share (R/W)
MaxUserCount	Maximum number of users allowed to work with share concurrently (R/W)

All properties marked as R/W can both be read and changed. To set the maximum user count to a limit of five users, use code like this:

```
' 24-45.VBS

Set net = WScript.CreateObject("WScript.Network")
local = net.ComputerName

Set share = GetObject("WinNT://" & local & "/LanmanServer/Public")
share.MaxUserCount = 5
share.SetInfo
MsgBox "Set max user to 5"
```

Automatically Restarting and Shutting Down

Through the API, your scripts can shut down or restart both your local machine and remote computers. Obviously, you need appropriate permissions to close a machine down remotely—it's necessary to be logged on as administrator.

Shutdown capabilities are provided by yet another COM object, called ntshutdown. Make sure you have installed it.

Shutting down a local machine

To shut down or reboot your local machine, use the ExitWindows method. It expects one optional parameter, as indicated in Table 24-9.

Table 24-9	Shutdown Options
Parameter	**Description**
0	Logoff
1	Shutdown
2	Reboot

In addition, Table 24-10 shows two values that enhance the basic reboot options.

Table 24-10	Shutdown Enhancements
Parameter	**Description**
4	Force: don't wait for programs to close
8	Power-off machine if possible

Remotely shutting down a machine

Use RemoteShutdown to send a shutdown request to another network machine. Remote shutdown will only be initiated if you have the appropriate rights on the remote machine. While shutdown is initiated, a dialog box warns the remote user.

As long as the dialog box is visible, AbortShutdown can cancel the shutdown request.

```
' 24-46.VBS

set tool = CreateObject("nt.shutdown")
set wshshell = CreateObject("WScript.Shell")

server = InputBox("Servername?")
result = tool.RemoteShutdown(server, "I'll shutdown your system!", _
5, true, false)
if result<>0 then wshshell.Popup "I am shutting down " _
& server & ". Hit OK within 5 secs to abort!", 5
tool.AbortShutdown server
```

Automatic logon

Windows NT Server/Windows 2000 Server require you to use a logon password. However, if your machine works in a safe environment, you may use automatic logon, too.

```
' 24-47.VBS

set wshshell = CreateObject("WScript.Shell")
key = "HKLM\Software\Microsoft\Windows NT\CurrentVersion\Winlogon\"
state = ReadKey(key & "AutoAdminLogon")
if state=1 then
     msg = "AutoLogon activated. Disable?"
else
     msg = "AutoLogon not activated. Enable?"
end if

answer = MsgBox(msg, vbYesNo + vbQuestion)

if answer = vbYes then
     if state=1 then
          DeleteKey key & "AutoAdminLogon"
          DeleteKey key & "DefaultUserName"
          DeleteKey key & "DefaultPassword"
          DeleteKey key & "DefaultDomainName"
          MsgBox "Done."
     else
          name = Ask("Username?")
          password = Ask("Password?")
          antwort = MsgBox("Logon to domain?", vbYesNo + vbQuestion)
          if antwort = vbYes then
               domain = Ask("Domain name?")
               wshshell.RegWrite key & "DefaultDomainName", domain
          end if
          wshshell.RegWrite key & "DefaultUserName", name
          wshshell.RegWrite key & "DefaultPassword", password
          wshshell.RegWrite key & "AutoAdminLogon", 1
          MsgBox "Done."
     end if
end if


function ReadKey(key)
     on error resume next
     ReadKey = wshshell.RegRead(key)
     if not err.number=0 then
          err.clear
          ReadKey = vbEmpty
     end if
end function

function DeleteKey(key)
     on error resume next
```

```
        dummy = wshshell.RegRead(key)
        if err.number=0 then
            wshshell.RegDelete key
            if not err.number=0 then
                MsgBox "Key """ & key & """: unable to delete!"
                err.clear
            end if
        end if
end function

function Ask(question)
    Ask = InputBox(question)
    if Ask="" then WScript.Quit
end function
```

Summary

This chapter provided some excellent tools for Windows NT management. You learned how to add and delete users, change group memberships, and do it all with fast API calls. This opens the door for timesaving batch-automation. You also learned about another COM object, which provides the methods to remotely or locally shut down or restart your system.

You also discovered ADSI, the new interface for all kinds of namespaces. You explored the object hierarchy and created tools to enumerate domains, groups, users, services, and even property sets. ADSI allows almost anything. It's your complete toolbox for professional administration.

This chapter concludes the long Windows scripting tour we started 24 chapters ago. Scripting has matured, and you now have both the inside knowledge and the tools to efficiently master any challenge — true scripting power at your fingertips.

Appendix A

When Bad Things Happen

True scripting fun almost always requires additional COM objects to spice up the basic sets of commands. Finding, or even programming, such script extensions isn't hard—you'll find numerous examples and full source code in this book. However, before you can use such extensions, you'll need to install them. This is where things can become tricky.

I Can't Install Some of the Script Components!

All scripts on CD automatically check whether or not the required COM objects are currently installed on your system. If a COM object is missing, the script won't sit silently. Instead, it will tell you which component is missing, and all you need to do is install the component from the companion CD.

But what if you can't get a COM object installed? What if some source code won't compile? On the next couple of pages, I'll provide you with a lot of undocumented background details that will help you understand (and resolve) those issues.

Details about COM Object installation

The easiest way to get a COM object working obviously is the use of the prepared install packages. All you need to do is call `SETUP.EXE`, and the Visual Basic installer takes care of everything else.

Unfortunately, the installer isn't very clever. It works most of the time, but not always, and sometimes, it may even have bad side effects.

The first step the installer needs to do is copying the `OCX` file to your system. The `OCX`-file is the "heart" of your COM object. The installer won't copy this file, though, if there's already a file of the same name stored in the Windows folder. It won't warn you, either. It just won't install the new `OCX` component but still report "success". So the first thing you should double-check is whether or not there are already `OCX` files of the name you are about to install.

Once the installer has successfully copied the OCX-file to your system, it registers the file automatically. Registering means that it will write all the important object information into the Windows registry. Most of the time, this works smoothly. However, on a Windows NT/2000 system, you may be required to have the appropriate permissions. On Windows 9x-systems, a corrupt registry may refuse to accept the new registration information. On Windows 98, you can always "refresh" your registry by launching the DOS mode and using `SCANREG /FIX`.

Once the `OCX` file is copied and registered, the installer copies a lot of additional files to your computer. Among these are the required Visual Basic run-time files. However, there can be other files, too. Some components require the services of other components. For example, some COM objects need access to the Common Dialog component, and others take advantage of Internet FTP or Kodak Imaging TWAIN components.

Whenever there are such "dependencies", the installer copies these files to your computer, too. It should make sure that it copies files only if they are missing, and only if there are no newer versions already installed. Unfortunately, due to the many service packs and add-ons Microsoft has published, this concept sometimes doesn't work. In the worst case, the installer overwrites newer files with older versions. This may cause your entire system to suffer.

Windows 2000 Installer problems

On Windows 2000, you may encounter another fascinating flaw—here, you can install one Visual Basic package only. Once you try to install a second one, Windows will complain about files it was unable to rename. Restarting Windows 2000 will enable you to install exactly one more package until the same error hits you.

Finding easy ways out...

The best approach therefore is to not use the Visual Basic installer technique at all. A much safer way is to load the source files and recompile the COM objects on your system. This way, no files are overwritten, and the resulting COM object is guaranteed to run on your system.

If you must use the VB installer technique, for example because you want to distribute your COM objects to some customers, always make sure you compiled the setup files on a system as similar as possible to the target systems. Don't compile on Windows NT when your target computers use Windows 98.

You can also fine-tune the install package. Just open the `SETUP.LST` file and remove any files you don't want the installer to distribute. This way, you can also combine more than one install package so your customer doesn't have to launch the installer multiple times.

Most of the COM objects really only require the `OCX` file. So you could distribute the `OCX` file with the VB 5 run-time files and register the OCX file manually using `REGSVR32.EXE`. This is the safest way to install your own COM objects because this way you have full control over which files are copied to the target system. If you know for sure that the VB 5 run-time files are already installed on the target system, then distributing `OCX` files only is a very slick method. `OCX` files are only a couple of hundred bytes in size and can easily be downloaded over the Internet.

If you want to get rid of `OCX` files some day, use `REGSVR32` again and take advantage of its options. `/u` will unregister any `OCX` file, and `/?` will pop up a dialog with all the options the command has to offer. Once an `OCX` file is unregistered, it can no longer be used because all the object information is removed from the Windows registry. The `OCX` file itself is still there, so you should delete it after unregistering it.

Using Commercial Installer Software

There's another alternative — . Instead of the free Visual Basic installer, you can always resort to a commercial installer such as InstallShield. If you need to distribute your COM objects on a commercial basis, these installers may well be worth the effort (and costs). The VB installer is suitable for home use only.

I can't compile the source code!

But what if you can't compile the source code in the first place?

I have checked the sources numerous times on numerous systems, so the reason for this behavior is not a design flaw. Most likely, the source code references external components that are missing on your system.

For example, if you use the Kodak Imaging tools to create your own little photocopy machine, your system may use a different version of the Imaging tools. The Visual Basic development environment won't be able to find the tools I used when I created the project. You'll see errors complaining about illegal properties or wrong arguments.

If this should happen to you, just remove the components and then add them again. By adding the components, you make sure the references are correct.

To do this, you right-click the toolbar window and choose Components. Now you'll see a list of all the components the project uses — components in use are marked with a checkmark. Click a component to see the true filename of the component.

Next, you can remove the components from the form or user control, and then add them again using another right-click into the toolbar window, choosing Components and Browse. Specify the filename you noted earlier.

Once the newly added components appear in your toolbox, you can place them onto the form or user control.

If you can't solve the problem, drop me a line: tob@compuserve.com. I'll be more than happy to assist you. Always bear in mind, scripting is like an adventure game. Don't expect everything to work as smoothly as a major appliance.

What's the fuss about "Automation Errors"?

Automation errors occur if the COM object your script uses isn't communicating right. Most of the time, this is due to version incompatibilities. For example, if you compile the Internet tools on a Windows 98 machine and try to use them with Windows 2000, you'll get an Automation error. This is why the prepared software packages were all compiled on Windows 2000. Since Windows 2000 is the latest Windows version, COM objects compiled on this system will generally work with all older Windows versions. If you do get automation errors, then recompile the code on your own machine.

Appendix B

About the CD-ROM

The CD-ROM included with this book contains the following materials:

- All scripts and component source code from the book
- Microsoft Windows Script Technologies Trial
- Adobe Acrobat Reader
- An electronic version of this book, *Windows Scripting Secrets*, in .pdf format

Scripts and Component Source Code

Don't type in all the scripts and sources! There's a much easier way: on this book's companion CD-ROM, where you'll find both the scripts and all the component source code.

Note

To compile and run the scripts and source code for this book, you will need the Visual Basic Control Creation Edition (VB CCE), which you can download from Microsoft at http://msdn.microsoft.com/vbasic/downloads/cce/, and Windows Scripting Host 2.0, which you can obtain at http://www.microsoft.com/msdownload/vbscript/scripting.asp?id=01.

Creating your own COM objects

After you have installed the Visual Basic Control Creation Edition (or if you already own Visual Basic), you can access the COM object source codes in the Code\Components directory. These are organized in subdirectories by project name: appactivate, capture, and so on. Open the .vbp files to see all the internal mechanics. There are no secret parts; I have provided full source code of any COM object introduced in this book.

Installing COM objects the easy way

If you don't like to compile COM objects yourself, take a look into the Install subdirectory. Here, you find setup packages for all COM objects. Just call setup.exe, and the Visual Basic installer will install all necessary files onto your computer.

Caution

However, before you install anything using the Visual Basic installer, make sure you have read the installer limitations outlined in Appendix A. The packages have been compiled with Windows 2000 to ensure they will work with as many Windows versions as possible. Still, using the VB installer may not install all components correctly on your system. There may even be cases where the installer replaces newer files with older ones, an intrinsic limitation of the VB installer, which is why you should pay attention to the following caveat. **On production systems critical to your business, you should avoid the VB installer packages and instead compile the COM objects yourself.**

Using scripts

All scripts are organized by chapter, and stored in the `Code/Scripts` subfolder. In contrast to the source code printed in the book, the scripts on CD also include a protection routine. It checks whether all of the required COM objects are installed on your system. This routine consists of two clearly marked parts, and you can remove those lines anytime if you don't need this kind of protection.

Changing and editing files

Note also that all files on CD by default have a write-protection attribute. If you want to change a file, you must copy it to your hard drive and remove the write protection attribute manually.

Overview: COM object list

All COM objects discussed in this book and used within the scripts are listed in the following table. In the left column, you find the COM object names scipts use to access the component. In the right column, you find the name of the component on CD. Search for this name both in `Code\Components` (source code) and `Code\Install` (setup packages).

Table A-1   COM Objects and Components

COM Object Name	*Component Name on CD*
`App.activate`	appactivate
`Cd.tools`	Cdtray
`Clip.board`	Clipboard
`Compress.files`	Compress
`Dialog.test`	Inputbox

COM Object Name	Component Name on CD
Dlg.tools	Comdlg
Dll.tobtools	Dll
File.versioninfo	Version
Filesystem.tool	filesys
Folder.tools	folderpicker
Format.tool	Format
Icon.handler	iconhandler
Iconpicker.tool	Iconpick
Iehelper.tools	Iehelper
Internet.communication	Internet
Listview.tool	Listview
Mci.manager	Mci
Memory.stats	Memory
Misc.information	Miscinfo
Modeless.dialog	Modeless
Module.spy	Spy
Nt.services	Ntservice
Nt.shutdown	Ntshutdown
Nt.user	Ntuser
Ole.bitmap	Capture
Ole.err	Oleerror
Os.version	Osversion
Process.id	Process
Property.tool	Property
Registry.update	Regupdate
Regtool.tob	Registry
Screen.tool	screen
Shellcopy.tool	Shellcopy
Timer.event	Timer
Tray.icon	Tray
Treeview.tool	Treeview

Continued

Table A-1 (continued)	
COM Object Name	**Component Name on CD**
Twain.manager	Scan
Typelib.decoder	Typelib
Web.dialog	Webdialog
Window.list	Windowlist
Window.list2	Windowlist2
Window.Manager	Winmanager

Microsoft Windows Script Technologies Trial

The CD-ROM includes the Windows Script Technologies Trial from Microsoft, which includes valuable add-ons and documentation. Included are:

- SCE10EN.EXE, which allows encryption of script files
- SCT10EN.EXE, which includes script components useful for developers who wish to include scripting capabilities into their applications.
- STE51EN.EXE, which helps install the latest version of Windows Scripting Host.
- VBSDOC.EXE, which includes VBScript help files.
- JSDOC.EXE, which includes JScript help files.
- WSHDOC.EXE, which includes Windows Scripting Host help files.

To install any of these items, go to the Windows Script Technology directory on the CD and double-click the appropriate executable file, then follow the setup instructions.

Adobe Acrobat Reader

Adobe Acrobat Reader is a helpful program that will enable you to view the electronic version of this book in the same page format as the actual book.

To install and run Adobe Acrobat Reader and view the electronic version of this book, follow these steps:

1. Start Windows Explorer (if you're using Windows 95/98) or Windows NT/2000 Explorer (if you're using Windows NT/2000), and then open the Adobe Acrobat folder on the CD-ROM.

2. In the `Adobe Acrobat` folder, double-click `rs40eng.exe` and follow the instructions presented onscreen for installing Adobe Acrobat Reader.

3. To view the electronic version of this book after you have installed Adobe Acrobat Reader, start Windows Explorer (if you're using Windows 95/98) or Windows NT/2000 Explorer (if you're using Windows NT/2000), and then open the `Windows Scripting Secrets` PDF folder on the CD-ROM.

In the `Windows Scripting Secrets` PDF folder, double-click the chapter or appendix file you want to view. All documents in this folder end with a `.pdf` extension.

Index

A

Abs function (VBScript), 50
AccountDisable method (Network object), 687
ActivateWindow method (WindowManager object), 371–372
  checking for focus, 375
Active Window Tracking, managing, 454
ActiveX controls
  as COM objects, 118
  controlling properties in, 140–141
  creating using VB CEE, 118
  form elements, preselecting 147
  modal window requirement, 522
  naming, 122–123
  OCX files for, 86
  security concerns, 118
  in scripts, 86
  testing, 123
  window container, modifying, 142–144
  windows, opening using, 132
  windows, resizing contents using, 144–146
  VB CCE coding assistance, 121–122
ActiveX Data Objects. *See* ADO (ActiveX Data Objects)
Add method (Network object), 680–681
AddHeader property (listview.tool), 209
AddPrinterConnection method (Network object), 490
AddUser method (NT User object), 672
ADO (ActiveX Data Objects). *See also* MDAC
  checking version, 646
ADO Database object (ADODB.Connection)
  ADO version, checking for, 646–647
  data, adding, 653
  data, viewing, 652
  databases, opening/querying, 649–651
  records, counting, 655
  records, deleting, 655–656
  tables, creating, 655–657
  tables, deleting, 657
  tables, viewing structure of, 651–652
  variable fields, retrieving, 654–655
ADODB.Connection object. *See also* Database Object
ADSI interface
  error messages, making readable, 676–677
  group types (table), 683
  groups, identifying members, 678
  network shares, managing, 690–692
  overview, 669–671
  passwords/user accounts, managing, 684–687
  users, group memberships, enumerating, 678
  users/groups, managing, 678–683
  Windows Services, managing, 688–690
Alias attribute (links), 239
AllowMultiselect flag, referencing, 191
AllUsersDesktop folder, 485
AllUsersPrograms folder, 485
AllUsersStartMenu folder, 485
AllUsersStartup folder, 485
animation effects
  built-in (table), 465–466
  combo box animation, 466
  cursor shadow effect, 466
  font smoothing, 474
  gradient captions, 467–468
  menu animation, 468–469
  selection fade, 471
  tooltips, 471–472

ANSI strings, Unicode string comparison, 214
anti-aliasing, enabling/disabling, 474
API (application programming interface) functions
  calling from COM objects, 127–129
Folder Picker dialog box wrapper, 198–200
  GetDiskFreeSpace, 226–229
  GetDiskFreeSpaceEx, 227–229
  for internal Windows commands, 125
  SHFileOperation, 250–252
  string handling, 213–215
AppActivate method (Shell object)
  with ForegroundLockTimeout, 333–335
  SendKeys method and, 332–333
  verifying window existence, 335
app.activate object, 333–335
appactivate.vbp, 334–335
Application object (Shell.Application)
  accessing files/folders using, 282
  displaying Properties page using, 282
  managing desktop windows, 381–382
  properties/methods (table), 273–274
Application property
  Application object, 273–274
  Folder object, 275
  FolderItem object, 276
  FolderItemVerb object, 286
  WebView object, 320
architecture
  of HTML dialog boxes, 545–546
  modular design (software packages), 349
  of windows, hierarchical, 384
Archive attribute (files/folders), 239
Argument property
  IShellLink object, 308
  Shortcut object, 291
arguments, 141–142
  adding manually, 41
  collections of, 41
  in custom dialog box wrappers, 196

default values, specifying, 142
  making optional, 142
  missing arguments, detecting, 142
  passing results using, 76–77
  passing arguments using drag-and-drop, 40–41
  as source of errors, 75
Arguments property (Shortcut object), 305–306
arrays, 55
  dynamic variable arrays, 54–55
  fixed variable arrays, 51–53
  long-integer arrays, retrieving, 449
  multidimensional arrays, 56
  shrinking/expanding, 55–56
arrows, shortcut. *See* shortcut arrows
Asc function (VBScript), 50
asynchronous execution
  of events, 509
  of programs, 355–356
Attributes property
  with File object, 237
  with File object, changing attributes, 240–241
  with File object, options, 239–240
  with Folder object, 231
  ShellFolder subkey value, 443
audio CDs
  identifying/launching CD, 631–632
  time formats, changing, 635–636
  tracks, controlling position remotely, 634–635
  tracks, identifying, 632–633
  tracks, recording individual, 642–644
audio files, playing
  MIDI files, 638–639
  WAV files, 640
automating
  automation objects, viewing, 98–99
  AutoPlay launch, 127
  desktop refreshing, 439–440
  DOS commands, 346–347
  objects for, viewing, 98–99
  REG file restorations, 411

remote machine logons, 694–695

scanning, 586–587

scanning tools, 586–587

script startup, links for, 300–301

undocumented object documentation, 105–108

Web browsers, closing of, 550–551

AutoNumber fields (databases), 654

AutoPlay, automatic launching, 127

AUTORUN.INF, 127

AvailableSpace property

Drive object, 220, 222, 225–226

IDrive object, 88

AVI (movie) files

output window style, customizing, 641–642

playing, 640–641

AVI video device type, 637

B

BackColor property, 142–144

background colors, windows, settings for, 143

backing up Registry contents, 255–259, 409–410

partial backups, 411

backslash (\\) character, in Registry key paths, 421

BackupFolder method, 255–259

batch files, script file comparison, 323–324

binary data, reading as string value in Registry, 418–419

binary files, encrypting, 65

bit-checking, 191

for file/folder attributes, 239–240

blinking cursors, size settings, 475

.bmp files. *See also* graphics files

file size, 597

renaming as .ico files, 622–623

BODY tag (HTML Web Browser template), modifying, 544–545

Boolean operators, searching for, 664

Boolean return values, retrieving information about, 448

boot mode, controlling, 498

borders, of windows, customizing, 456

BorderStyle property, 143

breakpoints, setting, 21

BrowseForFolder method, 203

with Folder Picker, 197, 200–201

launching program groups using, 325–327

with Application object, 273

buttonClick event (HTML dialog box), 173

buttons

creating, 596–597

event-handling code, adding, 136

preselecting, 37

radio, adding to web browser, 555–558

snap-to-button feature, 478

Start menu button, hiding, 386

on windows, enabling/disabling, 379–380

By Ref declarations

in custom dialog box wrappers, 196

passing arguments using, 75, 77

ByVal declarations, passing arguments using, 75

C

Cancel button (InputBox), enabling, 33

CancelButton property (Web Browser Dialog Box), 542

Capability command (multimedia devices), 636

Capture Window object, 390–392

CaptureScreenToClip method (Capture Window object), 390–391

capture.vbp, 390–392

CaptureWindowToClip method (Capture Window object), 391

CaptureWindowToFile method (Capture Window object), 391

capturing windows, 390–392

CascadeWindows method (Application object), 273, 382

cascading windows, 382

case-sensitivity, changing, 81

CBool function (VBScript), 49

CByte function (VBScript), 49

CCur function (VBScript), 49

CD-ROM drives. *See also* audio CDs
  API functions for, 126
  custom controls for, 126–127
  default, accessing, 628
  opening/closing, 125–127
  selected, accessing, 629–630
  status reports for, 630–631
  system support for, verifying, 628–629

CDate function (VBScript), 49–50

cdaudio device type, 637

CDbl function (VBScript), 49–50

cd.tools example project, managing CD-ROM drive, 126–127

centering forms (custom Web browser), 545

Change Icons dialog box, accessing icons, 613

ChangePassword method (NT User object), 673–674

ChangeSetting method (Registry Update object)
  for Active Window Tracking controls, 455
  GetASetting method comparison, 453
  icon spacing, changing, 453–454
  Windows settings, changing, 453

ChDir method (Internet Connection object), 573, 577

CheckFolder method
  with Folder object, 234
  with Version object, 265–266

check keyboard procedure, with custom Web browser, 552

child windows, locating/enumerating, 385–387

.chm (help) files, 115

Chr function (VBScript), 50

CInt function (VBScript), 49–50

Class-IDs, 92
  for virtual folders, viewing, 317–318
  Windows Recycle Bin, 436

Click events, adding to forms/dialog windows, 136–139

Clip.board object, 403

clipboards
  context menu, accessing, 403
  filenames, adding, 403
  window content, copying to, 390–392

clipboard.vbp, 403

CLng function (VBScript), 49–50

Close command (multimedia devices), 636

CloseHandle method (Internet Connection object), 562, 577

CloseInternet method (Internet Connection object), 577

closeTray method (cd.tools), 126–127

closing
  custom Web browser, automatically, 550–551
  IE (Internet Explorer) window, avoiding errors, 161–163
  objects, Quit method, 158
  programs, 356–357
  programs, as group, 341–342
  programs, individually, 342–344
  windows, 360

CLSID subkey (Registry), 92–94

CMD.EXE (DOS command interpreter), 344

Code view (VB CCE), 119–120

coding, custom COM objects, 121–122

colon (:) character, in command lines, 20

Color dialog box, flags (constants) for, 192–193

colors, window, changing, 457

Columns property (Index Server Query object), 661

COM objects
  accessing, 85

ActiveX controls as, 118
advantages of using, 124
CLSID information about, 93–94
creating, file.versioninfo example, 262–263
cross-Windows versions, Icon Picker example, 204–205
custom, registering, 150–151
DLL files for, 86
documentation for, 94–97, 157
features of, 86
filesystem.tool, 226–229
identifying, 157
IDispatch interface, 86
with Kodak Imaging tool (table), 582
MSComDlg.CommonDialog, 186–197
object type, 105
OCX files for, 86
Program Identifier, 93
property.tool, 286–288
real name for, finding, 156
scriptable, viewing, 100–105
Scripting.FileSystemObject, 86–87
with Scripting Host, 88–89
SHFileOperation, 250–252
system icons, 440
System.FileSystemObject, 219
viewing location/version information, 89–91
COM objects, custom, 135
arguments, optional, adding, 141–142
calling API functions from, 127–129
for CD-ROM tray API functions, 126
compiling/testing, 123, 134, 153
creating using Visual Basic, 117–118
distributing, 150–154
event handlers, adding to dialog windows, 136–139
modeless window displays, 136
naming control, 122–123
naming project, 122
for opening dialog boxes, 132–134
properties in, controlling, 140–141
registering manually, 150–151

storing, 138
testing, 123
VB CCE coding assistance, 121–122
window container modifications, 142–144
window contents, preselecting, 147
window contents, resizing, 144–146
ComboBox visual effect, enabling, 466–467
comdlg32.dll, 195
comdlg32.ocx, locating, 187, 194
comdlg.vbp, locating, 193
command lines
calling scripts from, 531
colon character in, 20
running scripts from, 41
using, 529
command window (Debug menu), 20
Command1_Click() procedure, opening/closing windows using, 137
commands
adding to context menus, 398–400
adding to New menu, 8–10
information about, viewing, 108–113
for multimedia devices (table), 636
new, accelerating visibility, 7
searching for, 111–113
Common Dialog COM, 186
accessing files using, 187
Color dialog box, 192–193
creating custom version, 193–197
Open File dialog box, 189–191
CommonControls1, 193
CompanyName property (version object), 264
CompareMode, changing case-sensitivity using, 81
compiling COM objects, 123, 133–134, 153, 196
Compress object, 269–272
Compressed attribute (files), 239
.compressed filename extensions, 270
compressed files, locating, 272

compressing
backup folders, 258
files, commercial tools for, 272
files, Compress object for, 269–271
files, compression options, 602–603
graphics files, 601–604
variable arrays, 55–56
CompressIt method (Compress object),
55, 269–272
compress.vbp, 269–272
ComputerName property (Network
object), 490, 676
computers, local, shutting
down/rebooting, 692–693
computers, remote
automatic logon, 694–695
shutting down/rebooting, 692–693
computers, slow, identifying, 496–497
%COMSPEC%, 41, 344
COMSPEC, 41
connect errors, FTP, trapping, 563–565
Connect method (Internet Connection
object), 577
ConnectFTP method (Internet
Connection object), 562, 577
accessing FTP server, 562
ConnectInternet method (Internet
Connection object), 562, 577
connection type, Internet, identifying, 575
ConnectionState method (Internet
Connection object), 575, 578
constants
button functions, 37
Folder Picker dialog box, 202
system dialog boxes, referencing in
scripts, 189–190
system-state icons, 38
VarType function, 47
container objects, checking for, 677–678
context menus (context menu
extensions)
calling, 283
for clipboard; adding filenames to, 403
commands, accessing, 284–286

debugging commands, adding, 19
for files/directories, adding commands
to, 401–402
for folders, adding commands, 398–400
entries, removing from, 401
script extensions for, 397–403
Send To Context, adding link to,
301–305
shell subkey for, 399
for system, adding commands to, 443
target files, accessing from links,
315–316
target files, showing location of,
318–329
viewing Class-IDs, 317–318
Control Panel folder
accessing, 279
applets in, accessing/running, 347–349
enumerating contents of, 281
ControlPanelItem method (Application
object), 273
Control_RunDLL API, 348–349
conversion functions (VBScript), 49–50
conversion tools, example script for,
59–60
Cool Switch window, size of, controlling,
481–482
Copy procedure
with File object, 237
with Folder object, 231
CopyHere method (Folder object), 275
copying files
backups, 255–259
to multiple destinations (MultiDest),
259
CopyMultiDest method, copying files to
multiple folders, 259
copyright information, retrieving, 264
Count property, 28, 112
counting, database records, 655
.cpl files (Control Panel items),
locating/running, 347–348
Create method (Network object), adding
new user accounts, 679–680

CreateBitmapIcon method (Tray Icon object), 520
CreateFolder property (Folder object), 236–237
CreateObject command, 85–86, 87, 106
  IDispatch interface, accessing, 324
  scriptable objects, identifying, 100
CreateShortcut method (Shortcut object), 290
CreateTextFile function
  with File object, 246–247
  with Folder object, 231
creating, database tables, 656–657
creating files, 246–247
CSCRIPT.EXE, 43
  DOS commands, launching, 530–536
  switching to automatically, 43–44
CSng function (VBScript), 49–50
CStr function (VBScript), 49–50
CTRL+ALT, for keyboard shortcuts, 13–14
CTRL+ALT+DEL, 15
  disabling. 461
CurrentUserCount property (shared folders), 692
Cursor Shadow visual effect, 465
  enabling, 467
cursors, blinking, size settings, 475
CurVer subkey, 92
custom commands, adding, 94–97
custom dialog boxes, creating/displaying, 540–541

D

DAT device type, 637
data, database
  adding, 653
  reading, 652
data retrieval
  functions/procedures, with, 72–81
  Dictionary object, using, 80
data transfers, 76–77
data types (Windows Registry), 429
databases

adding data, 653
ADO interface for, 645–646
AutoNumber fields, 654
Index Server with, 661–663, 666–667
managing using indexing, 658–660
opening/querying, 649–651
records, counting, 655
records, deleting, 655–656
sample.mdb example, accessing, 648–649
tables, creating, 655–657
tables, deleting, 657
variable fields, retrieving, 654–655
variable types (table), 655
viewing data, 652
viewing design/table structure, 651–652
date functions, 36
DateCreated property, 237
  with File object, 237
  with Folder object), 231
DateLastAccessed property
  with File object, 237
  with Folder object, 231, 234–236
DateLastModified property
  with File object, 237
  with Folder object, 231
dates
  asking for, 34–36
  identify weekday name for, 27
Debug command, adding to context menus, 19
Debug menu (Script Debugger), 19–20
debugging. *See also* error handling
  debug commands, adding to context menu, 19
  debugging timer, creating/using, 514–515
  scripts, Script Debugger, 15–18
  scripts, setting breakpoints, 21
decimal notation, 189
decision-making functions, 65–67
declarations, advantages of using, 83–84
declared variables, with VBScript, 46

declaring variable arrays
dynamic size arrays, 53–54
fixed-size arrays, 51–52
decompressing files, 271–272
decrypting files, 62–65, 129–131
default drives, controlling CD-ROM drives in, 628
default values, for arguments, specifying, 142
DEFRAG.EXE, preconfiguring, 329
Delete procedure
with File object, 237
with Folder object, 231
limitations of using, 250
DeleteFile method (Internet Connection object), 577
deleting
context menu entries, 401
database records, 655–656
database tables, 657
duplicate keyboard shortcuts, 295
files, sending to Recycle Bin, 253–254
folders, 234–236
invalid links, 291–293
list entries using ListView dialog box, 209–210
Registry keys/values, 420
Registry values, 414–415
system icons, enabling warning message, 445
.vbs scripts, 7–8
DelFromGroup method (NT User object), 675
DelUser function (NT User object), 673
Description property
with IShellLink object, 308
for shared folders, 692
with Shortcut object, 291
Desktop folder, 485
desktop icons
context menu commands, 443–445
managing, 440–442
spacing, modifying, 453–454
title wrap, enabling title wrap, 458

desktop keys
NameSpace, 437
searching for in Windows Registry, 431–432
DESKTOP.INI files/folders
changing folder icons and, 614, 618
customized, searching for, 623–626
desktops
changing Recycle Bin name, 435–436
dual-storage of, 438
hiding, 389
wallpaper, identifying, 450
keyboard shortcuts, launching from, 293
managing windows on, 381–382
NameSpace key, 437
refreshing automatically, 439–440
view options, setting manually, 389–390
device types, multimedia, 637
devices, multimedia, accessing, 127
DHTML object model, documentation, 174
dialog boxes/windows. *See also* forms; HTML documents
advantages of using, 186
appearance, variety in, 187
creating using COM objects, 131–132
creating using HTML template, 540
displaying text files in, 241–242
events, adding, 136–139
file access using, 187
FormatDrive, accessing, 259–262
HTML, components of, 545–546
Icon Picker, 203–206
in IE-based output windows, 168–170
Index Server, customizing, 664–665
ListView, 207–208
MsgBox function, 36–38
multi-line, 72–73
opening/closing, procedure for, 137
positioning on screen, 144
printing pictures from, 593–594
properties, controlling, 140–141

properties, setting, 142–144
Properties pages, 283
resizing contents, 144–146
system state icons, 38
title bars, removing, 143–144
user input into, saving, 138
dialog.ocx, 134, 135
dialog.text, 134
Dictionary objects
case-insensitivity, enabling, 81
contents of, enumerating, 82
multiple, using, 82
properties and methods (table), 82
values in, enumerating, 79
digitalvideo device type, 637
Dim function
for multiple array indexes, 56
for variable arrays, 51–52
Dir method (Internet Connection object),
577
limitations of, 573
FTP directories/subfolders, listing,
564–566
directory context menus, adding
commands to, 401–402
Directory attribute (folders), 239
DisableTimer event (Timer Control
object), 513–514
disabling
components, cautions about, 442
Registry-controlled script launching,
395–396
screen savers, 459–460
shortcut arrows, 478–479
snap-to-button feature, 478–479
user accounts, 687
visual/animation effects, 466–472
DisconnectInternet method (Internet
Connection object), 562, 577
disk tools, preconfiguring, 329
disks, storing compressed files on, 269
DisplayDialog function (Web Browser
Dialog Box), 542
displaying lists, ListView for, 207–213

display resolution, managing, 488–501
distributing custom COM objects,
150–154
dlg.tools project, 193–197
DLLRegister Server, 151
DLLs (dynamic link libraries), 86
contents, 129
functions in, finding, 507
structure, decrypting, 129–131
supported, checking for, 506
DLLUnregisterServer, 152
DLTS (Distributed Links Tracking
Service), Resolve method with, 312
Do. . .loop function (VBScript), 70–71
exiting prematurely, 71–72
document types, inserting into New
menu, 6
documentation
accessing/retrieving, 113–115, 182–184
for Icon Picker, 203–204
for Internet Explorer, 157
for Kodak Imaging tools, 583
manuals, HTML, generating, 176–181
for ListView dialog box, 212–213
for MSComDlg.CommonDialog,
187–188
for WinWord, 350–351
Documents menu, cleaning/maintaining
automatically, 487–488
manually, 485–487
DoEvents (VB CCE), 170–171
DoIt method (FolderItemVerb object), 286
domain names, identifying, 490–491
DOS commands, 529
automating, 346–347
executing using scripts, 324
piping commands, creating, 534–535
running using scripts, 344–347
writing/executing using script files,
529–530
DOS directory, viewing contents of,
345–346
DOS files, checking for, 266
DOS folder, converting to HTML, 59–61

DOS input/output streams
accessing, 529–530
compared with command-line
arguments, 42
tying scripts into, 42–46
DOS mode, 409–411
DOS window (DOS box)
handling scripts in, 42–46
launching, 41
Run command drag-and-drop features,
41
writing commands to, 529–530
DOS.vbs, 532–534
downloading files
FTP for, 567–568
repairing damaged file type
information, 604–606
Dr. Watson utility, troubleshooting
system crashes, 100–101
drag-and-drop operations
for desktop wallpaper, enabling,
475–476
passing arguments using, 40–42
script-loading using, 16–17
with Windows Run command, 41
drive context menus, adding commands
to, 398–399
Drive object
accessing, 220–222
AvailableSpace property, 220, 225–226
DriveType property, 224–225
FreeSpace property, 225–226
IsReady property, 223
relationship to Folder object, 230
SerialNumber property, 224
TotalSize property, 225–226
VolumeName property, 224
Drive property
with File object, 237
with Folder object, 231
drive space, available, determining,
225–226
DriveLetter property (Drive object), 222
drivers, multimedia devices, installed,

viewing, 637–638
drives
commands for, listing, 109–110
context menus, adding commands to,
401–402
formatting, 259–262
Properties pages, opening, 287–288
space on, determining, 87
viewing, 220–222
Drives collection, 51
DriveType property (Drive object), 51,
222, 224–225
DWebBrowserEvents2, viewing contents,
164
dword integers, returning, 449
dynamic arrays, 54–55
handling in scripts, 449
dynamic link libraries. *See* DLLs
(dynamic link libraries)

E

e-mail, repairing damaged file type
information, 604–606
early binding, 195
Edit command, editing scripts using, 5
Edit control (Imaging Tool object),
594–596
editing
graphics files, 592, 595–596
Registry entries, 412–415
scripts, 5, 11–12, 20–21
Editors, adding line-marking capability,
12–15
EjectPC method (Application object), 273
element collections, accessing, 542–543
elements (forms)
ordering, 133–134
positioning, automating, 146
preselecting, 147
selecting, 133
viewing properties, 140
empty folders, logging, 235
empty values, identifying, 33

empty variables, checking for, 36
emptydelete.txt (log file), 235
EmptyRecycler method (shellcopy.tool), 255
EnableTimer event (Timer Control object), 513–514
encrypting files
 binary files, 65
 random numbers for, 62
EndProcess method, 356
EndProgram method, 360
EnumChildWindows function (TreeView object), 387–389
EnumDir function, 78–79
EnumerateGroups method (NT User object), 674
EnumerateGroupUsers method (NT User object), 674
EnumInterfaces method, 511–512
EnumNetworkDrives method function (Network object), 490
 information in, 112–113
 viewing information about, 110
EnumPrinterConnections (Network object), 490
EnumUsers method (NT User object), 671
environment variables
 automatic conversions, 325
 %COMSPEC%, 41, 344
 saving script files in, 10
 %WINDIR%, 488
ERD folder (Windows 95), Registry backup information in, 409
err.clear command, 21
err.description command, 21
error-checking, adding to Format method, 261
error handling. *See also* debugging
 adding to functions, 76
 automation errors, 161
 avoiding illegal path names, 201
 error prevention/testing, 26–28
 event logging, 22–26
 finding errors, 11–15

launching programs correctly, 324–325
line-by-line script execution, 19–20
problems loading Icon Picker, 298
reenabling, 30
repairing damaged file type information, 604–606
resizing and, 146
Script Debugger for, 15–18
setting breakpoints, 21
stopping scripts, 15
turning off, 28–30
unpredictable errors, 28–29
variable declarations for, 83–84
VBScript variables, 46
error messages, 9
 ADSI, making readable, 676–677
 contents of, 11–12
 clear text, converting to, 147–150
 drive formatting activities, 261
 identifying errors, 15
 obtaining descriptions of, 21
 "Out of Memory", 33
 preventing displays of, 21
 during script development, 26
errors, types of
 from calling COM objects, 100–101
 FTP connect errors, trapping, 563–567
 invalid handles, 531
 ParseName function-related, 282
 in procedures/functions, 74–75
event handlers, adding to dialog boxes, 136–139
event logging, 22–26
event sinks, 510, 511
event_onClick event (HTML dialog box), 173
event_onQuit event (HTML dialog box), 173
events
 creating, timer control example, 513–514
 in custom HTML dialog box, 173–174
 halting scripts until firing of, 170–171

Continued

events *(continued)*
  in Internet Explorer, listing, 511–512
  in Internet Explorer, responding to, 161–163
  for modeless windows, 522–525
  public events, 514
  receiving, onQuit example, 510
  resize events, responding to, 145–146
  supported, viewing, 511–512
  for timer controls, 513–515
  for tray area icon displays, 516–522
  uses for, 509
executable files, launching using Run method, 324
executing script files, 4, 5
exit commands, placing in subroutines, 147
exit conditions, for looping actions, 70–71
Exit do keywords, 71–72
Exit keyword, 71–72
ExitWindows method (NT Shutdown object), 692
ExpandEnvironmentStrings method, Windows folder path information, retrieving, 488–489
expanding arrays, 55–56
ExpandIt method (Compress object), 269–272
ExpandText function (VBScript), 74–75
Explore method (Application object), 273
Explorer windows, 58
  backup files, accessing from, 258
  icons for, adding, 446–447
  view options, 389
  special folders/documentation access, 279–281
Export Registry command, 411
ExtendedProperty method (FolderItem object), 276
ExtensionDifferent flag, referencing in scripts, 191
ExtractIconEx method (Tray Icon object), 520

F

Favorites folder, 485
fax message tools, 579–580
fields (database tables), retrieving variable types for, 654–655
file access, 238
  Application object for, 282
  choosing programs for, 325
  Common Dialog object for, 187
  Explorer for, 317
  FileSystemObject object for, 281–282
File Attributes, 238–239
File menu, Save As dialog box, 10
File object
  opening/displaying text files, 241–242
  properties (table), 237
file templates, adding to New menu, 8
file types, key assignments, identifying, 402
FileDescription property (version object), 264
FileExists method (FileSystemObject object), 324
  with Imaging Tool object, 595
filemon utility (sysinternals.com), 427
filenames
  adding to clipboard, 403
  converting PIDLs to, 279
  finding using DOS commands with filters, 535–536
  quotation marks with, 41
FileOpenConstants, referencing in scripts, 189–191
FileRun method (Application object), 273
files
  binaries, encrypting, 65
  checking for, 28, 324
  compressing/decompressing, 269–272
  context menus, adding commands to, 401–402
  creating, 246–247
  DOS files, 266
  downloading/uploading, 562–574, 604–606

encrypting/decrypting, 62–65
icons, extracting from, 607–608
file attributes, reading, 239–240
graphics files, 579–580
help files, 113–115
icon files, 295–298
information about, retrieving, 266–268, 278–279
key assignments, 398–399
Property pages, 282–283, 287–288
properties, querying, 664
regedit files, 242–244
renaming, 247–248
script files, 244–246
sending to any destination, 301–305
sending to Recycle Bin, 252–253
shortcut arrows for, 479–480
16-bit Windows files, 266
target files, 315–316
templates for, 8
text files, 241–242
versions, information about, 262–264
write-protected, checking for, 240
Files property (Folder object), 231
FileSystem property (Drive object), 222
FileSystemObject object, 219
    accessing, 70
    Drive object, 220–226
    File object, 237–248
    FileExists method, 324
    folder/drive size information, 397–398
    Folder object, 230–237
    GetSpecialFolder method, 488
    with Imaging Tool object, 595
    methods and properties, 221
    text-file handling, 241
    Windows folder, accessing directly, 489
filesystem.tool COM object, ascertaining drive space using, 226–229
filesys.vbp, 226–227
FileType property (version object), 264
FileVersion property (version object), 264
file.versioninfo COM, creating, 262–263

filter flags, for enumerating user accounts, 672
Filter property (Network object), 683
filters, DOS commands, piping for, 535–536
FindComputer method (Application object), 273
FindFiles method (Application object), 273
finding. *See* searching
FireEvent method (Modeless object), 523
FireQuitEvent.ShowDialog method (Modeless object), 523
Fix function (VBScript), 50, 49–50, 62
fixed-size arrays, 52
flags (constants)
    AllowMultiselect flag, 191
    caption flashing controls, 379
    Color dialog box, 192–193
    EmptyRecycler method, 255
    enumerating user accounts, 672
    Folder Picker dialog box, 202
    Resolve method, 310
    SHFileOperation, 252, 254
    system dialog boxes, referencing, 189–190
    user account properties (table), 686
    WebView object, 320
flash count, identifying, 449
flashing title bars, for windows, 378–379
FlashWindowManually method (WindowManager object), 378
FlushIconCache method (Registry object), 479, 621
FlushIconCache method (Registry toolkit), 431
focus-lock, disabling, 333–335
focus() method, with custom web browser, 553
focus-owning windows, sending keys to, 332–333
FocusedItem property (WebView object), 320

focusit procedures, with custom web browser, 553

folder context menu, adding new commands, 398–400

folder access
Application object for, 274, 282
Folder object for, 230–231
Folder Picker for, 198–203

Folder object (FileSystemObject object), 230
CreateFolder property, 236–237
properties/methods, 231, 275
Size property, 232–234
with WebView object, 320

Folder Picker dialog box
launching program group, 325–327
access parameters, setting, 200–201
special flags, 202
wrapper for, 197–203

Folder2 object, 197, 275

FolderItem object, 276–277

FolderItem2 object, 277

FolderItemVerb object, 285–286

folders
adding/removing from index, 660
attributes of, reading, 239–240
checking for, 28
contents, viewing, 276–277
context menus for, adding commands, 398–401
in DESKTOP.INI, searching for, 623–626
empty, finding and deleting, 234–236
Fonts folder, 485
icons, changing/hiding, 614–619
local, synchronizing with Web folders, 569–574
MyDocuments folder, 485
name, viewing, 276
opening without knowing path, 57–58
querying, 664–665
shared, managing, 690–692
size, calculating, 232–234
special, accessing in Explorer, 279–281
virtual, viewing list of, 202

Font Smoothing visual effect, 466, 471–472

fonts
sample font page, 501–503
smoothing, enabling/disabling, 474
system, enumerating, 501

Fonts folder, 485

For each...next function (VBScript), 68–70

foreground window
accessing, 369–370
SendKeys method with, 335

ForegroundLockTimeout value (focus locks), 333–335

Form Layout window (VB CCE), 120

Format method, 260–262

FormatCurrency function (VBScript), 50

FormatNumber function (VBScript), 50

FormatPercent function (VBScript), 50

formatting
drives, 259–262
text, conversions, 59–61
variables, 50

format.tool object, 260–262

format.vbp, 259–260

Form_Resize procedure, adding to InputBox dialog window, 145–146

forms
controlling properties in, 140–141
designing in VB CEE, 132–134
for dialog windows, 132
elements for, selecting, 133
elements on, ordering, 133–134
HTML, centering, 545
resize events, responding to, 145–146

For...next function (VBScript), 68

FreeSpace property (Drive object), 220, 222, 225–226

frequency settings, managing, 500

FriendlyDir method (Internet Connection object), 577
FTP directories/subfolders, 564–566

FTP (file transfer protocol) servers
accessing, 562
connect errors, trapping, 563–567

directory listings, data in, 564–565

directory listings, retrieving, 562–563

files, downloading, 567–568

files, uploading, 568–569

methods for (table), 577–578

synchronizing local/Web folders, 569–574

ftp.microsoft.com, directory listings, retrieving, 562–563

full window drag, 466

controlling properties in, 474

verifying use of, 448

FullName property

with Shell object, 531

with Shortcut object, 291

functions

custom, creating, 73–74

dictionary objects with, 79–80

in DLLs, finding, 507

Internet Connection object (internet. communication), 577–578

lists of, building, 112

Network object (Script.Network), 490

of objects, viewing, 106–108

ordinal numbers as names of, 131

pitfalls, double variables, 74–75

popup enhancements, 38–39

return objects, 77

return values, 73, 76–80

searching for, 108–110

Shell Link object (table), 308

Unicode strings for, 204

WebView object, 319–320

G

GetActiveWindowName method, 335

GetSetting function (Registry Update object)

for Active Window Tracking controls, 455

ChangeSetting method comparison, 453

long-integer arrays, retrieving, 449

text strings, retrieving, 450

GetChildHandle method (WindowManager object), 385–386

GetDetailsOf function (Folder object), 275, 278–279, 281

GetDiskFreeSpace function, 227–229

GetDiskFreeSpaceEx function, 227–229

GetDrive function

adding, 87

file system, accessing, 220

help files/documentation, accessing, 114

GetExtendedError function (Internet Connection object), 578

GetFile function, 238

GetFile method (Internet Connection object), 578

GetFileVersion function

error messages with, 148

turning off error handling using, 28–30

GetFolder method (FolderItem object), 238, 277

GetForegroundWindowHandle method (WindowManager COM), 369–370

with CaptureWindow object, 390–391

window styles, changing dynamically, 374–374

window styles, current, identifying, 373

windows, moving, 376–377

windows, resizing, 377–378

GetIconAsLocation property (IShellLink object), 308

GetImageInfo method (Imaging Tool object), 603–604

GetLastError method (Internet Connection object), 578

GetLastErrorNumber method (Internet Connection object), 578

GetLink property (FolderItem object), 277

GetMemory method (Memory object), 491, 492

GetParentHandle method (WindowManager object), 384–385

GetRef method, with Web Browser Dialog Box, 546

GetSpecialFolder method (FileSystemObject object), 253–254, 488

GetSpellingSuggestions method (WinWord), accessing, 352

GetSystemInformation method, 503

GetSystemMetrics API function, wrapper for, 493–494

GetVersion method (version object), 262–263

GetVersion API function, wrapper for, 504

GetWindowCoordinates method (WindowManager object), 383–384

GetWindowFromProcess method (WindowManager object), 370–371, 374–376

GetWindowHandle method (WindowManager object), 368–369

GetWindowHandleFromClass method (WindowManager object), 369

GetWindowHandleFromCursor method (WindowManager object), 383–384

GetWinVer function (Registry toolkit), 418

.gif files, file size, 597. *See also* graphics files

global groups, 674, 675

global variables, 73

GoTo commands, adding to editors, 12–13

Gradient Captions visual effect, 465
    disabling, 467–468

graphics files
    buttons/icons from, 596–597
    editing, 592
    image quality, changing, 599–601
    loading/printing, 593–594
    printing, 590–592
    rotating images, 594–595
    scaling images, 595–596
    thumbnails/preview pages, 597–599
    viewing, tools for, 579–580

graphics, scanning
    automated, 586–587
    multiple images, 588
    saving image to disk, 585–586
    thumbnail previews, 589–590
    TWAIN driver support, verifying, 584

group accounts
    viewing members of, 678
    viewing using ADSI namespace, 676

Group property (Network object), 681–683

group types (ADSI), 683–683

groups
    adding users to, 680–681
    global, listing, 674
    global, managing, 675
    identifying members of, 678–679
    identifying membership in, 680
    removing users, 681
    viewing properties, 681–682

Groups method (Network object), 680

H

HandleEvents method, with timer control, 515

handles, window, 367

hard drives, formatting, 260–261

Height property (Web Browser Dialog Box), 542

help files
    downloading, 114
    for object functions, accessing, 113–115
    searching for, 114
    types of, 115

Help method (Application object), 273

Hex function (VBScript), 50

hexadecimal notation
    referencing colors, 192–193
    referencing constants, 189

HH.EXE, 115

Hidden attribute (files/folders), 239

hiding. *See also* automating
    desktops, 389
    script launches, 394–396
    Start menu button, 386

HKCR[backslash]CLSID key, icon storage in, 440
HKEY-CLASSES_ROOT (Windows Registry), 398, 409
  linking to, 94
  object information in, 93
  objects stored in, viewing, 98–100
HKEY_CURRENT_CONFIG (Windows Registry), 409
HKEY_CURRENT_ROOT (Windows Registry), 415–416
HKEY_CURRENT_USER(Windows Registry), 409, 434
HKEY_DYN_DATA (Windows Registry), 409
HKEY_LOCAL_MACHINE (Windows Registry), 409
  NameSpace key, 437
  program settings, storage of, 434
  searching for keys in, 431–434
.hlp (help) files, 115
host names (Internet servers), identifying, 575–576
HostByAddress method (Internet Connection object), 575–576, 579
HostByName method (Internet Connection object), 579
HostComputer property (shared folders), 692
hosting environment
  default, changing, 532–534
  identifying, 531
Hot Tracking visual effect, 466
Hotkey property
  with IShellLink object, 308
  with Shortcut object, 291
HTML code, embedding in script files, 244–246
HTML dialog boxes
  custom, creating, 171–174
  enabling Help button, script for, 546–547
HTML documentation manuals, generating, 176–181

HTML files
  converting DOS folder to, 59–61
  displaying in Internet Explorer, 158–159
  as HTMLDocument object, 174
  opening/choosing programs for, 325
  sample file, 159
HTML template (custom web browser)
  centering form, 545
  creating/displaying, 540–541
  modifying, 544–545, 547–550
  radio buttons, adding, 555–558
  results, retrieving from, 543–544
  template elements, accessing, 542–543
HTMLDocument object
  HTML page as, 174
  retrieving information about, 182–184
HTMLWindow2 object, viewing information about, 182

I

.ico (icon) files, 300, 622
icon caches, managing, 431
Icon Handler object (icon.handler)
  DESKTOP.INI folders, searching for, 623–626
  icons, available, accessing, 608–6131
  icons, extracting from files, 622–623
  icons, folder, changing, 614–619
  icons, system, changing/restoring, 619–621
Icon Picker dialog box
  selecting icons from, 298
  Windows system variations, 204
  wrapper for, 203–206
icon resource identifiers, 299
icon.handler object
  DESKTOP.INI folders, searching for, 623–626
  icons, available, 608–613
  icons, extracting from files, 622–623
  icons, folder, changing, 614–619
  icons, system, changing/restoring, 619–621

iconhandler.vbp, 608

IconLocation property (Shortcut object), 291, 295

iconpicker.tool, 204–205

iconpick.vbp, 204–205

icons
  adding to Explorer window, 446–447
  available, generating list of, 608–611
  available, selecting file from, 611–613
  cache for, enlarging, 431
  creating, 596–597
  custom, creating, 300
  desktop, adding context menu
    commands, 443–445
  extracting from files, 607–608, 622
  fixed resource identifiers, 299
  for folders, changing, 614–619
  hiding folders using, 619
  locating, 295–298
  Program menu, changing, 299
  Recycle Bin, hiding, 438
  script, adding arguments/files, 40–41
  shortcut arrows, changing, 480–481
  size, changing, 428–430
  spacing, changing, 453–454
  title wraps, enabling, 458
  in tray area, changing dynamically,
    520–522
  in tray area, for showing running
    scripts, 516–520

icons, system
  changing, 480–481, 619–621
  enabling warning message, 445
  finding/restoring, 440–442
  icon index, 481
  NameSpace key for, 437

identifiers, resource, 299

IDispatch interface, 86
  accessing using scripts, 324
  eliminating, 349

IDrive object, 87, 88

IE-based output window
  allowing input, dialog box setup,
    168–170

creating, 165–166
  HTML files, displaying in, 158–159
  resizing, 167–168

IE (Internet Explorer)
  automation errors, preventing, 161
  as COM object, 156
  components, viewing, 157
  contents, changing dynamically,
    159–161
  DHTML object model documentation,
    174
  documentation for, 157
  events in, responding to, 161
  real name for, finding, 156
  remote startup, 157–158
  titlebar text, customizing, 160
  TypeLibrary, 163–165
  as WebBrowser control wrapper,
    539–540

If statements (VBScript)
  compared with Select case, 67
  uses for, 66

If. . . then. . .else function (VBScript),
  65–66

IHTMLWindow2 object, viewing
  information about, 182

Image method (Imaging Tool object), 594

images. *See* graphics files

imaging controls, documentation for, 115

Imaging tool. *See* Kodak Imaging tool

Imaging Tool object (twain.manager),
  583–584. *See also* graphics files
  compressed files, viewing TIFF settings,
    603–604
  file type information, repairing
    automatically, 604–606
  scanned images, editing, 592
  scanned images, printing, 590–592
  scanning images, automated, 586–587
  scanning images, multiple scans, 588
  scanning images, saving image to disk,
    585–586
  scanning images, thumbnail previews,
    589–590

TWAIN driver support, verifying, 584

IMGADMIN.OCX. *See* Kodak Imaging tool

IMGEDIT.OCX, 582

IMGOCXD.HLP, 582

IMGSCAN.OCX, 582

IMGTHUMB.OCX, 582

Implemented Categories (COM objects), 94

index catalogs, accessing/managing, 659–660

Index Server
custom dialog box for, 665–666
enabling summary information, 666–667
features, 658–660
information categories (table), 662

Index Server Query object (ixsso.Query)
customizing search dialog box, 664–665
querying folders, 664–665
querying Index Server, 661–663
recycling, 663

indexes
in arrays, multiple, 56
managing databases using, 658–660

information categories
in Index Server (table), 662
in log files, 25–26

information management, 658

information, prompting for, 32–33

InfoTip value (tooltip text), 472–473

innerHTML property, 160

InProcServer32 information (COM objects), 93, 94

input type, testing for, 27

InputBox dialog window
automatic window closing, 147
designing in VB CEE, 132
example project, 132–134
Form_Resize() procedure, 145–146
for Registry edits, 413
text box element, preselecting 147

InputBox function, 32–33
arguments, 141–142
with custom web browser, 552–553

insertAdjacentHTML method, 160

installation scripts, 302

installing
Registry toolkit (registry.tobtools), 94, 97
screen savers, 463
Script Debugger, 16
Windows 2000 script debugger, 17–18

InStr function (VBScript), 57, 58

InStrRev function (VBScript), 57–58

Int function (VBScript), 49–50

integer values/arrays, long, retrieving, 449

Integer variable type, converting to, 50

internal objects, viewing functions/procedures, 106–108

InternalName property (version object), 264

Internet access. *See also* FTP
FTP connect errors, trapping, 563–565
FTP, uploading/downloading files, 562–574
Run method, limitations, 560
script extensions for, 559–560
using scripts, 560–561

Internet Connection object (internet.communication), 560
connection type identification, 575
connections, opening/closing 560–561
files, downloading/uploading, 567–569
FTP methods (table), 577–578
FTP server directories/subfolders, viewing, 563–567
host name identification, 575–576
IP address identification, 576
WinSock methods (table), 578–579

Internet Explorer. *See* IE (Internet Explorer)

Internet Explorer Script Debugger, 19

Internet Explorer shell view, WebView object, 319–320

Internet, Web sites, managing, 569–574. *See also* Web sites

Internet Wizard, disabling, 159

internet.communication object, 560
connection type, identifying, 575
files from Internet, downloading,
567–568
FTP methods (table), 577–578
FTP server directories/subfolders,
viewing, 563–567
host names, identifying, 575–576
IP addresses, identifying, 576
opening/closing connections, 561
uploading files from Internet, 568–569
WinSock methods (table), 578–579
InternetExplorer object
events in, listing, 511
Internet Connection object, 561
onQuit event, 510
OnVisible event, 511–512
internet.vbp, 560
InvokeVerb method (FolderItem object),
277, 284–286
InvokeVerbEx method (FolderItem
object), 277
IP addresses (Internet servers),
identifying, 576
is. . .() functions, checking information
using, 34–36
IsBrowsable property (FolderItem
object), 277
IsDate function
checking information using, 34–36
testing input type, 27
IsDebug property (version object), 264
IsEmpty function, checking empty
variables using, 36
IsFileSystem property (FolderItem
object), 277
IsFolder property (FolderItem object),
277
IShellLink object, 307–308
IsLink property (FolderItem object), 277
IsMissing function, detecting missing
arguments, 142
IsNumeric function, testing input type, 27
IsPatch property (version object), 264

IsPrerelease property (version object),
264
IsPrivate property (version object), 264
IsReady property (Drive object), 222, 223
IsRootFolder property (Folder object),
231
IsShortcut registry setting (Registry
Toolkit), 478–479
IsVer property (version object), 264
Items function (Folder object), 275
IWebBrowser (Internet Explorer object),
accessing remotely, 157–158
IWebBrowser2 interface, contents, 163
IWshCollection object
searching for, example script, 111–113
uses for, 112
ixsso.Query object
customizing search dialog box, 664–665
querying folders, 664–665
querying Index Server, 661–663
recycling, 663

J

JavaScript: keyword, with navigate
method, 160
JavaScript, WSH 2.0 (Scripting Host)
support for, 31–32
Join function, with variable arrays, 52
JPEG compression, 602
.jpg files, 602. *See also* graphics files
file size, 597
printing, 592

K

kernel32.dll, 361
key codes, Windows folder (table), 489
keyboard checker, activating in custom
web browser, 551–553
keyboard shortcuts. *See also* links;
shortcuts
assigning to form elements, 133
avoiding duplicate key names, 14
choosing output windows, 333–335

for desktop windows management, 382
duplicate, finding and deleting, 293–295
for line-numbering script, 13–14
menu underlines for, 469
system commands, 338
KeyExists method (Registry toolkit),
420–421
KeyPress event, adding to InputBox
dialog window, 147
keypress events, with custom web
browser, 550–553
keys (Windows Registry), 91
deleting, 420
enumerating values in, 416–417
file type main key, identifying, 402
file types, key assignments, 398–399
in HKEY_CURRENT_ROOT,
enumerating, 415–416
identifying using before/after
snapshots, 424–426
main, listing of, 409
path for, 421
searching for using Registry Editor, 431
undocumented, identifying using
RegMon, 427–428
verifying existence of, 420–421
keywords
with Dictionary object, 80
searching for function syntax, 109
KillProcess method, 356, 358
KillProgram method, closing windows
using, 360
Kodak Imaging tools
COM objects included with (table), 582
help/documentation for, 115
uses for, 579–580
wrapper for, 583

L

Last Known Good configuration
(Windows 2000), 410
launched windows, accessing, 370–371
launching
program groups, 325–327

programs, 328
programs, individually, 323–324
screen savers, 458–459
scripts, at intervals, 396–397
scripts, at logon, 393–394, 393–394
scripts, before logon, 396
LCase function (VBScript), 57
Leave method, with Web Browser Dialog
Box, 549, 554
Left function (VBScript), 57, 58
LegalCopyright property (version
object), 264
Len function (VBScript), 57
line-numbering script, 12–14
links
arguments for, optional, adding,
305–306
creating using Shortcut object, 290–291
icons for, customizing, 300
invalid, finding and deleting, 291–293
link files, accessing, 307–308
link files, creating, 289–290
resolving, 309–312
resolving, shortcuts for, 312–315
to Send To Context menu, adding,
301–305
target files, accessing Properties pages,
315–316
target files, controlling size, 306–307
uses for, 289–290
List Box visual effect, 466
disabling, script for, 468
lists
background sorting, 211–212
displaying, 207–213
removing entries from, 209–210
ListView dialog box
icon-containing files, selecting, 611–613
object model, 212
operating in background, 211–212
removing entries from, 209–210
viewing system file information,
266–268
wrapper for, 207–208

listview.tool component, 207–209
ListWindows function
  closing individual programs, 343–344
  closing running programs, 341
  creating, 341
  modifying to show executable names, 342–343
.lnk files, 289
LoadDialog function (Web Browser Dialog Box), 542
local folders, synchronizing with Web folders, 569–574
log files
  empty folders (emptydelete.txt), 235
  event logging, 22
  information categories, 25–26
  maintaining, 24
  time stamps, 25
  viewing, 23–24
.LOG files (Windows 9.x systems), finding, 22
LogEvent method, accessing/using, 22–23
logical errors, identifying, 15
LogIt procedure, event logging using, 22–23
logons. *See also* users
  automatic, to remote machines, 694–695
  names, identifying, 490–491
looping
  during data validation, 34–36
  with events, 515
  exit conditions, 70–71
  exiting prematurely, 71–72
  functions for, 67–72
  through variable arrays, 20
LTrim function (VBScript), 57
lz32.dll, decompressing files using, 269

M

Main window (VB CCE), 119
  Code view/Object view, 119
maintaining. *See* managing/maintaining

Make command, compiling objects using, 196
MakeDir method (Internet Connection object), 578
managing
  graphics files/images, 593–594
  log files, 24
  menu animation effects, 468–469
  systems, links for, 289
  systems, Windows NT/2000, 670
  Web sites, 569–574
MapNetworkDrive method (Network object), 490
Max Cached Icons key, 427–428
MaxButton property, 143
MaxRecords property (Index Server Query object), 661
MaxUserCount property (shared folders), 692
MCI Manager object (mci.manager), 626–627
  for audio CDs, 631–636, 642–644
  for AVI movie files, 640–641
  for CD-ROM drives, 628–631
  for MIDI files, 638–639
  for WAV files, 640
MCI (Media Control Interface), controlling, 626
mci.manager object, 626–627
  for audio CDs, 631–636, 642–644
  for AVI movie files, 640–641
  for CD-ROM drives, 628–631
  for MIDI files, 638–639
  for WAV files, 640
mciSendString API function, wrapper for, 626–627
  calling from COM objects, 127–128
mci.vbp, 626–627
MDAC (Microsoft Database Access Components), 644
  identifying version, 646–647
  updating, 646–647
Media Control Interface. *See* MCI (Media Control Interface)

Mem_load method (Memory object), 491

memory, managing, 491–493

Memory object (memory.stats)

current load, viewing, 492–493

usage statistics, retrieving, 491–492

memory. vbp, 491

memory.stats object

checking current load, 492–493

usage statistics, retrieving, 491–492

menu animation effects, delayed opening, 470

Menu Animation visual effect, 466, 468–469

Menu Underlines visual effect, 466, 469

menus

controlling using SendKeys, 338

Documents menu, cleaning/maintaining, 485–488

enabling/disabling, 380–381

message boxes, logging script activity using, 22

methods

Application object (table), 273–274

Dictionary object, 82

Folder object (table), 275

FolderItem object (table), 276

FolderItemVerb object, 286

Internet Connection object (internet.communication), 577–578

Link object (table), 308

Network object (Script.Network object), 490

Web Browser Dialog Box (web.dialog), 542

WebView object, 319–320

MetricsInformation method (Miscellaneous Information object)

properties/index values (table), 494–496

using, 494

Microsoft Database Access Components. *See* MDAC

Microsoft Office

MSComDlg.CommonDialog in, 186

WinWord spell-checker, accessing, 351–353

WinWord TypeLibrary, accessing, 349–351

Microsoft Script Debugger. *See* Script Debugger

Mid function (VBScript), 57, 58

MIDI (audio) files, playing, 638–638

MinButton property, 143

MinimizeAll method (Application object), 273

handling desktop windows using, 381–382

minimizing/maximizing windows

on desktops, 381–382

disabling, 380

at startup, 306–307

Miscellaneous Information object (misc.information), 493–494

boot mode, controlling, 498

font sample page, 501–503

MetricsInformation method, 494–496

mouse type, identifying, 497

networks, identifying presence of, 497–498

processors, identifying numbers of, 504

processors, identifying type, 503–504

slow systems, identifying, 496–497

miscinfo.vbp, 494

missing arguments, detecting, 142

modal window displays, 136, 522

Modeless object (modeless.dialog), creating/using, 522–525

modeless window displays, 136, 522

cautions about using, 525–526

controlling, script for, 524–525

icons lists, viewing using, 608

modeless.dialog object, 522–525

modeless.vbp, 522

ModifyDate property (FolderItem object), 277

modules

in currently running programs, viewing, 363–365

Continued

modules *(continued)*
    modular design (software packages),
        349
    purpose of, 124
module.spy COM
    listing currently running programs,
        362–363
    obtaining version information, 361–362
module.spy.vbp, 361
Monitor command, adding to .vbs file
        context menu, 19
monitoring programs, 357–358
more commands, piping using, 534–536
moricons.dll, system icons in, 295
mouse hover, timeout settings, 470–471
mouse type, identifying, 497
MouseDown events, 136
Move procedure
    with File object, 237
    with Folder object, 231
MoveHere method (Folder object), 275
movie (AVI) files
    customizing output window, 640
    playing, 640–641
moving windows, 376–377
MS Access sample database
        (sample.mdb), opening/querying,
        648–649
MS Word (WinWord)
    accessing spell-checker, 351–353
    accessing TypeLibrary, 349–351
MsComDlg.CommonDialog object
    accessing files using, 187
    generating documentation for,
        187–188
    locating, 186
    reasons for replacing, 193
MSDADC.DLL, identifying ADO version,
        646–647
msf (minutes-seconds-frames), 633
MsgBox dialog box
    behavior of, 37–38
    button-generating constants, 37
    buttons, adding to, 37

help files/documentation, accessing,
        113–114
    keeping on top, 38
    logging script activity using, 22
    system state icons, 38
    system-state icons, adding to 38
mshtml.tlb, viewing DHTML
        documentation in, 174–175
multi-line dialog boxes, Say procedure,
        72–73
MultiDest copying, 259
multidimensional arrays, 56, 79–80
MultiEdit property (listview.tool), 209
multimedia devices
    accessing, 127, 626–627
    defined, 626
    device types (table), 637
    generic commands for (table), 636
    installed, viewing list of, 637–638
MultiSelect property (Common Dialog
        object), 190–191
    with ListView dialog box, 208
MyDocuments folder, 485
myfilter.vbs, finding filenames using,
        535–536

N
Name property
    with File object, 237
    with Folder object, 231
    with FolderItem object, 277
    with FolderItemVerb object, 286
NameSpace key, 437
    Explorer window icons, adding,
        446–447
    Recycle Bin, hiding, 438
    system icons in, 442
namespace method (Application object),
        274
    accessing files/folders using, 282
namespaces, 675–676
naming. *See also* renaming
    COM objects, 122–123

path names versus shell naming
conventions, 281–282
navigate method, 158–160
NetHood folder, 485
Network object (WScript.Network)
ADSI namespaces, viewing contents of,
675–676
ComputerName method, 676
container objects, identifying 677–678
group members, identifying, 678
groups, managing, 680–683
passwords, managing, 684, 686–687
properties/methods/functions (table),
490
shared folders, handling, 690–692
user accounts, new, adding, 679–680
users, current, identifying, 490–491
users, managing, 684–685, 687
Windows Services, 688–690
networks
connections, viewing information
about, 112–113, 497–498
managing using ADSI interface, 678–687
restarting/shutting down computers,
692–695
shares, managing, 688–689
users/groups, managing, 490–491
New menu
automatic script startup, 8–9, 11
inserting .vbs document type into, 6–7
NewFolder method (Folder object), 275
newmore.vbs, 534–535
newvbsflle.vbs, 9–10
non-resizable windows, 143
Notepad editor window
accessing, script for, 369
writing scripts in, 3–5
NT Services object (nt.services),
controlling Windows Services, 688
NT Shutdown object (nt.shutdown)
with local machines, 692–693
with remote machines, 692–695
NT User object (nt.user)
accounts, deleting, 673

global groups, listing, 674
global groups, managing, 675
passwords, changing, 673–674
users, adding, 672–673
users, enumerating, 671–672
nt.services object, controlling Windows
Services, 688
nt.shutdown object
local machines, shutting
down/rebooting, 692–693
remote machines, automatic logon,
694–695
remote machines, shutting down,
692–693
nt.user object
accounts, deleting, 673
global groups, listing, 674
global groups, managing, 675
passwords, changing, 673–674
users, adding, 672–673
users, enumerating, 671–672
numbers, randomizing, 61–62
numeric content, sorting in ListView, 208

O
object functions, accessing
documentation, 113–115
Object view (VB CCE), 119
objects. *See also* API functions; COM
objects
automation, viewing, 98–99
closing, 158
in command searches, 109
components of, listing, 511–512
functions/procedures for, 106–110
scriptable, determining, 100–101
searching for, 111–113
Start-Objects, 106
undocumented, autodocumenting,
105–108
Oct function (VBScript), 50
OCX files, 86
OfflineStatus property (Folder object),
275

OKButton property (Web Browser Dialog Box), 542

OLE error messages
  converting to clear text, 147–150
  making readable, 676

OLEDB32.DLL, identifying ADO version, 646–647

OLEError function, 676

OLEerror.vbp, 148–149

onkeypress event, with custom web browser, 550

Onload property, with custom web browser, 550–553

OnQuit event
  with InternetExplorer object, 510
  responding to, script for, 161–163

OnVisible event (InternetExplorer object), 511–512

Open command (multimedia devices), 636

Open File dialog box
  accessing using script file, 187
  creating custom wrapper for, 195–196
  flags (constants) for, 189–191

Open method (Application object), 274

OpenAsTextStream method (File object), 237

opening menus, delay effects, managing, 470

OpenInternet method (Internet Connection object), 577

OpenTextFile method (File object), 241–244, 246–247

OpenTray method (cd.tools), 126–127

OpenWindow property, with IE-based output windows, 166

option //D (Scripting Host), 16, 18

option //X (Scripting Host), enabling script step-throughs, 18

optional keyword, 142

ordinal numbers, as function names, 131

OriginalFileName property (version object), 264

OS property (OS Version object), 264

OS Version object (os.version)
  DLLs, finding functions in, 507
  feature support, checking for, 506
  OSVersion method, 505
  WinKind method, 505–506

osversion.vbp, 504

OutOfDate property (Index Query Serer object), 663

overlay device type, 637

overlay icons. *See* shortcut arrows

P

packages, setup, Setup Wizard for, 152–154

Parent property
  with Application object, 274
  with Folder object, 275
  with FolderItem object, 277
  with FolderItemVerb object, 286
  with WebView object, 320

parent windows, viewing, 384–385

ParentFolder property
  with File object, 237
  with Folder object, 231

parentheses, placing arguments in, 75

ParseName method (Folder object), 275
  with Application object, 282
  with Folder object, 275

passwords
  changing on Windows NT/2000 systems, 673–674
  forcing changes in, 686
  prohibiting changes in, 686–687
  setting, 684

path names
  for DOS command interpreter, 344
  illegal, avoiding, 201
  for Registry keys, notation for, 421
  for running scripts, 41
  for special folders, viewing, 484–485
  versus shell's naming conventions, 281–282
  for Windows folder, 488

Path property
    with Drive object, 222
    with File object, 237
    with Folder object, 231
    with FolderItem object, 277
    with IShellLink object, 308
    in shared folders, 692
paths. *See* path names
Pause command (multimedia devices),
        636
PerlScript scripting language, WSH 2.0
        (Scripting Host) support for, 31
phrases, searching for, using Index
        Server, 664
pickfolder.vbp, 198–200
pictures, loading/printing, 593–594. *See
        also* graphics files
PIDLs (PathID lists), 279
piping commands
    creating, 534–535
    creating filters using, 535–536
    defined, 534
plain text files (.txt), saving script files
        as, 3–4
PlatformID
    identifying, 418
    retrieving, 505
Play command (multimedia devices),
        636
playing back
    AVI movie files, 640–642
    MIDI audio files, 638–639
    WAV audio files, 640
Popup function. 38–39
PopupItemMenu method (WebView
        object), 320
portmon utility (sysinternals.com), 427
power-saving features, enabling, 463–464
powering-off. *See* power-saving features
preconfiguring disk tools, 329
preselected buttons, 37
Preserve function, with array
        compression, 56
preventing errors, 26–28

previewing
    preview pages, thumbnails for, 597–599
    scanned images, 589–590
    windows, 391–392
printers, Property pages for, 287–288
PrintHood folder, 485
PrintImage method (Imaging Tool object),
        592
printing
    graphics files, 593–594
    scanned images, 590–592
procedures
    calling from Debug menu command
        window, 20
    for displaying windows, 134–135
    of objects, viewing, 106–108
    pitfalls, 74–75
    private variables in, 73
    searching for, 108–110
    VBScript, defining, 72
processes, currently running
    list of, viewing, 362–363
    ProcessIDs for, 355
    modules in, viewing, 363–365
process.id COM, 355
ProcessIDs, accessing directly, 355
processors, system, identifying processor
        type/numbers, 503–504
ProductName property (version object),
        264
ProductVersion property (version
        object), 264
ProgID
    CLSID key, components, 100
    CLSID key, WinWord, 351
    COM objects, 93
program groups
    custom, 325
    launching, script for, 325–327
    Startup Group, 301, 325
Program Identifier, 93
Program menu, changing icons on, 299
programs
    accessing modules in, 360–364
                                Continued

programs *(continued)*
  accessing using CreateObject, 349
  backdoor script access, 349
  closing as group, 341–342
  closing, EndProcess method, 356
  closing, individual, 342–344
  closing, KillProcess method, 356–357, 358
  in minimized windows, 359–360
  internal settings, protecting, 434
  internal settings, Registry storage, 434
  launcher scripts, customized, 323–324, 434
  list of, viewing, 339–341, 362–363
  modules in, 363–365
  monitoring, 357–358
  running synchronous, 358–359
  version information, obtaining, 361–362
Programs command, cautions about, 13
Programs menu, launching keyboard shortcuts from, 293
progress indicator, with EmptyRecycler method, 255
Project Explorer window (VB CCE), 119–120
properties, 139–140
  Application object (table), 273–274
  Dictionary object, 82
  Drive object (table), 222
  File object (table), 237
  Folder object (table), 231, 275
  FolderItem object (table), 276–277
  FolderItemVerb object, 286
  of form elements, viewing, 133
  of groups, group type, 682–683, 682–683
  of groups, viewing, 681–682
  Internet Connection object, 577–578
  Link object (table), 308
  Network object, 490
  screen properties, viewing information about, 183
  screen saver, changing, 461–463

  shared folders (table), 692
  Shortcut object (table), 291
  user accounts, 684–685, 686
  version object (table), 264
  Web Browser Dialog Box, 542
  WebView object, 319–320
Properties pages, 120, 315–317
  accessing, 286–288
  components in, viewing, 140
  displaying, 282–283
  keeping open, 284
  target files, accessing, 315–316
property-IDs
  for power-saving features, 464
  for Windows settings (table), 450–452
Property keyword, accessing properties using, 140–141
Property object (property.tool), 287–288
property.tool object, 286–288
public events, 514
PutFile method (Internet Connection object), 578

Q
QueryInxcomplete property (Index Query Server), 663
QueryMCIString method (MCI Manager object), 629
QueryTimedOut property (Index Query Server object), 663
Quick Format, 260–262
Quit method
  closing objects using, 158
  with QuitNow event, 521–522
  with Web Browser Dialog Box, 549
QuitNow event, 521–523
QuitOnDemand method (Tray Icon object), 517
quotation marks, with long filenames, 41

R
radio buttons, adding to custom web browser, 555–558

RAM, identifying amount available, 492–493

random numbers
encrypting/decrypting files using, 62–65
random number generator, 61–62

Randomize function (VBScript), 61–62
in decryption process, 62–65

RDISK.EXE utility (Windows NT), 410

Read Only attribute (files/folders), 239

ReadFile function, creating, 73–74

ReadKey function (Shell object), 411–412

ReadMCI method (MCI Manager object), 629

ReadOnly flag, referencing in scripts, 189–191

ready-to-use scripts, 26

rebooting local computers, 692–693

Recent folder, 485
cleaning out, 486–487

recompiling COM objects, 135

records (databases)
counting, 655
deleting, 655–656

RecordToWave method (MCI Manager object), 644

recreating Registry, on Windows 9.x systems, 411

Recycle Bin
access, controlling, 438–439
context menu commands, adding, 443–445
emptying, 255
function of, 253
icon, hiding, 438
name, changing, 435–436
warning messages, enabling/disabling, 445

Recycle function (shellcopy.tool COM), 252–253

recycling files, 252–253

ReDim function, 51
for dynamic variable arrays, 53–54
expanding/shrinking arrays, 55–56

RefreshMenu method (Application object), 274

RefreshWindowMetrics, 430

REG files, restoring automatically, 411

REG_BINARY(hexadecimal) data type, 429

RegDelete method (Registry toolkit), 420

REG_DWORD (integer) data type, 429

REGEDIT (Windows Registry)
accessing Registry content using, 408
accessing/using, 242–244
locating COM objects in, 91–92

RegEnum method (Registry object)
listing key values, 416–417
listing subkeys using, 415–416

registered owner, identifying, version-independent script for, 417–418

registering custom COM objects, 150–151

Registry, 420
automation objects, viewing, 98–100
backing up, 409–410
branches, exporting to REG files, 411
changes to, viewing, 427–428
COM objects in, locating, 91–92
context menu entries, deleting, 401
data types, 429
directory display, right/left pane contents, 409
editing entries in, 412–415
entries, reading, 242–244
file types, key assignments, 398–399
FlushIconCache method, 431
interface script, 428–429
location of, 408
program settings, 434
Registered Owner information, reading, 411–412
script editing control, disabling, 395–396
snapshots, comparing, 424–426
undocumented features, accessing using scripts, 428–430
uses/functions, 407–408

Continued

Registry *(continued)*
variable types, 418–419
variable types (table), 414
version-dependent scripts, 418–420
version-independent scripts, 417–418
Windows 9.x versus Windows NT/2000
systems, 409–412
Registry Editor (REGEDIT). *See also*
REGEDIT
key searches, 431
Registry-controlled script editing,
disabling, 395–396
Windows settings, changing, 452–453
Registry keys
changing values for, 429
deleting, 414–415, 420
display format, 408
in HKEY_CURRENT_ROOT file, 415–416
identifying, 424–426
reverting to original settings, 430
Run key, 394–396
Shell Small Icon Size key. changing,
428–430
subkeys, enumerating, 94–97
verifying existence of, 420–421
Registry settings
changes in, accepting, 430
defaults, reverting to, 430
hidden, uncovering, 424–426
Registry Toolkit (regtool.tob), 415
binary data, handling, 419–420
key values, listing, 416–417
Registry interface, creating, 428–429
shortcut arrows, managing, 478–481
stored values variable types,
identifying, 418–419
subkeys, listing, 415–416
writing version-independent scripts,
417–418
Registry Update object (registry.update)
Active Window Tracking user controls,
454–456
combo box animation, enabling, 466
CTRL+ALT+DEL, disabling, 461

cursor shadow effect, enabling, 466
cursors, blinking, size settings, 475
desktop icon spacing controls,
453–454
font smoothing, enabling/disabling, 474
full window drag, 448, 474
gradient captions, disabling, 467–468
list box animation, disabling, 467–468
menu animation effects, managing,
468–470
menu underlines, disabling, 469
screen savers, managing, 459–461,
463–464
selection fade, enabling/disabling, 471
snap-to-button feature, disabling, 478
system beep, controlling, 457–458
tooltips, enabling, 471–472
visual effects, disabling, 465
window borders, changing, 456
window colors, changing, 457
window icons, enabling title wrap for,
458
Windows property-IDs, accessing,
450–452
Windows settings, accessing, 448
RegMon utility, viewing Registry changes,
427–428
RegRead function
with Registry toolkit, 417–419
with Shell object, 412–415
Regsvr32.EXE, registering COM objects
using, 151
REG_SZ (text) data type, 429
RegWrite method
with Registry Toolkit, 419–420
with Shell object, 413–415, 419
RelativePath property (Shortcut object),
291
remote controls, for audio CDs, 634–636
RemoteShutdown (NT Shutdown object),
692–693
Remove method (Network object), 681
RemoveDir method (Internet Connection
object), 578

RemoveNetworkDrive method (Network object), 490

RemovePrinterConnection method (Network object), 490

removing context menu entries, 401

Rename command, adding to Recycle Bin context menu, 443–445

RenameFile method (Internet Connection object), 578

renaming. *See also* naming
  files/folders, 247–248, 619
  .vbs scripts, 7–8

Replace function (VBScript), 57

reports, CD-ROM drive status, 630–631

reserved words, Log, 23

Resizable property (Web Browser Dialog Box), 542, 545

Resize procedure (Modeless object), 523

resizing
  forms/dialog boxes, 145–146
  IE-based output window, 167–168
  window contents, 144–146
  windows, 143, 377–378, 381

Resolve dialog box, accessing using scripts, 313–315

Resolve method, 309–315

resolving links, 309–315

resource identifiers, for icons, 299

restoring Registry, on Windows 9.*x* systems, 411

results, passing using arguments, 76–77

RETURN keypress, closing web browser automatically, 550–551

return values, 76–77
  dictionary objects for, 79–80
  objects as, 87
  ShowWindow function, defining, 139
  system dialog box flags for, 190–191
  variable arrays for, 77–80
  for Windows property-IDs (table), 450–452

REXX scripting language, WSH 2.0 (Scripting Host) support for, 31

Right function (VBScript), 57, 58

Rnd function (VBScript), 61–62
  in decryption process, 62–65

Root Folder, enumerating files in, 220–221

RootFolder property (Drive object), 222

RotateLeft method (Imaging Tool object), 594

RotateRight method (Imaging Tool object), 594

Round function (VBScript), 50

RTrim function (VBScript), 57

Run command (Windows Start menu), drag-and-drop features, 41

Run key (Windows Registry), 394–396

Run method (Shell object), 531
  disk tools, preconfiguring, 329
  Internet access using, limitations, 560
  ProcessIDs with, 355–356
  ScanDisk utility, launching, 328–329
  spaces with, effects of, 324
  style limitations, 359
  uses for, 324–325
  window size/style settings, 327–328

Run method (Shell object), program-management
  closing/killing, 356–357, 360
  launching sequentially, 328
  launching using, 324
  monitoring, 357–358
  running synchronously, 358–359

run-time, changing properties during, 140

rundll32.exe, launching SHFormatDrive, 261–262

RunServices key, launching scripts before logon, 396

S

SAGE (System AGEnt), accessing, 329

sample.mdb (sample database)
  accessing, 648–649
  data, adding, 653
  data, viewing, 652
  opening/querying, 649–651
  records, counting, 655

Continued

sample.mdb *(continued)*
   records, deleting, 655–656
   table structure, viewing, 651–652
   tables, creating, 655–657
   tables, deleting, 657
   variable fields, retrieving, 654–655
Save As dialog box (File menu), 10
Save File dialog box, 188
Save method
   with Imaging Tool object, 594
   with IShellLink object, 308
   with Shortcut object, 291
SaveAs method (Imaging Tool object),
   594
   image quality, changing, 599–600
   options/parameters (table), 600–601
saving
   scanned images to disk, 585–586
   script files, 3–4, 10–11
ScaleToMax method (Imaging Tool
   object), 596
ScaleToPixelHeight method (Imaging Tool
   object), 596
ScanDisk utility, launching, 328–329
SCANDSKW.EXE, preconfiguring, 329
scanned images, compressing, 601–604
scanner device type, 637
scanning tools, 579–580
   automated scans, 586–587
   multiple scans, 588
   saving image to disk, 585–586
   scanned images, 590–592
   thumbnail previews, 589–590
   TWAIN driver support, verifying, 584
ScanTo method (Imaging Tool object),
   601–604
Scheduled Task Wizard, launching scripts
   using, 396–397
.scr files, searching for in Windows
   Registry, 432–433
screen coordinates, sizing windows
   using, 376
screen objects, viewing information
   about, 182–184

screen resolution
   available resolutions, identifying,
     498–499
   changing, 500–501
   current settings, identifying, 499
   frequency settings, changing, 500
screen savers
   currently running, verifying, 461
   disabling, 459–460
   launching, 458–459
   new, installing, 463
   power-saving mode, enabling,
     463–464
   settings/properties, changing,
     461–463
   timeout settings, 460
screen.tool object, 498
   frequency settings, 500
   screen resolution, managing, 499–501
screen.vbp, 498
Script Debugger (Microsoft), 15–18
   breakpoint setting, 21
   identifying logical errors, 15–16
   installing, 16
   launching, 16
   loading scripts into, 16–17
   in Windows 2000 systems, 17–18
script editing, Registry-controlled,
   disabling, 395–396
script extensions, compared with stand-
   alone programs, 121
script files, reading using File object,
   244–246
scriptable objects
   determining, 100–101
   listing, script for, 101–104
ScriptFullName procedure, 57–58
   with Web Browser Dialog Box, 545
Scripting Host. *See* WSH 2.0 (Scripting
   Host)
scripting languages, WSH 2.0 (Scripting
   Host) support for, 31
Scripting objects, documentation for, 114
Scripting.Dictionary object, 88

Scripting.FileSystemObject, 86–89, 107, 219
  adding error checking to formatting, 261–262
  Windows folder, accessing directly, 489
  Windows folder path information, retrieving, 488
SCRIPTOBJECTS.TXT, 101–104
scripts
  Active Window Tracking user controls, 455
  ADO databases, checking for ADO version, 646–647
  automation objects, viewing, 98–99
  birth date, asking for, 34–35
  Cool Switch windows, controlling size of, 481–482
  CTRL+ALT+DEL, deleting, 461
  frequency settings, identifying/modifying, 500
  identifying weekday names for dates, 27
  IDispatch interface, 86
  keyboard shortcut duplicates, finding and displaying, 293–295
  keys, sending, focus issues, 332–333
  modules, currently running programs, enumerating, 363–365
  mouse type, identifying, 497
  mshtml.tlb contents, viewing, 174–175
  random number generator, 61
  ReadFile function, 73–74
  registration functions, viewing, 150
  Resolve dialog box access, 313–314
  Say procedure, defining, 72
  Send To context menu, adding links, 301–305
  snap-to-button feature, disabling, 478
  software modules, accessing, 349
  tooltips, enabling, 471–472
  Windows editor, shortcut to 290
ADSI interface, 675–683
audio CDs/audio files, 631–633
AVI movie files, 640–641

CD-ROM drives, 628–631
COM objects, 85–91
context menus, 285, 398–399
Control Panel controls, 202–203
cursor-related, 466, 475
database-management, 651–657
debugging/error-handling, 15–21
DOS-related, 345–347, 529–530
drive management, 221–226
event-handling, 22–23, 509–513
executing, 54–55
font-related, 474, 501–503
graphics files (handling/managing), 592–599
hosting environments, 532–534
HTML documents, 158–161
Index Server, 661–665
launching, 8–11, 300–301, 393–397
ListView dialog box, 207–212
networks/network users, 190–191, 672–675
Open File dialog box, 190–191, 195–196
piping commands, 534–536
Properties pages, 282–288
scripts, SendKeys, 336–338
shortcut arrows, 478–481
user-related, 678–685
Web browser, custom. *See also* scripts, HTML documents, 545–551
Windows folder, 488–489
WinWord, 350–353
scroll bar, display options, 166
SCRRUN.DLL, Scripting objects in, 89
searching
  for compressed files, 272
  databases, 661, 665–666
  for help files, 114
  for internal/external commands, 108–110
  for invalid links, 292–293
  for keyboard shortcut duplicates, 293–295
  for objects and commands, 111–113
  for Registry keys, 431–434

security
backdoor script access, 349
encrypting/decrypting files, 62–65
Windows NT/2000 systems, 669–670
security risks, ActiveX controls, 118
Seek command (multimedia devices), 636
Select case function (VBScript), 67
Select Color dialog box, 188
Select Font dialog box, 188
/select, option (Explorer), opening
folders using, 58
Select Printer dialog box, 188
SelectedItems property (WebView
object), 318–320
Selection Fade visual effect, 466, 471
Self property (Folder object), 275
Send To Context menu, adding links to,
301–305
sending files, using links for, 301–305
SendKeys method (Shell object)
AppActivate method with, 332–333
controlling menus, 338
features, 330
key codes (table), 331–332
output windows, choosing, 333–335
wrapper for, 335–338
SendTo folder, 485
sequencer device type, 637
SerialNumber property (Drive object),
222, 224
ServicePause method (NT Services
object), 688
ServiceStart method (NT Services
object), 688
ServiceStop method (NT Services
object), 688
Set command (multimedia devices), 636
Set keyword, with COM objects, 87
SetDefaultPrinter method (Network
object), 490
SetFocus method, 147
SetIcon method (Web Browser Dialog
Box), 542
SetIconInternal method (Tray Icon
object), 520

SetIconLocation method (IShellLink
object), 308
SetTime method (Application object), 274
SetTimer event (Timer Control object),
513–514
setup packages, 151
Setup Wizard, 152–154
SETUP.EXE, for installing COM objects,
152
SetWindowCoordinates2 method, 376
Sgn function (VBScript), 50
ShareName property (Drive object), 222
sharing, on networks, managing using
ADSI interface, 690–692
shell file operation, SHFileOperation API
for, 250–252
Shell Link object (IShellLink), 307–308
shell naming conventions, versus path
names, 281–282
Shell object (WScript.Shell)
accessing Registered Owner
information, 411–412
Cool Switch windows, controlling size
of, 481–482
Documents menu, cleaning, 486–488
ExpandEnvironmentStrings method,
488–489
identifying current hosting
environment, 532–533
implementing event sinks, 511
programs, launching, 324
Run method, 324–329
screen savers, changing property
settings, 461–463
screen savers, installing new, 463
screen savers, launching, 458–459
SendKeys method, 329–344
SpecialFolders method, 484–485
Shell Small Icon Size key, 427–428
shell subkey (Windows Registry), 399
shell32.dll
accessing Shell.Application
documentation, 201–202
changing/restoring system icons,
619–621

Icon Picker documentation, 204
icons in, accessing, 481
SHFileOperation API, 250
system icons in, 295
Shell.application object, 273
desktop windows, managing, 381–382
files/folders, accessing, 282
Folder Picker, adding, 197
Properties pages, displaying, 282
properties/methods (table), 273–274
TypeLibrary information, 201–203
as wrapper, limitations, 197
shellcopy.tool object, 254
ShellFolder subkey
purpose of, 443
for system icons, 440
ShellSpecialFolderConstants.htm, 202
SHEmptyRecycleBin, 255
SHFileOperation API function
accessing, 250–252
backup operations, 255–259
MultiDest copying, 259
Recycle function, 252–253
shfileopstruct (SHFileOperation API),
250
SHFormatDrive API function, 259–262
SHObjectProperties API function,
286–288
shodocvw.dll, 201–202
shortcut arrows
appearance of, changing, 480–481
applying to files, 479–480
disabling, 478–479
Shortcut object
creating, 290
optional arguments, adding, 305–306
properties, 291
shortcuts. *See also* links
automatic switching to CSCRIPT.EXE,
44
changing icons for, 295–299
script-running, 6–7, 13, 393–395
ShortName property
with File object, 237
with Folder object, 231

ShortPath property
with File object, 237
with Folder object, 231
Show Help File dialog box, 188
Show method, 135
ShowButtons method (Web Browser
Dialog Box), 542
ShowColor method (CommonDialog
control), 188
ShowCommand property (IShellLink
object), 308
ShowFont method (CommonDialog
control), 188
ShowHelp method (CommonDialog
control), 188
with Web Browser Dialog Box, 545–546
ShowOpen method (CommonDialog
control), 188, 195–196
ShowPrinter method (CommonDialog
control), 188
ShowProp method (Property object),
287–288
ShowSave method (CommonDialog
control), 188
ShowWindow property
with Capture Window object, 391–392
creating, 134
defining return value, 139
optional arguments, 141–142
ShutdownWindows method (Shell
object), 274
single quotes, with SQL queries, 653
sixteen-bit Windows files, viewing,
265–266
size
of blinking cursors, settings for, 475
Cool Switch windows, controlling,
481–482
of folders/drive, ascertaining, 397–398
of graphical window elements,
identifying, 494–496
of windows, identifying/changing,
375–376
of windows, Run method settings,
327–328

Size property
with File object, 237
with Folder object, 231, 232–234
with FolderItem object, 277
snap-to-button feature, disabling, 478
SnapToDefButton, 478
software
backdoor script access, 349
modules in, 124
remote controls for, SendKeys, 329–344
running, ProcessIDs with, 355
sorting
background sorting, 211–212
ListView control for, 207–213
source code, ListView control, 212
space, drive, ascertaining, 225–226
spaces, with Run method, 324
SpecialFolders
in Explorer, accessing, 279–281
listing of, 280–281
for programs, 301
for startup, 301
Windows folder name and, 488
SpecialFolders method (Shell object),
484–485
spell-checker (WinWord), accessing,
351–352
spelling errors, testing for, 27
Split function, 53
NT User object, 671
with Registry Update object, 449
returning multiple values using, 78–79
with variable arrays, 52
SQL queries
single quotes with, 653
viewing/adding data, 652–653
Start Flash method (WindowManager
object), 378–379
Start menu button
adding scripts to 13
Documents menu,
cleaning/maintaining, 485–488
hiding, 386
Start menu, controlling using SendKeys,

338
Start-Objects, 106
start types (Windows Services), 690
StartMenu folder, 485
StartType property (Network object),
689–690
Startup folder, 485
Startup program group, 325
including scripts in, 301
launching scripts from, 393–394
startup scripts
launching, 300–301
startup window sizes/styles, 306–307
StartUpPosition property (Web Browser
Dialog Box), 545
Status command (multimedia devices),
636
Status property (Network object), 688
stepping through scripts, 18–20
Stop command (multimedia devices), 636
StopFlash method (WindowManager
object), 378–379
stopping scripts, 15
storage space, viewing available, 225–226
storing
COM objects, 91
compressed files, 269
data, Variant variable type and, 48
desktop objects, 438
MSComDlg.CommonDialog, 187
Registry backups, 409–410
snap-to-button feature information, 478
system icons, 440
user settings, 436
variable arrays, 51
StrConv function, converting string
formats using, 214
string handling
cutting excess lengths, 215
VBScript functions for, 56–57
Visual Basic commands for, 213–215
strings
converting one-dimensional arrays to,
79–80

extracting information from, 57–58

text, reading, script for, 450

using for return value, 77–80

StrPtr command, 214

structure, Windows shell, 250

styles of windows

changing dynamically, 374–375

identifying current, 372–374

sub. . .end sub, 72

SubFolders property (Folder object), 231

subkeys (Registry)

deleting, 420

enumerating, script for, 94–97

SubType property (version object), 264

Suspend method (Application object), 274

Synchronize method (Folder object), 275

synchronizing folders, locals folders with Web folders, 569–574

synchronous program execution, 357–359

SYSBCKUP folder (Windows 98), 410

sysinternals.com, 427–428

system

attribute (files/folders), 239

beep, controlling, 457–458

catalog (Index Server), 660

commands, keyboard shortcuts, 338

crashes, troubleshooting, 100–101

dialog boxes, 187–193

files, determining support for, 506

icons, 440–442, 619–621

menu, enabling/disabling, 380–381

snapshots, viewing running tasks using, 361

system-state icons, constants for, 38

SYSTEM32/CONFIG folder, Registry files in, 408

SYSTEM.DAT (Registry) files, 408

SYSTEM.INI, multimedia devices in, 638

SystemParametersInfo, changing Windows settings, 452–453

T

tables (database)

creating, 656–657

deleting, 657

fields in, variable types for, 654–655

viewing structure, 651–652

target files, size at opening, 306–307

TargetPath property (Shortcut object), 291, 295

cautions using, 306

TEMPLATE2.HTM (web browser object controls), 548

TEMPLATE3.HTM (onkeypress event), 550

TEMPLATE4.HTM (keyboard checker), 551–553

TEMPLATE6.HTML (radio buttons), 555–558

TEMPLATE.HTM (custom dialog boxes), 540–541

Templates folder, 485

templates, for files, 8

testing

custom COM objects, 123, 134

script, error prevention, 26–28

test.module (example COM object), 122–123

text editors, writing scripts in, 3–5

text handling

extracting information from strings, 57–58

format conversions, 59–61

VBScript functions for, 56–57

text strings, reading, 450

text, tooltips, changing, 472–473

TextStream objects, 529

thumbnail previews

scanned images, 589–590

using on preview pages, 597–599

windows, 391–392

TIFF files, 602

compression settings, viewing, 603–604

TileHorizontally method (Application object), 274, 382

TileVertically method (Application object), 274, 382

TileWallpaper key value, 476

tiling windows, 382

time formats, audio CDs, changing, 635–636

time stamps, in log files, 25

timeouts
  adding to queries, 38
  for mouse hovers, setting, 470–471
  for screen savers, setting, 460
  setting, 15

timer control, creating/using, 513–515

Timer Control object (timer.event), 513–514
  debugging timer, 514–515

Timer1_Timer procedure, for Timer Control events, 513

timer.event object, 513–514
  debugging timer, 514–515

TimerFired event (Timer Control object), firing timer control using, 514

timer.vbp, 513, 513–514

title bar, removing from dialog boxes/windows, 143–144

Title property
  with Folder object, 275
  with Web Browser Dialog Box object, 542

Toolbars (VB CCE), 118

Toolbox (VB CCE), 118

Tooltip Animation visual effect, 466, 471–472

tooltips
  animation effects for, enabling, 471–472
  changing text, 472–473

ToolTips, with Tree View tool, 389

TotalSize property (Drive object), 222, 225–226

Translate method (Internet Connection object), 578

tray area icons
  changing dynamically, 520–522
  for showing running scripts, 516–520

Tray Icon object, showing running scripts using, 516–520

tray.icon object, 516–520

TrayProperties method (Application object), 274

tray.vbp, 516

TreeView tool (treeview.tool), 387
  browsing system windows, 387–389
  ToolTip capability, 389

Trim function (VBScript), 57

troubleshooting
  Setup Wizard problems, 153–154
  system crashes, 100–101

tvtool.vbp, 387–389

TWAIN scanner driver
  dialog boxes, 586
  verifying support for, 584

twain.manager object, 583–584
  compressed files, viewing TIFF settings, 603–604
  file type information, repairing automatically, 604–606
  graphics files, managing, 593–599
  scanned images, editing/managing, 590–592
  scanning images, 585–590
  TWAIN driver support, verifying, 584

.txt files (plain text), saving script files as, 3–4

Type property, 105
  with File object, 237
  with Folder object, 231
  with FolderItem object, 277

TypeLibrary information, 93–94, 511–512
  accessing, WinWord example, 349–351
  DHTML object model, 174
  for IE, 157
  extracting information from, 105–106
  information categories (table), 511–512
  reading, 105

TypeName function (VBScript), 46–48

U

UCase function (VBScript), 57
undo feature, with Delete command, 250
undocumented objects
  autodocumenting, 105–108
  help/documentation for, 113–115
UndoMinimizeAll method (Application
    object), 274
  handling desktop windows using,
    381–382
Unicode strings
  ANSI string comparison, 214
  for undocumented functions, 204
UNIX commands, 529
unknown files, context menus for,
    401–402
unlocking user accounts, 687
unpredicatble errors, handling, 28–29
uploading files, 568–569
user accounts
  disabling, 687
  unlocking, 687
  viewing, 676
UserControl property, 119
  adding common dialog control
    wrapper, 194–195
USER.DAT (Registry) files, 408
UserDomain property (Network object),
    490
UserName property (Network object),
    490
UserProfile property (Network object),
    490
users
  account properties, changing, 684–685
  accounts, new, adding, 679–680
  group membership, identifying,
    678–680
  groups, 680–681
  input by, saving/validating, 138,
    553–554
  network, identifying current, 490–491
  passwords, setting/managing, 684,
    686–687

Recycle Bin access, controlling,
    438–439
users, Windows NT/2000 systems
  adding, 672–673
  changing passwords, 673–674
  deleting accounts, 673
  enumerating, 671–672
  global groups, listing, 674
  global groups, managing, 675

V

validating data
  checking information type, 34–36
  user input, in custom web browser,
    553–554
values
  arguments, specifying defaults, 142
  deleting from Registry, 414–415, 420
  empty, identifying, 33
  in keys, enumerating, 416–417
  long-integer, retrieving, 449
  viewing, 20
variable arrays
  declaring/using, 51–53
  dynamic size arrays, 54–55
  enumerating, 69–70
  looping through, 20
  multidimensional, 56
  returning multiple values using, 77–80
  shrinking/expanding, 55–56
variables
  converting, functions for, 49–50
  declared variables, 46, 83–84
  doubling in procedures/functions,
    74–75
  formatting, functions for, 50–51
  global scope for, 73
  in procedures, 73
  types, converting, 48–50
  types, in databases (table), 655
  values, viewing/changing, 20, 46–48, 60
  Variant variable type for, 46
Variant variable type (VBScript), 46

VarType function (VBScript), 46–48
VB CCE (Visual Basic Control Creation
     Edition), 117–118
  accessing StrPtr command, 214
  adding event handlers, 136–139
  CD-ROM tray API functions, 126
  Code view/Object view, 119–120
  Common Dialog COM, 193–197
  designing forms using, 132–134
  DoEvents, 170–171
  Form Layout window, 120
  Main window, 119
  MSComDlg.CommonDialog in, 186
  Object view, 119
  OLEError function, vdecoding error
     messages using, 148–149
  Project Explorer window, 119–120
  Properties window, 120
  Setup Wizard, 152–154
  starting new ActiveX control project,
     118
  Toolbars, 118
  Toolbox, 118
  wrapping SHFileOperation API, 250
VB (Visual Basic) programming language,
     creating COM objects using,
     117–118
vbArray constant, 47
vbByte constant, 47
vbCr constant, 78
vbCritical constant, 38
vbCurrency constant, 47
vbDataObject constant, 47
vbDate constant, 47
vbDouble constant, 47
vbEBoolean constant, 47
vbEmpty constant, 33, 47
vbError constant, 47
vbExclamation constant, 38
vbInformation constant, 38
vbInteger constant, 47
vbLong constant, 47
vbNull constant, 47
vbObject constant, 47

.vbp files, searching for in Windows
     Registry, 433–434
vbQuestion constant, 38
.vbs key (Registry), 398–400
.vbs (VBScript) files
  adding debugging commands, 19
  deleting, 7–8
  saving script files as, 4
  starting from New menu, 6–7
VBScript scripting language
  advantages of using, 31–32
  date/time functions, 36
  decision-making functions, 65–67
  Dictionary object, 80–82
  encrypting binaries, 65
  InputBox() function, 32–33
  IsDate() function, 34–36
  looping functions, 67–72
  MsgBox function, 36–38
  procedures, defining, 72
  random number generator, 61–62
  searching for intrinsic commands, 109
  text-handling functions, 56–61
  toolbox, 118
  undocumented string-handling
     commands, 214
  variable arrays, 51–56
  variables with, 46–56, 83–84
  Variant variable type, 46
vbSingle constant, 47
vbskco32.dll, compressing files using, 269
vbString constant, 47
vbSystemModel constant, 38
vbVariant constant, 47
vcr device type, 637
Verbs property
  accessing Context menu commands,
     285
  with FolderItem object, 277
version object
  creating, 262–263
  custom properties (table), 264
  viewing 16-bit Windows files, 265–266
versions, of software, identifying, 361–362

version.vbp, 262–264
video resolution
    available resolutions, identifying,
        498–499
    changing, 500–501
    current settings, identifying, 499
    frequency settings, 500
videodisc device type, 637
View mode, for desktops, setting
        manually, 389–390
ViewOptions property (WebView object),
        320
virtual folders, 317
    accessing in Explorer, 279–281
    viewing Class-IDs, 317–318
    viewing list of, 202
visible property, 158
Visual Basic 5.0 CCE. *See* VB CCE
Visual Basic Control Creation Edition. *See*
    VB CCE
visual effects, 465
    built-in (table), 465–466
    combo box animation, enabling, 466
    cursor shadow effect, enabling, 466
    font smoothing, enabling/disabling,
        474
    gradient captions, disabling, 467–468,
        467–468
    menu animation, managing, 468–469
    menu underlines, disabling, 469
    selection fade, enabling/disabling, 471
    tooltips, enabling, 471–472
Volume attribute (drives), 239
VolumeName property (Drive object),
        222, 224

W
WakeUp event (Modeless object), 523
wallpaper, desktop
    enabling drag-and-drop importation,
        475–476
    identifying, 450
    mode settings, 476–477

WallpaperMode, 476
warning messages, enabling in Recycle
        Bin, 445
WAV audio files
    playing, 638–638
    recording CD tracks as, 642–644
waveaudio device type, 637
web browser, custom
    accessing onkeypress event, 550
    adding radio buttons, 555–558
    automatic closing, 550–551
    creating/displaying template for,
        540–541
    validating use input, 553–554
Web Browser Dialog Box object
        (web.dialog)
    closing automatically, 550–551
    Help button, enabling, 545–546
    HTML template, controlling browser
        from, 547–550
    HTML template, creating/displaying,
        540–541
    HTML template elements, accessing,
        542–543
    keypress events, localizing, 551–553
    object controls, adding to template,
        548–550
    properties/methods (table), 542
    radio buttons with, 556–558
    user-entered data, retrieving,
        543–544
    user-entered data, validating,
        553–554
Web folders, synchronizing with local
        folders, 569–574
Web sites
    managing, 569–574
    MDAC updates, 648
    RegMon utility, 427
Web view, 202
WebBrowser control, 539–540
web.dialog object
    closing automatically, 550–551
                                Continued

web.dialog object *(continued)*
  Help button, enabling, 545–546
  HTML template, controlling browser from, 547–550
  HTML template, creating/displaying, 540–541
  HTML template elements, accessing, 542–543
  keypress events, localizing, 551–553
  object controls, adding to template, 548–550
  properties/methods (table), 542
  radio buttons with, 556–558
  user-entered data, retrieving, 543–544
  user-entered data, validating, 553–554
webdialog.vbp, 540
WebView object, 319–320
weekday names, for dates, identifying, 27
WhatIsIt function (Network object), identifying container objects, 677–678
Width property (Web Browser Dialog Box), 542
WINDIFF utility, comparing Registry snapshots using, 424–426
%WINDIR%, Windows folder in, 488
window container
  positioning on screen, 144
  properties for, setting, 142–144
  removing title bar, 143–144
window handles, 367
window IDs, 368
WindowManager object (window.manager)
  foreground windows, accessing, 369–370
  window components, accessing/managing, 383–387
  windows, accessing by name/class, 367–369
  windows, bringing to foreground, 371–372
  windows, launched, accessing, 370–371
WindowMove method (WindowManager object), 376–377

windows
  accessing by class name, 369
  accessing by name/ID, 368
  architecture, 384
  borders, customizing, 455
  bringing to foreground, 371–372
  child, locating/enumerating, 386–387
  closing/killing, 360
  content, capturing, 390–392
  core components, viewing, 383–384
  currently active, viewing, 334–335
  displaying, procedure for, 134–135
  flashing title bars, 378–379
  focus lock, disabling, 333–335
  focus-owning, sending keys to, 332–333
  foreground, accessing, 335, 369–370
  full window drag, controlling, 474
  hiding, 374–375
  launched, accessing, 370–371
  managing on desktops, 381–382
  minimizing/maximizing, disabling, 380
  moving, 376
  opening, 132
  output, IE-based, 165–168
  parent, viewing, 384–385
  previewing, 391–392
  resizing windows, 376–378, 381
  resizing contents, 144–146
  size of, identifying/setting, 306–307, 327–328, 376
  style, customizing, 359–360, 372–375
  style, Run method settings, 327–328
  verifying existence of, 335
Windows 2000 systems
  ADSI interface, 669–670
  ANSI support, 214
  calling scripts from command lines, 531
  DLTS (Distributed Links Tracking Service), 312
  DOS command script extensions, 533
  drag-and-drop limitations, 41
  event logging support, 22
  Folder2 object, 276

FolderItem2 object, 277
Icon Picker dialog box, 204
Index Server, 658–660
NameSpace key, 442
property-IDs (table), 450–452
running scripts like programs, 41–42
running tasks, viewing, 361
script debugger, 17
shell32.dll in, 202
special folders, 484
UNICODE strings, 214
user settings, storage of, 436
visual effects, disabling, 465
visual effects, identifying support for, 465
Web view integration, 202
Windows 95 systems, 10
    event logging support, 22
    scripts, stopping, 15
    special folders, 484, 485
    user settings, storing, 436
Windows 98 systems
    environment variables, 10
    special folders, 484
    user settings, storage of, 436
Windows 9.x systems
    DOS commands, interface for, 529
    Icon Picker dialog box, 204
    link-tracking in, 313
    LOG files, finding, 22
    programs, closing, 342–344
    property-IDs (table), 450–452
    Registry backups, 409–410
    Registry, restoring, 411
    rundll32.exe, launching, 261–262
    running tasks, viewing, 361
    ScanDisk utility, launching, 328–329
    script launch keys, 395
    scripts, launching, 396
    TargetPath property (Shortcut object), 306
Windows API (application programming interface), 125
Registry Update object wrapper, 448–481

SystemParametersInfo function, 448
Windows editor, shortcut to, 290
Windows Explorer, ListView, 207. *See also* Explorer window
Windows file transportation, SHFileOperation API, 250
Windows files, 16-bit, viewing, 265–266
Windows folder
    accessing directly, 489
    .exe files in, reading/storing, 54–55
    key codes (table), 489
    location of, identifying, 483
    scripts, saving in, 10–11
Windows function (Application object), 274
    internal, accessing, 125
Windows NT/2000 systems
    ADSI access, 675
    ADSI namespaces, viewing contents of, 675–676
    backup folders, compressing, 258
    calling COM objects, errors from, 101
    DOS command interpreter (CMD.EXE), 344
    events, logging, 24–25
    global groups, listing/managing, 674–675
    managing, 669–670
    programs, closing, 342–344
    Registry backups, 409–410
    Registry location, 408
    script launch keys, 395
    SpecialFolders, AllUsersStartup, 307
    users, adding/managing, 671–674
    WINDIFF utility, 425
Windows NT systems
    event logging support, 22
    Index Server, 658
    link-tracking in, 313
    running tasks, viewing, 361
    special folders, 484
    stopping scripts, 15
Windows Registry. *See* Registry
Windows Scripting Host. *See* WSH 2.0 (Scripting Host)

Windows Services
  browsing, 688
  managing using ADSI interface,
    688–690
  managing using API, 688
  start types (table), 690
Windows shell, 247–248
Windows system dialog boxes,
    advantages of using, 186
Windows system settings
  Active Window Tracking, managing,
    454–456
  changing, 452–453
  controlling properties, 452–453
  Icon Picker variations, 204
  icon spacing, 453–454
  icons, enabling title wrap, 458
  property-IDs (table), 450–452
  Resolve dialog box, accessing, 313–315
  system beep, controlling, 457–458
  system menu, enabling/disabling,
    380–381
  window colors, changing, 457
Windows versions, identifying, 504
WindowSize method (WindowManager
    object), 377–378
WindowStyle property (Shortcut object),
    291
WINHELP.EXE, 115
WinKind method (OS Version object), 505
Winmanager COM, 367
winmanager.vbp, 367–368
winmm.dll
  decrypting, 129–130
  displaying contents as HTML file,
    130–131
WinNT: identifier (ADSI), 675
WinsockInit method (Internet Connection
    object), 576, 578
WinsockQuit method (Internet
    connection object), 576, 578
WinType method (OS Version object),
    505
WinWord (Microsoft Office)

Registry snapshots, comparing, 426
  spell-checker, accessing, 351–353
  TypeLibrary for, accessing, 349–351
word wrapping, during editing, 12
work area, identifying current, 449
WorkingDirectory property
  with IShellLink object, 308
  with Shortcut object, 291
wrappers
  for Folder Picker dialog box, creating
    custom, 197–201
  MSComDlg.CommonDialog as, 186
  Open File dialog box, 195–196
  for SendKeys, 335–338
  shellcopy.tool object, 254
  for system dialog boxes, advantages,
    193
write-protection, checking files for, 240
write.vbs, adding data to databases, 653
writing scripts, simple example, 3–5
WScript object
  documentation for, 114
  general timeouts using, 15
  launching scripts using, 16
WScript.Arguments object
  automatic script launching using,
    393–394
  wallpaper, desktop, importing, 475–476
WSCRIPT.EXE
  running scripts in context menus, 400
  translating into CSCRIPT.EXE, 530–536
WScript.Network object, 89, 679–680
  ADSI namespaces, viewing contents of,
    675–676
  checking for containers, 677–678
  ComputerName method, 676
  groups, adding users, 680–681
  groups, managing, 681–683
  identifying group members, 678
  passwords, managing, 684, 686–687
  properties/methods/functions (table),
    490
  shared folders, managing, 690–692
  users, current, identifying, 490–491

users, managing, 680, 684–685, 687

Windows Services, managing, 688–690

WScript.Quit command, 21, 30

during data validation, 35

WScript.Shell object, 88, 411–412

Class-ID, 92

components, viewing, 105–106

Cool Switch window size, controlling, 481–482

Documents menu, cleaning automatically, 487–488

Documents menu, cleaning manually, 486

with event logging, 23

event sinks, implementing, 511

Popup function enhancement, 38–39

programs, launching, 324

Run method, 324

screen savers, launching/managing, 458–459, 461–463

Shell Link object (IShellLink), 307–308

Shortcut object, 290–291

SpecialFolders method, 484–485

Windows folder path information, retrieving, 488–489

WScript.StdIn object, accessing DOS Input streams, 529–530

WScript.StdOut object, accessing DOS Output streams, 529–530

WSH 1.0 (Scripting Host)

Count property errors, 28

WScript.Shell return objects, 106

WSH 2.0 (Scripting Host)

COM objects included with (table), 88–89

DOS Input/Output stream support, 42–46, 529

DOS version, 43

drag-and-drop capabilities, 16–17

error handling, re-enabling,30

error messages, 15, 21

event logging support, 22

features, 6

GetFileVersion feature, 262

hosting environment, identifying,531

Option //D, 16

Run method, 323–329

scripting language support, 31–32

SendKeys method, 329–344

setup, 4

.vbs file format for, 3–4

windows support limitations, 367

WScript.Shell return objects, 106

//X and ??D support, 19

WSH.LOG files, 22

WSHOM.OCX (WScript.Shell)

viewing components, 105–106

WScript objects in, 89

WSHShell object (WScript.Shell)

Cool Switch windows, controlling size of, 481–482

Documents menu, cleaning automatically, 487–488

Documents menu, cleaning manually, 486

ExpandEnvironmentStrings method, 488–489

implementing event sinks, 511

launching screen savers, 458–459

screen savers, changing property settings, 461–463

screen savers, installing new, 463

SpecialFolders method, 484–485

Y

yes-or-no questions, 36–38

Hungry Minds, Inc., End-User License Agreement

4. **Restrictions on Use of Individual Programs.** You must follow the individual requirements and restrictions detailed for each individual program in Appendix B of this Book. These limitations are also contained in the individual license agreements recorded on the Software Media. These limitations may include a requirement that after using the program for a specified period of time, the user must pay a registration fee or discontinue use. By opening the Software packet(s), you will be agreeing to abide by the licenses and restrictions for these individual programs that are detailed in Appendix B and on the Software Media. None of the material on this Software Media or listed in this Book may ever be redistributed, in original or modified form, for commercial purposes.

5. **Limited Warranty.**

   (a) HMI warrants that the Software and Software Media are free from defects in materials and workmanship under normal use for a period of sixty (60) days from the date of purchase of this Book. If HMI receives notification within the warranty period of defects in materials or workmanship, HMI will replace the defective Software Media.

   (b) **HMI AND THE AUTHOR OF THE BOOK DISCLAIM ALL OTHER WARRANTIES, EXPRESS OR IMPLIED, INCLUDING WITHOUT LIMITATION IMPLIED WARRANTIES OF MERCHANTABILITY AND FITNESS FOR A PARTICULAR PURPOSE, WITH RESPECT TO THE SOFTWARE, THE PROGRAMS, THE SOURCE CODE CONTAINED THEREIN, AND/OR THE TECHNIQUES DESCRIBED IN THIS BOOK. HMI DOES NOT WARRANT THAT THE FUNCTIONS CONTAINED IN THE SOFTWARE WILL MEET YOUR REQUIREMENTS OR THAT THE OPERATION OF THE SOFTWARE WILL BE ERROR FREE.**

   (c) This limited warranty gives you specific legal rights, and you may have other rights that vary from jurisdiction to jurisdiction.

6. **Remedies.**

   (a) HMI's entire liability and your exclusive remedy for defects in materials and workmanship shall be limited to replacement of the Software Media, which may be returned to HMI with a copy of your receipt at the following address: Software Media Fulfillment Department, Attn.: *Windows Scripting Secrets,* Hungry Minds, Inc., 10475 Crosspoint Blvd., Indianapolis, IN 46256, or call 1-800-762-2974. Please allow four to six weeks for delivery. This Limited Warranty is void if failure of the Software Media has resulted from accident, abuse, or misapplication. Any replacement Software Media will be warranted for the remainder of the original warranty period or thirty (30) days, whichever is longer.

(b) In no event shall HMI or the author be liable for any damages whatsoever (including without limitation damages for loss of business profits, business interruption, loss of business information, or any other pecuniary loss) arising from the use of or inability to use the Book or the Software, even if HMI has been advised of the possibility of such damages.

(c) Because some jurisdictions do not allow the exclusion or limitation of liability for consequential or incidental damages, the above limitation or exclusion may not apply to you.

7. **U.S. Government Restricted Rights.** Use, duplication, or disclosure of the Software for or on behalf of the United States of America, its agencies and/or instrumentalities (the "U.S. Government") is subject to restrictions as stated in paragraph (c)(1)(ii) of the Rights in Technical Data and Computer Software clause of DFARS 252.227-7013, and in subparagraphs (a) through (d) of the Commercial Computer – Restricted rights clause at FAR 52.227-19, and in similar clauses in the NASA FAR supplement, as applicable.

8. **General.** This Agreement constitutes the entire understanding of the parties and revokes and supersedes all prior agreements, oral or written, between them and may not be modified or amended except in a writing signed by both parties hereto that specifically refers to this Agreement. This Agreement shall take precedence over any other documents that may be in conflict herewith. If any one or more provisions contained in this Agreement are held by any court or tribunal to be invalid, illegal, or otherwise unenforceable, each and every other provision shall remain in full force and effect.

CD-ROM Installation Instructions

Each software item on the *Windows Scripting Secrets* CD-ROM is located in its own folder. To install a particular piece of software, open its folder with My Computer or Windows Explorer. What you do next depends on what you find in the software's folder:

1. First, look for a ReadMe.txt file or a .doc or .htm document. If this is present, it should contain installation instructions and other useful information.

2. If the folder contains an executable (.exe) file, this is usually an installation program. Often it will be called Setup.exe or Install.exe, but in some cases the filename reflects an abbreviated version of the software's name and version number. Run the .exe file to start the installation process.

3. In the case of some simple software, the .exe file probably is the software—no real installation step is required. You can run the software from the CD to try it out. If you like it, copy it to your hard disk and create a Start menu shortcut for it.

The ReadMe.txt file in the CD-ROM's root directory contains additional installation information, so be sure to check it.

For a listing of the software on the CD-ROM, see Appendix B.

Microsoft Product Warranty and Support Disclaimer

The Microsoft program on the CD-Rom was reproduced by Hungry Minds, Inc., under a special arrangement with Microsoft Corporation. For this reason, Hungry Minds, Inc., is responsible for the product warranty and for support. If your CD-ROM is defective, please return it to Hungry Minds, Inc., which will arrange for its replacement. PLEASE DO NOT RETURN IT TO MICROSOFT CORPORATION. Any product support will be provided, if at all, by Hungry Minds, Inc. PLEASE DO NOT CONTACT MICROSOFT CORPORATION FOR PRODUCT SUPPORT. End users of this Microsoft program shall not be considered "registered owners" of a Microsoft product and therefore shall not be eligible for upgrades, promotions or other benefits available to "registered owners" of Microsoft products.